The Evolution of Instit... Economics

The story of American Institutional Economics – from its emergence, through its interwar supremacy and to postwar decline – is rich and inter-esting but hitherto neglected. Understanding this history, including the achievements and failures, is a vital task for those involved in the recent revival of institutionalist ideas. Today, with the resurrection of pragmatist philosophy, key developments in psychology and the return of a non-reductionist Darwinism to the social sciences, the intellectual conditions for a revival and reconstruction of American Institutionalism are arguably in place.

Few are better qualified to provide an authoritative, wide-ranging account of the rise, fall and potential rebirth of institutional economics than Geoffrey Hodgson. This well-written and comprehensive study addresses the methodological and theoretical foundations of American Institutionalism, taking Thorstein Veblen's proposal for a 'post-Darwinian economics' seriously. In this and other respects, it challenges previous accounts of the nature, potential and contemporary relevance of American Institutionalism.

The Evolution of Institutional Economics will enhance the status of its author as one of the leading economists in the world. It will be read and re-read by economists, sociologists and philosophers.

Geoffrey M. Hodgson is Research Professor in Business Studies at the University of Hertfordshire, UK. He was formerly a Reader in Economics at the University of Cambridge, UK. His previous books include *How Economics Forgot History* (2001) and *Economics and Utopia* (1999), both available from Routledge.

A work of impressive interdisciplinary scholarship, *The Evolution of Institutional Economics* is simultaneously a well-written historical narrative and a sophisticated, astute contribution to the philosophy of the social sciences. ... Hodgson successfully sets the groundwork for the future development of economics as an evolutionary, truly *social* science.

Robert Aunger
King's College, Cambridge, UK

Geoffrey Hodgson has done more than anyone else to rehabilitate, indeed to reconstruct, the history-friendly evolutionary economics of the old American Institutionalists and the German Historical School. But he has not just recovered the intellectual paternity of institutional and evolutionary economics. He has also explored and improved its philosophical foundations. ... *The Evolution of Institutional Economics* is his crowning achievement.

Mark Blaug
University of Rotterdam, The Netherlands

Thought provoking and lucidly written, this book is a monument to Hodgson's outstanding efforts to reconstruct economics from a penetrating vision of the past. It offers an ingenious integrative analysis which clears the ground for a new approach to institutional economics that can contribute to a deeper understanding of the world in which we live, and will provide an enduring stimulus for theoretical discussions in the future.

Kurt Dopfer
University of St. Gallen, Switzerland

Occasionally, though rarely, an author offers more striking insight than that which might be gained from even the most diligent personal study. With *The Evolution of Institutional Economics* and *How Economics Forgot History*, Professor Hodgson has forcefully articulated the need to resurrect a research agenda for the social sciences which integrates the salient scientific categories of agency, structure and history in a meaningful and analytical manner.

Stephen Dunn
Department of Health, UK

This is a brilliant book about the rise, fall and potential renewal of the original institutional economics. The critiques of methodological collectivism and methodological individualism are particularly persuasive, and the book suggests a way forward for eschewing these dichotomous positions. Overall, this is an engaging, exciting and very well written work.

Phillip Anthony O'Hara
Curtin University, Australia

In this very stimulating and scholarly book, Hodgson shows how economics can end its painful isolation from the most creative findings of the other disciplines only by rejecting its own inconsistency between the traditional emphasis on scarcity and the implicit assumption of free rationality and free institutions. As Veblen and others have shown many years ago, rationality and institutions cannot be treated as a free lunch available to all economic systems. They are a costly product of human history. An economics that forgets history is necessarily silent on their emergence, and cannot explain their qualities and their limitations.

Ugo Pagano
University of Sienna, Italy

Geoff Hodgson's new book continues his search for a viable institutional economics. ... More than in any of his earlier works, he has put the problem of reconstruction on the table ... this book will engender a dialogue that will produce a revised and viable institutionalism – hopefully, too, an open and pluralist one.

Warren J. Samuels
Michigan State University, USA

The Evolution of Institutional Economics may be the best book ever written on the subject. It is a considerable intellectual achievement, not only in terms of analysis and synthesis, but also in terms of breadth and depth of learning. It focuses on the main unresolved issues and problems in institutional economics and offers a way to resolve them.

Rick Tilman
University of Nevada, Las Vegas, USA

This is a marvellous book! Hodgson's account of the rise and decline of American Institutionalism reads like a crime novel. And yet, in its breadth and deepness of ideas, explanations, and philosophical underpinnings it goes far beyond any history of economic thought. It provides a plea for returning to the Darwinian inspiration of Thorstein Veblen's research program for the social sciences. ... This book is possibly the most serious attempt to reinstate the evolutionary gist of American institutionalism since Veblen himself.

Ulrich Witt
Max Planck Institute, Jena, Germany

By the same author
Socialism and Parliamentary Democracy (1977)
Labour at the Crossroads (1981)
Capitalism, Value and Exploitation (1982)
The Democratic Economy (1984)
Economics and Institutions (1988)
After Marx and Sraffa (1991)
Economics and Evolution (1993)
Economics and Utopia (1999)
Evolution and Institutions (1999)
How Economics Forgot History (2001)

Economics as Social Theory
Series edited by Tony Lawson
University of Cambridge

Social Theory is experiencing something of a revival within economics. Critical analyses of the particular nature of the subject matter of social studies and of the types of method, categories and modes of explanation that can legitimately be endorsed for the scientific study of social objects, are reemerging. Economists are again addressing such issues as the relationship between agency and structure, between economy and the rest of society, and between the enquirer and the object of enquiry. There is a renewed interest in elaborating basic categories such as causation, competition, culture, discrimination, evolution, money, need, order, organization, power probability, process, rationality, technology, time, truth, uncertainty, value etc.

The objective for this series is to facilitate this revival further. In contemporary economics the label 'theory' has been appropriated by a group that confines itself to largely asocial, ahistorical, mathematical 'modelling'. *Economics as Social Theory* thus reclaims the 'Theory' label, offering a platform for alternative rigorous, but broader and more critical conceptions of theorizing.

The Evolution of Institutional Economics

Agency, structure and Darwinism in American Institutionalism

Geoffrey M. Hodgson

LONDON AND NEW YORK

First published 2004
by Routledge
11 New Fetter Lane, London EC4P 4EE

Simultaneously published in the USA and Canada
by Routledge
29 West 35th Street, New York, NY 10001

Routledge is an imprint of the Taylor and Francis Group

© 2004 Geoffrey M. Hodgson

Typeset in Palatino by
HWA Text and Data Management, Tunbridge Wells
Printed and bound in Great Britain by
TJ International Ltd, Padstow, Cornwall

British Library Cataloguing in Publication Data
A catalogue record for this book is available from the British Library

Library of Congress Cataloging in Publication Data
A catalog record for this book has been requested

ISBN 0–415–32252–9 (hbk)
ISBN 0–415–32253–7 (pbk)

To my PhD students – past, present and future.

Contents

Illustrations

Figures

Tables

Preface

My previous monograph – *How Economics Forgot History* – was about the limits of general theory in the social sciences. It favoured approaches that are sensitive to key differences in socio-economic systems through time and space. I explained how this problem of historical specificity had been recognized in the 1840s by Karl Marx and by members of the German historical school, and that it was at the centre of theoretical discourse in economics for 100 years. However, largely due to the catastrophes of Nazism and the Second World War, this vital problem in social science unfortunately disappeared from the principal agendas of research.

When I wrote *How Economics Forgot History* I planned a succeeding volume with a similarly historical narrative on the problem of agency and structure. But *How Economics Forgot History* did not announce that it was to be the first of two volumes. That might have tempted fate. I am not superstitious. But one cannot be too careful.

This is the previously unannounced second volume. The two volumes can be read in any order, but consideration of their order of publication is to be preferred. The theoretical focus here is on the interaction between the individual and society. The relationship between individual agency and social structure is uppermost and equal in importance to the problem of historical specificity for all the social sciences. It involves key questions of ontology and explanation. What is social structure and how does it relate to and affect individual agents? Do social structures have characteristics that are not found among the individuals involved? Is it possible and desirable to explain social structures in terms of individuals? Or to explain individuals in terms of social structures? Or are superior modes of explanation available?

Even at the end of the twentieth century, central issues in the analysis of the relationship between agency and structure remained incompletely resolved. The argument in the present book is that materials towards a solution to some of these unresolved issues lie in works that appeared – largely in the United States of America – principally from the 1890s to the 1920s. These materials have remained largely unrecognized and undeveloped. The past has become a foreign and unfamiliar country. But also these earlier approaches derived from a richer dialogue between the social sciences, biology and psychology. The earlier insights have been neglected partly because of the latterly acquired uneasiness among social scientists about importing ideas from biology.

Between the natural and the social sciences there remains a Berlin Wall. Modern mainstream economics wishes to retain its central idea of the primacy of choice, yet Darwinism requires that choice should also be subject to causal explanation. Modern sociology retains an impermeable boundary between the natural and the social, traceable in the writings of Karl Marx and Émile Durkheim, and becoming more widespread after the First World War. Sociologists fear that any importation of biological ideas would necessarily lead to obnoxious political conclusions, or undermine explanations that appeal to cultural factors. Such mistaken fears have led to indiscriminate rejection of earlier intellectual traditions, rather than a careful extraction of their powerful ideas.

The evolutionary and Darwinian approach to social theory that is proposed here does not explain social phenomena in biological terms. It does not see Darwinism as a moral justification of 'the survival of the fittest'. It does not see evolution as an optimizing or teleological process. It involves multiple levels of replication in the social as well as the biological sphere. This implies an irreducible hierarchy of different types of unit, including genes, individuals and social institutions. There are varied replicators and diverse units of selection at different levels. The picture is complex and non-reductionist. Hence Darwinism applies at the level of socio-economic evolution primarily through the selection of social structures rather than individual or biological units: selection at this higher level can sometimes work against the forces of genetic or individual selection. It does not deny the possibility of the inheritance of acquired characters at some (social) levels, but sees Darwinism as more complete than Lamarckism in explanatory power. It emphatically includes human intentionality but sees it as subject to a causal and evolutionary explanation. Darwinism involves more than variation, replication and selection – it invokes a universal and unrelenting search for causal and processual explanations.

But Darwinism does not provide a complete theory of everything, from cells to human society. Darwinism provides an over-arching framework of explanation, but without claiming to explain every aspect or detail. In insisting that evolution was dependent on its context, Darwin (1859, p. 314) himself declared: 'I believe in no fixed law of development'. Explanations additional to natural selection are always required to explain any evolved phenomenon. For example, natural selection alone cannot explain why some birds have dull, and others colourful, plumage. Different auxiliary explanations such as camouflage or competition for mates are required. Natural selection does not itself induce variability at the individual level, and additional theories are required to explain this.

The Darwinian framework has a high degree of generality, and it always requires specific auxiliary explanations. The metatheoretical framework of Darwinism provides a way of inspiring and organizing these explanations (Blute, 1997). As elucidated in more detail in the preceding volume (Hodgson, 2001c), there is no inconsistency between the general Darwinian and ontological commitments here and full recognition of the problem of historical specificity. Furthermore, this commitment to a general Darwinian framework does not overlook the important differences between the specific mechanisms of evolution in biology and in society.

Some significant Darwinian approaches to social theory appeared in the 1890s, in Britain and the United States. One of the contributors was Thorstein Veblen. Yet this aspect of his work is often neglected today. This book examines these lost arguments from an earlier economics and social theory, and shows how they can begin to resolve some of the theoretical problems that are at the top of the contemporary agenda.

In both this and the preceding volume there is a lengthy excursion into a neglected history of ideas. These explorations have the objective of bringing forgotten materials to light, to help in the construction of a new approach in the social sciences. Both books concentrate on almost exactly the same time period in their histories of ideas. *How Economics Forgot History* charted the rise of the German historical school and other related developments in economics, from the 1840s to the 1940s. This volume begins a little later, with the birth of Darwinism in 1859, and ends its historical narrative with the dramatic decline of American institutionalism just after the Second World War. It thus spans the period from the 1850s to the 1940s. The time periods are almost identical, and the central questions are related.

The narrative of *How Economics Forgot History* began in Germany. I considered the influence of the German historical school on American institutionalism, with specific regard to the problem of historical specificity. *The Evolution of Institutional Economics* moves from the Victorian England of Charles Darwin and Herbert Spencer to the rapidly industrializing America of the 1890s and after, in the quest of insights into theoretical problems of agency, structure, emergence and social evolution.

In both cases the historical narratives show how institutions, events and personal relationships influenced some crucial ideas. Matters of historical specificity, and of agency and structure, also pertain to the evolution of ideas themselves.

Some thinkers are important for both volumes, because they made significant contributions to the discourse on agency and structure, as well as to the problem of historical specificity. Among these names are John R. Commons and Frank Knight. Veblen also appears in both, but the treatment of his work is much more extensive here. Given this degree of temporal and personal overlap, there is some repetition of key facts or ideas. Some items that are summarized very briefly in one volume are discussed at length in the other. This repetition has been kept to a minimum, subject to the condition that one volume should be understandable with no prior reading of the other monograph.

Taken together, these two volumes can be compared to dramas or movies that repeat their coverage of a single set of events, but each time from a different point of view. On occasions, the two discourses collide on a central event or person, and repeat a few frames and phrases, only to move apart as the viewpoints again diverge.

This is, at best, a partial history of American institutionalism. It is an excursion through some institutionalist writings, relating to the problem of agency and structure. Lionel Robbins once remarked: 'an exhaustive history of Institutionalism – how dreary and voluminous that would be' (in Seckler, 1975, p. xi). Voluminous it would be, but I hope that this incomplete account will show that American institutionalism was far from dreary, and will inspire others to exhume still more buried ideas from its past.

A detailed discussion of the development of post-1945 institutional economics would take an additional volume, as long as the present one. It would have to tackle the contributions of leading figures such as John Kenneth Galbraith, K. William Kapp, Gunnar Myrdal and Karl Polanyi, as well as several important allied heterodox economists such as Nicholas Kaldor and Joan Robinson. I do not wish to belittle these postwar developments, but their inclusion in this volume is impossible.

Nevertheless, the present volume shows that by 1945 American institutionalism was fractured and diverse, and lacking a consensus on its own methodological and theoretical foundations. Despite the contributions of postwar theorists, these fractured foundations largely account for the failure of institutionalism to re-establish anywhere the prominence that it enjoyed in interwar America.

The aim of this work is not simply to unearth and understand old ideas but to recover materials from the past to help build something new. Although the inclusion of the latter aim may offend some historians, there are precedents in other histories of ideas. Most histories are written with a purpose in mind, even if it is more modest and less obvious. Essentially, this work is a discourse in methodology and social theory, using past ideas as raw material.

I am also keen to point out the modern relevance of many of the old institutionalist ideas. Hence, in my discussion of Veblen in particular, I occasionally quote modern authors who have (typically unknowingly) replicated the prescient insights of the founder of institutionalism. I hope the meticulous historian of ideas will not object to this practice in this context.

My ambitions for this history are greater than some because I believe that a great deal hinges upon an understanding of the changes in social science in the 1930s and 1940s. The boundaries and contours of both economics and sociology changed enormously, and not always for the better. The defeat and decline of the strong tradition of American institutionalism was a precondition for these changes. Understanding what went wrong is a precondition for putting it right.

We have inherited some pictures of American institutional economics from a number of latter-day interpreters. Some describe the school as 'not theoretical but anti-theoretical' (Coase, 1984, p. 230). Others, who are more sympathetic, declare a 'Veblenian dichotomy' between technology and institutions. Others deny any significant role for instinct psychology in Veblen's thought. Others would have it that institutionalism was founded on inductive or empiricist methods. Others see Clarence Ayres as a close intellectual descendant of Veblen. Others ignore or reject the explicit self-description of Frank Knight as an institutionalist. Others depict institutionalism as primarily an ideological and policy creed, neglecting both its huge ideological diversity and downplaying the integrity and meaning of Veblenian institutionalism at the theoretical level. And so on. The present volume shows that *all* these depictions are false.

Generally, we have not been well served by past accounts of the institutionalist movement. Adequate work in the history of ideas has been lacking. Allan Gruchy (1947, 1972) made some early and still useful attempts in this direction, but focused as much on matters of policy as on underlying theory and philosophy, entirely neglecting the Darwinian origins of institutionalism. Joseph Dorfman's (1934, 1949, 1959) contribution was monumental in its detail, but lacking in regard to methodology and theoretical depth. Adequate work on institutionalism as a whole has come much later, principally with the scholarly contributions of Malcolm Rutherford (1997, 2000a, 2000b, 2001, 2003). This present work is in part a history of institutionalism, but in many respects it is incomplete. Its central focus is on the methodological issues of evolution, agency and social structure. It is an attempt to reconstruct our vision of the past, as well as to construct an institutional economics for the future.

I have been writing about evolutionary ideas since the late 1980s. I must take the opportunity here to note some important changes in my viewpoint, particularly compared with my book *Economics and Evolution* (Hodgson, 1993) and some of my other publications drafted prior to 1999. These changes in my viewpoint occurred in the late 1990s, partly as a result of debates and discussions with Tony Lawson, Paul Twomey and several others. It was during this period that I became more interested in the application of a generalized Darwinian theory of evolution to socio-economic change, beyond matters of metaphor or analogy, but with the acknowledgement of key differences between biological and socio-economic evolution. In addition, after my departure from the University of Cambridge and my appointment to a Research Chair at the University of Hertfordshire at the end of 1998, I had the time to read much more widely and deeply, and develop my thinking about the issues raised in this book.

Consequently, for example, I was able to refine some key definitions, particularly of habits and institutions. I also sorted out my position on the tricky relationship between Lamarckism and Darwinism (Hodgson, 2001b). In particular, reading the work of philosophers or biologists helped me to understand more fully the philosophical implications of Darwinism with regard to causality and explanation. Reading more works by realist philosophers (especially Mario Bunge) further influenced my ideas on ontology, (in)determinism and causality.

I have moved some distance away from the Whiteheadian position with which I sympathized in *Economics and Evolution*. Although Alfred Whitehead remains for me a brilliant philosopher, I now find his quasi-vitalistic view of all matter to be unpersuasive. He attempted to resolve the dichotomies between material and vital, body and mind, causality and teleology, by an ontology grounded on the ubiquity of the organism. Whitehead's organicist ontology proclaimed teleology as a causal category. I now find this to be unconvincing. Some of the enduring aspects of Whitehead's thinking, such as his hierarchical ontology, are also found elsewhere, and I have discovered other layered ontologies that are more developed and appealing. There is much of value in Whitehead's organicism, but his anti-atomism would have better relied on concepts of relatedness and structure, rather than by investing atoms with the attributes of organisms.

It is on the question of causality that my view has changed most radically. Previously I remained agnostic on the possibility of an uncaused cause. For the reasons mentioned in Chapter 3, I now think that the notion of an uncaused cause is anti-scientific. But that does not mean that I have become a determinist, at least in some prominent senses of that term. My position on causality and determination in the present work is closer to that of much mainstream philosophy of science, at least in the postwar realist tradition of Bunge and others. Nevertheless, on several ontological questions I retain an open mind.

Despite my changes of view, there are a number of propositions that are common between *Economics and Evolution* and the present work. There is a shared stress on Darwinism, evolution, emergence and novelty. Similar conclusions are found in both works concerning the limits of analytical reduction and the partial autonomy of higher levels of analysis. These include a defence of the partial autonomy of macroeconomics and the use of institutions as units of analysis.

Acknowledgements

The author is very grateful to Howard Aldrich, Peter Allen, W. Brian Arthur, Glen Atkinson, Robert Aunger, Robert Bannister, Laure Bazzoli, Jeff Biddle, Marion Blute, Paul Dale Bush, Edmund Chattoe, Peter Corning, Peter Dickson, Michael Dietrich, Kurt Dopfer, Véronique Dutraive, Clare Eby, Ross Emmett, Sasan Fayazmanesh, Luca Fiorito, John Foster, Dan Hammond, Hella Hoppe, David Hull, Björn Johnson, Erkki Kilpinen, Charles Kindleberger, Thorbjørn Knudsen, Alexander Lascaux, John Laurent, Clive Lawson, Tony Lawson, Richard Lewontin, Stephen Nash, Julie Nelson, Richard Nelson, John Nightingale, Bart Nooteboom, Douglass North, Phillip O'Hara, Ugo Pagano, Pavel Pelikan, Michael Peneder, Jason Potts, Yngve Ramstad, Peter Richerson, Jochen Runde, Malcolm Rutherford, Warren Samuels, Mikael Sandberg, Peter Senn, Ralph Stacey, Rick Tilman, Marc Tool, Paul Twomey, Viktor Vanberg, Alex Viskovatoff, Jack Vromen, James Webb, Zhen Ye, Yuval Yonay, Bill Williams, Ulrich Witt, Harold Wolozin, John van Wyhe, anonymous referees and many others for critical comments, discussions and other assistance. I also thank archivists Mark Alznauer, Robert Chapel and Hannah Cowery, respectively at the University of Chicago, the University of Illinois at Urbana-Champaign, and the University of Bristol, for their invaluable help. I am also grateful to all those in the Routledge offices for their help, advice and encouragement.

This work draws on material from several previously published essays, from the *Cambridge Journal of Economics*, *Constitutional Political Economy*, *History and Philosophy of the Life Sciences*, *Journal of Economic Issues*, *Journal of Evolutionary Economics*, and from several volumes with editors Jeff Biddle, Leonardo Burlamaqui, Ana Célia Castro, Ha-Joon Chang, John Davis, Sasan Fayazmanesh, Edward Fullbrook, Steven Medema, Warren Samuels and Marc Tool (Hodgson, 1998a, 1998b, 1998c, 1998d, 2000a, 2000b, 2001a, 2001b, 2001d, 2002a, 2002b, 2002d, 2002e, 2003a, 2003b, 2003d, 2004). The author is grateful to the editors for their help and to the publishers for permission to use this material. The Association for Evolutionary Economics kindly granted permission to use material published in the *Journal of*

Economic Issues. All re-used material has been reworked, in some cases extensively.

Sadly in academia these days, few have sufficient time to read, think, research and write. However, since 1999 my personal circumstances have been exceptional. This book would not have been possible without the fantastic institutional support provided by the University of Hertfordshire. Particular thanks are due to Neil Buxton, Martin Timbrell and my colleagues in the Business School. Last but not least, I thank my family for their enduring love and support.

Dramatis personae principes

Alexander, Samuel (1859–1938)
Ayres, Clarence E. (1891–1972)
Bagehot, Walter (1826–1877)
Baldwin, James Mark (1861–1934)
Boas, Franz (1858–1942)
Broad, Charlie D. (1887–1971)
Burns, Arthur Frank (1904–1987)
Butler, Samuel (1835–1902)
Clark, John Bates (1847–1938)
Clark, John Maurice (1884–1963)
Comte, Auguste (1798–1857)
Commons, John Rogers (1862–1945)
Cooley, Charles Horton (1864–1929)
Copeland, Morris A. (1895–1989)
Darwin, Charles R. (1809–1882)
Davenport, Herbert J. (1861–1931)
Dewey, John (1859–1952)
Douglas, Paul H. (1892–1976)
Driesch, Hans (1867–1941)
Durkheim, Émile (1858–1917)
Ely, Richard T. (1854–1943)
Giddings, Franklin Henry
    (1855–1931)
Haeckel, Ernst (1834–1919)
Hamilton, Walton H. (1881–1958)
Hansen, Alvin (1887–1975)
Hobson, John A. (1848–1940)
Homan, Paul T. (1893–1969)
Hoover, Herbert (1874–1964)
Hoxie, Robert F. (1868–1916)
Hume, David (1711–1766)
Huxley, Julian (1887–1975)
Huxley, Thomas Henry (1825–1895)
James, William (1842–1910)

Kaldor, Nicholas (1908–1986)
Kant, Immanuel (1724–1804)
Keynes, John Maynard (1883–1946)
Knight, Frank H. (1885–1972)
Koopmans, Tjalling C. (1910–1984)
Kroeber, Alfred L. (1876–1960)
Kuznets, Simon (1901–1985
Lange, Oskar R. (1905–1965)
Lewes, George Henry (1817–1878)
Loria, Achille (1857–1943)
Malthus, Thomas Robert (1766–1834)
Marshall, Alfred (1842–1924)
Marvin, Walter T. (1872–1944)
Marx, Karl H. (1818–1883)
Mendel, Gregor Johann (1822–1884)
Mill, John Stuart (1806–1873)
Mills, Frederick C. (1892–1964)
Mitchell, Wesley Claire (1874–1948)
Morgan, Conwy Lloyd (1852–1936)
Myrdal, Gunnar (1898–1987)
Nourse, Edwin G. (1883–1974)
Peirce, Charles Sanders (1839–1914)
Pigou, Arthur C. (1877–1959)
Ritchie, David George (1853–1903)
Romanes, George J. (1848–1894)
Roosevelt, Franklin Delano
    (1882–1945)
Ross, Edward Alsworth (1866–1951)
Samuelson, Paul A. (born 1915)
Sellars, Roy Wood (1880–1971)
Slichter, Sumner H. (1892–1959)
Small, Albion W. (1854–1926)
Spaulding, Edward G. (1873–1940)
Spencer, Herbert (1820–1903)

Sumner, William Graham
(1840–1910)
Tarde, Gabriel (1843–1904)
Veblen, Thorstein B. (1857–1929)
Viner, Jacob (1892–1970)
Vining, Rutledge (1908–1999)
Wallace, Alfred Russel (1823–1913)
Ward, Lester Frank (1841–1913)

Watson, John B. (1878–1958)
Weber, Max (1864–1920)
Weismann, August (1834–1914)
Wheeler, William Morton
(1865–1937)
Whitehead, Alfred North (1861–1947)
Wundt, Wilhelm Max (1832–1920)
Young, Allyn A. (1876–1929)

Part I
Introduction

1 Nature and scope

What social science needs is less use of elaborate techniques and more courage to tackle, rather than dodge, the central issues. But to demand that is to
ignore the social reasons that have made social science what it is. To understand that we must first look more deeply into its history.

John Desmond Bernal, *Science in History* (1957)

The old or original institutional economics has had a very bad press. The
statement by Ronald Coase (1984, p. 230) that institutionalism was 'not theoretical but anti-theoretical' has been repeated uncountably by others, especially by 'new' institutionalists who are keen to maintain their
maximum distance from that older and unjustifiably cursed tradition.
Richard Langlois (1986, p. 5) wrote that: 'The problem with the Historical
School and many of the early Institutionalists is that they wanted an economics with institutions but without theory'. Oliver Williamson (1996b, p.
1792) similarly chimed: 'Where they differ is that older style institutional
economics was content with description, whereas newer style institutional
economics holds that institutions are *susceptible to analysis.*' Repeated so often by so many, this manifestly false allegation that the old institutionalism
was 'against theory' has regrettably stuck.[1]

Others, even more crudely, have resorted to *ad hominem* attacks. Lionel
Robbins (in Seckler, 1975, p. ix) wrote that institutionalism 'served as a
war-cry congenial to quite a number of muddled and slightly disturbed
spirits'. In fact, however, these allegedly 'muddled and slightly disturbed'
people were so numerous that they dominated American economics in the
interwar period, and their tradition remained prominent for a while after
the Second World War.

---

1 Rutherford (2001, pp. 180–2) has provided a useful selected list of interwar theoretical
   contributions of American institutional economics as a whole, thus rebutting its erroneous
   but widespread depiction as being 'atheoretical' or 'against theory'. For Perlman (1996, p.
   227) the idea that the original institutional economics was against abstract theory 'is a silly
   judgment, and has too often been made by people who ought to know better'.

However, suspicions are raised when many critics repeatedly and energetically dismiss the old institutionalism, without ever once providing any evidence that they have carefully read or analysed its texts. An experienced historian of ideas would smell that proverbial rat. A sociologist of religion would be reminded of the protective and palliative role of medieval incantations against heretics.

One reason why the German historical school was forgotten was the decline in the fraction of influential economists who could read or write in German. This explanation of decline does not apply to the American institutionalists.[2] Their works are in English and their articles are abundant in core journals of economics – such as the *Quarterly Journal of Economics*, the *Journal of Political Economy*, and the *American Economic Review* – from the 1890s to the 1950s. Any remotely curious academic can read this material by taking the volumes off the shelf of a half-decent library, or today by accessing the Internet.

Something odd and dubious is going on. What is at the root of this academic desire to demonize the old institutionalism without recourse to scholarly evaluation? One is drawn to the conclusion that something important and fundamental is at stake.

It is widely known that the old institutionalists were hostile to the narrow vision of economics as the 'science of choice' and the utility-maximizing version of 'economic man', which have prevailed for the second half of the twentieth century. So keen to dismiss these criticisms, many mainstream economists have resorted to the dismissive tactic of describing any broader version of their discipline, or any approach that is not based on individual utility maximization, as 'not economics'. This is a convenient riposte to those with a more pluralist and broad-minded conception of the subject, who would attempt to obtain jobs in prestigious departments of economics, or to publish their work in esteemed economics journals. Simply dismissing their work as 'not economics' saves all the time and trouble of reading, understanding and engaging with their ideas.

But this tactic does not work so well with institutionalism. In the United States, the heartland of modern orthodoxy, between the two World Wars the institutionalists themselves were the mainstream. Institutionalism has as big and as genuine a historical claim to be economics as neoclassicism. Institutionalists can appeal to history and rebut the 'not economics' slur. Against the institutionalists, the modern critics must try something else. Invented through whatever mixture of ignorance or malice, smearing institutionalism as 'against theory' works even better as a device to dismiss institutionalism from consideration.

---

2 The terms 'America' and 'American' are broader than, and not synonymous with, the United States. Institutionalism had a significant presence in Canada, and some influence in Latin America. I use the shorthand term 'America' to refer to a Western Hemispheric cultural and academic zone, within which the United States was the centre and by far the most important component.

At stake here, therefore, are rival conceptions of the nature and scope of economics as a discipline. Even if American institutionalism contained many erroneous or ill-formed ideas, its broad and institutionally grounded conception of the subject cannot be readily dismissed. Institutionalism offered an approach to the study of economic phenomena that drew not from one discipline but several. It appealed to psychology, anthropology, sociology, history and elsewhere, in an attempt to understand and explain the world as it is, has been, and may be. Its foremost concern was to understand the real world rather than to develop technique for its own sake.

It is not as if everything in the garden of mainstream economics is bringing healthy fruit. The last few years have witnessed enduring global poverty, dubious practices of reckless deregulation, prolonged recessions in Japan, Russia and elsewhere, growing indebtedness and extreme turbulence in financial markets. Many economists have ignored such problems, or otherwise they have often derived unimpressive or simplistic policy recommendations. Analytically, modern economic theorists have abandoned their previous promise to derive macroeconomics from microeconomic principles. Instead they have turned to game theory, but with limited results. Modern economists are often preoccupied with formal technique rather than understanding reality. They have privileged mathematical 'elegant toys', as Alfred Marshall (Whitaker, 1996, p. 280) would have called them, rather than effective policies. Although there are some successes in modern mainstream economics, heretics have no monopoly on failure. It is about time that the economics profession and other social scientists took a long and serious look at American institutionalism.

The new institutionalism

Williamson (1975) coined the term 'new institutional economics'. He and others helped to put the study of institutions back on the agenda. Previous publications in this intellectual tradition include Carl Menger's (1871) theory of the evolution of 'organic' or undesigned institutions, Ronald Coase's (1937) argument that the 'main reason why it is profitable to establish a firm … is a cost of using the price mechanism', and Kenneth Arrow's (1974) further development of the concept of transaction costs. The 'new institutional economics' now involves a massive literature, and Coase and Douglass North have each been awarded the Nobel Prize for their work in this genre.

Most new institutionalist writing has two important characteristics. First, there is a widespread view that institutions should be explained in terms of the interactions of individuals with given purposes or preference functions. The classic new institutionalist project is to explain institutions from a starting point of a set of given individuals. This focus on individuals as the ultimate elements in the explanation is clearly evident, for example, in North's (1981) theory of the development of capitalism, Coase's (1937) and Williamson's (1975, 1985) transaction cost analysis of the firm, and Schotter's (1981) game-theoretic analysis of institutions. In all these cases, the proposal is to start with given individuals and their interactions, and to move on to explain institutions. Second, there is an emphasis on the survival of specific institutional forms because they are alleged to lower 'transaction costs' relative to their alternatives.

The value of this work should not be denied. Substantial heuristic insights about the development of institutions and conventions have been gained on the basis of the assumption of given, rational individuals and by considering transaction costs. However, as explained in the following chapter, there are problems with the idea that explanations of institutions can start with given individuals in an institution-free 'state of nature'. Turning to transaction cost explanations, they too may have value, as long as the concept of a transaction can be clearly defined, and the associated costs can be specified adequately. However, the history of the transaction cost concept reveals a deep ambiguity over such issues (Klaes, 2000a, 2000b).

Accepting the value of many contributions in the new institutionalist genre, we are still required to explain some of the things that it takes for granted. In some circumstances it is legitimate to take the individual as given, as a simplifying abstraction. But individuals nevertheless remain to be explained. The task may be postponed, but it does not disappear. Similarly, the origins of the institutional structures that carry transaction costs also require an explanation. Furthermore, these deeper questions of explanation become vital once issues such as the influence of culture, the emergence and durability of institutions, and long-term economic development, become agendas of enquiry. It is important to understand how individual interactions lead to new institutional developments. But especially in the long term, it is also important to explain – at least in principle – how institutions or circumstances can affect individuals and alter their perceptions and goals.

Causal and evolutionary explanations are important with regard to the origin, development and coevolution of individuals and institutions. Generally speaking, the new institutional economics has so far made very limited use of evolutionary modes of explanation. Genuinely evolutionary theory is about the causal explanation of origin. It is here also that the old or original institutional economics comes in.

The original institutionalism

In America, the original institutional economics had an anomalous history and a shifting identity. It acquired its name in 1918 (Hamilton, 1919). At that time, a number of individuals were recognized as its intellectual leaders, including Wesley Mitchell and John Maurice Clark. But its towering inspiration was Thorstein Veblen, whose personal and professional life was marred by scandal, and who never occupied a senior academic position. John R. Commons was later also identified as an institutional economist, and American institutionalism reached its high point of influence in the 1920s and 1930s.

American institutionalism was highly diverse, but within it there were a number of persistent themes. One of these was a focus on the nature and evolution of key institutions and their role in the economy. Another was to use insights from psychology and elsewhere to understand how institutions shaped the dispositions and mentalities of individuals. Institutional economists also made a number of contributions to the conceptual and empirical foundations of macroeconomics and the theory of economic growth. They were also preoccupied with programmes of economic stabilization and welfare. A number of subdisciplines such as economics and law, labour economics, industrial economics, agricultural economics and industrial relations were highly influenced by institutionalism in the interwar period.[3]

This work is not intended to be a rounded history of American institutionalism. Instead, the aim is to look at its conceptual, philosophical and psychological foundations. It includes the story of how institutional economics acquired – and regrettably abandoned – a theoretical approach that provided a highly sophisticated understanding of the relationship between individual agents and social structures, and provided a meta-theoretical framework for understanding economic change.

American institutional economics was strongly influenced by both Marxism and the German historical school, but it was shaped still further and in more detail by developments in pragmatist philosophy and instinct–habit psychology in the last two decades of the nineteenth century. Just as significantly, Veblenian institutional economics was born out of Darwinism. Although institutionalism subsequently departed from much of its Darwinian heritage, a viable reconstruction of institutional economics involves a return to Darwinism.

In putting forward this view, I am concerned that a host of misunderstandings may emerge. I am also aware of professed misgivings that surround the question of Darwinism, even among heterodox or 'evolutionary' economists (Hodgson, 2002e). I explain at length in Chapters 3 to 8 below what Darwinism involves in this context. The opportunity is taken briefly here to state what Darwinism does *not* mean. Darwinism does *not* imply

- any form of racism, sexism, nationalism or imperialism,
- any moral justification of 'the survival of the fittest',

---

3 For overviews of the impact on subdisciplines of economics see Rutherford (2000a, 2000b, 2001). Not all these subdisciplines have adequate histories, but see McNulty (1980), Jacoby (1990) and Kaufman (1993, 1998).

- that militant conflict is desirable or inevitable,
- that human inequalities or power or wealth are desirable or inevitable,
- that cooperation or altruism are unfit or unnatural,
- that evolution generally involves optimization or progress,
- that social phenomena can or should be explained in terms of biology alone,
- that organisms can or should be explained in terms of their genes alone,
- that human intention is unimportant, or
- that human agency is blind or mechanistic.

As Darwinism does not mean any of these things, then what does it mean? In brief, as well as a theory of evolutionary selection, Darwinism means *causal explanation*, where a cause is understood as necessarily involving transfers of matter or energy. Divine, spiritual, miraculous or uncaused causes are ruled out. Explanations of outcomes involve connected causal sequences. Furthermore, Darwinism provides a specific framework for understanding the evolution of all open, complex systems, that have varied and replicating elements with different capacities to survive. Such processes of replication and selection are not confined to biology. Darwinian evolution can occur on multiple and irreducible levels. It can apply to social institutions and customs, as well as to individuals or genes. The history of the discovery and development of this insight is a foremost theme of this work.

We differ from plants and most animals, especially in our capacities for symbolic representation, language and culture (Donald, 1991). We prefigure many actions and consequences in our minds, and act intentionally. The mechanisms of socio-economic and biotic evolution are very different. In studying socio-economic evolution we are concerned with human welfare and well-being, and not merely with survival or fecundity. All these differences are vitally important. But it does not diminish the importance or analytical value of Darwinism one iota.

After it had lost sight of its Darwinian beginnings, institutionalism went into steep decline after the Second World War. Was this merely a coincidence? It is argued here that the causes of this decline were both internal and external. External events, such as the Second World War itself, had a major role. In addition, during the 1920s and 1930s, the climate of ideas changed, undermining the pragmatist philosophy, instinct–habit psychology and Darwinian ideas that were foundational to institutionalism.

Consistent with the biological idea of *paedomorphosis* in the evolution of a species (Hodgson, 2001c, p. 345), institutionalism must retrace its steps back to the early decades of the twentieth century, determine where it went wrong and take a different branching path. We must 'go back to Veblen' and develop things anew from there. The history of ideas is not a mere academic indulgence. It is an essential means of constructing an effective institutional economics for the twenty-first century.

It took nearly a hundred years for the implications of Charles Darwin's ideas in *The Origin of Species* (1859) to be accepted and fully understood within the scientific community. Philosophers have only recently appreciated the philosophical impact of Darwinism.[4] But the significance of Darwinism for the social sciences has been largely unrecognized since Veblen.

It may take one hundred years from Veblen's death in 1929 for him to be recognized by social scientists as one of the leading social theorists of all time. Yet this acknowledgement is hindered by Veblen's own failure to present his ideas in systematic form. Especially in the modern age of Darwin, the philosophical weight and robustness of Veblen's social theory exceeds that of, say, Max Weber or Talcott Parsons. Yet unlike these rivals, Veblen left us with no synthetic overview of his ideas. We have to extract them, like precious metal, from the veins of glittering insight that run sporadically throughout his works. Occasionally they have to be polished or repaired, but the treasure is nevertheless there for the taking.

I have an aversion to cults of personality and the uncritical veneration of any scientist or theorist. I am extremely uncomfortable with all types of cult or sect, including those in the academic arena. But it is my conviction that among social and economic theorists Veblen has not had his due. There is much more to Veblen than appears at first sight. He is much less of a social satirist or political propagandist, and much more of a philosopher and social theorist. At best, there are only two books of significance that concentrate on Veblen's underlying philosophy (Daugert, 1950; Dobriansky, 1957), as distinct from his other ideas or policy attitudes. Veblen is widely misunderstood and unappreciated. To use the term 'Veblenian social theory' is not to encourage another academic cult of personality. I do so to claim some concordance with Veblen's approach and to demonstrate that there is something more that we can learn from a theorist who has become largely marginalized and forgotten. I also emphasize that it is necessary to be critical; Veblen's several shortcomings and failures must be openly acknowledged.

The structure and content of this work

Two further chapters make up the introductory part of this work. Chapter 2 is on the relationship between agency and structure in social theory. This involves recent work by Roy Bhaskar, Anthony Giddens, Margaret Archer and others. After an exposition of the different viewpoints involved, it is suggested that an evolutionary perspective may have something to offer. But before this is elaborated, it is necessary to address several potential misunderstandings.

4　A survey of about one thousand academic philosophers organized by the *Philosopher's Magazine* put Darwin's *Origin of Species* as the third most important book in philosophy ever, after Plato's *Republic* and Kant's *Critique of Pure Reason* (*The Guardian*, 21 September 2001).

This is the role of Chapter 3. The two extremes of biological reductionism and complete evasion of biology are rejected. Several misunderstandings concerning Darwinism are addressed. For example, self-organization is a complement to, rather than a substitute for, Darwinian natural selection. As another example, socio-economic evolution may be Lamarckian, if suitably defined, but Lamarckism and Darwinism are not substitutes. Neither are they symmetrical in explanatory status: Darwinism is richer and more powerful.

Part II examines the origin and meaning of Darwinian ideas, and the early impact they had on the social sciences. Chapter 4 explains that the beneficial impact of Darwinism in social science has been neglected for fear of buttressing racist, sexist and imperialist ideas. While such abuses of biology have occurred, the history of 'Social Darwinism' is more complicated than often believed, and Darwin himself did not endorse such ideological views (Richerson and Boyd, 2001). This chapter also explores the important philosophical underpinnings of Darwin's scientific ideas. Chapter 5 introduces the central concept of emergence, and shows how early emergentist philosophy was stimulated and channelled by developments in Darwinian biology. Emergent properties are novel features that arise when elements come into combination, where such properties are not found in those elements on their own. Also introduced at this stage is the notion of a layered ontology. Finally, this chapter examines some early attempts to apply Darwinism to social evolution. Very few of these early attempts relied on a selection process involving structured social units, rather than mere aggregates of individuals.

Part III discusses Veblen's institutionalism and measures his achievement. Chapter 6 introduces Veblen and outlines the influences on his thought. In particular, the influence of Conwy Lloyd Morgan – a Darwinian student of Thomas Henry Huxley and pioneer of the concept of emergence – on Veblen is discussed in depth. Chapters 7 and 8 outline the foundations of Veblen's institutional and evolutionary economics, as they emerged in the 1890s. Veblen's achievement in this area includes his treatment of institutions both as units of evolutionary selection and repositories of knowledge. Veblen also stressed the role of habits and the ways that they can be shaped by institutional circumstances. This discussion leads to the introduction of the idea of 'reconstitutive downward causation' in a Veblenian context.

Chapters 9 and 10 criticize some of Veblen's ideas. Chapter 9 finds defects in his account of the 'instinct of workmanship' and its alleged conflict with pecuniary motives. Chapter 10 argues that Veblen's second book, *The Theory of Business Enterprise* (1904), contained two key research programmes, the first on the role of expectations and financial speculation in business cycles, the second on the alleged influence of the machine process on habits of thought. If it had been fully developed, then the former and more promising research programme could have upstaged John Maynard

Keynes by three decades. In contrast, the latter research programme was misconceived. Tragically, Veblen decided to concentrate on the latter rather than the former. Chapter 11 shows how Veblen's engagement with cutting-edge issues in philosophy and elsewhere had largely ceased by 1909. In particular he lost contact with key developments in emergentist philosophy in the 1920s. This missed connection was damaging for the institutionalist movement as a whole.

Chapter 12 considers the launch of institutionalism as a movement and its rise to prominence in the interwar period. It is also shown that the Veblenian foundations of institutionalism in philosophy, psychology and elsewhere were eroded by the rising behaviourist psychology and positivist philosophy, and were damaged by attempts to sever all remaining connections between biology and the social sciences. Shortly after the launch of institutionalism as a movement, it lost confidence in its theoretical underpinnings. This made the construction of a systematic theory for institutionalism much more difficult.

Part IV considers further developments in interwar American institutionalism by focusing on the contributions of four thinkers, namely John R. Commons, Wesley Mitchell, Frank Knight and Clarence Ayres. Three of these are conventionally described as institutionalists. The fourth person, Knight, is included because he accurately described himself as an institutionalist. The aim is not to review their work as a whole but again to focus principally on their treatment of the relationship between agency and structure. Their role in developing suitable foundations for institutional economics is highlighted. All four figures made important contributions, but none was able to develop further the Veblenian foundations of American institutionalism or provide an adequate alternative at that basic level. This part ends with a chapter on the external and internal reasons for the post-1945 decline of institutionalism. The internal reasons concern mainly the failure to develop adequate philosophical and psychological foundations. The external reasons include the major transformation of economics as a discipline during the Second World War.

Part V consists of three chapters. Chapter 19 reviews developments in philosophy, psychology, complexity theory and economics that can now help the revival of a Veblenian-style institutionalism. Chapter 20 shows some ways in which a Veblenian institutionalism can deal with some current problems in institutional theory and develop some insights concerning the nature of institutions. Chapter 21 concludes the book by briefly summarizing the lessons from this reconstructed history of institutional economics and by pointing to the task of constructing an institutionalism for the future.

2 Agency and structure

Back in 1982, a brief but brusque exchange ... took place between James Tobin ... and Robert Nozick ... Tobin exclaimed at Nozick: 'There is nothing more dangerous than a philosopher who's learned a little bit of economics.' To which Nozick immediately responded: 'Unless it's an economist who hasn't learned any philosophy.'

Terence Hutchison, 'On the Relations Between Philosophy and Economics' (1996)

What distinguishes a human agent from automata or insects is the developed capacity to reflect and deliberate upon the context, options, purpose and possible outcomes of action. As Karl Marx (1976, p. 284) wrote in *Capital:* 'what distinguishes the worst architect from the best of bees is that the architect builds the cell in his mind before he constructs it in wax'. This does not imply that all human behaviour is deliberate, but that human deliberation is possible. We should also acknowledge that some non-human animals might have very partially developed this capacity.

Alongside the concept of the agent, the concept of structure is central and essential to any viable social science. A social structure is a set of significant relations between individuals that can lead to causal interactions. Social structures can involve rules, norms, meanings, communication and much else. These relations can be acknowledged or unacknowledged by the individuals involved. Furthermore, social structures can survive the demise of particular individuals that once related to them. Accordingly, the study of human social systems is more than the study of human individuals, because society embodies relations and properties in addition to those of individuals themselves. Although structures frame and condition behaviours, they are neither reducible nor ontologically equivalent to them.

Broadly, the idea that society is more than a collection of individuals has a long pedigree. Indeed, it is much older than the individualistic notion that society is merely the sum of its members. Such atomistic conceptions date largely from the European Enlightenment of the late seventeenth and eighteenth centuries. Before that, the individual was generally regarded as being part of, or subordinate to, some greater entity or whole. For example, there is an ancient metaphor, traceable at least back to Plato and the Bible, that society is like a living organism in which the individual is a component. At the beginning of modern economics, the French physiocrat François Quesnay made use of the metaphor of blood circulating in the structure of the economic body (Foley, 1973). When Adam Smith wrote of the 'invisible hand' he was clearly suggesting that socio-economic systems have additional properties that are not reducible simply to the efforts of the individual minds and visible hands within them.

As modern social science developed in the nineteenth century, the idea of social structure strengthened and evolved. It found a prominent exponent in Marx, who fastened upon the architectural metaphors of structure and superstructure. Marx (1971, p. 20) wrote in 1859 in his famous Preface to *A Contribution to the Critique of Political Economy*:

> In the social production of their existence, men inevitably enter into definite relations, which are independent of their will, namely relations of production appropriate to a given stage in the development of the material forces of production. The totality of these relations of production constitutes the economic structure of society, the real foundation, on which arises a legal and political superstructure and to which correspond definite forms of social consciousness.

Law and politics thus rested on the 'economic' structure. While Marx failed to define what he meant by 'economic' here, in his writings the concept of a structure reached a high point of development. Instead of understanding social reality simply in terms of the wills and personalities of the individuals involved, his concept of structure hinted at the powerful interests, incentives and institutions that might constrain or mould individual human agency.

The idea of social structure also developed within the writings of the German historical school of economists. Some of the nineteenth-century German historicists used the old idea of society as an organism to connote the existence of social structure above constituent individuals (Hutter, 1994; Hodgson, 2001c). There the structure metaphor often assumed a biological form, like the physiology of an organism. Herbert Spencer (1877) likewise embraced an explicit concept of social structure and also described society as an organism. However, Spencer (1881, pp. 48–9) believed that 'the character of the aggregate is determined by the characters of the units' and that social structures emerge because of 'a proclivity towards the structure' in the 'substance' of each individual. Hence Spencer's notions of social structure or social organism did not amount to much more than the aggregate of individual attributes.

The French sociologist Émile Durkheim went much further, to emphasize that society is more than the sum of its parts. Durkheim developed his own distinctive argument that social facts were not reducible merely to individuals or their psychology. A concept of social structure is also traceable in the writings of Max Weber, but there it does not play such a strong and embracing role as in the works of Durkheim or Marx.

In some discourses the essential issues are addressed using different terms. A specific type of social structure, described as an institution, pervades the writings of institutional economists such as Thorstein Veblen, John R. Commons and Wesley Mitchell. A broad and inclusive conception of institutions is widely accepted by social scientists and is adopted here. We may define institutions broadly as durable systems of established and embedded social rules that structure social interactions.

The term 'rule' is broadly understood as an injunction or disposition, that in circumstances X do Y.[1] Hence it includes norms of behaviour and social conventions, as well as legal or formal rules. By their nature, institutions must involve some shared conceptions, in order to make rules operative. According to this definition, systems of language, money, law, weights and measures, traffic conventions, table manners, firms (and all other organizations) are all institutions.[2]

As Alan Wells (1970, p. 3) put it: 'Social institutions form an element in a more general concept, known as social structure.' The original institutional economists understood institutions as a special type of social structure with the potential to change agents, including changes to their purposes or preferences.[3] I have described this possibility as 'reconstitutive downward causation' and attempted to specify its causal processes (Hodgson, 2002a,

---

1 Rules are not necessarily explicit. As M. Weber (1978, p. 105) pointed out in 1907, rules are often followed 'without any subjective formulation in thought of the "rule"'. Hayek (1967, pp. 66–7) also emphasized non-articulated rules: 'it should be clearly understood that the term "rule" is used for a statement by which a regularity of the conduct of individuals can be described, irrespective of whether such a rule is "known" to the individuals in any other sense than they normally act in accordance with it.' However, Hayek (1979, p. 159) overly extended the term 'rule' to instincts, which are not necessarily culturally or socially embedded, as required in my definition of an institution. Notably, all culturally embedded rules are in principle codifiable, in which case breaches of rules can be more readily detected. In which case, mental representations of rules become significant (Searle, 1995). See Ostrom (1986) and Crawford and Ostrom (1995) for detailed analyses of the nature of institutional rules.

2 Note that Schmoller (1900, p. 61) defined an institution similarly as 'a partial order for community life which serves specific purposes and which has the capacity to undergo further evolution independently. It offers a firm basis for shaping social actions over long periods of time; as for example property, slavery, serfhood, marriage, guardianship, market system, coinage system, freedom of trade.' (Translated and quoted in Furubotn and Richter, 1997, p. 6.)

3 However, some institutionalists such a J. F. Foster (1981, p. 908) have misleadingly defined institutions as 'prescribed patterns of correlated behavior'. T. Lawson (2003a, pp. 189–94) rightly points out a difficulty in this conception: if institutions are behaviour, then how can changes in behaviour be explained? A related argument was devised by Aristotle in his critique of 'the Megaric view'. See footnote 29 on p.170 below.

2003b; Hodgson and Knudsen, 2004). These ideas will be addressed and developed in the present work.

Although it is familiar to Marxists and modern sociologists, the use of the term 'social structure' has not been universal in the social sciences as a whole. Its use, for much of the nineteenth and twentieth centuries, was not that frequent, and the term was rarely defined. During the twentieth century, it was largely within the rising discipline of sociology that the term began to be used more frequently. It was prominent in the work of some early American sociologists, such as Lester Frank Ward (1903), but others made less use of the term.

The American sociologist Talcott Parsons inherited a concept of structure principally from European forerunners – including Marx and Durkheim – and it retained a pivotal role in his theory of social action (Parsons, 1937). It was then developed by Robert Merton (1949) and in the 'structural sociology' of Peter Blau (1975) and others. Structure was given special attention by those influenced by Marxism, such as the Frankfurt School in Germany, and by the schools of structuralism in France founded by the anthropologist Claude Lévi-Strauss and by the Marxist theorist Louis Althusser.

It is disturbing to note that the agency–structure problem is evaded by some fashionable developments in contemporary social theory. In particular, there have been recent attempts by post-modernists and post-structuralists to dismiss or transcend this issue. In response, Nicos Mouzelis (1995, pp. 69–70) rightly assessed 'attempts to dismiss the agency–structure distinction ... either by conflating the two notions, or by ... deriving the one from the other' as leading to a theoretical impasse. Notably, many of these evasive attempts involve 'the reintroduction of the distinction by the back door ... by keeping the logic of the agent–structure dichotomy while expressing it through a different terminology'. The solution to the agency–structure problem is not to walk away from it, or to pretend it does not exist. Such strategies have notably ended up with the readmission of the problem in another form.

At the risk of oversimplifying matters, we may classify several types of treatment, or evasion, of the problem. The first group includes those approaches that claim that individuals are the ultimate explanatory or ontological elements. As noted in the next section, this 'methodological individualism' can itself be subdivided. A second group reverses the conflation: structures are regarded as the ultimate explanatory units. A succeeding section is devoted to this 'methodological collectivism'. A third group attempts what Margaret Archer (1995, p. 61) criticizes as a 'central conflation', by erecting a concept of 'structuration' that encompasses both structures and agents. This in some ways represents an advance on the preceding two positions. A fourth group shares with structuration theory the idea that agent and structure are mutually constitutive of each other. But in contrast to structuration theory, it disassociates agent from structure by insisting on their differences. However, this group limits the acknowledgement or explanation of their causal interaction in a manner explained below.

The fourth approach is more sophisticated than the preceding three. A primary aim of this book is to indicate that an institutional economics that builds on Darwinian and Veblenian ideas holds the promise of a fifth, superior approach. This would be both non-conflationary and causally interactive, in a fuller sense to be explained and explored at length. The key innovations in the fifth approach are to extend the requirements of causal explanation, and to place the issue in an over-arching evolutionary framework.[4]

Methodological individualism

There is a long-standing tradition in social theory, to attempt to explain social structures, institutions, and other collective phenomena, solely in terms of the individuals involved. This approach is promoted with mainstream economics and elsewhere. Some, even sociologists, simply take for granted 'the methodological individualism of scientific practice' (Lopreato and Crippen, 1999, p. 209) without even defining the phrase. But the substance and validity of 'methodological individualism' is widely contested. There is not even strict agreement on the definition of this term (Udéhn, 2001).[5]

Broadly, methodological individualism emphasizes the human agent over social structures. Ludwig Lachmann (1969, p. 94) asserted that methodological individualism means 'that we shall not be satisfied with any type of explanation of social phenomena which does not lead us ultimately to a human plan'. But very few social scientists would deny the role of individual intentions in the explanation of social phenomena. In another attempt Jon Elster (1982, p. 453) defined methodological individualism as 'the doctrine that all social phenomena (their structure and their change) are in principle explicable only in terms of individuals – their properties, goals, and beliefs'. Being less banal, this definition also is insufficiently precise, as it fails to clarify whether interactions between individuals or social structures are 'properties ... of individuals' or not. If individual

---

4 As well as the term 'evolutionary', the notion of 'causal explanation' itself requires specification and clarification. For useful accounts see Bunge (1959) and Lipton (1991). Some further remarks on causality are found below.

5 Schumpeter (1908, pp. 64–8, 77–9, 85–7, 154–5, 261, 541–7) first coined the term 'methodological individualism'. However, Schumpeter did not argue that *all* explanations in social science must necessarily and exclusively be in terms of individuals. Instead, he argued that it was the role of *economics* to start from given, rational individuals. For Schumpeter, this explanatory constraint was optional, once we moved outside 'pure economics'. As Udéhn (2001) shows, Schumpeter's use of the term is far from universal. The definition adopted in the present work is in terms of a general methodological injunction, rather than Schumpeter's methodological option or disciplinary demarcation criterion.

interactions or social structures are not 'properties of individuals', then this narrower and more meaningful notion of methodological individualism must be deemed inoperable, for the reasons given below.[6]

Much of the confusion in the debate over methodological individualism stems from whether methodological individualism means explanations (a) in terms of individuals alone, or (b) in terms of individuals plus individual interactions or social structures. If it were meant to mean (b), then few would disagree. Such an inclusive notion would not warrant the title of methodological individualism any more than the description 'methodological structuralism'. If social structures or interactions between individuals are also an essential part of the doctrine, then it is misleading to give the individual exclusive representation in the label.

Attempts to conflate socio-structural phenomena upon the individual generally flounder. There are three types of problem involved here, depending on the type of argument and version of methodological individualism involved. The first type of problem results from giving the individual too much of the explanatory burden. For example, Stephen Jones (1984) and Ekkehart Schlicht (1998) provide interesting theories of conformism and custom. However, the explanation of the emergence of customs and conventions depends crucially on an assumption that individuals exhibit 'rule preference' or a 'preference for conformism'. The problem of institutional emergence is thus 'solved' by making properties of institutions also the properties of individual preferences. In a manner reminiscent of Spencer's idea (1881, pp. 48–9) that social structures emerge because of 'a proclivity towards the structure' in each individual, the social phenomena are conflated upon the individual. The explanation carries force only because individuals have been obliged to take on board factors that properly relate to social structure. Crucially, what such theories do not explain is how individuals acquire these socially infused preferences.

There are many other examples of a similar conflation of social structures and their effects upon individuals. Howard Margolis (1982) and Kenneth Koford and Jeffrey Miller (1991), view institutions as resulting from features of individual preferences, such as for cooperation, for altruism, for conformism, or for the observance of social norms. Robert Frank (1988) and Amitai Etzioni (1988), emphasize individual emotions or add moral

---

6 Claimed supporters of some version of methodological individualism include Popper (1945, 1960), Hayek (1943, 1948, 1952b), von Mises (1949), Arrow (1968, 1994), Ghiselin (1974), Boudon (1981), Elster (1982), Coleman (1990), Furubotn and Richter (1997) and Schlicht (1998). Critics include Lukes (1973), Giddens (1984), Hodgson (1988), Bhaskar (1989), Douglas (1990), Kontopoulos (1993), Archer (1995), T. Lawson (1997, 2003b), Storper and Salais (1997), Bunge (1998) and Udéhn (2001). In apparently conciliatory statements, Sober (1981) and Kincaid (1997, 1998a) argue that the validity or invalidity of methodological individualism is ultimately an empirical issue. If that is the case, then the evidence is against the narrow version. No significant explanation of social phenomena in terms of individuals alone has yet been advanced. In practice there is always a social and relational residual that is not reduced entirely to individual terms.

norms in attempts to give individual preferences more substance and meaning. Still others propose the 'multiple self' in which the individual is treated like a social organization of multiple wills (Elster, 1986). Again, these works contain valuable insights. But the problem is that an augmented individual is constructed to carry the entire explanatory burden of social phenomena. As Archer (1995, p. 251) observes: 'What is going wrong here is the desperate incorporation of all emergent and aggregate social properties into the individual.' In all these cases, the key omission is a failure to explain how and why the individual acquires the assumed 'social' characteristics. It is not clear how these assumed individual characteristics could themselves be explained without reference to social relations or structures.

In a second case, it is fatally admitted that individuals can be somehow changed by social institutions, in which case the inevitable result is that narrow methodological individualism is abandoned. The injunction to explain all social phenomena solely in terms of given individuals founders, once it is admitted that social institutions can change individuals. For example, Friedrich Hayek (1943, 1948, 1952b) has been regarded by some as a promoter of methodological individualism. At the same time he admitted that people are formed by society, just as individuals (intentionally or unintentionally) form society through their combined actions. Thus Hayek (1948, p. 6) sought explanations of 'social phenomena ... through our understanding of individual action' but declared on the very same page that society is composed of 'men whose whole nature and character is determined by their existence in society'. As much as providing an 'individualistic analysis' of social phenomena, Hayek also conceded that individuals have to be understood in terms of their social circumstances. Hence the individual alone was not given ultimate explanatory primacy. This made it impossible for Hayek to be a methodological individualist, at least in the strict and narrow sense above. If it is believed that 'social phenomena' are explained by 'individual action' and the individual is 'determined by ... society', then the causality goes both ways. There is no warrant to describe this as 'methodological individualism' any more than 'methodological collectivism'.

The notion that individuals are socially determined must undermine any attempt to give the individual explanatory priority over social structures. The reason for this is that a socially determined individual cannot provide the ultimate explanatory bedrock that methodological individualism requires. Elster's suggestion that 'all social phenomena' have to be explained 'only in terms of individuals' is untenable if individuals themselves are then to be explained in terms other than individuals alone. If institutional influences on individuals are admitted, then these too are worthy of explanation. In turn, the explanation of those may be in terms of other purposeful individuals. But where should the analysis stop? The purposes of an individual could be partly explained by relevant institutions, culture and so on. These, in their turn, would be partly explained in terms of other individuals. But these individual purposes and actions could then be partly explained by cultural and institutional factors, and so on, indefinitely. We are involved in an apparently infinite regress, similar to the puzzle 'which came first, the chicken or the egg?' Such an analysis never reaches an end point.

It is simply arbitrary to stop at one particular stage in the explanation and say 'it is all reducible to individuals' just as much as to say it is 'all social and institutional'. The key point is that in this infinite regress, neither individual nor institutional factors have legitimate explanatory primacy. The idea that all explanations have ultimately to be in terms of individuals (or institutions) is thus unfounded. Once we admit that the individual is socially determined then we have an explanatory infinite regress, and neither individuals nor institutions can be the legitimate final term. Hence methodological individualism – in any adequately meaningful sense – has to be abandoned (Nozick, 1977; Hodgson, 1988).

In a third case – which is found in the 'new institutional economics' – attempts are made to explain the origin of institutions from interacting individuals, starting from an institution-free 'state of nature'. For example, Carl Menger (1871) pioneered a basic analysis of how institutions evolve. His chosen example was the institution of money. Menger saw money as emanating in an undesigned manner from the communications and interactions of individual agents. He started with a barter economy. The well-known problem with barter is the lack of a general 'double coincidence of wants'. To deal with this problem, traders look for a convenient and frequently exchanged commodity to use in their exchanges with others. Once such usages become prominent, a circular process of institutional self-reinforcement takes place. Emerging to overcome the difficulties of barter, a money commodity is chosen because it is frequent and convenient, and it is all the more convenient and frequent because it is chosen. This circular, positive feedback leads to the emergence of the institution of money.

Menger argued that there is a basic division between institutions that emerge spontaneously and those that result from a process involving overall, deliberate design. Menger's discussion of money has been interpreted as an attempt to show how some institutions could emerge spontaneously from the interactions of individuals in an institution-free 'state of nature'. This type of explanation is evident in the 'new' institutional economics of Oliver Williamson (1975, 1985), Richard Posner (1973), Mancur Olson (1965) and many others. This type of work is concerned to show how spontaneous institutions can emerge, simply out of the interactions of individuals, each pursuing their given purposes and preferences. Andrew Schotter (1981, p. 5) went so far as to define 'economics as the study of how individual economic agents pursuing their own selfish ends evolve institutions as a means to satisfy them' (emphasis removed). The stress is on a 'bottom up' approach: given a set of interacting individuals, how do institutions emerge?

The value of all this work should not be denied. Substantial heuristic insights about the development of institutions and conventions have been gained on the basis of the assumption of given, rational individuals. But even in its own terms there are serious problems with this approach. Alexander Field (1979, 1981, 1984) has advanced a fundamental criticism. In attempting to explain the origin of social institutions, the new institutional economics always has to presume given individuals acting in a certain context. Along with the assumption of given individuals, is the supposition of given rules of behaviour governing their interaction. What is sometimes forgotten is that in the presumed 'state of nature' from which institutions are seen to have emerged, a number of weighty rules, institutions and cultural and social norms have already been (implicitly or explicitly) assumed. These original institutions, rules and norms are unavoidable; even in an unreal 'thought experiment' we can never properly envisage an original 'state of nature' without them.

For example, in attempting to explain the origin of institutions through game theory, Field pointed out that several constraints, norms and rules must inevitably be presumed at the start. There can be no games without constraints or rules, and thus game theory can never explain the elemental constraints or rules themselves. As Field (1984) argued, game theory may be used to explain the emergence of some institutions, but to do so it has to assume at the beginning a significant number of rules and constraints. Even in a sequence of repeated games, or of games about other (nested) games, at least one game or meta-game, with a structure and payoffs, must be assumed at the outset. Any such attempt to deal with history in terms of sequential or nested games is thus involved in a problem of infinite regress: even with games about games about games to the *n*th degree there is still one preceding game left to be explained.

As another illustrative example, Williamson (1975, p. 20; 1985, p. 143) wrote that 'in the beginning there were markets'. However, the market itself is an institution. The market involves social norms and customs, instituted exchange relations, and information networks that themselves have to be explained. All market and exchange relations involve complex rules and thus markets cannot be an institution-free 'beginning'. As Viktor Vanberg (1986, p. 75) put it: 'What we call a market is always a system of social interaction characterized by a specific *institutional framework*, that is, by a set of rules defining certain restrictions on the behavior of market participants.' Like others, Williamson failed to explain the evolution of the firm from an institution-free 'state of nature'. In a comparative-statics approach, he implicitly assumed one institutional framework and explicitly attempted to derive another. Accordingly, the project of starting simply from given individuals was implicitly abandoned.

Numerous critical studies have confirmed a similar defect. In the claimed 'methodological individualism' of Karl Popper (1945), 'the social phenomena have not really been eliminated; they have been swept under the carpet' (Lukes, 1973, pp. 121–2). Likewise, in neoclassical economics, claims to implement 'methodological individualism' in fact reveal hidden assumptions concerning social structures (Kincaid, 1997). Mario Bunge (1998, p. 80) argued that proclaimed attempts of methodological individualism often have 'a hidden holistic component'. Similarly, Kyriakos Kontopoulos (1993, p. 79) noted that 'a methodological individualist strategy necessarily incorporates references to social relations'. As these critics have showed, claimed methodological individualists never start from individuals alone.

The strict and narrow methodological individualist has a problem of potentially infinite regress: attempts to explain each emergent layer of institutions always rely on previous institutions and rules. According to the Mengerian research programme, these in turn have to be explained. Unless an institution-free state of nature can be discovered, the idea of explaining all institutions in terms of individual interactions alone faces an infinite chain of links to be revealed.

There is a particular and fundamental reason why the idea of explaining all institutions in terms of the interactions of individuals, starting from an institution-free state of nature, must be abandoned. This is because *all* individual interactions depend unavoidably on some – at least rudimentary – form of language. Language itself is an institution. Individuals rely on customs, norms, and the institution of language, in order to interact. Interpersonal communication, which is essential to all stories of institutional emergence, itself depends on linguistic and other rules and norms.[7] The institution-free state of nature is unattainable, in minimally adequate theory as well as in reality.

Individual choice requires a conceptual framework to make sense of the world. The reception of information by an individual requires a paradigm or cognitive frame to process and make sense of that information. The acquisition of this cognitive apparatus involves processes of socialization and education, involving extensive interaction with others (Cooley, 1902, 1922; Mead, 1934; Fleck, 1979; Burge, 1986; Douglas, 1986; Hodgson, 1988; Bogdan, 2000). As well as language, these interactions require other, preexisting institutions. The means and mechanisms of our understanding of the world are necessarily acquired through social interaction. Cognition is a social as well as an individual process. Individual choice is impossible without these institutions and interactions. We cannot understand the

---

7 Bovill (1958) noted that the Moors and Ashanti traded salt for gold without a verbal language, by placing their products on opposite banks of the river and withdrawing, taking the merchandise back if the other offer was not deemed to be satisfactory. Nevertheless, even in this case there was a form of communication with shared interpretations and meanings. Otherwise trade would not be possible.

world without concepts and we cannot communicate without some form of language.

What is being contested here is the possibility of using given individuals as the institution-free starting point in the explanation. The above arguments show that attempts to start simply from individuals must actually start from individuals plus institutions. The canons of narrow methodological individualism may be proclaimed, but they are not followed.

All theories must first build from elements which are taken as given. However, the particular problems identified here undermine any claim that the explanation of the emergence of institutions can start from some kind of institution-free ensemble of (rational) individuals in which there is supposedly no rule or institution to be explained. Consequently, the project to explain the emergence of institutions on the basis of given individuals runs into difficulties, particularly with regard to the conceptualization of the initial state of nature from which institutions are supposed to emerge (Hodgson, 1998a).

Overall, while methodological individualism is a popular mantra, in narrow terms it is never actually achieved. Explanations are never reduced to individuals alone. The advocates of this approach fail to carry out their own prescriptions.

A reformulated project would stress the evolution of institutions, in part from other institutions, rather than from a hypothetical, institution-free 'state of nature'. Notably, in recent years, a number of significant studies have developed in this direction. Accordingly, Jack Knight (1992) criticized much of the new institutionalist literature for neglecting the importance of distributional and power considerations in the emergence and development of institutions. Even more clearly, Masahiko Aoki (2001) identified the problem of infinite regress in much of the former literature and developed a novel approach. He not only took individuals as given, but also assumed a historically bestowed set of institutions. With these materials, he explored the evolution of further institutions. With these studies, the goal of narrow methodological individualism is abandoned. Some institutions are taken as given, rather than attempting to conflate their explanation upon the individual.[8]

---

8   This is what game theory essentially does. A payoff matrix is assumed that expresses *not only* individual preferences *but also* institutional circumstances, rules or constraints. The starting point in game theory always involves – and unavoidably so – *both* individuals and institutions. As Shubik (1982, p. 8) put it, in game theory 'the rules of the game include not only the move and information structure and the physical consequences of all decisions, but also the preference systems of all the players'. However, the treatment of institutional constraints as given challenges the widespread but unelaborated genuflections to 'methodological individualism'. From a post-Darwinian and institutionalist viewpoint, a crucial question concerns the causal explanation of the presumed individual payoffs and their individual and institutional underpinnings. That which is assumed by the game theorist must at some stage be explained.

In sum, attempts to conflate explanations of social phenomena upon the individual have generally failed, because some 'social' aspect of the individual is simply assumed and cannot conceivably be explained without reference to social relations or structures, or because it is admitted that individuals are moulded by social circumstances, or because the theorist never actually starts from individuals alone.

Methodological collectivism

Today, warnings of the dangers of methodological collectivism (sometimes called methodological holism) are relatively commonplace.[9] By reversing the aforementioned (narrow) definition of methodological individualism, methodological collectivism can be defined symmetrically as the notion that *all* individual intentions or behaviour should be explained entirely in terms of social, structural, cultural or institutional phenomena.[10]

As with methodological individualism, we are concerned with doctrines that might come close to this extreme case. Hence methodological collectivism may suggest versions of 'structural determinism', 'cultural determinism', 'economic determinism' and 'technological determinism'. The versions that are close to methodological collectivism see individual thought or behaviour as being determined largely by structural, cultural or technological factors. In turn 'structure', 'culture', 'economy' or 'technology' are often seen as having a powerful logic and dynamic of their own. Social, cultural or technological systems are seen to dominate any individual motives or behaviours. Such systems are upheld to have their own teleology. They act somehow upon individual actors, who are dragged in their wake.

Examples or hints of methodological collectivism are found in Marxism, in the sociology of Durkheim, in structuralist or functionalist sociology or anthropology, and even in some versions of postmodernism. For instance, structure is asked to accomplish most or all of the explanatory work in the structuralist anthropology of Claude Lévi-Strauss (1962) and in the

---

9 The first appearance of the term 'methodological collectivism' may be in Hayek's (1943, p. 42) critique of attempts to treat 'social phenomena not as something of which the human mind is a part'. But this, misleadingly, is primarily an ontological rather than a methodological statement.

10 Note that such terms are sometimes used in different ways. For instance, Dugger and Sherman (1994, p. 107) claim that 'institutionalism relies on methodological collectivism rather than on methodological individualism. Since institutionalism is a cultural science, the individual is seen as a product of culture.' However, they immediately go on to write: 'The individual is not a cultural marionette, because individuals can and do transform their culture through collective action and even through individual action.' This somewhat qualifies the former statement and implies that explanations *entirely* in terms of social phenomena such as culture would be generally inadequate. Hence Dugger and Sherman do not advocate methodological collectivism in the strict sense that I define it here.

functionalist sociology of Talcott Parsons (1937). The 'postmodernist' Jean-François Lyotard (1984, p. 15) wrote: 'A *self* does not amount to much.' The tendencies in such accounts are to downgrade the human subject and to see everything that is human as entirely derivative from society.[11]

If Marx is accused of being a methodological collectivist, then his defenders will point out in response that he acknowledged the role of the individual. Nevertheless, there are some highly misleading passages. For example, Marx wrote in 1845: 'But the human essence is no abstraction inherent in each single individual. In its reality it is the ensemble of the social relations' (Marx and Engels, 1976a, p. 4). The danger in this assertion is that the individual could be regarded as no more than an expression of social relations. Similarly, in a section of the *German Ideology* written at about the same time, Karl Marx and Frederick Engels (1976a, p. 59) wrote: 'The ruling ideas are nothing more than the ideal expressions of the dominant material relations'. The similar pitfall here is that ideas and volitions could be seen simply as expressions of the 'material relations' of the social structure. These problematic formulations are not confined to their early works. In the 1860s Marx (1976, p. 989) described how the actions of the capitalist are 'no more' than the manifestation of capitalist structures:

> The *functions* fulfilled by the capitalist are no more than the functions of capital ... executed *consciously* and *willingly*. The capitalist functions only as *personified* capital, capital as a person, just as the worker is no more than *labour* personified.[12]

A similar idea is repeated in the third volume of *Capital*. Marx (1981, pp. 1019–20, emphasis added) wrote:

> The principal agents of this mode of production itself, the capitalist and the wage-labourer, are as such *simply* embodiments and personifications of capital and wage-labour – specific social characters that the social production process stamps on individuals, products of these specific social relations of production.

The problem here is that explanations of individual agency seem to be conflated entirely upon 'material relations' and 'social structures', without recognition of individual diversity, cultural variation or discretionary possibilities. Although multiple interpretations of these passages are possible,

---

11 Elements of postmodernism that lead to a downgrading of the human subject are criticized at length in Archer (2000, pp. 18–50).

12 This Marxist view of the capitalist as severely constrained by capitalist structures is contested in Hodgson (1999a) where I propose greater consequential differences between capitalist institutions and national cultures. Capitalists have a significant zone of discretion and their behaviour is not entirely dominated by capitalist structures. Consequently, an infinite variety of different types and trajectories of capitalism are possible.

Marx did not do enough to guard against a methodological collectivist interpretation.

A related difficulty in Marx's writing is his divination of social or 'productive forces' that, at least in some accounts, seem to have powers over and above individuals. For example, in the famous Preface to *A Contribution to the Critique of Political Economy* of 1859, Marx (1971, p. 21) wrote that 'the material productive forces of society come into conflict with the existing relations of production'. Such phrases have suggested that Marx was underplaying the role of the individual and making largely mysterious and undetailed 'productive forces' do the entire work of explanation of social change. On the other hand, the formulation in the Preface does have its relatively sophisticated defenders (G. Cohen, 1978). Furthermore, Marx and Engels (1975, p. 93) wrote in 1845 that 'history is nothing but the activity of man pursuing his aims'. But this apparent rejection of ontological collectivism was not enough to prevent his work being interpreted in methodologically collectivist terms.

Some of Marx's followers were less circumspect. For example, Nicolai Bukharin (1969, p. 40) wrote in a Soviet Russian textbook of 1921 that: 'Social phenomena determine at any given moment the will of the various individuals.' Much later, in his structural determinist account of Marxism, Louis Althusser gave explanatory priority to structure, while downgrading the human subject. He wrote: 'The true "subjects" are ... the relations of production' (Althusser and Balibar, 1970, p. 180). There are many similar Marxist examples of such a conflation of the individual with social relations or structures.

Turning to Durkheim, he too was strongly influenced by Marx but he reacted against the 'materialist' aspects of Marx's thought. Against Marx's notion that economic or material factors somehow determined individual thought or action, Durkheim (1982, p. 247) wrote in 1908: 'In social life, everything consists of representations, ideas and sentiments'. But in 1897 Durkheim (1982, p. 171) also insisted that:

> We believe it is a fruitful idea that social life must be explained not by the conception of it formed by those who participate in it, but by the profound causes which escape their consciousness. We also think that these causes must be sought mainly in the way in which individuals associating together are formed in groups.

But this clearly created a problem for Durkheim.[13] First, the character of these profound causes is not clear. To be consistent with the 1908 statement, these causes must also be 'representations, ideas and sentiments' – possibly those shared within groups or widely dispersed among society.

---

13 The following discussion draws heavily on Lukes's excellent introduction to a translation of Durkheim's *Rules of Sociological Method* (Durkheim, 1982).

Durkheim failed to resolve this problem and took refuge in unelaborated metaphorical phrases, such as 'collective forces' and 'social currents'. Durkheim (1982, p. 59, emphasis removed) defined his basic concept of the 'social fact' in the following terms:

> The social fact is any way of acting, whether fixed or not, capable of exerting over the individual an external constraint ... which is general over the whole of a given society whilst having an existence of its own, independent of its individual manifestations.

But there is a big difference between seeing such emergent phenomena as independent of *any one* individual, or external to *all* individuals. The above quotation is ambiguous. Permitted by such ambiguities and aided by his social metaphors, Durkheim sometimes slid towards a methodological collectivism, where society and 'social forces' somehow stand above and manipulate all individuals.

Like Marxism, Durkheimian sociology lacks a developed micro-theory of how social structures affect, and are affected by, individual purposes or dispositions. Marx seemed to make psychology redundant, by declaring that the human essence was nothing more than the 'ensemble of the social relations'. More explicitly, Durkheim (1982, p. 129) banned psychology from social science with his famous declaration in 1901 that 'every time a social phenomenon is directly explained by a psychological phenomenon, we may rest assured that the explanation is false'. The consequences of such neglects or prohibitions are highly damaging for social theory.

In the absence of a theory of how society may lead to the reconstitution of individual preferences or purposes, a temptation is to explain individual action primarily by reference to the *constraints* imposed by the evolving social organism upon the individual. Institutional constraints have effects, but without necessarily changing individual inclinations. For Durkheim (1982, p. 144) 'social life presents itself to the individual under the form of constraint'. His concept of 'constraint' seems to include anything from legal rules and their sanctions to matters of mere convenience, communication or coordination.

With such a concept of social constraint, there is some notion of the power that social institutions can hold over the individual. However, Durkheim's concept of social power is itself incomplete. As Steven Lukes (1974) argues in a classic study, power itself has multiple dimensions. One possibility is that power may be exercised by 'coercion, influence, authority, force or manipulation' (Lukes, 1974, p. 17) but these mechanisms do not necessarily involve the alteration of individual preferences, purposes or values. For Lukes, the overemphasis on the coercive aspect of power ignores the way that it is often exercised more subtly, and often without overt conflict. Lukes (1974, p. 23) thus wrote:

To put the matter sharply, *A* may exercise power over *B* by getting him to do what he does not want to do, but he also exercises power over him by influencing, shaping or determining his very wants. Indeed, is it not the supreme exercise of power to get another or others to have the desires you want them to have – that is, to secure their compliance by controlling their thoughts and desires?

Consider an example. If a criminal desists from crime, simply because they fear the risk of apprehension and punishment, then behaviour is changed through the force of deterrence and potential constraint. On the other hand, if someone persuades the criminal that wrongdoing is evil, and that there are morally superior ways of earning a living, then the released criminal will desist from crime, even if the constraints and perceived penalties are ineffective. The preferences and purposes of the criminal would have been changed through persuasion.[14]

Both Durkheim and Marx lacked an adequate account of how individual dispositions are moulded. Such accounts must necessarily include psychological mechanisms. In their absence the temptation is to place the emphasis on social constraints, rather than on the additional reconstitution of individuals themselves. This emphasis on constraints diminishes and denudes the concept of social power, including the dimension of power where individual purposes and preferences may be changed.

Many social theorists have criticized methodological collectivism for making the individual the mere puppet of social forces. In addition, it is argued here that the main problem is that methodological collectivism not only diminishes the individual, but it also pays insufficient attention to the processes and mechanisms by which the individual is fundamentally altered. One consequence of conflating the individual into the structure is to lose sight, not simply of the individual, but also of the mechanisms of social power and influence that may help to reconstitute individual purposes or preferences. It may appear paradoxical, but only by rescuing the individual from its conflation into the social, can the social determination of individuality be fully appreciated.

Part of the solution is to bring psychology back into the picture. But strangely this is absent from much of social theory. There is very little psychology in Marxism, partly because the subject was so underdeveloped during Marx's time. Durkheim himself bears part of the responsibility for the exclusion of psychology from the main currents of twentieth-century sociology. The influential Talcott Parsons (1937) was persuaded partly by Durkheim in this and other respects. Instead of psychology, and in a

---

14 Alternatively, Stigler and Becker (1977) would argue that no change in the preference function took place. Instead the persuader simply revealed new information to the actor. However, Stigler and Becker assumed a (meta-)preference function that is capable of accommodating an immense number of contingencies, certainly exceeding the computational and memory storage capacities of any human brain.

manner highly reminiscent of Durkheim, Parsons emphasized the power of social norms.[15]

Some influential neoclassical economists also abandoned psychology at about the same time. Lionel Robbins (1932) recast economics as 'the science of choice'. Individual ends were taken as given, economics was to be all about the rational choice of appropriate means. Because individual preferences were taken as given, psychology no longer had a significant role in this reconstruction of the subject (Hodgson, 2001c).

After their common rejection of psychological and other underpinnings, economics and sociology went their separate ways. Proclamations of methodological individualism were more prominent in economics, and of methodological collectivism in sociology. The social sciences as a whole were characterized as an apparent dilemma between an Adam Smith-like and incentive-driven view of action, on the one hand, and a Durkheim-like and norm-propelled view, on the other. In one discipline there appeared the 'self-contained', 'under-socialized', 'atomistic' and 'asocial' individual; in the other the individual seemed sometimes to be the 'over-socialized' puppet of 'social forces'.

However, despite the century-long battle between methodological individualists and methodological collectivists, they have much more in common than is typically admitted. Methodological individualism conflates the social upon the individual, thus losing sight of key mechanisms of social influence, and is consequently impelled to take the purposes and preferences of the individual as given. Methodological collectivism conflates the individual upon society and thereby lacks an explanation or adequate recognition of how individual purposes or preferences may be changed. The explanatory moves are different but the results are similar in some vital respects: there is no adequate explanation of how social institutions may reconstitute individual purposes and preferences. Typically, both approaches disregard the value and role of psychology in the explanation of social phenomena. Both methodologies end up with a diminished concept of social power, and an analytical overemphasis on overt coercion and constraint, rather than more subtle mechanisms of social influence.

Accordingly, as long as the debate within social theory simply moves back and forth along the line between these two positions then it will be incapacitated by a failure to examine, and escape from, their common presuppositions. They are two mutually implicated poles of a misconceived and unsustainable dualism; they have both demonstrably failed to bring social theory out of its twentieth-century impasse.

---

15 See Hodgson (2001c) for an account of how Parsons was also partly persuaded in this respect by his teacher Ayres. The institutional economist Ayres is discussed later and at length in the present work.

Reductionism and reduction

Methodological individualism and methodological collectivism are both different versions of reductionism, by which is meant the more general doctrine that all aspects of a complex phenomenon should be completely explained in terms of one level, or type of unit. This is a strong definition of reductionism, involving a universal imperative of explanation. But it is not lacking in adherents, such as Elster (1983, pp. 20–4): 'Generally speaking, the scientific practice is to seek an explanation at a lower level than the explandum. ... The *search for micro-foundations* ... is in reality a pervasive and omnipresent feature of science.' A major theme of this book is to criticize the reductionist view that such outcomes are generally attainable and always necessary.[16]

The definition here of reductionism in terms of explanation should be distinguished from ontological and epistemological reductionisms. Ontological reductionism involves the claim that wholes are nothing but their parts (or vice versa). Epistemological reductionism claims that we know of the whole entirely by knowledge of the parts (or vice versa). Such doctrines exist (and are vulnerable to criticism) but they are different from the definition here of reductionism in terms of explanations of nature and origin. We can find many pronouncements of (explanatory) reductionism. Biological reductionism proposes that (social) phenomena should be explained solely in terms of biological characteristics. Physical reductionism requires that (biological, chemical or other) phenomena should be explained solely in terms of physical characteristics. Neurological reductionism proposes that psychic phenomena should be explained entirely in neurological terms. Methodological individualism pursues universal explanations of social phenomena in terms of individuals, and methodological collectivism the reverse.

Reductionism should also be distinguished from reduction. Emphatically, some degree of reduction to elemental units is inevitable and desirable in science. Even measurement is an act of reduction. Science cannot proceed without some dissection and some analysis of parts. However, although some reduction is unavoidable, complete analytical reductions are generally impossible. They are beset by analytical explosions in the number of combinations of elements; they are cursed by the ubiquitous phenomenon of complexity. Complete analytical reductions are rarely, if ever, achieved.

---

16 Several authors have incorrectly identified Quine (1951) as the origin of the term 'reductionism'. Earlier uses include Urban (1926, p. 110) – who wrote of the 'revolt of Emergent Evolution against reductionism' – as well as Werkmeister (1937), Alpert (1938) and several others. The term is used in several different ways, but here I follow the usage of the term in classic presentation of the reductionist case, in Oppenheim and Putnam (1968), who advocated a reductionism in which explanations of phenomena were derived successively from scientific laws at lower ontological levels. Agazzi (1991) provides a useful set of essays on reduction and reductionism in science. See also Dupré (1993).

The strong version of reductionism criticized here cannot be refuted in principle, because any explanatory deficit might sometime be remedied in the future. In no science are the canons of reductionism strictly enforced. Yet the sciences achieve results. Although we can never be sure that some-day a missing explanation will be found, and a further explanatory reduc-tion might be possible, there is sufficient evidence from the sciences to undermine the reductionist dogma and to diminish reductionist ambi-tions. While reduction is a worthwhile and important aim, the sciences do not need 100 per cent reductionism to qualify as science.[17]

Few reductionists acknowledge a fateful consequence of their own doc-trine. If reductionism were viable, and complete analytical reduction to lower levels were possible, then the result would not be methodological in-dividualism but the dissolution of all sciences except subatomic physics. Everything would have be brought down and explained in its terms. There would be no mechanics, no thermodynamics, no chemistry, no biology and no social science. All sciences would be reduced to one. The reason why we have different sciences is that complete explanatory reduction is generally beyond reach, and multiple levels of explanation are both appro-priate and powerful. It should now be clearly seen that reductionist ambi-tions are at best, wildly optimistic, and at worst, dogmatic and diversionary.

Central conflation

In the 1980s, largely as a result of the stimulating work of Anthony Giddens (1976, 1979, 1984), debates on the problem of agency and struc-ture were given a welcome impetus. Giddens's 'structuration theory' is an attempt to steer a middle course between structural determinism and func-tionalism, on the one hand, and voluntarist, individualist and subjectivist formulations, on the other. Its attraction is to propose an alternative to the extremes of both methodological individualism and methodological col-lectivism. Giddens countered the widespread belief that the only alterna-tive to methodological individualism is the slippery slope to methodological collectivism, or vice versa. He argued that social theory should focus exclusively neither on the social totality nor simply on the ex-periences or behaviours of individual actors. Instead, social theory should

---

17 Dennett's (1995, pp. 80–3) condemnation of the sin of 'greedy reductionism' is confusing because reductionism by its nature is gluttonous. All reductionism is greedy, as it desires beyond possibility and need. According to Dennett, those who are guilty of 'greedy reductionism ... underestimate the complexities, trying to skip whole layers or levels of theory in their rush to fasten everything securely and neatly to the foundation'. However, such persons are not simply guilty of the sin of greed, but also of haste and sloppiness. Dennett's rejection of 'greedy reductionism' is essentially a doomed attempt to cleanse reductionism of its reckless deviants and to retain respectable reductionist credentials. Symptomatically, Dennett does not admit that complete explanatory reductions are generally unattainable in science. He is thus charged by his own indictment.

take its starting point as 'recursive social practice' and consider the ways in which such practices are sustained through time and space.[18]

At the heart of his structuration theory is the notion of 'duality of structure'. For Giddens, the idea of a duality is contrasted with that of a dualism. The two elements of a dualism are regarded as mutually exclusive or separable (Dow, 1990). By contrast, in a duality the parts are interdependent: each element may actually help to constitute or sustain the other. Giddens regarded agent and structure as a duality: where both human subjects and social institutions are jointly constituted in and through recurrent practices, and where no element has ontological or analytical priority over the other. In Giddens's theory, structure and agency are mutually and symmetrically constitutive of each other.

In structuration theory, the idea of structure is tied up with ongoing processes and capabilities. Structure is less an objective thing: more a 'virtual order' of 'transformative relations'. In short, Giddens (1982, p. 35) saw structures as 'recursively organized rules and resources'. For Giddens, agency is both free and constrained. Human beings are reflective of, and reactive to, their circumstances, as well as being conditioned by them. Equally, instead of the prominent idea that the 'structural properties of society form constraining influences over action ... structuration theory is based on the proposition that structure is always both enabling and constraining' (Giddens, 1984, p. 169).

Social life is reproduced by drawing upon social structures, just as social structures are reproduced (intentionally or unintentionally) through the practices of social life. Structure refers to the 'structuring properties' that make it possible for similar social practices to endure in time and extend in space. Hence, in structuration theory, 'structure' is as much a verb as a noun.

In the idea of structuration, no stress is placed on the existence of different ontological or analytical levels. Instead, agent and structure are regarded as different aspects of the same process. As Ian Craib (1992, pp. 3–4) put it in his commentary on Giddens, structure and agency are not treated as 'separate and opposing things in the world or as mutually exclusive ways of thinking about the world' but as 'simply two sides of the same coin. If we look at social practices in one way, we can see actors and actions;

---

18 As well as Cooley (1902), who is discussed later below, in some respects there are also similarities with the work of Bourdieu (1990) and Elias (1991, 2000), who attempted to escape similar dichotomies. The concept of *habitus* in the works of Bourdieu (1990) and Elias (1991) has some similarities with Giddens's concept of routinization. Storper and Salais (1997) have tried to synthesize the approach of Giddens with that of Bourdieu. Elias, like Giddens, emphasized process, and the mutual reconstitution of individual and society. American authors including Boas, Cooley, Ellwood, James, G. H. Mead, Small and Sumner influenced Elias. When Elias (2000, p. 455) wrote: 'concepts such as "individual" and "society" do not relate to two objects separately but to two different yet inseparable aspects of the same human beings', he suggested a dual aspect formulation, similar to that of Cooley and Giddens. For simplicity, we focus solely on the work of Giddens in this section.

if we look at them in another way we can see structures.' In fact, there is little to stop Giddens's duality of agent and structure collapsing into the more special case of a 'dual aspect theory', where agent and structure become different facets of a unity. As noted later below, other versions of dual aspect theory appear in the sociologies of Charles Horton Cooley (1902) and in attempted solutions to the mind–body problem.

What is missing in Giddens's account? In contrast to structuration and dual aspect theory, several philosophers have proposed an ontology in which reality is irreducibly layered: successively with physical, molecular, organic, mental, human individual and social layers.[19] Everything belongs to a level and each level has, within bounds, some autonomy and stability. However, no level is disconnected from others: each layer is linked to, and dependent upon, other layers. Such a stratified ontology is essentially absent from structuration theory. The individual and the social levels are conflated into the central ground of the recursive structure.

Essentially, in stratified ontologies, what separates one layer from another is the existence of *emergent properties* at the higher level. Units exist at higher levels that are not mere epiphenomena of lower-level units. A viable and irreducible hierarchical ontology depends upon the notion of emergent properties. As related in later chapters, the concept of emergent properties was developed by the philosopher George Henry Lewes (1875), the psychologist and philosopher of biology Conway Lloyd Morgan (1923), and several others. A property may be said to be *emergent* if its existence and nature depend upon entities at a lower level, but the property is neither reducible to, nor predictable from, properties of entities found at the lower level.[20]

Significantly, in his conflationary strategy, Giddens makes no significant or explicit use of the idea of emergent properties. Indeed, in one passage he rejected such a concept by suggesting that 'human actors ... do not come together *ex nihilo* to form a new entity by fusion or association' (Giddens, 1984, p. 171). This denial creates a serious problem. Central to Giddens's structuration theory are notions such as self-reflexivity and consciousness. But if neural entities 'do not come together *ex nihilo* to form a new entity by fusion or association', then how can human consciousness or self-reflexivity be explained? Arguably, consciousness is an emergent property of interactions in the human neurosystem. We have to rely on emergent properties to sustain notions such as consciousness and self-reflexivity, which are central to structuration theory. Likewise, the existence

---

19 See, for example, Broad (1925), Sellars (1926), Bunge (1973a, 1973b) and Bhaskar (1975). Emergentist philosophy is discussed later in the present work.

20 The idea of emergent properties is similar in some respects to the concepts of 'creative synthesis' (Wundt, 1895; Ward, 1903; Sellars, 1918, 1922) and 'synergy' (Ward, 1903; Ansoff, 1965; Corning, 1983, 2000a). The origin of, and relation between, these three concepts is discussed in later chapters below.

of a social structure depends upon emergent properties; otherwise it would be reducible to the individuals involved.

Third, a consequence of Giddens's rejection of emergent properties is not only the rejection of a higher and social level of analysis with their own emergent properties, but also the analytical neglect of the natural and physical world as the essential substratum and context of human activity. The denial of emergent properties forces structuration theory to accept a *single* level of reality, with nothing (social or otherwise) 'above' it, and nothing (natural or otherwise) 'below'. One consequence of this is the denudation of the concept of social structure. Another is the neglect of the natural and biological substratum of all human activity.

If structuration theory accepts a singular plane of being, then where is it? Giddens is explicit about this. For him, 'structure exists ... only in its instantiations of such [social] practices and as memory traces orienting the conduct of knowledgeable human agents' (Giddens, 1984, p. 17). Symptomatically, the formulation is repeated elsewhere: 'Structure exists only as memory traces, the organic basis of human knowledgeability, and as instantiated in action' (Giddens, 1984, p. 377). And again, in another work, for Giddens (1989, p. 256), structure 'exists only in a virtual way, as memory traces and as the instantiation of rules in the situated activities of agents'. An agent carries 'structural properties' in its memory, which may be transmitted through practice from one agent to another. Commentators on Giddens's theory thus observe that 'if structures have a locus of existence, it is in the heads of social actors' (Craib, 1992, p. 42). Richard Kilminster (1991, p. 96) made a similar point: '"structure" in Giddens' theory is *internal* to actors'.

A problem with the idea that social structure is entirely mental and internal is that it downplays the fact that structure consists not merely of persons or things, but also of interactive relations between persons, in a social and material context. Hence questions such as 'where is social structure?' are essentially misconceived, as a relation between two individuals separated in space has no singular, meaningful location. A relation is real, but it is an association, not a singular entity. Individuals may confront these structures, even if they do not have the memories, ideas or habits that are associated with them. Newborn infants face a social structure, even if they have little understanding of it. Rebels and heretics confront a social structure, when failing to follow its rules or adopt its associated ideas.

Overall, for structuration theory, the single level of being is human knowledge and action. Structuration theory either takes structure as mental and internal to actors, or it has few defences to prevent such a conflation. The problem with this modern solipsist philosophy is much the same as that which troubled Bishop George Berkeley in the eighteenth century, who was also tempted to find reality inside the mind. Berkeley asked: if the world consists merely of our knowledge or perceptions, then how do we explain the *persistence* of objects when we do not apprehend them?

Berkeley's solution was that they endured through time in the perception of God.

Similarly, Giddens had to explain the persistence of social structures. He searched for a secular solution to this Berkeleyian puzzle. He found it in the centrality and persistence of routinized practice. Indeed, for Giddens (1984, p. 60), the 'concept of *routinization*, as grounded in practical consciousness, is vital to the theory of structuration. ... An examination of routinization ... provides the master key'. But the next question is how can the existence of routinization itself be explained? Giddens's (1984, p. 50) answer seems essentially to lie in his concept of 'ontological security'. This allegedly has its origins 'in basic anxiety-controlling mechanisms' that in turn are acquired by the individual as a result of 'predictable and caring routines established by parental figures'.

However, this argument is incomplete and has a strong functionalist flavour: the replication of routines is explained in terms of their function. The explanation for the persistence of routines is seen as the search for ontological security, which in turn results from the persistence of (parental) routines. However, no adequate explanation is given for the persistence of these 'caring routines established by parental figures'. These routines may be handed down from generation to generation, but why would this be so? No adequate explanation of the origin or persistence of routines is given, and Giddens's discussion of ontological security does not provide it.[21]

Despite these omissions, the stress on routinization in structuration theory has affinities with the 'evolutionary economics' of Richard Nelson and Sidney Winter (1982, 2002), which – redolent of the institutionalism of Veblen and Commons – also stresses routines. However, Giddens (1984, pp. 228–43) has been a critic of evolutionism in the social sciences and has rejected 'evolutionary' ideas in that domain.[22]

Related to Giddens's abandonment of evolutionary theory is his inadequate treatment of historical time. This defect has been identified by 'critical realists' Roy Bhaskar (1989) and Margaret Archer (1995). For Bhaskar and Archer, but not for Giddens, human agents and structures are not different aspects of the same things or processes, but *different entities*. Although structures, of course, contain individuals, and structure and agent

21 Another problem with Giddens's explanation in terms of 'ontological security' is that a highly stable ontology could have unstable, chaotic or unpredictable outcomes. Also routines themselves can have highly disruptive effects, for example when they are embodied in a military organization. What might matter most for the agent would be epistemological rather than ontological security.

22 In teleological and pre-Darwinian terms, Giddens (1979, p. 233) described evolution as 'social change as *the progressive emergence of traits that a particular type of society is presumed to have within itself from its inception*'. This epigenetic or 'unfolding' conception of evolution is non-Darwinian and very different from the evolutionary economics of Veblen (1899a, 1919a) or of Nelson and Winter (1982). These accounts see economic evolution as an ongoing, imperfect and non-teleological process of competitive selection, acting upon a varied population of institutions, habits, customs and routines. Evolution in this conception is not necessarily progressive, and is not vulnerable to Giddens's critique.

are interdependent, they are different and distinct. This separation of actor and structure stems from the fact that, for any particular actor, social structure always exists prior to her engagement with the world.[23] As Bhaskar (1989, p. 36) wrote:

> people do not create society. For it always pre-exists them and is a necessary condition for their activity. Rather, society must be regarded as an ensemble of structures, practices and conventions which individuals reproduce and transform, but which would not exist unless they did so. Society does not exist independently of human activity (the error of reification). But it is not the product of it (the error of voluntarism).

Hence any given individual is preceded by the social structures into which they are born. In recognizing the temporal priority of structure, Bhaskar and Archer took their cue from Marx. In 1852, Marx (1973, p. 146) wrote that: 'Men make their own history, but not ... under circumstances they themselves have chosen but under the given and inherited circumstances with which they are directly confronted.' Durkheim made a similar point at the beginning of the twentieth century. In his *Rules of Sociological Method*, Durkheim (1982, p. 51) pointed out that the social actor must learn pre-existing beliefs, laws, customs and so on: 'if they existed before he did, it follows that they exist outside him. The system of signs ... the monetary system ... the credit instruments ... practices ... all function independently of the use I make of them.' In a particularly useful study of social structure, Kyriakos Kontopoulos (1993, p. 211) similarly insisted that 'institutions are "always already there" and, thus, become the parameters of new actions and systems of interaction'.

It is in the work of Archer that the implications of the temporal priority of structure over the individual are drawn out most clearly. Following Marx, Durkheim and Bhaskar, Archer (1995, p. 72) wrote: 'This is the human condition, to be born into a social context (of language, beliefs and organization) which was not of our making.' She criticized Giddens's structuration theory as involving a 'central conflation' because it conflates structure and agency into processes acting together at a single level. Giddens's duality of structure wrongly treats structure and agency as not only mutually constitutive but also *conjoined*.

Archer thus exposed a major difficulty in structuration theory: it cannot incorporate historical time. Because it resists untying structure from

---

23 There was an earlier, insufficiently acknowledged but contrasting tradition in American philosophy describing itself as 'critical realism'. This is discussed in a later chapter below. See also Sellars (1908, 1916, 1922), Drake *et al.* (1920), Bode (1922), Moore (1922) and Werkmeister (1949). By 'critical realism' in the contemporary context I refer to the writings of Bhaskar (1975, 1989), Archer (1995, 2000) and others. C. Lawson (1994, 1996), T. Lawson (1997, 2002, 2003a, 2003b), Runde (1998) and others have applied insights from this perspective to economics.

action, it cannot recognize that structure and agency work on different time intervals. As individuals, we are born into a set of structures that are not of our making. Acting within them, they may be changed or sustained by our actions. We then bequeath them to others. However, Archer did not conflate individual into structure, giving the latter the sole burden of explanation. Indeed, the reproduction of social structure depends upon the actions of the individuals involved. She aimed for 'a theoretical approach which is capable of *linking* structure and agency rather than *sinking* one into the other' (Archer, 1995, p. 65).[24]

However, the differentiation of structure from agent is valid if structure is seen as external to any given individual, but not if it is regarded as external to *all* individuals. Structure does not exist apart from all individuals, but it may exist apart from any given individual. In some accounts – such as Durkheim's – this distinction is not always given sufficient stress. The danger, as a consequence, is that the concept of structure may be reified.

Non-conflation but incomplete explanation

In her alternative approach to social theory, Archer (1995, p. 91) proposed a 'morphogenetic cycle' involving first (a) a given structure, then (b) social interaction, then (c) structural elaboration or modification. The cycle then indefinitely repeats itself through these three phases. She criticized other approaches for downplaying particular phases of this cycle. For example, methodological individualism misses out the first step (a) and then moves simply from (b) to (c). In contrast to both methodological individualism and methodological collectivism, all three elements in the cycle are important.

To recapitulate: as acknowledged above, the work of Giddens was a major attempt to transcend the dichotomy between methodological individualism and methodological collectivism. However, Bhaskar and Archer criticized Giddens for conflating structure and agency. They developed an approach that likewise transcended the dichotomy between methodological individualism and methodological collectivism, but emphasized that structure and agency were different entities. Like Marx and Durkheim, it asserted that structures historically pre-exist each individual. Archer thus developed her 'morphogenetic' approach that moved cyclically, from

---

24 Archer (1995, 2000) also introduced the terms 'upwards conflation' and 'downwards conflation'. By 'upwards conflation' she meant accounts where 'structure is held to be the creature of agency' (Archer, 1995, p. 84) and by 'downwards conflation' she referred to theories where structural forces drive the system and 'agents are never admitted to touch the steering wheel' (Archer, 1985, p. 81). However, her terminology is ambiguous as the reverse choice of terms could apply. Devolving structural explanations down to the characteristics of individuals (methodological individualism) could just as well be described as 'downwards conflation', just as methodological collectivism could be described as 'upwards conflation'.

structure to social interaction, back to the (modified) structure. A process of structural evolution was suggested.

While the Archer–Bhaskar critical realist approach is an important advance, there are problems with it. In particular, while there is a general account of structural change, there is as yet no account of how individuals are changed. We are told how structures evolve, but there is no parallel explanation of the changes to individuals. In contrast to methodological collectivism, individual agency is rightly retained and emphasized. Bhaskar (1989, p. 80) and other critical realists have argued repeatedly that 'intentional human behaviour is caused' but 'it is always caused by reasons, and that it is only because it is caused by reasons that it is properly characterized as intentional'. But in critical realism there is no adequate explanation of the causes of reasons or beliefs. So far, the account of agency in critical realism is incomplete (Faulkner, 2002).

Bhaskar (1975, pp. 70–1) endorsed an 'ubiquity determinism', meaning that every event is caused. Yet critical realism has so far failed to apply this universal principle to individual reasons or beliefs. It recognizes rightly that beliefs are part of social reality, but does not give an account of the cultural, psychological or physiological causes of beliefs or reasons themselves. In critical realism there is a general explanation of structural change, but so far no equivalent explanation of how individual agents acquire or change their beliefs, reasons, purposes or preferences. The possibility of such changes may be admitted, but as yet there is no indication in critical realism of how such changes may be explained.

As a result of this omission, a temptation is to adopt a schema in which structure somehow channels individual activity with a sufficiency to explain it, thus putting the emphasis on the role of structures as constraints on individuals. Instead, what is required is an account of individual agency that includes an explanation of how structures can lead to fundamental changes in individual reasons, beliefs or purposes.

Critical realism rightly insists that structure and agency are different entities, but in making this disassociation, a partial and inadequate account is so far provided of their interaction. There is a general account of the causal connection from individuals to structures, but not one from structures to individuals, which shows how beliefs or reasons are formed or changed. That is why I characterize the position of Bhaskar (1989) and Archer (1995) as a case of non-conflation but incomplete explanation.

While critical realism has articulated an important critique of the work of Giddens, there is a gap in the theories of Bhaskar and Archer: there is no explanation, even in principle, of the evolution of reasons or beliefs. However, this limitation is not unique to critical realism: in social science as a whole, many other approaches share this defect.

For instance, a similar problem can also be found in the writings of Marx. There is no adequate explanation in Marxism of individual motivations. They are assumed to spring in broad and mysterious terms from the relations and forces of the system. A capitalist is said to act as a capitalist because he occupies a capitalist role within the social structure. A worker is said to act as a worker because she is obliged to take that social position. Explanations of individual action within Marxism characteristically devolve upon structure. Although Marx and Engels often rightly acknowledged that structures themselves are the result of human activity, they often describe how in a class-divided society people become prisoners of these structures. Within Marxism, the connection between social structure and individual action is made by the presumption of rational reflection upon their perceived interests acting under the constraints of social structures. Here too, structure bears the burden of the explanatory work. There is no explanation of how particular perceptions of interests and interpretations of situation may arise.

We require an explanation of how individual intentions or preferences may change. Without such an account, a danger is that structural constraints are called upon to do the main work of explaining human behaviour. As a result, the disconnection of agency and structure may end up explaining the individual solely by reference to structure, thus conflating the individual into the structure, as criticized above. In contrast, if there is a causal and psychological explanation of how structures can affect or mould individual purposes or preferences, then the role of the individual is placed alongside that of structure and becomes part of a more ample, two-way explanation. Such a spiral of causation from structure to individual, and from individual to structure, does not deny individuality; but it places the individual in their proper place within the ongoing process of social transformation.

However, while Marxism and critical realism have an inadequate explanation of individual motives, they are better than many other approaches in their recognition of the powerful role of social structures over individuals, while simultaneously attempting to retain a concept of agency. In many other cases there is an inferior explanation of structural powers and an equally inadequate explanation of individual transformations. Both methodological individualism and methodological collectivism come into this doubly defective category.

Also, much of mainstream economics has exhibited these twin failings. There are too few attempts to explain individual preference functions. Similarly, Austrian school economists take the purposes of individuals as given and do not regard their explanation as the task of economics or any other social science. As Hayek (1948, p. 67) wrote: 'If conscious action can be "explained", this is a task for psychology but not for economics ... or any other social science.' Like many others, Hayek shunned one of the central problems of social science – to explain human motivation.[25]

Likewise, methodologically collectivist attempts to explain individuals exclusively in terms of social structures also typically fail to provide an adequate account of human motivation. It is often simply assumed that roles or cultures or institutions affect individuals, without explaining how such social structures work their magic on individual motivations. Some have turned to behaviourist psychology, in the belief that its mechanisms of stimulus and response provide the answer. But behaviourism fails to address the inner springs of cognition and deliberation, overlooks the fact that beliefs are part of social reality, and makes the agent a puppet of its social environment.

Veblenian institutional economics relied on the non-behaviourist psychology of William James and others. The concepts of instinct and habit pointed to a fuller account of how individual motivations evolved. However, by the interwar period, instinct–habit psychology had become displaced by behaviourism. Behaviourists such as John B. Watson eschewed consciousness and intentionality as 'unscientific' concepts because they could not be observed directly. Veblen did not embrace behaviourism, but many other institutionalists, including Mitchell, adopted behaviourist psychology in the 1920s. Others, such as Commons, failed to develop any theory of human motivation. Frank Knight placed himself in an idiosyncratic minority by criticizing behaviourism while retaining many institutionalist ideas. For Knight, economics had to address both individual intentions and social institutions. In contrast, Clarence Ayres went with the flow of opinion, by embracing behaviourism and arguing that technology and institutions largely conditioned individuals. The initial, Veblenian, promise of a resolution to the problem was lost.

What is required is a framework within which the transformation of *both* individuals and structures can be explained. This approach must involve explanations of possible causal interaction and reconstitution, both from individual to structure and from structure to individual. This would mean an explanation of the evolution of individual purposes and beliefs, as well as an explanation of the evolution of structures. Preferences or purposes would be endogenously formed. Their co-evolution must be examined, without conflating one into the other. Such an evolutionary analysis provides the means by which social theory may escape from its unsustainable dichotomies and make further progress.

The development of social theory in the last quarter of the twentieth century has prepared the ground for the building of such an approach. In

---

25 While Hayek excluded the explanation of individual motivations simply as a consequence of disciplinary demarcation, von Mises excluded them on the grounds of perceived limits to explanation. Von Mises (1949, p. 16) argued that such phenomena as thoughts and feelings 'cannot be analyzed and traced back to other phenomena' and thus upheld an 'insurmountable methodological dualism'. However, even if thoughts and feelings defy explanation, as a result of the complexity of causes involved, this does not deny the fact that they are *caused*. Furthermore, in some cases, causes can be identified. For example, enduring personality traits may relate to experiences in childhood. In addition, we can partly explain particular mass political sentiments by economic or political events. For example, the rise of Nazism can be partly explained by the punitive reparations imposed after the First World War, plus subsequent unemployment and inflation.

particular, the transcendence of the old dichotomy between methodological individualism and methodological collectivism has created space for more sophisticated developments, including those mentioned above.

To bring evolution in, we have to learn from biology. But what we learn is not purely biological. Darwinian evolutionary theory points to a causal explanation of process, focusing both on causal links and changes at the microscopic level and their consequences in terms of transformations in structures, populations and species. This general Darwinian imperative of causal explanation requires that the evolution of individual purposes and beliefs must be explained as well as acknowledged. Ultimately, in principle, Darwinian evolutionary theory assumes no entity or characteristic as given. The emphasis is not on fixed units or relations but on the causal explanation of processes and transformations.

In particular, as elaborated in Chapter 4 below, Darwinism involves an ontological commitment to variation among members of a population. In regard to the social sciences, this 'population thinking' reinforces the premise that there is significant variation in personality and purposes between individuals, and that these variations matter in the explanation of social phenomena. Methodological individualists have long acknowledged this variation. Population thinking is another antidote to both methodological collectivism and any central conflation. But Darwinism does not sustain methodological individualism either. Not only does it insist that the individual has to be explained, but it also sustains higher levels of theorising and analysis above that of the individual.

However, the mere mention of biology will cause many social theorists to run for cover, or to reach for their guns. This prejudice among social theorists is a huge barrier to further advance. The next chapter is an attempt to forestall some likely misunderstandings and misconceptions.

3 Objections and explanations

Encouraged by superficial notions of evolution,
Which becomes, in the popular mind, a means of disowning the past.
                                        T. S. Eliot, 'The Dry Salvages' (1941)

While the promise appears of an evolutionary approach to the problem of structure and agency, there is continuing resistance to the intrusion of evolutionary or biological ideas in social theory. On the other hand, there is a minority of enthusiasts who seem to believe that biology can explain everything human. As Erkki Kilpinen (2000, p. 33) rightly remarks: 'Modern thought (post-modern, too, for that matter) tends to reduce action either to biology or to anything-but-biology: socio-biology and deconstructionism are today's Scylla and Charybdis.'

One extreme position is the notion that social and economic behaviour can be explained largely in terms of biological characteristics, such as genes. Such a sociobiological view is rejected here, for several reasons given in this book. Even in biological terms it is widely criticized. The other extreme position is that biology is largely irrelevant to the study of human society, and that social scientists may forever consider economies or societies as if they were separated from the ecosystem and the biotic world. This view is widespread among many sociologists and economists.

This book steers between these two extremes. Both extreme views neglect the interactions between humanity and nature; they constrain scientific enquiry by limiting investigation into the complex causal interactions between nature and human society. One view overrides the causal influence of the social environment. The other neglects that human beings, like other organisms, have evolved from other species, and that human capacities must be partly explained in evolutionary terms.

For much of the twentieth century, discussion by social scientists of biology or evolution was taboo. The horrifying, racist pseudo-biology of the Nazis helped to reinforce the academic view that biological ideas should be entirely separated from the social sciences. Consequently, since the

1920s, a large number of psychologists and social scientists have proclaimed that human behaviour is entirely a product of human culture or the social environment. But even if all relevant human behaviour could be explained entirely in cultural or environmental terms, this would not justify such a Berlin Wall between biology and the social sciences. There are many reasons for this, and we may consider just a few.

First, whether they are largely determined by nature or by nurture, human mental and physical capacities are bounded, and the explanation of their limits is a matter for the science of human evolution. Human beings are not infinitely malleable but rather special. An explanation of human abilities and limitations must involve an understanding of the human psyche, and how that has evolved.

Second, human beings interact with the ecosystem and other organisms. An understanding of how humans have evolved in interaction with their environment is not only an important topic for scientific enquiry in its own right, but also a vital means of preserving a sustainable ecosystem and limiting damage to the natural environment.

Third, science develops by the transfer of ideas and metaphors from one sphere to another. Just as the economist Thomas Robert Malthus inspired Charles Darwin, the social sciences can gain ideas and inspiration from biology. This does not mean that any or every idea in one sphere is useful in another. Neither does it mean that social and biological mechanisms are similar. The whole point about metaphors is that they are inexact. It simply means that some such ideas and metaphors can be inspirational, and for this reason the sciences should not be sealed off from one another.

Fourth, since the famous launch of sociobiology by Edward O. Wilson in 1975, a growing group of researchers have attempted to explain many human capacities and behaviours in evolutionary terms. This diverse and rapidly growing literature varies both in quality and in line of argument. Some researchers attempt to explain human and social phenomena entirely and crudely in terms of genes. This line of research neglects emergent properties and causal powers at the cultural and social level. Others see the evolution of human society partly in terms of units of information or 'memes' (Dawkins, 1976). This concept also has its problems, including a persistent vagueness concerning its meaning and its mechanisms of replication. Characteristically, these literatures have been impoverished by limited contact and conversation with social scientists. Fault lies on both sides. But by rejecting biology outright, many social theorists have been the more insular. Relatively few social scientists provide evidence that they understand much biology or evolutionary theory.

Partly as a result of inadequate dialogue from sociologists and social theorists, sociobiology has been led by amateurs in social theory. As interest in the interaction between the biotic and the social has grown outside mainstream social theory, we have seen the emergence of new extra-disciplinary research groups and networks, some of which claim no allegiance to sociobiology. There is a now almost an alternative social science, separate from the traditional disciplines of sociology and economics, and with little knowledge of its predecessors. As long as the more traditional social scientists remain with their heads in the sand, they will be ill equipped to deal with this emerging set of rival doctrines. Continuing insularity could mean both the impoverishment of the social sciences and the further development of erroneous or naïve versions of evolutionary social theory. To avoid these outcomes, it is essential that social theorists have an improved and less reactionary understanding of evolutionary theory, and that the new social evolutionists appreciate and understand the rich heritage of the social sciences.

It is appropriate at this point to address some additional misconceptions that have helped to divert social theorists from addressing some relevant insights from evolutionary theory. We confine ourselves to some prominent misconceptions and objections, with brief responses and counter-arguments. Later chapters of the present work will expand on some of these points.

Darwinism means neither optimization nor reductionism

Even in economics, where evolutionary ideas have become common, several misconceptions persist. The recent interest in evolutionary theories in economics derives largely from the works of Richard Nelson and Sidney Winter (1982), Kenneth Boulding (1981), Friedrich Hayek (1988) and a few others. There was a brief former flurry of interest in evolutionary themes, including works by Armen Alchian (1950) and Milton Friedman (1953). Still earlier, as discussed below in the present book, evolutionary ideas were found in economics in the 1880–1930 period.

We consider the interventions of Alchian and Friedman first, partly because they have been highly influential among mainstream economists. In different ways, both Alchian and Friedman used evolutionary theory to conflate explanations of economic processes onto one level of analysis. Alchian (1950) proposed that even if firms never actually attempted to maximize profits, 'evolutionary' processes of selection would ensure the survival of the more profitable enterprises. Friedman (1953) amended this, by seeing 'natural selection' as grounds for assuming that agents act 'as if' they maximize, whether or not they consciously do so. Both of these arguments have been subjected to detailed criticism. They rely on an overly simplistic concept of competition and fail to demonstrate that some kind of optimal behaviour does indeed result.[1]

---

1   E. Penrose (1952) pointed out that Alchian implausibly assumed that firms cannot know the conditions of survival but economists can. Friedman's evolutionary argument was criticized in Winter (1964), Boyd and Richerson (1980), Schaffer (1989), Hodgson (1994, 1999b) and Dutta and Radner (1999).

It is a serious misconception to see evolution as always leading to either static or optimal outcomes (Veblen, 1899a; Hodgson, 1993; Cohen and Stewart, 1994; J. Potts, 2000). Such results occur under restricted conditions only. In an open system, equilibria are always temporary. Some contrasting outcomes involve positive feedbacks and are highly sensitive to initial conditions. Possibly suboptimal phenomena such as lock-in and path dependence are now widely acknowledged.[2]

More generally, evolution does not drive towards some goal or destination. Instead it carries the baggage of its past, in a typically haphazard, ongoing process of adaptation and selection. It is important to dispense with all mistaken notions of evolution as an optimizing, goal-driven or necessarily progressive process. Darwin (1871, vol. 1, pp. 166–77) himself emphasized: 'we are apt to look at progress as the normal rule in human society; but history refutes this. ... We must remember that progress is no invariable rule.'

But that is not the only prominent misconception. In addition, many social scientists react to the mention of 'evolution' or 'Darwinism' as an indication that the explanation of social phenomena is about to proceed in purely biological terms. They mistake these labels as inevitable indicators of an unavoidable biological reductionism in which social phenomena – from social culture to economic performance – are purportedly explained largely in terms of human genes.

In fact, there is an ongoing discussion within biology itself as to the possibility of other additional units and levels of selection. Charles Darwin (1859, pp. 235–42) himself explained that sterile insects (such as worker ants) had evolved because integrated family communities (with sterile and non-sterile members) had themselves become whole units of selection. Concerning human society, Darwin (1859, pp. 422–3; 1871, vol. 1, pp. 59–61, 106) argued that natural selection operates upon the elements of language as well as on individuals. Darwin (1871, vol. 1, p. 166) also proposed that tribal groups with moral and other propensities that served the common good would be favoured by natural selection. Darwin seemed to endorse a version of group selection, and perhaps hinted at the natural selection of institutions, as well as the natural selection of individuals. Several modern biologists have argued that evolutionary selection occurs at higher levels: not simply on genes, but on individuals, groups and even species. Darwinian anthropologists such as Robert Boyd and Peter Richerson (1985) and William Durham (1991) have developed a two-level theory where there is transmission at the level of both culture and the genes.

Even Richard Dawkins, who attained fame with his hymn to genetic reductionism in *The Selfish Gene* (1976), proposed an additional level of

2 Gould (1980), David (1985, 1994, 2001), Dosi *et al.* (1988), Arthur (1989, 1994), North (1990), Hodgson (1993), H. P. Young (1996).

selection in the last chapter of this work, with his idea of a cultural 'meme'. It is difficult to propose cultural 'memes' and remain a genetic reductionist, because that would require an explanatory reduction of all memes to genes. Despite his genetic reductionist starting point, Dawkins was driven by the logic of his own argument to adopt multiple-level selection theory (Hull, 1980, 1981). Dawkins (1983, p. 422) thus wrote: 'It is also arguable that today selection operates on several levels, for instance the levels of the gene and the species or lineage, and perhaps some unit of cultural transmission.'[3]

Given that evolutionary selection can operate at the group and cultural levels, the invocation of evolutionary ideas in social science does not imply that explanations of social phenomena have to be, or can be, reduced to properties and changes at the level of the genes. There are other possible units of replication. Units such as habits, routines, customs and institutions themselves endure through time and replicate by imitation, even if their features are not sustained with the same fidelity as the coding in the DNA. There is variation even between similar units of these types, and the selection environment favours the survival of some over others. Emergent properties and causal relations at higher levels imply that the analysis of these higher-level selection processes cannot be explained entirely in terms of lower-level units. The processes and time-scales involved at higher levels may be so different from those at lower levels that much of the explanation of higher-level phenomena must be in higher-level terms.

Later chapters of this book will examine further the application of Darwinian principles to social theory. Several authors over the last 150 years have proposed that Darwinian evolution takes place within society, not simply metaphorically, analogically, or by extension of lower-level phenomena. Darwinian evolution literally takes place at the level of society itself, operating on social as well as biological units. The necessary conditions for Darwinian social evolution include the existence of varied replicating entities, and some differences in their capacities to survive in any given situation. These replicating entities might include social rules or routines. If Darwinian social evolution were shown to work at this level, it would not require the invocation of biological reductionism. Such a notion of replication on multiple levels permits accounts of social evolution involving social rather than biological elements. Darwin's theory implies neither global optimization nor biological reductionism (Hodgson, 1993; Khalil, 1997).

A wide variety of views have been gathered under the term 'Darwinism', including reactionary doctrines described as 'Social Darwinism' and

---

3 Multiple levels of evolution have also been considered by Lewontin (1970), Arnold and Fristrup (1982), Brandon and Burian (1984), Eldredge (1985), L. Buss (1987), Goertzel (1992), Depew and Weber (1995), Maynard Smith and Szathmáry (1995, 1999), Brandon (1996), Sober and Wilson (1998), L. Keller (1999), Kerr and Godfrey-Smith (2002) and Henrich (2004).

the genetic reductionism of today. It must be emphasized that the use of the term Darwinism here should not be taken to imply any of these things. The term 'Darwinian' is used here to describe the general and causal theory of evolution, involving variation, inheritance and selection, which is at the centre of the classic works by Darwin (1859, 1871). More details of the Darwinian theoretical core will be elaborated at a later stage.

The limits of sociobiology

As sociology has lost its consensus over core presuppositions, some sociologists have established formerly alien doctrines such as methodological individualism and individual utility maximization (Coleman, 1990). Strong antibodies would have repulsed these invaders in the 1940–80 period. But the crisis of modern sociology is so severe that doctrines as alien as biological reductionism have now established themselves within. The lure of reductionism is such that several economists (Becker, 1976; Hirshleifer, 1977, 1985; Tullock, 1979; Robson, 2001a, 2001b, 2002), and even some modern sociologists, have proposed that much human behaviour can be explained in terms of our genetic inheritance.

Joseph Lopreato and Timothy Crippen (1999) diagnose the crisis in modern sociology and creditably propose an injection of Darwinism. However, their recommendations come too close to a form of biological reductionism. Lopreato and Crippen (1999, p. 77) propose at some '*ultimate level*' that: 'Organisms tend to behave in ways that maximize their inclusive fitness.' But they ignore the work of Darwinian cultural evolutionists from Veblen (1899a, 1919a) to Boyd and Richerson (1985) who argue that when cultural transmission enters the picture such maximization of genetic fitness will typically be diverted or overlaid by other factors. Even if humans 'ultimately' behave in ways that maximize their inclusive genetic fitness, this tells us very little about variations in human behaviour, between different cultures or across short periods of time. It tells us something concerning survival, sexuality and reproduction, where some of the strongest instinctive pressures have evolved. Some very broad conclusions may be drawn concerning gender and family relations.[4]

But an infinite number of feasible social structures – and patterns of mating and childcare – could ensure the reproduction of the human species. Social theory is concerned with the explanations of differences within the broader set of possibilities. Furthermore, inclusive fitness theory tells us less about non-familial social structures, particularly those that have emerged only in the last few thousand years, and have not been subject to the same type or longevity of evolutionary selection pressure as those where sex and human reproduction are paramount. Human societies vary

---

4   See the extensive evidence cited in Lopreato and Crippen (1999).

culturally and institutionally through time and space. The lonely hour of 'ultimate' genetic determination never comes.

The leading sociobiologist Edward O. Wilson (1978, p. 167) declared:

> Can the cultural evolution of higher ethical values gain a direction and momentum of its own and completely replace genetic evolution? I think not. The genes hold culture on a leash.

What is wrong with this statement? No matter how much we may (rightly) insist that cultural evolution is (extremely) important, it would be absurd to suggest that it can 'completely replace genetic evolution'. The final sentence is more problematic. If it means that culture is determined by the genes and can be explained largely in terms of the genes, then it is false. But Wilson himself admitted that the leash is 'very long' (1978, p. 167). It is more appropriate to point out in response to Wilson that analysis at the genetic level is chronically limited as a basis for explaining detailed human behaviour. Wilson bypasses the task of explaining many varied actual and possible behaviours that lie within the ample limits of genetic restraint. The laws of gravity also hold culture and behaviour on a leash, but it would be absurd to conclude from this truism that we can largely explain human behaviour with the laws of physics. Human genetic constraints were established long ago in our evolution. While knowledge of these constraints is important, and they do tell us something about human behavioural dispositions and possibilities, on their own they explain little of our culture or behaviour in a modern complex society.

Wilson (1978, p. 153) admitted that human 'social evolution is obviously more cultural than genetic'. This is why his sociobiology is at best of highly limited use for social science. The task of social science is to explain particular behaviours or phenomena within the very wide zone provided by genetic and physical constraints. Social science examines further constraints and causal mechanisms, which themselves cannot be reduced solely to biological terms. The genes help to form the substrata of human nature. But they do not constitute human nature as a whole. Our genes tell us something of our fundamental human nature, as presented at our birth, but they tell us nothing of the specific and varied cultural contexts in which vital human dispositions are channelled and formed. In particular, through processes of socialization and learning, we develop a cognitive structure by which to interpret and respond to the data received by our senses. The initial basis of this structure is genetic, but subsequent neural development is much a result of our interactive experiences in a social and natural context. It is a major task of the social scientist to understand the implications of the cultural processes of socialization and learning for human behaviour and potential.

We have to pay much more attention to levels of replication or selection above that of the gene. Human genetic evolution has taken place in a human cultural environment. *One consequence is that social selection can often override the pressures of genetic selection.* For example, the European physiognomy is much less suited than that of Aborignines to the Australian climate. European Australians suffer a much higher rate of skin cancer, for example. Yet European-type institutions dominate the continent. These institutions have been selected despite the unsuitedness of some European genes. The genetic advantage of the Aborigines in relation to the natural environment has been overridden by selection at the institutional level. The importance of additional levels of selection above that of the gene means that genes cannot tell the whole story.

These additional levels of replication or selection at the social level are not trivial. Taking Darwinism seriously at the cultural and institutional level means much more than 'memes' such as catch-phrases or pop songs. If there are replicators of information in the social domain, then they will be structured entities, acknowledging the structural and institutional nature of knowledge itself (Langlois, 2001). Darwinism at the social level involves the selection of different types of institutional structures, upon which the survival or prosperity of nations or populations (along with their genes) can sometimes depend. Evolution at the social level involves social relations and structures, and more than mere information of a social kind.

Wilson's highly limited concept of culture is symptomatic of the kind of problem that has appeared when biologists have entered the social domain, but with insufficient appreciation of social theory. For Wilson (1978, p. 78) 'cultural change is the statistical product of the separate behavioural responses of large numbers of human beings'. On the contrary, culture is not merely the average and variance of individual characteristics; it is also a system involving structured, interactive relationships between individuals. Consequently, culture is not reducible to the statistical properties of a mere aggregate of individuals; culture involves relations between individuals and emergent properties that are not reducible to individuals alone. That is what gives rise to higher levels of selection, above genes and the individual. Just as our genes loosely affect cultural possibilities, our culture has had an effect on our genetic endowment (Boyd and Richerson, 1985; Durham, 1991).

For much of the twentieth century, sociology rightly emphasized culture but wrongly ignored its biological and genetic limits and preconditions. At the other extreme, a small minority of social scientists have surrendered to sociobiology. In both cases, a careful articulation of the interactive relationship between the cultural and genetic aspects of humanity has been lacking. At both extremes, an adequate discourse on emergent properties and ontological levels has been absent. A major purpose of this book is to outline the achievements of Veblenian institutionalists, evolutionary theorists and emergentist philosophers in establishing a multiple-level evolutionary theory, where both social culture and human instincts are acknowledged.

Biology is not a means of legitimating universal market competition. Markets themselves are neither the universal solution to the problem of scarcity nor the exclusive domain of human competition (Hodgson, 2001c). Furthermore, competition itself is not universal in the biological sphere (Kropotkin, 1902; Lewontin, 1978; Augros and Stanciu, 1987; Sober and Wilson, 1998). Also some psychologists see evolution as a challenge to some versions of individual rationality (Cosmides and Tooby, 1994a, 1994b; Plotkin, 1994, 1997; Cummins and Allen, 1998).

While some social scientists relapse into reductionism, many sociologists resist any suggestion that the social sciences can learn from biology. They have been trained to believe that biology and psychology simply cannot be used to help explain social phenomena. Some will follow Durkheim (1982, pp. 32–3) in his *Rules of Sociological Method* of 1901 and 'separate the psychological domain from the social one' while separating the social from the biological as well. Many will react against past abuses of biology in social theory – when it has been called upon to support nationalism, imperialism, racism and sexism – and draw the mistaken conclusion that all biological explanations and metaphors have thus to be cast out of the discipline. They will ignore the fact that no reputable theory in biology gives any support whatsoever to any form of discrimination. Neither can we reasonably conclude from biology that our genes largely determine our fate. Even genetic reductionism has to admit that the social environment is an important determining factor, including in individual development.

The general resistance of sociologists to biology is both unjustified and deleterious. As a handful of authors have suggested, part of the disabling crisis of modern sociology is its inability to overcome its own compartmentalization from biology and other sciences. Instead of the language of compartmentalization and rejection, the pressing task is to give psychology and biology some appropriate and limited explanatory scope, restricted by the recognition of emergent properties at the social level, and enhanced by a revived and inclusive framework of social theory.[5]

Is self-organization an alternative to Darwinian evolution?

John Foster (1997) and Ulrich Witt (1997) have proposed that the theory of self-organization provides a basis for evolutionary thinking in economics.

---

5 Van den Berghe (1990), Halton (1995) and Lopreato and Crippen (1999) have addressed this crisis in sociological thought. Modern sociologists who have embraced evolutionary or even Darwinian ideas include Blute (1979, 1997), Runciman (1989, 1998), Kontopoulos (1993), Aldrich (1999) and Chattoe (2002). In particular, Hirst and Woolley (1982), Lenski and Lenski (1987) and Maryanski and Turner (1992) have argued that sociological studies should also take account of the physical environment and the biological inheritance of human beings. Influential organizational studies such as McKelvey (1982), G. Carroll (1984), Hannan and Freeman (1989), Singh (1990) and Hannan and Carroll (1992) have also been inspired by evolutionary biology.

Foster took the more extreme position, to argue that self-organization is a superior alternative to any 'biological analogy'. Foster (1997, p. 444) wrote:

> Once we abandon biological analogy in favour of an economic self-organization approach ... then we are no longer interested in the microscopic details of selection mechanisms, but in the endogenous tendency for acquired knowledge and skills to interact to create increases in economic organization and complexity.

Foster has alluded to modern versions of such an approach, as in the works of Ilya Prigogine and Isabelle Stengers (1984), Daniel Brooks and E. O. Wiley (1988), David Depew and Bruce Weber (1995), Stuart Kauffman (1993, 1995), Weber and Depew (1996), Weber *et al.* (1989) and Jeffrey Wicken (1987).

Clearly, several of the above authors were critical of some presentations of Darwinian theory. For example, Depew and Weber (1995) noted the changing agendas and shifting emphases of Darwinian enquiry over the years. Others like Brooks and Wiley (1988), B. Weber *et al.* (1989) and Wicken (1987) were keen to generalize evolutionary explanations and integrate insights from thermodynamics such as the entropy law. Kauffman (1993) made a powerful argument that natural selection alone cannot explain the origin of complex organisms. Systems involving non-linear interactions involve a large number of possible states, most of which would have little survival value. Kauffman argued that processes of self-organization channel systems into more restrictive possibilities, some of which can have evolutionary benefits.

However, in contrast to Foster (1997), none of these modern authors cited above saw his argument as an alternative to Darwinian theory. Wicken (1987) wrote of 'extending the Darwinian paradigm', not exterminating it. Depew and Weber (1995) considered 'Darwinism evolving', not Darwinism abandoned. Weber and Depew (1996, p. 51) wrote:

> the very concept of natural selection should be reconceived in terms that bring out its dynamical relationships with chance and self-organization. In our view, Kauffman's recent work, as expressed in *The Origins of Order*, does just this.

Note here that what is involved is a revision of natural selection theory, not its negation. Kauffman (1995, p. 8) himself called for a 'revision of the Darwinian worldview' not its abandonment. As Kauffman (1993, p. 644) also related:

> I have tried to take steps toward characterizing the interaction of selection and self-organization. ... Evolution is not just 'chance caught on

the wing'. It is not just a tinkering of the ad hoc, of bricolage, of contraption. It is emergent order honored and honed by selection.

The last sentence is worthy of reflection and emphasis. Kauffman did not conceive of his theory as an alternative to Darwinism (R. Lewin, 1992, pp. 42–3). On the contrary, once self-organized systems and subsystems emerge, natural selection does its work by sorting the more adapted from the less. Kauffman explained this in detail. Natural selection acts upon these self-organized structures once they emerge. Far from being an alternative to natural selection, self-organization requires it: in order to determine which self-organized units have survival value. As Gary Cziko (1995, p. 323) argued:

> the laws of physics acting on nonliving entities can lead to spontaneous complexity, but nothing in these laws can guarantee *adapted* complexity of the type seen in living organisms … Of all the complex systems and structures that may self-organize due to the forces of nature, there can be no assurance that all or any of them will be of use for the survival and reproduction of living organisms.

In a sense, Witt (1997, p. 489) was correct in his assertion that self-organization 'provides an abstract, general description of evolutionary processes' but natural selection is no less abstract, nor less general. Indeed, self-organization involves an ontogenetic evolutionary process, in that it addresses the development of a particular organism or structure. (In biology, ontogeny refers to the growth and development of single organisms, where the genetic material is given.) This does not rule out the possibility that ontogeny can also involve the natural selection of entities *within* the organism. For example, the growth of many organisms involves the natural selection of immunities, neural patterns and (often beneficial) bacteria in their gut (Edelman, 1987; Plotkin, 1994). Likewise, the growth of a firm may involve the internal selection of habits or routines (Nelson and Winter, 1982). Hence some descriptions of self-organizing processes involve some (phylogenetic) selection of constituent components of the emerging structure.

However, accounts of self-organization or ontogeny do not *necessarily* involve selection or phylogeny. By definition, phylogeny means the existence and evolution of a whole population, within which selection occurs. Hence natural selection is *always* phylogenetic as well as ontogenetic, in that it addresses the evolution of whole populations of organisms or structures, as well as the development of individual organisms. In general, ontogeny *may* incorporate phylogeny but does not necessarily do so (consider the examples in the preceding paragraph); but phylogeny *always* incorporates ontogeny.

Furthermore, from the point of view of the overall evolutionary process, complete evolutionary descriptions require a phylogenetic account of the selection of ontogenetically developing units. Hence while self-organization is important (and perhaps essential), it cannot provide a *complete* evolutionary description. This must involve phylogeny as well as ontogeny. If we are confined to ontogeny then our description of the overall evolutionary process is incomplete; it does not address the differential survival and fecundity of different (self-organized) structures or organisms. Consequently, self-organization may be an important part of evolution and ontogenetic development, but it cannot replace natural selection.

Self-organization theorists have shown how complex structures can emerge without design, but these structures are themselves subject to evolutionary selection. Some will survive longer and be more influential than others: selection will operate. We have every reason to see these issues as relevant to economic evolution. Conscious choices, competitive pressures, market forces or environmental constraints operate on technologies, institutions, regions and even whole economies. All of these contain self-organized structures, but this neither precludes nor demotes the role of evolutionary selection.

Yngve Ramstad (1994) also argued that biological analogies are inappropriate for economics. One of his reasons is based on the argument of John R. Commons that institutional evolution involves 'artificial' rather than 'natural' selection. This is critically discussed in Chapter 13 below, where it is established that artificial and natural selection are not mutually exclusive, and the former always relies on the latter; so we do not have to deal with this objection here.

The Lamarckian confusion

Many social scientists have described social evolution as 'Lamarckian'.[6] In fact, the relationship between Darwinism and Lamarckism is more complicated than many have assumed. One of the most important ideas in 'Lamarckism' – although it pre-dates the 1809 work of Jean-Baptiste de Lamarck by centuries – is the admission of the possibility of the inheritance of acquired characters. This idea was popularized by Lamarck and influentially endorsed by Auguste Comte and Herbert Spencer. The nineteenth-century Darwinians did not rule out the possibility of the inheritance of acquired characters. Even in the first edition of *Origin of Species*, Darwin (1859, pp. 82, 137, 209) himself endorsed this idea. Darwin never denied a

---

6 Among those that have made the claim that social evolution is Lamarckian are Popper (1972a), Hirshleifer (1977), Gould (1980), Simon (1981), McKelvey (1982), Medawar (1982), Nelson and Winter (1982), Gray (1984), Boyd and Richerson (1985), Hayek (1988), C. Freeman (1992), Metcalfe (1993) and Hodgson (1993). However, Boyd and Richerson (1985), Metcalfe (1998) and Hodgson (2001b) uphold that social evolution is *both* Darwinian and Lamarckian.

limited role for the inheritance of acquired characters and in his later life he gave it increasing rather than decreasing attention and approval. Hence Lamarckism (in this sense) and Darwin's doctrine are not necessarily mutually exclusive. We now know that the possibility of the inheritance of acquired characters is non-existent (or highly limited) at the level of genetic evolution. In contrast, it has been argued by many that acquired characters can be passed on and inherited in the social domain.[7]

Just as there are differences between Keynesianism and the doctrines of Keynes, and Marxism and the ideas of Marx, we must draw a distinction between Lamarckism and Lamarck's own views. Lamarck (like Darwin) was a philosophical materialist and saw intention or volition as rooted in material causes (Boesiger, 1974; Lamarck, 1984). Hence Lamarck did not see will or purpose as ultimate drivers of evolution. It was not Lamarck himself but later 'Lamarckians' that made unexplained will or purpose so central to a depiction of evolutionary change.[8]

But Lamarck and the Lamarckians had something important in common: they all believed in the inheritance of acquired characters. Hence there are grounds to define Lamarckism primarily in terms of the inheritance of acquired characters. Three working definitions of Darwinism, Lamarckism and Weismannism (or neo-Darwinism) are suggested in Table 3.1.

Two internal problems with the Lamarckian theory of the inheritance of acquired characters – even in the social sphere – are that we further require

Table 3.1   Definitions of Darwinism, Lamarckism and Weismannism

Term	Definition
Darwinism	A causal theory of evolution in complex or organic systems, involving the inheritance of genotypic instructions by individual units, a variation of genotypes, and a process of selection of the consequent phenotypes according to their fitness in their environment.[9]
Lamarckism	A doctrine admitting the possibility of the (genotypic) inheritance of acquired (phenotypic) characters by individual organisms in evolutionary processes.
Weismannism (or neo-Darwinism)	A doctrine denying the possibility of the (genotypic) inheritance of acquired (phenotypic) characters by individual organisms in evolutionary processes.

7   The idea that Lamarck's theory necessarily involves organisms willing their own adaptations probably originally emanates from a 1830 caricature of Lamarck's views by G. Cuvier (R. Richards, 1987, p. 63). It does not derive from Lamarck himself (Burkhardt, 1984, pp. xxx–xxxi).

8   The genotype is the genetic coding of an organism. The phenotype is the organism's behavioural propensities and manifest attributes. The phenotype is an outcome of the genotype and the organism's environment.

9   But even this proposition should be treated with extreme care. A problem is defining what we mean by a 'characteristic' in the social domain and what is to be treated, by contrast, as analogous to the gene (Hull, 1982; Hodgson, 2001b; Knudsen, 2001).

an explanation of (a) what inhibits or prevents injuries or other disadvantageous acquired characters from being inherited, and (b) why organisms seek to adapt to their environment. Lamarckism simply assumes that only advantageous acquired characters will be inherited. In addition, some Lamarckians presume a voluntarism of will, but the origin of this will itself remains unexplained. A causal explanation of why organisms strive for advantage or improvement is lacking.

As Richard Dawkins (1983, 1986), Helena Cronin (1991), Henry Plotkin (1994) and others have pointed out, these gaping holes in Lamarckian theory have to be filled by a Darwinian or other explanation. Darwinian natural selection helps to explain how advantageous characters are favoured. Organisms seek to adapt to their environment in terms of the production of variations of genotype, leading to different behaviours, some of which involve successful adaptations. Upon these varieties, natural selection does its work. Even if acquired characters were inherited, natural selection would be required to ensure that the advantageous rather than the disadvantageous characters were passed on. Even if it is valid, then Lamarckism requires Darwinism as an explanatory crutch.

Insofar as organisms are purposeful, this capacity too has evolved through natural selection. Darwinism thus points to an evolutionary explanation of the very origin of will or purpose itself. Hence overall, Darwinism is a more general and powerful theory than Lamarckism. If social theory can be legitimately described as Lamarckism, in the sense of admitting the possibility of inheritance of acquired characters, then this Lamarckism must be nested within a Darwinian theory (Hodgson, 2001b; Knudsen, 2001).

Accordingly, Lamarckism is not an alternative to Darwinism, even in the social sphere. It is erroneous to see them as rivals because Lamarckism depends on Darwinian natural selection to complete its explanations. Even if we can talk of acquired characters being inherited in the social domain – and this idea itself is far from straightforward (Hull, 1982; Hodgson 2001b) – then this does not undermine the greater explanatory importance of Darwin's theory.

Darwinism does not exclude intentionality

Another frequent objection to the use of these ideas in social science is that Darwinian evolution is 'blind' and ignores the conscious intentions and plans of human individuals. Because intentionality is a vital concept for the social sciences, this may seem the most important objection, and thereby its rebuttal is vital. Famously, in response to Alchian (1950), Edith Penrose (1952) argued that Darwinian theories of evolution excluded the deliberative and calculative behaviour that was characteristic of human action in the economic sphere. However, this hard-and-fast distinction between humans and other organisms is difficult to reconcile with the fact that humans evolved gradually from other species. If conscious intentions are unique to humans, then when and how in evolutionary time were these cognitive privileges bestowed upon humanity? To avoid a religious or mystical answer, we have to assume that these cognitive attributes themselves evolved through time, and existed to some degree in pre-human species.

A crucial point emerges here. It is part and parcel of Darwin's underlying philosophy that all intention has itself to be explained by a causal process. This causal explanation has to show how the capacity to form intentions has itself gradually evolved in the human species, and also how individual intentions are formed in the psyche. For Darwin, natural selection is part of these causal explanations. There can be no first and 'uncaused cause'. However, the fact that intentions are somehow caused or determined does not mean that human agency is any less substantial or real (Vromen, 2001). Human intentions are part of social reality and social interactions involve human expectations concerning the intentions of others. None of these points is undermined by the recognition that intentions themselves are caused.

From a Darwinian philosophical perspective, all outcomes have to be explained in a linked causal process. There is no teleology or goal in nature. Everything must submit to a causal explanation in scientific terms. In his prescient essay on the impact of Darwinism on philosophy, John Dewey (1910a, p. 15) wrote: 'Interest shifts ... from an intelligence that shaped things once for all to the particular intelligences which things are even now shaping'. Instead of God creating everything, the Darwinian focus is on how everything, including human intelligence and intentionality, was created through evolution. Intentionality is still active and meaningful, but it too has evolved over millions of years. Likewise, in their textbook on biological evolution, Theodosius Dobzhansky *et al.* (1977, pp. 95–6) wrote:

> Purposefulness, or teleology, does not exist in nonliving nature. It is universal in the living world. ... The origin of organic adaptedness, or internal teleology, is a fundamental, if not the most fundamental problem of biology. There are essentially two alternative approaches to this problem. One is explicitly or implicitly vitalistic. ... However, ... this is a pseudo-explanation; it simply takes for granted what is to be explained. The alternative approach is to regard teleology as a product of evolution by natural selection.

As Daniel Dennett (1995, p. 205) reported, Darwin turned the traditional doctrine of intentionality upside-down: 'intentionality doesn't come from on high; it percolates from below, from the initially mindless and pointless algorithmic processes that gradually acquire meaning and intelligence as they develop'.

Accordingly, Penrose (1952) and others were wrong to suggest that Darwinian theories of evolution necessarily excluded deliberative and calculative behaviour.[10] On the contrary, in the social context, deliberation and selection coexist. Furthermore, as Darwin insisted, intentions, calculations and preferences have themselves to be explained by the methods of science. Darwinism invokes both a theory of natural selection and a universal commitment to causal explanations. This brings us right back to the aforementioned central lacuna in modern social theory – the widespread and enduring failure to provide an adequate causal explanation of human intentionality and human motives.

It might be objected that there is more to human purposefulness than goal-driven behaviour. After all, ants and robots are purposeful in that sense. A key point about social interactions is that we gauge and impute the intentions of others, in order to understand and anticipate their behaviour. Social action is intersubjective and reflexive. It is very much about meanings, interpretations of meaning, and imputations of meaning to the behaviour of others. Regrettably, some enthusiasts of Darwinism have overlooked these issues. But there is nothing in Darwinism that rules out their inclusion. On the contrary, if interpretations of meaning and intention are causally efficacious, then there is a Darwinian imperative to understand their role. Furthermore, the capacities to think, interact and interpret have themselves evolved and must also be understood in evolutionary terms (Bogdan, 1997, 2000).

Some theorists of social evolution believe that the 'Lamarckian' is preferable to the 'Darwinian' label because the former preserves human intentionality. There is a deep irony here, because Lamarck himself, as noted above, was a philosophical materialist and saw human will as formed by material causes. No version of 'Lamarckism' offers an escape from the need to provide a causal explanation of intentionality.

Not only is there nothing in Darwinism that excludes or undermines the reality of human purposes and intentions, but also Darwinism itself, as explained in later chapters, promoted an emergentist tradition in philosophy that underlined the status and reality of human intentionality. In contrast, many so-called 'Lamarckians' broke from the materialism of Lamarck and proposed an unsustainable dualist ontological position where intentions arose mysteriously from the mind, themselves being incapable of causal explanation.

It might be objected that the explanation of human motives denies the reality of choice. This will be discussed further below. At this stage it is pointed out that causal determination of choices does not imply an absence of the subjective awareness of choice. Neither does it imply that choice is

---

10 In conversations with the present author before her death in 1996, Penrose had revised her opinion. She was deeply fascinated with evolutionary explanations of human consciousness, and did not take human deliberation as given or for granted.

unreal. Very small causal influences can have big effects and can thus cause the individual to act otherwise. Finally, the notion that choice or any other phenomenon is uncaused is unacceptable, for reasons explored later.

It is not being argued here that every theory or explanation in the social sciences has to include an explanation of all the motives or preferences of the individuals involved. No theory can explain everything. For some purposes and in some circumstances, it can be legitimate to take the purposes or preferences of the individuals involved as given. All theories involve abstractions. In some cases it can be legitimate to abstract from the influences on, and changes in, individual preferences and purposes. In which case, human intentions become the elemental forces in the particular theoretical explanation. But even in this case, the assumptions concerning human intentions should be consistent with what we know about human evolution and individual development. Furthermore, the use of a simplifying assumption in one theory does not rule out the need for another theory to explain those elements that are taken as constant or given. Intentions and preferences still have to be explained at some stage. Explanations of human motives should use resources from biology, psychology and anthropology, as well as from other social sciences.

The ambiguous bogeys of mechanism and determinism

Some social scientists may object that the argument here is 'mechanistic' or 'deterministic'. The social sciences are satiated with rebuttals of 'mechanistic' and 'deterministic' doctrines, but these words are themselves rarely and poorly defined. Others, in contrast, enthusiastically take up the idea that human beings are 'mere machines', as a warrant for their version of scientific enquiry. Their opponents see such 'mere machines' statements as sufficient condemnation of the approaches involved. Yet rarely is the 'mere machines' idea clarified and explored further. Both enthusiasts and critics fail to adequately define their terms.

Consider the words of Richard Dawkins (1976, pp. x, 2, 21–5), who described humans as 'survival machines', 'machines created by our genes' or 'robot vehicles blindly programmed' to preserve their genes. These phrases are designed to shock. But all shock and explanatory value is lost when it is realized that Dawkins did not explain adequately what he meant by a machine. He would admit that humans have consciousness and purpose, but provided minimal exploration of the meaning of these terms. Yet he also repeatedly ascribed 'ruthless' will and purposefulness to the 'selfish gene'. Dawkins denuded the human individual of purposefulness, but only by repeatedly ascribing intentionality to the genes. For him, genes are purposeful but humans are mere machines. But he failed to explain the difference. A consequence is that the concept of intentionality is undermined. With both enthusiasts and opponents of 'mechanistic' doctrines, rhetoric triumphs over substance.

Among those social scientists that emphasize consciousness and choice, things are only slightly better. Economists typically make a song and dance about choice. But only the maverick economists reflect upon its substance and definition (Shackle, 1961, 1976; Buchanan, 1969; Loasby, 1976; T. Lawson, 1997). Sociologists write of human agency and self-reflection, but the underlying presuppositions are inadequately explored.

To proceed further, some definitions must be attempted. A provisional definition of a 'mechanism' is a structure involving causal connections but lacking an adequate capacity for self-reflection and intentionality. A minimal feature of intentionality is the capacity to prefigure a goal in conscious thought. Leaving further important questions on one side, it is already clear, with this rough definition of a mechanism, that the Darwinian theoretical approach embraced here is not mechanistic. This is because Darwinism does not deny intentionality, at least in the sense of the existence of consciousness and prefiguration. Darwinism simply asserts that human intentionality is itself caused, and in turn it requires some causal explanation.

In contrast, despite its verbal emphasis on 'choice', much of mainstream economics is mechanistic in the sense of lacking adequate notions of human self-reflection, intelligence, intentionality or will. This is because human agents are often modelled as automata, with limited cognitive or learning capacities, reacting crudely to stimuli from their environment that are somehow unambiguous. Furthermore, some mainstream economists claim that the same basic model of human agency, based on utility maximization, also applies to lower organisms, including 'honeybees, ants and schooling fish' (Landa, 1999, p. 95), or even bacteria (Tullock, 1994). This simply confirms the observation that the degree of intelligence and self-reflection found in human beings is not encompassed by a standard and allegedly ubiquitous utility function. To overcome the limitations of 'mechanistic' models of human agency, significant attention must be given to factors such as the number and complexity of stimuli, cognitive processes, interpretative ambiguity, and so on (Bandura, 1986; Hodgson, 1988; Simon *et al.*, 1992; Witt, 2000; Loasby, 2001; Vanberg, 2002).

Other writers see the term mechanistic as denoting something very different, such as an emphasis on quantitative rather than qualitative factors of change. Again, the approach adopted in the present work is not mechanistic, even in this alternative sense. Both qualitative as well as quantitative changes are emphasized here. Still other writers associate 'mechanistic' with an atomistic ontology, in which entities are said to possess qualities independently of their relations with other entities. Others use the term 'mechanistic' to describe systems whose functional specification denies variation or diversity in the functional parameters. But again, the approach adopted here is not mechanistic in any of these senses.

The Darwinian ideas that every event is caused, and that even human motivations have to be subjected to causal explanation, will provoke in some quarters the accusation of 'determinism'. This too is misleading and at least in some senses mistaken. The very word 'determinism' connotes a confusing multiplicity of meanings. Essentially, there are at least three different versions of 'determinism', as briefly described below.

1 **Predictability Determinism.** Determinism is sometimes defined as the epistemological doctrine that 'any event can be rationally predicted, with any desired degree of precision, if we are given a sufficiently precise description of past events, together with all the laws of nature' (Popper, 1982, pp. 1–2).
2 **Regularity Determinism.** A different definition of determinism is the notion that any given set of circumstances and state of the world must lead to a *unique* outcome: 'given A, B must occur' (Blanshard, 1958, p. 20). Regularity determinism involves a denial of randomness and chance in the universe. This is an ontological rather than an epistemological notion: it says nothing about what we may be able to know or predict.
3 **The Principle of Determinacy.** Another definition of determinism is the notion that *every event has a cause* (Urmston, 1989). This is again an ontological statement about the world, otherwise known in philosophy as 'the principle of universal causation' or 'ubiquity determinism'. As Mario Bunge (1959, p. 26) put it, the 'principle of determinacy' means: 'Everything is determined in accordance with laws by something else'.

These crucial differences require that the ambiguous word 'determinism' be defined whenever it is used. The principle of determinacy is central to Darwinism and is adopted here.[11] But the other two versions are rejected. There is nothing in Darwinism that involves any commitment to the first two versions of determinism. Furthermore, these three versions of determinism are logically independent: one does not flow from the other. Predictability determinism – the dream of Laplace – is itself countered by the realization of analytical and computational limits in the face of complexity, and even of the limits of mathematics itself (Gödel's Proof), and more recently by theories of computability, chaos and complexity. There are nonlinear systems with such a high degree of sensitivity to initial conditions that no amount of accurate measurement of the appropriate parameter values can provide a sufficiently accurate prediction (the Butterfly Effect). Predictability in the human domain is also confounded by the logical problem of predicting future knowledge or creativity. If prediction led us to

---

11 Note the difference with Hodgson (1993) where I was equivocal over the adoption of the principle of determinacy. I was then needlessly worried that this principle might be incompatible with free will and genuine choice. Bunge (1959), Bhaskar (1975), Earman (1986) and Auyang (1998) have rightly argued that predictability determinism is quite different from the principle of determinacy.

know future knowledge, then it would be present knowledge, not knowledge confined to the future (Popper, 1960, 1982).

The principle of determinacy does not mean that the future is inevitable, at least in the sense of unavoidable. As Dennett (2003) pointed out, knowledge of causal determination enhances rather than diminishes the possibility of avoiding an outcome. Determinacy does not mean inevitability.

The principle of determinacy does not rule out the possibility of statistical determination, where effects are stochastic but with regular statistical properties. Statistical laws are still laws. If outcomes were statistically determined, and statistical determination was not merely apparent but real, then the second proposition – regularity determinism – would strictly and generally be false. But the third proposition would not be undermined.

Even if determination is not statistical but links one set of causes with one set of effects, then there are still objections to regularity determinism. Roy Bhaskar (1975) rightly rejected regularity determinism on the grounds that it would work only if it were confined to a closed system, and most systems are in fact open. The possibility of exogenous disturbances undermines regularity determinism in specific systems.

Would regularity determinism apply to the universe as a whole? Given that the universe is interconnected and systems are open, the regularity 'given A, B must occur' could not be specified A corresponded to a complete description of all the possible influences on B, from throughout the universe. In practice, the statement 'given A, B must occur' will itself be indescribable in its massive scope and complexity. Strictly, with unlimited interconnectedness, the 'given A, B must occur' statement will only pertain if A is a complete description of the state of the universe. The idea of regularity determinism cannot apply to any limited description of the world, and complete descriptions are unattainable. Consequently, even if regularity determinism applied to the universe as a whole, it would offer little epistemological guidance for science.

Having rejected or disabled the first two versions of determinism, the (third) principle of determinacy is retained. Indeed, it is a necessary foundation for science. A theological definition of a miracle is something that happens without a scientifically explicable cause. If science admits the possibility of an event without a cause, then it has abandoned its own mission. We can retain a broad view of the nature of science, but the quest for meaning and explanation is indispensable to any version of the scientific enterprise. Of course, we cannot prove the unfeasibility of an uncaused cause. In general, proofs of causality, or of its absence, are impossible. But science is nevertheless obliged to search for causal explanations, and determinacy must thus be assumed. In many circumstances, prediction will be impossible. Nevertheless, the quest for some kind of causal explanation must remain. To behold a first and uncaused cause is to issue licence at that point to abandon the quest.

Darwinism is thus incompatible with the idea of George Shackle (1976) that human intentionality is an 'uncaused cause'. A problem with Shackle's position is that it involves an investigatory closure. Once we affirm an 'uncaused cause' we say that science should explain this much, but no more. We may move so far down the causal chain, but no further. We arrive at a causal and explanatory roadblock, policed by the adherents of the 'uncaused cause'. Admittedly, all ontological commitments involve dogma in the sense that they cannot be directly verified by experience. But the principle of determinacy is preferable to the 'uncaused cause' in that it does not place dogmatic bounds on the scope of scientific enquiry and explanation. The preferable ontological commitment is one that rules out miracles and denies any no-go zones for science. The roadblock must be opened, even if the road ahead is treacherous and complex.[12]

How can a first and 'uncaused cause' be compatible with the recognition that other outcomes are caused? How is this special causal void to be explained? Is it ubiquitous to nature, or does it lurk merely in a mammalian neural system? Or is it unique to humans? How can evolution explain its sudden appearance?

The uncaused cause is sometimes defended as the requirement of real choice. If our choices are determined, how could we have acted otherwise? Choice may be seen to lack substance if there was no alternative. But crucially, two situations of choice are never identical in all details. Even if two situations are very similar, we could act differently because of slight influences with sufficiently magnified effects. For instance, the very fact that we are reflecting upon the possibility of 'acting otherwise' may be sufficient for us to make a different choice. A multiplicity of conflicting causal influences acts upon our decisions, with complex feedbacks and interactions. In some cases, our own deliberations can have big effects. Complexity, emergence and sensitivity can make choice real, despite the fact that it is determined.

Dewey (1894, pp. 338–9) notably responded to the proposition of an uncaused ego with the insistence that 'it becomes necessary to find a cause for this preference of one alternative over the other'. He continued: 'when I am told that freedom consists in the ability of an independent ego to choose between alternatives, and that the reference to the *ego* meets the scientific demand with reference to the principle of causation, I feel as if I were being gratuitously fooled with'. For Dewey, in full Darwinian spirit, the need for causal explanation could not be abandoned.

Some authors argue that if our will is determined then we can hardly be held responsible for our choices and our actions. It is alleged that as a result

---

12 My own position has changed on this issue. Hodgson (1993) failed to decisively reject the notion of an uncaused cause. However, I also noted that chaos theory suggests that even if the world is deterministic, it may appear as entirely spontaneous and free. I now believe that the admission of the possibility of an uncaused cause is not only unnecessary but also untenable, for the reasons given here.

of such 'determinism' there can be no basis for morality or law. Two brief responses are appropriate here. First, if our will is determined, then moral pressure and legal sanctions still can have an effect on our actions. Consequently, there is no ground for abandoning morality or law. Second, even if, on the contrary, our will was an 'uncaused cause', then we would be no more responsible for the capricious and spontaneous processes that led to our actions. The 'uncaused cause' adds nothing extra to the importance of morality or law. They are important in any case.

For example, a philosophically minded murderer might claim that his decision to pull the trigger of his gun was caused by events beyond his control. Another might claim that her intention to murder appeared spontaneously (or uncaused) in her mind. The first murderer is just as responsible for the murder as the second. In both cases the prosecution would argue that the (caused or uncaused) inclination to kill should have been resisted by the murderer, so that the murder did not take place. The principle of determinacy does not diminish the burden of individual responsibility.[13]

The position adopted here does not rule out some notions of novelty, nor even of 'free will'. A number of philosophers – including the Greek scholastics, David Hume and Jean-Paul Sartre – have argued that an idea of free will is compatible with the principle of determinacy. In philosophy, this position is known as 'compatibilism'. It upholds that even if our choices are determined then that does not rule out the reality of the process of choice. It is beyond the scope of this work to establish the possibility of compatibilism. I simply note that the Darwinian position stated here admits ground for the 'compatibilist' argument that 'choice' and 'free will' can be reconciled with the proposition that every event is determined. The human will is a real cause, but it is a proximate rather than an ultimate cause (Mayr, 1982).[14]

If novelty simply refers to unpredicted outcomes then we have no difficulty admitting such possibilities, even if every event is caused. We now know from chaos theory that even if every event is determined, the world is still often unpredictable. Randomness and apparent indeterminacy remain. Novelty may be caused, but it will often appear as entirely spontaneous and free. Prior causes always exist, but the complexity of the system may make them especially difficult to identify. In open, complex, non-linear systems all sorts of novelties are possible. What are ruled out of the picture are novel effects that do not themselves obey actual scientific laws.[15]

---

13 For a discussion of related ethical themes, in the context of Darwinism, see J. Richards (2000).
14 On compatibilism see Sterba and Kourany (1981), Dennett (1984), Honderich (1993) and Vromen (2001).
15 On the compatibility of novelty with the principle of determinacy see Bunge (1959, ch. 8). Vromen (2001) rightly argues that evolutionary theory cannot be rejected on the grounds that it fails to predict novelty. If novelty involves unpredictability then it is unpredictable by *any* theory.

A note on causation

Aristotle identified four types of causality: the formal, material, efficient and final. His notion of 'cause' was somewhat broader than the modern meaning. It included assertions of the origin, nature, form and material constitution of a phenomenon. In much modern usage, a narrower sense of the word is invoked: causes are always taken to mean the specific factors leading to an effect. As Jochen Runde (1998, p. 154) put it: 'a cause of an event [includes] anything that contributes, or makes a difference, to the re-alization of that event in one or more of its aspects'.

Within this narrower and more dynamic meaning of 'cause', two of Ar-istotle's categories remain: 'efficient' and 'final' causality. Efficient causal-ity is similar to the concept of causality in the modern natural sciences. The word 'efficient' here does not necessarily refer to an optimal (or any other particular type of) outcome. It simply means capable of having an effect. Final causality, or 'sufficient reason', is teleological in character: it is di-rected by an intention, purpose or aim. Hence, within this narrower notion of a cause, Aristotle promoted a causal dualism. Much later, René Des-cartes retained a similar division, with his dualistic separation of physical matter from the independent, volitional and supposedly immaterial hu-man soul.[16]

This distinction persists in modern thought, where the natural sciences embrace descriptions of cause and effect involving matter and energy, and the social sciences find their causal fuel in human intentions, purposes or beliefs. The compartmentalization of the natural from the social sciences encourages a form of dualism with two different conceptions of cause.[17]

Here the attempt at reconciliation proceeds in materialist terms. The modern natural sciences admit no cause that does not involve the rearrangement or transformation of physical matter or energy. We may call this the 'materialist condition of causality'.[18] According to this view, all causes involve movements of matter and transfers of energy or momen-tum, as a necessary but not sufficient condition of it being a cause.

16 See Bunge (1980) and Stich (1983, 1996).
17 Mainstream sociology has typically taken it for granted, or even by definition, that 'action' is motivated by reasons based on beliefs. Others have criticized the adoption of such a 'folk psychology' that explains human action wholly in these terms. The critics point out that such explanations are a mere gloss on a much more complex neurophysiological reality. These dualistic and 'mind-first' explanations of human behaviour are unable to explain adequately such phenomena as sleep, memory, learning, mental illness, or the effects of chemicals or drugs on our perceptions or actions (Bunge, 1980; Stich, 1983; P. M. Churchland, 1984, 1989; P. S. Churchland, 1986; A. Rosenberg, 1995, 1998; Kilpinen, 2000).
18 Aristotle's concept of 'material cause' was quite different. It referred to the material make-up of an object as part of the explanation of its nature. There is a striking lack of consensus, even among philosophically inclined social scientists, over the terms involved here. An alternative to imposing the 'materialist condition of causality' would be to use Aristotle's phrase 'efficient causality'. But the intention here is to escape from the Aristotelian causal framework. Furthermore, 'efficient' can easily be misunderstood, especially by economists.

In philosophy, the precise definition and logical form of a causal statement is highly complex and still unresolved (Sosa and Tooley, 1993; Salmon, 1998). The 'materialist' condition imposed here, however, is to some degree independent of this philosophical debate. Although, at least at the social level, we cannot understand causality completely in terms of identifiable material relations, all relevant causal relations involve movements of matter and transfers of energy or momentum. In physics and elsewhere, causes are not fully understood, but all causes satisfy this materialist condition of matter–energy transfer.

Intentions can satisfy the materialist condition of causality if intentions are understood as involving transfers of matter or energy, including at the neural level. Indeed, any action or communication involves movements of matter and transfers of energy or momentum. Notwithstanding the fact that they are caused, intentions themselves are causes. Intentions are real but do not require an entirely different kind of causality. The causes and effects of intentions have to be explained, in terms that include the important role of mental prefiguration and judgement. They are special causal mechanisms but not an entirely separate (teleological) fundamental type of cause.

The fact that the sciences are still saddled – well over two millennia after Aristotle – with more than one version of causality, is rarely a subject for discussion. The wall between the natural and the social sciences has averted us from this question. Yet when dialogue does occur between the biologist and the social scientist then the problem emerges.

The development of quantum physics – particularly in the so-called Copenhagen interpretation – has sometimes prompted a rejection of causal explanation in the terms outlined here. However, statistical determination, as expressed in probabilities, does not imply the absence of a cause. Charles Sanders Peirce gave the name 'tychism' to the doctrine of the probabilistic nature of causation. However, even if outcomes are stochastic, statistical determination is still involved. Statistical determination or tychism does not mean indeterminacy. Quantum physics does not necessarily lead to an abandonment of some standard principles of causal determination (Bunge, 1959).

Quantum physics may be consistent with a non-statistical version of causal determination. We may not be able to offer precise predictions of the motion of subatomic particles simply because of our ignorance of all the causes that bear upon them. As Bertold Brecht had a character explain in his play *Me-Ti*: 'Their movements are difficult to predict, or cannot be predicted, only because there are too many determinations, not because there are none.' The same may be true of the subatomic quanta. Albert Einstein and others were concerned about the abandonment of strict causation by the quantum physicist for some form of stochasticity, and remarked that he could not believe 'in a God who plays dice'. Einstein retained faith 'in complete law and order'. Consequently, Einstein *et al.* (1935) argued that explanations of quantum phenomena had to be completed by the addition of 'hidden variables' (Salmon, 1998). This issue remains controversial in physics (Cushing, 1994).

Determined, non-linear systems can simulate stochastic behaviour. Ian Stewart (1989) has thus conjectured that chaos theory can thereby bridge the gulf between the apparent randomness of the quanta and the operation of causal laws. The throw of a die leads to apparently random effects, but that does not rule out the outcome being a unique result of a specific combination of prior circumstances and events. Similarly, random number generators in computers use multiplication and numerical truncation to generate a series of (pseudo-)random numbers. Apparent stochastic behaviour may be an aggregate outcome of non-probabilistic causal processes operating at lower, micro levels.

However, for the purposes of this book, no ruling is necessary, or will be made, over the admissibility or otherwise of statistical or stochastic determination. The minimum core ontological position maintained and defended here involves the principle of determinacy or universal causation (proposition three above), and a commitment to a singular overall type of materialist causality that can connect diverse domains. The principle of statistical determination is ruled neither out nor in. The rise of chaos and complexity theory, has given a recent fillip to Einstein's proposition that strict rather than statistical determination is everywhere at work. But it is not necessary to take a position on this here.

Forward to the past

The previous chapter pointed to an evolutionary approach, in which the transformation of agents as well as structures is explained. The case is made that this approach should be Darwinian, in that social phenomena are also subject to principles of variation, replication and selection. This evolutionary and Darwinian approach to social theory recognizes emergent properties in the social domain and does not attempt to explain the social in entirely biological terms. It does not see evolution as an optimizing or teleological process. Evolution occurs on multiple levels, including the social as well as the biological. It emphatically includes human intentionality but sees its emergence as subject to a causal and evolutionary explanation. Human agency is a cause, but it is a cause in turn that has to be explained. Darwinism involves more than variation, replication and selection – it invokes an unrelenting search for causal explanations.

Remarkably, such an approach to social theory was partly developed in the 1890s, particularly in the United States, but also drawing on publications from Germany, Britain and France. The works of a connected group of British thinkers including Charles Darwin, Thomas Henry Huxley, George Henry Lewes and Conwy Lloyd Morgan were of particular importance. Within a few years, all of the ideas described in the preceding paragraph were present. Yet this extraordinary episode in American social theory is largely neglected by the social theorists of today.

One of the principal authors of this Darwinian transformation of social theory in America was Thorstein Veblen. His work synthesized the evolutionary theory of Darwin, the instinct–habit psychology of William James and William McDougall, and the pragmatist philosophy of James and Charles Sanders Peirce. Fatefully, however, Veblen did not build up his insights into a systematic and comprehensive treatise. Nevertheless, Veblen's works were widely cited, and he influenced a number of other important thinkers. The evolution and nature of this brilliant, neglected but incomplete synthesis is explored below.

However, as explained in Parts III and IV, the intellectual environment of American academia began to change rapidly and substantially after 1914. In philosophy, pragmatism was displaced by positivism, and instinct–habit psychology was replaced by behaviourism. Meanwhile, the inheritors of Veblen's legacy failed, partly because of the less favourable intellectual environment in the interwar period, to complete a theoretical system for institutional economics.

Remarkably, however, the present philosophical and psychological environment is more conducive to the revival and development of the original, Veblenian project. This book is an attempt to contribute to this task.

The next two chapters examine some key issues that are related to Veblenian thought. One chapter discusses the impact of Darwinian and Spencerian evolutionary ideas on psychology and the social sciences. The other addresses the concept of emergence and some of its implications. Chapters 6 to 10 will focus more specifically on Veblen's contribution.

Part II
Darwinism and the Victorian social sciences

4   Charles Darwin, Herbert Spencer and the human species

It has taken 100 years to appreciate fully that Darwin's conceptual framework is, indeed, a new philosophical system.

Ernst Mayr (1964)

To understand the character of the evolutionary social science that emerged at the end of the nineteenth century, it is necessary to appreciate the huge influence of two British pioneers of evolutionary thinking: Charles Darwin and Herbert Spencer. Their versions of evolutionary theory were very different. But both of them had an enormous, global influence.

Darwin studied at the University of Edinburgh and subsequently obtained a degree at the University of Cambridge. His father was a successful country physician. His grandfather was Erasmus Darwin and his great uncle was the industrialist Josiah Wedgwood. Darwin married his cousin, Emma Wedgwood, the granddaughter of the pottery entrepreneur. With these connections he needed no academic affiliation or stipend, and had the financial means to be an independent writer and researcher.

For Darwin, the evolution of species was principally a result of repeated natural selection of variants that were better adapted to survive and procreate in their environment. The inspiration for Darwin's theory of natural selection came partly from economics. His early notebooks (Gruber, 1974; Vorzimmer, 1977) show that in 1838 and 1839 Darwin read Adam Smith's *Theory of Moral Sentiments*. Darwin was also influenced by his friend Charles Babbage, who wrote an important text *On the Economy of Machinery and Manufactures* (Babbage, 1832; Schweber, 1977, 1980; Hodgson, 1993). In 1838, when Darwin was on the verge of his theoretical breakthrough, he also read the famous *Essay on the Principle of Population* by Thomas Robert Malthus (Schweber, 1977; Hodge and Kohn, 1985). Malthus depicted a picture of species superfecundity in the face of enduring resource scarcity, upon which Darwin developed his own theory of natural selection.

Darwin delayed the publication of his theory for fear of the reaction to its materialistic philosophy and anti-creationist message. When he realized that Alfred Russel Wallace had independently formulated the principle of natural selection, Darwin was prompted to rush the *Origin of Species* into print. The *Origin* was published in 1859 and the *Descent of Man* in 1871. The first edition of 1250 copies of the *Origin* sold out on the day of publication, followed by a 3000 print run of the second edition that was sold in a few weeks. This work received instant and massive attention, and volumes of sales that would be the envy of many an author even today.[1]

In 1859 a minority of the British scientific establishment believed that humans or other species evolved. Largely due to Darwin, many became evolutionists. By the 1870s the evolutionists had the upper hand and their opponents were a diminishing minority. This transformation of opinion was assisted by important institutional and cultural developments in Victorian society. Britain was still in the throes of rapid industrial development, massive urban expansion and political reform. Science was becoming more secularized and less obedient to the church. The founding and expansion of institutions of higher learning in London began to challenge the dominance of conservative ideas from Oxford and Cambridge. The Darwinians became influential in the learned societies, effectively taking over the prestigious Royal Society of London for the Promotion of Natural Knowledge in the 1870s.

But while the scientific establishment began to accept that species had evolved, Darwin's particular evolutionary theory, with the concept of natural selection at its centre, remained highly controversial for another 60 years, even among leading biologists. After the 1860s, most of the criticism of the general idea of the evolution of species came from people who were not scientists. But among the scientific community the criticism of the theory of natural selection, actually increased. The scientific and philosophical core of Darwin's work was not fully appreciated, at least until well into the twentieth century.

The general idea of evolution pre-dates Darwin. Before 1859, several people had already suggested that the story of the creation in *Genesis* was not literally true, that fossils were evidence of species evolving over perhaps millions of years, and humankind had somehow evolved from the apes. The general idea that all species had been derived from a smaller number of ancestors had been put forward in the eighteenth century or earlier (Lovejoy, 1936). Jean Baptiste de Lamarck had published his *Philosophie Zoologique* in 1809, also proclaiming the idea of the evolution of species (Lamarck, 1984).

---

1 See the more detailed discussions of the ideas of Darwin and Spencer in Hodgson (1993), Dennett (1995) and La Vergata (1995). The influence of Malthus was also crucial for Wallace. Wallace attended the Grammar School in the small town of Hertford, where at the nearby East India College Malthus had been the first Professor of Political Economy in Britain.

However, the *Origin of Species* gave an enormous boost to this broad idea, and provoked the reaction of Christian fundamentalists. Darwin's contribution was widely referred to as 'the ape theory'. At that time, less attention was given to the truly novel aspects of Darwin's work, including its distinctive but largely implicit philosophical outlook and its revelation of mechanisms of natural selection. In these respects, Darwin's theory was highly original and not merely an extrapolation of previous doctrines. Darwin became famous for ideas that were not his own, while his truly original contribution was largely overlooked.[2]

Spencer was from a family of religious nonconformists. The son of a schoolteacher, he had no university education. From 1837 he worked as a civil engineer, first on the London to Birmingham railway and then on the Birmingham to Gloucester line. Intrigued by the fossils exposed by railway cuttings, he became a convert to Lamarck's evolutionary theories (Spencer, 1904, vol. 1, p. 176). When the Birmingham to Gloucester railway was completed in 1841, he was discharged from his job. But Spencer was delighted, because it released him from employment and gave him the opportunity to develop a career in writing.

From 1848 to 1853, Spencer was a sub-editor on *The Economist*. But he had free time for his writing. He published a number of articles, including one in 1852 that proposed a conception of natural evolution that was superficially similar to Darwin's but lacked a detailed explanation of the mechanisms involved. Spencer's *Social Statics* (1851) was an immensely successful work that combined scientific pretension with a dose of individualist and free market ideology. In 1857 he planned a system of 'synthetic philosophy' covering biology, psychology, sociology and ethics. His central evolutionary idea was the progressive transformation of the homogenous into the heterogeneous; in nature and society there was increasing variety and more complex organization. To this he added the law of conservation of energy and other ideas from mid-nineteenth century physics. Numerous volumes followed, most of them being reprinted several times. Spencer achieved worldwide fame, but he was particularly popular in the United States of America, where from 1860 to his death in 1903, over 368,000 copies of his books were sold (Spencer, 1904, vol. 2, p. 113 n.).

In Britain, Spencer's devotees included Samuel Butler and Alfred Marshall. The creative use in Marshall's *Principles* (1890) of Spencerian biological ideas has received some discussion elsewhere (Thomas, 1991; Hodgson, 1993; Laurent, 2000). The Irish Australian William Hearn (1863)

---

2 Glass *et al.* (1959, p. vi) wrote that some of the alleged forerunners of Darwin 'were hardly evolutionists: others, in their own eyes, not evolutionists at all. Some, who lived in the period after 1859, even hated the Darwinian teaching and fought it vehemently.' Concerning claims that natural selection was discovered before Darwin, the biologist Mayr (1985b, p. 769) argued that 'virtually all of these so-called prior cases of natural selection turn out to be a rather different phenomenon, which is only superficially similar to selection.' The closest precursors of the Darwinian theory are discussed in Dennett (1995, pp. 28–34, 49).

applied Spencerian evolutionary principles to economics and the American neoclassical economist John Bates Clark laced his *Philosophy of Wealth* (1885) with organic metaphors and images taken from Spencerian biology.

Spencer did not like being described as a Darwinist because he believed that he had published a valid theory of evolution prior to Darwin. It was Spencer, not Darwin, who coined the term 'survival of the fittest'. It was not until 1866, after the first edition of the *Origin of Species* had appeared, that Darwin was persuaded by Wallace to use Spencer's phrase, rather than 'natural selection', in key passages in that work (Waters, 1986, pp. 207–8). Furthermore, it was Spencer, not Darwin, who popularized the term 'evolution'. Darwin did not introduce the word until the sixth edition of the *Origin of Species*, and then he used it only sparingly.

Before he was forced by critics to retreat, Spencer identified the 'survival of the fittest' with an individualist ideology and an optimal equilibrium state. In contrast, for Darwin, the fitter were essentially those who had the relatively greater capacity to adapt to prevailing environmental conditions. For many Darwinians, including Petr Kropotkin (1902) and Thorstein Veblen (1899a), it was unjustified to equate fitness with either individualism or optimality. But Spencer's individualism was resolute.

In style, methodology and content, the writings of Darwin and Spencer were very different. Darwin's works are driven by a searching curiosity. He set out the empirical phenomena in detail and endeavoured with caution and modesty to find causal explanations. He referred to many other studies and was careful to give other contributors due credit. In contrast, Spencer erected bold, general laws and principles, using evidence as little more than sparse ornamentation. Furthermore, Spencer was much more keen than Darwin to claim apparent political and ideological implications for his theories.

Spencer (1904, vol. 1, p. 289) openly admitted that he simply stopped reading a book when he reached a point of fundamental disagreement. Consequently, he engaged in few exercises of critical comparison. Compared with Darwin, Spencer cited other authors less frequently, and did little to compare his theoretical system with any rivals. In his *First Principles*, which appeared three years after the *Origin of Species*, Spencer only briefly acknowledged Darwin. Spencer (1893) persistently argued that natural selection did not provide an adequate explanation of the evolution of species.

In the 1850s, Spencer became part of a consequential network of British intellectuals, centred on London. The particular significance of this group for the later development of institutional economics will become more apparent below. Spencer met the writer and philosopher George Henry Lewes in 1850 and they became close friends. Spencer also became a companion of Thomas Henry Huxley after their first meeting in 1852, several years before Huxley became a famous advocate of Darwinism.

Unlike Darwin, Spencer and Lewes, Huxley held an academic position. From 1854 he lectured in natural history at the newly founded Royal School of Mines, which became part of the University of London. After the publication of the *Origin* in 1859, Huxley became a foremost advocate of the idea of human evolution, earning the nickname of 'Darwin's bulldog'. His famous debate with Bishop Samuel Wilberforce occurred in Oxford in 1860. Darwin's radical doctrine of evolution was announced to the world, and no science would be untouched.

The eclipse of Darwinism

But it was not plain sailing for Darwin's theory. Even some of Darwin's disciples, including Huxley, were not convinced that natural selection was the principal evolutionary mechanism (Kottler, 1985). Huxley also gave less emphasis than Darwin to the importance of adaptation. As Michael Ruse (1979, p. 223) put it: 'But, for all his emotional identification with Darwin, Huxley put evolution first and natural selection second.'

Darwin himself had no adequate explanation of the sources of variation in individuals or of the mechanisms of inheritance. Gregor Mendel published his famous paper in 1866. But it was not until the early twentieth century that his genetic researches were discovered by mainstream biologists. Mendelian genetics were not successfully synthesized with Darwin's theory until the 1940s. Prior to this time, the gaps in Darwin's theory made it vulnerable to attack. The mechanisms of transmission of similarities and variations were not understood. It was doubted that step-by-step natural selection could explain the evolution of a complex organ such as the eye, or an entirely new species of organism.

In an attempt to explain variation and inheritance, Darwin elaborated a theory of 'pangenesis' in his book *Variation of Animals and Plants Under Domestication* (1868). Darwin conjectured that the cells of the body throw off minute particles or 'gemmules' that gather together in the sexual or germ cells of the organism. Gemmules were messengers to the germ cells, carrying information concerning the characteristics of the parts of the body from which they had come. As a result, the sexual or germ cells would contain information representing the living body in which they were carried. Through sexual reproduction, this information would be passed on to the cells of the offspring, which could then develop the inherited characteristics. Lamarckian inheritance would thus be possible. Darwin had no direct evidence of pangenesis and his hypothesis proved to be totally ungrounded.

Critics of Darwin complained that natural selection could account for neither the origins of variations nor the presumed speed of evolution. In further attempts to deal with these problems, successive editions of Darwin's *Origin* were increasingly Lamarckian. Elsewhere too, support grew rather than diminished for Lamarckian doctrines. A strong group of

Lamarckians emerged in America in the 1870s, under the leadership of biologists such as Edward Drinker Cope and Alpheus Hyatt (Pfeifer, 1965; Richardson and Kane, 1988). On the whole, the American Lamarckians were vitalists, believing in the 'life force' as the driver behind evolution. In that respect they differed from the doctrine of Lamarck himself.

Darwin had been hugely influential in persuading the wider public of the fact of human evolution from the apes, but his particular theory of natural selection was rejected or downplayed by many in the scientific community. The acknowledgement of evolution led to doctrinal discord rather than consensus among scientists.

Another challenge to Darwin's theory came from Sir William Thomson (later known as Lord Kelvin) in a series of papers published from 1862. Using the classical laws of heat production and radiation, he calculated that the Earth had existed for a few million years. This was not enough time for the evolution of life and complex organic species to take place by natural selection. Unto his death, Darwin regarded this as the most serious objection to his theory. However, as it turned out much later, Lord Kelvin was in error. He had neglected the heating effects of radioactive decay. Scientists now believe that the Earth has existed for about 5000 million years.

Other objections to Darwin's theory emerged. For example, it was argued that any favourable mutation in a population would be overwhelmed and diluted through the breeding of the affected individual organism with others (Jenkin, 1867; Bennett, 1870). According to this view, a beneficial mutation would not endure for long enough to be favoured by natural selection. In the next generation it would be greatly diluted by the sexual combination of two parents, only one of which would be likely to have this mutation. It was widely assumed by scientists that each offspring blended in some near-medial proportion the characteristics of its parents. We now know this assumption to be false. Blending inheritance can maintain variation as long as a large enough source of hereditable dissimilarity exists. But as a result of the Jenkin–Bennett criticism, Darwin was again forced to put more stress on the envisaged possibility of a Lamarckian inheritance of acquired characters, although he never abandoned his central principle of natural selection. In contrast, Spencer (1893) continued to regard the Jenkin–Bennett argument as one of the decisive objections to relying on natural selection as a primary explanation of evolution.

The limits of natural selection were also questioned by some of Darwin's supporters. Wallace, who was Darwin's ally from 1859, came to the conclusion that natural selection could not account for the relatively rapid development of the human mind. In other respects, Wallace had more enthusiasm for the theory of natural selection than other Darwinians, such as Huxley. In contrast to Huxley, Wallace defended natural selection as the *primary* mechanism in the evolution of species. But Wallace had doubts concerning its ability to explain the origin of human mental capacities. The development of the complex human brain in just a few million years – with its immense capacity for extensive reflection, abstract analysis and intricate communication – is indeed amazing. Wallace doubted that natural selection could explain this phenomenon.

How could the evolution of the human mind be explained? Significantly, in the nineteenth century, many scientists believed that the more primitive societies were populated by humans who represented an intermediate stage in evolution, between apes and 'civilized' humans. For example, Spencer (1868, vol. 1, p. 50) believed that 'the civilized European departs more widely from the vertebrate archetype than does the savage'. Of course, this widespread but erroneous view was tied up with racism.

In significant contrast, Darwin (1971, vol. 1, pp. 232–3) noted 'the numerous points of mental similarity between the most distinct races of man'. For him the evidence suggested 'similar inventive or mental powers'. More extensively, and on the basis of his own extensive anthropological studies in South America, East Asia and elsewhere, Wallace (1869, 1870) similarly argued that there was little difference in the development of the human brain in different ethnic groups, and even between civilized humans and the most primitive savages. Today, such a proposition would seem both tenable and unremarkable, as well as being applauded for its anti-racist and anti-imperialist sentiments. Indeed, Wallace's progressive and egalitarian views have been much commended ever since.

Wallace also cited archaeological studies of early hominoids and their reports of brain sizes not much less than those of modern humans. Both through time and across races, there was relatively little difference in the mean size of the human brain.

However, Wallace saw this proposition of commensurate brain size as a problem for the theory of natural selection, to which in other contexts he adhered strictly and without reservation. His belief that primitive peoples were very close in brain development to more civilized humans removed any possibility of regarding primitive groups as representatives of a lower or intermediate stage of human evolution. The evidence suggested relatively little variation in human intelligence, in time or ethnic space, but a large gap between humans and apes. Wallace came to the conclusion that natural selection could not account for this gap.

Wallace reasoned further that if modern humans were capable of great technological and social achievements, then earlier humans were capable of similar feats. Hence much of the brain capacity and mental powers of earlier humans in less developed societies must have been unused. Wallace insisted that the principle of natural selection could not account for the appearance of an organ of much greater capacity or utility than was required for the survival of the species at that time. Natural selection cannot anticipate future needs. Earlier hominoids seemed to have brains much larger than required for survival, so natural selection could not account for human mental capacities.[3]

Wallace (1870, p. 188) was thus led to declare: 'We should then infer the action of a mind, foreseeing the future and preparing for it.' Wallace concluded that some superior, spiritual intelligence had guided the evolution of humans, but not other species. He believed that human intelligence had a unique origin in the 'unseen universe of Spirit'. As far as the explanation of the evolution of the human mind was concerned, Wallace removed natural selection and replaced it with spiritualism.[4]

Unlike Darwin and Huxley, Wallace did not see the human mind as emerging from complex developments and interactions in the human nervous system. For Wallace (1870, p. 365), no amount of additional neural capacity could itself bring about the phenomenon of a conscious mind:

> But this greater and greater complexity, even if carried to an infinite extent, cannot, of itself, have the slightest tendency to originate consciousness in such molecules or groups of molecules. ... You cannot have in the whole, what does not exist in any of the parts.

Note here the implicit denial of emergent properties. But instead in embracing spiritualism in reaction to the problem of body and mind, Wallace was no isolated crank. Spiritualism swept Europe and America from the 1850s. Many Victorian intellectuals, including Francis Galton and Sir Arthur Conan Doyle, also embraced the creed.

After the publication of the 1869 paper by Wallace, Darwin wrote to his friend, expressing surprise that his explanation of human evolution had privileged humans above other species. The key point of difference was not whether Wallace was right or wrong concerning the similar level of cerebral development of all human races. With the benefit of hindsight he was clearly right. The point of dispute was his unwarranted appeal to the *deus ex machina* of spiritual intelligence in the explanation of human evolution. Darwin remarked that he 'differed grievously' from Wallace on this point, seeing 'no necessity for calling in an additional and proximate cause in regard to man'. In this letter to Wallace, Darwin referred to their joint parentage of the theory of natural selection: 'I hope that you have not murdered too completely your own and my child' (Marchant, 1916, pp. 197–9).

Even if we deride Wallace's spiritualism, we should still take the problem that led him to its adoption with some seriousness. Indeed, many reputable developments in twentieth-century social science are redolent of

---

3 In 1871 Huxley (1894, vol. 2, pp. 120–86) responded to this argument with the claim that survival in a hunter–gatherer society involved detailed knowledge and considerable intelligence. Hence early humans had no significantly greater redundancy in brain capacity than those in developed societies.

4 For more detailed discussions of Wallace's ideas see G. Jones (1980), Kottler (1985), R. Richards (1987), Blitz (1992) and W. Coleman (2001). In an essay of 1878, Engels (1964, pp. 51–62) criticized Wallace's spiritualism.

Wallace's doctrine that natural selection does not apply to human society or the human mind. In much of twentieth-century social science, as in the work of Wallace, humans are privileged above other species. In this sense, much of twentieth-century social science is closer to Wallace rather than to Darwin. With a few notable exceptions, neither economists nor sociologists have paid much attention to the evolutionary origins of human intelligence or preferences. Typically, in twentieth-century economics, preference functions are taken as given. In much of twentieth-century sociology, the biological origins of human capacities are similarly ignored. Generally, the problem of the evolutionary origin of human capacities was not answered but abandoned by social scientists. At least Wallace should be credited with attempting an answer.

Samuel Butler (1878) published an influential attack on Darwin's theory, arguing that natural selection could not account for the evolution of complex organisms. Quoting from second-hand sources rather than Lamarck himself, Butler developed a version of Lamarckism where both 'want or desire' and 'inherited memory' aided the evolutionary process. Proposing that Darwinism reduced human beings to purposeless machines, he attempted to restore teleological causation to biology, mistakenly attributing such a volitional notion to Lamarck.

Butler did not understand that Darwin had attempted to explain human intentionality, not to belittle it. Yet his criticism of Darwin became widely adopted. George Bernard Shaw (1921) replicated it several decades later in the famous Preface to *Back to Methuselah*. Butler's idiosyncratic doctrine that memory is inherited from parents to offspring would today find few adherents. But some of his other views survive. Many share his mistaken belief that Lamarck saw changes to organisms as resulting from their own volition. Likewise repeated today is the false idea that Darwin's theory of natural selection depends on a view that human beings are purposeless automata. Butler and others are responsible for their dissemination.

Partly because of the perceived limitations of Darwin's theory, and because Spencer had seemingly achieved a much more complete synthesis of scientific knowledge, Spencer overshadowed Darwin in the 1880–1900 period, in both America and Europe. To some extent, Darwinism was in eclipse in the scientific community. The particular emphasis on natural selection, and other detailed features of Darwin's theory, had a restricted influence, even in the natural and the social sciences that embraced the general idea of evolution (Allen, 1968; Bowler, 1983, 1988; Sanderson, 1990). The idea that natural selection was the motor of evolution was not widely accepted until after the First World War.

In the nineteenth century, the problem of explaining the relatively rapid and recent evolution of human intellectual capacities seemed to give the advantage to those such as Butler and Spencer who believe in the possibility of acquired character inheritance. These Lamarckians argued that the development of human capacities was cumulative, in the sense that acquired capacities in one generation could be handed down immediately to the next. By this accumulation of adaptations, Lamarckism could seemingly account for a much more rapid rate of evolution than natural selection. The evolution of human civilization was explained largely by the presumed rapid biological evolution of the human species.

For Spencer and many other nineteenth-century theorists, social evolution operated ultimately in terms of human biological characteristics. It was widely believed that social progress ultimately depended on the biological factors of human inheritance. Consequently, the speed of the underlying evolution of the human organism constrained the pace of socio-economic development. Spencer (1881, pp. 400–1) thus argued that 'society cannot be substantially and permanently changed without its units being substantially and permanently changed ... social evolution ... is limited by the rate of organic modification in human beings'. Accordingly, for Spencer, explanations of socio-economic evolution could be reduced largely and ultimately to changes in the human organisms that composed the population. Hence, in modern parlance, Spencer adopted a form of biological reductionism. He emphasized the effect of the social environment on individual development but saw the social environment as an outcome of individual biological capabilities.

The apparent strength of Spencer's theory was, by the use of a Lamarckian mechanism, that it could encompass both biological and social evolution. On closer inspection, however, there were gaps in Spencer's theory. For example, there was no explanation of the proclaimed tendency of all evolving systems to become progressively more complex. In supporting his presumption of evolutionary progress, Spencer appealed to universal evolutionary laws. But these laws were themselves given inadequate causal justification. In reaching for ultimate explanations, Spencer (1862) was obliged to fall back on to the mystical notion of a universal and unknowable motive force, an inaccessible 'Ultimate Cause', working generally in the direction of progress (Wiltshire, 1978). While Spencer proclaimed mysterious teleological laws of endogenous change, Darwin in contrast focused on the incremental, processual, causal mechanisms and exogenous conditions of development.

Crucially, nineteenth-century biologists had a much more limited understanding of the detailed processes of evolution than today. The Darwinians were at a disadvantage because they were unable to point to the precise mechanisms of replication and transmission. Their insistence on step-by-step, causal explanations could not yet be exemplified in the details of evolution itself.

There are several reasons why this episode in the history of Darwinism is important. It shows that the Darwinians were grappling with problems of human mental and social development in an attempt to reconcile the growth of human mental capacities and human civilization with the causal process of natural selection. Fortunately, this issue was to remain on the agenda into the early decades of the twentieth century, and to stimulate the idea of emergent properties. As shown in the next chapter, the continuing dialogue between biology, philosophy and social theory produced ostensible solutions to the problems raised by Wallace and others. In the meantime we return to the development and reception of Darwinism in the late nineteenth and early twentieth centuries. Given widespread and persistent misconceptions in this area, it is necessary to examine both the reception of Darwinism among social scientists and the misleading use of the 'Social Darwinism' label.

Mythologies of social Darwinism

The fame of Darwin was such that phrases such as the 'struggle for existence' and the 'survival of the fittest' were often applied to social phenomena. Supposedly Darwinian ideas were associated with every conceivable political stance, from pacifism to militarism, from socialism to individualism, from liberalism to conservatism (Himmelfarb, 1959, p. 407). Social Darwinism has been linked with eugenics; but conservatives, liberals and socialists alike adopted eugenic policies.[5]

Huxley wrote extensively on the ethical implications of Darwinism. He steered away from extreme doctrines of individual competition or group collectivism. Huxley (1894, vol. 1, p. 272) wrote in 1871: 'If individuality has no play, society does not advance: if individuality breaks all bonds, society perishes.' Henry Drummond (1894) interpreted Darwinism in a way that emphasized the role of the environment in human development. He argued that the poor were largely impoverished by their living conditions and lack of education. In accord with Darwin in his *Descent of Man*, Drummond saw the positive evolutionary role of human altruism and cooperation. Such progressive Darwinian ideas do not fit many of the modern caricatures of 'Social Darwinism'.

Benjamin Kidd and Lester Frank Ward have both been described as 'Social Darwinists'. But both opposed eugenics, and Ward was a particularly vociferous opponent of racism. He was not alone; the American church minister Charles Loring Brace (1863) used Darwinism to argue for a notion of common racial origins and against racism and slavery. 'Social Darwinism' lacked a unique and identifiable political salience, and in academic circles its use was relatively rare until the 1930s.

---

5   Liberals and socialists such as E. Aveling, E. Bellamy, C. H. Cooley, J. B. S. Haldane, J. Huxley, J. M. Keynes, H. J. Laski, J. Needham, G. B. Shaw, C. P. Snow, B. Webb, S. Webb and H. G. Wells counted themselves as followers of eugenics (Paul, 1984). Critics included F. Boas, B. Kidd and L. F. Ward. The position of prominent eugenicists on social reforms was complex. In their popular textbook on *Applied Eugenics*, Popenoe and Johnson (1918) advocated inheritance taxes, birth control, the abolition of child labour and compulsory education, but opposed minimum wage legislation and socialism. The purpose of this note is not to excuse eugenics, but to demonstrate that support for this doctrine was far from confined to conservatives, elitists, or racists.

The now forgotten but once fashionable French sociologist Gabriel Tarde (1884) was one of the few in academic circles who used the term 'Social Darwinism' approvingly. Tarde (1890, 1903) attempted to apply Darwinism to an analysis of imitative behaviour in human society. But this usage was relatively primitive and innocent, and without strong ideological connotations. Hence Tarde does not appear in modern demonologies of 'Social Darwinism'.

The first significant appearance of the term 'Social Darwinism' in a leading academic journal in the English language was in a review of a book first published in Italian by the socialist economist Achille Loria (1895).[6] But Loria's use of the term was quite different from that of Tarde's. One chapter of Loria's work is a critique of 'Social Darwinism', by which Loria meant the misapplication of the term 'struggle for existence' to humanity, as a mistaken justification for nationalism, militarism and war. However, Darwin himself had never used his theory in explicit support for any political ideology. While Darwin wrote of the 'struggle for existence', he never used it as a justification for war. The idea that nature somehow justifies human aggression was not Darwin's. Instead, the idea is found in folklore and mythology, and thus pre-dates Darwin by millennia.

Kropotkin (1902) argued convincingly that Darwin's 'struggle for existence' had been wrongly invested by some with a particular and overly narrow meaning. Kropotkin (1902, p. 22) wrote: 'The conception of struggle for existence as a factor of evolution, introduced into science by Darwin and Wallace, has permitted us to embrace an immensely wide range of phenomena in one single generalization' including 'intellectual progress and moral development'. Kropotkin saw this 'struggle for existence' as broadly and generally 'a struggle against adverse circumstances'. This is an accurate and commendable interpretation of Darwin's concept. Kropotkin (1902, p. 72) argued at length that 'natural selection continually seeks out the ways precisely for avoiding competition as much as possible'. Such broad and appropriate interpretations of the Darwinian notions of 'natural selection' or 'struggle for existence' necessarily imply neither individualist competition nor any form of warfare.[7]

What are arraigned – mostly by critics – under the term 'Social Darwinism' are ideas that have either little connection with Darwinism or are not

---

6 According to the JSTOR Internet database of journals (in social science, history, philosophy and statistics), the terms 'Social Darwinism', 'Social Darwinist' or 'Social Darwinists' appear in only 21 articles or reviews in the entire 1870–1931 period, and only nine times before 1916. Out of these nine earlier references, eight are critical of 'Social Darwinism', or are reviews of works that are critical of 'Social Darwinism'. In the years from 1925 to 1931 inclusive, the term simply does not appear. Parsons (1932) reintroduced the term, and the menace of Nazism stimulated its further use. The only article or review found in this entire academic database clearly and explicitly advocating 'Social Darwinism' in any sense was by the eugenicist D. C. Wells (1907). After Hofstadter (1944), and until the present day, mentions of 'Social Darwinism' were plentiful but entirely dismissive and critical.

exclusively represented by it. People such as Herbert Spencer and William Graham Sumner – who have been frequently described as Social Darwinists – were not close followers of Darwin's doctrine. Spencer's differences with Darwin have already been noted. Sumner occasionally adopted Spencer's phraseology of the 'survival of the fittest' and less often Darwin's term 'natural selection', and used them in an imprecise exoneration of individualism, inequality and market competition. However, despite today being widely described as a 'Social Darwinist', there is relatively little Darwinism in Sumner's writings (Bannister, 1973, 1979; N. Smith, 1979). In his most important treatise, Sumner (1906) mentioned Darwin only once. Sumner's disciple Albert Galloway Keller (1923, p. 137) remarked that his teacher 'did not give much attention to the possibility of extending evolution into the societal field'.[8] More generally, the American sociologist Ward (1907, p. 292) protested that he had 'never seen any distinctively Darwinian principle appealed to in the discussions of "social Darwinism"'.

Several followers of Darwin harboured racist, imperialist and sexist ideas. For example, Joseph Le Conte (1892) was President of the American Association for the Advancement of Science when he published a book arguing that the 'negroes' were an inferior and doomed race. In Germany, the respected academic biologist Ernst Haeckel was an enthusiastic advocate of a Darwinism mixed with racist sentiments. Haeckel (1874) published a book containing a diagram depicting African people as closest in type to apes.[9] Similarly, the American anthropologist Daniel Shute (1896, p. 127) exclaimed that 'the Caucasian stands at the head of the racial scale and the Negro at the bottom'. But such obnoxious propositions are neither contained in, nor implied by, Darwin's own writings.

However, Darwin's attitudes to women were typical of his time. Darwin (1871, vol. 2, p. 316) proposed with no supporting evidence that: 'Man is more courageous, pugnacious, and energetic than woman, and has more inventive genius.' Huxley (1900, p. 449) campaigned for the extension and upgrading of female education, but was still of the view that the intellectual potential of women was less than that of men.

---

7   Contrary to Hawkins's (1997, pp. 178–80) unconvincing attempt to exclude Kropotkin from his definition of 'Social Darwinism', Kropotkin's explanation of cooperation flowed directly and explicitly from his notions of 'struggle for existence' and 'natural selection'. Hawkins interpreted these terms in a narrow sense that Kropotkin rejected. In establishing these concepts in a broad and inclusive sense, Kropotkin's text is close to the modern technical concept of selection (Price, 1970, 1995; Sober, 1984; Sober and Wilson, 1998; Knudsen, 2002; Henrich, 2004).

8   Keller (1915, 1923) himself applied much more resolutely the Darwinian principles of variation, selection and inheritance to Sumner's 'folkways' and social evolution. Like Veblen, Keller identified analogous principles and mechanisms in the social domain.

9   Haeckel's diagram is reproduced and criticized in Gould (1978, p. 215). Racist views were widespread at the time but Darwin himself did not replicate them. Notably, writing in the years 1874–81, Engels (1964, pp. 211–12, 309–12) approved of Haeckel's (1874) book. Engels passed over its obnoxious depiction of African inferiority without comment, and saw Haeckel's concentration on 'adaptation and heredity' as a superior and sufficient alternative to Darwin's own theory of natural selection.

But Darwin was neither a jingoist nor a racist (Richerson and Boyd, 2001). He was a progressive liberal. On his travels to South America he was outraged by human slavery and he criticized the treatment of native peoples by the Spanish and Portuguese. In 1882 he signed a petition protesting against the persecution of the Jews in Russia. He extolled neither selfishness nor competition. Referring to social cooperation, Darwin (1871, vol. 1, p. 162) wrote: 'Selfish and contentious people will not cohere, and without coherence nothing can be effected.' The cavalier use of the term 'Social Darwinism' associates him with scientific and ideological doctrines that he never proclaimed. Darwin suffered the fate of all those that achieve fame for their ideas: he was misrepresented.[10]

Compare the true views of Darwin on race with those of Karl Marx and Friedrich Engels. In the *Neue Rheinische Zeitung* on 13 January 1849 (edited by Marx and Engels) Engels proclaimed that 'the disappearance from the face of the earth ... of entire reactionary peoples' such as the Slavs would be a 'step forward' (Marx and Engels, 1977, p. 238). In his letter to Engels of 7 August 1866, Marx with apparent approval cites a claim that 'the common negro type is only a degeneration of a far higher one' (Marx and Engels, 1987, p. 305). Racist statements such as these are not found in Darwin's writings.

Under the label of Social Darwinism a number of myths have been promoted. It associated Darwinism with a number of propositions that bear no necessary or logical relation to this scientific theory, and it fed on the limited assimilation and misunderstandings of Darwinian theory prior to the First World War (Bowler, 1983, 1988). Contrary to myth, there was no clear school of Social Darwinists, instead it was a term originally and largely applied by anarchists, socialists and pacifists to the views they opposed (Bannister, 1979). By the 1940s, widespread political views, from anarchists such as Kropotkin, through liberal free traders such as Spencer and Sumner, to more militant nationalists and racists such as Haeckel were conflated together under the single, misleading label of Social Darwinism.

Another, fatal myth was to presume that a theoretical position could itself be evaluated in terms of the political views of its proponents. On the contrary, no matter how distasteful (or attractive) the political views of individuals proposing a theoretical analysis, this has no bearing on whether the theoretical explanation of cause and effect is actually true or false. The choice of priorities for scientific research is partly and unavoidably a political decision. But the scientific evaluation of scientific theories or results is not.

Not only have multiple insights been rejected on the grounds of the obnoxious political views of their proponents, but also a whole tradition of attempting to apply Darwinian ideas to social science, or to gain insight

---

10 This is not to deny some of the ramifications of Darwin's wider views, explored by Desmond and Moore (1991) and R. Young (1985).

from biology concerning the human condition, has been consigned to obscurity. This is despite the fact that the political views of many of the promoters – Kropotkin, Ritchie, Veblen and Ward included – were far from individualism or conservativism. All have been casualties of the ongoing campaign against Social Darwinism, and the attempt to remove any discussion of biology from social science.

Another, related myth was to see any relationship between biology and the social sciences as inevitably negative or unsound. This myth gained strength in the 1930s when Anglo-American sociology tried to break entirely from biology. To consolidate and justify its independence and isolation from the natural sciences, it exaggerated and misrepresented the previous impact of Darwin's ideas on the social sciences. One of the leading manufacturers of this myth was Parsons (1932, 1934, 1937) who began to broadly identify 'Social Darwinism' with almost any application of ideas from biology to the study of human action. Given further impetus by the horrors of Nazism, the effect of the myth was to break off much interdisciplinary conversation between the social sciences and biology. This outcome had a dramatic and adverse effect on the development of the social sciences (Cravens, 1978; Degler, 1991; Weingart *et al.*, 1997; Hodgson, 1999b).

Several of these myths of Social Darwinism were given credibility by the classic work on *Social Darwinism in American Thought* by Richard Hofstadter (1944), where the skills of a great historian were deployed in the ideological war effort against fascism and genocide. However, Hofstadter's thesis has been systematically challenged by several critics, including Robert Bannister (1979) and Donald Bellomy (1984). In America there were relatively few instances where Darwinism was used to support capitalism, imperialism, racism or war. A more prominent ideological use of Darwinism in the 1880–1940 period was as a justification of progressive reform rather than conservative reaction. Hofstadter had lumped together all sorts of views under the vaguely defined label 'Social Darwinism' and failed to note the crucial differences in both analysis and orientation between Darwinism and Spencerism. As Raymond Wilson (1967, p. 93) confirmed: 'No more than a small handful of American business leaders or intellectuals were "social Darwinists" in any sense precise enough to have a useful meaning.'

As a result of these myths, the uncritical modern use of the phrase 'Social Darwinism' is imprecise and highly misleading. No adequate consensus exists on the meaning of the term 'Social Darwinism' and it has little descriptive value. This is not to deny the important influence of the Darwinian world-view, or the rhetorical significance of its importation into discourses concerning human society. Part of the revolutionary significance and attraction of Darwinism was to require that humankind should be considered as a part of nature. Darwinism also emphasized scarcity and the struggle for life. But the idea that the term 'Social Darwinism' represented a coherent doctrine in additional (theoretical or ideological) respects is false.[11]

Broadly 'evolutionary' ideas appeared in the works of Henry Maine (1861), Edward Tylor (1871), Lewis Henry Morgan (1877) and several others. Tylor (1871, p. 7) wrote notably that 'institutions which can best hold their own in the world gradually supersede the less fit ones'. But this was in the context of a non-Darwinian and teleological view of cultural development. They assumed a series of preordained stages through which civilization and culture had to pass, suggesting that history had a definite path or goal. History for them was the progressive unfolding of immanences. While they attempted to erect general theories of cultural development, they failed to produce an adequate causal story of the alleged single-track progress of civilization. Whether describing social development as an evolution from 'status to contract' or 'barbarism to civilization', these writers registered a common commitment to progress and a limited appreciation of Darwinism (Bannister, 1979; Bowler, 1988; Sanderson, 1990). Some classic evolutionists distanced themselves entirely from Darwin's work. Passing references to 'struggle', 'fitness', and even 'natural selection' in their books showed the influence of Darwinian or Malthusian terminology, but no deep commitment to Darwinism.

The mythology of Social Darwinism has helped to bury a generation of important social theorists. The modern student of sociology will hear much of Émile Durkheim and Max Weber. Even Comte will be mentioned – after all, he invented the word 'sociology'. But there will be much less of Herbert Spencer. His contribution is as overly neglected today as it was overly praised in his lifetime. And they will probably learn nothing of the ideas of the once fashionable Frenchman Gabriel Tarde (1890, 1899, 1903), or of highly influential Americans such as Lester Frank Ward (1883, 1893, 1903), Franklin Giddings (1896), Edward Ross (1901), Charles Horton Cooley (1902, 1922) or William Graham Sumner (1906). Of course, with a century of hindsight we can find many flaws in these works. But there is not a shred of justification for the exclusion of this entire generation of social theorists from the historical annals of sociological theory. Largely thanks to the myths of 'Social Darwinism', they have been excluded because they considered the interaction between the social and the biotic

---

11 In terms similar to Parsons (1937), Hawkins (1997) elaborated an extremely broad definition of 'Social Darwinism' that could apply to anyone who believes that principles of evolution in nature have anything to do with human society. At the same time, Hawkins mistakenly associated Darwinism with narrow notions of 'struggle for existence' and 'natural selection' that excluded cooperation or equality. He used the term 'biological determinism' without defining it adequately, and without considering the possible application of Darwinian evolutionary principles to *social* or *cultural* units and mechanisms. Neither Veblen nor leading modern theorists of cultural, economic or organizational evolution were discussed, while modern sociobiology was sweepingly maligned. For a devastatingly critical review of Hawkins's book see Johnson (1998).

spheres. By the 1930s, such interactions became highly unfashionable in sociology.[12]

Many of these earlier theorists did not reduce explanations of social phenomena largely to biological terms. Consider Giddings, who from 1894 was a professor of sociology at Columbia University. He was an advocate of United States imperial expansion, but he did not derive his imperialism from biology. Giddings (1896, p. v) believed 'that sociology is a psychological science, and that the description of society in biological terms is a mistake'. To describe him as a 'Social Darwinist' is thus misleading.

Ward could hardly be further from the standard depiction of 'Social Darwinism'. Dubbed 'the father of American sociology' (Faris, 1950) and 'the American Aristotle' (Chugerman, 1939), he was born in Illinois into a relatively poor family. After service in the Civil War, he worked as a US Government paleobotanist. In 1906, Ward was elected as the first president of the newly founded American Sociological Association. Like many others at the time, he brought ideas from biology into the social sciences. In this and several other respects there are similarities between Ward and Marshall – who was one year younger than Ward. The foremost influences over both authors were Georg Wilhelm Friedrich Hegel and Herbert Spencer. Both authors had a defining influence on their subject. Both authors were Lamarckians. But Ward – in contrast to Marshall and especially Spencer – stressed that evolution was often wasteful, rather than leading generally or automatically towards perfection. He did not see existing circumstances as actually optimal or in the automatic process of becoming so.

Ward (1883, 1893, 1903) argued at length that the outcome of evolution, whether in nature or society, was rarely, if ever optimal. Hence the use of evolutionary theory in the social sciences could not be used to justify an economic policy of laissez-faire. Enlightened government intervention was required to guide the more spontaneous processes of social evolution on a relatively beneficial course. In particular, free markets do not necessarily maximize human welfare. Accordingly, his emphasis on suboptimality in social evolution helped to lay the theoretical groundwork of the welfare state.

As well as being an opponent of racism, Ward denied that women were inferior to men in their intellectual abilities. He argued that men had subjugated women because of their inherently greater physical size and strength. Once again, evolution led to suboptimal outcomes. For Ward the manifest subjugation of women was not evidence, even from an evolutionary perspective, of its efficiency, desirability or natural foundation.

---

12 The names of Thomas and Znaniecki (1920), Bentley (1908) and others should be added to this lost generation. Kilpinen (2000) convincingly argues that a further reason why this generation was forgotten was because it was infused with pragmatist notions of action that became unfashionable in the interwar period and were neglected by subsequent generations of sociologists, from Parsons (1937) to Giddens (1984).

In *Pure Sociology*, his most important theoretical work, Ward (1903) developed a hierarchical ontology in which the social levels depended upon the psychological and biological levels below, but could not be analytically reduced to them. (This discerning and outstanding work influenced Veblen, as revealed later below.) In his *Applied Sociology*, Ward (1906) attacked eugenics and argued that social environment and conditioning were most important in human development. With his rejection of biological reductionism and his stress on the importance of the social environment, Ward again defied the caricatures of Social Darwinism.

From 1892 Charles Cooley taught in the sociology department at the University of Michigan. Modern sociologists might also dismiss him hastily because of his firm advocacy of a Darwinian 'evolutionary point of view' and his frequent citations of Darwin. Like many radicals at the time, Cooley (1918) supported some aspects of eugenics. For these reasons, Cooley today would be widely written off. But far from the portrayals of 'Social Darwinism', Cooley (1902, 1922) developed a theory of the individual in society that emphasized the social basis of cognition and learning. Again the phrase 'Social Darwinism' conceals and distorts much more than it reveals.

Overall, the label of 'Social Darwinism' is unhelpful and misleading. It serves the purpose of tolerating 'Darwinism' in biology but entirely excluding it from social science. It lumps together and dismisses a whole host of varied and important developments in the 1870–1914 period that in some way developed or maintained links between biology and the social sciences. We should be critical of racist, sexist and imperialist ideologies, but these emanate neither from the act of linking biology with the social sciences, nor from the principles of Darwinism. Just as nuking entire cities is not a good solution to the problem of urban crime, it is not a good strategy to deal with abuses of biology in the social science by severing all links with the science of life.

It would be better if the use as a descriptive term of the highly ambiguous and imperfectly grounded phrase 'Social Darwinism' were discontinued. It would be clearer and more effective if authors criticized more directly the readily identifiable and less ambiguous ideological ills of racism, sexism, imperialism or eugenics. If biological reductionism is also to be a target, then let us describe it by its name. If some promoters of sociobiology or evolutionary psychology attempt to explain the social entirely in biological terms, then let us critically evaluate that methodology, and identify the irreducible properties of the social domain. Let us stop telling false histories, and henceforth call things by their proper names.[13]

---

13 For a development of the ideas in this section see Hodgson (unpublished).

Darwinism and causality

Darwin not only proclaimed that species had evolved, but also searched for the processual and causal mechanisms of evolution. For Darwin, science involved a commitment to causal explanations. However, even disbelievers in the idea that species had evolved, such as the Cambridge scientists William Whewell and Adam Sedgwick, believed that science involved causal explanation (Ruse, 1981). Such creationist opponents simply held that the explanation of the origin of species was a matter of theology, not science; the creation of species was a miracle that must be attributed to no other cause but God. Against this view, Darwin's life work was marked by an ambition to extend the realm of scientific causal explanation into areas that were deemed taboo by religious doctrine.

Even before his theory of natural selection was properly formulated, Darwin considered that the origin of the human species, and its unique capacity for reflection and rational deliberation, could in principle be explained by science. In 1838 Darwin jotted in his 'Notebook C': 'Why is thought, being a secretion of the brain, more wonderful than gravity a property of matter? It is our arrogance, it our admiration of ourselves' (Barrett *et al.*, 1987, p. 291). Darwin rejected explanations of natural phenomena in terms of design, to focus instead on the detailed causes that had cumulated in the emergence of elaborate phenomena over long periods of time.

It has been suggested that Darwin delayed the completion and publication of his *Origin of Species* for several years for fear of hostility to his materialist philosophical views.[14] In any case, a search for materialist causal explanations permeates all his work. When Darwin (1859, p. 167) expressed a profound ignorance of the mechanisms that led to variations in organisms, he did not believe that variations emerged spontaneously, in the sense of being without a cause. Darwin (1859, p. 209) asserted that such 'accidental variations' must be 'produced by ... unknown causes' rather than embracing a notion of a spontaneous, uncaused event.

Darwin (1871, vol. 1, p. 131) wrote similarly of 'a large class of variations which may be provisionally called spontaneous, for they appear, owing to our ignorance, to arise without any exciting cause'. Note that Darwin did not believe that the variations arose without a prior cause. He simply argued that 'owing to our ignorance' they 'appear' to be 'spontaneous'. Darwin (1883, vol. 2, p. 282) wrote: 'No doubt, each slight variation must have its efficient cause'. Even when the causal mechanism was elusive or unknown, he believed that it was the task of the scientist to attempt to discover it.

The frequent suggestion that Darwin's theory *necessarily* involves or implies a stochastic, tychist or probabilistic concept of causality is ungrounded. Darwin himself believed in a notion of causality that involved the transfers

---

14 See Gruber (1974, p. 202), Schweber (1977, pp. 310–15), Gould (1978, pp. 21–7) and Ruse (1979, pp. 184–5). R. Richards (1987, pp. 152–6) has suggested additional or alternative reasons for the delay.

of physical matter or energy. He upheld that relatively simple mechanisms of cause and effect could, given time and circumstances, lead to amazingly complex and varied outcomes. He relied on this intuition, rather than any notion of statistical or stochastic determination. But his belief in the principle of determinacy would not be negated if causes were in fact stochastic (Bunge, 1959). Within Darwinism, we can remain agnostic on the question of probabilistic, statistical, tychist or stochastic determination.

Darwin upheld that complex effects could be explained in terms of a detailed succession of step-by-step causal mechanisms. A process of change was an accumulated sequence of causal mechanisms. Darwin (1859, p. 43) wrote of the supreme importance of 'the accumulative action of Selection'. Darwin's adopted maxim, *'natura non facit saltum'* (nature does not make leaps) was in part an appeal to this method of detailed, sequential causal explanation. In one of the several places in the *Origin* where he repeats this ancient motto, Darwin (1859, p. 471) wrote: 'As natural selection acts solely by accumulating slight, successive, favourable variations, it can produce no great or sudden modification; it can act only by very short and slow steps.' Darwin did not simply argue that natural selection worked slowly, he also – and more importantly – upheld that each step in the process was liable to causal explanation.

This doctrine applied even to the most sophisticated and complex outcomes of evolution, such as the eye and human consciousness. Likewise, there were no miraculous leaps in the evolution of human intentionality. Like all human attributes, they must have been prefigured in the species from which humans are descended. Darwin (1859, p. 208) thus wrote: 'A little dose ... of judgement or reason often comes into play, even in animals very low in the scale of nature.' In a paper of 1874, Huxley (1894, vol. 1, pp. 236–7) elaborated and generalized Darwin's argument as the 'doctrine of continuity':

> The doctrine of continuity is too well established for it to be permissible to me to suppose that any complex natural phenomenon comes into existence suddenly, and without being preceded by simpler modifications; and very strong arguments would be needed to prove that such complex phenomena as consciousness, first made their appearance in man. We know, that, in the individual man, consciousness grows from a dim glimmer to its full light, whether we consider the infant advancing in years, or the adult emerging from slumber and swoon. We know, further, that the lower animals possess, though less developed, that part of the brain which we have every reason to believe to be the organ of consciousness in man; ... [they] have a consciousness which, more or less distinctly, foreshadows our own.

The upshot is that humans combine conscious reasons and purposes with less conscious, habitual or autonomic actions. In addition, Huxley had similar views to Darwin concerning causality and the aims of science. In a lecture of 1868, Huxley declared that there was no escape 'from utter materialism and necessarianism'. For Huxley the idea of an uncaused and spontaneous event was absurd and unacceptable. Science was nothing less than an ongoing endeavour to reveal the causes behind phenomena. Huxley (1894, vol. 1, pp. 158–9) wrote:

> any one who is acquainted with the history of science will admit, that its progress has, in all ages meant, and now, more than ever, means, the extension of the province of what we call matter and causation, and the concomitant gradual banishment from all regions of thought of what we call spirit and spontaneity.

Similarly, George Romanes – a friend of Darwin and Huxley, a Cambridge graduate, and sometime professor of physiology at the Royal Institution – also insisted that Darwinism above all meant causal analysis. For Romanes (1893, p. 5), taxonomy and the accumulation of facts were the means, but not the goal, of science. 'Not facts, then, but causes or principles are the ultimate objects of scientific quest.' In another passage, Romanes explained that a goal of Darwinism was to extend the type of causal explanation that was applicable to mechanical phenomena into the organic world. Romanes (1893, p. 402) argued that Darwinism

> seeks to bring the phenomena of organic nature into line with those of inorganic; and therefore to show that whatever view we may severally take as to the kind of causation which is energizing in the latter we must now extend to the former. ... the theory of evolution by natural selection ... endeavours to comprise all the facts of adaptation in organic nature under the same category of explanation as those which occur in inorganic nature – that is to say, under the category of physical, or ascertainable, causation

Although it was prevalent in the nineteenth century, it should not be assumed that the Darwin–Huxley–Romanes view of causation was universal. On the contrary, Darwinians had to contend with the highly influential positivism of Comte (1853). Comte believed that science rested essentially on perceptible phenomena. David Hume had famously and rightly argued that events, but not causes, could be observed. Accordingly, for Comte the search for causes was futile, because they could not be discerned in our experience. Comte argued that such unobservables as causal connections were 'metaphysical' and beyond science. For Comte, instead of causal explanation, science must search for empirical regularities to derive laws.

The result was ironic. The Darwinians (with their emphasis on evolution) were opposed on one side by the creationists, acting in the name of religion. In addition, the Darwinians (with their emphasis on causation) were opposed on the other side by the stricter Comteans, acting in the name of science. From a strict Comtean perspective, Darwinism seemed to occupy a metaphysical no-man's-land between religion and science.

However, Comte's influence, even among his disciples, was never total. Despite his admiration for Comte, John Stuart Mill openly proclaimed some metaphysical principles in the first and subsequent editions of his *Logic* (1843). In particular, Mill upheld the validity of the law of universal causation: that every event is caused. Mill also thought that this law was applicable to the social sciences.

Lewes similarly attempted to escape from the Comtean legacy. While Comte saw the search after causes as futile, because they could not be observed, Lewes (1874, p. 307) believed that 'the search after efficient causes is not only justifiable, but may be successful'. For Lewes (1875, p. 388), like Mill and Darwin: 'Every event that happens has a cause, everything that exists is a cause.' Lewes believed in a single type of causation. Every outcome had to be explained in terms of a materialist cause. Human will was also itself caused. The mind was not simply the brain, but the mind had a physical basis. The attribution to volition of a separate category of causality was not acceptable to Lewes (1875, p. 401). Not only did he support the Darwinian theory of evolution, his philosophical position on causality was also close to that of Darwin. Other relevant aspects of Lewes's position are discussed in the next chapter.

Accordingly, in the second half of the nineteenth century, a philosophical alternative to Comtean positivism began to emerge, which was based on Darwinism. Its central tenet was that every event is determined in accordance with laws by something else, and in turn the outcome becomes a beginning for the next link in the causal chain. Furthermore, these laws of change are matters for scientific investigation. Darwin claimed to discover laws that applied to the natural world. He was candid, however, about the limits of his own efforts and the huge agenda of future enquiry.

Darwinism and variety

At the centre of Darwin's theory is the idea of selection working upon variety. Here is a key difference between Darwin, on the one hand, and Lamarck and Spencer, on the other. Lamarck and Spencer argued that variation was largely a result of multiple adaptations to the environment. In contrast, for Darwin 'variation was present first, and the ordering activity of the environment ("natural selection") followed afterwards' (Mayr, 1982, p. 354). For Lamarck, the environment was the principal agent of change. In contrast, Darwin argued that change resulted from a combination of variation and environmental selection, which in turn might lead to a change in environmental circumstances.

A philosophical innovation in Darwin's thinking was his ontological commitment to variety; where the understanding of the essence of something involved its placement in a population of similar but not identical entities. In contrast, within Platonic and Aristotelian 'typological essentialism', entities are regarded as identifiable in terms of a few distinct characteristics, which represent their essential qualities. In typological thinking, species are defined in terms of a few distinct characteristics that establish their essence. Accordingly, all variations around the ideal type are regarded as accidental aberrations.

Darwin abandoned the Platonic or Aristotelian version of essence to replace it by something quite different. For Darwin, the essence of any type included its potential to exhibit or create variation. Accordingly, an understanding of an item must also consider the *population* of similar entities in which that variation is present or possible. This is what Mayr (1963, 1964, 1976, 1982, 1985a, 1985b, 1992) called 'population thinking'. In population thinking, species are understood in terms of a distribution of characteristics, whereas in typological thinking variation is a classificatory nuisance. In Darwinian evolution the idea of variation encapsulated in population thinking is of paramount interest because it is upon variety that selection operates. This means that we cannot model an evolutionary system simply by focusing on the average or representative features of a population. Summarizing a complex system in terms of average or representative components neglects the variety that is essential to system behaviour and evolution.

Darwin's 'population thinking' demarcates Darwin's theory from the essentialist mechanics of Isaac Newton. But in several respects, Darwin came from a Newtonian starting point. Darwin and Newton shared a concern for causal explanation, for explanatory unification and for law-like statements. Furthermore, Darwin's natural selection concept was analogically and metaphorically treated as a 'force'. However, at a critical point, Darwin departed from Newton. As Silvan Schweber (1985, pp. 48–9) explained:

> Darwin abandoned the Newtonian model of dynamical explanations in important respects and came to a novel conceptualization of dynamics for biological systems. ... Living systems were infinitely more complicated than Newton's planetary system. Biological 'elements' had characteristics that were changing in time: they had a history. All the interactions of organisms whether with one another or with the environment were non-additive, non-instantaneous and exhibited memory. It was the ahistorical nature of the objects with which physics dealt that gave the Newtonian scheme the possibility of a simple, mathematical description. It was precisely the *historical* character of living objects which gave biological phenomena their unique and complex features.

There are profound differences between the biological and the physical sciences (Mayr, 1985a; Schweber, 1985). In Darwinism the focus is not on singular essences but on variety. Its ultimate emphasis is not equilibrium but continuous and unending change, even if some Darwinians are tempted to use equilibrium models. As it will be shown below, the Darwinian emphasis on novelty and variety proved inspirational for some American philosophers.[15]

Problems of mind and will

Darwinism brought not only human evolution, but also the human mind and consciousness onto the agenda of science (R. Richards, 1987). Science proceeds by extending the domain of causal explanation. As more of the human psyche could be explained by natural selection, Darwinism brought the frontier of scientific enquiry to the inner workings of the human mind.

The Darwinians pointed to reasons why consciousness and intention had themselves evolved. As Romanes (1883, p. 272) argued, the evolutionary advantage of intention and judgement in conscious organisms was 'probably that of supplying to natural selection variations of ancestral instincts which are not merely fortuitous, but intentionally adapted to the conditions of the environment'. Conscious reflection on novel circumstances and behavioural choices provided a better evaluation of threats and opportunities. It led to behaviour that enhanced the organism's chances of survival. This in turn led to the selection of organisms that were more skilled in their conscious deliberations.

Among humans, bipedalism enabled the development of manipulative skills – including the use of tools, weapons and fire – that in turn promoted more complex mental development through evolutionary selection (Childe, 1951; Bronowski, 1973). The repertoire of cognitive problems was massively enlarged with the development of cooperative social structures, with rules concerning individual interactions, and linguistic communication (Cummins, 1998). Environmental factors, manipulative capacities, social structures, and language all interacted together to promote further mental development through natural selection.

But at this point we open a Pandora's Box of philosophical problems, confronting interminable disputes over free will and the nature of mind and consciousness. However, this is not primarily a work on the philosophy of mind or causation, but on the philosophical foundations of institutional economics, with causation among its basic building blocks. The strategy here will be to search for a minimal core position, rather than to explore the philosophical problems of mind and causation in all their details. This minimal core position is based on Darwinism.

---

15 Another prevailing and important feature of Darwinian evolutionary processes is irreversibility. However, this is also a feature of thermodynamic systems. See Dosi and Metcalfe (1991) and Mani (1991).

Darwin's followers addressed the evolution of mind and consciousness. In 1874 Huxley (1894, vol. 1) wrote an essay in which he argued that animals had a degree of consciousness. But he treated mind as an epiphenomenon, without its own causal powers. Mind and matter were linked, but only by degrading or relegating the role or powers of mind. The problem, which Huxley could not adequately resolve, was to retain the Darwinian notion that mind and consciousness were caused outcomes, while also upholding that mind could itself be a cause. Huxley grappled with these problems at length and reached convoluted and even self-contradictory conclusions (Blitz, 1992).

Two American philosophers, Charles Sanders Peirce and William James, addressed this problem. Given their special importance for American institutionalism, we shall discuss these philosophers in more detail. For them, Darwinism was not simply a doctrine of evolution but a view of the world with philosophical implications (Wiener, 1949). Although they expressed reservations about some aspects of Darwinism, they looked favourably upon its central principles of variation and natural selection. Particularly attractive was Darwin's idea that selection worked on infinite variety as its natural material, and variety was replenished by a creative spawning of novelty. For Peirce and James, Darwinism meant an emphasis on novelty or chance as the source of variety, which were not found in the theories of Lamarck or Spencer (James, 1880; Peirce, 1891, p. 168; 1935, pp. 15–16). Both James and Peirce 'made use of Darwin to uncover spontaneity in nature' (Russett, 1976, p. 77).

However, Peirce and James did not adopt Darwin's tenet that, while the causes of variation were unknown, this was simply 'owing to our ignorance' and 'each slight variation must have had its efficient cause'. Darwin acknowledged the limitations of our knowledge but upheld that even unexplained outcomes were caused. Instead, Peirce and James saw variation and novelty in nature as evidence of some kind of universal indeterminism.

In particular, Peirce (1892) argued that natural laws were defied by frequent infinitesimal departures, thus revealing the irregularity and spontaneity of the universe. Peirce argued that 'mechanical' notions of determination could not account for 'all the variety and diversity in the universe'. However, as Bunge (1959, p. 23 n.) put it: 'The whole of his celebrated criticism of [scientific] legality relied on the erroneous identification of scientific law with *mechanical* law.' Peirce's arguments rule out neither law-like determination in general nor stochastic determination in particular. Peirce did not show that variety and diversity are uncaused or undetermined. Causal processes can readily generate even random variations. Peirce's argument is ineffective against the principle of determinacy.

For James, a major incentive for his indeterminism was a concern to underline the reality of the human will. In similar vein to Peirce, William James attacked 'determinism' in a lucid and challenging essay first published in 1894. The notion of determinism that he rejected was essentially the 'regularity determinism' discussed in Chapter 3 above. James (1897, p. 150) wrote:

> What does determinism profess? It professes that those parts of the universe already laid down absolutely appoint and decree what the other parts shall be. The future has no ambiguous possibilities hidden in its womb: the part we call the present is compatible with only one totality. Any other future complement than the one fixed from eternity is impossible. The whole is in each and every part, and welds it with the rest into an absolute unity, an iron block, in which there can be no equivocation or shadow of turning.

James (1897, p. 292) saw determinism as implying a block universe involving 'the absolute block whose parts have no loose play'. Rejecting this form of determinism, James (1897, pp. 150–1) went on to define the indeterminism that he favoured:

> Indeterminism, on the contrary, says that the parts have certain amount of loose play on one another, so that the laying down of one of them does not necessarily determine what the others shall be. It admits that possibilities may be in excess of actualities, and that things not yet revealed to our knowledge may really in themselves be ambiguous. Of two alternative futures which we conceive, both may now be really possible; and the one becomes impossible only at the very moment when the other excludes it by becoming real itself. Indeterminism thus denies the world to be one unbending unit of fact. It says there is a certain ultimate pluralism in it.

Regularity determinism cannot apply to any open system. But the rejection of regularity determinism does not undermine the principle of determinacy. The argument that the parts of the universe 'have certain amount of loose play on one another, so that the laying down of one of them does not necessarily determine what the others shall be' reminds me of my childhood Meccano set. With Meccano nuts, bolts and holed metal rods and plates, one can construct a toy vehicle or building. If the nuts and bolts are not tightened sufficiently then the 'loose play' in the system could make it wobbly and unrobust. But this 'loose play' is readily explicable, within an entirely mechanical conception of the connections and forces involved. James's argument is not successful in undermining even the most transparent and mechanical form of determination. Both James and Peirce were at fault in their rejection of the principle of determinacy.

James went further to assert an ontological pluralism of multiple possible states of the universe, all of which are potentially real. For James, alternative possibilities, including mutually exclusive outcomes, were part of the whole truth. James (1897, p. 152) admitted, however, that no fact of

observation could clinch this matter, one way or the other. James's assertion of multiple possibilities was essentially an attempt to establish the reality of free will (1897, pp. 155–64, 180–2). On James's ontological pluralism
I shall propose an agnostic position here.

There is a way of retaining multiple possibilities without necessarily
adopting James's ontological pluralism. No discrete system is entirely
sealed off from external influences, and some of these influences can have
highly significant effects. Hence a number of near-identical systems, in
near-identical situations, can generate very different effects. In this sense,
looking among a population of similar units, multiple possibilities exist.
This applies whether or not, for the universe as a whole, there are multiple
possible futures as proposed by James.[16]

The existence of multiple possibilities among a population of similar
units enlarges the real opportunity for variety and enhances 'population
thinking'. This vital ingredient to Darwinism moves us away from the relative simplicity of Newtonian mechanics to a much more complex, varied
and evolving world, where path dependence and history are paramount.

The seven philosophical pillars of Darwinism

Darwinism is associated with the ideas of variation, inheritance and selection. Moreover, underlying this theory of evolution are seven philosophical principles that are even more fundamental to Darwinism. Some but not
all of these principles were explicit in Darwin's work. Some are best formulated in terms of twentieth-century philosophical concepts. But all of them
are at the core of a suitably modernized Darwinism. Four of the points are
ontological (concerning being) and three are methodological (concerning
explanation). The first four concern the nature of the world and its causal
connections, irrespective of the state of our knowledge (or ignorance) of
the way the world works.

A first Darwinian philosophical principle – the principle of determinacy

This is otherwise known in philosophy as 'the principle of universal causation' or sometimes 'ubiquity determinism'. Its rough and ready expression
is 'every event has a cause', and more precisely, *everything is determined in
accordance with laws by something else* (Bunge, 1959).

The principle of determinacy does not imply that events are necessarily
predictable, or that any one set of events will always lead to the same, regular outcome. These versions of 'determinism' are not adopted here.

---

16 For at least two reasons, the principle of determinacy does not imply a block universe.
First, it does not mean 'that everything in the world is connected with *everything* else in *all*
respects; nor does causal determinism assert that everything is *causally* connected with
everything else' (Bunge, 1959, p. 98). Second, it leaves open the possibility of stochastic
determination.

'Mechanistic' views are said to exclude intentionality, but here intentionality is acknowledged and included. The principle of determinacy upholds that intentions are caused, but this does not diminish the reality or responsibility of will or choice. The alternative and unacceptable view of an uncaused cause would not make us responsible for our actions, as they would result from capricious and spontaneous processes beyond our knowledge and control.

A second Darwinian philosophical principle – emergentist materialism.

This principle will be explained in more detail in later chapters, but due to its importance it is mentioned here. Emergentist materialism rejects multiple and independent forms of being, where one type of substance (notably mind) is treated as entirely separate from and independent of another (notably matter). Instead of being a ghost in the machine, the mind is understood in terms of emergent properties of organized matter. Human intentions are regarded as emergent properties of materialist interactions within the human nervous system (Bunge, 1980). However, because of emergent properties, it is difficult to explain specific mental phenomena entirely in neural or other physical terms. Hence emergentist materialism limits or excludes reductionism.

A third Darwinian philosophical principle – population thinking

This entails an ontological commitment to variety; where the understanding of the essence of something involves not only the singular entity, but also its membership of a population of similar but non-identical entities. The essence of a type necessarily includes its potential to exhibit or create variety. Accordingly, the understanding of any item must also consider the population of similar entities in which that variation is present or possible. This 'population thinking' does not abandon the philosophical notion of essence but endows it with a special and enriched meaning. On the basis of population thinking, the Darwinian emphasis on variation is established (Mayr, 1976, 1982).

A fourth Darwinian philosophical principle – the doctrine of continuity

A species is a causal and evolutionary outcome of accumulated gradations and variations, with organisms that inherit and preserve most of their characteristics through time. It is upheld that complex outcomes are the result of accumulated, incremental changes. Miraculous leaps and teleological determination are excluded. This means that human intentionality has itself evolved gradually through time. Also conscious intentions themselves coexist in the mind with less conscious, habitual and autonomic actions. In general, continuity involves mechanisms of inheritance upon which slight generational variations are accumulated. Darwin's treatment of inheritance is thus grounded on this principle.

A fifth Darwinian philosophical principle – cumulative causal explanation

The idea of causal explanation is applied sequentially to these step-by-step developments. Accordingly, explanation of change involves tracing causal processes by focusing on their key processual algorithms. Even if every step in a process cannot be determined in detail, the algorithmic process helps to provide an explanation. The key algorithmic process emphasized by Darwin was natural selection. However, as emphasized above, the concept of selection in Darwinism necessarily invokes neither competition nor militant struggle.

A sixth Darwinian philosophical principle – the principle of evolutionary explanation

It follows from the above that any behavioural assumption, including in the social sciences, must be capable of cumulative causal explanation in evolutionary terms, or at least be consistent with a scientific understanding of human evolution. Other sciences are not mere extensions of biology, but they must be consistent with an acceptable version of it. In particular, if there are biological constraints or influences on human capacities or behaviours, then they should be neither contradicted nor negated by assumptions at the psychological or social levels.

A seventh Darwinian philosophical principle – the principle of consistency of the sciences

This is a generalization of the sixth principle: any scientific assumption or principle at a specific ontological level must be consistent with a scientific understanding of all lower ontological levels. For example, the social sciences are not reducible to psychology, biology, chemistry or physics, but they must be consistent with acceptable versions of these sciences.

A forceful modern plea for the consistency of the sciences is by Edward O. Wilson (1998), who rightly criticized economics for its failure to incorporate insights from other sciences. But Wilson proposed a degree of reductionism that is not inherent in the seventh principle, and does not give sufficient acknowledgement of emergent properties and irreducible levels of analysis. Contrary to Wilson's *Consilience*, the seventh Darwinian philosophical principle does not involve a commitment to reduce all sciences to one.[17]

What happens when assumptions or principles at one level are inconsistent with those at other levels? It would be reasonable to suggest that, in the absence of any strong reason to the contrary, assumptions or principles at lower levels take priority over assumptions or principles at all higher levels. No assumptions or principles at any higher level can violate, override or supersede the operation of any physical law. Similarly, chemical determination has priority over biological laws, biological determination has priority over the psychic, and psychic determination has priority over social laws.

Simplifying abstractions in science, such as the treatments of bodies as single particles in mechanics, may be strictly false but nevertheless do not overturn scientific principles at any level. However, there are examples of inconsistencies between different scientific discourses. For example, the post-1945 synthesis between 'Walrasian' microeconomics and 'Keynesian' macroeconomics predicted market-clearing full employment at the microeconomic level but possible unemployment equilibria at the macroeconomic level. This inconsistency was rightly challenged. Either the 'Walrasian' microeconomics or 'Keynesian' macroeconomics had to go. Inconsistencies exist within and between other sciences, but they are always a cause for concern, and await resolution in one way or another.

These Darwinian philosophical principles are central to Veblenian institutional economics. But they contain some philosophical leeway. Consider an eighth issue, over which the present work is agnostic. The principles above are compatible with notions of either statistical or non-statistical causation. In the case of statistical causation or tychism, a cause can lead to multiple possibilities, even in the same circumstances and with the same causes (Bunge, 1959). Commonly cited examples of statistical causation include the throw of a die or the disintegration of a radioactive atomic nucleus. However, in general, as noted above, statistical causation may all be a result of non-statistical causation in non-linear systems (Stewart, 1989). No attempt is made to resolve these issues here. For the purposes of the present work it does not matter whether statistical causation with multiple possible outcomes is admitted as such, or randomness is regarded as a consequence of non-linearities and non-statistical causation. Precise prediction may be impossible in cases of statistical or non-statistical causation, but neither of these two causal stances rules out the possibility of explanation. Hence, at least as far as we go in this book, a stance on the issue of statistical versus non-statistical causation is of little consequence.

---

17 Wilson (1998, p. 226) wrote: 'The central idea of the consilience world view is that all tangible phenomena, from the birth of the stars to the workings of social institutions, are based on material processes that are ultimately reducible, however long and tortuous the sequences, to the laws of physics.' Wilson's reductionist goal is rejected here. Oddly, Wilson (1978, p. 11) elsewhere mentioned 'novel, emergent phenomena' but acknowledged neither the anti-reductionist consequences nor the irreducibility of the social or other ontological levels.

5 Precursors of emergence and multiple-level evolution

A syllable is not merely the sum of its letters ... nor is flesh just fire + earth. For after dissolution, the compounds – flesh or the syllable – no longer exist; but the letters do, and so do fire and earth. The syllable, then, is something on its own – not merely the letters ... but something else besides. Similarly, flesh is not merely fire and earth, hot and cold, but something else besides.

Aristotle, *Metaphysics*

Chapters 6 to 8 show how the core principles of Darwinism spurred the rise of Veblenian institutional economics in America in the 1890s. But some essential and preliminary topics remain to be discussed before we land for an enduring stay on American shores. First we return to the 1870s, and address two key problems then faced by Darwinism. The narrative in this chapter discusses the works of some British authors and takes us up to the mid-1890s.

The two problems concern the attempts by Darwinians to explain the evolution of the human species and of human society. The first of these two problems has been raised already. Darwinism upholds that intelligent life in general and human consciousness in particular has evolved out of earlier and more primitive organisms. Accordingly, how do we explain the evolution of human consciousness? We have noted that Alfred Russel Wallace came to the conclusion that it could not be explained by natural selection. In contrast, most Darwinians, including Thomas Henry Huxley, emphasized the physical basis of mind. However, in asserting this materialist view, Huxley reduced mind to a mere epiphenomenon of matter.

Ernst Haeckel, a German sympathizer of Darwin, faced a similar dilemma. But instead of reductionist materialism, his reductionist inclination was to endow all matter with psychic qualities. In other words, he proposed a form of panpsychism. Huxley and Haeckel were driven by their understanding of the Darwinian law of continuity to propose some kind of single-level ontology. Although they took opposite views, in emphasizing continuity they both obscured the distinction between matter and mind. The problem of understanding the evolution of mind from matter forced them to declare that either mind was matter, or that matter was mind. In contrast, Wallace resolved the issue in the case of humankind by entirely abandoning the doctrine of continuity.[1]

Neither Wallace's materialist–spiritualist dualism, Haeckel's panpsychism nor Huxley's reductionist materialism were satisfactory. Dissatisfaction with Darwinian attempts to resolve the ancient philosophical conundrum of the relationship between body and mind led to forms of vitalism, Lamarckism and mysticism.

The second problem also helped to sustain Lamarckism into the early decades of the twentieth century. The problem existed because several leading social theorists – including Herbert Spencer and Alfred Marshall (1923, p. 260) – believed that the march of human civilization and its social institutions were 'the products of human nature and cannot change much faster than human nature changes'. Marshall and others resolved this problem by presuming that the rate of change of biological human nature 'is increasing constantly and rapidly'.

From this point of view – which we now know to be erroneous – the spectacular rise of human civilization and technology in the last few thousand years could and had to be explained in large part by changes in human nature. Insofar as humankind had leapt forward in its achievements, this would have to correspond to similar leaps in the biotic constitution of human beings. How could such rapid changes in human nature come about?

The Lamarckians had a ready answer to this problem. They proposed a circular process of positive feedback, in which advancing human capacities gave rise to more advanced institutions, thus encouraging greater human development through learning and environmental stimulation.[2] Crucially, from a Lamarckian perspective, every step forward in individual human development could be passed on to others through the inheritance of acquired characters. Hence the circular feedback process was boosted by the fact that each generation could build cumulatively on the characteristics acquired in and handed down from the preceding generation of individuals. In this way, social development and individual biotic evolution kept in step with one another. Within Lamarckism, reductionist explanations of the development of human society in terms of human biology seemed possible.

As noted above, many Darwinians, including Darwin himself, did not deny the possibility of the inheritance of acquired characters. A difference

1 Similarly, in the 1890s, Peirce promoted an idealism where all matter was regarded as a form of rigidified mind. Peirce claimed 'that physical phenomena are fundamentally mental' (Hookway, 1985, p. 143).
2 Spencer (1862) used the term 'multiplication of effects' for what we now call 'positive feedback'.

between the Darwinians and the Lamarckians was over the relative degree of emphasis given to the additional mechanisms of natural selection. In the 1870s, the balance of argument shifted in favour of Lamarckism. Natural selection did not seem to be able to account for the rapid evolution of the human species that was necessary to explain the equivalently rapid rise of human civilization in biologically reductionist terms.

The emergence of George Henry Lewes

At this point, George Henry Lewes made a major and prescient contribution.[3] Lewes wrote extensively on the physical basis of mind and on the philosophy of science. In his philosophical volumes, entitled *Problems of Life and Mind*, Lewes (1874, 1875, 1877, 1879) grappled with both of the aforementioned Darwinian difficulties.

Lewes adhered to a materialist and monist ontology, upholding that all phenomena are made up of matter. He rejected idealism in philosophy and vitalism in biology. However, he argued that although mind had a physical basis, its properties could not be reduced to those of matter alone. He explained that varied factors, when combined together in a complex system, could lead to properties that cannot be found among the component properties in isolation. These additional properties were described as 'emergents'. This is the passage by Lewes (1875, p. 412) in which the term first appears:

> Thus, although each effect is the resultant of its components, the product of its factors, we cannot always trace the steps of the process, so as to see in the product the mode of operation of each factor. In the latter case, I propose to call the effect an emergent. It arises out of the combined agencies, but in a form which does not display the agents in action.

The general term 'resultant' refers to any amalgamation of effects, including additive combinations. For Lewes, an 'emergent' was a special kind of resultant. Lewes (1875, p. 413) argued that emergents resulted from the interaction of varied components: 'with emergents, … instead of adding measurable motion to measurable motion, or things of one kind to other individuals of their kind, there is a co-operation of things of unlike kinds.' Lewes (1875, p. 414) used this illustrative example: 'Unlike as water is to oxygen or hydrogen separately, or to both when uncombined, nothing

---

3 Lewes was born in London but spent much of his restless youth in France and Germany. Fluent in French and German, he was familiar with the works of Hegel, Goethe and Comte. After his return to England he eventually made a living through his writing, as did his famous partner Mary Ann Evans (George Eliot). She dedicated her novel *The Mill on the Floss* to Lewes. By 1870, with the huge success of her novels, the couple enjoyed financial security.

can be more like water than their combination, which is water.' In other words, the properties of water were not contained in hydrogen or oxygen on their own, or when together uncombined. We can swim in and drink water, but with their uncombined components we can do neither.

In sum, for Lewes, an emergent was a property of a system that could not be traced and explained in terms of its components or their interactions. Lewes developed an idea that was traceable as far back as Plato in his *Theaetetus* and Aristotle in his *Metaphysics*: that a whole can be greater than the sum of its parts. Similarly, there is the so-called 'law of the transformation of quantity into quality', which was laid down by Georg Wilhelm Friedrich Hegel in his *Logic* of 1830 (Hegel, 1976) and subsequently taken up by Karl Marx and Frederick Engels. Likewise, Auguste Comte (1853, vol. 2, p. 181) wrote in the 1830s of irreducible properties: 'Society is no more decomposable into individuals than a geometrical surface is into lines, or a line into points'. With his idea of 'heteropathic' causation John Stuart Mill (1843, bk. 3, ch. 6, para. 2) also hinted at a notion of emergence. To illustrate this, Mill also used the example of water as a 'chemical' combination of substances giving rise to a substance with different properties. But Mill's discussion of heteropathic causation did not apply it to mental or evolutionary phenomena. The idea of emergent properties is also foreshadowed in the work of Lewes's friend and contemporary, the Scottish philosopher Alexander Bain (1870).[4]

Part of Lewes's personal contribution was to clarify and broaden the idea of emergents to social and mental, as well as physical phenomena. He coined the noun 'emergent'. Later authors used the terms 'emergent property' and 'emergence' and they became enduring concepts in several sciences.

Lewes emphasized that emergents were outcomes of the interaction of dissimilar factors. His argument amounted to more than the maxim that 'the whole is greater than the sum of its parts'. The whole is more than its parts because it includes the relations between those parts. Lewes said that the whole could have further additional properties, as a result of those relations and the combination of different component elements. Moreover, Lewes's argument was different from the Hegelian law of 'the transformation of quantity into quality'. Lewes argued that emergents were not an outcome of the aggregation of similar and additive factors but of the interaction of dissimilar elements. Lewes posited that complex combinations of elements could lead to properties not traceable in the elements themselves, although each complex depended upon its constituent parts.

A key significance of this concept was to open up the possibility of qualitative novelty in the evolutionary process. Evolution could become more than aggregation and continuous transformation; it would become possible to conceive of new properties and forms, including the emergence of

---

4   It is also likely that Peirce was influenced by Bain (1859, 1870).

mind, without abandoning a commitment to the material basis of existence, and without reducing mind to matter, or vice versa.

Lewes also pointed to an ontological hierarchy of levels, which is now commonplace in the philosophy of science. Matter takes different forms – atomic, molecular, organic, neurophysiological and so on. Elements at any higher level always depend upon their constituent and lower-level components, but at the higher levels there are emergents that cannot be deduced from lower-level properties.

Lewes made use of this terminology to argue that mind and consciousness were emergents, upon physical and neurophysiological foundations. He thus proposed a position that was superior to both the spiritualism of Wallace and the mental epiphenomenalism of Huxley. The idea that mind was an emergent, and upon a materialist foundation, was later developed and debated by a number of authors, some of which are noted later in the present work.

Lewes, emergence and social evolution

As well as tackling the problem of the physical basis of mind, and offering a preliminary solution to it, Lewes also pondered the relationship between the evolution of human nature and the evolution of civilization. He thus addressed the two Darwinian problems mentioned above. Just as Lewes did not believe that the mind could be explained entirely in physical or neurophysiological terms (although the mind depends for its existence on neural matter), he also did not believe that human society could be explained entirely in terms of the biotic characteristics of its individual members (although society depends for its existence on the biotic vitality of those individuals). He thus pointed to an *emergent level* of social evolution.

Indeed, Lewes connected the two problems and their responses, by taking the concept of mind at the individual level and proposing the concept of the 'General Mind' at the social level. For Lewes, the 'General Mind' was not a mystical entity, but his choice of term betrayed an enduring Hegelian influence on his thought. It had an equivalent ontological status to ideas such as 'organizational learning' and 'collective action' that are commonly used today. But we must allow Lewes (1879, vol. 1, pp. 161–2) to speak for himself:

> The experiences of each individual come and go; they correct, enlarge, destroy one another, leaving behind them a certain residual store, which, condensed in intuitions and formulated in principles, direct and modify all future experiences. The sum of these is designated as the individual mind. A similar process evolves the General Mind – the residual store of experiences common to all. By means of language the individual shares in the general fund, which thus becomes for him an impersonal objective influence. To it each appeals.

We all assimilate some of its material, and help to increase its store. Not only do we find ourselves confronting Nature, to whose order we must conform, but confronting Society, whose laws we must obey. We have to learn what Nature is and does, what our fellow-men think and will, and unless we learn aright and act in conformity, we are inexorably punished.

The central idea here is that society creates a store of intuitions and experiences that are condensed in customs and laws, formulated through the medium of language. These customs and laws are social emergents, standing above the individual. They are formed by individuals, but they also form a social environment to which each individual adapts. The individual is obliged to conform to these customs and obey these laws, or suffer adverse consequences. Not only do these customs and laws emerge out of individuals and their interactions, but also they coerce and impose sanctions upon individuals. The causation works both ways. Lewes's exposition involves a notion of social structure that is not reduced to individuals. Neither is the individual explained entirely by structure. Enlarging on these points, Lewes (1879, vol. 1, pp. 164–5) continued:

Customs arise, and are formulated in laws, the restraint of all. The customs, born of the circumstances, immanent in the social conditions, are consciously extricated and prescribed as the rules of life; each new generation is born in this social medium, and has to adapt itself to the established forms. Society, though constituted by individuals, has a powerful reaction on every individual. 'In the infancy of nations,' said Montesquieu, 'man forms the state; in their maturity the state forms the man.' It is thus also with the collective Experience of the race fashioning the experience of the individual. It makes a man accept what he cannot understand, and obey what he does not believe. His thoughts are only partly his own; they are also the thoughts of others. His actions are guided by the will of others; even in rebellion he has them in his mind. His standard is outside. ... If he does not feel what all feel, he is thrown out of account, except in the reckoning of abnormalities. Individual experiences being limited and individual spontaneity feeble, we are strengthened and enriched by assimilating the experiences of others. ... The nation affects the sect, the sect the individual. Not that the individual is passive, he is only directed; he, too, reacts on the sect and nation, helping to create the social life of which he partakes.

Lewes proposed here an articulation of actor and structure, where each was conditioned by, and dependent upon the other. His position was antithetical to the twin reductionisms of methodological individualism and methodological collectivism. However, while seeing this mutual interdependence of actor and structure, Lewes did not regard the relationship between them as symmetrical. For Lewes, the past dominated the present; we all adapt to a world that existed before our birth. Those now dead largely created this world, but the living can in some respects change it. Lewes (1879, p. 166) wrote:

> Civilisation is the accumulation of experiences; and since it is this accumulated wealth which is the tradition of the race, we may say with Comte that the Past more and more dominates the Present, precisely as in the individual case it is the registered experiences which more and more determine the feelings and opinions. Human knowledge is preeminently distinguished from Animal Knowledge by this collective experience.

Building on Comte's insight that actors that are dead dominate social life, Lewes realized that collective experience likewise bound the individual to the past. As Karl Marx (1973, p. 146) wrote in 1852: 'The tradition of the dead generations weighs like a nightmare on the minds of the living.' This insight breaks the symmetry of actor and structure by bringing in the key ingredient of time (Archer, 1995).

It is also important to note that Lewes's development of the concept of an emergent, his attempted solution to the mind–body problem, and his derivation of a temporally located concept of society that was not reducible to individuals, were all prompted in part by the Darwinian framework of his thought.

Let us take stock of what Lewes proposed concerning the problem of agent and structure. First, Lewes argued that agent and structure are mutually constitutive of each other. In particular, social structures can affect individual beliefs, preferences and aspirations. Through social structures and customs, we are pressured (albeit often incompletely) not only to acquiesce and to conform but also to 'feel what all feel' and adopt the beliefs and preferences of others. The accumulated experiences of all 'more and more determine the feelings and opinions'. I have already introduced the term *reconstitutive downward causation* to describe the possibility that social structures can change individual preferences to some degree. This notion admits an enhanced concept of social power and is established below as one of the essential characteristics of institutional economics.

Second, Lewes pointed to the fact that the social store of custom and tradition is made up essentially of 'collective experience' and accumulated knowledge, built up with the growth of human civilization and accessible in part by means of language and learning. Hence Lewes pointed to the insight that social institutions are not simply rules and constraints, but also *repositories of social knowledge*. He indicated that institutions could accumulate experience and knowledge in some way. This general notion of institutions as a kind of social memory became a keystone of early American institutional economics.[5]

Several theorists, including Marx, saw social structures reconstituting individual preferences or beliefs. For example, in the third volume of *Capital*, Marx (1981, p. 1020) wrote of 'specific social characters that the social production process stamps on individuals'. But this notion is less well developed in Marx's writings. Also, compared with Lewes, the more dramatic omission is that Marx did not articulate a conception of social institutions as repositories of social knowledge. Indeed, the concept of knowledge in Marx's work is one largely of natural-scientific or technical knowledge. Marx did not fully recognize that social interactions require and sustain other forms of knowledge that are an essential part of individual adaptation within society. These other forms of knowledge are partly expressed in customs, rules and other protocols of behaviour. Part of this rich heritage of knowledge is built up in the centuries of accumulated common law. Marx lacked a developed concept of custom, and he saw common law as something conservative, to be swept aside in social revolution, rather than carefully sifted and partially retained. Following Lewes, custom became a central concept in American institutional economics, thus expressing an important difference between Marxism and institutionalism.[6]

Lewes's notion that social institutions acted as emergent repositories of social knowledge resolved a particular problem that had perplexed Wallace and others concerning the evolution of the human species. Wallace had concluded that different races, whether in primitive or civilized circumstances, were at similar levels of intellectual potential. But he then could not explain the relatively rapid evolution of human civilization in some regions, while other humans remained in a savage state. Lewes proposed civilization itself could evolve at a rate much faster than the physiological and mental capacities of humans themselves, as knowledge and experience were accumulated. Human capacities could not be understood in terms of the human brain alone. Human abilities also depended on the structured environment of social interactions between individuals. The growing knowledge that was embedded in social structures provided an environment in which individuals could realize more and more of their

---

5   Other social theorists recognized social evolution as in part an accumulation of experiences and ideas. Such hints are found, for example, in Buckle's *History of Civilization in England* (1858) and in an essay of Huxley (1894, vol. 7, pp. 155–6) from the 1860s. But neither author placed social evolution in the context of emergent properties, as Lewes had done.

6   Note the valid criticism of Marx by Commons (1925, pp. 686–7): 'Here is the culminating oversight of Karl Marx in his theory of socialism … namely, the failure to see the importance of custom, and what in Anglo-American jurisprudence is named the common law … between the individual and the state is a supreme principle of stabilization by custom, which both regulates the individual proprietor, on the one hand, and overrides the arbitrary will of the state, on the other hand.' Veblen's criticisms of Marx, including on the matters of human knowledge, motivations and habits, will be outlined later below.

intellectual potential, possibly without such a rapid growth in individual human capabilities.

However, Lewes did not give enough emphasis to this argument because he retained, like Darwin himself, strong Lamarckian inclinations. If the inheritance of acquired individual human characters were possible, then the mechanism outlined in the last paragraph was not necessary to explain the growth of human civilization. It could be explained by acquired character inheritance alone. An additional mechanism, where the evolving social environment itself stimulated individual development, would not be essential. For this reason the full impact of Lewes's additional argument was not realized, even by Lewes himself.

Several other issues were not sufficiently clarified in Lewes's work. He articulated only partially an ontology of different levels. The nature of social institutions and structures was not examined in any depth. Furthermore, Lewes did not elaborate any psychological mechanism through which individual feelings, beliefs or aspirations could be remoulded by their institutional or social circumstances. Yet he made a significant start. Others would build on Lewes's ideas. Partly under the stimulation of further debates within biology, they would receive further development. Eventually – but alas largely unattributed – they would flourish in America.

In regarding institutions as repositories of social knowledge, and in pointing to emergent properties as key features of a social ontology, Lewes paved the way for a multi-level theory of selection and evolution, in which social evolution was a part. The significance of these insights will be elaborated later below. Above all, by suggesting a notion of reconstitutive downward causation in the social context, and by recognizing institutions as repositories of social knowledge, Lewes must be acknowledged as a forgotten grandfather of American institutional economics, at least in its Veblian genre.

Just as Lewes's ideas had emerged from a largely Darwinian problematic, the further development of this important line of thought was stimulated by an important advance in biology. At this stage it is important to outline this key development. It will become clear how and why this had an important impact on the social sciences. In that context, later below, we can then relate the story of how the spirit of Lewes crossed the Atlantic.

The Weismann barrier

After Darwin's death in 1882, some further scientific developments in biology had major and lasting consequences on both the natural and the social sciences. In the 1880s the German biologist August Weismann carried out a series of experiments at Freiburg University to test the Lamarckian principle of the inheritance of acquired characters. These studies convinced him of the fallacy of the Lamarckian principle and prompted him to develop an alternative theory of inheritance. Weismann (1889, 1893) also saw impossible complications in Darwin's theory of pangenesis. He did not believe that it was possible that the gemmules could carry information concerning parts of the phenotype to the germ cells and accumulate this information in a sufficiently coherent and effective manner.

Instead of seeing the body or phenotype as the source of variation, Weismann concentrated on the germ cell and its reproduction as the basis of deviation and change. Weismann suggested a 'germ plasm' that would carry the genotypic information and would itself be largely immutable. Pangenesis depended on a Lamarckian 'top down' transmission of information from phenotype to genotype. In contrast, Weismann regarded inheritance as an entirely 'bottom up' process, from genotype to phenotype. All changes in the genotypical characteristics of the population of a species would come about by sexual recombination, by natural selection on varying genotypes, and to a lesser extent by random mutation. In contrast, according to Weismann's theory, the acquired characteristics of an organism would not affect its germ plasm or genotype. This became known as the Weismann barrier; it prevented the characteristics of the organism affecting its germ plasm.

By the early 1890s, Weismann's works were translated into English and widely discussed. Weismann guided evolutionary biology along a path of enquiry that was vindicated in general terms by the development of Mendelian genetics in the early years of the twentieth century. Weismann's inspiration eventually triumphed with the synthesis of Darwinism and Mendelism in the 1940s.

Defending his Lamarckian position, Spencer (1893) critiqued Weismann. Spencer again raised the point that natural selection could not on its own account for the presumed rate of evolution. Weismann argued in response that there was no apparent means through which an acquired character could be passed on to offspring. The debate with Weismann dented Spencer's reputation and gave the Darwinian theory a new lease of life. Weismann put the Lamarckian idea of the inheritance of acquired characters on the defensive.

But these outcomes exacerbated the problem that had perplexed social scientists for decades. While they were trapped within a biological reductionist paradigm, social scientists after Weismann had even greater difficulty in explaining the mismatch between, on the one hand, the slow rate of evolution of human mental capacities and, on the other hand, the enormous and rapid advances in civilization and technology in the last few millennia.

As noted above, the Lamarckians had avoided this problem by insisting on the possibility that newly acquired habits and other characteristics could readily be passed on genetically from generation to generation. But Weismann's contribution had seemingly ruled out this option. He argued that the evolution of the human genotype had been slow, and any assistance from the inheritance of acquired characters had to be ruled out. As a result of Weismann's work, it now seemed even more difficult to explain the evolution of civilization within a Darwinian framework.

This created an apparent paradox: despite tremendous advances in civilization and technology in the last few millennia, in *biotic* and *genetic* terms humankind had evolved only to a very slight degree. Genetically, humans had changed very little in the centuries that had witnessed enormous advances in science, technology and civilization. To nineteenth-century intellectuals disposed to emphasize the biological determination of social phenomena, how could such a mismatch be explained? Weismann's arguments posed severe problems for both the Lamarckians and the biological reductionists.

Weismann's work had an immediate impact, and was widely cited in the academic journals of philosophy, anthropology, sociology and economics. In his highly popular – but idiosyncratic and confused – book on *Social Evolution*, Benjamin Kidd (1894) referred to Weismann several times, gave some of his conclusions cautious approval, and noticed the impetus they had given to the Darwinian school. Alfred Marshall wrote to Kidd on 6 June 1894 to express his admiration for the book. However, Marshall remained a Lamarckian and a Spencerian. In this letter to Kidd, Marshall admitted that he had read part of the 1893 controversy between Weismann and Spencer 'without being convinced' of Weismann's arguments. Marshall could not accept that 'two men alike at birth', one of whom lives a healthy and one an unhealthy life, each could have similar children of equal health and potential (Whitaker, 1996, p. 114). Marshall remained convinced that the social experiences and acquired characteristics of the parents would inevitably affect their children. Even in later editions of his *Principles*, Marshall retained his adherence to a number of Spencerian and Lamarckian doctrines. In particular, Marshall (1949, p. 206) clung stubbornly to his belief that 'children of those who had led healthier lives, physically and morally' would 'be born with a firmer fibre' and would 'acquire more wholesome instincts'. Marshall did not believe that the more healthy offspring could be explained by the influence of the environment alone (Groenewegen, 1995, pp. 484–6).

Like Marshall, the leading American sociologist Lester Frank Ward (1891, 1892) attacked the Weismann doctrine. From his Lamarckian viewpoint, he claimed that if Weismann were correct then evolution would have not proceeded beyond protazoa. When applied to human society, Ward also argued that 'natural selection' could not account for the lasting inefficiencies and dysfunctional institutions of human society. In the 1890–1914 period, Weismann's results were not a comfort to social scientists but a challenge.

The examples of Kidd, Marshall and Ward show that the debate between the (Lamarckian) transmissionists and the (Darwinian) selectionists in the 1890s was far from confined to biology. It was realized immediately that whether Weismann was right or wrong would have major effects on the social as well as on the natural sciences. Among the several issues at stake was whether or not changes in human nature and mental capacities could be seen as the direct driving forces in social evolution. If Weismann were right, then the pace of evolution of inherited human nature would be restricted to the process of natural selection. Social science would then again have the problem of explaining the relatively rapid rise of human civilization in a few thousand years. The evolution of human civilization could not be explained in terms of the concomitant evolution of inherited human nature. A huge question emerged that could not be readily answered in the existing Darwinian scheme.

Conwy Lloyd Morgan

Our story returns to that group of British intellectuals around Darwin and Spencer, who had developed and promoted evolutionary theory from the 1850s to the 1880s. Conwy Lloyd Morgan was born in London. He studied mining and metallurgy at the Royal School of Mines. After obtaining his degree, and a short period as a tutor for a wealthy family in Chicago, he became a graduate student under Huxley, by whom he was profoundly influenced. After a few years at the Diocesan College at Rondebosch in South Africa, Morgan returned to England to take up a lectureship at University College in Bristol in 1883. In the following year he was elected to the Chair of Geology and Zoology, and in 1887 as the Principal of University College. Morgan spent the rest of his career at that institution, which became the University of Bristol in 1909. After one year as the first Vice-Chancellor of the new university, he resigned from administrative work to continue his research. In 1920, he retired from the university and became an Emeritus Professor of Psychology.

Morgan was a friend of George Romanes, and was his literary executor after his untimely death. Especially during his early years in Rondebosch and Bristol, Morgan was a prolific writer, producing ten books and many journal articles in a dozen years. In some places Morgan (1891) referred extensively to Lewes's works. In some early writings, Morgan (1885, 1891, 1894) rejected Weismann's arguments. However, Morgan (1891, pp. 480–503) also developed the idea that human progress could be accounted for by an evolving social environment, rather than by a brain puffed-up by inherited Lamarckian capabilities. He thus realized that Weismann's doctrine did not necessarily lead to pessimistic conclusions. In 1892 he tried to persuade Wallace that there was 'no cause to despair. Human progress is still possible' (Burnham, 1972). Inspired by Weismann's 1894 Romanes Lecture on 'The effect of external influences on development', Morgan became fully persuaded that Weismann's central thesis was correct. Morgan set to the task of dealing with the problems thrown up by the assumed validity of the Weismann doctrine, including the problem of reconciling the slow pace of biological evolution with the much more rapid evolution of human society (Morgan, 1896a, 1896b). However, it was some time before Morgan developed these insights into a theory of emergent evolution.

In some of his earliest works, Morgan (1885, 1891) devoted himself to the problem of consciousness in animals and humans, and made a pioneering contribution to comparative psychology. He proposed that learning by experience involved choice among rival strategies and ideas, analogous to the natural selection of organisms. In 1899 he was the first fellow to be elected to the Royal Society of London for work in psychology. Morgan argued against Huxley's treatment of consciousness as an epiphenomenon of the brain. Morgan also rejected Wallace's appeal to the supernatural as an explanation of the evolution of human mental capacities. He also attempted to avoid the panpsychism of Haeckel and others (Blitz, 1992; Costall, 1993). Instead, Morgan developed a more sophisticated ontology where mind was not reduced to body alone, and consciousness was seen as emerging from the interaction of complex neural phenomena. In this context, although Lewes influenced him, Morgan did not use the word 'emergent' at this time. For Morgan, evolution was not a mechanical process; it reflected the organism's intentional relationship with its environment.

Morgan also published a series of articles in leading philosophical journals such as the *Monist* and *Mind*. Like Lewes, but against Comte, Morgan argued that metaphysical presuppositions were essential to human thought and enquiry, but they could not be derived by generalization from observation or experience. They simply had to be assumed. Foremost among these presuppositions was the realist commitment to the existence of a material universe, whether or not humans perceived it. But Morgan went further to uphold a religious faith in God as the first cause and Creator of the universe, as a deity who subsequently did not intervene causally in the world.

Morgan addressed the problem of explaining a sufficiently rapid pace of evolution within a Darwinian framework. As noted above, this was a pressing problem at that time because a prominent Lamarckian objection to Darwinism was that evolution would happen too slowly and haphazardly without the inheritance of acquired characters. The Lamarckians claimed that the allegedly 'blind' and 'random' principles of Darwinism could not explain the rate and effectiveness of biotic evolution. In the USA, the psychologist James Mark Baldwin addressed the same problem.

In the same year, Baldwin (1896) and Morgan (1896a, 1896b) both published arguments that attempted to show how biological evolution could be hastened without the inheritance of acquired characters. Morgan was relatively unlucky, for the phenomenon acquired the name of the 'Baldwin Effect'.[7] Eventually, Baldwin was unlucky too, for as Darwinism became

---

7 R. Richards (1987, pp. 403–4) gave some reasons, other than luck, why the effect was so named.

ascendant after the 1930s, some thinkers dismissed the Baldwin–Morgan arguments because they seemed to smack of Lamarckian heresy. However, in fact the Baldwin–Morgan theories were devised to rebut Lamarckism and rescue Darwinism.

Morgan and Baldwin pointed out that natural selection acted on the phenotype rather than the genotype. Natural selection operated on all the phenotypical characteristics of the organism, whether they were inherited or acquired. As a result, the benefits of favourable inherited characteristics could be nullified by acquired characteristics that were deleterious, and unfavourable inherited characteristics could be cancelled out by acquired characteristics that were favourable. The most beneficial outcome for the organism would be when a beneficial inherited characteristic was supplemented by a beneficial acquired characteristic.

Hence any organism with an inherited propensity to develop beneficial acquired characteristics under specific conditions would doubly benefit. Natural selection would favour inherited mechanisms to acquire particular characteristics when they were beneficial. Although acquired characteristics could not themselves be inherited, the inherited capacity to acquire particular characteristics would be passed on. Natural selection may not simply lead to the development of species which are more adapted to their environment, but also to species with capacities to respond by further adaptation to likely future changes in the environment.

For example, if we do manual work, then the skin on our hands thickens. However, our children will not inherit skin of this extra thickness. Nevertheless, we pass on, through our genes, the capacity to grow thick skin in response to manual work. Over time, considering the population as a whole, natural selection may favour those with a genetic disposition to grow thicker skin more readily. Accordingly, an acquired character is not inherited directly. But through natural selection the capacity to acquire that character spreads through the population as a whole. There is no Lamarckian inheritance, and no breach of the Weismann Barrier. An adult does not pass on the acquired attribute of thick skin to its offspring. The infant's skin is thin and vulnerable. It will stay so, unless the hands are used. However, from a broader perspective the process *appears* Lamarckian, as an acquired character spreads among the population through time.

The significance of these proposals by Morgan and Baldwin in the 1896–1914 period was not simply to protect the arguments of Weismann from attack by the Lamarckians. It also suggested that evolution operated on secondo-rder capacities. Natural selection did not simply privilege beneficial inherited characteristics, but also inherited propensities to acquire beneficial characteristics. The Morgan–Baldwin arguments established the evolution of evolvability as a second-order aspect of natural selection and pointed to multiple levels in the evolutionary process.

Morgan and Baldwin proposed that this effect could speed up the process of evolution. In particular, if a genetic ability to adapt to, and learn from, a social culture evolved, then young humans would learn to deal with the complexities of advanced culture, just as manual work leads to a thickened skin. However, the evolution of evolvability does not necessarily speed up the pace of evolution to a degree that explains the rapid evolution of civilization in the last few thousand years. The problem is that genetic evolution, even if it involves the evolution of adaptability, is still extremely slow.

There were differences between the accounts of Morgan and Baldwin, and further problems in both their theories. Some time later, the British Darwinian biologist Conrad Waddington (1953, 1969, 1976), followed by John Campbell (1987) and Christopher Wills (1989), revived and refined their arguments. These developments, starting in the 1890s, reveal 'evolvability to be the greatest adaptation of all' (Depew and Weber, 1995, p. 485).[8]

Prelude to multiple-level evolution

As noted previously, Darwin foreshadowed multiple-level selection theory by proposing that natural selection operates on whole communities of insects, on the institution of language, on human groups, as well as on individuals. Following Darwin, some supposed a 'struggle for existence' between races and nations. But typically it was not made clear whether groups were selected because of their structural characteristics, or because of the characteristics of the individuals that comprised the group. In the latter case the individuals, not the group, would be the unit of selection, even if the account were presented in terms of a group, race or nation. Loose reference to the selection of a group did not mean that the group was fully established as a unit of selection.

Well before Darwin, it was commonplace to attribute to society the characteristics of a natural organism. This idea of a 'social organism' was popular among the German historical school (Krabbe, 1996; Hodgson, 2001c). It was employed at length by Herbert Spencer (1877, 1881), and by John Bates Clark (1885), Alfred Marshall (1890), John Hobson (1902) and many others. However, while the loose idea of 'natural selection' of 'social organisms' appeared, the mechanisms of this presumed selection process were inadequately clarified. Spencer, for instance, was reluctant to make 'social organisms' into full-blown units of selection, partly because of the individualistic bias in his theory. Despite social organism rhetoric, for

---

8 Morgan saw the organism making an 'intelligent choice'. But this choice is itself inadequately explained by natural selection. An objection to Baldwin's formulation was that if individual adaptations were sufficient to preserve an organism, then there is no reason why any related congenital variation should be favoured by natural selection. The Baldwin Effect depends upon the luck of fortuitous mutation after habits are established. In contrast, Waddington's (1953, 1969, 1976) 'genetic assimilation' works through progressive selection of the appropriate capacity to respond to stress. See also Dennett (1995, pp. 77–80), Hardy (1965, pp. 161–70), Maynard Smith (1975, pp. 303–7), Mayr (1960, pp. 371–7), Piaget (1979, pp. 14–21), R. Richards (1987, pp. 398–404, 480–503).

Spencer the units of selection were individuals. In contrast, Sidney Webb (1889, p. 53), the leading Fabian socialist and co-founder of the London School of Economics, adopted the terminology of the 'social organism' but insisted that 'the units selected are not individuals but societies'. But he was also unclear of the mechanisms or criteria of selection, other than to allude to the competitive struggle between nations for access to raw materials and for supremacy in world markets.

In fact, Webb blocked a multiple-level selection theory with his unwarranted denial of selection at the level of human individuals. Spencer blocked it too, by effectively making the individual the exclusive unit of selection in the social context. In general, the mere terminologies of group struggle or the social organism are not sufficient to establish multiple or higher level units and processes of selection.

Generally, the prevalence of Lamarckism discouraged the development of a multi-level selection theory. Lamarckians such as Spencer argued that acquired human characteristics gave rise to social structures and circumstances, which might in turn lead to more acquired characters. But, for Spencer, selection and replication operated on the biological level only. In this Lamarckian scheme, no higher level of selection was required to account for the evolution of culture or institutions. The evolution of civilization was derived from the accumulation of individual characteristics. Lamarckian ideas did not prohibit multi-level evolutionary theory, but they made its development less compelling.

John Bates Clark (1887, p. 46) was strongly influenced by Spencer and had used the term 'economic Darwinism'. But by this he meant 'a struggle for existence between competitors of the new and predatory type and those of the peaceable type' which was no more than a loose application of the principle of selection to economic competition. Even Marshall, who laced parts of his *Principles* (1890) with ideas taken from Spencerian evolutionary biology, did not develop the idea of natural selection of social institutions. In the few passages where he mentioned a concept of selection, it was upon individuals not institutions (Marshall, 1949, pp. 167–8). Reflecting their Spencerian dispositions, in the cases of both Clark and Marshall the principle of selection was underdeveloped and played a lesser role.

Those that were described as sociologists and evolutionists rarely extended the principle of selection to social customs, groups or institutions. For example, Gabriel Tarde (1890, 1899) searched for some kind of uniformity that was distinctly social, and could not be reduced to biological or physical terms. This he found in the 'laws of imitation'. He saw imitation as a mechanism of 'social memory' and noted its similarities with biological inheritance. But Tarde did not see this memory as a property of social structures or institutions. Neither did he provide an adequate social equivalent of natural selection.[9]

Achille Loria (1895, 1897) argued against the application of the Darwinian principle of selection to social life. The analyses of Otto Ammon (1895) and Georges Vacher de Lapouge (1896, 1897) addressed individual selection, not the selection of social units. Even when Lapouge emphasized the term 'social selection' he meant the selection of ethnically defined individuals in the context of their social environment.[10] Carlos Closson was from 1892 to 1895 a colleague of Veblen's at the University of Chicago. He translated an essay of Lapouge into English and published similar accounts of 'social selection' himself (Closson, 1896a, 1896b). What Closson meant by 'social selection' was similar to the notion of Lapouge, involving the selection of neither groups nor institutions but merely of individuals in a social milieu. For Closson, Lapouge and many others, the quality of human civilization depended principally on the capacities of the human individuals within it.

Walter Bagehot (1872) wrote of inheritance and natural selection in the social sphere. But his emphasis was on the struggle between nations, not a process of selection involving additional social units. He considered the role of imitation and the 'cake of custom' but did not emphasize their institutional integument as itself a unit of selection. Nevertheless, Bagehot and William James (1880) considered the natural selection of ideas in human learning and in the development of science. They were thus among the first to consider an evolutionary epistemology. James (1880, p. 441) opened his essay with the observation of a 'remarkable parallel ... between the facts of social evolution on the one hand, and of zoölogical evolution as expounded by Mr. Darwin on the other'. However, despite this fruitful hint, his discussion was largely confined to the selection of ideas in the heads of individuals. Oliver Wendell Holmes (1881) had taken inspiration from Darwin in his analysis of the evolution of law.[11] Subsequently Samuel Alexander (1892) and Benjamin Kidd (1894) wrote on the natural selection of ethical principles. Albeit limited in their robustness or scope, the works referenced in this paragraph were exceptional in bringing the principle of selection into the social domain, and considering units of selection other than individuals alone.

However, against attempts to extend Darwinian principles to the social sphere, some Darwinians, such as Huxley (1894, vol. 9), argued at length

9 Veblen was highly dismissive of a voguish work by Tarde (1890, 1899), which had been praised by Baldwin, Small and Ward, among others. Veblen (1900b, p. 363) criticized Tarde's 'elastic', 'ambiguous', and superficial formulations, noting that 'the volume may contribute materially to curtail the vogue of M. Tarde's sociological doctrines'. Veblen (1902, p. 147) was also critical of another of Tarde's works, describing its theoretical foundations as 'behind the times'. Like other writings by Tarde, its 'penchant for system making and symmetry gives it an air of completeness and definitiveness which is not borne out by substantial results' (Veblen, 1902, p. 147). A century later, Tarde has been escribed as a 'forefather of memetics' (Marsden, 2000).

10 The writings of Ammon and Lapouge were preoccupied with explanations of social phenomena in terms of alleged racial characteristics. Lapouge's studies of 'Aryanism' were later fêted by the Nazis.

11 With Dewey, James and Peirce, Holmes was a member of the 'Metaphysical Club' founded in 1872 in Cambridge, Massachusetts (Menand, 2001).

that natural selection did not and should not operate at the level of human society. Huxley proposed that the 'struggle for existence' should not and could not be applied to political doctrines in human society. He argued that social and political policy should work not *with* but *against* the 'struggle for existence'.

Although Huxley was right to be highly cautious about drawing political conclusions from Darwinism, his argument created an unwarranted dichotomy between nature, on the one hand, and human society and ethics, on the other. While Huxley did not entertain the possibility that Darwinian principles might apply to the analysis of social evolution, he undermined his own dichotomy by acknowledging the reliance of humans on their natural environment. Like many others at that time, he associated Darwinism with a negative, competitive and restrictive notion of the 'struggle for existence', in contrast to a broader Darwinian notion of selection. As a result, Huxley's argument further discouraged the development of any multiple-level evolutionary theory that might include a social and non-biological level. Huxley's attempt to prevent any ideological abuses of Darwinism resulted in a roadblock for scientific enquiry.

Henry Drummond (1894), Benjamin Kidd (1894), John Dewey (1898) and Petr Kropotkin (1902) all opposed Huxley's false dichotomy between nature and human society. They argued that Darwinism still applied to human society and human evolution: there was no preventative barrier between the natural and the social. But none of these critics clearly established social structures as additional units of selection. At best, Kropotkin (1902) wrote loosely of the natural selection of social groups. Kidd (1894, p. 43) wrote of human 'societies' and 'the survivals of the fittest' in the same sentence, but did not establish any notion that social structures were themselves subject to selection processes as well as individuals. In terms redolent of Lewes, Drummond (1894, pp. 191–2) pointed out that with social species such as humans, and with the development of language, a new level of evolutionary transmission had emerged: 'Evolution, up to this time, had only one way of banking the gains it won – heredity. ... But with the discovery of language there arose a new method of passing on a step in progress.' When a person 'learned anything he could pass it on; when he became wise wisdom would not die with him, it was banked in the Mind of humanity'. This suggested an additional level of evolutionary transmission and inheritance, but did not examine the units of selection and processes of replication in more detail. Like others, Drummond failed to consider the 'natural selection' of social structures or institutions.

A difficulty placed in the way of a Darwinian theory of social evolution was the absence thus far of a hierarchical ontology. In the 1890s, beyond the suggestions made by Lewes, Morgan and a few others, there was no developed notion of an emergent property. Accordingly, the idea of higher levels of reality, each associated with specific emergent properties, causal powers and laws, was underdeveloped and rudimentary at best.

In 1895 the idea of selection operating on social institutions or customs had not yet developed much beyond the hints already provided by Darwin in the *Descent of Man*. The furthest advances in the application of Darwinian ideas to the evolution of human society had been made by Bagehot (1872), Drummond (1894) and a few others.

Two parallel developments had to fuse together to provide the conceptual and philosophical basis for a multi-level selection theory, applicable to socio-economic evolution. The first was the realization that the mechanisms of replication and selection could apply to both nature and society. The second was the establishment of a hierarchical ontology consistent with monism, which would permit a rigorous account of replication and selection operating on social units above, and in addition to, natural organisms. This second development required a notion of emergent properties. This combination of ideas was prefigured, but did not emerge fully, in the nineteenth century. Among the heralds of such a theory of social evolution, we may count Lewes and Morgan. A third and neglected name will be mentioned below. The fourth name is the main subject of Part III of the present work.

Preliminary moves in the development of a hierarchical ontology had been provided by Lewes (1879, vol. 1, pp. 164–5) and Morgan (1896a, p. 340) but neither proposed a theory of social evolution involving selection of units at the social level. While Darwin had discussed the selection of morality and customs in his *Descent of Man*, he discussed neither hierarchical ontologies nor emergent properties. Morgan's own adoption of a hierarchical ontology was to come later on, in the second decade of the twentieth century. Even then it was limited with respect to social phenomena.

David George Ritchie

After Darwin and prior to 1895, applications of Darwinian natural selection to social phenomena typically saw the units of selection as individuals, rather than social structures or institutions. The clearest and greatest exception was the brilliant philosopher David Ritchie. He was born in Jedburgh on the Scottish borders. Educated in philosophy at the University of Edinburgh, from 1878 to 1894 he was a fellow and tutor at Oxford, where Thomas H. Green and Arnold Toynbee influenced him. He corresponded with Alexander and was inspired by Alexander's (1892) theory that Darwinian selection could be applied to the evolution of ethical ideas. In 1894 Ritchie became a professor of logic and metaphysics at St Andrew's University. Politically he had liberal, feminist and social democratic sympathies.[12]

---

12 Ritchie was a member of the Fabian Society until 1893, when it resolved to support the formation of a Labour Party separate from the Liberals. For further biographical details see Latta (1905) and Nicholson (1998).

In his book *Darwinism and Politics* (1889) Ritchie argued that Darwinism did not support totalitarianism, conservatism or laissez-faire. Ritchie (1889, p. 59) upheld that in human societies 'language and social institutions make it possible to transmit experience quite independently of the continuity of race'. In other words, cultural transmission functioned alongside, and in addition to, what today we describe as genetic inheritance. As a result, Ritchie argued: 'An individual or a nation may do more for mankind by handing on ideas and a great example than by leaving numerous offspring.'[13]

In the second edition of this book, Ritchie (1891) added an essay 'Natural selection and the history of institutions' and argued that Darwinian principles of variation, heredity and selection applied to the evolution of social institutions as well as to organisms. Ritchie repeated that language and institutions are social mechanisms through which adaptations and knowledge may be inherited. He wrote of a struggle between 'institutions, languages, ideas' as well as a struggle between individuals. But here, as elsewhere, Ritchie warned that although Darwinian principles applied to social evolution, they must always be used carefully, with meticulous acknowledgement of the differences in the mechanisms involved.

In a later article, originally read at the University of Cambridge,[14] Ritchie developed these ideas in more depth. Ritchie understood that Darwinism above all involved a commitment to causal explanations. In particular, against the doctrine of Wallace, Ritchie (1896, p. 170) believed that human mental capacities were a result of natural selection:

> Consciousness and reflection *may* be explained *historically* as the result of natural selection. Our simian ancestors who first happened to have brains which enabled them to adapt means to ends, instead of simply following their instinctive tendencies, got a great advantage over their less reflective brethren.

With this commitment to Darwinian evolutionary explanations, Ritchie (1889, 1896) forensically examined the conditions under which the principle of selection might be extended to the social sphere. Although he regarded biology as a better source of ideas for the social sciences than physics or chemistry, he repeatedly warned against the casual and uncritical use of biological terms in a social context. Ritchie argued that there was not simply a process of struggle in society between individuals, but between different 'social organisms' including the family, social

---

13 Note also the similarity with modern 'dual inheritance' theories of evolution, involving transmission at both the genetic and cultural levels (Boyd and Richerson, 1985; Durham, 1991).

14 It is possible but not proven that this presentation influenced the young Pigou, who eleven years later was to publish a remarkable paper on a similar theme, discussed briefly in Chapter 11.

organizations, nations and so on. This second-level struggle vastly complicated the processes of social evolution and selection. For instance, as
Ritchie pointed out, one individual might simultaneously belong to several social units or institutions. Accordingly, the processes of selection at a
social level might conflict with each other, as well as with the natural selection of individuals.

Ritchie pointed out that natural and social evolution differed in other respects. For instance, selection in the natural world works through the
death of the unfit. In contrast, in the social sphere, it is not simply through
'the slow and deadly process of natural selection that the various elements
in our civilization have been produced, preserved, and diffused'. Repeating some of the points in his *Darwinism and Politics*, Ritchie (1896, pp.
168–9) argued that in social evolution 'a great many habits are due to imitation and not to instinct, i.e., they are transmitted in the *social inheritance* of
the race, and are not dependent on *heredity*, in the biological sense'. For
Ritchie, this developed capacity to imitate involved a degree of consciousness and reflection. In these circumstances both 'the *habit* may be changed
without the extinction of the *race* ... customs and institutions may perish
without the necessary destruction of the race that practiced them' and 'customs and institutions may be handed on from race to race, and may long
survive the race from whom they originated' (Ritchie, 1896, p. 170). The life
span of the social units of selection could be entirely non-coextensive with
the lives of the human individuals that sustained them.

While carefully acknowledging these important differences, Ritchie still
regarded the theory of selection as being applicable to the social domain.
Despite detailed differences of evolutionary mechanism, the 'range' of
Darwinian theory could be extended from the biological to the social
sphere. In a prescient passage, Ritchie (1896, pp. 170–1) wrote:

> But in asserting that human society presents many phenomena that
> cannot be accounted for by natural selection in its purely biological
> sense, I am not denying the truth of the theory, but rather extending its
> range. There is going on a 'natural selection' of ideas, customs, institu-
> tions, irrespective of the natural selection of individuals and of races.

This quotation contains a path-breaking recognition that Darwinian
principles could be applied to social evolution and to non-biological units
of replication or selection. The idea of 'extending the range' of Darwinian
principles outside the biological sphere tallies with what was later described by Richard Dawkins (1983) as 'Universal Darwinism'.[15]

---

15 Darwin (1859, pp. 422–3; 1871, vol. 1, pp. 59–61, 106) himself hinted at this broader
application of Darwinian principles to non-biological phenomena. Before Ritchie,
Bagehot (1872), James (1880), Alexander (1892), Drummond (1894) and others developed
such applications. Veblen (1899a), D. Campbell (1965) and Cloak (1975) further developed
the idea. All this was long before Dawkins (1983) coined the term 'Universal Darwinism'.

A key innovation by Ritchie was to recognize that the units of replication or selection could be social entities such as customs and institutions, rather than individuals alone. This is possibly the first explicit appearance of the idea of a natural selection of customs, institutions or social structures in the English language. There were several earlier applications of natural selection to social phenomena, but none of them so clearly made customs or institutions the explicit units of selection. Ritchie, like Lewes, was an institutionalist before its time.

For Ritchie, selection worked at different levels, and sometimes in conflicting ways. In human society it involved 'artificial selection' as well as 'natural selection'. Furthermore human beings had a capacity to use their intelligence 'to ends that are of no obvious or immediate practical utility' (Ritchie, 1896, p. 170). For these reasons, Ritchie (like Ward and Veblen) did not regard evolution as an optimizing process and he thus elaborated the theoretical grounds for some degree of state intervention and welfare provision (Ritchie, 1901).

Ritchie was highly critical of the misuse of the Lamarckian doctrine in the social sphere, especially when it was proclaimed as an alternative to the principle of selection. Ritchie (1901) provided some of the most acute criticisms of Spencer's Lamarckism. Spencer's attempts to derive a political doctrine from his evolutionary theory were devastated by Ritchie's exposures of their flaws and inconsistencies.

Highly prescient as it was, Ritchie's framework lacked a notion of emergent properties. Without this, his multi-level theory was vulnerable to a biological reductionist critique in which the higher level would be explained entirely in terms of the lower. Furthermore, he had no detailed psychological theory, and he did not emphasize that institutions are repositories of knowledge. Sadly, Ritchie did not live long enough to participate in these later developments. He died in 1903, at the age of 49. So passed away one of the most extraordinary social philosophers ever to emerge in Britain. Ritchie's work must rank as one of the first and most successful attempts to extend Darwinian principles to human society, its culture and its institutions. Yet today he is largely forgotten by evolutionists and social theorists.[16]

To the New World

In 1895 Morgan was invited to deliver a course of Lowell lectures at Boston, Massachusetts. He set sail for the USA, on a planned visit to several cities, including Chicago, where Veblen was then employed. As explained below, this visit was a likely spur to Veblen in his creation of a

16 Thoemmes Press and P. Nicholson must be congratulated for bringing out a six-volume collection of Ritchie's (1998) works. Ritchie's ideas have received some attention from political philosophers, but less so in the respects highlighted here.

post-Darwinian evolutionary economics. The intellectual tradition from Darwin through Lewes to Morgan would make its connection with the embryonic elements of American institutionalism. This episode will be discussed in the next chapter. Like Morgan, we leave Europe for American shores. Our narrative from henceforth will be centred in the New World.

Part III

Veblenian institutionalism

6 The beginnings of Veblenian institutionalism

> The growth of a large business is merely a survival of the fittest. ... The American Beauty rose can be produced in the splendor and fragrance which bring cheer to its beholder only by sacrificing the early buds which grow up around it. This is not an evil tendency in business. It is merely the working out of a law of nature and a law of God.
>
> John D. Rockefeller, Junior, quoted in Ghent (1902)

> it is ... only by injecting a wholly illegitimate teleological meaning to the term 'fittest' as used by Darwin and the Darwinists that the expression 'survival of the fittest' is made to mean a survival of the socially desirable individuals.
>
> Thorstein Veblen, Review of *Socialisme et Science Positive* by Enrico Ferri (1896)

In 1860 the population of the United States was 31 million. By 1913, it had more than tripled to 97 million. From 1871 to 1913, the US gross domestic product grew at an average annual rate of 4.3 per cent, while its population grew by 2.1 per cent. By 1913, the US had the highest level of gross domestic product per capita in the world. From 1870 to 1913, US exports multiplied more than sevenfold in real terms, while German exports increased less than sixfold, and British exports little more than tripled. In that period, average gross investment in fixed capital was over 20 per cent of gross national product (Scheiber *et al.*, 1976). An Industrial Revolution was under way, rapidly transforming the US from a predominantly rural and agricultural, to a largely urban and manufacturing society. In 1880 just over a quarter of the US population lived in urban places. By 1920, more than half of the population lived in towns or cities. The period from the Civil War to the First World War was one of rapid population growth and economic development, with substantial increases in productivity and average income. The US became the industrial and financial centre of the world capitalist economy (Maddison, 1964, 1991). The emergence of institutional economics in this period of rapid structural and cultural change was no accident (Mayhew, 1987).

At the end of the Civil War, universities in the United States were few in number, disposed towards subjects such as theology and law, and lacking in any significant graduate programme of study. As the country expanded rapidly in population and economic output, so too grew the economic means and the perceived economic need for a modern tertiary education system. The first US university to have a graduate programme was Johns Hopkins, founded in 1876. Between 1880 and 1914, a number of new universities such as Stanford and Chicago were established, and older institutions such as Yale and Harvard were modernized. By the 1920s, the USA was to rival Germany as a powerhouse of university research, in the social as well as the natural sciences (Hofstadter and Hardy, 1952; Veysey, 1965).

However, many US universities remained under the control of governors or trustees who were disposed towards the interests of corporate business, intolerant of critics of the capitalist order, required high 'moral standards' of their faculty and students, or disallowed any challenge to their version of Christianity. The Stanford family financed Stanford University from the profits of their railroad business. The University of Chicago received a large founding endowment of $30 million from the oil tycoon John D. Rockefeller, Senior. The universities were often at the behest of the captains of faith or business. Such authorities were to create professional difficulties for many American academics, including leading economists such as Henry Carter Adams, John R. Commons and Thorstein Veblen.

Nevertheless, a distinctive US intellectual tradition began to take shape. Of course, European ideas were highly influential. Before 1914, the most highly developed university system was not in Britain or France, but in Germany. Leading American economists – such as H. C. Adams, John Bates Clark, Richard T. Ely and Edwin R. A. Seligman – went to Germany in the 1870s to study under members of the German historical school (Hodgson, 2001c).

The German connection was also important in psychology. William James studied psychology in Berlin, where he was impressed by German theoretical advances and experimental methods (Perry, 1935). James had planned to study at the University of Leipzig under the psychologist Wilhelm Wundt, but he had to return to America because of ill health. On returning to the United States, James in 1876 established the first psychological laboratory in North America. James Mark Baldwin was also a proponent of the new experimental psychology emanating from Germany. In 1889 Baldwin moved to Toronto to found the first psychological laboratory in the British Empire. Between 1876 and 1894, several other leading American psychologists went to study under Wundt (Boring, 1950, pp. 272–3).

Between 1885 and 1905, a number of scholarly associations were founded, including the American Economic Association in 1885, the American Psychological Association in 1892, the American Anthropological Association in 1902 and the American Sociological Association in 1905. Several influential scholarly journals were established even before 1900, including the *American Journal of Psychology* in 1887, the *Quarterly Journal of Economics* in 1887, the *Journal of Political Economy* in 1893, the *American Journal of Sociology* in 1896 and *American Anthropologist* in 1899. The academia that Veblen entered as a young man was one of multiple influences, plural perspectives, vibrant activity and rapid expansion.

Enter Thorstein Veblen

Thorstein Veblen was born in Wisconsin in 1857, the fourth son and sixth child of Norwegian immigrants who had arrived in the United States in 1847. The family moved to Minnesota when Thorstein was a young boy. He saw the development of the railroads and the conversion of Midwest farms from virtual self-sufficiency to cash crops.

Fluent in French and German, Veblen read widely in the social and natural sciences. In the 1870s, when he was a student at Carleton College, Veblen read Herbert Spencer. However, when he was at Johns Hopkins University for a semester in 1881, Veblen was taught by the formidable pragmatist philosopher and critic of Spencer, Charles Sanders Peirce. During the 1880s, and especially during his years at Yale University, Veblen came under the additional influence of William Graham Sumner. Spencer visited Yale University in 1882, when he was at the highest point of his enormous influence in the United States, and when Veblen was a postgraduate student under Sumner's tutelage.[1]

Sumner's (1885, 1906) publications ranged from monetary theory to anthropology. In economics he proposed a limited role for the state, although in contrast to Spencer he supported trade unionism and some welfare measures. In a later work, based on his lectures at Yale, Sumner (1906) stressed the subtle influence of uncodified patterns of behaviour or 'folkways', handed down from generation to generation. Sumner (1906, p. 2) wrote: 'Men begin with acts, not with thoughts.' He emphasized the replication of customs through imitation, with little reflection or conscious design. But he had no developed psychological or evolutionary theory to back up this insight.[2]

---

1 See Dorfman (1934, pp. 30, 43–6), Riesman (1963, p. 19), Edgell (1975, 2001), Edgell and Tilman (1989), Eff (1989), Murphree (1959) and Perlman and McCann (1998, pp. 526–38). Despite Spencer's popularity among American intellectuals, his alleged atheism led Yale President Noah Porter to attempt to ban his works from the university.
2 Some remarkable modern studies have, like Sumner's, examined the striking transmission through the generations of virtually unchanging, and often uncodified, role structures and behavioural dispositions. See Todd (1985), Fischer (1989) and Salamon (1992). As noted in Chapter 4, the widespread description of Sumner as a 'Social

In contrast to both Spencer and Sumner, Veblen was much more sympathetic to socialism. An early article published by Veblen (1919a, p. 387) in 1892 addressed Spencer, and was 'offered in the spirit of the disciple'. However, Veblen began to reject many of Spencer's arguments, including on the question of the feasibility of socialism. The Spencerian influence waned and was replaced by Darwinism.[3]

Veblen completed a doctoral thesis at Yale University, in which he compared Spencer and Kant (Dorfman, 1934, p. 46). One of Veblen's (1884) very early articles was on Kant, and the Kantian influence remained. Generally, Veblen's economics and social theory were guided by his understanding of philosophy. As Stanley Daugert (1950, p. 1) remarked: 'Not until we understand Veblen's philosophy can we assess fully the extent of his contributions to our knowledge of economic processes.'

Veblen read Marxist literature avidly, and it had a profound and enduring impact on his thought. He became a sympathetic but penetrating critic of Marxism. When it appeared posthumously in 1894, Veblen greeted with biting sarcasm Marx's claimed completion of his theory of surplus value in the third volume of *Capital* (Dorfman, 1934, pp. 116–17). But his interest in Marx and other social theorists also helped to persuade Veblen to seek an academic career as a social scientist rather than as a philosopher. Veblen's lack of religious belief also made it more difficult for him to obtain a post in an academic department of philosophy.

In 1888, during a six-year spell of unemployment, Veblen married his first wife Ellen Rolfe. They had met as undergraduates at Carleton College; she was the niece of the college president. After working for a year at Cornell University, in 1892 Veblen took up a junior post in the Department of Political Economy at the newly formed University of Chicago. This university adopted a research-oriented policy by reducing the teaching loads of its faculty (Oberschall, 1972). Despite some dissatisfaction with this institution, Veblen remained there for fourteen years. It was the first time that he had lived in a city. He saw the sharp divisions between Chicago's gushing wealth and its grinding poverty, as well as some of its outbursts of industrial and civil unrest.

In the new university, most of the burden of editing the Chicago-based *Journal of Political Economy* 'fell upon Veblen's shoulders' (Dorfman, 1934, p. 95). 'It was in Chicago that Veblen had the most sympathetic and stimulating colleagues and where most of his best work was done' (Riesman, 1963, p. 18). There many thinkers, including his friend and leading biologist Jacques Loeb, influenced him. Loeb advocated a positivist and

---

Darwinist' is misleading, because Sumner did not place his insights in a developed Darwinian framework (Bannister, 1973, 1979; N. Smith, 1979).

3   In later writings Veblen went further in his critique of Spencer. For instance, he noted the incompatibility between Spencer's atomistic individualism and a genuinely evolutionary and 'post-Darwinian' conception of socio-economic change (Veblen, 1908a, p. 159 n.; 1919a, p. 192 n.). See Hodgson (1993, pp. 127–8).

reductionist version of Darwinian theory, arguing that all living phenomena could and should be ultimately explained entirely in terms of their
physical and chemical constituents. Although Veblen never embraced
Loeb's reductionism or positivism, Loeb 'appears to have helped give
Veblen his life-long credo that only a social science shaped in the image of
post-Darwinian biology could lay claim to being "scientific"' (Riesman,
1963, p. 19).[4]

Chicago had the first university department of sociology in the world,
headed by Albion Small, a disciple of Lester Frank Ward. Small had also
studied the works of the German historical school in Leipzig and Berlin in
the 1870s. He founded and edited the *American Journal of Sociology*. 'No
other early sociologist labored as hard and as faithfully as Small to establish sociology as a fully constituted profession' (Martindale, 1976, p. 128).

Another colleague at Chicago was the pragmatist philosopher George
Herbert Mead. Mead had addressed Kant's argument that the conditions
of objective knowledge had to be found in concepts held by the knowing
subject prior to experience. He pointed out that Kant gave no explanation
of the origin and development of those preconceptions (Joas, 1991).[5] For
Veblen, this provided a further entrée for an evolutionary analysis of categories and habits of thought (Fontana *et al.*, 1992). However, as shown
later, Veblen's Kantian framework of thought impaired some of his other
arguments.

The philosopher John Dewey came to Chicago in 1894 and remained
there until 1902. The academic careers of Veblen and Dewey thus over-
lapped, as they had done briefly at Johns Hopkins University in the early
1880s and were later to do so again, after the First World War at the New
School for Social Research in New York. However, there are only a few definite traces of the influence of Dewey on Veblen (Tilman, 1996, 1998).[6]

In his famous essay on 'the reflex arc concept', Dewey (1896) provided a
critique of one of the assumptions that would later be central to behaviourist psychology. For Dewey, the stimulus–response mechanism was flawed
because stimuli are not given data. The actions and dispositions of the
agent are necessary to perceive the stimulus. Stimulus and response cannot be separated, because action is necessary to obtain a stimulus, and the
response invokes further stimuli. Hence 'the distinction of sensation and

4   On Veblen and Loeb see Rasmussen and Tilman (1992, 1998). Notably, both Loeb and
    Veblen (1914, pp. 324, 334) resolutely opposed the anti-materialist vitalism of Bergson
    (Tilman, 1996, p. 79). After the appearance of the English edition of *Creative Evolution* in
    1911, the Frenchman's ideas became influential in America. In response, Loeb made
    strenuous efforts to resist his dualism of matter and mind (Tilman, 1996, p. 105 n.).
5   Mead, like Sumner, emphasized that action precedes thought. Mead (1934, p. 18) later
    wrote using the language of emergence: 'consciousness is an emergent from behavior; that
    so far from being a precondition of the social act, the social act is the precondition of it'.
    Meanings and preconceptions were formed in an ongoing process of social interaction.
6   I have found only two explicit references to Dewey in Veblen's (1923, p. 16 n., p. 291 n.)
    writings.

movement as stimulus and response respectively is not a distinction which can be regarded as descriptive of anything which holds of psychical events or existences as such' (Dewey, 1896, p. 369).

Veblen (1900a, pp. 246–7) replicated part of this argument with approval, but without mentioning Dewey by name. Under the influence of Dewey, Veblen (1900a, pp. 246–7) noted the 'modern catchword' of 'response to stimulus' and pointed out that 'the reaction to stimulus' is conditioned also by 'the constitution of the organism' which 'in greater part decides what will serve as a stimulus, as well as what the manner and direction of the response will be'. This passage clearly demarcates Veblen from behaviourist psychology, where the stimulus itself is seen as sufficient to condition a response. In contrast, Veblen saw the human agent as discretionary, with 'a self-directing and selective attention in meeting the complex of forces that make up its environment'. For Veblen, as with James, part of this discretionary and selective capacity was moulded by habits and instincts. While Dewey made some partial accommodations to behaviourism in the interwar period, Veblen never abandoned instinct–habit psychology and he showed no enthusiasm for behaviourism.

The leading American anthropologist Franz Boas was in Chicago in the 1890s. He radically transformed anthropological presuppositions and approaches, including the concept of culture. For Sir Edward Burnett Tylor (1871) and Lewis Henry Morgan (1877) the word 'culture' was virtually a synonym for 'civilization', and they both embraced a teleological and unilinear notion of its development (Sanderson, 1990). Boas criticized their stage-by-stage schemes of 'cultural evolution' and introduced the modern anthropological meaning of the word 'culture' into the English language (Stocking, 1968). Boas saw culture and social environment as the major influence on human character and intelligence. His writings from the 1890s referred not to culture in a singular sense but to a plurality of different cultures.

Veblen read widely in anthropology and broadly followed Boas's usage of the term culture. It is likely that Boas (1894) influenced Veblen with his insistence that the evolution of culture and civilization did not simply track the evolution of the human mind and body. But Boas did not explain in sufficient detail how institutions or culture evolved. Like Boas, Veblen rejected universal schemes of social or cultural evolution, as developed by Spencer and others. Veblen knew Boas in Chicago, and occasionally referred to his work.[7]

Veblen was familiar with the writings of the pragmatist psychologist and philosopher William James. The *Principles of Psychology* (James, 1890) was a permanent influence on Veblen and many other thinkers. Like Veblen's former teacher Charles Sanders Peirce, James was critical of

---

7 According to Tilman (1996, p. 69 n.) there was a correspondence between Veblen and Boas in 1919. See also Edgell (2001, p. 103).

Spencer, rejecting his utilitarianism and his metaphysics. From James's Darwinian viewpoint, the appearance of Weismann's (1889, 1893) studies obliged him to elaborate more clearly the difference between inherited and acquired characters, and between instincts and habits. Hence the concept of habit became central to James's work.

Although Veblen did not embrace all their philosophical arguments, the ideas of James and Peirce had a formative and fundamental influence upon him, establishing Darwinism not merely as a biological but also as a philosophical and methodological creed. In particular, within a Darwinian theoretical approach, James provided Veblen with a psychological emphasis on habit and instinct. The Jamesian influence remained paramount in all his works.

Veblen's criticisms of Marxism

While editing the *Journal of Political Economy*, Veblen frequently reviewed works on Marxism and socialism. Overall, Veblen published 21 items in the years 1893–1897 inclusive. No less than 17 of these were book reviews in that journal. In turn, 11 of these 17 were reviews of books, mostly in German or French, concerned primarily with socialism or Marxism.[8] In a review of Max Lorenz's *Die Marxistische Socialdemokratie* (1896), Veblen noted that its author (Lorenz, 1896, p. 50) had found a crucial defect in Marxian theory. In response, Veblen (1897b, p. 137) wrote:

> While the materialistic interpretation of history points out how social development goes on – by a class struggle that proceeds from maladjustment between economic structure and economic function – it is nowhere pointed out what is the operative force at work in the process. It denies that human discretion and effort seeking a better adjustment can furnish such a force, since it makes man the creature of circumstances. This defect reduces itself ... to a misconception of human nature and of man's place in the social development. The materialistic theory conceives of man as exclusively a social being, who counts in the process solely as a medium for the transmission and expression of social laws and changes; whereas he is, in fact, also an individual, acting out his own life as such. Hereby is indicated not only the weakness of the materialistic theory, but also the means of remedying the defect pointed out. With the amendment so indicated, it becomes not only a theory of the method of social and economic change, but a theory of social process considered as a substantial unfolding of life as well.

Lorenz and Veblen suggested that Marxism lacked an adequate theory of human agency. Veblen developed his criticism of Marxism in later

---

8   See the list of Veblen's publications in Dorfman (1934, pp. 519ff.).

works, while retaining a strong Marxian influence in his thought. Veblen (1901a, pp. 225–6) observed that the theory of human motivation in Marxism is largely one of rational appraisal of class interest, without any explanation of how the criteria and procedures of rationality themselves evolve. Still later, Veblen (1906b, pp. 581–2) emphasized the point that any rational appraisal of interests does not itself explain how people acquire their beliefs and seek particular objectives. Veblen (1907, p. 308) brought Darwinism into his critique:

> Under the Darwinian norm it must be held that men's reasoning is largely controlled by other than logical, intellectual forces; that the conclusion reached by public or class opinion is as much, or more, a matter of sentiment than of logical inference; and that the sentiment which animates men, singly or collectively, is as much, or more, an outcome of habit and native propensity as of calculated material interest.

This crucial emphasis on habit as a key mechanism by which social conditions affect individual preferences and beliefs, distinguished Veblen from Marx.[9] Veblen rightly argued that the mere class position of an individual as a wage labourer or a capitalist tells us very little about the specific conceptions or habits of thought, and thereby the likely actions, of the individuals involved. Individual interests, whatever they are, do not necessarily lead to accordant individual actions. As Veblen (1907, p. 309) pointed out, and as sophisticated Marxists such as Antonio Gramsci (1971, pp. 163–5) later emphasized, the members of the working class could perceive their own salvation just as much in terms of patriotism or nationalism as in socialist revolution. The class position of an agent – exploiter or exploited – does not itself lead to any particular view of reality or pattern of action. Marxism lacked an explanation of how structures or institutions affected individual purposes or inclinations. Abram Harris (1932, p. 743) later suggested that in Marx's writings this was 'the weakest link in his chain of reasoning'.

Veblen's (1897b, p. 137) above-cited 'amendment' to Marxism in his review of Lorenz (1896) had a number of remarkable features. In this short passage, some crucial and innovative elements of his reasoning can be detected. First, in Veblen's short 1897 review there was an emphasis on the 'causes and principles' that are central to Darwinism. The 'materialistic' interpretation of history lacked an explanation of 'the operative force at

---

9   In an attempt to synthesize Veblen and Marx, O'Hara (2000, p. 49) tried to draw the sting out of Veblen's critique of Marxism, but missed the key point that Veblen found lacking in Marxism any explanation of the causal mechanisms by which social structures may affect human attitudes or behaviour. It is true that both Veblen and Marx saw 'structural conditions which fundamentally condition human behavior in groups'. But the question is *how* social structures affect preferences or behaviour. Veblen found this mechanism in his theory of habit. Marx proposed no equivalent mechanism.

work in the process'. The crucial point was that it did not explain how so-cial forces impel individual actors to think and act. Veblen addressed this hiatus in his subsequent work.

Second, Veblen rejected the proposition that the individual is *'exclusively* a social being, who counts in the process *solely* as a medium for the transmission and expression of social laws and changes' (emphasis added). In other words, Veblen dismissed the idea that the individual's ac-tions are formed entirely by his or her socio-economic circumstances.

Third, although Veblen rejected explanations exclusively in terms of systemic wholes, he did not replace this doctrine with methodological in-dividualism, and thereby attempt to explain socio-economic phenomena exclusively in terms of individuals. Hence Veblen did not deny that a hu-man is 'a social being' or 'a medium for the transmission of social laws and changes'. He simply rejected an exclusive stress on social determination, and asserted that the human agent is *'also* an individual, acting out his own life as such' (emphasis added). This suggests that humans mould their cir-cumstances just as they are moulded by them.

Fourth, for Veblen in 1897, explanations of socio-economic evolution must involve individual agents as well as institutions and structures. However, the evolution of individuality must itself be explained: 'a theory of social process considered as a substantial unfolding of life as well'.

Fifth, this need for an explanation of origin led Veblen to conceive the individual in both biological and socio-economic terms. Humans are biotic as well as social beings, so their biology cannot be ignored. Socio-economic evolution must thus be regarded 'as a substantial unfolding of life as well'. However, socio-economic phenomena were not seen as reducible to the bi-otic substratum. The 'theory of the social process' had to be compatible with, but also more than, the theory of the evolution of human life.

Accordingly, from Veblen's evolutionary and Darwinian perspective, individual and social structure were in a process of coevolution, rather than one being the determinant of the other. Veblen's insistence on the evo-lution of individuality also led to critiques of some of the central proposi-tions of orthodox economics, as outlined in later chapters.

Furthermore, while Veblen shared many of Marx's perspectives, in-cluding the idea that individuals were moulded by their social circum-stances, he departed from Marx on key points. In particular, for Veblen, the fact that social institutions could profoundly affect individuals did not mean that individuals were infinitely impressionable. Consider Veblen's extensive invocation of instinct and his repeated discussions of the inher-ent conservatism and inertia of institutions. Much more than Marx, Veblen pointed to the biological, structural and historical limits to human mallea-bility. His discourse on human nature was not reduced to a discourse on social structure; it additionally involved human evolution and institu-tional history.

Nevertheless, his interchanges with Marxism were a major source of intellectual stimulation. We can detect this change in the 1890s. By 1898, Veblen had switched mainly from reviewing books to the creative outpouring of a remarkable series of original academic works. He became less a critic and more an innovator. Veblen's *Theory of the Leisure Class* of 1899 was followed by his *Theory of Business Enterprise* in 1904. It was also from 1898 to 1909 that Veblen produced an extraordinary series of classic articles, mostly in the *Quarterly Journal of Economics*, the *American Journal of Sociology* and the *Journal of Political Economy*.[10] These foundations of Veblenian institutional economics are examined in the next two chapters.

Veblen, emergence and the rejection of reductionism

In the late 1890s, Veblen made a series of contributions that established the possibility of an evolutionary economics that would break from the static, teleological and individualistic limitations of preceding doctrines. Veblen's evolutionary economics was announced in his 1898 essay 'Why is Economics not an Evolutionary Science?' and his 1899 book *The Theory of the Leisure Class*. Veblen had a sophisticated understanding of biological theory, but he rejected biological and physical reductionism. Veblen also rejected the idea that social phenomena could be explained in terms of either the individual or society alone. Instead he embraced an evolutionary and interactive pattern of explanation along Darwinian lines, involving multiple levels of analysis and pointing implicitly to emergent properties.[11] In these years, Veblen's thought underwent a theoretical revolution, stimulated by a number of debates in biology and social theory.

On 23 January 1896, Veblen wrote to his former graduate student Sarah Hardy that he had 'a theory' that he wished to propound:

> My theory touches the immediate future of the development of economic science, and it is not so new or novel as I make it out to be. ... Economics is to be brought in line with modern evolutionary science, which it has not been hitherto. The point of departure of this rehabilitation, or rather the basis of it, will be the modern anthropological and psychological sciences ... Starting from this preliminary study of usages, aptitudes, propensities and habits of thought (much of which is already worked out in a more or less available form) the science, taken

---

10 These essays are collected together in two volumes (Veblen, 1919a, 1934).

11 T. Lawson (2003a, p. 201; 2003b, p. 329) rejected the proposition that 'Veblen held a theory of emergence' and attributes this proposition to me. If this proposition means that Veblen assimilated emergentist philosophy, then it is clearly false, and I agree with Lawson. Instead, what I am trying to say is that Veblen's multiple-level evolutionary theory depended upon, and paved the way for, a concept of emergence which Veblen himself did not elaborate. Furthermore Morgan, who influenced Veblen, made hints in that same direction. But emergentist philosophy was not well developed until the 1920s, so Veblen could hardly assimilate it fully.

generally, is to shape itself into a science of the evolution of economic institutions. (Quoted in Jorgensen and Jorgensen, 1999, p. 194.)

In this letter, Veblen hinted at a sudden innovation in his thinking, inspired by others. He was referring to some of the key ideas that were to appear later in *The Theory of the Leisure Class*. But Veblen did not go further into details. The phrase 'evolution of economic institutions' in this letter does not necessarily imply a concept of evolutionary *selection* or 'selective elimination' of institutions, which was to first appear in Veblen's (1897a, p. 390) published writings in June 1897, and was also manifest in the *Leisure Class*.

There is a strong possibility that Conwy Lloyd Morgan helped to inspire these developments in Veblen's thinking. In early 1896, Morgan delivered a lecture at the University of Chicago, entitled 'Habit and Custom: A Study in Heredity' (Dorfman, 1934, p. 139). Some key points of this talk were published in Morgan's (1896a) book *Habit and Instinct*. Dorfman does not tell us whether Veblen attended this lecture or was even availed of its content. And Morgan's visit to Chicago was probably a few days after Veblen's letter to Hardy. Nevertheless, Morgan's imminent visit to Chicago might have prompted Veblen's interest in the ideas of the visiting lecturer.[12]

A hypothesis is that Morgan's visit to the United States provided a key stimulus in the development of Veblen's theory of socio-economic evolution. His letter to Hardy of 23 January 1896 suggests that Veblen was already thinking of ways to extend ideas from 'modern evolutionary science' to economics. But Morgan's visit to Chicago would have been an important additional spur. Although it was some years later that Veblen (1914, p. 30 n.) first referred to Morgan, it was with definite approval, showing that Veblen was familiar with Morgan's 1896 book.

In contrast to Spencer and Ward, Morgan contended in his United States lectures that acquired habits are not inherited. Rejecting Lamarck in favour of Weismann, Morgan then asked: if human beings had evolved only slightly in genetic terms, then what had evolved in the last millennium or so of human society? In this period, human achievements have been transformed beyond measure. Morgan's (1896a, p. 340) answer to the puzzle was as follows:

---

12 Morgan was in the United States from late 1895 until February 1896. A letter from George Peckham (1896) to Morgan suggests that the Chicago visit was shortly before or after Morgan's lecture at the University of Urbana-Champaign (noted in the university records for 3 February 1896). Urbana-Champaign is only 150 miles from Chicago. From 10 to 31 January, Morgan was lecturing in New York City or Boston. (See R. Richards, 1987, pp. 398–9, and issues of *Science* from June 1895 to February 1896 for information on Morgan's US tour.) It is also possible that Veblen attended some of Morgan's lectures in New York City, Boston or Urbana-Champaign, or received accounts of their content. Veblen did have the inclination and resources to travel, for he visited England in the summer of 1896, on a mission to meet William Morris (Jorgensen and Jorgensen, 1999, pp. 65–6).

This is that evolution *has been transferred from the organism to the environ-ment*. There must be increment somewhere, otherwise evolution is im-possible. In social evolution on this view, the increment is by storage in the social environment to which each new generation adapts itself, with no increased native power of adaptation. In the written record, in social traditions, in the manifold inventions which make scientific and industrial progress possible, in the products of art, and the recorded examples of noble lives, we have an environment which is at the same time the product of mental evolution, and affords the condition of the development of each individual mind to-day. No one is likely to ques-tion the fact that this environment is undergoing steady and progres-sive evolution. It is not perhaps so obvious that this transference of evolution from the individual to the environment may leave the *faculty* of the race at a standstill, while the *achievements* of the race are pro-gressing by leaps and bounds.

This passage was clearly inspired by the ideas of George Henry Lewes (1879, pp. 164–6) concerning the repository of 'collective experience', as quoted in the preceding chapter.[13] Essentially, Morgan brought to America Lewes's idea of the social environment as a storehouse of knowledge. What Morgan added to Lewes's account was an insistence, in line with the work of August Weismann, that human biotic and mental capacities could not evolve so rapidly as to account for the evolution of human civilization. With Morgan's acknowledgement of the Weismann barrier, Lewes's argu-ment was given more prominence and emphasis.

In the Lamarckian view, acquired habits could be accumulated and passed on by human genetic inheritance, as well as by imitation or learn-ing. Following Weismann, Morgan rightly denied that the human genetic endowment was evolving so rapidly. There is no evidence that the human brain and human mental capacities have changed significantly in well over 30,000 years of human evolution. This fact has to be reconciled with the ap-pearance and more rapid development of human civilization in the last few thousand years.

Morgan's understanding of human evolution hinted at an *emergent level* of socio-economic evolution that was not explicable exclusively in terms of the biological characteristics of the individuals involved. Evolution oc-curred at this emergent level as well, and without any necessary change in human biotic characteristics. Accordingly, the crucial concepts of emer-gence and emergent properties were liberated by the Weismannian insis-tence of a barrier between acquired habit and biotic inheritance. Because of the Weismann barrier, Darwinians such as Morgan were driven to con-sider the biological and the social spheres as partially autonomous, but

---

13 The idea that the social environment itself evolved was originally stated by Morgan (1891, pp. 480–503).

linked, levels of analysis. As Robert Richards (1987, p. 404) put it, Morgan 'extended the reach of evolution from the instincts of animals to the achievements of advanced civilization'. But he did this by establishing the concept of emergence, and without reducing the social to the biological.

In later works, Morgan and others developed the philosophical idea of emergence (Blitz, 1992). However, despite his considerable later contribution, Morgan himself never developed the concept of the social as an emergent level. Others accomplished this task, as discussed in Chapter 10 below. Nevertheless, Morgan's early statements of 1896 concerning the 'transference of evolution from the individual to the environment' clearly hinted at a social level of evolution that could not be explained simply in terms of the evolution of individuals alone. As this social environment itself evolved, the Darwinian process of natural selection brought about very slight changes in the human organism. Slow, phylogenetic evolution (that is, involving changes in the genetic material) was thus possible, over tens of thousands of years. This long-run evolutionary process would in part be driven by behavioural and cultural change.[14]

However, in the time scale of hundreds of years these *phylogenetic* changes were too gradual to play any significant influence on social evolution itself. Nevertheless, the rapid changes in the social environment were a moving target for the *ontogenetic* development of each human individual. Significantly, the actual ('phenotypic') development of any particular organism depends, additionally, on the stimulation and nutrition it receives from its environment.

For example, the average height of the population of developed countries has increased in the last few hundred years. But no significant genetic change has caused this. The explanation lies in the improvements in diet and living conditions. It is almost entirely a result of individual ontogeny under improved environmental circumstances, rather than of the phylogenetic evolution of the human species. If a society condemned a segment of the population to strenuous labour, then their physique would alter accordingly. If a society provided higher standards of education, nutrition or health care, then the development or lifespan of individuals could be improved.

None of these acquired characteristics would be transmitted to human progeny by genetic inheritance. Above all, the reproduction and survival of the relevant 'environmental' features of the socio-economic system would ensure the replication or enhancement of well-developed muscles, educated minds or healthy bodies into the next generation. It is primarily the social system that would preserve or develop the capacity for change,

---

14 The idea of behavioural changes driving evolution is important in non-human as well as human biology. Darwin hinted at the idea in the *Origin*. Note the discussion above of the 'Baldwin Effect', the similar arguments of Morgan (1896a) himself, and Mayr (1960). For some striking examples in human evolution see Durham (1991).

not significantly the human genotype. As Veblen (1914, p. 18) wrote later, in terms redolent of Morgan:

> The typical human endowment of instincts, as well as the typical make-up of the race in the physical respect, has according to this current view been transmitted intact from the beginning of humanity ... On the other hand the habitual elements of human life change unremittingly and cumulatively, resulting in a continued proliferous growth of institutions. Changes in the institutional structure are continually taking place in response to the altered discipline of life under changing cultural conditions, but [instinctive] human nature remains specifically the same.

The possible influence of Morgan may be detected in other passages in Veblen's (1899a, pp. 188–92, 220; 1914, pp. 38–9) work. All these should be compared with Morgan (1896a, p. 340) quoted above. However, without any explicit mention of Morgan by Veblen in the 1890s, this evidence is circumstantial rather than decisive. It is possible that others who were thinking along similar lines separately influenced both Morgan and Veblen. From the evidence available it is difficult to confirm or deny this. However, it is clear and significant that by 1897 Veblen was thinking of institutions as the objects of selection in socio-economic evolution. This dating is consistent with Morgan's visit to Chicago in 1896.[15]

Prominent theorists such as Spencer (1881, pp. 400–1) and Marshall (1923, p. 260) argued that economic institutions could change only as fast as the evolution of human nature. Veblen differed, by making use of Morgan's suggestion of multiple levels of evolution. However, Morgan did not make the objects and mechanisms of socio-economic evolution clear. He did not identify any social units of selection, their sources of variation or any selective process at the social level. He simply indicated the possibility of 'storage in the social environment' through the written record, in social traditions, technology and art. This was, nevertheless, a highly significant point. Morgan's conception of 'environmental' evolution implied that, despite change, some degree of inertia and continuity in environmental conditions was necessary, so that appropriate ontogenetic development could occur. In short, the means of preservation of information were necessary for learning. It was left to Veblen to make the crucial next step: institutions were revealed as objects of selection in socio-economic evolution. What was enormously significant was that Veblen did not accept that culture or institutions could be explained solely in biological terms. As Veblen (1909a, p. 300) wrote a few years later:

---

15 Veblen (1925, p. 48) later wrote that: 'There is little if anything in the way of heredity to distinguish this generation ... from the generations of men that have gone before, say, during the past 10,000 years or so.' One of the few scholars to notice the strong influence of C. L. Morgan on Veblen is Tilman (1996, pp. 73–5, 79–83).

> If ... men universally acted not on the conventional grounds and values afforded by the fabric of institutions, but solely and directly on the grounds and values afforded by the unconventionalised propensities and aptitudes of hereditary human nature, then there would be no institutions and no culture.

Veblen thus suggested that if socio-economic phenomena were determined exclusively by biological factors, then the concepts of institution and culture would be redundant. Culture and institutions are irreducible to biological factors alone. Veblen thus broke decisively from biological reductionism. Consistent with this interpretation, the concepts of cultural and institutional evolution were developed in *The Theory of the Leisure Class*.[16]

However, Veblen failed to buttress this argument with an explicit or sufficiently well-developed concept of emergent properties. On this, Morgan had provided no more than a hint of what was to come later in emergentist philosophy. Without such a concept, Veblen's evolutionary theory had insufficient defences against a reductionist argument that institutions and culture could themselves be explained entirely in terms of the preferences or other characteristics of individuals. Obversely, there was little defence against attempts to divide the social sciences from biology and psychology, which were to become widespread after the First World War. As well as dividing one ontological level from another, the concept of emergence also links them together. It provides defences against biological or individualistic reductionism and from any unwarranted separation of the social sciences from biology or psychology. Veblen lacked these necessary fortifications.

Institutions as units of evolutionary selection

Morgan's argument gave socio-economic evolution a degree of autonomy from biological inheritance. With the intervention of Morgan and others, the scene was set for Veblen's intellectual revolution: the concept of the Darwinian selection of institutions, at an additional level of evolution. The history of institutional economics is full of strange twists and turns. Its unintended and unacknowledged intellectual paternity, resulting from the ejaculations of a relatively obscure psychologist–biologist–philosopher of Welsh descent while on a foreign tour, is indeed one of the most curious.

---

16 Later Veblen (1914, p. 16) pointed out that cultural evolution could override genetic evolution to the point that the survival of a population was in jeopardy: 'any given racial stock may dwindle and decay for no other reason than the growth of its culture has come to subject the stock to methods of life widely different from those under which its type of man originated and made good its fitness to survive'. This implied an irreducibility of cultural evolution to genetic evolution, which Veblen only partially theorized.

It is thus perhaps no accident that about the time of Morgan's visit to Chicago the idea of a Darwinian process of selection of institutions began to develop in Veblen's work. This idea began to surface in two book reviews of Marxist texts, which appeared in the *Journal of Political Economy* in December 1896 and June 1897. The first of these two reviews was of a work by the Italian socialist and criminologist Enrico Ferri (1896, 1906), which attempted to show that Marxism was compatible with the evolutionary approaches of both Darwin and Spencer. Ferri's eclectic and superficial amalgam of Darwin, Spencer and Marx melded the 'struggle for existence' with the 'class struggle', by arguing that struggle between classes overshadowed rivalry between individuals or nations. Veblen (1896, p. 99) extended Ferri's argument by noting that the 'struggle for existence, as applied within the field of social evolution, is a struggle between groups and institutions rather than a competition ... between the individuals of the group'.

Even more poignantly, in yet another book review, Veblen (1897a, p. 390) saw in Antonio Labriola's (1897, 1908) Marxism the doctrine that the 'economic exigencies' of the industrial process 'afford the definitive test of fitness in the adaptation of all human institutions by a process of selective elimination of the economically unfit'. But these were Veblen's words, not Labriola's. Labriola had no intention of applying Darwinism to social evolution. Veblen made the additional and substantial theoretical leap of applying the principle of selection to institutions, and not merely to individuals or groups. Extrapolating Labriola's 'tedious' and uninspiring work for his own purposes, Veblen (1897a, p. 391) saw a 'materialist ... conception of the evolution of social structure according to which the economic activities, and the habits bred by them, determine the activities and the habitual view of things in other directions than the economic one'. Veblen briefly suggested the possibility of an amended version of Marxism that might be 'affiliated with Darwinism', while providing his own meaningful theoretical hint of a process of selection of social institutions and of individual habits of thought. While these ideas were absent from Labriola's lacklustre volume, nevertheless it helped Veblen to make the intellectual leap of applying the principles of Darwinian selection to emergent social structures or institutions.

Veblen went further than Morgan, and Lewes before him. For Veblen, the institutional structure of society was not merely 'the environment', as Morgan had put it. Veblen indicated that 'the environment' consisted of institutional elements that were themselves, like organisms, subject to evolutionary processes of selection. Darwinism was interpreted not narrowly in terms of individuals being selected in a fixed environment, but in an environment that is changed in its interaction with those creative individuals. As Veblen (1898b, p. 391) put it: 'The economic life history of the individual is a cumulative process of adaptation of means to ends that cumulatively change as the process goes on, both the agent and his environment being at any point the outcome of the last process.' Veblen (1898b, p. 393) concluded that 'an evolutionary economics must be a theory of a process of cultural growth as determined by the economic interest, a theory of a cumulative sequence of economic institutions stated in terms of the process itself'.

This was essentially the core theoretical project of *The Theory of the Leisure Class*. In January 1895 Veblen described this book as being at least 'half written' in 'first draft' but he 'had to rewrite it completely a number of times' prior to its publication in February 1899 (Dorfman, 1934, p. 174; Jorgensen and Jorgensen, 1999, pp. 192). Whenever it was written down, the appearance of the Darwinian phrase 'natural selection' in the *Leisure Class* was extremely significant and played a crucial role in Veblen's argument. In a key passage, Veblen (1899a, p. 188) declared:

> The life of man in society, just like the life of other species, is a struggle for existence, and therefore it is a process of selective adaptation. The evolution of social structure has been a process of natural selection of institutions. The progress which has been and is being made in human institutions and in human character may be set down, broadly, to a natural selection of the fittest habits of thought and to a process of enforced adaptation of individuals to an environment which has progressively changed with the growth of community and with the changing institutions under which men have lived. Institutions are not only themselves the result of a selective and adaptive process which shapes the prevailing or dominant types of spiritual attitude and aptitudes; they are at the same time special methods of life and human relations, and are therefore in their turn efficient factors of selection. So that the changing institutions in their turn make for a further selection of individuals endowed with the fittest temperament, and a further adaptation of individual temperament and habits to the changing environment through the formation of new institutions.

It was no accident that Darwin's phrases 'natural selection' and 'struggle for existence' appeared here. Veblen (1899a, p. 207) wrote also in the same work of 'the law of natural selection, as applied to human institutions'. Apparently without of the influence of David Ritchie (1889, 1896), but with the probable inspiration of Morgan, Veblen became the second writer after the publication of the *Origin of Species* to apply with some rigour Darwin's principle of selection to the evolution of customs and institutions.

The decisive implication was that Darwinism could be applied to human society without necessarily reducing explanations of social phenomena entirely to individual psychology or biology. Once we consider the natural selection of *institutions*, and in turn treat institutions as emergent properties in the social realm, then that road is opened. Regrettably, however, Veblen did not go far enough down this route.

In sum, there is strong circumstantial evidence that a crucial but hitherto unacknowledged influence came during or immediately after the visit to Chicago by the British biologist and philosopher Morgan. As a Darwinian opponent of the Lamarckian theory of biological inheritance, Morgan argued that it was not human individuals that had 'evolved' significantly in the last few centuries, but their social environment. The evidence is circumstantial but the timing is beyond dispute. Crucially, it was shortly after Morgan's visit to Chicago that the idea of an evolutionary process of selection of institutions first appeared in Veblen's (1896, pp. 99–100; 1897a, p. 390) work.

7   The Darwinian mind of Thorstein Veblen

Where do these
Innate assumptions come from? Not from what
We think truest, or most want to do:
Those warp tight-shut, like doors. They're more a style
Our lives bring with them: habit for a while,
Suddenly they harden into all we've got
                                   Philip Larkin, 'Dockery and Son' (1963)

In this and the following chapter I outline the foundations of Veblen's institutional and evolutionary economics, as it emerged in the period from 1896 to 1909. With one exception, Veblen's most important published works appeared in twelve crammed years from 1898 to 1909 inclusive. They include his *Theory of the Leisure Class* (1899a) and *The Theory of Business Enterprise* (1904). Fifteen of the eighteen classic essays collected together in Veblen's *Place of Science in Modern Civilization* (1919a) appeared in those dozen years. The foremost theoretical work that lies outside this period is the *Instinct of Workmanship* (1914), which Veblen himself regarded as his most important work. It laid out more completely than any other the psychological foundations of his approach. However, this later volume was planned as early as 1900, and five of its seven long chapters were probably drafted by 1911 (Dorfman, 1934, p. 197; Jorgensen and Jorgensen, 1999, pp. 140, 207). Consequently, it will be considered largely as a product of those energetic earlier years. In addition, Veblen's *Higher Learning in America*, although published in 1918, was drafted by about 1904 (Veblen, 1918, p. v; 1973, p. 141). Other works after 1909, especially his *Imperial Germany* (1915), are also of importance, but they are less concerned with the further development of theoretical and conceptual foundations and more with applications of his ideas.

Chapter 9 will take a critical look at Veblen's ideas on the instinct of workmanship and pecuniary motives. Discussion of Veblen's work on the role of science and the machine process will be postponed to Chapter 10.

The main subject of this and the next chapter is Veblen's contribution to a Darwinian social theory, his insights on how Darwinism can transform the social sciences, and his contribution to the philosophical and psychological foundations of institutional economics.

But first, what happened to Veblen himself in the period up to 1909? Both his academic and his personal life are relevant to understand the conditions of his creativity. Employment at the Department of Political Economy at the University of Chicago was not secure. In the 1890s the university trustees sacked two people from the department for their leftist political views. Veblen's own position was always vulnerable. As for his personal life, his marriage was no longer a happy one. In 1896 he professed to one of his previous graduate students – Sarah Hardy – that he was in love with her, knowing that she was engaged to someone else. Five weeks later he confessed this declaration to his wife, pronouncing that their marriage had been an 'awful mistake'. Two months later he asked her for a divorce. But she resisted and they remained married in name until 1912.[1]

In these disruptive and depressing circumstances, the immense quality and importance of Veblen's written output is all the more remarkable. To the surprise of both its author and publisher, the *Theory of the Leisure Class* was highly successful, and attracted a wide readership. Some of its phrases, including 'conspicuous consumption' and 'conspicuous waste' entered the popular vocabulary. Much of this fame was, as John Hobson (1936, p. 16) noted, 'chiefly due to its satirical commentary upon the upper classes' rather than to its scientific content. Yet Veblen always meant the work to be appreciated as an evolutionary contribution to social and economic theory, as suggested by its original subtitle: *An Economic Study in the Evolution of Institutions.*[2]

The evolutionary and Darwinian aspects of the *Leisure Class* have received insufficient attention, partly because of a failure of many commentators to appreciate the intellectual environment of the 1890s and thereby the substance and stature of Veblen's intellectual achievement. In addition, subsequent institutional economists endorsed the interwar schism

---

1 See Jorgensen and Jorgensen (1999, esp. pp. 27–8, 54–64, 141). Ellen willed her body to scientific research and poignantly requested that a copy of her autopsy report be sent to her former husband (Eby, 2001, p. 263). The autopsy of 1926 revealed that Ellen Veblen had an underdeveloped vagina. Biology matters.

2 In later reprints the subtitle was shortened to *An Economic Study of Institutions.* Contrary to Dorfman (1934, p. 323) this change was made earlier than 1912. A 1908 edition in the possession of the present author has the shorter subtitle. Dorfman speculates that the change was to remove the confusion that the *Leisure Class* was 'concerned with the genealogical pedigree of institutions rather than with the present-day functioning of business enterprise, of modern capital'. No plausible reason for the change of subtitle is available, and it is also not clear whether Veblen or his publisher originally suggested the change. However, it is evident that Veblen (1914, pp. 17–19, 49; 1919b, pp. 5, 40, 57) never abandoned evolutionary themes and biological terms (such as 'mutation' and 'selection'), even in his later writings.

between biology and the social sciences, and eschewed the Darwinian origins of institutionalism.[3]

In 1900 – at the age of 43 – Veblen was appointed to the rank of assistant professor. But his position in Chicago remained untenured, insecure and relatively underpaid. In 1904, unproven rumours erupted of an affair between Veblen and the wife of a faculty member. Provided by Veblen's wife with what might have seemed to be corroborative evidence of the affair, and enraged by Veblen's written disapproval of any ties between universities and big business, the university president made it clear that he wished Veblen to leave. In order to preserve the new 'splendor and fragrance' of this Rockefeller-financed university, and to remove the corrupting whiff of scandal, Veblen was one of the 'early buds' that had to be sacrificed.

Veblen wrote to Lester Frank Ward, asking for his help in his application for the post of chief of the Division of Documents at the Library of Congress at Washington, DC. Ward (1900) had written a very favourable review of *The Theory of the Leisure Class* and had described the book 'as one of the most brilliant productions of the country'. Ward nominated Veblen to the prestigious *Institut International de Sociologie*, which was limited to 100 members, including at that time Alfred Marshall, Carl Menger, Eugen von Böhm-Bawerk, Adolph Wagner, Alchille Loria and Gustav Schmoller. But the job application was unsuccessful (Dorfman, 1934, pp. 254–7; Jorgensen and Jorgensen, 1999, pp. 78–84).

To his relief, in 1906 Veblen secured a post at Stanford University. Initially he found its atmosphere and governance much more conducive than Chicago. He was given a higher salary and allowed 'to teach as little as he wished and devote his time to writing' (Dorfman, 1934, p. 269). There Veblen continued to find intellectual stimulation, with colleagues such as Allyn Young in the Department. While at Stanford, Veblen produced and published a number of highly significant articles.

He was briefly reconciled with his wife Ellen, who joined him in nearby Palo Alto. But the marital repair was not permanent. Veblen had already started a discreet affair with another of his former Chicago students, Ann Bradley Bevans. Twenty years his junior, with children by a previous marriage, she was destined to become Veblen's second wife. She wrote repeatedly to Ellen Veblen urging her claim on Ellen's husband. Bevans claimed that she alone could make Veblen more productive as an economist and bring him world fame (Eby, 2001, p. 279). Thus knowing of her husband's enduring relationship with Bevans, a vengeful Ellen Veblen sent a dossier of letters to the president of Stanford in 1909. They included information on Veblen's imagined or real extra-marital affairs with Hardy, Bevans and others. Eventually, the president asked for his resignation. Veblen obliged.

---

3   Veblen had copies of Darwin's *Origin, Descent* and *Voyage of the Beagle* in his personal library on Washington Island, as well as four of Spencer's volumes (Edgell, 2001, pp. 67, 74).

Ellen Veblen also wrote to the authorities at Chicago and Columbia, alluding to her husband's extra-marital behaviour. For a while, Veblen believed that no university would ever hire him again.[4]

Nevertheless, in 1911, Veblen moved to the University of Missouri. Young helped Veblen to find a position, declaring in writing that 'Veblen is the most gifted man whom I have ever known' (Dorfman, 1934, p. 299). Herbert Davenport, his friend and former Chicago student and colleague, had become the head of the economics department at Missouri. Veblen's contract had to be renewed annually, and his Stanford salary of $3000 was reduced at Missouri to $2000 a year.[5] Nevertheless, Veblen stayed there until 1918 when he resigned from academia, to take up jobs first as a government official and next as editor of *The Dial* (Jorgensen and Jorgensen, 1999). Both of Veblen's marriages were childless, although he was a devoted stepfather to the children of his second wife. He and Bevans married in 1914. Tragically, she had a miscarriage in 1915. A brain tumour caused her madness and death in 1920. From 1919 to 1926, Veblen taught at the New School for Social Research, in New York (now New School University). When John Hobson met Veblen in Washington, DC in 1925, the Englishman described him as 'a beaten man' (Veblen, 1973, p. 275). Veblen died in California in 1929.

Veblen's most creative and brilliant years, from 1896 to 1909, were also years of suffering in his personal life and of persecution in his career. 1896 was the year in which his marital relationship broke down, and 1909 was the year in which he returned to a stable and devoted sexual partnership. Similarly, his academic troubles began in the late 1890s and lasted until 1911. After 1909 – and contrary to the promise of Ann Bevans – domestic emotional stability and support would divert Veblen's surplus energies into his adopted family and away from his academic work. He wrote to Wesley Mitchell on 3 August 1910: 'Domestic circumstances, interesting enough in their way, are all there is time for' (Jorgensen and Jorgensen, 1999, p. 135). Subsequently, he went through a divorce and a second marriage. Then the outbreak of war in 1914 diverted his scholarly attention from theoretical fundamentals to matters of imperialism and peace.

---

4 Jorgensen and Jorgensen (1999) have provided the best and most reliable account of Veblen's personal life as a whole. They and Edgell (2001) correct some of the distortions in Dorfman (1934). However, Eby (2001) has skilfully cast Ellen Veblen in a more sympathetic light. It is possible that Veblen had attempted to reconcile himself with his wife Ellen at least partly in an attempt to keep up appearances of marital propriety at Stanford, and to protect his academic position there, while carrying on his affair with Bevans. Notably, Veblen himself indicated that his *Higher Learning in America* (1918, p. v) was a critical reaction to his bitter experience of academic misgovernment at Chicago. While Ellen had responded to marital problems by attacking an individual – her husband – Veblen's foremost response was to address the institutional pathologies that had enhanced his suffering.

5 In 2002 prices, this would be equivalent to a reduction from about $59,000 to about $39,000 per year.

Prior to 1909, Veblen's intense creativity in the face of adversity is explicable in terms of someone who retreated into the solitude of his study and threw himself into his writing.[6] He then found solace and refuge from the emotional and institutional storms around him. His very own 'instinct of workmanship' was energized in a context of personal pain and unfulfilment. The spurs to creativity are often mysterious. In this period of personal distress, Veblen produced a major revolution in social and economic thought, even if in some crucial aspects it was flawed or incomplete.[7]

Veblen on ontological commitments and positivism

Against positivism and empiricism, Veblen rejected the view that science could be founded on experience or experiment alone, without additional presuppositions that themselves are not grounded in observation. Veblen (1900a, p. 241) thus rejected the Comtean attack on metaphysics, asserting instead that the 'ultimate term or ground of knowledge is always of a metaphysical character'. For Veblen (1900a, p. 253), 'a point of view must be chosen' and consequently the 'endeavor to avoid all metaphysical premises fails here as everywhere'. Evidence can always be interpreted in different ways: 'No substantial agreement upon a point of knowledge is possible between persons who proceed from disparate preconceptions' (Veblen, 1904, p. 344). Veblen understood that experience alone could not be the foundation of knowledge, as all knowledge also depends on preconceptions, some of which are unavoidably 'metaphysical'. For Veblen, unlike the positivists, 'metaphysical' was not a term of abuse. Veblen rightly held that some 'metaphysical presuppositions' were necessary and unavoidable for science.[8]

In particular, one of Veblen's principal criticisms of positivism concerned the need in science to impute causal relations. As David Hume had rightly pointed out in the eighteenth century, no causal connection can itself be observed. The imputation of causal connections must always involve preconceptions by the analyst, and such imputations cannot be derived from experience or data alone. These mental constructions were

---

6 Is there any other explanation for Veblen's declining academic output? Veblen suffered from poor health, but this weakness was manifest long before 1909. Many of his maladies were blamed on an overdose of calomel (otherwise known as mercurous chloride, which can decompose into the poisonous forms of metallic mercury or mercuric chloride) that he had been prescribed in his early thirties (Dorfman, 1934, p. 306). What of mind–body dualism? Unwittingly but brilliantly, Veblen refuted it thus.

7 Veblen was aged 35 when he arrived at Chicago, and 52 in 1909. This phase of life is often one of maximum academic creativity. However, mere age is no strong reason why a thinker as creative and engaging as Veblen, with the time, resources and encouragement to research and write, should have subsequently reduced his output.

8 See Veblen (1900a, pp. 241, 253; 1904, pp. 311, 314, 344; 1906a, pp. 596–7; 1914, pp. 260, 336). The unavoidability of some 'metaphysical presuppositions' is now accepted as the consensus view among modern philosophers of science. See Quine (1953), Kuhn (1970), Popper (1972b), Caldwell (1982) and many others.

unavoidable to science but themselves indemonstrable by its data. So far, this argument is unassailable. However, Kant went even further, by arguing that causal connections were essentially mental constructions held by the researcher. This Kantian position is questionable because it challenges the real status of a cause.

In his early article of 1884 on Kant, Veblen followed the German philosopher in his argument that the 'reflective judgement is continuously reaching over beyond the known, and grasping that which cannot come within experience' (Veblen, 1934, p. 179). As Stanley Daugert (1950, p. 36) established, Veblen's philosophy retained a 'Kantian bias'. Some of the limitations of Veblen's modified Kantianism and its causal ontology are discussed in Chapter 10 below. What particularly concerns us here is Veblen's valid, post-Humean stance on the epistemological status of a cause.

Veblen did not endorse Comte's argument that, because they cannot be discerned in experience, any search after causes would be futile. Against empiricism, Veblen (1906a, p. 597) appropriately identified the 'preconception of causation' as necessary for 'the actual work of scientific enquiry'. Veblen (1908b, p. 398 n.) elaborated:

> Causal sequence … is of course a matter of metaphysical imputation. It is not a fact of observation, and cannot be asserted of the facts of observation except as a trait imputed to them. It is so imputed, by scientists and others, as a matter of logical necessity, as a basis of systematic knowledge of the facts of observation.

Veblen (1914, p. 260) repeated, in a similar vein: 'The principle, or "law," of causation is a metaphysical postulate; in the sense that such a fact as causation is unproved and unprovable. No man has ever observed a case of causation.' Veblen (1904, p. 67) himself followed 'a habit of apprehending and explaining facts in terms of material cause and effect'. This involved a materialist ontology: 'Its metaphysics is materialism and its point of view is that of causal sequence.'

Veblen (1904, p. 371) asserted that 'the endeavor of the Positivists ... to reduce scientific theory to a system of accountancy has failed.' Also in opposition to many positivists, Veblen rejected regularity determinism. He pointed out that the thesis 'that like causes produce like effects, or that effect is, in some sense, of the same character as the cause, has fallen into decay as holding true only in such tenuously general terms as to leave it without particular force'. Overall, Veblen clearly distanced himself from positivism.[9]

Veblen on Darwinism and Lamarckism

Despite his extensive knowledge of biology, Veblen was too careful to commit himself in the then ongoing and unresolved debate over Lamarckism. Whether acquired characters could be inherited or not was in part an empirical question, to be answered by biological research. These issues were far from resolution in the biology of the 1890s and early 1900s; too little was understood of the mechanisms of genetic inheritance. Veblen did not wish to build his theory on what might be shifting scientific sands, and he took from Charles Darwin what he rightly regarded to be most decisive and enduring: the Darwinian principle of selection and the emphasis on causation. Veblen remained neutral on the question of whether or not acquired characters could be inherited. The outcome of this controversy did not affect key parts of his argument. Veblen (1899a, pp. 190, 192) thus wrote:

> For the present purpose, however, the question as to the nature of the adaptive process – whether it is chiefly a selection between stable types of temperament and character, or chiefly an adaptation of men's habits of thought to changing circumstances – is of less important than the fact that, by one method or another, institutions change and develop. ... For the immediate purpose it need not be a question of serious importance whether this adaptive process is a process of selection and survival of persistent ethnic types or a process of individual adaptation and an inheritance of acquired traits.

But while Veblen (1899a, p. 248) admitted the possibility that differences 'in temperament may be due in part to a difference in the inheritance of acquired traits', he was not neutral between the theories of Darwin and Lamarck. Veblen (1904, p. 369) wrote: 'Darwin set to work to explain species in terms of the process out of which they have arisen, rather than out of the prime cause to which the distinction between them may be due.' What Darwin had tried to do, albeit without complete success, was to provide a processual explanation of the origin of species where the causal mechanisms involved were fully specified. Veblen (1904, p. 369 n.) continued in a highly perceptive footnote: 'This is the substance of Darwin's advance over Lamarck, for instance.' On this basis of more adequate causal explanations of process, Veblen rightly judged Darwin to be superior to Lamarck.

In 1901, the Dutch biologist Hugo De Vries published *Die mutationstheorie* in German. He noted the forgotten genetic discoveries of Gregor Mendel and proposed his own 'mutation theory'. This work

---

9 Contrary to Bush (1999, p. 128), I do not regard Veblen as a positivist. Also in opposition to Bush, the proposition that there is a distinction between judgements of fact and judgements of value does not itself imply an adherence to positivism, in either its Comtean or logical positivist versions. I quote Veblen's own explicit opinions on the distinction between facts and values in Chapter 18 below.

caused a big stir, and was welcomed with enthusiasm by Veblen's Chicago colleague, Loeb. The rediscovery of Mendelian genetics eventually led to the modern neo-Darwinian synthesis in biology and the victory of the Darwinians over the Lamarckians. But this did not occur until the 1940s, long after Veblen's death. Three years after De Vries, Veblen (1904, p. 149) mentioned the concept of mutation. But it was not until 1910 – a year after the publication of the English translation of De Vries's book – that Veblen started work on a paper that explicitly incorporated some of De Vries's ideas.[10] Accordingly, neither Mendel nor De Vries played a significant part in the Veblenian theoretical revolution of 1896–1909.

Veblen, Darwin and causation

Charles Hodge (1874, p. 52) – an American religious critic of Darwinism – had rightly argued that the most important distinguishing feature of Darwinism was neither the notion of evolution nor that of natural selection but the rejection of 'teleology, or the doctrine of final causes'. For Hodge this condemned Darwinism as atheistic, leaving no space for the guidance of God. In contrast, for Veblen, the Darwinian rejection of teleology became the necessary basis of a scientific and 'post-Darwinian' approach to economics and social science. There is abundant evidence that Veblen understood Darwinism partly and fundamentally in terms of a commitment to detailed and sequential causal analysis. For example, Veblen (1898a, pp. 375–8) wrote:

> Any evolutionary science ... is a close-knit body of theory. It is a theory of a process, of an unfolding sequence ... of cumulative causation. The great deserts of the evolutionist leaders ... lie ... in their having shown how this colorless impersonal sequence of cause and effect can be made use of for theory proper, by virtue of its cumulative character.

This insistence on explanation in terms of a cumulative causal sequence was repeated in several works (Veblen, 1898b, pp. 381, 384, 386; 1900a, p. 266; 1904, pp. 67, 313, 314, 365). Although Darwin himself did not use the term 'cumulative causation', it is important to underline the way that Veblen (1904, p. 370) saw it as linked with Darwinism:[11]

> [Darwin's] inquiry characteristically confines itself to the process of cumulative change. His results, as well as his specific determination of

---

10 Dorfman (1934, p. 295). This paper was published three years later (Veblen, 1913). Veblen (1914, pp. 16–18, 21–5, 69, 140; 1915, pp. 277–8; 1925, p. 51) repeatedly referred to Mendelian genetics in his later works.

11 James (1880, p. 453) used similar words: 'It is only following the common-sense method of a Lyell, a Darwin, and a Whitney to interpret the unknown by the known, and reckon up cumulatively the only causes of social change we can directly observe.'

the factors at work in this process of cumulative change, have been questioned; perhaps they are open to all the criticisms levelled against them as well as a few more not thought of; but the scope and method given to scientific enquiry by Darwin and the generation whose spokesman he is has substantially not been questioned, except by that diminishing contingent of the faithful …

Veblen (1907, p. 304) also wrote:

in the Darwinian scheme of thought, the continuity sought in and imputed to the facts is a continuity of cause and effect. It is a scheme of blindly cumulative causation, in which there is no trend, no final term, no consummation. The sequence is controlled by nothing but the *vis a tergo* of brute causation, and is essentially mechanical.

The ambiguous words 'blindly' and 'mechanical' in the above quotation might cause some confusion. There is no warrant for assuming that for Veblen they meant a lack of individual purpose or will, but they could encourage such a misinterpretation. Veblen must be criticized for using such terms, at least in an unqualified manner. Nevertheless, his key point of emphasis was one of causal sequence. Veblen (1919a, p. 37) visited this theme persistently, as in these words published in 1908:

The characteristic feature by which post-Darwinian science is contrasted with what went before is a new distribution of emphasis, whereby the process of causation, the interval of instability and transition between initial cause and definitive effect, has come to take the first place in the inquiry; instead of that consummation in which causal effect was once presumed to come to rest. This change in point of view was, of course, not abrupt or catastrophic. But it has latterly gone so far that modern science is becoming substantially a theory of the process of consecutive change, realized to be self-continuing or self-propagating and to have no final term.

In the same year Veblen (1908a, p. 159 n.) wrote of 'the field of cumulative change within which the modern post-Darwinian sciences live and move and have their being'. A few commentators on Veblen have recognized this crucial Darwinian focus on causal processes in Veblen's writings. As Karl Anderson (1933, p. 602) put it, modern science for Veblen 'demands an explanation of things in terms of cause and effect, and postulates that the causal relationship has neither starting-point nor stopping-point but runs in an endless sequence'. Similarly, Idus Murphree (1959, p. 312) remarked that Veblen 'thought of the Darwinian method as one that revealed the impersonal sequence of mechanical cause and effect and dispensed with a search for universal purposes and belief in a "natural order"'.

Veblen and others sometimes described this emphasis on detailed, step-by-step causal explanation as part of the 'genetic' method. Veblen (1903, p. 655) explained the 'genetic' method of 'modern science' as applied to social phenomena:

> This method is the genetic one, which deals with the forces and sequence of development and seeks to understand the outcome by finding how and why it has come about. The aim is to organize social phenomena into a theoretical structure in causal terms.

The term 'genetic' like 'genesis' refers to causal origin or determination.[12] The word 'genetic' had been widely used in methodological or scientific contexts in the nineteenth century, and it should not be confused with the modern biological term 'gene'. The 'gene' concept was first introduced into biology in 1909 by Wilhelm Johannsen. It would thus be an appalling error to interpret Veblen's use of the term 'genetic' as an accommodation to genetic reductionism!

In Veblen's writing there was the same emphasis on the detailed and processual nature of Darwinian evolution as in the modern work of Daniel Dennett (1995). Although Veblen did not use the word, he had as much appreciation as Dennett of the nature of Darwinian evolution as an 'algorithmic' process. Veblen used phrases such as 'genetic theory', 'cumulative causation', 'theory of a process, of an unfolding sequence' and 'impersonal sequence of cause and effect' to connote the same idea. This Darwinian focus on algorithmic processes is both revolutionary and highly modern; it directs attention to ongoing processes rather than static equilibria alone.[13]

However, while Veblen coined the term 'cumulative' causation, he used it primarily to refer to cumulative sequences of cause and effect.[14] With other authors, the term 'cumulative causation' took on the different meaning (in modern parlance) of non-linear processes of positive feedback. For instance, in his classic article on 'increasing returns' Allyn Young (1928, p. 533) wrote that: 'change becomes progressive and propagates itself in a

---

12 The German term *genetisch* also alludes to origins and is found in the eighteenth-century writings of Herder and Schiller. Apparently, the word 'genetic' in this same general (and not particularly biological) sense was introduced into English by Carlyle (Hayek, 1988, p. 147).

13 However, the differences between Dennett and Veblen should not be overlooked. For example, Dennett's (1995) devotion to the vague concept of the 'meme' as the unit of cultural evolution contrasts with Veblen's pragmatist insistence on habit as the basis of ideas and essence of culture, and with his emphasis on emergent institutions as units of selection. One of the problems with 'memetics' is that the causes of meme replication are unexplained, while Veblen explained the replication of institutions in terms of the psychological mechanisms of individual habit formation. Furthermore, Veblen's (1909a, p. 300) strictures against reductionism have no adequate parallel in Dennett (1995). See footnote 17 on page 30 above.

14 A possible exception is where Veblen (1904, p. 368) wrote of 'complex' processes 'in which any appreciable deviation may forthwith count in a cumulative manner'.

cumulative way'. One of his students was Nicholas Kaldor, who made extensive use of Young's positive-feedback notion of 'cumulative causation' (Kaldor, 1985). Gunnar Myrdal (1939, 1957) independently took the idea of cumulative causation from the positive feedback mechanisms in the monetary economics of fellow Swedish economist Knut Wicksell.[15]

On matter, mind and human intentionality

Veblen attempted to reconcile the reality of human will and intentionality with science and causal explanations. In his first published article of 1884, Veblen (1934, p. 175) noted the contradiction between 'freedom of the person' in Kant's *Critique of Practical Reason* and 'the notion of strict determinism' found in his *Critique of Pure Reason*. Veblen saw in Kant the idea that 'in order to free activity, a mediation between the two was likewise indispensable'. Veblen's subsequent writing also involved an attempt to mediate between 'freedom' and 'determinism', but one that was consistent with Darwinian principles. Veblen neither denied nor underestimated the significance of human intentionality, but saw it as a result of evolution. Darwin rejected religious and teleological explanations of origin or destiny. Veblen rejected them too, while attempting to leave an intermediate place for 'teleology' in human purposeful behaviour. He retained the idea that persons were purposeful, but Veblen (1898c, pp. 188–93) placed this proposition within an evolutionary framework:

> Like other animals, man is an agent that acts in response to stimuli afforded by the environment in which he lives. Like other species, he is a creature of habit and propensity. But in a higher degree than other species, man mentally digests the content of habits under whose guidance he acts, and appreciates the trend of these habits and propensities. ... By selective necessity he is endowed with a proclivity for purposeful action. ... He acts under the guidance of propensities which have been imposed upon him by the process of selection to which he owes his differentiation from other species.

Hence Veblen followed Darwin and regarded human intentionality as a capacity that had itself evolved through natural selection. As Veblen (1899a, p. 15) put it in another work, the capacity of humankind to act with deliberation towards ends was itself a result of natural selection:

> As a matter of selective necessity, man is an agent. He is, in his own apprehension, a centre of unfolding impulsive activity – 'teleological'

---

15 However, Åkerman (1932, 1938, 1942) – another Swede – was influenced by Veblen's writings and his concept of cumulative causation while studying at Harvard in 1919–20. Perhaps Myrdal was also influenced by Åkerman, and thus indirectly and additionally by Veblen as well.

activity. He is an agent seeking in every act the accomplishment of some concrete, objective, impersonal end.

Despite this, Veblen is widely misunderstood as underestimating the actuality or significance of human intentionality and purposefulness. On the contrary, Veblen (1898b, p. 391) insisted: 'Economic action is teleological, in the sense that men always and everywhere seek to do something.' The fact that such purposeful behaviour itself emerged through evolutionary selection does not mean a denial of the reality of purposeful behaviour. Instead, Veblen consistently tried to reconcile a notion of individual purposefulness (or sufficient reason) with his materialist idea of causality (or efficient cause).

Intentions can be causes, but intentions are always caused. The evolution of human intentionality, and its development within each human being, has to be explained in terms of materialist causes and evolutionary selection. As noted above, this is an aspect of the Darwinian doctrine of continuity. Accordingly, like Darwin, Huxley, Lewes and Morgan, Veblen rejected a dualist or Cartesian ontology that separated intentionality completely from matter and materialist causality. Veblen (1909b, pp. 624–5) saw such a dualism as unacceptable for the following reason:

> The two methods of inference – from sufficient reason [or intention] and from efficient [or materialist] cause – are out of touch with one another and there is no transition from one to the other: no method of converting the procedure or the results of the one into those of the other.

Others since have echoed Veblen's argument against the idea of separate types of cause, and against the related Cartesian dualism of matter and mind. For example, Barry Hindess (1989, p. 150) asked pertinently: 'If human action is subject to two distinct modes of determination, what happens when they conflict, when intentionality pushes one way and causality pushes another?' We do not and cannot know the answer, because to reach it would involve the reconciliation of irreconcilables. John Searle (1997, pp. xii–xiii) similarly remarked: 'dualism ... seems a hopeless theory because, having made a strict distinction between the mental and the physical, it cannot make the relation of the two intelligible'. Mario Bunge (1980, p. 20) put it in a nutshell: 'Dualism is inconsistent with the ontology of science.'

Veblen perceived the consequences for the social sciences of this mistaken dualism. For example: 'The immediate consequence is that the resulting economic theory is of a teleological character – "deductive" or "a priori" as it is often called – instead of being drawn in terms of cause and effect' (Veblen, 1909b, p. 625). His solution, following Darwin, was to place human intentionality in an evolutionary context. At least in principle, consciousness had to be explained in Darwinian and evolutionary terms. As Veblen (1906a, p. 589) alluded: 'While knowledge is construed in teleo- logical terms, in terms of personal interest and attention, this teleological aptitude is itself reducible to a product of unteleological natural selection.' In the following passage, Veblen (1909b, p. 625) explained in more detail:

> The modern scheme of knowledge, on the whole, rests, for its defini- tive ground, on the relation of cause and effect; the relation of suffi- cient reason [or intention] being admitted only provisionally and as a proximate factor in that analysis, always with the unambiguous reser- vation that the analysis must ultimately come to rest in terms of cause and effect.

But this does mean that intentionality (or sufficient reason) is nonexistent or unimportant. On the contrary, Veblen (1909b, p. 625) acknowledged 'that the relation of sufficient reason enters very substantially into human conduct. It is this element of discriminating forethought that distinguishes human conduct from brute behavior'. Veblen (1909b, p. 626) then went on to observe and approve that 'modern science at large has made the causal relation the sole ultimate ground of theoretical formulation'. Veblen saw 'the relation of sufficient reason as a proximate, supplementary, or inter- mediate ground, subsidiary, and subservient to the argument from cause to effect'.

In sum, while human intentionality is real and consequential, and a nec- essary element in any causal explanation in the social sciences, intentions themselves had at some time to be explained. As Veblen (1909b, p. 626) put it, explanation could not be confined to the 'rationalistic, teleological terms of calculation and choice' because the psychological beliefs and mecha- nisms that lay behind deliberation and preferences had also to be ex- plained in terms of a 'sequence of cause and effect, by force of such elements as habituation and conventional requirements'. By acknowledg- ing the need for such causal explanations, Veblen rejected both the as- sumption of the given individual in neoclassical economics and the opposite error of regarding human agency as entirely an outcome of mys- terious social forces.

As well as to Darwin, Veblen's treatment of intentionality owed a great deal to the then emerging tradition of American pragmatism. Hans Joas (1996, p. 158) succinctly summarized the pragmatist contribution in this area:

> The alternative to a teleological interpretation of action, with its inher- ent dependence on Cartesian dualisms, is to conceive of perception and cognition not as preceding action but rather as a phase of action by which action is directed and redirected in its situational contexts. Ac- cording to this alternative view, goal-setting does not take place by an

act of intellect *prior* to the actual action, but is instead the result of a reflection on aspirations and tendencies that are pre-reflexive and have *already always* been operative. In this act of reflection, we thematize aspirations which are normally at work without our being actively aware of them. But where exactly are these aspirations located? They are located in our bodies. It is the body's capabilities, habits and ways of relating to its environment which form the background to all conscious goal-setting, in other words, to our intentionality. Intentionality itself, then, consists in a self-reflective control which we exercise over our current behavior.

Although Veblen rarely spelt out such matters in sufficient detail, I submit that this pragmatist conception of action is entirely consistent with his own expressed views, and its adoption is explicable in terms of his knowledge of the ideas of Peirce, James and Dewey. In this pragmatist view, intentionality is not denied but placed in the context of habits of thought and behaviour.

Veblen's position on intentionality has been the subject of some misunderstanding. David Seckler (1975, p. 56) came to the verdict that Veblen 'teeters between free will and determinism'. But Seckler did not define these terms adequately. Sure enough, Veblen can be criticized for sometimes describing a Darwinian causal process as 'mechanical'. This can give the impression that intentionality or purposefulness is excluded. But Veblen acknowledged the reality of purposeful behaviour. While Seckler (1975, p. 86) accepted the 'methodological dualism' of Ludwig von Mises (1949) and others, Veblen (1898b, p. 386) argued in contrast that the dualist position of the Austrian school should be dissolved by bringing purposes and preferences within the orbit of scientific explanation. What Seckler failed to understand was that Veblen was trying to overcome the problems of dualism. Veblen was not trying to dispense with human will but to reconcile it with materialist causality. Admittedly, Veblen was not entirely successful in formulating this position. But Veblen's shortcomings are no excuse for ignoring his efforts in that direction.

Richard Langlois (1986, p. 4) alleged that Veblen 'wished to rid economics of any sort of human intelligence and purpose'. Similarly, in an incisive essay on Veblen, Malcolm Rutherford (1998a, pp. 475–6) saw problems emanating from Veblen's non-teleological notion of explanation in the social sciences:

Following Darwin, [Veblen] sought an evolutionary theory that was free from teleology and ran in purely causal terms. He was aware that individuals acted in a goal-directed manner, but he wanted to present institutional change as unintended result – as a result of a causal process that did not rely on intentionality or on the appraisal of one institutional scheme as compared to another.

Rutherford is one of the best interpreters of Veblen, and Langlois is an incisive theorist. But both writers distort Veblen's position here. Neither Veblen nor Darwin dismissed intentionality, but saw teleological or goal-directed behaviour as explicable in causal terms. Contrary to Rutherford, Veblen's explanation of action and institutional change did involve intentionality. It should be clear from the quotations above that Veblen saw intentionality as part of the explanation of institutional change. Veblen recognized purposeful behaviour but saw it as ultimately explicable in causal terms.[16]

Veblen outlined the problem of reconciling human volition and causality but failed to develop an adequate and non-reductionist philosophical framework in which human intentionality, monism and causality could be reconciled; without reducing mind to matter, or matter to mind. In retrospect, a missing conceptual tool was an explicit and developed concept of emergence in the context of a layered ontology. Modern philosophers make much use of these concepts in their treatment of the mind–body problem (Bunge, 1980; Sperry, 1991). However, emergentist philosophy did not come to maturity until the 1920s, at the very end of Veblen's life.

The principle of evolutionary explanation

Veblen used the idea of an unbroken historical chain of cause and effect to undermine the presuppositions of mainstream economics. His use of Darwinian methodological injunctions led to a powerful critique. Ultimately, because the human agent was a subject of an evolutionary process, he or she could not be taken as fixed or given. A causal account of the interaction between the individual and social structure had to be provided. This causal account should not stop with the individual, but it should also attempt to explain the origin of psychological purposes and preferences.

Veblen argued that a problem with mainstream economics was that it provided a causal and evolutionary explanation neither of 'rational economic man' nor of his given preference function (Argyrous and Sethi, 1996; Hodgson, 1998a). How did such rationality and preferences appear in human evolution? What causes and processes brought them into being? How and when are they formed in the development of each human individual? For Veblen, such an escape from evolutionary principles was impossible. Darwinism meant not only a critique of Divine intervention, but it also required a rejection of immanently conceived preference functions. As a result, the universal assumption in neoclassical economics 'of a passive and substantially inert and immutably given human nature' (Veblen, 1898b, p. 389) had to be criticized.

---

16 Statements by Broda (1998, p. 222) that with Veblen 'individual intentions are reduced to their institutional conditioning' leading to a 'neutralization of the individual' are unsupported by any quotation from Veblen's text, and denied by several passages above.

Veblen upheld that utilitarian and hedonistic explanations of human behaviour were inadequate because they did not encompass an evolutionary and causal explanation of the origin of the assumed behavioural characteristics. The neoclassical assumption of given preferences side-steps an explanation of the origin and initial acquisition of those preferences. The assumption that individuals are selfish requires an explanation of the evolution of selfishness. In general, postulates about human behaviour at the socio-economic level themselves require explanation in evolutionary terms.

Veblen thus challenged the narrow definition of economics as 'the science of choice'. At a particular level of abstraction, it may be appropriate to consider the consequences of individual choices with fixed preferences, but the Darwinian perspective also obliges us eventually to consider the origin and evolution of those preferences. If economics is confined to fixed preferences, which are simply assumed at the outset, then it has to admit that it is limited in scope and that the narrow-defined 'economic approach' cannot explain everything. It would be better if the scope of economics were broadened, to include the explanation of the origin and variation of preferences themselves. Individual preferences have to be placed in the context of both individual development and the evolution of the human species.

Once we address human evolution, we must consider the possibility that at least some versions of 'rational economic man' would not emerge through evolutionary selection. As Veblen (1898c, p. 188) wrote with characteristic irony:

> But if this economic man is to serve as a lay figure upon which to fit the garment of economic doctrines, it is incumbent upon the science to explain what are his limitations and how he has achieved his emancipation from the law of natural selection.

Veblen rightly argued that if 'economic man' is assumed then his evolution must be explained. Veblen (1898c, p. 187) criticized the neoclassical assumption of an 'aversion to useful effort' or disutility of labour, on the grounds that it was inconsistent with the reality of human survival. This particular argument is criticized in Chapter 9 below. What concerns us here is Veblen's valid and more general methodological injunction that any assumptions concerning the human agent must be capable of explanation in evolutionary terms: the assumptions of economics and other social sciences should be consistent with Darwinism and our understanding of human evolution. This does not imply that all explanations have to be reduced to instincts. One of his underlying arguments is that any assumptions made concerning human nature or motivation should be consistent with those human attributes that have resulted from natural selection over hundreds of thousands of years. In this respect Veblen followed William

James (1890), who made a supreme effort to reconcile psychology with the insights of Darwinism.

Veblen thus upheld what has been termed above the (Darwinian) principle of evolutionary explanation. This principle demands that any behavioural assumption in the social sciences must be capable of causal explanation along (Darwinian) evolutionary lines, and be consistent with our understanding of human evolution. The social sciences are not a mere extension of biology, but they must be consistent with it. Mere consistency allows widespread scope for various propositions, but Veblen suggested that some assumptions, in particular those concerning 'economic man', may not satisfy this requirement. In the above manner, and by extending physical notions of causality to the social realm, Veblen upheld a principle of consistency of the sciences.

But Veblen did not sufficiently go into details. In examining the validity of his proposition that 'natural selection' would not give rise to 'economic man' we must distinguish between at least two versions of the latter. A first, narrower, version depicts 'economic man' as orientated solely towards his own pecuniary gain. A second, broader, version simply regards 'economic man' as rational, in the sense that his behaviour conforms to the standard axioms of utility theory and can be 'explained' in terms of the maximization of his own utility.

As argued at length elsewhere (Hodgson, 2001c), the problem with the second and broader version is not that the evidence contradicts it, but that every actual and conceivable piece of evidence can be fitted into the theory. Even the results of modern experiments with human subjects that are depicted as a challenge to the standard theory can be fitted into some tortured version of utility-maximizing behaviour. These experiments do not and cannot show that people are not maximizing their utility, because utility is never measured. Even apparent preference transitivity can be explained away, because the compared choices always take place in (at least slightly) different contexts, thus rendering two apparently identical choice elements as in fact different. There is no conceivable piece of evidence concerning behaviour that cannot in principle be 'explained' by the thesis of utility-maximizing behaviour. Consequently, the theory has little genuine explanatory power.[17]

---

17 Accordingly, modern attempts to demonstrate that evolutionary selection leads to human agents that conform to the standard axioms of expected utility theory (Binmore, 1994, 1998a; Robson, 2001a, 2001b, 2002) do not carry so much force as might appear at first sight. The axioms are formally consistent with *any* behavioural outcome (Hodgson, 2001c, ch. 16). The axioms formally exclude the possibility of inconsistent preferences or behaviour. On Monday I preferred beef to chicken. On Tuesday my choices were reversed. But this apparent inconsistency can be explained away by differences in the state of the world, such as a BSE scare announced on Tuesday morning. Because of the complexity of the decision context, it is generally impossible to take all (perceived) factors into account and thus demonstrate a case of preference inconsistency. Utility functions can be fitted to any behavioural outcome and thereby explain little. A genuinely Darwinian approach must locate the real dispositions that help to cause the behaviours,

By contrast, the first and narrower version of 'economic man' can in principle be undermined by evidence. Evidence suggests that people do not always act to maximize their pecuniary rewards, or that sometimes they derive considerable pride and satisfaction from their labours. Here the results of many modern experiments with human subjects, which suggest that people do not always maximize expected monetary gains, are of great relevance. There is strong evidence that people often act in ways that are inconsistent with the maximization of expected monetary rewards. Unlike the second and broader version, the first and narrower definition of 'economic man' is capable of falsification.[18]

Addressing the broader version of 'economic man', it is difficult to provide an evolutionary explanation of how each individual acquired a complex but unchanging utility function. This utility function would have to have the remarkable capability of determining a preference with respect to goods and activities that are beyond the comprehension of the infant at birth, or have not even yet come into being. Even if such a utility function is capable of fitting empirically with all such present and future preferences, then it does so as a static device, defying novelty, evolution and the workings of time.

The principle of evolutionary explanation also challenges the role-driven picture of the individual in much of twentieth-century sociology. Even if the individual were to be explained in terms of social roles, then it would also be necessary to explain how those roles, and the individual disposition to conform to them, evolved. Such an account would be forced to consider both the psychology of individual motivation and the social mechanisms by which roles are created and reproduced. It would thereby undermine its own pre-eminent emphasis on social roles.

I am responsible for giving the principle of evolutionary explanation a name, but I am not the originator of the idea. Darwin, James and Veblen formulated it. Modern evolutionary psychologists have revived the idea. They have provided evidence that human beings are not particularly good at abstract logical arguments. However, reflecting the fact that humans have evolved in a social setting, our rational capacities are greater when

---

rather than the triumphant exclamation of ultimately empty, *ex post* conceptual generalizations. Notably, endorsements of standard utility theory contrast with modern evolutionary economics (Nelson and Winter, 1982; Bowles, 2002) and Darwin's (1871, vol. 1, pp. 97–8) own view that his theory of human behaviour undermined utilitarian explanations based on selfishness or the maximization of happiness.

18 This does not denote a commitment to a Popperian philosophy of science. I do not uphold that science should consist of falsifiable propositions alone. But there is a big difference between falsifiable and non-falsifiable versions of 'rational economic man' and their explanatory powers. Non-falsifiable statements may fit all possible phenomena. If they have value, it is conceptual or analytical, rather than in terms of empirical description. In contrast, falsifiable statements would be negated by specific outcomes. A minimal reading list on the experimental evidence against some falsifiable versions of 'economic man' would include Kahnemann *et al.* (1982), V. Smith (1992), Kagel and Roth (1995), Field (2001) and Henrich *et al.* (2001).

logical rules are placed in a social context. Our minds are more tuned to socially contextualized rules than to abstract logical reasoning. More generally, our knowledge makes use of 'modular' intelligence or 'fast and frugal' heuristics, rather than extended, intricate computations that consume as much as possible of the available information. The human mind bears the marks of its evolutionary context and origins.[19]

Leda Cosmides and John Tooby (1994a, p. 68) argued that human intentionality must be studied in an evolutionary context: 'The human brain did not fall out of the sky, an inscrutable artefact of unknown origin, and there is no longer any sensible reason for studying it in ignorance of the causal processes that constructed it.' This has led to a critique of prevailing versions of rationality and intentionality in the social sciences. Among these is the separation of thought from its neural and material context. As Denise Cummins (1998, p. 31) put it: 'The Cartesian fantasy is that mind is pure intellect, the engagement in pure thought for its own sake. But evolution doesn't work that way.'

Cosmides and Tooby (1994b, p. 327) rejected the widespread assumption 'that rational behavior is the state of nature, requiring no explanation'. They went on to criticize what they call the Standard Social Science Model, where the mind harbours general cognitive processes that are 'context-independent' or 'context-free'. The key argument in this modern literature is that postulates concerning the rational capacities of the human brain must give an explanation of their evolution according to established Darwinian principles of evolutionary biology (Cummins and Allen, 1998).

However, some evolutionary psychologists have gone too far in making claims for their approach. A number of biological reductionists have got onto the bandwagon, making all sorts of claims concerning gender roles and much else. They have argued that psychology must be *reduced* to evolutionary biology by suggesting that psychological – and perhaps social – phenomena are explicable largely in biological terms. They have belittled the role of culture and proposed a single-level selection theory, centred on the gene. This group has grabbed the headlines, giving the wrong impression that they are representative of evolutionary psychology as a whole. In contrast, another group of evolutionary psychologists has upheld that psychology must be *consistent* with our understanding of human biological evolution and have developed evolutionary psychology in an explicitly non-reductionist manner.[20] Largely ignoring this second group, some critics of evolutionary psychology have misleadingly concentrated their attack entirely on its flawed and reductionist versions.[21]

It is regrettable that discussions of attempts to reconcile the biological, psychological and social sciences repeatedly require such qualifications

---

19 See D. Buss (1999), Cosmides and Tooby (1994a, 1994b), Cummins (1998), Gigerenzer *et al.* (1999), Plotkin (1994, 1997), Sperber (1996), Todd and Gigerenzer (2000) and Weingart *et al.* (1997).

and caveats. The essential point is this: following Darwin, James and Veblen, the principle of evolutionary explanation requires that theories and assumptions in psychology and the social sciences should be consistent with our knowledge and understanding of human evolution.

Instincts and habits

For many twentieth-century social theorists, the mere mention of instinct was taboo. The modern revival of instinct–habit psychology will be addressed in a later chapter. I shall also criticize Veblen's unwarranted and unsuccessful attempts to over-extend the explanatory role of instinct in the social domain. But these errors do not undermine Veblen's valid and enduring insight that an understanding of the roles of both instinct and habit is necessary for social science.

Instincts are inherited behavioural dispositions that, when triggered, give rise to reflexes, urges or emotions. Instincts are not fixed behaviours; they are dispositions that can often be suppressed or diverted. There is clear evidence for some human instincts. There are instinctive reflexes to clutch, suckle, and much else. In particular, after Noam Chomsky (1959) first doubted the behaviourist view that language could develop simply through stimulus and response, it has been conclusively demonstrated that language cannot be learned simply through interaction with the environment. Newborn babies inherit the means of recognition and imitation of some vocal sounds, as well as some elemental understanding of linguistic structure (Pinker, 1994). Although the development of language is impossible without extensive social interaction (Brown, 1973), it is also impossible without priming instincts.

The removal of all instincts would result in the tragic absurdity of a newborn with no guidance in its interaction with the world. Bombarded by sensations, but lacking any goal or impulse, it would be overwhelmed

---

20 For instance, Plotkin (1994, p. 176) wrote: 'What saves intelligent behaviour from such a reductionistic account is the presence of selectional processes in the mechanism of intelligence.' In sum, 'intelligent behaviour ... cannot be reductively explained by genetics or genetics and development'. Plotkin and other evolutionary psychologists recognize a major role for culture, as well as genetic make-up, in human development. Ben-Ner and Putterman (2000) also argue that evolutionary psychology does not lead us to the biological reductionism that some of the popularizers have promoted.

21 For example, the critique of evolutionary psychology by Rose and Rose (2000) was confined to reductionist versions only, neglecting the explicitly non-reductionist statements of Plotkin (1994) and others. Rose and Rose (2000) also overlooked some important differences between evolutionary psychology and E. Wilson's (1975, 1978) sociobiology. While many sociobiologists assumed that observed behaviour is biologically adaptive in the present, evolutionary psychologists started with the weaker assumption that evolved psychological mechanisms were fitness enhancing in the past, and not necessarily adaptive in the current environment. Sociobiology often attempted to reduce explanations of social behaviour to the genetic level, whereas the non-reductionist wing of evolutionary psychology explicitly excluded the possibility of reducing such explanations to the genes.

by sensory stimuli, but with no disposition for selective attention. The newborn infant could do little else but engage in a random and directionless search through effectively meaningless sensations. If the newborn mind was like a blank slate, then the infant would have inadequate means of structuring its interaction with the world or of learning from experience, and the slate would remain blank.

Instincts are aroused by circumstances and specific sensory inputs. Particular circumstances can trigger inherited instincts such as fear, imitation or sexual arousal. It is beyond the point to argue that acquired habit or socialization are much more important than instinct. Emphatically, many of our dispositions and much of our personality are formed after birth. But the importance of socialization does not deny the necessary role of instinct. Both instinct and habit are essential for individual development. Inherited dispositions are necessary for socialization to begin its work. Obversely, much instinct can hardly manifest itself without the help of culture and socialization. Instinctive behaviour and socialization are not always rivals but often complements: they interact with one another. The degree to which we are affected by our social circumstances is immense, but that is no ground for the banishment of the concept of instinct from social theory.

Veblen inherited principally from James (1890) an emphasis on the role of both habit and instinct in human thought and action. The primary reason for placing habits and instincts within the study of human cognition and behaviour is a Darwinian insistence that human mental capacities have evolved out of preceding, less conscious and less deliberative forms, in our pre-human ancestors. In particular, the human capacity to reason must have been prefigured in earlier stages of evolution (Darwin, 1859, p. 208). Once again, the doctrine of continuity is relevant here. (See Chapter 4.) Furthermore, the conscious elements of the human mind have necessarily been built upon, and must operate through, less conscious mental mechanisms. In evolution there was no sudden appearance of reason, nor sudden banishment of instinct and habit.

In his *Theory of the Leisure Class* Veblen articulated a relationship between human biological instincts and socio-economic evolution. The Darwinian imperative of survival means than the human individual has particular traits, the most 'ancient and ingrained' of which are 'those habits that touch on his existence as an organism' (Veblen, 1899a, p. 107). In addition: 'With the exception of the instinct of self-preservation, the propensity for emulation is probably the strongest and most alert and persistent of the economic motives proper' (Veblen, 1899a, p. 110). On such assumptions concerning human nature, Veblen built his inspirational account of the runaway process of status emulation in modern society.

Although the concepts of instinct and habit are prominent in Veblen's works of the 1890s, his most extensive treatment of these concepts is in his *Instinct of Workmanship* (1914). Here the ideas of the British psychologist

William McDougall (1908) also came into play, alongside the earlier and more important influence of James. Lamarckians such as McDougall did not see instincts as entirely inherited but as gradually modified by habitual behaviour. McDougall was a Lamarckian to the end, even rejecting the prevalent doctrine of August Weismann. In his Lamarckism the distinction between habit and instinct was blurred. As Darwin (1859, p. 209) himself claimed, if the inheritance of acquired characters occurs, 'then the resemblance between what originally was a habit and an instinct becomes so close as not to be distinguished'. Darwin provided a satisfactory definition of neither habit nor instinct, despite his frequent use of these terms. James was more precise on this question, and criticized Darwin for regarding instincts as accumulated habits. With the benefit of Weismann's researches, James clearly distinguished between instincts and habits; the former can be biologically inherited, the latter cannot.

Following James, Veblen saw habit and instinct as distinct and central categories. Veblen (1914, pp. 2–3) argued that an 'inquiry into institutions will address itself to the growth of habits and conventions, as conditioned by the material environment and by the innate and persistent propensities of human nature'. He continued: 'for these propensities, as they take effect in the give and take of cultural growth, no better designation than the time-worn "instinct" is available'. Veblen (1914, p. 13) upheld that 'instincts are hereditary traits'. Throughout his writings, Veblen generally saw instinct as an 'innate and persistent' propensity. He distinguished it from habit, which is a propensity that is moulded by environmental circumstances.

However, for Veblen, instincts were not mere impulses. All instincts involve intelligence, and the manifestation of many instincts means the presence of an intention behind the act. As Veblen (1914, pp. 3, 32) insisted: 'Instinctive action is teleological, consciously so ... All instinctive action is intelligent and teleological.' In this respect, Veblen contrasted his notion of instinct with the idea of a 'tropism' in the work of Loeb. Foreshadowing behaviourist psychology, Loeb (1900, 1912) was less concerned to impute consciousness and intention to these springs of action. In this respect, Veblen (1914, p. 4) differed from Loeb and followed McDougall (1908) in regarding actions as consciously directed towards ends:

> The distinctive feature by which any given instinct is identified is to be found in the particular character of the purpose to which it drives. 'Instinct,' as contra-distinguished from tropismatic action, involves consciousness and adaptation to an end aimed at.

Veblen (1914, p. 9) put 'the instinctive proclivities into close relation with the tropismatic sensibilities' but also stressed the conscious and purposeful character of instinct. The problem was to explain the origin of consciousness and purpose out of an assembly of tropismatic reflexes. Understandably, Veblen did not successfully square the circle here, and the phenomenon of consciousness remains a central problem for science.[22] Nevertheless, Veblen linked instinct with intelligent behaviour and saw instincts as part of the apparatus of reason. Veblen (1914, pp. 5–6) wrote:

> The ends of life, then, the purposes to be achieved, are assigned by man's instinctive proclivities; but the ways and means of accomplishing those things which the instinctive proclivities so make worth while are a matter of intelligence. It is a distinctive mark of mankind that the working-out of the instinctive proclivities of the race is guided by intelligence to a degree not approached by other animals. But the dependence of the race on its endowment of instincts is no less absolute for this intervention of intelligence; since it is only by the prompting of instinct that reflection and deliberation come to be so employed, and since instinct also governs the scope and method of intelligence …

However, some of Veblen's formulations on instinct have caused confusion. On the one hand, Veblen (1914, pp. 2–3, 13) stated that instincts were 'innate and persistent … propensities' and 'hereditary traits'. On the other hand, a few pages later, Veblen (1914, p. 38) wrote that: 'All instinctive behavior is subject to development and hence to modification by habit.' Several authors have seized on this latter sentence as evidence that by instinct Veblen did not mean fixed and inherited dispositions. Instead, he here seemed to suggest that an individual's instincts could be altered by an individual's development and environment. This would seem to contradict the earlier statement in the same work that instincts were 'innate and persistent'.

But the contradiction disappears when it is realized that in the first passage (Veblen, 1914, pp. 2–3) Veblen refers to 'instinct' and in the latter (Veblen, 1914, p. 38) he refers to 'instinctive behavior'. The instincts of an individual cannot be changed; but 'instinctive behavior' can. Behaviour promoted by instincts can be modified or repressed, through constraints or countervailing habits or reflection. The sexual instinct, for example, is biologically inherited and innate, but can take a variety of behavioural forms, depending on cultural and other influences.[23]

In another passage in the same work, Veblen (1914, p. 85) wrote of 'pliancy and tractability common in some degree to the whole range of

---

22 See, for example, Davies and Humphreys (1993), R. Penrose (1994) and Searle (1997).
23 Mitchell (1914, 1936) was one of the first of a long list of wishful thinkers who, to this day, have seized upon this apparent ambiguity, arguing that by instinct Veblen did not or should not really mean 'innate and persistent … hereditary traits' but malleable individual dispositions moulded by the environment. This wishful thinking became especially popular with those who tried to turn Veblen into a behaviourist. But this reading has no clear support in Veblen's texts, and goes against his adoption of the Jamesian distinction between habit and instinct. After all, if instincts can be moulded by environmental circumstances, there is less of a difference between instincts and habits. Yet Veblen did not treat these words as interchangeable.

instincts'. These words are ambiguous. Given that all fixed instincts yield behaviours of types that depend conditionally on circumstantial triggers, the alleged 'pliancy' of instincts may mean no more than their 'compliance' with the situation. For those determined to find evidence that Veblen saw instincts as malleable, his single unelaborated allusion to 'pliancy and tractability' is perhaps the best they can find. But yet again, even these words do not contradict Veblen's insistence that instincts are 'innate and persistent … hereditary traits'.

Veblen retained a necessary place for both instinct and habit – nature and nurture – in his explanation of human behaviour. Human deliberation and habits of thought are shaped by the social culture. But 'it is only by the prompting of instinct' that human cognition and deliberation come into play. Instincts help to spur emotions that drive many of our actions and deliberations. Veblen saw instincts as not only the basis of human purposes and preferences, but also as the primary drives and prompts of intelligent deliberation and action. Instincts focus activity on specific ends, and help to shape the means of their pursuit. Inherited nature is necessary for nurture to function. Nature and nurture are not rivals but complements.

But if instinct can bear such a burden, what is to stop natural selection eventually creating sophisticatedly programmed instincts that are sufficiently flexible to deal with most circumstances? If instincts are so powerful, why do they not evolve to provide the complete apparatus of human cognition and action? If this happened, then no major role would be left for habits, as instincts would be sufficient for survival. In addressing these important questions, Veblen (1914, p. 6) argued that instincts on their own were too blunt or vague as instruments to deal with the more rapidly evolving exigencies of the human condition. Habits, being more adaptable than instincts, are necessary to deal with 'the larger body of knowledge in any given community' and the 'elaborate … ways and means interposed between these impulses and their realisation'. With intelligent organisms dealing with complex circumstances, instincts remain vital, but the modificatory power of habits becomes relatively more important. The social and natural environment is too inconstant to allow the natural selection of sufficiently complex and refined instincts to take place. Habits are acquired, additional and necessary means for instinctive proclivities to be pursued in a changing social and natural environment. As Veblen (1914, pp. 6–7) put it:

> The apparatus of ways and means available for the pursuit of whatever may be worth seeking is, substantially all, a matter of tradition out of the past, a legacy of habits of thought accumulated through the experience of past generations. So that the manner, and in a great degree the measure, in which the instinctive ends of life are worked out under any given cultural situation is somewhat closely conditioned by these elements of habit, which so fall into shape as an accepted scheme

of life. The instinctive proclivities are essentially simple and look directly to the attainment of some concrete objective end; but in detail the ends so sought are many and diverse, and the ways and means by which they may be sought are similarly diverse and various, involving endless recourse to expedients, adaptations, and concessive adjustment between several proclivities ...

Instincts are 'essentially simple' and directed to 'some concrete objective end'. Habits are the means by which the pursuit of these ends could be adapted in particular circumstances. In comparison to instinct, habit is a relatively flexible means of adapting to complexity, disturbance and unpredictable change.[24]

Veblen saw habits, like instincts, as essential for conscious deliberation. Habit is not opposed to reason but part of the act of deliberation itself. In turn, the habit-driven capacity to reason and reflect upon the situation could give rise to new behaviours and new habits. Habits and reason can interact with one another in an ongoing process of adaptation to a changing environment. This capacity to form new habits, aided by both instincts and reason, has helped to enhance the fitness of the human species in the process of natural selection.

Veblen explained how processes of habituation give rise to 'proximate ends' in addition to any 'ulterior purpose' driven by instinct. He gave the example of the habit of money acquisition in a pecuniary culture. Money – a means – becomes an end in itself; and the pursuit of money becomes a cultural norm. But pecuniary motives are not innate to humankind: they are culturally formed. Veblen (1914, p. 7) then began to elaborate how habits, acquired anew by each individual, could in effect be transmitted from generation to generation, without any assumption of acquired character inheritance at the individual level:

Under the discipline of habituation this logic and apparatus of ways and means falls into conventional lines, acquires the consistency of custom and prescription, and so takes on an institutional character and force. The accustomed ways of doing and thinking not only become an habitual matter of course ... but they come likewise to be sanctioned by social convention, and so become right and proper and give rise to

---

24 Veblen's argument resonates with the recent theory that capacities for sophisticated habit formation and cultural growth emerged among humans to deal with a changing and unpredictable climatic and natural environment. Environmental change, particularly climate change, is now emerging as a major explanation of the evolution of both intelligence and culture among humans (R. Potts, 1996; Richerson *et al.*, 2001; Calvin, 2002). The capacity to form sophisticated and adaptable habits is not found to the same degree among other species because of the relatively more sophisticated development of social structures among early humanoids. As Darwin (1871) himself expounded, habituation and sociality are linked together. See modern studies such as Tattersall (1998) and Klein and Edgar (2002).

principles of conduct. By use and wont they are incorporated into the current scheme of common sense.

Veblen (1899a, p. 246) had written earlier that 'the scheme of life, of conventions, acts selectively and by education to shape the human material'. Similarly, Veblen (1914, pp. 38–9) explained that 'the habitual acquirements of the race are handed on from one generation to the next, by tradition, training, education, or whatever general term may best designate that discipline of habituation by which the young acquire what the old have learned'. In terms redolent of Lewes and Morgan, Veblen saw conventions, customs and institutions as repositories of social knowledge. Institutional adaptations and behavioural norms were stored in individual habits and could be passed on by education or imitation to succeeding generations. As noted above, Veblen thus acknowledged processes of 'dual inheritance' or 'coevolution' (to use modern terms) where there was evolution at both the instinctive and the cultural levels, with their different means of transmission through time.[25]

Veblen (1914, p. 39) wrote: 'handed on by the same discipline of habituation, goes a cumulative body of knowledge'. Veblen (1914, p. 53) also emphasized that habits were the mechanisms through which the individual was able to perceive and understand the world: 'All facts of observation are necessarily seen in the light of the observer's habits of thought'. In other words, habits of thought are essential to cognition. Habits are acquired through socialization and provide a mechanism by which institutional norms and conventions are pressed upon the individual. This aspect of 'reconstitutive downward causation' will be discussed further in the next chapter.

Nevertheless, from the acquisition of language to elemental acts of imitation and socialization, the primary thoughts and behaviours that begin to form habits require instinctive impulses for their initialization. These instincts and habits power our emotional drives. We are riven with dispositions and preconceptions: some inherited, some acquired. These dispositions and preconceptions do not entirely determine our thoughts and actions, but they create the reactive mechanisms leading to possible behavioural outcomes.

The outcome was that Veblen emphasized the *double weight of the past* on human deliberation and decision-making. First, the natural selection of instincts over hundreds of thousands of years has provided humans with a set of basic dispositions, albeit with substantial 'variations of individuality' (Veblen, 1914, p. 13) from person to person. The newborn infant comes into the world with these fixed and inherited propensities. But, second, the world of the child is one of specific customs and institutions into which he or she must be socialized. The individual learns to adapt to these

---

25 See Boyd and Richerson (1985) and Durham (1991).

circumstances, and through repeated action acquires culturally specific habits of thought and behaviour. These customs and institutions have also evolved through time; they are the weight of the past at the social level. The weight of instinct results from the phylogenetic evolution of the human population. Habituation is the mechanism through which the weight of social institutions can make its mark on the ontogenetic development of each individual.

In Veblen's writings, the term 'habit' suggests a propensity or disposition, not behaviour as such. Veblen often coupled the words 'habit and propensity' or 'propensities and habits' together. Veblen meant that habit is also a propensity, alongside other propensities, such as instincts. The most decisive passages on this question are the following. Veblen (1898b, p. 390) wrote of 'a coherent structure of propensities and habits which seeks realization and expression in an unfolding activity'. Here habit is tied in with other propensities and 'seeks realization', suggesting that habit itself is a disposition, rather than behaviour. Even more clearly, Veblen (1898c, p. 188) remarked that 'man mentally digests the content of habits under whose guidance he acts, and appreciates the trend of these habits and propensities'. Here habits are not actions, but the dispositions that guide them.

Veblen's usage was consistent with the pragmatist philosophers and instinct psychologists, who saw habit as an acquired proclivity or capacity, which may or may not be actually expressed in current behaviour. Repeated behaviour is important in establishing a habit. But habit and behaviour are not the same. If we acquire a habit we do not necessarily use it all the time. It is a propensity to behave in a particular way in a particular class of situations.[26]

Consider these words of Veblen's contemporaries. James (1892, p. 143) proclaimed: 'Habit is thus the enormous fly-wheel of society, its most precious conservative agent.' Likewise, James Mark Baldwin (1894, p. 30) saw habits as dispositions, when he wrote that 'the great practised habits of the organism get confirmed by stimulation again and again'. The pragmatist sociologists William Thomas and Florian Znaniecki (1920, p. 1851, emphasis added) criticized 'the indistinct use of the term "habit" to indicate any uniformities of behavior. ... A habit, inherited or acquired, is the *tendency* to repeat the same act in similar material conditions.' Thomas was an acquaintance of Veblen in Chicago. Also treating habit as a propensity, McDougall (1908, p. 37) wrote of 'acquired habits of thought and action' as 'springs of action' and saw 'habit as a source of impulse or motive power'. Elsewhere, in his defences against the behaviourist invasion, McDougall

---

26 T. Lawson (2003b, p. 333) interprets Veblen differently, 'as using the term habit to indicate certain (repeated) forms of action' but does not give any textual evidence to support this interpretation. On the contrary, the passages from Veblen quoted here suggest a view of habits as propensities or dispositions. Furthermore, Veblen was immersed in a pragmatist milieu where a dispositional interpretation of habits was pre-eminent.

(1924) explicitly emphasized the conceptual difference between dispositions and behaviour. As John Dewey (1922, p. 42) put it: 'The essence of
habit is an acquired predisposition to *ways* or modes of response.' The use
of habit is largely unconscious. Habits are submerged repertoires of potential behaviour; they can be triggered or reinforced by an appropriate stimulus or context.[27]

Many thinkers have difficulty accepting the idea of habit as a disposition. They prefer to define habit as behaviour. A source of the problem is a
reluctance to remove reason and belief from the exclusive driving seat of
human action. The 'mind-first' conception of action pervades social science. If habits affect behaviour then it is wrongly feared that reason and belief will be dethroned. The concern is that volition would be replaced by
mechanism. However, from a pragmatist perspective, reasons and beliefs
themselves depend upon habits of thought. Habits act as filters of experience and the foundations of intuition and interpretation. Habit is the
grounding of both reflective and non-reflective behaviour. But this does
not make belief, reason or will any less important or real.[28]

Other considerations are important here. Modern philosophy of science
is predominantly realist in its inclination. Central to most strands of modern realist philosophy is the distinction between the *potential* and the *actual*,
between dispositions and effects, where in each case the former are more
fundamental than the latter. This distinction is traceable back to Aristotle.[29]
Science is about the discovery of causal laws or principles. Causes are not
events; they are generative mechanisms that can under specific conditions
give rise to specific events. For example, a force impinging on an object
does not always make that object move. The outcome also depends on

---

27 The conception of a habit as a propensity or disposition is also found in modern works
such as Camic (1986), Margolis (1994), Murphy (1994), Kilpinen (2000) and others. James
(1890), Royce (1903) and Dewey (1922) are among the enduring classic pragmatist
writings on habit.

28 The treatment of habit here contrasts with neoclassical analyses where habit is seen as
based upon, and derivable from, rational behaviour (Lluch, 1974; Phlips and Spinnewyn,
1984; Becker and Murphy, 1988; Becker, 1992). This treatment of habit lacks an adequate
explanation of the particular preference functions that are assumed to be foundational.
Note also that Becker's (1992) definition of habit as serially correlated behaviour is very
different from that of a programmed disposition or propensity, as adopted here.

29 Aristotle (1956, p. 35) noted that '"habit" means a disposition' but can also be used to
denote an activity. Aristotle (1956, pp. 227–8) criticized Eucleides of Megara – a disciple of
Socrates – and his school 'who maintain that a thing *can act* only when it *is acting*. But the
paradoxes attending this view are not far to seek. … A man will not be, for example, a
builder unless he is building; for to be a builder is to be able to build. Now if a man cannot
have an art without having at some time learned it, and cannot later be without it unless he
has lost it, are we to suppose that the moment he stops building he has lost his art? If so,
how will he have recovered it if he immediately resumes building? The same is true of
inanimate objects. … The Megaric view, in fact, does away with all change. On their
theory that which stands will *always* stand, that which sits will *always* sit; … Since we
cannot admit this view … we must obviously draw a distinction between potentiality and
actuality.' I have also applied this argument to the definition of a routine (Hodgson,
2003c).

friction, countervailing forces, and other factors. Causes relate to potentialities; they are not necessarily realized in outcomes. As Veblen (1899c, p. 128) himself put it: 'The laws of nature are ... of the nature of a propensity.' Hence there must be a distinction between an observed empirical regularity and any causal law that lies behind it.[30] In this work and elsewhere, the word habit is used to describe a disposition or propensity, and is distinguished from behaviour.

The primacy of instincts and habits over reason

Habit comes before belief and reason. The following pragmatists emphasized this insight. Charles Sanders Peirce (1878, p. 294) declared that the 'essence of belief is the establishment of habit'. Josiah Royce (1969, vol. 2, p. 663) announced in his 1902 presidential address to the American Psychological Association: 'The organization of our intelligent conduct is necessarily a matter of habit, not of instantaneous insight.' Dewey (1922, p. 30) similarly remarked that the 'formation of ideas as well as their execution depends upon habit'. In the pragmatist view, habit supports rather than obstructs rational deliberation; without habit, reason is disempowered (Kilpinen, 1999, 2000).

With ample cues such as these, Veblen adopted a pragmatist theory of action in which activity and habit formation precede rational deliberation. For the pragmatist, activity itself does not require reason or deliberation; we only have to consider the habitual or instinctive behaviour of non-human animals to establish this truth. According to the Darwinian principle of continuity, but contrary to much of twentieth-century social science, the uniqueness of humanity does not lie in any relegation of instinct or habit, but in the critical supplementary deployment of conscious rational deliberation when a striking problem or novel situation demands it. Reasons and intentions emerge in continuous process of interaction with the world, while we are always driven by habits and other dispositions. As Veblen (1919a, p. 38) wrote in 1908: 'habits of thought are an outcome of habits of life'. Veblen (1919b, p. 15) later explained:

> History teaches that men, taken collectively, learn by habituation rather than precept and reflection; particularly as touches those underlying principles of truth and validity on which the effectual scheme of law and custom finally rests.

Reason is intimately connected with doing, because activity is the stimulus for habits of thought, and because reason and intelligence are deployed to guide action through problems and difficulties. Intelligence is 'the selective effect of inhibitive complication' (Veblen, 1906a, p. 589). In

---

30 See for example Bhaskar (1975), Harré and Madden (1975) and Popper (1990).

less cryptic words, deliberation and reason are deployed to make a choice when habits conflict, or are insufficient to deal with the complex situation. In turn, these particular patterns of reason and deliberation themselves begin to become habituated, so that when we face a similar situation again, we may have learned to deal with it more effectively. Reason does not and cannot overturn habit; it must make use of it to form new habits. Veblen (1906a, p. 588) wrote that 'knowledge is inchoate action inchoately directed to an end; that all knowledge is "functional"; that it is of the nature of use'. Knowledge is an adaptation to a problem situation; it stems from and assists activity.[31]

As Daugert (1950, pp. 35–6) observed: 'Veblen appears to be using the concept "habits of thought" as he formerly used the word "mind" to describe the process by which the adaptation of phenomena takes place.' For Veblen, as Daugert explained, our concepts evolve in interaction with the world: 'Ideas or concepts, that is, habits of thought, are thus not merely the passive products of our environment but are active, dynamic, and creative instruments searching for conduct adaptable to changing circumstances.'

Instinct is prior to habit, habit is prior to belief, and belief is prior to reason. That is the order in which they have evolved in our human ancestry over millions of years. That too is the order in which they appear in the ontogenetic development of each human individual. The capacity for belief and reason develops on a foundation of acquired instinctive and habitual dispositions. That too is the order in which they are arranged in a hierarchy of functional dependence, where the current operation of reason depends upon belief, belief depends upon habit, and habit depends upon instinct. Lower elements in the hierarchy do not entirely determine the higher functions, but they impel them into their being, where they are formed in their respective natural and social context. The lower elements are necessary but not sufficient for the higher (Margolis, 1987; Murphy, 1994).

Accordingly, Veblen (1914, p. 30 n.) recognized 'that intellectual functions themselves take effect only on the initiative of the instinctive dispositions and under their surveillance'. By adopting this view, the false 'antithesis between instinct and intelligence will consequently fall away'. Veblen saw Darwinism as implying that habit and instinct were the basis of motivation; they impelled and dominated any rational calculation of individual interests or objectives. As noted already, this was the basis of Veblen's fundamental criticisms of both Marxism and neoclassical economics.

Consider two contrary views of the place of habit. Richard Ault and Robert Ekelund (1988, p. 442) criticized Veblen for overlooking that habits 'are themselves the product of past adaptations driven by economic

---

31 Margolis (1994) has also shown that the most cerebral and deliberative of human activities, the pursuit of science, also depends on habits of thought.

calculations'. This 'mind first' criticism overlooks the fact that 'economic calculations' themselves rely on habits (and instincts). Ault and Ekelund rightly point out that the outcomes of decision and reason may sometimes give rise to habits. However, contrary to Ault and Ekelund, habits are always required for decision and reason, but habits themselves do not necessarily rely on deliberation.

While Ault and Ekelund tried to give priority to deliberation over habit, Tony Lawson (2003b, p. 48) regarded them as symmetrical. He argued that discursive reflection and habits 'require, and causally condition, each other. Although everything in the social world turns on human practice, no feature of social life warrants explanatory/analytical priority.' This symmetrical treatment of deliberation and habit is wrong. Reason always requires habit to begin to operate. But the reverse is not always the case, because although sometimes decisions lead to habits, we often form habits as the result of non-discursive impulses such as instincts. Furthermore, habits precede reason in our evolutionary past: we are descended from organisms that had no developed capacity to reason. Habit has both ontogenetic and phylogenetic priority over reason, and instinct has both ontogenetic and phylogenetic priority over habit.

When the human species evolved its capacity to reason, its dependence on instinct and habit did not decline. Darwin (1871, vol. 1, p. 37) wrote: 'Cuvier maintained that instinct and intelligence stand in an inverse ratio to each other; and some have thought that the intellectual facilities of the higher animals have been gradually developed from their instincts. But ... no such inverse ratio really exists.' In comparable terms to Darwin and Veblen, John Hobson (1914, p. 356) proposed 'to break down the abruptness of the contrast between reason and instinct and to recognize in reason itself the subtlest play of the creative instinct'. Similarly, Charles Horton Cooley (1922, p. 30) also emphasized that reason 'does not supplant instinct' and 'reason itself is an instinctive disposition ... to compare, combine, and organize the activities of the mind'.

In contrast, Émile Durkheim (1984, pp. 262, 284) wrote in 1893 that: 'It is indeed proven that intelligence and instinct always vary in inverse proportion to each other ... the advance of consciousness is inversely proportional to that of the instinct.' As the social sciences broke from biology in the interwar period, this false antithesis between intelligence and instinct became commonplace in twentieth-century social science.[32]

But the breach with biology is slowly being repaired. Remarkably, with developments in modern psychology and elsewhere in the 1980s and 1990s, the views of Darwin, Veblen, Cooley and Hobson on instincts – rather than those of Durkheim – now seem remarkably modern. For

---

32 Even Hayek (1988, pp. 16–17), who increasingly adopted ideas from biology, believed that a 'gradual replacement of innate responses by learnt rules increasingly distinguished man from other animals' and typically regarded instincts as 'atavistic', 'ferocious' or 'beastly'.

instance, Howard Margolis (1987, p. 29) has pursued the hierarchy of instinct, habit and reason in the following terms:

> The output of the brain ... would then consist of some blending of instinct, habit, and judgment, all subject to errors and limitations, but on the whole sufficient to make the brain capable of survival in the environment in which it operates. There is a natural hierarchy in the three modes (instinct, habit, judgment). Habits must be built out of instincts, judgment must somehow derive from instinct and habits.

The idea that reason is in part a manifestation of instinct, and that instinct and reason are complements, has again found its time a century after James, Veblen and Cooley. Cosmides and Tooby (1994b, p. 330) wrote of 'reasoning instincts' and Henry Plotkin (1994, p. 165) has explained that:

> Rationality and intelligence are extensions of instinct and can never be separated from it. The doctrine of separate determination is completely wrong. ... *Instinct is the mother of intelligence.*

Instinct is not the antithesis of reason, but one of its preconditions. By freeing the conscious mind from many details, instincts and habits have an essential role. If we had to deliberate upon everything, our reasoning would be paralysed by the weight of data.

Arthur Reber (1993) has argued that implicit learning of an unconscious character is ubiquitous even in humans and higher animals. This is partly because higher levels of deliberation and consciousness are recent arrivals on the evolutionary scene and came after the development of more basic mechanisms of unconscious learning in organisms. There was no cause or possibility for evolution to dispense with habits and instincts once human reasoning emerged. It built upon them, just as human bipedal physiology built upon the modified skeletal topology of a quadruped. Earlier structures and processes, having proved their evolutionary success, are likely to be built upon rather than removed. Hence earlier evolutionary forms can retain their use and presence within the organism. They will do this when they form the building blocks of complex further developments. That being the case, we retain instincts and unconscious mental processes that can function independently of our conscious reasoning. As some animal species developed more complex instincts, they eventually acquired the capacity to register fortuitous and reinforced behaviours through the evolution of mechanisms of habituation. In turn, upon these mechanisms, humans built culture and language. Our layered mind, with its unconscious lower strata, maps our long evolution from less deliberative organisms. Consistent with the evolutionary doctrine of continuity, habits and instincts are highly functional evolutionary survivals of our pre-human past.

Paul Twomey has explored in detail the parallels between Veblen's 'economic psychology' and much of modern psychology and cognitive science. The perspective that Veblen inherited from Peirce, James and others 'stressed the active and multi-tiered nature of the mind in which instincts, habits, and conscious reasoning are all significant for understanding human behaviour' (Twomey, 1998, p. 437). Many of the ideas of the early pragmatists and instinct psychologists have today made a comeback. 'Modern research has tended to lessen the priority of the conscious, deliberating aspect of the mind' (Twomey, 1998, p. 441). Accordingly, neurologists such as Antonio Damasio (1994) have undermined the Cartesian barrier between body and mind, and accordingly between intentional and materialist causality. The phenomenon of the mind cannot be understood from the functioning of the brain alone. Mind and reason are both also inseparable from the body and its environment (A. Clark, 1997a, 1997b). This environment includes the institutions within which people act. Beliefs and intentions are, in part, formed and changed through interactions with others (Lane *et al.*, 1996). We think and act in and through the contexts of our activities. The idea of the human will as the ultimate, context-independent source of all intention and belief is untenable.

Consequently, any attempt to define rationality in an entirely context-independent manner will be inadequate. In an ongoing process, people act, perceive, reason, make decisions, and act again. They try to do the best with their knowledge in the circumstances. But the cognitive frames and criteria, which they use in their perceptions and deliberations, necessarily precede and mould the reasoning process. Rationality itself depends on prior social and psychological props.

It is not the notion that humans act for reasons that is being attacked here. Humans do act for reasons – but reasons and beliefs themselves are caused, and have to be explained. It is proposed here that reasoning itself is based on habits and instincts, and it cannot be sustained without them. Furthermore, consistent with the evolutionary doctrine of continuity, instincts and the capacities to form habits, developed through a process of natural selection that extends way back into our pre-human past.

8 Veblen's evolutionary institutionalism

> As institutions are beliefs which are shared and established in the group, the history of institutions is really the history of knowledge.
>
> Murray G. Murphey (1990)

This chapter addresses some of Veblen's central ideas on human agency and institutional evolution, on the basis of the philosophical and psychological foundations outlined in the previous chapter. It is shown that Veblen steered a course away from both methodological individualism and methodological collectivism, while emphasizing the weight of the past on human cognition and action. Institutions, for Veblen, were partly repositories of knowledge. Through identifiable psychological mechanisms, institutions can also affect individual dispositions, but without eliminating the reality and relative autonomy of human agency. Finally, it is shown how Veblen placed these ideas within a Darwinian framework of institutional evolution, alongside biological evolution at other levels.

The rejection of both methodological individualism and methodological collectivism

The strongest definition of methodological individualism is the injunction that socio-economic phenomena must be explained exclusively in terms of individuals. Methodological collectivism is symmetrically defined here as the injunction that socio-economic phenomena must be explained exclusively in terms of socio-economic wholes, structures, institutions or cultures. Veblen used neither term, but implicitly rejected both doctrines.

As we have seen, Veblen critiqued the overemphasis in Marxism on the structural determination of individual agency. Veblen's attempted solution to this problem was to conceive of both agency and structure as a result of an evolutionary process. In particular, he saw human agency and purposefulness as a result of evolution at both biological and social levels. Purposeful behaviour is the result of both inherited instinct and the cultural and material environment of the individual. This leads to the formation of habits, which act as the grounding of purposes and beliefs.

One of Veblen's clearest statements of his general position on methodological individualism and methodological collectivism was made in his article on 'The Limitations of Marginal Utility' in the *Journal of Political Economy*. Because of its importance regarding this central methodological question in social theory, the relevant passage will be quoted almost in its entirety. Veblen (1909b, pp. 628–9) started by pointing out that the assumption of given individuals under given institutional conditions would lead to static outcomes:

> Evidently an economic inquiry which occupies itself exclusively with the movements of this consistent, elemental human nature under given, stable institutional conditions – such as is the case with the current hedonistic economics – can reach statical results alone; since it makes abstraction from those elements that make for anything but a statical result.

Veblen (1909b, p. 629) then made it clear that institutions serve not merely as constraints, but also they affect the very wants and preferences of individuals themselves:

> Not only is the individual's conduct hedged about and directed by his habitual relations to his fellows in the group, but these relations, being of an institutional character, vary as the institutional scene varies. The wants and desires, the end and the aim, the ways and the means, the amplitude and drift of the individual's conduct are functions of an institutional variable that is of a highly complex and wholly unstable character.

This statement amounts to a strong assertion of the reconstitutive power of institutions over individuals. Institutional changes affect individual 'wants and desires'. Preferences are endogenous, rather than exogenously given. This amounted to a notion of reconstitutive downward causation, in everything but name. Nevertheless, he acted immediately to forestall any misunderstanding that this strong downward causation amounted to a methodological collectivism. He did not believe that the social wholes entirely determine the individual parts. Veblen (1909b, p. 629) made it absolutely clear that the individual was still causally effective, that institutions were a product of individuals in a group, and institutions could not exist without individuals:

> The growth and mutations of the institutional fabric are an outcome of the conduct of the individual members of the group, since it is out of the experience of the individuals, through the habituation of

individuals, that institutions arise; and it is in this same experience that these institutions act to direct and define the aims and end of conduct. It is, of course, on individuals that the system of institutions imposes those conventional standards, ideals, and canons of conduct that make up the community's scheme of life. Scientific inquiry in this field therefore, must deal with individual conduct and must formulate its theoretical results in terms of individual conduct.[1]

However, the above passage does not amount to an assertion of methodological individualism, as defined here.[2] Instead, Veblen upheld that individuals could not be removed from the picture, and he placed the individual in its social context. Veblen (1909b, pp. 629–30) insisted that a complete and detailed causal explanation – that is what he meant by 'a genetic theory'[3] – means an explanation of how the individual acquires relevant habits of thought and behaviour:

> But such an inquiry can serve the purposes of a genetic theory only if and in so far as this individual conduct is attended to in those respects in which it counts toward habituation, and so toward change (or stability) of the institutional fabric, on the one hand, and in those respects in which it is prompted and guided by the received institutional conceptions and ideals on the other hand.

Veblen (1909b, p. 630) then went on to criticize those mainstream economists who 'disregard or abstract from the causal sequence of propensity and habituation in economic life and exclude from theoretical inquiry all such interest in the facts of cultural growth'. By emphasizing 'cumulative causation' and 'continuity of cause and effect' Veblen broke from any idea that explanations could ultimately be reduced to one type of entity or level. No such reduction is admissible within his Darwinian framework because all such elements have themselves to be explained in causal terms. As the

---

1 As a representative critic, Khalil (1995, pp. 555–6) asserted: 'Inspired by Veblen's legacy, old institutional economists generally tend to view the preferences of agents as, in the final analysis, determined by cultural norms.' This may be true of some old institutionalists, but it was not true of Veblen who insisted that social science must 'formulate its theoretical results in terms of individual conduct'. From an evolutionary perspective, as Veblen understood well, there is no 'final analysis'. Despite its subtitle, Khalil's (1995) article is essentially about neither Veblen nor his true legacy, but about versions of institutionalism that became prominent in America after Veblen's death. See in particular the chapters on Ayres, later in the present work.

2 In contrast, Rutherford (1984, p. 345) quoted two of the above three sentences in isolation and concluded that Veblen was a methodological individualist. Either Rutherford was wrong, or he was using a different definition of the term. Veblen does not state that explanations must *exclusively* be in terms of individuals. An appreciation of Veblen's broader methodological position is gained by placing the above statement in the context of the passages that precede, succeed and qualify it.

3 See Veblen's (1903, p. 655) own definition of the 'genetic' method, as quoted on page 152 above.

philosopher of biology Elliott Sober (1981, p. 95) put it: 'Causality, in virtue of its transitivity, gives aid and comfort neither to the holist nor to the individualist. The causal chain just keeps rolling along.'

In sum, by rejecting both the individual and society as the ultimate unit of explanation, Veblen distanced himself from both methodological individualism and methodological collectivism. His solution was to adopt an evolutionary framework of explanation, in which there is an asymmetry between actor and structure. The nature of this asymmetry will be explored below. Above all, Veblen's position does not give solace to any form of (biological, cultural, structuralist or individualist) reductionism.[4]

Referring to the discussion in Chapter 2 above of different perspectives in modern social theory, Veblenian institutionalism shares with several other modern perspectives – including critical realism (Bhaskar, 1989; Archer, 1995) and structuration theory (Giddens, 1984) – the endorsement of the following four propositions:

1 **The dependence of social structures upon individuals**. Social structures would not exist if individuals ceased to exist. Individuals through their actions may create, confirm, reproduce, replicate, transform or destroy social structures, either intentionally or unintentionally.

2 **The rejection of methodological individualism**. Nevertheless, social structures cannot be explained entirely in terms of individuals and their relations. They are not reducible, in an ontological or an explanatory sense, to individuals alone.

3 **The dependence of individuals upon social structures**. For their socialization, survival and interaction, individuals depend upon social structures, and individual behaviour is significantly affected by its socio-structural context.

4 **The rejection of methodological collectivism**. Nevertheless, individual behaviours cannot be explained entirely in terms of the social structures in which they are located. Such reductionist explanations are invalid.

These four propositions are implicit in the writing of Veblen. They mean that individuals and social structure are *mutually constitutive*. These four propositions are elemental for any viable and non-reductionist social theory. But much more is required, as indicated below.

---

4   Whether Veblen was a 'holist' depends on the definition of the term. If it connotes explanation entirely in terms of collectives or social wholes then Veblen was not a holist. But that term is used in many other different ways. In fact, its usage has become so widespread and wide-ranging, and generally at variance from that of Smuts (1926) who originated the term, that it is best not used at all.

Temporal asymmetry and the weight of the past

Veblen shared with Auguste Comte, Karl Marx, George Henry Lewes, Émile Durkheim and others the insight that we are born into a world of many institutions that are not of our making. Hence there is a temporal asymmetry: although structures depend for their existence on a *group* of individuals, for each *single* individual, several structures precede agency. As noted in Chapter 2 above, this insight rules out the central conflation of Giddens (1984) where actor and structure are seen as facets of a combined process. Giddens's structuration theory treats structure and agency as not only mutually constitutive but also conjoined. On the contrary, while people can change and be changed by social structures, they do not choose or create the structures and institutions into which they are born. Agents and structures are not different *aspects* of the same things or processes but different *entities*.

Veblen recognized this temporal asymmetry and the weight of the past on human decisions and actions. For example, Veblen (1898b, pp. 392–3) wrote of economic evolution in the following terms:

> the base of action – the point of departure – at any step in the process is the entire organic complex of habits of thought that have been shaped by past processes. The ... expression of each is affected by habits of life formed under the guidance of all the rest.

Similarly, in *The Theory of the Leisure Class*, Veblen (1899a, p. 191) argued:

> The institutions – that is to say the habits of thought – under the guidance of which men live are in this way received from an earlier time; more or less remotely earlier, but in any event they have been elaborated in and received from the past.

Again, Veblen (1914, pp. 6–7) explained in *The Instinct of Workmanship*:

> The apparatus of ways and means available for the pursuit of whatever may be worth seeking is, substantially all, a matter of tradition out of the past, a legacy of habits of thought accumulated through the experience of past generations.

By rejecting the given individual as a fundamental explanatory unit, Veblen focused on the weight of history on individual expectations and choices. Veblen (1915, p. 132) thus wrote of the 'restraining dead hand' of the past. To take the individual as given would be to amputate his or her past; to take institutions as given would cut off another causal process. The Veblenian restoration of mechanisms by which the past bears upon the present has major implications for economic and social theory. It demarcates the whole tradition of institutional economics not only from the mainstream assumption of given preference functions, but also from those in the Keynesian tradition who emphasize expectations of the future without also paying heed to the formation of expectations by means of acquired understandings and cognitions (Hodgson, 1988). To take stock at this point, we note Veblen's concordance with a fifth proposition for social theory, which adds to those on page 179:

5 **The temporal priority of society over any one individual**. Individual interactions with society are engagements with something already made. In this sense, several social structures pre-date any one individual. As individuals we do not make society: it is there in some form at our birth, bearing the marks of the past practices of former generations. This temporal cleavage establishes social structures and society as entities distinct from individuals (or mere aggregates of individuals), at least because of the structural legacy bequeathed by past actors, and separates structure and agency as distinct but interconnected objects of investigation.

Social structures can be changed, but the starting point is not of our choosing. This fifth proposition breaks the conceptual symmetry of actor and structure and opens the door to time and history (Archer, 1995; Eby, 1998). Several modern social theorists would endorse the five propositions above; they are also consistent with some versions of Marxism. We now move into additional territory where Veblen's contribution is even more distinctive, as well as being of huge relevance to economic and social theory today.

Institutions as repositories of social knowledge

Possibly through ideas inherited from George Henry Lewes and hints provided by Conwy Lloyd Morgan, Veblen took up and developed the notion that social groups and institutions carry accumulated knowledge and experiences from the past. Accordingly, Veblen argued that the social complex of interacting individual habits constituted a social stock of largely intangible knowledge that could not be associated with individuals severally. As Veblen (1898d, pp. 353–4) put it:

Production takes place only in society – only through the co-operation of an industrial community. This industrial community ... always comprises a group, large enough to contain and transmit the traditions, tools, technical knowledge, and usages without which there can be no industrial organization and no economic relation of individuals to one another or to their environment. The isolated individual is not a productive agent. What he can do at best is to live from season to season, as the non-gregarious animals do. There can be no production without technical knowledge; hence no accumulation and no wealth to be owned, in severalty or otherwise. And there is no technical knowledge apart from an industrial community.

Many economists uphold that production is entirely a result of owned factors of production – such as land, capital and labour – whose owners can be remunerated accordingly. Veblen developed an enduringly relevant critique of this mainstream notion. Veblen (1921, p. 28) argued that production depended on a 'joint stock of knowledge derived from past experience' that itself could not become an individually owned commodity, because it involved the practices of the whole industrial community. Veblen (1898d, p. 354) continued:

> Since there is no individual production and no individual productivity, the natural-rights preconception that ownership rests on the individually productive labor of the owner reduces itself to absurdity, even under the logic of its own assumptions.

However, it is not Veblen's critique of mainstream economics that primarily concerns us here, but his contribution to the foundations of economic and social theory. Veblen's (1908a, 1908c, 1908d) devastating critique of the concept of capital in economic theory is best encountered by reading the original essays. We focus here on Veblen's (1908c, pp. 539–40) argument that learning and experience are accumulated within a community:

> These immaterial industrial expedients are necessarily a product of the community, the immaterial residue of the community's experience, past and present; which has no existence apart from the community's life, and can be transmitted only in the keeping of the community at large.

Veblen (1914, p. 103) repeated this point, again and again, here referring to technological knowledge and its storage in the social group:

> Technological knowledge is of the nature of a common stock, held and carried forward by the community, which is in this relation to be conceived as a going concern. The state of the industrial arts is a fact of group life, not of individual or private initiative or innovation. It is an affair of the collectivity, not a creative achievement of individuals working self-sufficiently in severalty or in isolation.

Nevertheless, he made it clear that the collective domain of knowledge devalues neither the role of the individual, nor the fact that knowledge is always held by individuals and is a matter of individual experience. As Veblen (1908c, p. 521) put it:

> The complement of technological knowledge so held, used, and trans-mitted in the life of the community is, of course, made up of the ex-perience of individuals. Experience, experimentation, habit, knowledge, initiative, are phenomena of individual life, and it is nec-essarily from this source that the community's common stock is all de-rived. The possibility of growth lies in the feasibility of accumulating knowledge gained by individual experience and initiative, and there-fore it lies in the feasibility of one individual's learning from the expe-rience of another.

The individual and the social aspects of knowledge are connected, be-cause the social environment and its 'common stock' of experience provide the means and stimulus to individual learning. The social environment is the result of individual interactions, but without this social environment the individual would be stultified. Learning is thus potentially a process of positive feedback between individual and society. The above quotations make it clear that Veblen saw the social domain as the site of a potential storehouse of knowledge. But Veblen took the argument one significant step further. In the *Leisure Class*, Veblen (1899a, pp. 193–4) wrote:

> Any community may be viewed as an industrial or economic mecha-nism, the structure of which is made up of what is called its economic institutions. These institutions are habitual methods of carrying on the life process of the community in material contact with the material en-vironment in which it lives. When given methods of unfolding human activity in this given environment have been elaborated in this way, the life of the community will express itself with some facility in these habitual directions. The community will make use of the forces of the environment for the purposes of its life according to methods learned in the past and embodied in those institutions.

This brought his concept of a social institution into the picture. Veblen stated here that institutions are social structures, involving individual hab-its and engaged with a material environment.[5] He wrote of members of a community making use of their social and material environment for their purposes, according to methods learned in the past and embodied in their social institutions. The latter quotation is one of Veblen's clearest state-ments that institutions function as repositories of social knowledge.

---

5 Searle (1995), Aunger (2000, 2002) and others emphasize the material component of institutions. Material objects and circumstances can provide vital cues for thoughts and actions that are essential to individual interactions within institutions.

He also discussed some of the mechanisms and means by which this knowledge is stored. Veblen (1906a, p. 592) wrote of 'habits of thought that rule in the working-out of a system of knowledge' being 'fostered by ... the institutional structure under which the community lives'. Veblen not only identified an environment of stored knowledge that is conducive to learning – as was the case with Lewes and Morgan – but also saw it as structured and made up of institutions. These institutions are the expression and outcome of the interaction of habituated individual behaviours, but cannot be reduced to the behaviours of individuals alone.[6]

However, Veblen did not develop his analysis of the institutional aspect of social knowledge much further. In the absence of a stratified ontology and a developed concept of emergence, social theorists would always be wary of terms like 'social memory' and the notion that knowledge could be associated with routines, organizations and institutions, as well as with individuals. Veblen's idea was the germ of a research programme that took many decades to be further developed. Although there were occasional prior appearances, similar conceptions did not begin to become popular again until the 1980s, when in economics Richard Nelson and Sidney Winter (1982) described routines as 'organizational memory' and sociologists such as Barbara Levitt and James G. March (1988) rehabilitated the concept of 'organizational learning'. But none of these key works from the 1980s refers to Veblen.

Mechanisms of reconstitutive downward causation

Especially with the hindsight of a century or more, one has to be especially careful not to attribute to Veblen an insight or concept that is not actually in his writing. With this warning in mind, this section addresses earlier ideas with terms that are of later origin. This is the notion of 'downward causation', coined in psychology by Nobel Laureate Roger Sperry (1964, 1969, 1976, 1991) and taken up by Donald T. Campbell (1974b) and others.

In its literature, the notion of 'downward causation' has weak and strong forms. Campbell (1974b, p. 180) saw it in weaker terms of evolutionary laws acting on populations: 'all processes at the lower levels of a hierarchy are restrained by and act in conformity to the laws of the higher levels'. Here evolutionary processes help to reconstitute populations but not necessarily individuals. In the weaker version of downward causation, applied to human society, structures act primarily as deterrents or constraints upon individual action. They may channel or redirect human behaviour, but without changing individual purposes or preference

---

6 Sadly Veblen never provided an adequate definition of an institution. T. Lawson (2003b, pp. 332–3) has shown clearly that Veblen's (1909b, p. 626) words 'settled habits of thought common to the generality of men' does not appear in its context as a definition of an institution. This corrects my (Hodgson, 1998a, p. 179) earlier mistaken suggestion that these words amount to a definition.

functions. An example of (weak) downward causation is a 'particle in a fluid being carried away by the current' (Auyang, 1998, p. 65). Another example of (weak) downward causation is natural selection operating on a population of organisms.

A stronger notion, which is here described as 'reconstitutive downward causation' involves both individuals and populations not only restrained, but also changed, as a result of causal powers associated with higher levels. Sperry (1991, pp. 230–1) also suggested a strong interpretation of downward causation in the social context. He recognized, for example, that 'higher cultural and other acquired values have power to downwardly control the more immediate, inherent humanitarian traits'.

Veblen considered both strong and weak forms of downward causation, although he did not use that terminology. Veblen (1899a, p. 212) considered the powers of an institution over individuals in the following terms:

> So soon as it has won acceptance as an authoritative standard or norm of life it will react upon the character of the members of the society which has accepted it as a norm. It will to some extent shape their habits of thought and will exercise a selective surveillance over the development of men's aptitudes and inclinations. The effect is wrought partly by a coercive, educational adaptation of the habits of all individuals, partly by a selective elimination of the unfit individuals and lines of descent.

In recognizing that institutions can 'shape … habits of thought' and enforce a 'coercive, educational adaptation' on individuals, Veblen was adopting a strong and reconstitutive sense of downward causation. However, in the same passage Veblen recognized the weaker form of downward causation involving 'selective elimination of the unfit individuals'. Veblen (1899a, p. 246) repeated both versions in several places, writing for instance that 'the scheme of life, of conventions, acts selectively and by education to shape the human material'.

The idea of downward causation has been criticized for supposing that higher-level processes somehow cause lower-level physical laws to be violated (Kim, 1992). In terms of the interaction of agency and social structure, objections would rightly be raised against the idea of 'social forces' or 'economic laws' themselves acting directly upon the intentions of agents. Sperry's proposition that 'cultural and other acquired values have power to downwardly control … inherent humanitarian traits' requires clarification in this respect, to avoid such objections. If the social or cultural can affect the individual, then it does so through causes that operate upon the individual at the psychological level. If it is to be acceptable, the concept of reconstitutive downward causation does not rely on unexplained or mysterious types of cause or causality.

In clarifying his position, Sperry (1991, p. 230) rightly insisted that 'the higher-level phenomena in exerting downward control do *not disrupt* or *intervene* in the causal relations of the downward-level component activity'. This could usefully be termed Sperry's Rule.[7] It ensures that emergence, although it is associated with emergent causal powers at a higher level, does not generate multiple types or forms of causality at any single level. Any emergent causes at higher levels exist by virtue of lower-level causal processes.

Sperry's Rule excludes methodological collectivism. Instead, Sperry's Rule obliges us to explain particular human behaviour in terms of causal processes operating at the individual level, such as individual aspirations, dispositions or constraints. Where higher-level factors enter, is in the more general explanation of the system-wide processes giving rise to those aspirations, dispositions or constraints.

Accordingly, at the level of the human agent, there are no magical 'cultural' or 'economic' forces controlling individuals, other than those affecting the dispositions, thoughts and actions of individual human actors. People do not develop new preferences, wants or purposes because mysterious 'social forces' control them. Following Veblen, what have to be examined are the social and psychological mechanisms leading to such changes of preference, disposition or mentality. It is through these mechanisms that social power is exercised over individuals.

What does happen is that the framing, shifting and constraining capacities of social institutions give rise to new individual perceptions and dispositions. Upon new habits of thought and behaviour, new preferences and intentions emerge. Veblen (1899a, p. 190, emphasis added) was specific about the psychological mechanisms involved: 'The situation of today shapes the institutions of tomorrow through a selective, coercive process, *by acting upon men's habitual view of things.*'

The crucial point here is to recognize the significance of reconstitutive downward causation on *habits*, rather than merely on behaviour, intentions or preferences. Clearly, the definitional distinction between habit (as a propensity or disposition) and behaviour (or action) is essential to make sense of this statement. But a second point is also of vital significance. Habit and instinct are foundational to the human personality. Reason, deliberation and calculation emerge only after specific habits have been laid down; their operation depends upon such habits. In turn, the development of habits depends upon prior instincts. Instincts, by definition, are

---

7 This could be developed by using Humphreys's (1997, p. 7) proposition that 'allows higher level events to causally affect 0-level events if the former are part of causal chains that begin and end at the 0-level'. An 0-level event is an event at the lowest ontological level. But Humphreys points out that his argument could be reformulated to 'allow similar possibilities for causal chains beginning and ending at higher levels than 0'. Humphreys (1997) provides a powerful reply to Kim (1992) and a rigorous formulation of the idea of emergence that escapes some of its recent criticisms. See also Humphreys (1989).

inherited. Accordingly, reconstitutive downward causation upon instincts is not possible. (However, in the weaker sense, 'downward causation' upon instincts is possible, simply because instincts exist and evolve in consistency with higher-level principles, such as the laws of evolution.) Reconstitutive downward causation works by creating and moulding habits. Habit is the crucial and hidden link in the causal chain.

Clearly, institutions may directly affect our choices, by providing incentives, sanctions or constraints. For example, we decide to drive within the speed limit because we see a police patrol car. However, this particular intention is explained in terms of the *existing* preference to avoid punishment. This explanation does not itself involve a reconstitutive process. In contrast, to provide a reconstitutive causal mechanism, we have to point to factors that are foundational to purposes, preferences and deliberation as a whole. This is where habits come in. By affecting habits, institutions can indirectly influence our purposes or preferences. As long as we can explain how institutional structures give rise to new or changed habits, then we have an acceptable mechanism of reconstitutive downward causation.

In this manner it is possible to avoid both methodological individualism and methodological collectivism. By acting not directly on individual decisions, but on habitual dispositions, institutions exert downward causation without reducing individual agency to their effects. Furthermore, upward causation, from individuals to institutions, is still possible, without assuming that the individual is given or immanently conceived. Again and again Veblen described how institutional changes acted upon individual habits of thought and behaviour. The concept of habit was central to his understanding of how institutions affect individual dispositions and behaviour, and how social power is exercised.[8]

The broader idea that social institutions can in some way affect individual purposes or preferences became thematic for institutional economics as a whole. For example, Wesley Mitchell (1924a, p. 24) saw money as an institution that 'makes us all react in standard ways to the standard stimuli it offers, and affects our very ideals of what is good, beautiful and true'. John R. Commons (1934a, p. 698) likewise made it clear that 'not only the physical framework of the body, but also the spiritual framework of the mind, becomes institutionally habituated to the dominant ways of doing things'. Although this broad idea is thematic for institutionalism, it is not confined to it. For example, Alfred Marshall (1890) wrote repeatedly in his *Principles* of 'the development of new activities giving rise to new wants' (Marshall, 1949, p. 76). But no one was more careful than Veblen to specify

---

8 Bourdieu (1990) takes a similar line with his rather pretentious concept of *habitus*. Bourdieu and Wacquant (1992, p. 122) go so far as to indicate that *habitus* is practically equivalent to the term habit in its pragmatist meaning. But it would be even better to call a habit a habit. In their influential sociological text, Berger and Luckmann (1966, p. 70) emphasized that all 'human activity is subject to habitualization' but failed to specify the nature of habit itself.

the causal mechanisms of habituation, through which institutions can affect the very personality of the individual. A general statement of reconstitutive downward causation follows. This sixth principle of social theory, is actually an extension of the third principle on page 179 above:

6 **Reconstitutive downward causation**. The causal powers associated with social structures may not simply impede or constrain behaviour, but may also affect and alter fundamental properties, powers and propensities of individuals. When an upper hierarchical level affects components at a lower level in this manner, this is a special and stronger case of 'downward causation' that we may term as *reconstitutive downward causation*. Those particular social structures that have the capacity for substantial, enduring and widespread reconstitutive downward causation upon individuals are termed *institutions*.

The third principle asserts that social structure can affect individual behaviour. The sixth principle goes further, by upholding that social structure can also affect the fundamental properties of the individual. Taken together, the third and sixth principles are the symmetrical counterpart of the first principle; for the first principle upholds – less controversially – that individuals can help to reconstitute the fundamental properties of some social structures.

Variation, inheritance and selection

The task that remains in this chapter is to sketch Veblen's extension of Darwinian evolutionary theory to the evolution of institutions. Veblen understood that the process of Darwinian evolution had three important aspects. First, there must be sustained variation among the members of a species or population. Variations may be random or purposive in origin, but without them, as Darwin insisted, natural selection cannot operate. This is the concept of variation. Second, there must be some mechanism of heredity or continuity, through which offspring have to resemble their parents more than they resemble other members of their species. In other words, there has to be some mechanism through which individual characteristics are passed on through the generations. Third, natural selection itself operates either because better-adapted organisms leave increased numbers of offspring, or because the variations or gene combinations that are preserved are those bestowing advantage in struggling to survive. This is the concept of the struggle for existence. Consider these three features in turn, as they appear in Veblen's work.

For Veblen (1900a, p. 266) a Darwinian science must address 'the conditions of variational growth'. Veblen (1901b, p. 81) saw a 'Darwinistic account' in economics as addressing 'the origin, growth, persistence, and variation of institutions'. Veblen (1899a, p. 217) also referred to 'a selection between the predatory and the peaceable variants'. This indicated that for Veblen, and in conformity with Darwin, variation exists prior to (as well as after) evolutionary selection.

Veblen did not provide a full account of the sources of variation of social institutions. In general, Veblen (1909b, p. 628) saw cultural variation as cumulative: 'The growth of culture is a cumulative sequence of habituation' but 'each new move creates a new situation which induces a further new variation in the habitual manner of response' and 'each new situation is a variation of what has gone before and embodies as causal factors all that has been effected by what went before'.

For Veblen, the 'instinctive propensity' of 'idle curiosity' was also a major ongoing source of variety and invention. 'This instinctive curiosity' may 'accelerate the gain in technological insight' as well as 'persistently disturbing the habitual body of knowledge' (Veblen, 1914, p. 87). Note here that Veblen was again disposed to bring in an instinctive explanation of social outcomes. Especially to the modern reader, this is not so convincing. But the validity or otherwise of this point should be a matter not of prejudice against the concept of instinct but of scientific investigation.[9]

Veblen also used the metaphor of mutation, applying it to social and economic institutions. The first appearances of the use of the term 'mutation' in an institutional context in Veblen's writings are 'business capital and its mutations' (Veblen, 1904, p. 149), 'effects of these institutions and of the mutations they undergo' and 'growth and mutations of the institutional fabric' (Veblen, 1909b, pp. 627–9). Ten years later Veblen (1919b, pp. 5, 40) wrote of 'the mutation of habits' and proposed that 'the state of the industrial arts has been undergoing a change of type, such as followers of Mendel would call a "mutation"'. Writing much later, the anthropologist John Pfeiffer (1969, p. 304) saw – in Veblenian fashion – that human restlessness and curiosity represent 'for cultural evolution what genetic mutation represents for organic evolution, a built-in source of novelty and increasingly complex patterns of life – the source, indeed, of the human spark'.

We now turn to the second Darwinian concept, the question of inheritance. It is clear from the *Leisure Class* that the institution was regarded as the unit of relative stability and continuity through time, ensuring that much of the pattern and variety is passed on from one period to the next. Veblen (1899a, p. 191) wrote:

> Institutions are products of the past process, are adapted to past circumstances, and are therefore never in full accord with the

---

9   One of the earliest references to 'idle curiosity' is in Veblen (1906a, p. 590). Dyer (1986) argued convincingly that Veblen's crucial inspiration for the concept was Peirce's idea of 'musement'. Veblen (1914, p. 85 n.) noted that James and McDougall upheld the idea of an instinctive search for knowledge.

requirements of the present. ... At the same time, men's present habits of thought tend to persist indefinitely, except as circumstances enforce a change. These institutions which have so been handed down, these habits of thought, points of view, mental attitudes and aptitudes, or what not, are therefore themselves a conservative factor. This is the factor of social inertia, psychological inertia, conservatism.

This relative stability and durability of habits and institutions made them key objects of evolutionary selection in the socio-economic sphere. But Veblen did not examine the processes or institutional replication or inheritance in sufficient detail.

Third, turning to the concept of selection, Veblen (1898c, p. 188; 1899a, pp. 188, 207; 1900a, pp. 241, 261, 217; 1906a, p. 589) poignantly but infrequently applied the specific phrase 'natural selection' to habits of thought or to social institutions. Nevertheless, the concept of selection is common and persistent in his works. Words such as 'select', 'selection' and 'selective', used in the Darwinian sense of a process of sifting and preservation of fortuitous adaptations, are used with conspicuous frequency. I have counted well over a hundred appearances. A large number of these appearances concern the selection of institutions, customs or habits of thought. Confining ourselves to the *Leisure Class* (Veblen, 1899a) alone, the following examples are a small sample:

> In whatever way usages and customs and methods of expenditure arise, they are all subject to the selective action of this norm of reputability; and the degree in which they conform to its requirements is a test of their fitness to survive in the competition with other similar usages and canons. (p. 166)

> There is a cumulative growth of customs and habits of thought; a selective adaptation of conventions and methods of life. (p. 208)

> Social evolution is a process of selective adaptation of temperament and habits of thought under the stress of the circumstances of associated life. The adaptation of habits of thought is the growth of institutions. ... a process of selection ... a selective process ... (pp. 213–4)

> Wherever the pecuniary culture prevails, the selective process by which men's habits of thought are shaped, and by which the survival of rival lines of descent is decided, proceeds proximately on the basis of fitness for acquisition. (p. 241)

This and much other textual evidence on Veblen's use of the concept of selection, along with his understanding of the importance of variation and inheritance in the Darwinian theory, decisively favours an interpretation of his work as one in which Darwinian principles are applied to the analysis of social evolution.

It must again be emphasized that Veblen's Darwinian economics did not involve the assertion that economic evolution can or must be reduced substantially to biological terms. Furthermore, Veblen's use of Darwinian terminology was not confined to metaphor. Veblen made it abundantly clear that he believed that socio-economic systems actually evolved in a manner consistent with the Darwinian concepts of variation, inheritance and selection. Veblen did not believe that the application of Darwinian theory was confined to nature. In his social theory, his use of Darwinian theory was much more than mere word play. The difference between natural and social evolution was in the units of selection and in the details of the evolutionary processes, not in the exclusion of variation, inheritance or selection from the social sphere. Variation, inheritance and selection are present and real in both the social and the natural context.[10]

The relatively infrequent appearance of the phrase 'natural selection' does not undermine the claim that Veblen was an evolutionary economist in a Darwinian genre. As mentioned above, he used the concept of selection frequently. But it remains to consider why Veblen did not often choose to attach the adjective 'natural' to the abundant instances of 'selection' or 'selective process' in his work. We may guess why. First, and most obviously, Veblen was concerned with the evolution of society, and not of the non-human, natural world. As his attention was directed at society rather than nature, the term 'natural' was dropped. Second, the 'natural selection' of institutions could be misinterpreted by the reader in terms of 'nature' doing the selecting, or that the selection was taking place according to 'natural' rather than economic or other social criteria. Third, economists and others who advocated a 'natural' order, or 'natural rights', were the persistent objects of Veblen's (1899c; 1901a; 1908a; 1914, pp. 258–60, 289–98, 340–3) devastating criticism. Resistance to the likely interpretations of the word 'natural' as 'normal' or 'predestined' could have led to the rejection of the term, especially when the word 'selection' on its own would do. Hence there are several possible reasons why Veblen more frequently used the word 'selection' rather than 'natural selection'. As a result, the marginalization of the word 'natural' in his writing should not be taken to imply that Veblen lost any of his Darwinian inspiration.

Incidentally, for different reasons, Darwin himself was uneasy about the phrase 'natural selection'. It was suggested to him that the word 'selection' invoked the image of 'nature's Guiding Hand', or even one of God being the selector. Darwin thus conceded: 'I suppose "natural selection" was a bad term' (Desmond and Moore, 1991, pp. 458, 492). For this reason

---

10 For discussions of the Darwinian character of Veblen's work see Harris (1934), Daugert (1950), Hill (1958), Murphree (1959), Russett (1976), Dugger (1984), Edgell and Tilman (1989), Tilman (1992, 1996) and many others. See Jennings and Waller (1998) for a contrary but unconvincing view.

Darwin sometimes used the words 'descent with modification' instead. He ultimately preferred the term 'natural preservation' (Ruse, 1979, p. 208). Both Darwin and Veblen were hesitant about the use of the term 'natural selection' but for different reasons. Darwin feared that the word 'selection' could suggest a Godly selector. Veblen was concerned that the term 'natural' would buttress false conceptions of a natural or optimal order in the economy or society. Hence Darwin cultivated the word 'natural' and Veblen economized and used the word 'selection' alone.[11]

An underdeveloped theory of institutional evolution

While Veblen generally saw institutions as units of selection in a process of economic evolution, he did not make the context, criteria or mechanisms of selection entirely clear. Prompted by the notion that the social 'environment' itself evolves, Veblen (1899a, pp. 188–98) moved towards, but did not complete, a causal analysis of that evolutionary process. Insofar as an evolutionary analysis exists, we have to impute it from passages such as the one quoted above, where Veblen (1899a, p. 191) wrote that the 'selective adaptation can never catch up with the progressively changing situation in which the community finds itself at any given time'. This suggests a process of imperfect institutional adjustment and cultural lag. But it does not sufficiently explain the evolution of the 'progressively changing situation' in which institutions are selected.

Nevertheless, Veblen was clearly attempting to move towards a theory of institutional evolution. In its time and context, this sketchy and preliminary analysis of institutional evolution in the *Leisure Class* was a major achievement, standing significantly above such precursors as those of Bagehot, Lewes, Tarde, Morgan and Ritchie. Having started this research programme, however, he failed to move it forward. Cynthia Russett's (1976, p. 153) verdict was apposite and accurate:

> If Veblen failed to develop an evolutionary methodology, he also failed to develop a comprehensive evolutionary theory to explain in detail how institutions evolve in the cultural environment and what sorts of interaction occur between economic activity and institutional structures. Veblen was something of an intellectual butterfly, and he often lacked the patience to elaborate his ideas into a coherent system. But he teemed with fragmentary insights, and these can be pieced

---

11 Dobriansky's (1957) critique of Veblen failed to appreciate Darwinism. For example, Dobriansky (1957, p. 93) falsely upheld that natural selection implied both *uniformity* and *finality*, entirely contrary to its true meaning in terms of *variety* and *process*. Dobriansky grasped neither the philosophical significance of Darwinism nor its central place in Veblen's thought. Not uniquely, a critic thought he was attacking Veblen; but the critique carries more weight against other 'Veblenians'. Daugert (1950) is superior and more accurate in its philosophical treatment of Veblen.

together to suggest the outlines of a Veblenian scheme of cultural evolution – what might be called a 'pre-theory' of cultural change.

Endless speculation is possible on the reasons for Veblen's failure. But we may focus on two points. First, as discussed in Chapter 10, Veblen was quickly diverted into other channels of enquiry. As it turned out, some of these were unfruitful. Others were of some value, but did not fill the lacuna in his theory of institutional evolution. Second, while Veblen established a multiple-level evolutionary theory by considering the replication and selection of human institutions as well as of human individuals, it is striking that whenever he saw a remotely plausible explanation of a social phenomenon in terms of instincts rather than in terms of institutions he rarely failed to seize the opportunity. For instance, Veblen inflated the instinct of workmanship, and its explanatory role in social evolution, to dimensions that challenge credulity. I shall argue in the following chapter that some of Veblen's instinct-based theories, including the alleged role of the instinct of workmanship, are misconceived even in Darwinian terms. Sometimes Veblen pushed his instinct-based explanations too far.[12]

However, while Veblen overemphasized the explanatory role of instinct at the social level, it is imperative that we do not overreact by removing the concept in its entirety from social science. As explained above, the concept of instinct is necessary for an adequate theory of institutional evolution, notwithstanding the fact that explanations of institutions and other social phenomena cannot be reduced to instinctive terms.

The tragedy was that the majority of social scientists in the twentieth century, including leading institutional economists, were persuaded to ditch the concept of instinct by 1940. The concept of instinct was taboo in the social sciences for over fifty years. After Veblen's death, the challenge for the next generation of institutional and evolutionary economists was to

---

12 Such challengeable explanations involving inherited biological characteristics have led several authors to accuse Veblen of 'racism'. Ayres (1952, p. 25) wrote of Veblen: 'worst of all, perhaps, was his tentative addiction to racism. He was somehow persuaded that "the dolicho-blond race" was possessed of certain peculiar propensities which shaped its culture – an idea which present-day anthropologists most decisively reject'. However, while Veblen's speculations concerning 'the dolicho-blond race' are implausible and empirically ungrounded they do not amount to racism. As Tilman (1992, p. 161) pointed out, such allegations of racism ignore both the ideological and scientific context of Veblen's own time and, more importantly, the fact that Veblen never expressed animosity towards any race in his writings. No supposition of racial differences in Veblen's writings was ever seen by him as grounds for racial discrimination or repression. Indeed, such a deduction would be illegitimate, as normative statements about human rights are not logically deducible from empirical statements about human differences, or from theoretical statements about the causes of human attributes or behaviour. Veblen's accusers seem to uphold that all propositions concerning non-superficial dissimilarities between different ethnic groups are racist, and that any critique of racism is dependent upon the denial of any such dissimilarities. On the contrary, an unconditional opposition to racism, independent of the validity or otherwise of any proposition concerning ethnic similarities or dissimilarities, is stronger and more resilient than any conditional anti-racist stance.

complete the task of elaborating a theory of institutional evolution along the lines suggested by Veblen. The outcome of this banishment of a central concept was that the project could hardly be commenced, let alone completed.

Veblen's lack of an explicit and developed concept of emergence further compounded the problem and facilitated his explanatory regresses from institutions to instincts. The concept of emergence is bound up with the type of hierarchical ontology that is the grounding of multiple-level evolutionary theory. As elaborated in Chapter 11 below, a group of emergentist philosophers made major strides in this direction in the 1920s. Veblen was dissuaded by his Kantian upbringing from going down this road. Kantianism makes ontological statements matters of analytical expediency, rather than commitments concerning the essentials of the real world. A substantial move away from Kantianism towards a non-empiricist realism is a prerequisite of a viable emergentist discourse.

A related weakness in Veblen's work is his failure to articulate adequately a concept of a self-organized social structure or spontaneous order. He understood very well that social outcomes are often unintended and unplanned. Veblen (1903) was familiar with the concept of the 'spontaneous development of society' as developed by Lester Frank Ward (1903) and others. He saw many institutions as emerging without overall prior design or legal decree. But he did not give enough theoretical attention to the evolution of emergent social patterns or structures with properties that are not found among the individuals involved. In his writing, social institutions sometimes appear as additive resultants of a combination of individual habituations. Veblen's failure to assimilate fully a concept of emergence may help to explain his failure to develop adequately the notion of 'self-organized' or 'spontaneous' social orders.

9 The instinct of workmanship and the pecuniary culture

> Much of the work of Thorstein Veblen may be considered an astute rework-
> ing of Marx for the academic American public of his day ... Veblen's poli-
> tics are masked by ironic distaste for pronouncements of ideals, but
> probably he was at heart an anarchist and syndicalist.
>
> C. Wright Mills, *The Marxists* (1963)

The purpose of this chapter is to evaluate two prominent, enduring and related themes in Veblen's writing. They are the presumed explanatory and
normative role of the 'instinct of workmanship' and the alleged dichotomy
between pecuniary and industrial motives. The character of this critique of
the instinct of workmanship must be made clear. It is not derived from any
distaste for the concept of instinct, or from a dislike of evolutionary or biological ideas in social science. This is not an external but an internal critique, in that important ideas in Veblen's writing are evaluated principally
in his own Darwinian and evolutionary terms.

The Darwinian framework of Veblen's argument

Veblen's thematic idea of 'an instinct of workmanship' appeared as early
as 1898 and was never abandoned. On the basis of the aforementioned
Darwinian principle of evolutionary explanation, Veblen argued that any
assumptions concerning human nature and agency must be consistent
with our understanding of human evolution. Accordingly, in his article on
'The Instinct of Workmanship and the Irksomeness of Labor', Veblen argued that if 'economic man' is assumed then his evolution must be explained. Veblen (1898c, p. 187) discussed the neoclassical assumption of an
'aversion to useful effort', seeing the notion of a disutility of labour as inconsistent with the reality of human evolution. Veblen (1898c, p. 187) thus
wrote:

> A consistent aversion to whatever activity goes to maintain the life of
> the species is assuredly found in no other species of animal. Under the
> selective process through which species are held to have emerged and
> gained their stability there is no chance for the survival of a species
> gifted with such an aversion to the furtherance of its own life process.

No species will evolve a 'consistent aversion' to activities necessary for
its survival. Hence, if humans had consistently avoided useful work, then
the species would not have survived. In contrast, hundreds of thousands
of years of human evolution must have led to the selection of some propensity to engage in work that was useful for survival. This is the basis of his
idea of an 'instinct of workmanship'. Veblen (1898c, p. 194) argued: 'By selection and by training, the life of man, before a predaceous life became
possible, would act to develop and to conserve in him [an] instinct of workmanship.'

In *The Theory of the Leisure Class*, Veblen (1899a, p. 15) again saw this instinct as an outcome of evolutionary selection. He saw humans as 'possessed of a taste for effective work, and a distaste for futile effort' with 'a
sense of the merit of serviceability or efficiency and of the demerit of futil-
ity, waste, or incapacity. This aptitude or propensity may be called the instinct of workmanship'. This idea that evolutionary selection has given rise
to an instinct of workmanship was repeated elsewhere by Veblen (1914, p.
17) when he argued that 'selective survival' depended on 'relative fitness
to meet the material requirements of life'.[1]

Veblen argued that the 'instinct of workmanship' remained necessary in
any economic system, including capitalism. Although capitalist pecuniary
incentives had become powerful, modern productive labour still depended on a degree of attention and care that would be inadequately promoted by monetary incentives.

While the inherited instinct of workmanship fortunately persisted,
other habitual motives were selected at the cultural level. Veblen (1899a, p.

---

1 Veblen (1914, pp. 14–18) seemed to admit that evolutionary selection could equally have
given rise to a bellicose instinctive propensity to pillage the resources of other tribal
groups. In an attempt to show how such a predatory instinct could be displaced by the
instinct of workmanship, Veblen developed a dubious theory that the 'European racial
stocks' that 'make up the population of the Western nations' are more of a 'hybrid mass'.
He rightly pointed to the rapid pace of cultural evolution, and proposed more
questionably that this European 'hybrid mass' had relatively more genetic diversity to
cope with these changes. For some unclear reason, modern Europeans were in their
circumstances less selected for their 'fighting capacity' and more for their 'relative fitness
to meet the material requirements of life'. The alleged adaptability to changing
institutional conditions of this European 'hybrid mass' somehow led to the selection of the
more stable 'instinct of workmanship'. Veblen thus suggested that this instinct was most
well developed among these 'hybrid' peoples of European descent. But he gave no further
evidence to support this highly questionable and threadbare argument. The idea that the
European population is more hybrid than the natives of other continents is contradicted
by modern DNA research. And both logic and evidence are lacking from the argument
that hybridity in racial origines results in instincts of workmanship rather than predation.

238) wrote: 'Life in a modern industrial community, or in other words life under the pecuniary culture, acts by a process of selection to develop and conserve a certain range of aptitudes and propensities.'

Coming into conflict with the inherited instinct of workmanship, incongruent habitual motives were selected and replicated in a capitalist culture. The capitalist environment selected propensities towards pecuniary gain rather than useful productivity. Consequently, Veblen saw a clash between the pecuniary culture engendered by capitalism and the necessary care and diligence in its process of production, still sustained to some degree by the enduring instinct of workmanship. This was part of his famous dichotomy between business and industry, between making money and making goods. The pecuniary culture of capitalist business undermined the conditions of productive and useful industrial work. As Veblen (1899a, p. 241) put it:

> Wherever the pecuniary culture prevails, the selective process by which men's habits of thought are shaped, and by which the survival of rival lines of descent is decided, proceeds proximately on the basis of fitness for acquisition. Consequently, if it were not for the fact that pecuniary efficiency is on the whole incompatible with industrial efficiency, the selective action of all occupations would tend to the unmitigated dominance of the pecuniary temperament. The result would be the installation of what has become known as the 'economic man,' as the normal and definitive type of human nature. But the 'economic man,' whose only interest is the self-regarding one and whose only human trait is prudence, is useless for the purposes of modern industry.

By 'economic man' in this context, Veblen meant individuals who minimized their productive effort because of their marginal disutility of labour. He argued that if such an 'economic man' emerged as the norm, then the productivity of industry would suffer. If the human race had been persistently grabbing money and shirking work, then it would have become extinct. But capitalism, according to Veblen, exacerbates these tendencies toward extinction. Within capitalism, as Veblen (1901a, p. 210) put it: 'The ground of survival in the selective process is fitness for pecuniary gain, not fitness for serviceability at large.' By promoting pecuniary incentives over the instinct of workmanship, capitalism was seen to undermine its own foundations.[2]

Veblen not only placed his argument in a Darwinian framework, but also he was keen to avoid the misconception that it meant an optimizing

2 As well as the obvious parallel here with Marx's position, note also the similarity with Schumpeter's (1942) claim that a contractarian system undermines its necessary culture of devoted service, and K. Polanyi's (1944) similar proposition that markets are corrosive of the social fabric. What is distinctive about Veblen's argument, however, is its Darwinian framework of evolutionary selection.

process. Veblen (1901a, p. 217) thus criticized 'a doctrine of natural selection; according to which all disserviceable or unproductive, wasteful employments would, perforce be weeded out'. Note that here Veblen criticized a particular and optimizing version of 'natural selection', not the idea in general. Earlier Veblen (1899a, p. 166) had similarly considered circumstances where 'the more obviously wasteful usage or method stands the better chance of survival'. Accordingly, Veblen argued that a capitalist culture led to the selection of attributes of pecuniary acquisition rather than productive efficiency.[3]

Would an instinct of workmanship be selected in evolution?

While Veblen's adoption of Darwinian principles in the socio-economic domain is endorsed here, in detail Veblen's argument was flawed in several respects. Some of the conclusions that Veblen claimed to adduce from Darwinian principles are unconvincing in Darwinian terms. As outlined below, Veblen made three connected and crucial mistakes. I shall argue that there is a good reason for an instinctive propensity for useful activity or 'instinct of workmanship' to evolve in animals, but most vitally in species without culture or institutions. Furthermore, in all species there are good reasons for an additional and partly offsetting instinctive aversion to energetic activity to also evolve. Consequently, Veblen's claim that the instinct of workmanship contradicted the neoclassical assumption of a diminishing marginal utility of labour was invalid.

The first of Veblen's mistakes was to belittle the role of compensating inducements and incentives. Consider Veblen's attempted critique of the neoclassical assumption of work-shirking 'economic man'. More accurately, neoclassical economists argued that the individual would avoid work *unless forced or induced to do so*. Veblen ignored these matters of compensating incentive and inducement. Even with a supposed marginal disutility of labour, it is easy for a neoclassical economist to explain increased effort by increased inducements. A marginal disutility of labour simply requires the payment of sufficient and compensating utility to induce work. Veblen failed to give a good reason why a dislike of labour is inconsistent with an evolutionary explanation.

Veblen's second mistake was to overlook the possibility of the selection and evolutionary survival of an aversion to labour. Leaving aside the contentious concept of a marginal disutility of labour, there are plausible reasons for an aversion to labour to also evolve. Such an aversion could be selected because it would reduce the expenditure of energy and effort.

3 Edgerton (1992) provided many examples of maladaptive practices in pre-industrial and industrial societies. He thus confirmed the ubiquitous suboptimality of social evolution, as earlier stressed by Veblen (1899a) and Ward (1883, 1893, 1903).

Such economies of effort might bestow greater fitness on the individual, by reducing exhaustion or energy inputs. Accordingly, most animal species have an instinct for rest and sleep.

However, Veblen was right to suggest that a life wholly of unproductive repose would lead to extinction. There must be inducements to occasional productive activity, triggered by hunger or whatever. Hence the existence of an aversion to energetic activity would not mean that individuals would always avoid work. For this reason, and contrary to Veblen, any species could evolve a 'consistent aversion' to energetic activity, as long as a compensating productive activity was triggered when survival was at risk. Veblen overlooked both compensating inducements to work, and consequently a possible reason for an aversion to labour to evolve. Hence the evolutionary foundation of his 'instinct of workmanship' is in question.

We may criticize the supposed marginal disutility of labour on the grounds that it ignores the satisfaction that individuals may gain from creative, intrinsically interesting, socially rewarding, or morally favoured work. Nevertheless, an aversion to sustained physical exertion, repetitive labour or drudgery may still remain, and be selected in an evolutionary process.

A preliminary and rudimentary guide to the evolution of different propensities and aversions to work can be obtained by looking at the evolution of other species, especially apes. In such cases it is clear that several different and sometimes conflicting instincts are involved. When prompted by hunger, animals may devote much time and energy to the search for food. On the other hand, animals can also spend much time in sleep, idleness or play, which could also be explained in evolutionary terms through the fitness advantages bestowed by economies in energy and effort.

The third vital mistake was to disregard the possibility that productive activity may have been the result not only of instincts, but also of their combination with habits that were formed in particular social or institutional settings. In which case, the role of instincts may be less important than particular social institutions in maintaining human productive activity. Humans are social animals, with culture and institutions. We may trace back their sociality to our simian ancestors. As a result, the possibility exists that selection operates not only on the single level of instincts but also at the level of human social institutions. After all, Veblen (1899a, p. 188) himself pioneered the concept of the 'natural selection of institutions' as well as of individuals.[4]

As long as there was social structure and social culture, the survival of the human race did not necessarily depend on *instincts* conducive to

---

4 Because this is an *internal* critique of Veblen's argument, there is no need to go into the detailed controversies over 'institutional selection' or 'group selection' here. See the references to works favouring multiple levels of selection in Chapter 3 above. On group selection see Sober and Wilson (1998), Bergstrom (2002) and Henrich (2004).

productive activity. The evolutionary bottom line for a society is that instinctive or culturally engendered propensities to useful work must outweigh instinctive or culturally engendered propensities to avoid labour. All that is required is that the *combined net effect* of cultural transmission and the inheritance of instincts lead to propensities to engage in work that can sustain the life process. As long as there are reproducible social structures with cultural inducements that ensure that the requisites of human life are obtained, then humanity can survive.

Species without culture or institutions may lack these compensating cultural mechanisms. Hence there must in acultural species be an *instinct* for life-preserving activity, even if it exists alongside an instinct for rest and sleep. But once a social culture evolves, selection pressure for an *instinct* of workmanship could be alleviated by the creation of *cultural* mechanisms that promote life-enhancing activity. Once a culture is established – however rudimentary – systems of sanction and reward themselves provide non-instinctive behavioural inducements. Humans and their ancestors have lived socially for many millions of years; hence the selection pressure for an *instinct* of workmanship has been correspondingly diminished and overshadowed by the selection of behavioural inducements at the *cultural* level.

Human survival could thus depend on the successful reproduction of social structures or institutions with such positive attributes, and of individuals that complied with their cultural norms or rules. This conformity may itself depend in part on instincts. But instinct is not the whole story. Without good reason, Veblen's explanation devolved entirely to the instincts what could be partly explained in cultural and institutional terms. Despite his insight into 'the natural selection of institutions' he here saw instincts as the sufficient explanatory element. This exclusive explanatory reduction was unjustified and flawed.

Note that this argument is not one in principle against the explanation of any aspect of human behaviour in terms of instincts. Whether instincts matter in particular instances is a question to be resolved largely by empirical enquiry. On the contrary, Veblen is criticized here for ruling out in principle, and without empirical warrant, the possibility of an explanation of a propensity to work in terms of culture.

Jacques Loeb endorsed Veblen's idea of an instinct of workmanship. Loeb (1900, p. 197) argued that: 'We are instinctively forced to be active in the same way as ants or bees.' However, ants and bees have no proper social culture. Their individual personalities and their behaviour are entirely programmed by their instincts. In contrast, human personality and behaviour, although built on instincts, is very much formed and moulded by cultural circumstances, which can provide inducements to productive activity. Loeb – a biological reductionist – omitted culture from the picture. Strangely, in this particular instance, Veblen committed the same error.

Essentially, the survival of a society depends on its capacity to produce the means of life and to replicate itself. As Veblen understood, society can be immensely inefficient or wasteful and still survive, as long as the condition in the preceding sentence is satisfied. But we cannot derive an instinct of workmanship from this condition.[5]

Veblen's achievements in this area include his principle of evolutionary explanation and his valid insistence that human evolution must have somehow led to the selection of (social or individual) propensities to produce the means of human survival, despite any attendant inefficiency or waste. His mistake was to overlook the fact that these propensities could be cultural, alongside any additional and limited 'instinct of workmanship'. Despite Veblen's path-breaking discussion of the 'natural selection of institutions', his analysis of multiple levels of evolutionary selection did not go far enough.

Elsewhere (Hodgson, 2001c) I have proposed 'the provisioning principle' to express the necessary condition of the survival of a human society as the capacity of that society to replicate habits, routines and institutions that could help to provide the means of sustaining human life. Such habits, routines and institutions could themselves be selected in an evolutionary process, internally within the society itself, or externally through rivalry with other societies. This major amendment to Veblen's approach replaces the 'instinct of workmanship' with 'the institutionalized propensity to provision for human needs' as a surviving feature of selection in social evolution.

On the basis that it was exclusively and universally favoured by evolutionary selection for human fitness and survival, Veblen (1899a, p. 99) argued that 'the instinct of workmanship ... is the court of final appeal in any question of economic truth or adequacy'. After revealing the flaws in Veblen's argument, it becomes clear that this normative standard cannot serve in the manner that Veblen suggested (O'Hara, 1999). If there is a universal normative standard by which to judge the adequacy of social institutions, then it is in terms of their capacity to sustain or enhance the means of human life. In broad terms, this is close to the idea of 'instrumental valuation' proposed by John Dewey and later institutionalists (Dewey, 1939; Bush, 1987; Tool, 1995) and to modern theories of human and social needs (Maslow, 1954; Thomson, 1987; Doyal and Gough, 1991; Corning, 2000b).

Pecuniary versus industrial motives

Veblen assumed that a culture of pecuniary gain worked against the instinct of workmanship and thereby against industrial motives or industrial institutions. These supposed conflicts were thematic for Veblen's work

---

5 Given Veblen's predispositions to both Darwinism and instinct theory, it is surprising that he did not adopt or adapt Darwin's (1871) theory of social instincts.

and took a number of forms. In the *Leisure Class,* Veblen (1899a, p. 208) proposed a dichotomy between 'pecuniary or industrial institutions'. In his
Theory of Business Enterprise, Veblen (1904, p. 158) further dwelt on the idea
of a 'discrepancy, not uncommonly a divergence, between the industrial
needs of the community and the business needs of the corporation'.

This 'discrepancy' was later misrepresented by some of his disciples as
the 'Veblenian dichotomy' between *all* 'technology' and *all* 'institutions'.
Instead, as quoted in the previous paragraph, Veblen saw a dichotomy between two types of institution, the pecuniary and the industrial. As argued
in Chapter 17 below, Veblen never proclaimed a general dichotomy between 'technology' and 'institutions'. Although he did describe some particular cases where the two came into conflict, he also described cases
where one facilitated the other. The true general dichotomy in Veblen's
writings was not between technology and institutions, but instead between the alleged imperatives of workmanlike 'industry' and of predatory
'business'. Another passage in *The Theory of Business Enterprise* goes into
more detail. Veblen (1904, pp. 41–2) wrote:

> In common with other men, the business man is moved by ideals of
> serviceability and an aspiration to make the way of life easier for his
> fellows. ... Motives of this kind detract from business efficiency, and an
> undue yielding to them on the part of business men is to be deprecated
> as an infirmity. Still, throughout men's dealings with one another and
> with the interests of the community there runs a sense of equity, fair
> dealing, and workmanlike integrity;

One of his important insights here was, along with Gustav Schmoller
(1900) and others, to recognize that business people have mixed and complex motives, and that the 'self-seeking motive is hemmed in and guided at
all points in the course of its development by considerations and conventions that are not of a primarily self-seeking kind' (Veblen, 1901b, p. 92).
This idea of mixed motives was consistent with the notion of an inner battle, within the psyche of the business person, between motives of diligence
and service on one side, against the foremost business imperative to make
money.

But what is difficult to accept is the idea that 'ideals of serviceability' always 'detract from business efficiency'. No argument is given to support
this. It would be countered by abundant evidence that, within limits, ideals
of serviceability can actually help the success of a business in some contexts. Of course, the achievement of profit is necessary for the survival of
business enterprise. However, a business that makes the maximization of
its profits its exclusive explicit objective is likely to fail. This has been described as the 'paradox of profit' (Bowie, 1988). The more a business becomes obsessed with profits over its service to customers, the less likely its
obsession will be realized. Businesses have to maintain a measure of

goodwill; the overt pursuit of greed and self-interest can undermine the necessary trust and respect.

Sometimes Veblen took the alleged dichotomy between business and industry to untenable extremes. In a later work, Veblen (1923, p. 278) proclaimed that 'any intrusion of business strategy into the conduct of industry will be sabotage'. This argument is flawed. It does not follow from the existence of two different systems of value that one will necessarily 'sabotage' the other. Different value systems can in principle be entirely consistent with each other, even if it is improbable in this case. The more likely situation in this context is that the two value systems are partially compatible but in some respects they can come into conflict. But this does not amount to the 'sabotage' of one by the other.

Veblen was right to suggest that a single-minded devotion to pecuniary gain could undermine necessary care and attention to detail. But the suggestion that pecuniary motives always and necessarily undermine efficiency is untenable. Following a pecuniary motive does not generally mean that the means of human life are thereby undermined. Pecuniary motives can sometimes lead to useful and beneficial outcomes.

The evaluation of institutions that employ pecuniary motives involves an analysis of complex interactions between different forces. Most if not all institutions rely on a mix of different stimuli and motives. In addition, from a Darwinian perspective, no institution is likely to be 'absolutely fit' in all circumstances. What matters in evolutionary terms is fitness relative to others, with respect to specific social and natural *context*. Similar remarks apply to the evaluation of the capacity of an institutional set-up to provision for human needs.

Consequently, the evaluation of an institution employing pecuniary motives depends in part on the demonstration of viable alternatives. Another question is whether pecuniary motives always detract from useful and efficient production. Even if comprehensive central planning of a complex industrial economy were possible, it would not necessarily mean that there was a universal conflict between industrial and pecuniary motives or institutions. We have no good reason to follow Veblen and assume such a universal antagonism between these two factors.

Veblen (1898c, p. 194) wrote: 'Self-interest, as an accepted guide to action, is possible only as the concomitant of a predatory life.' This simplistic statement overlooks the possibility than self-interest, when channelled and constrained by appropriate institutions and cultural settings, can lead to productive rather than predatory outcomes. Similarly, Veblen (1899a, p. 241) exaggerated to the point of error when he proclaimed that any self-interested motive 'is useless for the purposes of modern industry'. Again he overlooked the possibility that a limited degree of self-interest, especially when enlightened and in a suitable institutional and cultural framework, can have positive benefits in some circumstances.

Veblen (1901a, p. 216) rightly warned against the apologetic uses of economic theory by those inclined to see the pecuniary and market mechanisms as entirely beneficial:

> Expressions constantly recur in economic discussion which imply that the transactions discussed are carried out for the sake of the collective good ... Such expressions are commonly of the nature of figures of speech and are serviceable for homiletical rather than scientific use. They serve to express their user's faith in a beneficent order of nature, rather than to convey or to formulate information in regard to the facts.

But Veblen simply inverted the apologetic position, by proposing that erroneous views such as pecuniary motives always and everywhere 'detract from business efficiency' and always and everywhere amount to 'sabotage'. For 'faith in a beneficent order of nature' Veblen substituted an equally unfounded universal faith that the pecuniary order always defied human nature. For the universal apologetics for the pecuniary and market mechanisms, Veblen substituted the unconvincing view that they were universally dysfunctional.

Indeed, it was against the spirit of Veblen's own work to evaluate pecuniary or self-interested motives independently of their cultural or institutional context. Veblen followed both Marxists and pro-marketeers in evaluating pecuniary and market institutions with an unambiguous and unchanging moral sign. Marxists have proclaimed that the mere existence of pecuniary incentives will themselves encourage acquisitive individual behaviour, with no further reference to the role of ideas and culture in helping to form the aspirations of social actors. This de-cultured viewpoint has difficulty explaining the contrasting versions of consumerism that prevail in different capitalist societies (Hodgson, 1999a). In giving all pecuniary motives a negative sign, Veblen slipped back into the Marxian view, without following the logic of his own critique of Marxism.

Veblen's distinction between the pecuniary and the industrial is close to Marx's distinction between exchange value and use value. Marx inherited this distinction from Aristotle, Adam Smith and David Ricardo. However, for Marx and the classical economists, exchange-value and use-value were two aspects of a commodity, not two dichotomized motives or employments. Veblen pushed his similar distinction between the pecuniary and the industrial to unwarranted and dichotomous extremes.

It has been shown here that Veblen's belief in a conflict between industrial and pecuniary motives rested in part on his mistaken conviction in a universal 'instinct of workmanship' that served as 'the court of final appeal in any question of economic thruth or adequacy'. This chapter has revealed internal flaws in the Darwinian argument that Veblen used to uphold a universal 'instinct of workmanship'. The argument here that incentives to work are not necessarily instinctive – and are more importantly to do with compensating inducements – links with the proposition that industrial and pecuniary motives are not necessarily dichtomous. Veblen's dichotomy was also sustained by a mistaken treatment of workmanship, industry and technology independently of matters of organization, culture, perception and incentive. These problems are raised in the next chapter.

Instead of asserting a primary dichotomy between 'business' and 'industry', Veblen should have evaluated the mechanisms of business enterprise in detail, showing where they could serve human needs, where they were defective, and where they were deleterious. As in the case of Marx, Veblen was unable to propose a feasible industrial system, without such pecuniary motives, as an alternative to capitalism. This limitation in his policy stance is raised again in Chapter 10 below.[6]

Nevertheless, Veblenian institutionalism can survive the removal of these flaws. This is especially the case because the faulty arguments presented by Veblen have been shown to a large degree to be inconsistent with his evolutionary and Darwinian framework. A Veblenian institutionalism can be reconstructed on these evolutionary and Darwinian principles.

---

6 Relevant here is the longstanding 'socialist calculation debate', which suggests that it is not possible to establish a complex industrial economy without some use of markets or monetary exchange. These issues have been discussed at length elsewhere (D. Lavoie, 1985; Steele, 1992; Hodgson, 1999a).

10 A wrong turning

Science and the machine process

Two roads diverged in a wood, and I –
I took the one less travelled by,
And that has made all the difference.

Robert Frost, 'The Road Not Taken' (1916)

Veblen turned to the problem of explaining the origins of modern scientific culture.[1] He argued, in brief, that the growth of modern science was itself stimulated by the rational 'habits of thought' that were said to be associated with the spread of machines. Such a discussion of the impact of machines and technology protruded into his second book, *The Theory of Business Enterprise* (Veblen, 1904). This machine-powered explanation of 'the place of science in modern civilization' was the title of an essay published in 1906, which incidentally Veblen himself considered to be his best (Dorfman, 1934, p. 260).

This preoccupation with technology and its cultural effects became an enduring feature of his writing, but has led to repeated accusations of 'technological determinism'. Technological determinism is widely attacked, but much less frequently defined.[2] More careful discussions acknowledge that technology itself involves human knowledge and social relations, and recognize that both the physical and social aspects of production are entwined. Technology is embedded in social relations, but this does not rule out enquiries into the possible influences of technology on human thoughts, behaviours and social structures. The ill-defined

---

1 A shorter version of this chapter appeared in Hodgson (2004).
2 For definitions and discussions of 'technological determinism' see G. Young (1976), Cohen (1978), Miller (1981), Sherwood (1985), Pfaffenberger (1988). The institutionalist J. F. Foster (1981, p. 932) advocated 'technological determinism' but defined it unusually in normative terms, as the need for policy solutions that are in 'instrumentally efficient correlation with the technological aspects of the [social] problems'. The fact that 'technological determinism' is used in multiple (positive and normative) ways, even within institutional economics, underlines the need for careful definition, whenever the term is used.

accusations of 'technological determinism' should not be used to silence such investigations.

The following section outlines Veblen's views on the impact of the machine process. The section after that considers some of the philosophical underpinnings of Veblen's position. Yet another section criticizes Veblen's argument that mechanization leads to particular habits of thought. The penultimate section draws out some related criticisms of Veblen's underdeveloped ideas on work organization and systems of socio-economic coordination. The fifth section concludes the chapter.

The impact of the machine process

In his *Theory of Business Enterprise*, Veblen (1904, pp. 153–4, 185–267) erected an elaborate theory of industrial depression and the business cycle, based on his dichotomy between industrial and pecuniary employments. Very briefly, Veblen saw business fluctuations and industrial depressions as rooted in the credit mechanism and business psychology, with their cycles of boom, bust and possible recovery. This analysis had business speculations and expectations at the centre, against the counterpoint of the increasing potential productivity of mechanized industry. Against the prevailing view that industrial recessions in market economies would automatically bring about the mechanisms of recovery, Veblen stressed that the forces that created depressions would feed cumulatively on their own results.

Veblen (1904, p. 185) criticized Karl Marx and Mikhail Tugan-Baranovsky for approaching the analysis of business cycles from 'the mechanical facts of production and consumption; rather than, from the side of business enterprise – the phenomena of price, earnings, and capitalization'. Veblen saw the source of capitalist crises in the financial institutions that promoted the excessive and irrational exuberance of the speculators. He focused on the institutional basis of earnings and capitalist expectations, rather than 'mechanical facts of production and consumption' such as Marx's rising 'organic composition of capital'. Consequently, it has been rightly argued by some commentators (Vining, 1939; Raines and Leathers, 1996) that Veblen brilliantly foreshadowed the theory of business fluctuations and employment in the later work of John Maynard Keynes (1936).[3]

However, instead of blazing a trail that could have earned him the fame and prestige of an American Keynes, after 1904 Veblen analysed the causes of business fluctuations no further. Instead, in several publications, he subsequently devoted a greater part of his energy to a secondary theme that had emerged in a late and subsidiary chapter of *The Theory of Business Enterprise*

3 Although Veblen's theory of business cycles was substantial and original, it was partly inspired by others, particularly Hobson (1896), who was cited by Veblen (1904) in several places. Keynes (1936) also acknowledged the seminal importance of Hobson's work in this area.

(Veblen, 1904, pp. 302–73) concerning the supposed impact of the machine process on prevailing ideas in modern civilization. The macroeconomic theory of business fluctuations and unemployment was unfortunately 'the road not taken'. Veblen took the wrong turn, and erected a theoretically implausible and philosophically misconceived theory of cultural change, driven by the machine process.

This judgement, of course, is with the benefit of hindsight. The most important global economic event of the nineteenth century was the Industrial Revolution. In 1904, the Great Crash and the Great Depression were yet to come. Veblen addressed mechanization as one of the most significant processes of his time, as Keynes in the 1930s faced the devastation of capitalism in crisis. Veblen's wrong turning was highly understandable in the circumstances, but tragic nevertheless.

Further reasons for his less productive choice of theoretical project require some consideration, but the first task must be to outline Veblen's theory of the impact of the machine process. In several works, Veblen focused on the transition from 'handicraft' production to the 'machine process' established in modern factories by the Industrial Revolution. Veblen (1914, p. 241) saw 'the logic of the machine process' as 'a logic of masses, velocities, strains and thrusts, not of personal dexterity, tact, training, and routine'. According to Veblen (1904, pp. 66–7), the 'machine process' inculcates and enforces a number of 'habits of thought', first involving 'a standardization of conduct and of knowledge in terms of quantitative precision'. Veblen (1904, p. 306) argued:

> The machine process pervades the modern life and dominates it in a mechanical sense. Its dominance is seen in the enforcement of precise mechanical measurements and adjustments and the reduction of all manner of things, purposes and acts, necessities, conveniences, and amenities of life, to standard units.

For Veblen (1904, p. 312): 'The discipline exercised by the mechanical occupations, in so far it is a question here, is a discipline of the habits of thought.' According to Veblen (1904, p. 67), the machine process 'inculcates a habit of apprehending and explaining facts in terms of material cause and effect'. Veblen believed that the people most likely to be affected in this way were not necessarily the machine operatives, but skilled mechanics, supervisors and engineers (Layton, 1962; Rutherford, 1992; Knoedler and Mayhew, 1999; Edgell, 2001). Veblen (1904, p. 313) argued that these habitual ideas of material cause and effect would develop primarily

> among those who are required to exercise what may be called a mechanical discretion in the guidance of the industrial processes, who ... are required to administer the laws of causal sequence that run

through material phenomena, who therefore must learn to think in the terms in which the machine processes work.

Veblen (1904, 1906a, 1914) repeated these arguments in several places, but never provided an adequate explanation of how the machine process assisted the growth of these particular preconceptions or habits of thought. Insofar as he supplied an explanation, it relied on a concept of 'matter-of-fact' knowledge, which he explained all too briefly in the following terms. For Veblen (1906a, pp. 585, 598) 'matter-of-fact' meant 'impersonal, dispassionate insight into the material facts with which mankind has to deal' and he wrote of 'that matter-of-fact inquiry that constitutes scientific research'. He then proposed an evolutionary theory by which 'matter-of-fact' habits of thought are selected in a 'struggle for existence' against those habits of lesser efficacy or fitness. This evolutionary aspect of Veblen's (1906a, p. 586) argument is apparent in the following passage:

> A civilization which is dominated by this matter-of-fact insight must prevail against any cultural scheme that lacks this element. This characteristic of western civilization comes to a head in modern science, and finds its highest material expression in the technology of the machine industry. ... The cultural structure clusters about this body of matter-of-fact knowledge as its substantial core.

Sure enough, countries that are more technologically advanced are likely to win out in economic or military struggles. But it is not clear why technological advances should always be associated with 'matter-of-fact' habits of thought. Some reservations concerning this supposed correlation are expressed later below.

Veblen (1904, p. 67) mentioned that such habits of mind were 'both a cause and an effect of the machine process'. The cultural effects were deemed to be deep and wide-ranging: 'In the nature of the case the cultural growth dominated by the machine industry is of a sceptical, matter-of-fact complexion, materialistic, unmoral, unpatriotic, undevout' (Veblen, 1904, p. 372). Veblen's analysis worked in both directions: habits of thought affected technology just as technology affected habits (Rutherford, 1984).

For many years, Veblen was absorbed with this questionable hypothesis concerning the impact of the machine process on habits of thought. But he sometimes qualified and circumscribed his analysis. For instance, Veblen (1904, pp. 309–10) wrote:

> Of course, in no case and with no class does the discipline of the machine process mould the habits of life and thought fully into its own image. There is present in the human nature of all classes too large a residue of the propensities and aptitudes carried over from the past and working to a different result. The machine's régime has been of

too short duration, strict as its discipline may be, and the body of inherited traits and traditions is too comprehensive and consistent to admit of anything more than a remote approach to such a consummation.

Here he admitted that the effects of the machine process could be delayed and remote. Furthermore, in his book on *Imperial Germany*, Veblen (1915, p. 237) considered the possibility of a cultural backlash that would 'dispel the effects wrought by habituation to the ways and means of modern industry and the exact sciences'. For Veblen there was no single, determined outcome, as history 'teaches that there is always another way, and that one should not underrate the cultural efficiency of a tenacious adherence to archaic institutions in the face of any eventuality'. Veblen was too careful a thinker than to propose a close or direct connection between technology and ideas. Hence any accusations of Veblen of 'technological determinism' have to be somewhat qualified.

The philosophical problematic

To understand Veblen's focus on the machine process we must appreciate his own philosophical preconceptions and concerns, and in particular the influence of Immanuel Kant. Prior to Kant, David Hume had rightly and famously argued that causal connections, whether they exist or not, cannot themselves be observed. As a result, the principle of universal causation – that every event is caused – cannot be derived directly from experience. Kant then argued that causal links had to be imputed by the observer, as a necessary condition of all rational enquiry. Up to this point, the Kantian position is incontestable. The problems arise when we consider the ontological status of causal relations. Although Kant did believe in the existence of a world beyond our senses, his idea of causation was not something resident in the nature of things but part of the necessary classificatory and explanatory principles. In effect, causation had no objective reality; it was all in the mind.

This Kantian influence remained with Veblen, although in important respects it was modified by his Darwinism. Veblen (1914, p. 260) wrote: 'The principle, or "law," of causation is a metaphysical postulate; in the sense that such a fact as causation is unproved and unprovable.' This is a clear recognition of the problem revealed by Hume and Kant. Veblen often repeated the valid point that some *a priori* assumptions are necessary for science. By insisting on the prior necessity of 'metaphysical premises' Veblen was rightly emphasizing the need for ontological commitments that could not be established by empirical data. In the subsequent century, scientists unlearned this truth in their long excursions through versions of positivism, only to rediscover the inescapable priority of ontology in the closing decades of the twentieth century. Veblen's insistence on the unavoidability of 'metaphysical presuppositions' and the priority of ontological commitments was thus vindicated after many years of denial.[4]

But if, as Veblen rightly believed, causal explanation was essential to science, and no causal connection could be established simply by data, then the pressing problem was to determine how science could establish and select a particular causal explanation. If causation was a matter of 'metaphysical premise' or 'imputation', then how could the scientist decide which causal explanation to presume or impute? If the known facts could not provide the answer for the scientist, then how should the decision be made? A problem in the Kantian scheme was that it left the choice of causal explanation as a rather arbitrary and individual matter for the scientist, and offered no criteria by which the validity or value of different causal explanations could be assessed. Generally, the problem of arbitrariness dogs any attempt to apply Kantian philosophy to the natural and social sciences.

Charles Sanders Peirce argued that truth was not an individual matter but one for a community of scientists. Accordingly, for Peirce, truth was the ultimate consensus that emerged as the result of enquiry and debate between scientists, once all empirical and explanatory problems had been resolved. It appears, however, Veblen was not satisfied with this line of argument. It is here where Charles Darwin came in.

James (1880) had hinted that Darwin's concept of selection would apply to ideas as well as biological organisms. In other words, Darwinian principles could be applied to the evolution of knowledge as well as the origin of species. James thus foreshadowed the 'evolutionary epistemology' of Karl Popper (1972a), Donald T. Campbell (1974a) and others.

Veblen should also be given credit as a founder of evolutionary epistemology. Veblen (1900a, p. 261) wrote of 'the work of natural selection, as between variants of scientific aim and animus and between more or less divergent points of view'. Crucially, he also applied Darwinism to the particular problem of choice of 'metaphysical premises'. Veblen (1900a, p. 241) insisted: 'The ultimate term or ground of knowledge is always of a metaphysical character.' But he then concluded: 'It is subject to natural selection and selective adaptation, as are other conventions.' Veblen thus proposed the application of evolutionary selection to ontological as well as empirical propositions. This was a clear philosophical synthesis of Kant, Darwin, Peirce and James.[5] All metaphysical preconceptions and empirical

---

4 As noted in Chapter 18, the contributions of Quine (1951) and others undermined the logical positivist dismissal of metaphysics, by showing that all empirical statements require ontological presuppositions.

5 In his critique of Veblen, Dobriansky's (1957) then-unfashionable emphasis on Peirce and his philosophical realism was commendable and prescient. However, Dobriansky falsely attributed to Veblen an 'extreme' and 'empiricist' refusal of metaphysical presuppositions that was repeatedly and explicitly denied by Veblen (1900a, pp. 241, 253; 1904, pp. 311, 314, 344; 1906a, pp. 596–7; 1914, pp. 260, 336) himself.

conjectures were subject to a struggle for survival in the open forum of the critical scientific enquiry.

Veblen took from Darwin the insistence on detailed causal explanations of phenomena. Everything must submit to a causal explanation in scientific terms. Veblen's acknowledged 'metaphysical premises' included the idea of 'efficient cause' or 'cause and effect'. How could these 'metaphysical premises' be verified? His attempted solution was to see these metaphysical ideas on causality as being an outcome of the rise of the machine process itself. The earlier, handicraft era had fostered different views on cause and effect, in which something analogous to the designs and intentions of the craftsperson were supreme. According to Veblen (1904, p. 365), handicraft production encouraged a view in which 'the effect is treated as a finality, not a phase of a complex sequence of causation ... but rather as an unfolding of a certain prime cause in which is contained, implicitly, all that presently appears in explicit form'. However, as a result of the mechanization of production, quite different views on causation prevailed. Veblen (1904, p. 311) wrote:

> The machine technology takes no cognizance of conventionally established rules of precedence; it knows neither manners nor breeding ... Its scheme of knowledge and of inference is based on the laws of material causation, not on those of immemorial custom, authenticity, or authoritative enactment. Its metaphysical basis is the law of cause and effect, which ... has displaced even the law of sufficient reason.

Hence Veblen attempted to resolve the Kantian problem of arbitrariness by appealing to the ideational outcomes of the evolution of mechanized production. His metaphysical premises were not justified simply because they were modern, but because they somehow were part of the cultural circumstances somehow generated by the machine age. Veblen (1906a, p. 598) thus wrote of the modern scientist:

> the canons of validity under whose guidance he works are those imposed by the modern technology, through habituation to its requirements ... His canons of validity ... are habits of thought imposed on him by the scheme of life current in the community in which he lives; and under modern conditions this scheme of life is largely machine-made. In the modern culture, industry, industrial processes, and industrial products have progressively gained upon humanity ... they have become the chief force in shaping men's daily life, and therefore the chief factor in shaping men's habits of thought. Hence men have learned to think in the terms that the technological processes act.

If this argument were successful then Veblen would have solved two vital theoretical problems at a stroke. First, if Veblen had shown how the machine process affects our thoughts then he would have provided a vital and aforementioned 'weakest link' in Marx's theory of social change, which was identified by Veblen himself and discussed in Chapter 6 above. We might begin to explain how individual ideas and motivations are partly moulded by material circumstances. It would be shown how those engaged in the machine process come to challenge specific social institutions. Second, with this argument Veblen also attempted to resolve the Kantian philosophical problem of how allegedly arbitrary metaphysical premises could be grounded or justified. Veblen was playing for high theoretical stakes. But ultimately, as argued below, his argument failed.

In his effort to resolve these important theoretical problems, Veblen strained his argument to the limit, particularly by claiming that mechanical action can not only condition but also itself invoke a particular manner of thought. Veblen rightly pointed out that modern human culture is dominated by industrial processes and products, but did not explain how these cause changes in habits of thought. It is likely that we are profoundly affected by our day-to-day experiences of machines, but any process of moulding our thoughts depends on much more than this. Any sensual experience is processed through a mental apparatus of cognitive framing and interpretation, which is not itself provided by the machine, but bestowed by a specific culture. As a result, a variety of interpretations of any given (mechanical or other) experience are possible. Above all, different social cultures harbour different interpretations and meanings of any given experience. The machine does not mould our ideas in a singular pattern, as Veblen seemed to suggest.

But Veblen's general line of reasoning is not without force or subtlety. Veblen's strategy was to convince others of his own ontological commitments by claiming that they too had been caused by modern material circumstances. The causal principle applied not only to the social and economic world but also allegedly to Veblen's own theory about that world. The self-referentiality of his theory was subdued, but has not gone unnoticed (Samuels, 1990).[6]

Veblen (1904, p. 319) then went on to argue that the notion of causality promoted by the machine process was at odds with explanations of the social order in terms of 'natural rights' or 'habits of recourse to conventional grounds of finality or validity'. Depending as it did on the conventions of law and property, the world of business enterprise appealed to its allegedly 'natural' and 'conventional' foundations to legitimate its existence. As Veblen (1904, p. 318) put it:

---

6 However, it does not follow from this proposition that observers are entirely prisoners of their own interpretative frameworks, or that any framework is as good as any other. See T. Lawson (2002, 2003b) for critical discussions of 'postmodernist' or 'relativist' interpretations of Veblen, and an interpretation of his work that places it closer to modern philosophical realism.

The ultimate ground of validity for the thinking of the business class is the natural-rights ground of property – a conventional, anthropomorphic fact having an institutional validity, rather than a matter-of-fact validity such as can be formulated in terms of material cause and effect … Arguments which proceed on material cause and effect cannot be met with arguments from conventional precedent or dialectically sufficient reason, and conversely.

According to Veblen, the disparities between the rising materialist and causal modes of explanation, on the one hand, and antiquated explanations based on arbitrary conventions or alleged 'natural rights', on the other, would lead to challenges to the latter. Like Karl Marx (1867) and Joseph Schumpeter (1942), Veblen saw capitalism as undermining its own ideological and institutional supports, but for different reasons. Veblen (1904, p. 374) argued:

Broadly, the machine discipline acts to disintegrate the institutional heritage, of all degrees of antiquity and authenticity – whether it be the institutions that embody the principles of natural liberty or those that comprise the residue of more archaic principles of conduct still current in civilized life. It thereby cuts away that ground of law and order on which business enterprise is founded.

Veblen's theory of the machine process provided another scenario in which capitalism is undermined by the very productive activity that it has unleashed. Mechanization encouraged 'matter-of-fact' habits of thought that in turn undermined the conventional 'natural rights' of property and contract. Hence 'industry' came into conflict with 'business' institutions. These grand historical implications were part of the appeal of the Veblenian theoretical edifice.

But Veblen was also just as much concerned to use his theory of the machine process to resolve the Kantian dilemma of choice of preconceptions. This was no obscure matter of arcane philosophy. At stake was the very justification of the premises that economic science had to choose in order to understand the world. Such premises were required to evaluate other doctrines, to develop new theories and to enable empirical and theoretical enquiry to proceed.

Kant influenced a number of other social scientists, notably Alfred Marshall, Max Weber and Frank Knight (Hindess, 1977; Hodgson, 2001c). In its acknowledgement of metaphysics, Kantianism represented a relatively sophisticated position. However, with the rise of positivism and empiricism in academic circles during the first half of the twentieth century, anyone who argued that some metaphysical presuppositions were necessary for science would find dwindling supporters.

These days, at least in the philosophy of science, the situation has changed radically. It is now commonplace to accept that science requires some premises that cannot themselves be verified by, or built directly upon, data or experience. However, this assertion today is not framed predominantly in Kantian terms. The prevalent stance is some modern form of philosophical realism. In the last few years, sophisticated varieties of realist philosophy have also established themselves in economics and sociology. Within this broad, modern realist tradition, it has been demonstrated that it is possible to establish key ontological presuppositions that are consistent with the possibility of scientific enquiry. Within the more prominent versions of modern realism, the choice of presuppositions is not merely a matter of individual imputation, as Kant would have it, but disciplined by the recognition of a world beyond our senses, in which events are subject to causes and laws.[7]

As Veblen rightly recognized, the search for universal premises itself faces the limits of diversity and complexity in the real world. Social science should be sensitive to historically or geographically specific phenomena. However, this does not mean that universal presuppositions can be avoided in their entirety. Some universal ontological commitments, particularly concerning causality and uniformity in nature, are necessary for science to proceed at all (Hodgson, 2001c).

Veblen attempted to establish his presuppositions of universal causation and Darwinian evolution on the basis that they themselves were a historically contingent product of the machine age. His implicit metatheory included the proposition that such preconceptions are historically specific. But Veblen's metatheory is itself universal and hence does not fit into Veblen's own historically contingent scheme. An internal contradiction appears in his thought.

There is a parallel here in discussions concerning relativism. The relativist upholds that all propositions are relative or contingent. But this is itself a universal statement. Even historical relativism requires some absolute and universal presuppositions. For the 100 per cent relativist, there is no escape from this paradox. Modern philosophical realism is free of such contradictions and paradoxes.

A source of Veblen's problem was his Kantianism. Veblen recognized the need for metaphysical postulates but treated them as contingent and potentially arbitrary tools of thought, rather than ontological presuppositions stemming from an understanding that a real world actually exists beyond our senses. In a doomed synthesis of Kant and Darwin, he then attempted to use evolutionary theory to justify the conceptions of causality

---

7   On philosophical realism see Aronson (1984), Bhaskar (1975), Bunge (1973a), Cartwright (1989), Chalmers (1985), Harré (1986), Humphreys (1989), Leplin (1984), Manicas (1987) and Popper (1990). For applications of realist philosophy to the social sciences see Archer (1995), Bhaskar (1989), T. Lawson (1997, 2003b), Mäki (1998, 2001, 2002), Outhwaite (1987), Sayer (1984) and Searle (1995).

in modern science. But his use of evolutionary theory itself involves preconceptions. He was caught in a self-referential methodological tangle.

From a realist stance, where presuppositions concern a real world beyond our senses, a different picture emerges. If universal causation is valid and real then it is genuinely universal. If every event is caused, then that stricture applies to events before, during and after the machine age. Furthermore, if the principles of Darwinian evolution apply to all populations of entities where there is selection, variety and replication, then these principles do not apply to the machine age alone.

How can machines affect thoughts?

Having discussed the philosophical underpinnings of Veblen's theory, we now dissect the theory itself. Veblen (1904, p. 310) wrote: 'The machine technology rests on a knowledge of impersonal, material cause and effect.' In addition: 'The discipline exercised by the mechanical occupations ... is a discipline of the habits of thought' (Veblen, 1904, p. 312). Hence, as noted above, he argued that the machine process engendered 'matter-of-fact' attitudes and some general propositions concerning causation. According to Veblen (1904, pp. 66–7), the machine age encourages 'a standardization of conduct and of knowledge in terms of quantitative precision and inculcates a habit of apprehending and explaining facts in terms of material cause and effect'.

Veblen believed that engagement with machines gave rise to habits of thought that involved 'matter-of-fact' attitudes and habits of explanation 'in terms of material cause and effect'. The problem here is not the primacy that Veblen gave to habit in his theory. Furthermore, it is also reasonable to suggest that the machine process has affected, in interaction with social culture, our habits of thought and behaviour in some ways. In particular, when working with machines, some knowledge of specific causes and effects is required of the skilled operator or engineer.

Veblen (1904, p. 322) rightly acknowledged that conservative and conventional habits of thought would be found in both 'industrial' and 'business occupations'. But he nevertheless exaggerated the degree to which 'machine technology' could help to undermine 'conventionally established rules of precedence' (Veblen, 1904, p. 311) such as the rights of property. Here Veblen allowed the mistaken suggestion that industry could function without any rules or conventions, or that conventional rules are always antithetical to industrial norms.

On the contrary, technology itself depends on the accumulated tradition of experiment and trial, with complex arrangements that cannot be causally dissected or optimized in every detail. Modern studies have shown that engineering is a partially conservative evolutionary process: it progresses through evolutionary selection upon established usages and conventions (Rosenberg and Vincenti, 1985; Vincenti, 1990).

A particular problem concerns the specific 'matter-of-fact' and causal habits of thought that Veblen saw as being engendered by the machine. It has been argued above that Veblen faced the philosophical problem of grounding or justifying his own presuppositions concerning causality. My suggestion here is that this lacuna forced him to seek an implausible solution to his Kantian dilemma. The idea that machines especially promote 'matter-of-fact' attitudes, and explanations 'in terms of material cause and effect' does not stand up to even moderate theoretical and historical scrutiny.

First, the concept of 'matter-of-fact' is itself extremely vague. Does it mean grounded on facts and experience rather than ungrounded metaphysical presuppositions? This question involves an untenable dichotomy, because the facts never speak for themselves. As Veblen (1900a, p. 253) himself recognized: 'The endeavor to avoid all metaphysical premises fails ... everywhere.' Metaphysical and other preconceptions are required to make sense of any empirical fact. Being 'matter-of-fact' unavoidably brings in metaphysics as well. Furthermore, the same facts are often capable of different interpretations, depending on the metaphysical and other premises involved.

The idea that the machine process engenders habits of thinking 'in terms of material cause and effect' is at least slightly more precise concerning the purported outcome. However, the connection itself is no more convincing. Practical involvement, even with machines, does not itself make the philosophically complex and physically mysterious nature of causality clear. The skilled machine operator or engineer may learn the mechanisms of the machine, but that does not provide a specific and detailed understanding of causal ontology.

For example, until a few hundred years ago, scientists believed in an Aristotelian conception of causality and motion where objects require the continuous application of force in order to move. In contrast, Newton asserted that particles would continue on the same course and with the same velocity, until they were impeded or disturbed. Newton's laws of motion were not obvious; it took an exceptionally gifted intellect, in special circumstances, to discover them. Indeed, when the canals were built in the eighteenth century, an observer could have deduced that continuous power was required to move the canal boats. From this observation Aristotle, rather than Newton, might seem to be vindicated. In contrast, when the railways were built, a railway train would move downhill without any power. With railway technology, Newton rather than Aristotle might seem to be right. Very different notions of causality and motion might be encouraged by different industrial phenomena.

Furthermore, even from a Newtonian standpoint, not everything is 'matter-of-fact'. For example, the cause moving a railway train down the track was far from clear or plainly 'matter-of-fact'. Even today, physics has difficulty explaining the force of gravity. When we observe the moon in the sky we may take its suspension for granted. But the explanation of its position again depends on the mysterious and far-from-obvious force of gravity. Explanations of gravity in the physics of Isaac Newton and Albert Einstein are very different and the nature of gravity remains problematic to this day.

The Industrial Revolution not only involved mechanical linkages but also heat, chemicals and (later on) electricity. The nature of heat and its causes are also not obvious, and false theories of heat were believed until the second part of the nineteenth century. In particular, the principle of conservation of energy is not directly observable. The steam engine was operating well before the principles of thermodynamics were properly formulated. Simple observation of most chemical processes reveals little of cause and effect. For example, iron or steel manufacture involves relatively obscure chemical reactions and metallurgical transformations. Metal technology resulted largely from trial and error, rather than full rational cognizance of the chemical processes. Electricity and magnetism are similarly mysterious, at least without modern scientific theories and presuppositions. In short, it is not immediately obvious how machines involving heat, electricity or chemical reactions work. The machine operator or engineer is not provided and privileged with an explanation by virtue of being in close contact with the machine.

Consider some historical evidence from the early nineteenth century, when numerous machines were being introduced in Britain. Commonplace reactions to mechanization were often far from causally focused or 'matter-of-fact'. When the machine-breaking movement emerged in England in 1811, these 'Luddites' sang a song entitled 'General Ludd's Triumph' – from which the following is an extract – against the mechanical looms and knitting frames that had apparently cost them their jobs (Hammond and Hammond, 1920, pp. 259–60):

> These Engines of mischief were sentenced to die
> By unanimous vote of the Trade;
> And Ludd who can all opposition defy
> Was the grand executioner made.

Rather than their employers or the social system, the Luddites blamed the machine for their plight. In the nineteenth-century world of the machine, this was not the only case of misplaced causal attribution. The Industrial Revolution was often associated with outbursts of religious fervour, rather than rational appraisals of cause and effect. Edward Thompson (1968, pp. 418–30) has described the rantings and hysteria at the time of the Methodist revival of the early nineteenth century. As Lewis Mumford (1934, p. 284) elaborated:[8]

the emotional fervor of Wesley's Methodism spread like a fire in dry grass through the very depressed classes that were subject to the new factory régime. The direct reaction of the machine was to make people materialistic and rational; its indirect action was often to make them hyper-emotional and irrational. The tendency to ignore the second set of reactions because they did not logically coincide with the claims of the machine has unfortunately been common in many critics of the new industrial order: even Veblen was not free from it.

There may be a grain of truth in Veblen's supposition that mechanization encouraged some presuppositions and habits of thought concerning cause and effect. But as the British institutional economist John Hobson (1936, p. 29) commented, Veblen 'overstressed' the 'technological factor ... as a transforming medium. Though machinery has undoubtedly influenced our ways of thinking and our attitude to the services, it has been less revolutionary than Veblen is disposed to think.' Hobson (1926, p. 348) also rightly pointed out that machines have a repetitive quality that could also encourage conservative habits of thought:

> The defect of machinery, from the educative point of view, is its absolute conservatism. The law of machinery is a law of statical order, that everything conforms to a pattern, that present actions precisely resemble past and future actions.

But while machines themselves have the quality of relentless and unchanging sequential repetition, their increasing use in production was accompanied historically by huge social upheavals. In reaction against these effects, the machine itself was blamed for social ills. The social dislocations of mechanized industry and agriculture fostered multiple religious and millennarian movements of intense fervour. As noted above, Veblen accepted the possibility of an 'archaic' or conservative resistance to the habits of thought engendered by the machine process. But he did not see its possible effect as a desperate communal cry for meaning and salvation, in the midst of its relentless rhythm and its accompanying social disturbance.

Even if mechanization promoted the particular idea that every event is caused, this as such does not exclude beliefs such as that God is a cause, or the machine is a social agent. In particular, religious beliefs persist today among many scientists and engineers. Even at the cost of inconsistency, humans are highly capable of partitioning their thoughts concerning the world around them. Some people impute materialistic causality in one sphere, but God and spirituality in another. The United States, the world's leading industrialized country, where the development of the machine

---

8 Diggins (1978, p. 91) referred to Mumford as 'Veblen's greatest anthropological disciple'. See Long (2002). Mumford was a student of Veblen at the New School.

process has reached its apogee, is one of the most religious of developed countries. Yet such religious beliefs are inconsistent with the exclusively materialistic version of causality embraced by Darwin and Veblen. According to opinion poll evidence, almost half of Americans believe that humans were created by God, and did not evolve from apes.[9]

Veblen (1914, p. 180) once argued that the 'pecuniary culture' results in 'a deflection from matter-of-fact to matter of imputation'. With the result that: 'Theological preconceptions are commonly strong in the pecuniary culture'. If elaborated, this argument might explain the American disposition towards religion on the basis of the American disposition towards money. But the success of American industry would, according to Veblen, undermine such religious sentiments. Furthermore, the US is the clear world leader in most areas of scientific research. Accordingly, while they have embraced religion, Americans have not been entirely 'deflected' from 'matter-of-fact' issues. The Veblenian argument leads us into contradictions that are difficult to reconcile.

The institutional economist Robert Hoxie was a former student of Veblen and an early critic of Veblen's theory (Fishman, 1958; McNulty, 1973; Rutherford, 1998a). Hoxie (1917) noted that Veblen's argument would imply that trade unionists, being close to the machine process, would be less inclined to accept the 'natural-rights ground of property' than their employers. However, in his studies of US trade unions, Hoxie found that this was not strictly the case. A prominent motive among trade unionists was to secure the maximum possible pecuniary return for their toil. Trade unions entered into the pecuniary world of business and bargained over matters of money. Workers were as much concerned with remuneration as ideas of physical causation. Malcolm Rutherford (1998a, p. 475) argued that in the face of this critique Veblen himself modified his views, as in his *Engineers and the Price System* (1921), by placing more emphasis on educated engineers rather than machine workers as possible agents of social change.[10]

Science involves the relentless and unbounded pursuit of integrated and consistent causal explanations. However, the machine does not itself engender such a pursuit. A culture that gives rise to science is grounded on habits of secularism, rationalism and scepticism. The institutions and values of a pluralist society sustain it. It requires sufficient income above subsistence to provision its research activity. Particular habits of thought and

---

9 In November 1997 the Gallup Organization polled a representative sample of adult US residents on their views on the origin of the human species. As many as 44 per cent agreed with the creationist statement: 'God created human beings pretty much in their present form at one time within the last 10,000 years or so.' Only a small minority accepted an evolutionary explanation without any divine intervention.

10 The events leading to Hoxie's suicide are discussed in McNulty (1973), Nyland (1996) and Hodgson (2001c). McNulty noted Hoxie's disillusionment with Veblen's theory as a factor causing his depression. Nyland documented how Hoxie's disenchantment with his own and Commons's research on Taylorism caused a more immediate personal crisis.

institutions are necessary to establish 'the place of science in modern civilization'. In this explanation of the institutional, cultural and economic preconditions of science, the machine is no longer the centrepiece of the argument.

Reactions to mechanization are, in part, culturally specific. Although Veblen often recognized the role of culture, his allegedly universal story of the effects of mechanization created a problem in his own analytical scheme. There is nothing inherent in mechanization *per se* that leads to a specific behavioural or ideational outcome. We observe machines, but our understanding of them depends on our preconceptions. Mechanical action cannot itself bequeath ideas of ontology or logic.

Veblen and the organization of the economy

As noted above, Veblen (1904, p. 158) created a dichotomy 'between the industrial needs of the community and the business needs of the corporation'. The idea that there can be a conflict or tension between the two can be accepted. But there are no grounds to see this conflict as one of universal incompatibility. The relationship between corporate business and human need is much more complex, and it is naïve to ascribe either universal antagonism or universal harmony. Another problem arises if we imagine that industry can exist and function without some kind of organized business structure (public, private or whatever). Industry requires some kind of organization and management of production, alongside the essential, institutionalized mechanisms of coordination and distribution in the economy as a whole.

Veblen's neglect of this crucial organizational issue precisely paralleled his arguments concerning the machine process. In the case of the latter, the machine was considered in unwarranted separation from the social institutions in which it was embedded. With his dichotomy between 'business' and 'industry', it was suggested by Veblen that the needs of industry could be considered as if they were matters divorced from the business institutions required to administer or coordinate production. In both cases, industry or technology became strange, independent forces, acting somehow separately from the institutions in which they were embodied. The institutionalist John Maurice Clark (1925, p. 57) criticized Veblen in this respect:

> As for the technical processes, neither Veblen nor anyone else has ever shown how social efficiency can be organized on a technical basis alone. ... Veblen's antithesis [between business and industry], valuable as it is as a challenge to orthodoxy, cannot serve the purposes of a constructive search for the line of progress. This calls for an evolution of our scheme of values, not for a 'technocracy' which ignores value.

Veblen (1921, p. 100) declared: 'Twentieth-century technology has outgrown the eighteenth-century system of vested rights.' But Veblen did not describe the system of economic organization and coordination that was appropriate for twentieth-century technology. Even when he got closest to discussing these matters of economic organization and coordination, Veblen's statements were sorely lacking. For example, Veblen (1921, p. 156) advocated 'a disallowance of absentee ownership' because it has been 'proved to be noxious to the common good'. But again he was silent on the system of ownership or organization that would replace the absentee owner of industrial assets. In a characteristic passage, involving mock-innocent and muted provocation, Veblen (1923, p. 278) wrote:

> The calculus of business is a calculus of money-value, which is not a mechanical or material fact; whereas the calculus of industry is a calculus of mechanical, tangible, material values. From which it follows that any intrusion of business strategy into the conduct of industry will be sabotage.

The problems begin in the first sentence and spill over into the second. Contrary to Veblen, industry is not merely a matter of 'mechanical, tangible, material values'. It is also a matter of social organization and human psychological motivation. The 'calculus of money-value' may have some inhibiting, distorting or other effects on productivity. But the removal of this monetary calculus would bring industry to a halt, unless it was replaced by some other feasible system of entrepreneurial, managerial and workforce motivation. Veblen offered us no practicable alternative. He saw the negative effects of the monetary calculus, but, largely blind to the central questions of industrial organization and motivation, he failed to acknowledge that the monetary calculus nevertheless provides powerful incentives, as well as distorting priorities. Veblen failed to examine any alternative system of economic organization, allocation and coordination.

Veblen was not alone in this respect. The same flaws are found in the writings of Marxists and other radicals. To this date, all proposals of alternatives to the existing capitalist order are highly limited in their detail, and lacking in an elaboration of feasible alternative incentive structures and systems of allocation. Such omissions and defects limit the stature of both Veblen and Marx as economic thinkers, despite their major achievements. Veblen did not go as far as Marx in treating technology as a separate 'force' but he did likewise neglect the incentive structures that are tied up with any actual or alternative system of production.[11]

In 1911, Frederick Winslow Taylor published his famous *Principles of Scientific Management*. Like many other radical thinkers at the time, Veblen

---

11 For a critical discussion of Marx's rare and limited statements on the economic organization of socialism or communism, and of two recent proposals for the organization of a socialist economy, see Hodgson (1999a, ch. 2). See also Steele (1992).

welcomed Taylorism because he thought that it would help to rationalize production, raise productivity, increase output, and enhance the material conditions of the working classes. Contrary to his widespread modern depiction as a villain, Taylor himself was a progressive who believed in higher pay for workers, improved working conditions and a reduction in working hours. In addition, the Taylorist movement was not generally anti-union. It had neither the intention nor the outcome of general workforce deskilling. For many thinkers, Taylorism was a progressive and technocratic solution to economic challenges.[12]

But Taylorism had its problems, and it is again symptomatic that Veblen did not acknowledge them. These problems concern the limits of mechanical specification of the work process and some inhibition of workforce motivation (Vroom and Deci, 1970). In a particularly astute and prescient critique of Taylorism, Hobson (1914, p. 219) noted that even routine work 'still contains a margin for the display of skill, initiative and judgement'. Hobson (1914, pp. 219–20) further argued:

> Indeed, were the full rigour of Scientific Management to be applied throughout the staple industries, not only would the human costs of labour appear to be enhanced, but progress in the industrial arts itself would probably be damaged. ... The large assistance given to technical invention by the observation and experiments of intelligent workmen, the constant flow of suggestion for detailed improvements, would cease. The elements of creative work still surviving in most routine labour would disappear.

Hobson recognized the matters of motivation and innovation that were neglected in Veblen's account of work and the machine process. Although Veblen's support for Taylorism was far from damning or catastrophic, it betrayed a neglect of important matters of human perception and motivation. Hobson's diagnosis was much superior in this respect.

What was catastrophic about Veblen's overall contribution to economics was not simply the lack of an integrated theoretical system but also his failure to understand adequately the motivational and organizational realities of a pecuniary and market economy. Other than vague allusions to an undetailed anarcho-syndicalism or a 'Soviet of engineers', Veblen was largely silent on the key questions of economic organization and coordination. Veblen (1921, p. 144) wrote minimally of an 'industrial directorate' of experts, 'working in due consultation with a sufficient ramification of sub-centers and local councils' in the apparent belief that obtainable and

---

12 See Tichi (1987), Wrege and Greenwood (1991), Nyland (1996), Guillen (1997), Knoedler (1997) and Bruce and Nyland (2001). Commons opposed Taylorism, but for challengeable reasons. Veblen (1904, p. 313 n.) did not believe that the machine process would lead to deskilling or 'a deterioration or numbing of ... intelligence'. He saw this as 'too sweeping a characterization of the change brought on by habituation to machine work'.

centralized knowledge and expertise were sufficient to deal with all the problems of conflicting claims and economic allocation in a modern complex economy. Of a possible system to replace that of predatory business institutions, Veblen provides no more than the haziest outline (Hodder, 1956; Rutherford, 1992). This lacuna in his thinking was also typical of many radicals and Marxists, but ultimately damaging. No theoretical approach in economics can claim supremacy unless it understands these problems and has adequate answers to them. The greatness of Veblen's economics is significantly limited by this defect. Some later institutionalists – such as John R. Commons, Morris Copeland and Wesley Mitchell – were more cognizant of these problems. While advocating substantial government intervention in economic matters, they understood the indispensability of some markets and the impossibility of any solution based on comprehensive planning alone.

Concluding remarks

In short, Veblen argued that the spread of the machine process engendered 'matter-of-fact' habits of thought and particular ontological presuppositions concerning causality. However, detailed arguments and historical evidence indicate that machines do not affect thoughts in the way that Veblen proposed. It has also been suggested here that Veblen developed this flawed argument because of problems in his Kantian position and his unsuccessful attempt to reconcile Darwin with Kant. Replacing Kantianism by a suitable modern version of philosophical realism would remove this particular problem and provide a stronger foundation for both Veblen's Darwinism and his presuppositions concerning causation.

However, the machine process does have an impact on our thoughts and behaviour, just as any new technology, when deployed in a social setting, can change habits and routines. For example, the development of the factory system encouraged employers to devise new institutions of management and production. It also brought workers together in large groups. It revolutionized conceptions of timekeeping and stimulated the emergence of collective organizations and ideologies. Technology does matter. The blanket accusation of 'technological determinism' is typically too imprecise. Veblen's general view that technology can have effects on institutions is acceptable. But the particular effects that he outlined, and his neglect of institutional incentive structures, are more problematic. Veblen's theory of the influence of the machine process is one of the weakest parts of his legacy.

11 Missed connections

Creative synthesis and emergent evolution

Long lost, late won, and yet but half-regained.
                    Percy Bysshe Shelley, 'Ode to Naples' (1820)

In this chapter we discuss the development of the ideas of emergence and creative synthesis in the philosophy and social theory of the early twentieth century. The idea of emergent properties appeared in psychology and philosophy, in dealing with the mind–body problem. It also came into view in sociology, when addressing the relationship between the individual and society. It was detectable at least in outline in the works of several early sociologists, even before the philosophy of emergence was fully articulated. The tragic outcome was the failure of Veblenism to connect with these developments, even at a time when Veblen was still alive.

Proto-emergentism: Franklin Henry Giddings

Franklin Giddings was a prominent early American sociologist. In his enthusiasm for Darwinism he was atypical, given the then predispositions of American thinkers towards Lamarckism (Stocking, 1962, 1968; Pfeifer, 1965). Several years before Thorstein Veblen, in a publication of the American Economic Association, Giddings (1888, pp. 29–47) characterized the preceding economic theory as non-evolutionary and pre-Darwinian. In his *Principles of Sociology*, Giddings (1896, p. 417) emphasized the concept of natural selection and explicitly rejected any notion of 'uncaused causes'. For Giddings: 'Sociology is an attempt to account for the origin, growth, structure, and activities of society by the operation of physical, vital, and psychical causes, working together in a process of evolution' (1896, p. 8). Giddings (1896, p. 116) saw imitation as 'the chief social factor of economic life' and entertained a concept of 'artificial selection' (1896, p. 414) in the social sphere. He criticized Spencer for his depiction of society as 'a physical organism' and emphasized that a 'society is an *organization*, partly a product of unconscious evolution, partly a result of conscious planning' (1896,

p. 420). Significantly, Giddings (1896, pp. 132–3) recognized George Henry Lewes's (1879, pp. 161–5) carefully formulated concept of a 'general mind' (as noted in Chapter 5 above). Giddings (1896, p. 134) wrote:

> The social mind is a concrete thing. It is more than any individual mind and dominates every individual will. Yet it exists only in individual minds, and we have no knowledge of any consciousness but that of individuals. ... The social mind is the phenomenon of many individual minds in interaction, so playing upon one another that they simultaneously feel the same sensation or emotion, arrive at one judgement and perhaps act in concert. ... A wave of feeling may surge through a crowd, and expand itself in an almost purely reflex act, as when an audience bursts into applause.

In his emphasis on unplanned social outcomes, in his incorporation of the work of Lewes, and in his two-level treatment of the interaction of human minds in society, Giddings prefigured a concept of emergent properties. As in Giddings's appropriate example of a crowd, its behaviour can readily be considered as an emergent property of the interactions of its individual members.

Proto-emergentism: Émile Durkheim

In France, at about the same time, Émile Durkheim was developing a very different version of sociological theory, with a schism between social theory on the one hand, and psychology and biology on the other. Principally for this reason, after Anglophone sociology turned away from biology, Durkheim's influence became far more enduring than any pre-1914 American sociologist. But it is not necessary to discuss Durkheim in detail here. The point of this brief visit to France is to note that Durkheim too was prefiguring a concept of emergence. In 1901, Durkheim (1982, pp. 39–40) wrote in his *Rules of Sociological Method*:

> The hardness of bronze lies neither in the copper, nor the tin, nor in the lead which have been used to form it, which are all soft or malleable bodies. The hardness arises from the mixing of them. The liquidity of water, its sustaining and other properties, are not in the two gases of which it is composed, but in the complex substance which they form by coming together. Let us apply this principle to sociology. If, as is granted to us, this synthesis *sui generis*, which constitutes every society, gives rise to new phenomena, different from those which occur in consciousness in isolation, one is forced to admit that these specific facts reside in the society itself that produces them and not in its parts – namely its members.

In the above passage, Durkheim clearly presented a notion of novel properties that arise when elements or factors are combined, these new properties being absent from the components of the synthesis taken severally. Like Giddings, Durkheim saw crowd behaviour as a significant evocation of new properties of social wholes. Durkheim (1982, pp. 53, 56) wrote:

> Those individuals who are normally perfectly harmless may, when gathered together in a crowd, let themselves be drawn into acts of atrocity. ... An outburst of collective emotion in a gathering does not merely express the sum total of what individuals share in common, but something of a very different order ...

Durkheim was dead and Giddings had retired from academia before the terminology of emergence became properly established in philosophy in the 1920s. Although the term 'emergent property' was not yet in currency, leading early sociologists such as Giddings and Durkheim explained how the combination of individuals together in a social structure gave rise to new properties, and saw this phenomenon as central and significant for social theory.

Dual aspect theory: Charles Horton Cooley

Charles Horton Cooley was originally trained as an economist and taught by Henry Carter Adams. Walton Hamilton (1919, p. 318) saw Cooley as one of the 'leaders' of American institutionalism (alongside Adams, Veblen and Mitchell). Similarly, Joseph Dorfman (1963, p. 41) considered Cooley as the 'fourth founding father of institutional theory' (after Veblen, Commons and Mitchell). In his most important book on *Human Nature and the Social Order*, Cooley (1902, 1922) was influenced by the concept of the 'social self' in the work of William James (1890). Partly reflecting the influence of James, Cooley (alongside Giddings) was atypical among American sociologists in being more inclined to Darwin than Lamarck. Cooley argued that both our means of understanding the world and our personality are necessarily formed in interaction with others, in a structured social context. The individual mind emerges through social communication. In stressing the social constitution of the self, Cooley inspired George Herbert Mead (1934).[1]

However, in emphasizing the social nature of individuality, Cooley conflated the individual with society. For Cooley (1902, pp. 1–2; 1922, p. 37): '"society" and "individuals" do not denote separable phenomena, but are simply collective and distributive aspects of the same thing'. For Cooley, both the individual and society are abstractions of a single life

---

1 Cooley (1902) influenced J. M. Clark (1918) and H. Simon (1957, 1996). See Chapter 12 below.

process. In some ways this is similar to the 'central conflation' in the modern work of Anthony Giddens (1984), as discussed in Chapter 2 above. They are both examples of a 'dual aspect' theory. An objection to dual aspect theory is that any given agent is preceded by historically given social structures. Hence agency and structure are not different aspects of the same thing but are separable in time. This was argued by George Henry Lewes (1879) and before him by Auguste Comte (1853). Accordingly, society constitutes an emergent level, dependent upon but ontologically different from the individual. Lester Frank Ward (1903) and others pioneered this concept of an emergent social level, as we shall see below.

Dual aspect theory appeared previously in attempts to deal with the mind–body problem. In this context, both Spencer and Thomas Henry Huxley had adopted a dual aspect formulation. Huxley (1896, vol. 1, p. 351) had written of 'mental and physical phenomena' as 'merely diverse manifestations' of a tentatively proposed 'substratum'. Likewise, Cooley saw society and the individual as different 'aspects of the same thing'. The problem with a dual aspect ontology in these contexts is that it conflates and confuses the different entities that it is trying to relate to each other. As in the later work of Giddens, Cooley's conflation was also mentalistic, in that he regarded the underlying processes and structures as essentially in the mind.

If society and the individual are different aspects of the same thing, then statements concerning the social nature of the individual are eroded of meaning. If dual aspect theory were valid, then it would be just as true to say that the social was individual in nature. The terms 'individual' and 'social' have to represent different phenomena for the social character of individuality to be fully appreciated.

Creative synthesis and a layered ontology: Lester Frank Ward

Ward's Lamarckism has already been noted. His psychology was essentially pre-Jamesian, emphasizing the principles of pleasure and pain rather than impulse, habit and learning. Nevertheless, his work in sociology places him among the titans. In 1903, Ward published one of the greatest works of twentieth-century sociology. This work is not without its limitations, but its almost entirely uncited status today is shamefully unwarranted. With its exposition of a multi-layered ontology and a more elaborate prefiguration of the concept of emergence, it is a significant advance over Giddings, Durkheim and Cooley. Albion Small wrote to Ward in 1903: 'we all know that you are head, shoulders, and hips above us in many respects scientifically. You are Gulliver among the Lilliputians' (Stern, 1947, p. 719). But the next generation of Lilliputians banished Gulliver from their sociological island.

In his 1903 book, Ward favourably cited Thorstein Veblen's *Theory of the Leisure Class*. What also makes Ward's book particularly important for the history of institutionalism is the fact that it was both favourably reviewed and repeatedly cited with approval by Veblen (1903, 1904, 1906a). Veblen (1903, p. 655) described Ward's work as a 'great treatise':

> *Pure Sociology* is a captivating volume … Dr. Ward succeeds in what others have attempted. He has brought the aims and methods of modern science effectively into sociological inquiry. … The aim is to organize social phenomena into a theoretical structure in causal terms.[2]

Unfortunately, Veblen did not make much use of Ward's theoretical contribution and we are obliged to discuss it in the absence of further comment from Veblen. Ward foreshadowed emergentist philosophy by considering forces or components that can sometimes combine together and lead to novel outcomes. He used the term 'synergy' to refer to the energetic combination of different forces. Ward (1903, p. 171) wrote:

> I have at last fixed upon the word *synergy* as the term best adapted to express its twofold character of *energy* and *mutuality*, or the systematic and organic *working together* of the antithetical forces of nature.

This was not the first use of the term 'synergy' but its prominence in Ward's work was highly significant.[3] Ward (1903, pp. 183–5) employed it in the following context, where he examined the creation and importance of social structures and institutions:

> Social structures are the products of social synergy, i.e., of the interaction of different social forces … whose combined effect, mutually checking, constraining, and equilibriating one another, is to produce structures. … We may therefore qualify Darwin's severe formula of the struggle for existence and look upon the whole panorama rather as a *struggle for structure*. … The most general and appropriate name for social structures is human institutions.

The second of Ward's proto-emergentist terms was 'creative synthesis'. This phrase also appeared before 1903, but typically in a looser, descriptive sense. The German psychologist and philosopher Wilhelm Wundt was one

---

2   According to the JSTOR database, citations to Ward's book declined rapidly in frequency after the First World War. Small (1903–4) made some important criticisms of Ward's work. A brief appreciative discussion of the philosophy underlying Ward's thought is by A. Nelson (1968). Some reasons for the declining popularity of these earlier thinkers, and the subsequent amnesia of Anglophone sociology, are discussed below and in Hodgson (2001c).

3   The term 'synergy' comes from the Greek *synergos*. Before Ward (1903) it appeared in Maudsley (1887). More recently, Ansoff (1965), Haken (1977, 1983), Corning (1983), Maynard Smith (1989) and Maynard Smith and Szathmáry (1995, 1999) promoted it or its derivatives.

of the first to use it as a key theoretical concept. Ward himself quoted the following translation from Wundt (1895, vol. 2, p. 274):

> There is absolutely no form which in the meaning and value of its content is not something more than the mere sum of its factors or than the mere mechanical resultant of its components.

This would be a particularly strong version of emergence, because it suggested that emergent properties are present in *any* combination of components. Most emergentist philosophers did not go this far. Wundt also inspired the vitalist biologist Hans Driesch, who also used the term 'creative synthesis' in works published in German from 1903 (Driesch, 1908, vol. 2, pp. 82, 169, 238). Durkheim also cited Wundt in his works, and it can thus be conjectured that Durkheim's prototypical concept of emergence was also drawn from this German well.[4]

Ward devoted a whole section of his book to 'creative synthesis'. Ward (1903, pp. 79–96) argued at length that components or forces when brought together could lead to phenomena with novel properties. He deployed this argument to the emergence of consciousness in the higher organisms and the creation of human social structures. For Ward (1903, p. 237): 'Progress results from the fusion of unlike elements.'

In a related context, Ward attempted to improve upon the famous taxonomy of the sciences pioneered by Comte. Comte arranged the sciences according to their perceived degree of generality. His classification moved from the most general to the particular and concrete. Mathematics was regarded as the most general science, followed by astronomy, physics, chemistry, biology and sociology. Ward (1903, p. 124) criticized Comte because he 'had no idea of creative synthesis'. Comte's positivism kept him away from all such metaphysical speculation. Instead, for Ward, the hierarchical arrangement of the sciences should relate to levels of reality, each level involving new resultants from the creative syntheses of their constituent elements at a lower level. As Ward (1903, p. 90) put it: 'The natural order of the sciences is due to the fact that the more complex phenomena of the higher sciences are the creative products of phenomena of a lower order.'

Hence Ward used his concept of creative synthesis to develop a hierarchical ontology. This was one of the very first moves in this direction. At its simplest, Ward (1903, p. 94) proposed four ontological layers: the physical, the vital, the psychic, and the social. The physical involved matter. The vital concerned living organisms, involving vital properties that were not found in matter in general. The next level, the psychic, addressed organisms with nervous systems sufficiently developed to give rise to

---

4   Wundt (1895) also used the term 'critical realism'. See the discussion of this term below. Wundt was also a forerunner of the *Gestalt* theory of the early 1900s, represented by Wertheimer, Köhler and Koffka. Instead of individual sensations, they saw people as perceiving an 'emergent whole'.

consciousness. The social level applied to the properties of structures of interacting conscious organisms. The domain of sociology was at this fourth level. It addressed additional properties not found at the lower levels.

Nevertheless, while sociology considered properties created at the highest level, those properties were a result of the creative synthesis of elements at lower levels. Hence the sciences 'grow out of one another' (Ward, 1903, p. 96) instead of each science being entirely separate. Ward (1903, p. 101) thus wrote of the 'biologic origin of the subjective faculties' and also insisted that 'sociology must have a psychologic basis'.

Clearly, the concept of creative synthesis was not confined to human society. Creative syntheses occurred throughout nature and before the existence of humankind. These outcomes were not designed. Concerning human society, the social order could have undesigned effects as well as planned results, resulting from the creative synthesis of individual interactions. In sociology, Ward (1903, p. 186) thus made 'the distinction between natural and artificial, or between spontaneous and factitious institutions'. But he immediately added: 'although really one class is as natural as the other, and both are partly spontaneous and partly factitious'. Ward (1903, p. 188) used the example of language: 'Language is among the earliest of human institutions, and was certainly spontaneous.'

Redolent of the earlier work of Carl Menger (1871), Ward stressed both designed or 'factitious' institutions, on the one hand, and 'spontaneous' or 'autogenetic' institutions, on the other. As indicated in the previous paragraph, Ward's important emphasis on spontaneous institutions derived principally from his concept of creative synthesis. However, unlike Menger, he emphasized that all institutions were themselves partly made up of constructed as well as spontaneous elements. Furthermore, unlike many latter-day members of the Austrian school, he did not regard the existence of spontaneous orders as an excuse for minimizing government intervention in the economy. Ward (1883, 1893, 1903) persistently argued that social and economic evolution, if left on their own, would generally produce suboptimal results. He thus provided grounds for judicious government intervention. Ward (1903) also explained at length that structures and institutions were not merely constraints, but their solidity provided an essential springboard for dynamic behaviour.

In sum, in a highly significant prefiguration of the concept of emergence, Ward allied his concepts of 'creative synthesis' and 'synergy' within a hierarchical ontology. He thus created the basis for social sciences that were connected to biology and psychology, as well as addressing social properties and structures that could not be reduced to psychological or biological terms alone. Foremost among the structures of human society were social institutions, which arise partly through spontaneous and undesigned processes. But these emergent outcomes were rarely optimal, suggesting grounds for government intervention.

The potential importance of Ward's work for the subsequent development of institutional economics was enormous. Ward had begun to provide the material to fill some major gaps in the foundations of institutional economics as developed by Veblen. Tragically, however, Ward's work was not given the attention it deserved, and after the First World War it fell into neglect.

Ward and Veblen communicated: but no creative synthesis

In his review of Ward's *Pure Sociology*, Veblen (1903, p. 655) described himself as 'one who is not himself a lifelong specialist in the science' of sociology, and saw Ward's work as having a limited potential impact for economics. This betrayed more about Veblen than it did about Ward. Ward's sociological volume is relatively philosophical in content. Hence Veblen's remarks suggest a lack of involvement in developments in both philosophy and sociology, at least after the turn of the century. Despite his fruitful philosophical training, Veblen cited few philosophers other than Kant. In addition, despite the fact that Veblen today is widely – if misleadingly – described as a 'sociologist' or 'economic sociologist', he showed only a marginal interest in the emerging discipline of sociology. Veblen cited a few anthropologists, but Ward was the only major sociologist to receive a significant mention in his writings.

A striking fact emerges from an analysis of Veblen's citations of other authors. After 1914 he cited relatively few new works. Veblen's citations show that his years of magnificent productivity – from 1896 to 1909 – drew largely on the great intellectual store that he had built up in the 1880s and 1890s. In those years, personal difficulties impelled him into writing, but after he brought out his ideas he did not fully replenish his intellectual warehouse. Veblen's 1903 review of Ward's book is the first clear indication of a man dangerously out of touch with developments in fields that were close to his own. In later years this deficit would become more evident. In the works that followed *The Instinct of Workmanship* (Veblen, 1914) he made fewer citations of the works of others, and he often repeated his earlier ideas. In the last sixteen years of his life, Veblen lost touch with the pulse of intellectual life and with the new ideas that were closest to his own specialisms and achievements. This was to have deleterious consequences not only for his own intellectual progress but also for institutional economics as a whole. If Veblen had made more of key developments in philosophy and the social sciences, then he would also have prepared the ground for his followers, of which fortunately, and with justification, there were many. Any reconstruction of institutional economics must connect with the developments in philosophy that – although Veblen and his followers largely neglected them – are vital to complete the Veblenian foundations.

Social evolution: Arthur Cecil Pigou

For completeness, we review two further contributions to the theory of socio-economic evolution, which appeared subsequent to Veblen's breakthrough in this field in the late 1890s. First, in an entirely forgotten paper, the young Arthur Pigou addressed social evolution and welfare in the light of the rediscovery of Mendelian genetics. Against his Cambridge teacher Alfred Marshall, he abandoned the Lamarckian doctrine of acquired character inheritance in biology. Pigou (1907, p. 360) wrote: 'the *original properties* of a child are not likely to be affected to any important extent by the circumstances in which the parents' lives have been passed'. Pigou (1907, p. 361) then pointed out that there was a difference between (what we now call) genotype and phenotype, the former being unaffected by acquired characters of the latter: 'The entity which biology declares to be unaffected by ancestral environment [genotype] is a different entity from that to which the concept of progress applies [phenotype].'

Significantly, Pigou (1907, p. 361) proposed then that evolution proceeded along two tracks. He referred to 'processes of evolution' in both 'the physical world' and 'the world of ideas'. With this acknowledgement of dual inheritance, Pigou (1907, p. 362) argued: 'Changes in ancestral environment start forces which modify continuously and cumulatively the conditions of succeeding environments, and through them the human qualities for which the current environment is in part responsible.' Hence the evolution of the social environment could bring about significant improvements in individual human phenotypes without changes in their genotypes.[5]

For Pigou this conclusion had important policy implications. After Weismann undermined Lamarckism in biology, some eugenicists argued that welfare provision could be wasteful because the evolution of society could only proceed on the basis of the evolution of the gene pool, and improvements in the social environment would not significantly improve the genetic stock. Pigou countered this argument with his dual inheritance theory. Although the social environment could not significantly affect genotypes, it could have major effects on human phenotypes: 'Progress – not merely permanent, but growing – can be brought about by methods of social reform with which breeding and gametes have nothing whatever to do' (Pigou, 1907, p. 362).

For reasons akin to those of Ritchie and Veblen, and similarly prompted by the developments brought about in biology by Weismann and others, Pigou thus broke from the biological reductionism that persisted in the minds of several Lamarckians, including Marshall. Marshall was not against social reforms, but he believed that they also worked directly on the genes (or gametes) as people acquired beneficial characters. Pigou

---

5   Pigou did not cite the similar but fuller arguments of Ritchie or Veblen.

made the reformist policy inclinations of Cambridge economics consistent with sounder biological principles. This was an opening for a post-Darwinian economics in Cambridge. But alas, this post-Darwinian road was not taken.[6]

Social evolution: James Mark Baldwin

James Mark Baldwin obtained a first degree and doctorate from Princeton in the 1880s. He subsequently emerged as a leading figure in experimental psychology, being one of the first to apply Darwinian principles to associative learning. He was a founding member of the American Psychological Association in 1892 and its sixth president in 1897. He taught psychology at Toronto (1889–1893), Princeton (1893–1903) and Johns Hopkins (1903–9). He met Conwy Lloyd Morgan in New York in 1896, where they discovered they had simultaneously elaborated the argument now known as the 'Baldwin Effect'.

Caught up in a personal scandal after the police arrested him with an African–American woman during a raid on a Baltimore brothel – thus breaking multiple taboos within contemporary US society – Baldwin had to leave the USA in 1909. He briefly held a post at the National University of Mexico, and took up residence in Paris in 1910. His landmark work on mental development in children included, for the first time in psychology, experiments with children, including his own daughter. His work on child development greatly inspired Jean Piaget, among others. Baldwin was one of the first experimental psychologists to apply Darwin's theory of evolution to his theories of development (Boakes, 1984; R. Richards, 1987; Murray, 1988).[7]

In his *Darwin and the Humanities* (1909), Baldwin attacked Spencerian and vitalistic theories of evolution and characterized Darwinism as the imposition of causal and law-like explanations. Addressing the evolution of societies, Baldwin (1909, p. 44) saw groups as possible units of selection. In similar terms to Morgan, George Henry Lewes and others, he saw the 'absorption of the social tradition' as a key mechanism of social evolution (Baldwin, 1909, p. 52). He thus hinted at the wider application of Darwinian principles. Baldwin (1909, p. 55) wrote that 'Darwin struck upon a law of universal application in nature'. Like Walter Bagehot, William James and Thorstein Veblen, he acknowledged the possibility of a natural

---

6   In 1908, at the age of 30, Pigou was appointed as Marshall's successor to the chair of economics at Cambridge. I have argued elsewhere that his huge generational leap was significant in depriving the small Economics Department in Cambridge of sufficient knowledge of past traditions in social science, thus reinforcing the insularity of the Cambridge tradition in economics (Hodgson, 2001c, pp. 109–12).

7   Piaget retained the idea that the intellectual development of the human child was an interaction between inherited cognitive predispositions and its environment – describing his view as 'genetic epistemology' – during the decades when others maintained a hermetic divide between biology and psychology.

selection of ideas as the grounding of an evolutionary epistemology. One of Baldwin's key innovations was to extend the theory of natural selection to the theory of human development and learning.[8]

Baldwin considered the basis of social integration and solidarity, and emphasized the importance of self-reflective behaviour at the social level. But although he saw social groups as possible units of selection, he had no developed notion of institutions or social structures. Essentially he applied Darwinism to the natural but not to the social world. Unlike Veblen, Baldwin (1909, p. 83) was an enthusiast of 'a thorough-going positivism of method' and intimated a dislike for 'metaphysical' speculation while sometimes unwittingly indulging in it himself. From this stance he was not receptive to the emergentist philosophy of Morgan and others, and did not see the road it opened to a multiple-level selection theory. Overall, Baldwin's contribution to the Darwinian theory of social evolution was less important than that of Ritchie or Veblen.

'New realism' and 'critical realism' in America

Major developments took place in American philosophy in the second decade of the twentieth century. They are briefly reviewed here to show their connections with the growing emergentist philosophy and their importance for institutional economics. A major event was the declaration of six young realist philosophers, mostly from leading university departments of philosophy. Edwin B. Holt, Walter T. Marvin, W. P. Montague, Ralph Barton Perry, Walter B. Pitkin and Edward Gleason Spaulding published their 'program and first platform' in 1910. Therein they vigorously attacked idealist philosophy and asserted that a reality exists, independently of any knowledge we may or may not have of that reality (Holt *et al.*, 1910). This sparked a lively debate in the leading philosophical journals, which helped to invigorate the realist tradition in American philosophy.

The American 'new realists' were influenced by pragmatism. John Dewey immediately responded to the 'program' of the six realists, expressing several points of agreement and a few of disagreement. Dewey (1910b, pp. 553–4) wrote: 'so far as realism means anti-idealism, I agree with it ... knowledge always implies existences prior to and independent of their being known'. However, Dewey differed from the six realists over their use of the concept of 'external relations'. This led to a set of responses and rejoinders, particularly involving Dewey and Spaulding. Eventually these

8 Baldwin is thus celebrated today as a precursor of 'Universal Darwinism' (Plotkin, 1994, pp. 64–6). However, as noted above, the idea of applying Darwinian principles to non-biological evolving systems, given the existence of replication, variation and selection, dates from Darwin himself and is also found in the nineteenth-century works of Bagehot (1872), James (1880), Alexander (1892), Drummond (1894), Ritchie (1896), Veblen (1899a) and others. Ritchie and Veblen went much further than Baldwin by stressing the selection of social institutions.

two authors were able to express their joint agreement on a number of key points (Dewey and Spaulding, 1911).[9]

Subsequently, Spaulding (1912) published a critique of the dualist philosophy of Henri Bergson (1911). Herein Spaulding developed a theory of the relation between parts and wholes that was essential to the forthcoming emergentist philosophy. He argued that wholes might be found to have properties that are not possessed by their component parts. This suggested an ontology involving different levels of reality, each with distinguishing properties. Spaulding's 1912 statement attracted attention partly because of his association with the lively debates concerning the 'new realism'. Heavily influenced by Driesch, Spaulding (1906) quoted Driesch's concept of 'creative synthesis' and his discussion of how wholes may acquire properties that are not contained in their parts. Just as Ward had brought the German concept of 'creative synthesis' into American sociology, Spaulding did the same, three years later, for American philosophy. Spaulding subsequently repeated this term and continued to argue that an organization of parts has characteristics that are qualitatively different from the characteristics of the parts alone.

Spaulding's work was quickly taken up by Morgan and others (Blitz, 1992, pp. 86–8). Another of the six 'new realists' to influence Morgan and make a major contribution to the development of emergentism was Walter Marvin, who was strongly influenced by Bergson and emphasized chance and spontaneity in nature. Although his hierarchical ontology was no overall advance on that of Ward, Marvin (1912, pp. 143–4) introduced the general idea of an ontology of layers into American philosophy.

A second important development in American philosophy occurred independently at about the same time. Still in his twenties and even younger than Marvin and Spaulding, Roy Wood Sellars (1908, 1916) introduced the term 'critical realism' into Anglophone discourse. The term had also been used in German by Wundt (1895). In his version of critical realism, Sellars promoted a non-reductionist scientific naturalism. He opposed naïve and empirical realism, believing that reality could not be appraised directly through our senses. He developed a layered and structured ontology and defended realism against various forms of positivism. Sellars (1918) also borrowed from Wundt and Ward the term 'creative synthesis', employing it extensively in his later writings. This was essentially a concept of emergence by another name. Sellars attracted a group of critical realists, including George Santayana and Arthur Lovejoy. Some of these philosophers were influenced by pragmatism (Drake *et al.*, 1920).[10]

By the 1920s, Sellars (1922, 1926) had embraced evolutionary ideas and was engaged in substantial discussions with the British emergentist

---

9   See Tiles (1988, ch. 6) for a discussion of Dewey's distinctive brand of realism.
10 R. W. Sellars taught at the University of Michigan and was the father of Wilfred Sellars, another famous American philosopher.

philosophers including Samuel Alexander and Conwy Lloyd Morgan. Another crucial link was made between two allied traditions of philosophical realism, both crucial for the development of post-Darwinian, evolutionary or institutional economics. In that same decade, emergentist philosophy burst into flower. This development is briefly summarized in the next section, focusing on the key elements that are necessary for a post-Darwinian theory of socio-economic evolution.

The flowering of emergentist philosophy

The ideas that stimulated emergentist philosophy flowed from Wundt and Driesch in Germany, from Bergson in France, and from Lewes in England, to sociologists Giddings and Ward in America, to the American new realist philosophers, and back across the Atlantic to Morgan in Bristol.

Also inspired by the emphasis on creativity and novelty in Bergson's (1911) theory of evolution, Morgan worked to incorporate these elements, while rejecting Bergson's dualist ontology and his vitalist doctrine of spontaneity. 'It was in the crucial year of 1912 that Lloyd Morgan completed the intellectual journey that resulted in the theory of emergent evolution' (Blitz, 1992, p. 92). Further influenced by both Marvin and Spaulding, Morgan (1913) proceeded to develop a three-layered ontology, involving the physico-chemical, the organic and the mental. In this hierarchy, the higher levels were grounded on those below, but involved novel and qualitative emergent properties, resulting from a creative synthesis of lower-level elements. The crucial stage in this confluence of ideas was the combination of emergent properties with a layered ontology. What was most important about Morgan's contribution was his placement of these ideas in the context of a Darwinian evolutionary process involving the creation of qualitative novelties. A theory of emergent evolution was born.

Both Morgan and Sellars had a friend and correspondent in the Australian-born philosopher Samuel Alexander, who was for many years a professor of philosophy at the University of Manchester in England. Alexander (1920) published his own major treatise on *Space, Time and Deity*, and therein acknowledged Morgan's priority in the development of its core emergentist ideas. Subsequently, Morgan (1923, 1926) set out a full account of his theory of emergent evolution in two volumes. A vital part of his argument was an attempt to merge the idea of qualitative novelty in evolution with the aforementioned Darwinian 'doctrine of continuity'. Both materialist monism and the motto *natura non facit saltum* had to be reconciled with a theory of creative evolution, but without uncaused causes or implausible saltationist breaks.

Morgan took the term 'resultant' from Lewes to describe general combinations of effects that were the necessary but not sufficient grounding for emergence. Emergent properties were special resultants, involving properties that were not predictable from the constituent parts. Morgan also employed the term 'supervenience' to denote the possibility of elements at a higher level affecting those at a lower. Emergents were not mere epiphenomena; they could themselves have a causal role that was extended to parts at a lower level. This idea was much later described as 'downward causation' (Sperry, 1964, 1969, 1976, 1991; D. Campbell, 1974b). Accordingly, Morgan believed that organic matter could affect its physico-chemical elements. But it was unclear how causal powers at one level could affect elements at another level.[11]

Morgan (1923, p. 6) defined emergence in terms of limits to prediction: 'What ... one cannot predict ... is the emergent expression of some new kind of relatedness among pre-existent events.' As David Blitz (1992, p. 99) has observed, 'the predictability of knowledge was an epistemological consideration, while the status of novelties as reducible or emergent was ontological'. Morgan overlooked the possibility that some properties might be unpredictable today, yet predictable by the science of tomorrow. The supposed emergent properties might become explicable or predictable in terms of lower level elements, and by definition they would no longer be emergent. Consequently, emergent properties would no longer be permanent characteristics of reality but mere symptoms of the underdevelopment of science.

There were further problems in Morgan's account. In his attempt to reconcile the doctrine of continuity with the emergence of novelty, Morgan moved away from Darwin's strictly non-teleological notion of causality, to revert almost to a pre-Darwinian notion of evolution as an 'unfolding' of pre-given forms (Morgan, 1923, p. 111). Darwin's conception of causality was displaced by a teleological notion of immanence or preformation, and relatively less explanatory weight was put on Darwinian processes of selection. Outcomes were seen as there at the beginning, hidden and compacted, but to be unfolded in a display of emergent novelty. This gave his emergentist philosophy a distinctly teleological and pre-Darwinian flavour.[12]

One reason for Morgan's rehabilitation of teleology was his preoccupation with theology. In terms similar to those of Alexander (1920), Morgan desired to place God in his emergentist scheme. For these two British philosophers, the ultimate emergent property was the Deity. God was at the apex of the ontological hierarchy, as the supreme and transcendent

---

11 Note that Morgan's use of the term 'supervenient' was very different from that of Kim (1978, 1993) and others who have used it to denote the situation where the identity of two or more entities at the macro level does not assume identity at the constituent micro level, but identity at the micro level does guarantee identity at the macro level (Kincaid, 1998b). For example, identical structured sets of individuals may produce the same social outcomes, but identical social outcomes are not necessarily produced by identical structured sets of individuals. In contrast to Morgan and Wheeler, Kim and others saw the modern concept of supervenience as an alternative to emergentism.

12 In an early essay, Morgan (1896c) had symptomatically denied that natural selection was the chief factor in explaining human evolution.

property of mind. For Alexander and Morgan, the very unpredictability of emergence was the mark of God, and evidence of insurmountable limits to scientific enquiry. For them, the ultimate understanding of emergent properties had to be in theological rather than scientific terms. God was 'the ultimate philosophical explanation, supplementary to scientific interpretation' (Morgan, 1923, p. 9).

Morgan wished to retain mind as the scientific ultimate, and theological penultimate, under God. Three decades earlier Morgan (1896a, p. 340) had considered 'social evolution ... by storage in the social environment to which each new generation adapts itself'. Yet he had never developed this prescient and inspiring insight into a notion of emergent properties and causal powers at the social level. God had stood in the way. For Morgan, mind instead of society had to be ontologically supreme, to prepare the ground for the omniscient and omnipresent mind of the Creator. In a single essay Morgan (1919) briefly considered social evolution in emergentist terms, but was reluctant to take this further. The development of the idea of society as possessing emergent properties and causal powers that were not reducible to its individual members was left to others in the emergentist tradition.

However, Morgan's combination of emergent properties with a hierarchical ontology, while emphasizing the evolution of novelty, was an outstanding achievement. It provided the means to transcend both the ontological dualism of the vitalists and the reductionism of the mechanistic materialists. In the same way it prepared the philosophical ground for a sociology and an economics that were based on material reality but not entirely reducible to its terms. It is only through the adoption of some version of emergence, as pioneered by Lewes and Morgan, that meaningful and irreducible social sciences are possible. In this respect Morgan was unaware of the full significance of the philosophy that he had created, or of the next steps required to make an adequate social science possible.

Understandably, Morgan's theological gloss on emergentist philosophy provoked a reaction to emergentism by atheistic and agnostic philosophers, including Bertrand Russell (1927, 1931). It is also possible that some American institutional economists were put off by the appearance of God behind a Darwinian mask. Following the precedent of Alfred Russel Wallace, Morgan revived a form of mysticism within what was supposed to be Darwinism.

An important attempt to rescue emergentist philosophy from theology was made by the English philosopher Charlie Broad (1925), who emphasized that organic and mental properties were determined by the organization of matter, and no extra vitalistic or spiritual qualities were required. Broad was the first explicit philosopher of emergent properties to adopt a consistently materialist ontology. Broad's (1925, p. 61) superior definition of emergence is worth considering here:

Put in abstract terms the emergent theory asserts that there are certain wholes, composed (say) of constituents *A*, *B*, and *C* in a relation *R* to each other; that all wholes composed of constituents of the same kind as *A*, *B*, and *C* in relations of the same kind as *R* have certain characteristic properties; that *A*, *B*, and *C* are capable of occurring in other kinds of complex where the relation is not of the same kind as *R*; and that the characteristic properties of the whole *R(A, B, C)* cannot, even in theory, be *deduced* from the most complete knowledge of the properties of *A*, *B*, and *C* in isolation or in other wholes which are not of the form *R(A, B, C)*. The mechanistic theory rejects the last clause of this assertion.

Broad steered emergentist philosophy away from God and towards a concept of relations or structures. Broad placed the burden of explanation of emergent properties on the role of relations or structures in combining together elements in different ways. Accordingly, mind had to be understood as a property emerging from the (complex) organization and causal interaction of neural matter. Both the matter and its structural organization were of importance. Social structures were understood as having emergent effects and causal powers. However, just as Broad steered British emergentism back towards materialism, emergentist philosophy was overwhelmed by a number of attacks, principally from positivists. Consequently, Broad's (1925) book represents the last major work in the British emergentist tradition (McLaughlin, 1992; Horgan, 1993).

There was a colloquium on emergentist philosophy within the Sixth International Congress of Philosophy, held at Harvard University in September 1926. Representatives of American pragmatism, American critical realism and German philosophy of psychology met at Cambridge, Massachusetts. Participants included Dewey, Driesch, Lovejoy, Sellars and Whitehead. The proponents of 'emergent properties' and of 'creative syntheses' compared and merged their ideas.[13]

The Harvard entomologist William Wheeler (1926, 1928) made a significant contribution at this colloquium. Wheeler referred to Lewes, Wundt, Morgan, Spaulding, Sellars, Broad and *Gestalt* psychology. His stance as a philosophically-inclined entomologist prompted him to consider the meaning and properties of the social, not only among social insects but also with regard to human societies. Criticizing sociology for avoiding this issue, Wheeler (1926, pp. 435) proposed that 'there is a much greater wealth of emergents at the social level than is commonly supposed' and 'the peculiarities of social emergence bear an interesting analogy to those of mind'. Wheeler (1926, p. 437) thus argued that 'the social is a correlate as well as an emergent of all life in the sense in which Morgan speaks of mind as being both a correlate and emergent of life'. Like Broad, Wheeler (1926,

---

13 A. Whitehead moved in 1924 from London, England to take up a chair in philosophy at Harvard University. Whitehead (1926, p. xxiii) noted his debt to Morgan (1923) and Alexander (1920).

p. 438) attempted to steer emergentist philosophy away from theology: 'I fail to understand why Alexander and Morgan select deity as the supervenient level next to mind, since their general scheme of emergent evolution most naturally demands the social as the next level in ascending order.'

In embracing emergent properties at the social level, Wheeler did not endorse social or vital forces that were separate from the individuals involved. Considering all forms of organization or structure, Wheeler (1926, p. 438) emphasized 'that the organization *is entirely the work of the components themselves* and that it is not initiated and directed' by other forces, such as a deity or Bergson's *'élan vital'*.[14]

Although this account of emergents at the social level was sketchy and incomplete, and did not adequately elaborate the distinctive features of human societies, Wheeler was one of the first two advocates of emergentist philosophy to elaborate explicitly the social as an ontological level with its own emergent properties. A problem that Wheeler failed to notice, however, was that mind clearly has emergent properties – such as consciousness and self-reflectivity – which are not possessed by societies. This means that the ontological hierarchy has to be amended in a manner that acknowledges that some properties may be lost, as well as others gained, in the movement from lower levels to the higher.[15]

Significantly, Wheeler (1921, p. 64) at least once referred to Veblen. Ironically, the wheel had turned full circle. Years earlier, Veblen had come into contact with some of Morgan's proto-emergentist ideas, and with Ward's layered ontology and 'creative synthesis'. Yet Veblen was to eschew this cutting-edge philosophy, just as it produced some of its most impressive emergentist constructions. Wheeler's citation of Veblen was an echo of earlier links, which to the disadvantage of institutional economics had been all but forgotten.

Another emergentist philosopher to establish a social level in a layered ontology was Sellars (1926). Here for the first time he also adopted the Lewes–Morgan terminology of emergence. Sellars (1922, 1926) argued that emergent properties were functions of the increasing complexity of the structured organization of matter and had nothing to do with God or the supernatural. Sellars thus criticized the accounts of emergence by Alexander and Morgan for their theological trappings. While evolution conformed to the doctrine of continuity, emergence meant the creation of a hierarchy of different ontological levels. Each higher level was

14 See also Wheeler (1930, 1939). Wheeler's work on insects was a significant influence on the entomologist E. O. Wilson (1971, 1975). However, Wilson's work is marked by the desire to explain social phenomena largely in reductionist and biological terms.

15 In a paper published in the proceedings of the Sixth International Congress of Philosophy, Lovejoy (1927, pp. 25–6) distinguished between 'indeterminist' and 'determinist' theories of emergentism. Horgan (1993) argued that Broad and other British emergentists were 'determinists', in the sense that they saw emergents as subject to causal laws.

characterized by a greater complexity of organization and interaction of its component parts. This concept of complexity made God redundant. In terms very similar to Ward twenty years earlier, Sellars identified matter, life, mind and society as the four basic layers in his ontology.

What was also significant in this work was the confluence of the British and American versions of emergentism and the standardization of their terminology. Sellars (1959, p. 2) later related how in the early 1920s Alexander brought Sellars's (1922) book *Evolutionary Naturalism* to the attention of both Morgan and Whitehead. In response, Morgan (1927, pp. 302–9) inserted an appendix in the second edition of his *Emergent Evolution*, sympathetically discussing Sellars and his 'critical realism'.

In Sellars's (1927, p. 224) version of evolutionary naturalism there was a refusal to reduce the organism to 'a mere mechanical system'. Purposeful behaviour was an emergent and teleological form of causality in general: 'There are qualitatively different systems in nature with different modes of causality. This teleology is a characteristic feature of human organisms.' Sellars (1959, p. 1) persisted with the idea of 'levels of causality' resulting from a 'structural enlargement of the category of efficient causality' where 'the mode, or technique, of causality is tied in with pattern or organization'. Sellars thus saw reason and purpose as real, emergent forms of a single 'efficient causality' within an ontology that was materialist and monist.

Also in the 1920s a number of other emergentist, quasi-emergentist and emergentist-inspired schemes emerged, including those in the works of Jan Smuts (1926), John Dewey (1926) and George Herbert Mead (1932, 1934, 1938).[16] But unfortunately most contemporary institutional economists and social theorists neglected these emergentist developments.

The importance of emergentist philosophy

The promise of emergentist philosophy was the resolution of the problem of the relationship between the sciences, granting them all a degree of autonomy within a consistent whole, and without the complete reduction of any one science to another. By the 1920s, the social sciences had largely escaped from biological reductionism. But they required a philosophical framework through which they could still absorb suitable insights from other sciences, including from psychology and Darwinian evolutionary theory. Emergentism would allow the social sciences to avoid reductionism but still retain links with, and draw ideas from, biology and psychology. Emergentist philosophy held out the promise of conversation, consistency and coexistence between the social and the other sciences, but without reductionism.

For Veblenian evolutionary economics, the development of emergentist philosophy was crucial. Veblen tried to turn economics into an

---

16 See Blitz (1992) for a review of these and related contributions.

evolutionary science, in particular by importing the insights of Darwinism. At the same time, Veblen rejected biological reductionism, saw institutions as units of selection in social evolution, and elaborated a causal and explanatory discourse at the level of the social. The further development of this project required the philosophical resources of emergentism to help justify the analysis of causal powers at the social and individual levels, without wholesale reduction to biological terms. Veblen advanced his 'post-Darwinian economics' and surpassed biological reductionism, but this construction would remain in the air, unless its relationship with the sciences at lower levels could be established in terms of emergent properties.

A similar requisite applied to the social sciences as a whole. Without emergentist philosophy, both economics and sociology faced a number of unsatisfactory choices. One such option would be to build these social sciences directly on those insights and categories from human biology or psychology. If this option were taken, then there would be great difficulty in addressing emergent properties of institutions, cultures or socio-economic systems that did not fit readily into a biological or psychological matrix. Some prominent proponents of neoclassical economics, from Alfred Marshall to Gary Becker, have attempted versions of this reductionist approach.

Another unsatisfactory option would be to retreat into subjectivism, and reconstruct the social sciences in terms of the subjective choices of given individuals. The claimed advantage of this route, developed particularly by economists of the Austrian school, is that by taking the individual as given, the causal explanation of the individual is no longer required. The cost, however, is that all explanatory links between the social and economic, on the one hand, and the psychological and the biological, on the other hand, are ignored or broken. Hence the advantage of this route is illusory; it is achieved only through the partial abandonment of causal explanation. The core element of the individual is taken as given and no longer explained.

A third unsatisfactory option would be to attempt to overcome the individualistic and subjectivist biases of the first two approaches by shifting the entire analysis upwards to the social, cultural or socio-systemic level. Any psychological or biological roots to individual or group behaviour would be downplayed or ignored, to develop an analysis exclusively in higher-level terms. This was essentially the route taken by Talcott Parsons in sociology, and by Clarence Ayres and others in post-1945 versions of the original institutional economics. Without adequate explanation, the connecting ladders between the social and individual levels were pulled up. These connections were destroyed in the hubbub of attacks on instinct psychology and the vaguely defined bogey of 'Social Darwinism'. These approaches inverted individualistic reductionism by proposing another wholesale explanatory reduction to structural, cultural or similarly collective terms. One form of reductionism was replaced by another.

This methodological collectivism was later to meet its downfall. Its failure to incorporate an adequate emergentism caused sociology to flip from one extreme to another. Hence among the wreckage of Parsonian sociology in the 1980s, James Coleman (1990) led a whole cohort of sociologists back to methodological individualism and the second option above.

The fourth, more satisfactory option, for the social sciences in general and institutional economics in particular, involves emergentist philosophy. The consequences of the failure of institutional economics to accommodate and develop emergentist ideas in explicit terms are explored in some of the following chapters. Veblen's failure in this regard has been discussed already. It was in part a tragedy of timing. In many respects Veblen's ideas for a 'post-Darwinian' social science were decades ahead of their time. And Veblen died just three years after some emergentists had explicitly posited a social level in their ontological hierarchy, even if it had been foreshadowed before.

I argue in Chapter 14 below that Veblen's adoption of higher levels of analysis, with its unarticulated links with emergentist philosophy, had a major consequence in the interwar period. This was no less than the development of modern macroeconomics. Veblen's student, Wesley Mitchell, tried to justify an analytical focus on higher ontological levels; he tried to erect a partially autonomous macroeconomic level of analysis. This was an important consequence of the Veblenian legacy.

But unfortunately, explicit discussions of the concept of emergence (or of 'creative synthesis') by early institutional economists are extremely rare, involving about five authors. The first mention is in a philosophical essay by Morris Copeland (1927) that considered 'the part–whole relation'. Copeland (1927, p. 96) noted a 'renewed emphasis on the part–whole relation'. He mentioned the works of Bergson, Whitehead and the *Gestalt* school, and 'Lloyd Morgan's conception of an emergent as something more than the additive resultant of the constituents'. But Copeland did not refer to these ideas any further.

Copeland failed to embrace emergentism at a high point of its development because he was heading philosophically in a very different direction. Copeland (1927, p. 104) saw parts and wholes as not 'real in their own right' but 'mere constructs of convenience'. In seeing concepts as simply tools of thought, not as attempts to grasp or represent the essential structures and processes of reality, Copeland thus distanced himself from philosophical realism, which is a necessary but not sufficient condition for emergentist philosophy. Instead, Copeland argued in favour of predictive instrumentalism, where success in prediction is seen as the test and value of a theory, foreshadowing the famous stance of Milton Friedman (1953).

The remaining mentions of emergence by institutionalists or their sympathizers are equally underdeveloped. The New Zealand economist Ralph

Souter (1933) mentioned the concept of emergence in his doctoral dissertation at Columbia University.[17] Three years later, in his book on *Veblen*, the British institutional economist John Hobson (1936, pp. 215–6) wrote: 'Emergent evolution brings unpredictable novelties into the processes of history, and disorder, hazard, chance, are brought into the play of energetic action.' But he neither referred to any theorists of emergent evolution by name, nor developed these ideas.

For the maverick institutionalist Frank Knight (1948, p. 42) 'man ... seems the product of "emergent evolution," in which many new traits have been successively superimposed upon an extending series without, in the main, eliminating the earlier'. But he declined to develop this proposition much further, other than to mention emergent evolution again in a few places (Knight, 1948, p. 51; 1960, p. 43; 1964, p. 303). For Knight, the emphasis in his use of the term 'emergent evolution' was on the novelty and unpredictability of emergents, and less on the layered ontology, or on the Darwinian evolutionary context.

Finally, in his posthumously published book, John R. Commons (1950, p. 135) briefly cited the terms 'holism' and 'emergent evolution'. Commons rightly saw Jan Smuts (1926) as the originator of the term 'holism' and cited his works. However, without attempting to explain their meanings, Commons wrongly treated the concepts 'holism' and 'emergent evolution' as equivalents. He did not seem to be aware that Smuts had explicitly differentiated his concept of 'holism' (which had a meaning very different from prominent usages today) from the concept of emergence in the work of Morgan and others. For Smuts (1926, p. 321 n.) 'the character of wholeness, the tendency to wholes' was 'more fundamental' than 'emergence or creativeness'. Commons's misguided treatment of holism and emergence as equivalents betrayed a limited understanding of these philosophical terms.

That is all. With these small exceptions, the crucial developments in emergentist philosophy passed unnoticed by institutional economists. No institutionalist attempt was made to incorporate emergentism, at least until long after the Second World War. Most other economists and sociologists also ignored the concept of emergence, at least until the 1970s.[18] When the term has been used, it has rarely been probed or examined in detail. Its meaning was often garbled and unclear.[19] Especially lacking are considerations of past problems and debates surrounding emergentism. Social

---

17 See Hodgson (2001c) for a discussion of Souter's role and ideas.
18 The 1970s was the first decade with ten or more citations of the terms 'emergent property' or 'emergent properties' in articles in sociology journals in the JSTOR database. These terms are even more rarely cited in economics.
19 Parsons's (1937) muddled and misleading use of the term 'emergent property' is criticized in Hodgson (2001c). On the subsequent history of emergentism in sociology see Sawyer (2001).

science as a whole has been impoverished by its relative ignorance of both the philosophy of science and the history of ideas.

After 1926, emergentism came under increasing attack. It suffered the onslaught of positivism and endured a marginalized existence for many years. To his great credit, Sellars (1955, 1959) persisted with his approach, and witnessed the beginnings of its return to popularity in the postwar period. Sellars was one of the most important bridges between the classical era of emergentist philosophy and the post-positivist philosophy of today.

Veblenian institutionalism on emergentist foundations

To complete this chapter, I list the elements of a Veblenian-style institutionalism that incorporates emergentist philosophy, particularly in the non-theistic and materialistic (or naturalistic) versions of Broad, Sellars and others. The intention here is to indicate what might have been created if the opportunity had then been grasped, rather than to explore all the components rigorously and in depth. The first 19 features are explicit or implicit in Veblen's works (for detailed explanations see Chapters 4, 6, 7 and 8 above). To begin, Veblen's own institutionalism involved the following six negative positions:

1 A rejection of positivism and empiricism.
2 A rejection of regularity determinism.
3 A rejection of biological reductionism as unviable.
4 A rejection of methodological individualism as unviable.
5 A rejection of methodological collectivism as unviable.
6 A rejection of evolution as a teleological or necessarily optimizing process.

Veblen's institutionalism also adopted the following doctrines or principles:

7 The principle of universal causation or determinacy.
8 The Darwinian doctrine of continuity.
9 The Darwinian principle of cumulative causal explanation.
10 The extension of Darwinian principles to socio-economic evolution.
11 The principle of evolutionary explanation.
12 The principle of consistency of the sciences.
13 The temporal and ontological primacy of instincts and habits over reason.
14 The dependence of social structures upon individuals.
15 The dependence of individuals upon social structures.
16 The temporal priority of society over any one individual.

17 The possibility of reconstitutive downward causation.
18 Institutions as units of evolutionary selection.
19 Institutions as repositories of social knowledge.

However, the following important and connected elements were unclear, underdeveloped or absent in Veblen's works. They have been discussed in the present and previous chapters, and are vital for a Veblenian theoretical system rebuilt on emergentist foundations:

20 Population thinking, as a Darwinian ontological commitment.
21 An irreducible and layered ontology, including physical, vital, mental and social levels.
22 Emergent properties, associated with complexity of structure and causal interactions between dissimilar components.
23 Emergent properties as a source of novelty in evolution.
24 Consciousness and intentionality as irreducible emergent properties of the nervous system, its components and their interactions.
25 Human social interaction as involving extensive intersubjective interpretations of intention and meaning, leading to particular emergent properties of human society.
26 The possibility of spontaneous order or emergent self-organization in social and other systems.
27 The existence of important emergent properties at the level of social and macroeconomic structures.

Propositions 20–27 are not arbitrary additions to the preceding 19. For instance, proposition 20 is an essential component of the Darwinian perspective adopted by Veblen. Likewise, propositions 21 and 22 – involving emergent properties and a layered ontology – are an essential underpinning to other propositions, such as the rejection of reductionism inherent in propositions 3–5 above.

Despite the fact that propositions 20–27 were not developed adequately in Veblen's works, some of them found incomplete parallels in institutionalist writing. In particular, as explained in Chapter 14, the key contribution of Mitchell and others to the development of modern macroeconomics can be seen as a substantial move in their direction of proposition 27. In failing to embrace emergentist philosophy in the 1920s, institutionalist theory was significantly weakened. But institutionalism as a whole was far from dead or obsolete. Indeed, it was yet to reach the zenith of its influence.

12 The launch of institutional economics and the loss of its Veblenian ballast

There is the economic life process still in great measure awaiting theoretical formulation.

Thorstein Veblen, 'Why Is Economics Not an Evolutionary Science?' (1898b)

Prior to 1918, institutional economics had not emerged as an identifiable school of economic thought. Yet by that time, Thorstein Veblen's works had achieved an immense popularity in America. Among economists, Veblen was widely admired as an incisive thinker and a forensic critic of received wisdom. Citations in leading academic journals to Veblen's works increased substantially, including from core journals in economics, reaching a high frequency in the interwar period (see Table 18.1 below). Part of the enduring appeal of Veblen's works was his analytical treatment of the driving processes of American capitalism, from the rituals of consumption to the powers of technology. His underlying philosophical arguments and his fusion of economics with Darwinism received less attention. For many, Veblen was seen primarily as a critic of the existing order and a pioneer of a new American political radicalism. Although Veblen never provided a detailed policy analysis, and his political views were vague and covert in his writings, he also became an icon of radical economic reform. As the US emerged from the First World War and faced the tasks of economic revitalization, Veblen's iconic status was further enhanced.

The problem of social control

Rarely, if ever, is a school of economic thought formed by theory alone. Classical, Marxian, Keynesian and Austrian economics all had their distinctive policy agenda. Institutionalism found its policy stance in the desired 'social control' of the untamed forces of business, while promoting a government system of social welfare.

An early pioneer of the American concept of 'social control' was Edward Alsworth Ross. While at Johns Hopkins in the late 1880s and early 1890s, Ross was influenced by both the economist Richard Ely and the sociologist Lester Frank Ward. Ross married Ward's niece and dedicated his seminal work *Social Control* (1901) to Ward. He was in some respects an agrarian populist, but notably hostile to Chinese and Japanese immigration. Ross accepted a job in the 1890s at Stanford University. But his controversial views against oriental immigration and 'cheap labour' drew the disfavour of Jane Stanford – the university co-founder and benefactor – and in 1900 he was dismissed (Stern, 1946, p. 742). Ross was subsequently at the University of Nebraska (1901–6) and the University of Wisconsin (1906–37). *Social Control* was admired by US President Theodore Roosevelt and by institutional economists such as Richard Ely, Wesley Mitchell, Walton Hamilton and John Maurice Clark.

Ross (1901) argued that many social arrangements arise spontaneously 'without design or art'. He stressed the deep, undesigned and durable roles of custom, imitation and social power in preserving the social order. He believed that 'natural moral motives' were sufficient in many situations to give rise to social order, without the extensive use of the state or statute law. However, by contrast, in a relatively complex society, the 'natural' or spontaneous mechanisms of order were insufficient and unreliable: 'Men are therefore in chronic need of better order than the natural moral motives will provide' (Ross, 1901, p. 59). In a complex society, the inherited impulses and dispositions of humanity were insufficient to bring civilized order and further progress. Systematic controls were required to tame destructive and discordant human impulses. Ross thus pointed to the possibility of the disruption or breakdown of order.

A limitation of Ross's analysis was his underestimation of the role of culture in shaping human dispositions. Although instincts and 'natural moral motives' are important – and the extent of their importance is largely a matter of empirical investigation – they are always overlaid by culturally formed propensities and motives. Although Veblen too emphasized instincts, he differed from Ross in giving greater emphasis to this formative role of culture, and the superiority of Veblen's analysis in this respect was widely acknowledged.

In policy terms, Ross avoided the extremes of libertarianism and statism. Libertarians uphold that social order can always arise spontaneously, with little or no assistance from the state. They often regard the state as disruptive and dysfunctional. At the other extreme, statists see the state as the solution to many social or economic problems, including the maintenance of social order. Ross avoided these two extremes by simultaneously emphasizing the spontaneous mechanisms of social order and proclaiming their limits. Where spontaneous organization failed, the government had to step in. But at the same time, such intervention should acknowledge and rely upon the importance of custom and imitation. Like Ward, Ross used his analysis to justify a degree of government intervention.

Other leading American social theorists promoted similar ideas. Charles Ellwood was an admirer of Veblen and a colleague at the University of Missouri (Dorfman, 1934, p. 310). Ellwood (1912, pp. 355–61) followed Ross and Ward and adopted a distinction between a 'spontaneous' or 'natural' order, on the one hand, and a 'social order', on the other. He saw a 'spontaneous' order as underpinned by instinct, habit, custom and tradition. In contrast, a 'social order' was said to involve consciously formulated regulations and institutions, designed to ensure the conformity of the individual to the behaviour of the group.

These works appeared in the context of a progressive and reforming movement in the United States in the early decades of the twentieth century. By the outbreak of the First World War, there was a prominent group of leading social scientists arguing for welfare measures and some degree of state intervention in the American socio-economic system (A. Davis, 1967). This movement was given a major boost by the First World War. Successive US governments set up a number of research institutes to examine the 'social problem' and assess the deprivations of the American poor. An increasing number of academic social scientists were trained and recruited for statistically based social research. The growing links between government and university social scientists helped to develop and crystallize both economics and sociology as professions (Martindale, 1976; Bernstein, 2001). Conservative or laissez-faire ideas were relatively marginalized. In contrast, an interventionist policy spirit was ascendant in both economics and sociology. Such interventionist sentiments were sustained in the 1920s and 1930s (Barber, 1988).

In Britain, John Hobson (1896, 1902, 1914) had long been preoccupied with the development of the theoretical foundations of reformist and progressive government policies. In an extensive review of Hobson's *Work and Wealth* (1914), the American institutionalist Hamilton (1915, p. 568) applauded its preoccupation with planning and welfare:

> Hobson is concerned with a state of well-being that can be attained only by conscious effort. It must be reached by careful planning, not by the automatic operation of a let-alone principle. He is, therefore, compelled by his problem to set up an elaborate standard of social welfare, appraising in their complex mutual relations all the elements of a well-ordered social whole.

Hamilton (1915, p. 583) saw *Work and Wealth* as an important 'attempt to reduce the current social reform movement to a definitive theoretical statement'. Hamilton, like others at that time, saw the struggle for social reform as taking place in the realm of economic theory as well as in overt matters of policy. He saw a task of the economic theorist to draw out the 'theory implicit in progressivism' that would replace the individualistic assumptions of 'neo-classicism'.

Hence policy sentiments in the 1900–18 period formed an agenda for theoretical economics in America. In particular, the political agenda of 'social control' was said to require criticism of the individualist assumptions of neoclassical economics, investigations into the causes and cures of business cycles, and studies of industrial concentration and control. Significantly, by 1904, Veblen had addressed all these theoretical issues in his writings. He was thus an available figurehead for this growing movement of economists. In this policy-driven context, it is understandable (even if regrettable) that less attention was given to other important aspects of Veblen's work, including his philosophical arguments and his adoption of Darwinian evolutionary ideas.

Following Veblen: Wesley Mitchell and John Maurice Clark

Wesley Mitchell came to the University of Chicago in 1892 and graduated in 1896. In 1897, when he was a graduate student of Veblen, Mitchell was awarded a travelling fellowship to Europe. After studying in Halle, and with Carl Menger in Vienna, Mitchell returned to Chicago and obtained his PhD in 1899. Mitchell read the works of the German historicists and developed interests in monetary economics, psychology and business cycles. The influence of Veblen was uppermost and enduring.[1]

Mitchell taught as an instructor at Chicago from 1901 but left for the University of California at Berkeley in 1903. While criticizing the idea of 'rational economic man', Mitchell (1910) originally wanted to apply William McDougall's instinct theory to economics. Mitchell (1910, p. 201) wrote:

> More fundamental is the great problem of accounting for economic rationality itself. … As such it is the central problem of economics – not a solid foundation upon which elaborate theoretical constructions may be erected without more ado. Even if economists are justified in starting with this assumption, they are not justified in stopping before they have made it a problem. And when they treat it as a problem they will find themselves working back to habits, and from habits back to instincts.

Mitchell here repeated Veblen's Darwin-inspired imperative that the causal origins of rationality must eventually be explained. More

---

1 Mitchell was broad-minded enough to accept ideas from elsewhere, including from some works of the Austrian School. Mitchell (1917, p. 115) wrote: 'Austrian theory in general and Wieser's version in particular is agreeably realistic; it deals with human planning, not with mathematical abstractions.' But Mitchell (1917) went on to criticize Austrian theory for not having an adequate explanation of the psychological, institutional, cultural and historical factors that shape individual plans and aspirations.

specifically, Mitchell (1910, pp. 202–3) argued that depictions of economic rationality overlooked the cultural transmission of knowledge and over-estimated individual powers of understanding and analysis:

> it would be far beyond the power of any human brain to beat out of the tangled maze of experience, unassisted, more than an infinitesimal portion of the concepts which the civilized races have accumulated. ... By formal and informal education he is gradually taught to compre-hend and to use a more or less considerable fraction of those concepts which prevail ... Social concepts are the core of social institutions. The latter are but prevalent habits of thought which have gained general acceptance as norms for guiding conduct. In this form the social con-cepts attain a certain prescriptive authority over the individual. The daily use by all members of a social group unremittingly molds those individuals into common patterns without their knowledge, and occa-sionally interposes definite obstacles in the path of men who wish to act in original ways.

For Mitchell (1910, p. 216), economics had been misled into an abstract description of rational economic man. The real problem for economics was to understand the institutional and cultural contexts in which individual capabilities were moulded:

> its leading problem is to account for the actual human types which are found in every nation, by tracing the processes by which habits and in-stitutions have grown out of instincts, and by examining the fashion in which the new acquisitions and the old traits combine in controlling human conduct.

Mitchell then argued that the rational, calculative mentality was histori-cally specific; it was a product of the rise of a monetary exchange economy. As Allyn Young (1911, p. 415) commented, Mitchell had shown how 'the money concept itself has been an active factor in giving purpose, system and rationality to economic activity'. Mitchell sent McDougall a copy of his 1910 article. McDougall replied, but was sceptical that his ideas would be taken up by the economics profession (Tilman, 1996, p. 103 n.).

Nevertheless, the assault on 'rational economic man' and the campaign within economics for recognition of the insights of psychology continued. In a subsequent article on this theme, written from his new academic posi-tion in Columbia University, Mitchell (1914, pp. 1–2) lamented that econo-mists such as Vilfredo Pareto, Joseph Schumpeter and Philip Wicksteed had seen the 'proper policy' for economics as 'non-intercourse with psy-chology'. Mitchell then made an extensive case for the use of psychology, mentioning Sigmund Freud and drawing heavily on the works of Werner Sombart and Thorstein Veblen.

John Maurice Clark made another forceful plea for the study of psychology by economists. The third son of John Bates Clark was strongly influenced by Thorstein Veblen, John Hobson, Alfred Marshall, Charles Horton Cooley, John R. Commons and Wesley Mitchell (Hickman, 1975; L. Shute, 1996). While a professor at the University of Chicago, J. M. Clark (1918) published his article on 'Economics and Modern Psychology' in the *Journal of Political Economy*. It is a forgotten classic, with enduringly modern themes. Clark recognized that decision 'involves effort of attention'. Rational deliberation is costly and it is constrained by scarce human mental capacities. Clark (1918, p. 25) wrote:

> A good hedonist would stop calculating when it seemed likely to involve more trouble than it was worth, and, as he could not in the nature of the case tell just when this point has been reached, he would make no claim to exactness for his results.

This argument did not simply allude to the problem of the 'cost of information'. Clark also undermined the proposition of global rationality by showing that, because of imperfect information, even if the rational calculator had reached an optimum 'no claim to exactness' could be made. In several respects this discussion reminds us of the concept of 'bounded rationality' in the work of Herbert Simon (1957). Sidney Winter (1964, p. 264) likewise observed: 'There must be limits to the range of possibilities explored, and those limits must be arbitrary in the sense that the decision maker cannot *know* that they are optimal.' As Mark Pingle (1992, p. 8) put it: 'The paradoxical difficulty facing the consumer when optimizing is costly in that it is not possible to make an optimal choice and know that the choice made is optimal.' However, these modern engagements with the limits of rationality under conditions of limited brain capabilities and information do not acknowledge Clark's earlier account.

Clark (1918, pp. 23–4) recorded some precedents for the idea that choice and deliberation could be too burdensome, including a discussion in the work of Cooley. Cooley (1902, pp. 33–34; 1922, pp. 69–70) had written: 'The exhausting character of choice, of making up one's mind, is a matter of common experience. … An incontinent exercise of choice wears people out, so that many break down and yield even essentials to discipline and authority.' Clark also acknowledged that William James expressed similar ideas in his *Psychology* (1900, p. 431) when he noted that deliberation over complexities could be so taxing that we 'feel that even a bad decision is better than no decision at all'. Hence Simon's concepts of bounded rationality and satisficing behaviour find an earlier parallel in the work of an 'old' institutional economist.[2] Signalling the further influence of both

---

2   Although Simon (1996) had no recollection of reading Clark's (1918) paper before the present author sent him a copy in 1996, the founder of modern behavioural economics did acknowledge the likely influence of Cooley and James on his ideas.

James and Veblen, Clark (1918, pp. 26–7) also stressed the importance of habits in economic decision-making:

> But if human nature is so largely dynamic there remains one static element, namely, habit. And indeed it is only by the aid of habit that the marginal utility principle is approximated in real life, for only so is it possible to have choosing which is both effortless and intelligent, embodying the results of deliberation or of experience without the accompanying cost of decision which, as we have seen, must prevent the most rational hedonist from attaining hedonistic perfection. For habit is nature's machinery for handing over to the lower brain and nerve centers the carrying on of work done first by the higher apparatus of conscious deliberation.

In this passage Clark went much further than the commonplace observation that habit 'helps economize on the cost of searching for information' (Becker, 1992, p. 331). With his argument that 'it is only by the aid of habit that the marginal utility principle is approximated in real life', Clark proposed that even if agents were utility maximizers, then the capacity to maximize utility could only appear on the basis of previously acquired habits and capabilities. Habit precedes rational deliberation, and provides its necessary grounding.

As well as a common interest in psychology and its relevance for economics, both Clark and Mitchell made major contributions to the theory of business fluctuations. Mitchell's *Business Cycles* (1913) was an attempt to develop the empirical and theoretical grounding for the theory of business fluctuations in Veblen's *Theory of Business Enterprise* (1904). In another neglected essay, Clark (1917) introduced the acceleration principle into economic literature and anticipated the modern accelerator–multiplier theory of the business cycle. More famously, the multiplier–accelerator principle was later developed and formalized by Roy Harrod (1936) and Paul Samuelson (1939).[3]

To some degree, Clark and Mitchell saw the standard Marshallian apparatus of price theory as necessary for economic analysis.[4] They took it for granted that institutionalism had to make use of some Marshallian-type tools, while they criticized some of the more extreme or 'unrealistic' assumptions found in the neoclassical tradition, such as individual utility maximization, universal diminishing returns, static equilibrium, perfect competition or perfect information. Modified Marshallian notions of cost

---

3   Shackle (1967, pp. 264–6) noted Clark's contribution, but also pointed out that other authors had anticipated Clark with similar ideas, namely A. Aftalion in 1913 and C. F. Bickerdike in 1914. Fiorito (2001) has cast still more light on Clark's achievement in this area.

4   Marshall himself was much more of a subtle and dynamic theorist than he is sometimes caricatured. See Jensen (1990) and Niman (1998) for sympathetic interpretations.

are evident, for instance, in Clark's (1923) theory of 'overhead costs' (Fiorito, 2003). Regarding the neoclassical legacy, Veblen is often depicted as taking a contrasting and more iconoclastic position. However, in lectures delivered in 1926–7, Mitchell (1969, vol. 2, pp. 685–6) pointed out:

> Veblen himself at times makes casual, implicit use of orthodox economic theory. For instance, if the theorist looks ... in *The Theory of Business Enterprise* ... he will find Veblen explaining how a rise in prices at the beginning of a period of prosperity spreads from its source to other lines of industry ... In that discussion he is taking for granted that the reader ... understands the theory of prices as expounded in the ordinary text books ... in ordinary terms of supply and demand theory. In short, his theory of the expansion phase of business cycles runs in terms ... of changes of conditions of supply and demand.

Indeed, when Veblen (1892, 1893, 1905) analysed price levels he acknowledged the effects of supply and demand. He did not throw the concepts of supply and demand overboard. Veblen differed more strikingly from neoclassical economic theory in his rejection of concepts such as the utility-maximizing agent, and in his critique of a normal or natural level of profits, wages, prices or employment. J. M. Clark and Mitchell also rejected these ideas, but endorsed other aspects of Marshallian theory.[5]

The launch of institutional economics

In the summer of 1918, under the initiative of president Irving Fisher, the American Economic Association (AEA) set up a Committee on Cooperation in Economic Research with Walton Hamilton as its secretary and Allyn Young as its chairman. A primary aim was to address the key problems of economic development after the First World War. A prominent concern of this committee was to make economic theory relevant for postwar policy. In addition, Hamilton and others had planned to consolidate support within the Association for an economics more oriented to the realities of institutions, culture and psychology, and had adduced the support of Veblen and Mitchell for this project (Barber, 1988; Rutherford, 2000b).

On 11 November 1918, the armistice was signed that ended hostilities in the First World War. A few days later, in December, across the Atlantic, at the annual meeting of the AEA, the term 'institutional economics' was first used in a public forum. This was in a paper delivered by Hamilton (1919). The leading active promoters of institutionalism in the immediate post-

5   Similarly, Commons (1931, pp. 648, 656) admitted elements of orthodox price theory and made scarcity a central concept (Biddle and Samuels, 1998). Likewise, Hamilton (1923) criticized the idea of a natural 'law' of supply and demand but – especially when dealing with practical matters – Hamilton (1918, 1944) adopted a concept of scarcity and accepted without question that supply and demand affected prices.

1918 period were Hamilton, Clark and Mitchell. Joseph Dorfman (1974, p. 28) believed that 'Hamilton should be credited with having played the role of chief promoter'.[6]

Many American economists then rejected the idea of immutable economic laws that made government intervention nugatory. In his AEA presidential address to his colleagues, Fisher (1919, p. 21) proclaimed: 'It is given to us as to no previous generation of economists to share in fixing the foundations for a new economic organization and one which shall harmonize with the principles of democracy.' The consensus was that economics should be empirically grounded, rather than being a deductive exercise based on challengeable assumptions concerning human nature or market competition. It was in this distinctly post-classical, forward-looking and practically-minded context that institutional economics was born.

Henry Carter Adams and Charles Horton Cooley had taught Hamilton at the University of Michigan. He mentioned them, along with Veblen and Mitchell, as the 'leaders' of the emerging American institutional economics. Hamilton's (1919) institutionalist manifesto is important not simply as a historical document, but also as an incomplete working definition of the institutionalist approach at the point where it became widely influential.

In contrast to some modern misconceptions of the 'old' institutionalism as 'atheoretical' or even 'anti-theory', Hamilton (1919, pp. 309–11) argued that '"institutional economics" is "economic theory"'. It 'alone meets the demand for a generalized description of the economic order. Its claim is to explain the nature and extent of order amid economic phenomena'. He claimed that institutional economics alone could unify economic science by showing how parts of the economic system related to the whole. Institutional economics was not defined in terms of any normative stance. Hamilton declared: 'It is not the place of economics to pass judgements upon practical proposals' (1919, p. 313). However, part of its genuine appeal as a theory was the claim that it could be used as a basis for relevant economic policies.

For Hamilton (1919, p. 317) the 'most important' omission of neoclassical theory was its neglect of 'the influence exercised over conduct by the scheme of institutions under which one lives'. Hamilton saw institutional economics as filling this gap. The influence of institutions was not seen as merely constraining behaviour. The idea that institutions form and change individuals, just as individuals form and change institutions, was seen as a central tenet of institutionalism. Hamilton's 'bare outline of the case for institutionalist theory' accepted that 'institutional theory is in process' and stressed the pressing task of relevant, theoretical development.

Institutional economics, from Veblen to John Kenneth Galbraith (1958, 1969), has consistently emphasized some of Hamilton's themes. It has

---

6   Hamilton (1916, p. 863 n. 5) previously mentioned that Hoxie had described himself as an 'institutional economist' (McNulty, 1973; Rutherford, 1997, 2000b).

always striven for policy relevance. But, more fundamentally, it has also stressed the role of institutions in economic life, the qualitatively transformative nature of economic activity, and the way in which those institutional and structural changes both affect and reconstitute human purposes, preferences, psychology and behaviour.

Institutionalists do not have a very good record in defining and agreeing among themselves upon the essentials of their approach. I submit, however, that there is a core idea in institutionalism that above all others helps to define its identity. The idea that institutions can be reconstitutive of individuals is arguably the most fundamental characteristic of institutional economics. Obviously, institutions themselves differ, in time and in space. However, individuals themselves are also likely to be radically affected by these differences. Different institutions can act as more than constraints on behaviour: they may actually change the character and beliefs of the individual.

As a result, much of the 'new' institutional economics of Oliver Williamson (1975) and others is not 'institutional economics' in the stronger sense of involving the reconstitution of individual preferences by institutional circumstances. This is because most 'new' institutionalists cling on to an irreducible notion of the rational individual that Veblen, Commons, Mitchell, Hamilton and others were keen to replace or explain. Much of the 'new' institutionalism sees behaviour as 'the result of conscious endeavor by individuals who knew thoroughly their own interests'. But this is Hamilton's (1919, pp. 316–17) own characterization of the very type of economics that institutionalism sought to supersede. For Williamson, for example, the character and purposes of individuals do not change as they move from institution to institution, even from a caring family to a ruthless capitalist firm. In contrast, 'old' institutional economists stress that institutions and culture can mould individual preferences or purposes.[7]

Although he was very much concerned to develop institutional economics as an instrument for 'the problems of control', Hamilton did not define institutional economics in terms of any specific policy stance. In practice, institutionalism was adopted by policy-makers from a variety of policy viewpoints, from socialism through social democracy to moderate conservatism.

What is also worth noting at this stage is the extent to which Hamilton (1919, p. 316) emphasized the contributory importance of 'modern social psychology' to the understanding of human behaviour. More specifically, Hamilton criticized those economists that had 'overlooked … instinct and impulse'. Hence by 'modern psychology' Hamilton meant instinct–habit psychology. Similarly, at that time, the institutionalist Carleton Parker (1918) argued that economic behaviour had to be understood in terms of

---

7 However, there are signs of a shift in thinking among some new institutionalists. See, for example, North (1994, 1995).

inherited impulses and instincts. The institutionalist Lionel Edie (1922) also stressed the role of instincts in powering economic behaviour.

However, as explained below, even by 1918 the philosophical and psychological pillars of institutionalism were fractured by academic critics. Furthermore, within a few years, even among institutionalists, faith had been lost in the Veblenian research programme, and its attempt to place economics and the social sciences within an encompassing Darwinian and evolutionary paradigm. This early theoretical crisis within institutionalism in the interwar period was not obvious to everyone but it proved catastrophic for its future development. These problems were partly obscured by policy preoccupations. The 'problem of social control' and postwar reconstruction remained on the agenda, to be followed by the crisis of economic policy in the Great Depression of the 1930s.

Institutionalism permeated the teaching programmes of many American universities. By 1931, more than six comprehensive texts treating economics from an institutionalist standpoint were available, along with several other institutionalist monographs and anthologies. These texts emphasized the economic importance of institutions, that institutions could be changed by policy interventions, that any prevailing institution is not necessarily optimal, that many institutions serve business or pecuniary interests, and that new institutions were required for 'social control' in their era. On the policy front, J. M. Clark (1926) published his *Social Control of Business*, and several other institutionalist works addressed this theme (Rutherford, 2000b).

The subsequent careers of Hamilton, Clark and Mitchell are indicative, both of the high status accorded to institutionalism in the interwar period and of the priority given to economic policy and its statistical grounding. In 1924, Walton Hamilton was named Director of the new Brookings Graduate School, formed in tandem with the Institute for Government Research, in Washington, DC. In 1934, he was an influential member of the National Industrial Recovery Board. Clark served, for example, on the National Resources Board of the US Government in the 1930s. Mitchell's prestige was the greatest of the three, and his substantial influence on successive US governments is discussed below in Chapter 14.

From the early 1920s until the 1950s, institutionalists were involved in US government initiatives in the economy. Several were active in the inspiration, development and promotion of President Franklin Roosevelt's New Deal (Stoneman, 1979; Wunderlin, 1992; Schwartz, 1993; Barber, 1994, 1996; Bernstein, 2001). With the US entry into the Second World War in 1941, institutionalists participated with other economists in the government administration of the war economy. Galbraith served as the deputy administrator in the US Office of Price Administration. In 1946, the institutionalist Edwin Nourse was appointed by the Executive Office of the US President as the chair of the first-ever Council of Economic Advisors. He was followed in that position by two other institutionalists, Leon

Keyserling (from 1949 to 1953) and Arthur F. Burns (from 1953 to 1956). For a third of a century, institutionalism was not primarily a creed of marginalized dissidents, but in the forefront of professional activity and US government policy advice.

There was concordant recognition for institutional economists from the profession. Mitchell became AEA president in 1924. He was notably preceded in that position by John R. Commons in 1917 and Herbert Davenport in 1920, and was followed by several other institutionalists and their sympathizers, such as Allyn Young in 1925, Thomas Adams in 1927, Edwin Gay in 1929, J. M. Clark in 1935, Frederick Mills in 1940, Sumner Slichter in 1941, Edwin Nourse in 1942, Albert Wolfe in 1943 and several other institutionalists after the Second World War. Mitchell and J. M. Clark were the first recipients – in 1947 and 1952 – of the AEA Francis A. Walker Medal, awarded every five years 'to the living American economist who in the judgement of the awarding body has during his career made the greatest contribution to economics'. Simon Kuznets, who was Mitchell's former colleague at the National Bureau of Economic Research, won the Nobel Prize in 1971.

Veblen also received belated recognition from the establishment within the economics profession. In 1925, a petition with over two hundred signatories was circulated requesting the nominating committee of the AEA to select Veblen as President. The signatories included future AEA presidents Morris Copeland, Paul Douglas, Edwin Gay, Alvin Hansen, Frank Knight, Frederick Mills, Edwin Nourse, Sumner Slichter, Jacob Viner and Albert Wolfe. Veblen declined the honour (Dorfman, 1934, pp. 491–2, 553; Jorgensen and Jorgensen, 1999, pp. 169, 174, 261).

The banishment of biology

Veblen provided several unsystematized components of an incipient theoretical core for institutional economics as it emerged as a school after the First World War. Institutionalism became a broad and diverse movement, and not all of its members subscribed to such fundamental philosophical or psychological presuppositions. But, at the time, no prominent institutionalist advanced any rival or alternative set of core ideas to replace those provided by Veblen. Yet, as early as 1914, and in several different ways, these foundations were being undermined by major developments in American social science.

Movements in Western psychology and social science in the early twentieth century began to question the notion that there was any biological or instinct-based determination of human behaviour. Clearly, this would have major implications for Veblenian institutionalists who had embraced instinct–habit psychology and proposed the extension of Darwinian ideas to social science. This section discusses this breach between biology, on the one hand, and anthropology and sociology, on the other. The following section deals more directly with the implications for Veblenian institutional economics.

Some ideologically motivated scientists regarded variations in aptitude and behaviour as rooted largely or wholly in human biology, and drew racist, imperialist or sexist conclusions. In this context, liberal academia became increasingly disturbed by the ideological conclusions that were being drawn by some from biology. A major factor behind this shift of opinion was the First World War. Witnessing the greatest human slaughter in history, liberal and radical academics reacted against the prominent belligerent rhetoric of 'race struggle' and the 'survival of the fittest' (Nasmyth, 1916). A representative critic was Ralph Barton Perry, one of the aforementioned American 'new realists'. In his *Present Conflict of Ideals*, Perry (1918) argued that ideas of racial superiority and the natural status of conflict had been used to justify the war. Perry thus attacked all associations between biology and the social sciences. Darwinism was accused of a circularity of logic and a 'strong tendency to favor the cruder and more violent forms of struggle, as being more unmistakably biological' (Perry, 1918, p. 145). Others even more crudely blamed the war on a German militarism allegedly inspired by an amalgam of ideas from Nietzsche, Weismann and Darwin (Bannister, 1979, pp. 239–41). But Friedrich Nietzsche had no great affection for Darwinism, and the proposition that the scientific ideas of Weismann or Darwin can be used to justify German nationalism or militarism is totally unfounded.[8]

Franz Boas, a Jewish immigrant from Germany, was influential in debunking some of the pseudo-scientific ideas of the racists. Boas was motivated by liberal views and a strong anti-racism. In a number of careful and influential studies he showed that social and environmental conditions were as least as important as the genetic legacy in individual human development. Boas (1894) argued that if one race were more civilized than another, then we cannot conclude that their biologically inherited capacity for civilization was the greater. He saw culture and social environment as the major influence on human character, potential and intelligence. By the end of the First World War, a number of sociological and anthropological textbooks were in existence promoting Boasian views. Significantly, however, Boas did not deny that there were natural and genetic influences on human characteristics and behaviour. He just saw social culture as far more important. Boas's views on such matters were similar to Veblen's: together they stressed the causal roles of both culture and instinct.

Largely under the influence of Boas's research, a number of leading American sociologists and anthropologists became convinced of the importance of nurture over nature. But many went further than Boas. During the 1900–20 period, sociologists such as Charles Ellwood, Carl Kelsey and

---

8 The notion that Nietzsche inspired aspects of militarism or fascism still remains controversial (Golomb and Wistrich, 2002).

Howard Odum moved away from the idea that innate biological factors accounted for human behaviour, to the notion that human characteristics were entirely malleable and that the environment was the overriding influence. Leading American sociologists had abandoned the concept of instinct by the 1920s (Cravens, 1978).

Alfred Kroeber, a highly influential student of Boas, went much further than his teacher. In a number of articles published in the *American Anthropologist* between 1910 and 1917 he declared that social science should be separated, in both method and substance, from biology. For Kroeber, the Weismann barrier and the consequent decline of Lamarckism in biology somehow became an excuse for the separation of biology from the social sciences. In Kroeber's (1915, 1917, 1923) view, biological inheritance had no significant part in the history of humankind; independence from biology was indispensable for understanding the meaning and use of the concept of culture.

Indeed, the growing acceptance of Weismann's arguments had created difficulties for many anthropologists and sociologists. By ruling out the inheritance of acquired characters, it became evident that the genetic constitution of humankind had changed very slowly, as a result of natural selection only. Consequently, any social scientist inclined towards biological reductionism would have to presume that the progress of human civilization was equally slow. Those that adopted Weismann's conclusions would have a further choice, between *either* accepting multiple ontological levels and emergent properties (and explaining the more rapid evolution of culture and civilization on the lines suggested by David Ritchie, Conwy Lloyd Morgan, Thorstein Veblen and Arthur Pigou), *or* rejecting the links between biology and culture in their entirety. Partly because of the underdevelopment of emergentist philosophy and dual inheritance theories at that time, many such as Kroeber took the second choice. The first choice – also consistent with Weismannism – was not so clearly visible. Hence it became the view that anthropology and sociology should have nothing to do with any kind of biology. Culture was entirely separated from instinct. Any biotic influence on human characteristics and behaviour was ruled out. All biological analogies were deemed inappropriate, even dangerous, for social science.

Consequently, the ideas of Lamarckian sociologists such as Ward were attacked on two fronts. First it was pointed out that the Weismann results had discredited his Lamarckian biology. Second, Ward and others were attacked for maintaining links between sociology and biology. As Lamarckism became discredited, both the biology and the Lamarckism were jettisoned, even to the point of eschewing Darwinians such as Giddings and Cooley. As a result, these early American sociologists rapidly declined in influence, to be eclipsed by the rising 'non-biological' approaches in social science (Stocking, 1962, 1968; Cravens, 1978).

completely neglects Reform Darwinism and its discrediting.

Margaret Mead continued Kroeber's line of argument. In 1928, she published a classic plea for the supremacy of culture over biology in her *Coming of Age in Samoa*. By the 1920s, the views of Kroeber and Mead had become widely accepted by American social scientists. Ruth Benedict, a former student of Boas, later consolidated the victory with the publication in 1934 of the equally influential work *Patterns of Culture*.[9]

Even the existence of a sexual instinct in humans and other organisms came under attack. The influential University of California at Berkeley psychologist Zing Yand Kuo asserted that all sexual appetite was the result of social conditioning. In an extreme statement of the environmentalist position, Kuo argued that all behaviour was not a manifestation of inherited factors but a result of environmental conditioning or stimulation (Degler, 1991, pp. 157–9).

In the interwar period in America, links between the social sciences and biology were axed, and even biological metaphors became suspect (Cravens, 1978; Degler, 1991; Weingart *et al.*, 1997).[10] In the 1930s, with fascism rampant in Europe and in East Asia, those in liberal Western academia that continued to assert that biology could explain some differences in human behaviour lost the academic argument and became tainted by accusations of racism, imperialism and sexism. It was overlooked that the earlier links between sociology and biology had coexisted with a variety of views, from the laissez-faire individualism of William Graham Sumner to the radical egalitarianism of Ward. The effects of this intellectual shift were felt through the Western academic world.

Hostility to racism, imperialism, sexism or the abuse of science is commendable. But the existence of racist pseudo-science does not itself imply an absence of causal connections between nature and society, or between genes and human capabilities or behaviour. These causal connections are matters of scientific enquiry. A scientific position on these questions cannot be justified on ideological or normative grounds. Just as racists and sexists had allowed their ideology to mangle their science, some anti-racists or anti-sexists did the same. Ideology distorted science on both sides. The type of social science that eventually prevailed in liberal academia was much less obnoxious in ideological terms. But its theoretical explanations and causal stories were highly questionable and often lacked sufficient empirical corroboration (Degler, 1991).

There was a strong ideological motivation behind the shift of opinion among liberal American academics. These intellectual changes were much

---

9   See the powerful critique of M. Mead's work by D. Freeman (1983, 1992).
10 Earlier social scientists, such as Karl Marx and Émile Durkheim, had also limited the use of biology in their theories. In America, Patten (1894) attacked Ward's 'biologism' and in Britain, Spiller (1914) urged the removal of the 'Darwinian incubus' from sociology. However, Ward remained an influential figure until the 1920s, and other leading sociologists such as Hobhouse also retained links with biology. The sociological reaction against biology did not gain its full momentum until the 1920s.

to do with the ideological commitment of liberal Americans to individualism, democracy, personal liberty and equality of opportunity (Cravens, 1978; O'Donnell, 1985; Degler, 1991). At the time, this egalitarian ideology of the intelligentsia was confronted by a number of illiberal enactments by federal and state legislatures. For example, Chinese and Japanese immigrants into the US were virtually barred in 1882 and 1907 respectively. Eugenic sterilization laws were first enacted in Indiana in 1907 and followed by 1933 by twenty-nine other US states (Eggen, 1926). Eugenicists lobbied the US House Committee on Immigration and Naturalization for the exclusion of southern and eastern Europeans. The 1924 Johnson–Reed Immigration Act further restricted immigration into the US on ethnic criteria, largely favouring those from Northern Europe, while entirely banning others including the Japanese.

Liberal academia had something to campaign against, and many used their expertise to scrutinize the flimsy assumptions behind such racist legislation. Some went further, to deny that differences in biological characteristics were significant in explaining human behaviour. There was a particularly strong reaction within academic anthropology against its associations with biology (Stocking, 1968, pp. 297–9). However, the denial of the causal relevance of biological characteristics 'was not supported by the evidence' but seemed to 'fit quite well with a number of basic American values' (Stocking, 1968, pp. 306–7). The choice between viewpoints was made on different grounds, including matters of ideology. The choice of cultural theory by academics is not itself immune from the influence or provocation of academic or national cultures.

There is a widespread American ideological belief that all individuals can and should shape their own individual destiny. Much of the impetus behind behaviourist psychology, for example, derived from a conception that human minds were of equal potential, and differed principally from one another because of differences in conditioning by their environments. John B. Watson (1924, p. 104), the founder of behaviourism, boasted that he could turn each of 'a dozen healthy infants' into 'any type of specialist … doctor, lawyer, artist, merchant … beggar-man and thief, regardless of … tendencies, abilities, vocations and race'. The enthusiastic entry on 'Behaviorism' in the 1930 edition of the *Encyclopaedia of the Social Sciences* symptomatically declared: 'At birth human infants, regardless of their heredity, are as equal as Fords … each ready to respond to its appropriate stimulus' (Kallen, 1930, p. 498). This image of the Ford production line elegantly but perhaps unwittingly combined two prominent American tenets: faith in technology and the original equality of humankind.

In contrast, the older instinct–habit psychology and Darwinian evolutionary theory suggested to many that genes or instincts entirely determine behaviour, over which the individual has no further control. This misinterpretation of Darwinism survives today, despite the fact that it has been exposed to severe criticism. There is nothing in Darwinism that denies or excludes reflections and intentions that can resist or override many elemental impulses. Nevertheless, such misconceptions of Darwinism helped to bring about the marginalization of instinct–habit psychology and Darwinian evolutionary theory in the social sciences. Furthermore, the general recognition of inherited biological characteristics in Darwinian biology was difficult to reconcile with the naïve and extreme environmentalism that prevailed in Anglophone academia from the 1920s to the 1950s, in which the behavioural significance of variations in any inherited characteristic was largely denied.

The same period saw important changes in prevailing conceptions of method and approach in social science. Versions of positivism had grown in popularity in all sciences and had been given a further impetus by Ernst Mach and others in the 1890s. It was argued that the social sciences had to gain 'scientific' credentials, and that this should be done by imitating the empiricist and deductivist methods that were believed to be in operation in the natural sciences. The ideological abuses of biology were seen as a grave warning. For many, such as Max Weber in Germany, they were an impetus to render social science 'value free' (Hennis, 1988).

The further rise of positivism had profound effects on sociology. As the earlier generation of theorists was marginalized by some for their dalliances with biology, they were also criticized by positivists for their inclusion of 'metaphysical' concepts such as 'social forces' or the 'social mind'. For example, Edward Hayes (1907, p. 651) declared that sociology should have 'nothing to do with any metaphysical concepts that may be thought to underlie social phenomena'. Among others, Franklin Giddings, Lester Ward, William McDougall and Albion Small were implicated in these attacks. According to Hayes, to refer to 'social forces' was to resort to a metaphysical explanation, much like the discredited 'vital force' in biology. This positivist argument proved to be so persuasive that when Hayes (1911) developed his argument in a conference paper 'one commentator thought he was kicking a dead horse' (D. Ross, 1991, p. 347).

In particular, the attacks on Ward's (1903) work had tragic effects: his development of emergentist philosophy in the language of 'creative synthesis' was lost and forgotten for sociology. More generally, emergentism faced opposition from those sociologists and anthropologists who were suspicious of any kind of links between biology and human society, including those links within the layered ontology of emergentism. By 1911, it also faced opposition from positivist sociologists who criticized as 'metaphysics' any such ontological discussion. The diminution of emergentist discourse would help pave the way for both individualist and collectivist varieties of reductionism in the social sciences in the coming decades.

For example, by the 1920s, influential sociologists such as Floyd Allport (1924, 1927) could be found arguing for a version of reductionism where groups and institutions were to be explained solely in terms of individual behaviour, understood in terms of the canons of behaviourist psychology.

In response, the social interactionists argued that the individual was no more a fixed unit than the group, and that social stimulation and social relationships affected behaviour.

Moves to create sociology as a discipline largely free of ties with biology or psychology were evident even before the First World War (Cravens, 1978). Eventually, in the 1930s, under the leadership of Talcott Parsons, American sociology dramatically cut all of these ties and declared itself as a mature, independent and supreme discipline (Hodgson, 2001c).

The abandonment of Veblenian psychology and philosophy

Even before 1918, the psychological and philosophical foundations of institutionalism had already come under sustained assault from within the American scientific community. As early as 1909, the president of the American Psychological Association (APA), Charles Judd, criticized the works of James and McDougall and the very idea of instinct. Several leading psychologists argued that instinct provided no explanation that could be verified by experiment. Knight Dunlap (1922) attacked instinct psychology in his works and in his 1922 presidential address to the APA, because it relied on concepts that allegedly had no expression in 'concrete facts'. For instincts, Dunlap substituted manifest feelings. In an increasingly positivistic intellectual climate, critics of instinct-based theories of human nature pointed to the flimsiness of the empirical evidence and the difficulties of experimental verification. Many of these criticisms were summarized in an influential book by the sociologist Luther Bernard (1924).

John Dewey, George Herbert Mead and Jacques Loeb taught John B. Watson at Chicago. Watson (1936, p. 274) wrote of his lessons with Dewey: 'I never knew what he was talking about then, and unfortunately for me, I still do not know.' Watson moved to Johns Hopkins in 1908. When James Mark Baldwin resigned his Johns Hopkins chair in 1909 – after being arrested by police in a brothel – the young Watson assumed Baldwin's prestigious duties as editor of the *Psychological Review*. After gaining academic prominence as a result of this scandal, Watson (1913, 1914, 1919) announced the new behaviourist psychology, arguing on the basis of animal experiments that environmental conditioning was primary and instinct a secondary concept. Although several American psychologists initially resisted the behaviourist elimination of mind as a matter of scientific concern (Samelson, 1981), the behaviourist ethos of experimentation swept over the discipline. By 1919, 'what had been ... a sort of rebellious sideshow among the academic psychologists took on the dimensions of an intellectual revolution' (Kallen, 1930, p. 497). Eventually, Watson and other behaviourists entirely abandoned the concept of instinct. They alleged that consciousness, intention, sensation and introspection were 'unscientific' concepts because they could not be observed directly. Behaviourism promoted a positivist vision of science and concentrated instead on empirically manifest behaviour. They disregarded everything that could not be directly measured and tested by experiment as unscientific. This tied in closely with a growing general adherence to positivism amongst social and natural scientists. The emphasis on measurement and experiment in behaviourist psychology gave it an aura of positivistic and dispassionate objectivity (O'Donnell, 1985; S. Lewin, 1996).

Especially when compared with biological reductionism, a commendable aspect of behaviourism was its recognition of the role of the culture and the environment in shaping human behaviour. But behaviourism did not pioneer the idea of cultural influence. Instinct–habit psychology, as used by Veblen and others, was well equipped to understand the impact of cultural and institutional conditions on human capabilities. Indeed, because instinct–habit psychology did not treat the individual as a mere puppet of social conditions, their power to shape individuality could be better appreciated.

Hamilton (1919, p. 317) had criticized those economists that had 'overlooked the part that instinct and impulse play in impelling … economic activity'. But within a very short period of time this Jamesian and Veblenian viewpoint was itself under attack. With the rapid ascent of behaviourism in the 1920s, the idea of instinctive behaviour in human beings was sidelined. Just thirty years after the heyday of William James, the concept of instinct had virtually disappeared from American psychology.

For example, the sociologist Ellwood (1918) – a sometime admirer and colleague of Veblen – criticized habit-based theories of culture (including Veblen's) because they did not sufficiently acknowledge the distinctive features of human society. Ellwood argued that if habit was so important as the basis of culture then how could it explain the lack of a developed culture among lower animals? Ellwood did not appreciate the fact that the capacity to form habits was even more important and varied in humans than in other species, and that habit was a necessary but not sufficient feature of culture. In contrast, some psychologists and sociologists who had strongly criticized instinct psychology retained a place for habit in their analysis (Kantor, 1922b; Bernard, 1924). But this intermediate position was short-lived. In a philosophy journal, Charner Perry (1928, p. 269) wrote: 'Instinct as category is now become suspect, and habit seems to be its heir.' Under the influence of behaviourism, habit became simply a reference to established or repeated behaviour, rather than underlying dispositions. Its explanatory value was thus challenged. By the late 1930s, the pragmatist concept of habit had also followed instinct into virtual oblivion, in psychology and in the social sciences more generally (Camic, 1986; Degler, 1991). In America, many sociologists and economists abandoned the psychological ideas that had underpinned Veblenian institutionalism.

Generally, a positivistic and technocratic drift among the social sciences marginalized the earlier pragmatist philosophy of Charles Sanders Peirce and William James. The philosophical underpinnings of Veblenian institutionalism were partly eroded by an increasing commitment to positivism in the social sciences.

Behaviourism depicts the mind as a *tabula rasa* upon which environmental influences are imprinted. However, no individual can act in the world without means of selecting the most important from the flood of sensory stimuli that reach the brain. Behaviourism, like empiricism, upholds that meaning is inherent in the data themselves. In contrast, Veblen and others were aware that mental preconceptions were necessary to frame and select the more important data. Instinct makes the first selective moves. Then on top of instincts we develop more sophisticated habits of cognition, particularly through interaction with others. These habits can supplement or override instincts. The rise of behaviourism and the abandonment of instinct–habit psychology meant the adoption of an empiricist concept of learning. There was no explanation of how an individual could cope with the varied mass of data reaching the brain.

Veblen applied natural selection to the evolution of institutions and adopted a Darwinian commitment to explanation in terms of cumulative cause and effect. However, until the 1940s, Darwinism itself remained highly controversial, even within biology. Furthermore, the breaking of the links between the Anglophone social sciences and biology in the early part of the twentieth century meant that Darwinism became an unpopular theme for social scientists. All this was catastrophic for the further development of Veblenian institutionalism. The institutionalists themselves discarded its Darwinian agenda.

Overall, these shifts in psychology, philosophy and the social sciences, and the consequent abandonment of the essence of Veblenian economics, severely damaged the methodological and conceptual nucleus of American institutionalism, even during its heyday in the 1920s and 1930s. While its influence and success on the American scene obscured these core theoretical and methodological problems for a while, they made it increasingly difficult for American institutionalism to withstand the assault from the rising neoclassical and formalistic economics that emerged in the late 1930s.

We can see signs of these shifts and changes of thinking in the writings of leading institutionalists. Early on, Mitchell (1914, p. 22) chided Veblen for upholding that instincts were 'hereditary traits' and for neglecting that instincts 'have important acquired elements in addition to the elements which are inherited'. Mitchell did not understand that instincts (at least by a post-Weismann definition) were entirely inherited. He thus abandoned a key aspect of Veblenian psychology. The institutionalist Albert Wolfe (1924, p. 472) later praised Mitchell's 1914 essay as looking 'to behavioristic psychology as a promising basis for economics as a science of behavior'. Mitchell (1925, p. 6) himself applauded the 'rapid' moves in psychology towards 'an objective conception and quantitative treatment of their problems'. Eventually, Mitchell (1936, p. xlix; 1937, p. 312) lost all confidence in both Darwinism and instinct–habit psychology as foundations for institutionalism: 'The Darwinian viewpoint is due to be superseded in men's minds: the instinct–habit psychology will yield to some other conception of human nature.' Discussing Mitchell's views, the institutional economist Allan Gruchy (1972, p. 43) explained approvingly, and with an apparent genuflection to positivism: 'Mitchell did not follow Veblen in emphasizing the instinctive basis of human behavior, because instincts cannot be objectively analyzed'. Gruchy did not mention that Mitchell (1910, 1914) had earlier embraced instinct–habit psychology. But Mitchell's shift towards behaviourism was entirely consistent with his empiricist frame of mind.

J. M. Clark (1918) mentioned instincts several times in his most important essay on economic psychology. Subsequently he paid them little attention. By 1932, he could declare that institutional economics 'has a natural kinship with behaviorism' (Kiekhofer *et al.*, 1932, p. 105). It seems that Clark's early and highly productive interest in psychology waned after 1918 because, as he shifted to behaviourism, he was unsure of the scientific grounding of his earlier position.

John Dewey (1922, p. 104) also expressed some reluctance in using the term 'instinct' and generally switched to the word 'impulse' instead. Where Dewey (1922, pp. 106–9) retained the term 'instinct' he gave it an unclear meaning, even suggesting in one passage that human instincts could change more rapidly than social customs or institutions. At the same time, his concept of habit was broadened to take up many of the roles that instinct psychologists had previously accorded to instincts. In response, William McDougall (1924) argued convincingly that instincts were still essential to Dewey's own argument, and should not be abandoned.

In his *Logic*, Dewey (1938, p. 143) still wrote of knowledge as 'mediated through certain organic mechanisms of retention and habit' but neither 'instinct' nor 'impulse' appears in the index of that book. In a later work, not only is the concept of instinct absent, but also habit plays an insignificant role (Dewey and Bentley, 1949). By then Dewey had abandoned instinct–habit psychology.

In the 1920s and 1930s, leading American institutionalists also rejected instinct–habit psychology and key elements of Darwinism. The Veblenian research programme of building a 'post-Darwinian' economics was dropped. The institutionalist and future AEA president Joseph Spengler (1950, p. 249) wrote: 'Evolutionism as such has not played a prominent part in American economic thought since 1930'. When Clarence Ayres emerged as the *de facto* leader of American institutionalism after 1945, what were seen as the embarrassing elements of its Veblenian legacy had already been abandoned.

As one of the earliest critics of instinct–habit psychology, Ayres (1921a, p. 561) described the 'prolific and varied instinct literature' as 'largely self-refuting. ... When instincts fall out, institutions get their due'. Ayres was in the vanguard of the movement among social scientists to ditch the concept of instinct in its entirety. Ayres (1958, p. 25) later proclaimed: 'the very notion of instincts is now scientifically obsolete'. Although Ayres was right to point out that Veblen failed to define instinct adequately, instinct–habit psychology remained foundational to Veblen's position.[11]

In one passage, Ayres (1951, p. 48) could be accused of rewriting the history of his own movement: 'Institutionalism has been identified with behaviorism as long and as consistently as it has been identified at all.' This overlooks the huge chasm between Veblen's instinct–habit psychology and behaviourism. Perhaps Ayres was redefining behaviourism in very broad terms, as any psychology that recognized the potential influence of environmental or social conditions on behaviour. But this would not explain or justify Ayres's assault on the very idea of instinct, or the wholesale rejection by institutionalists of instinct–habit psychology in the 1920s. No one has adequately explained why instinct rules out the possibility of environmental or cultural influences, and Veblen's work testifies that the ideas of instinct and cultural influence can coexist.

While most institutionalists abandoned instinct–habit psychology, there were a few exceptions. One was Rexford Tugwell (1922, 1930, 1949). While applauding the scientific and empirical emphasis in behaviourism, he noted that without some elemental and instinctive drives, learning and reason would be disabled.[12] Unlike most institutionalists, both Tugwell and Copeland (1931, 1958b) persisted in raising themes from evolutionary biology, sometimes using relevant biological ideas and analogies in their writings.[13]

In other ways, however, Copeland went with the stream. Copeland (1921, 1924, 1925, 1926) embraced behaviourist psychology with increasing enthusiasm, applauding its emphasis on observability and prediction (Asso and Fiorito, 2003a). In terms very different from James and Veblen, Copeland (1926, p. 245) argued in behaviourist terms that: 'Knowing is a form of psychological response to stimulus'. Copeland (1927, p. 104) also wrote: 'The merits or demerits of ... analysis are for the scientist questions of the success they yield in predicting and controlling ... the proof of an analysis – or a synthesis – is in the predictions it will enable us to make.'

---

11 Later chapters of the present work examine differences between the ideas of Veblen and Ayres.
12 Tugwell became an advisor to President F. D. Roosevelt. For an account of Tugwell's contribution to economic policy development, to the neglect of his philosophical and psychological ideas, see Gruchy (1972, pp. 62–70). Gruchy's (1947, 1972) work also includes discussions of several other institutionalists that are not addressed in detail here.
13 Much later Copeland (1981, p. 2) abandoned such themes, when he wrote: 'there seems to be nothing in the socio-economic evolutionary process that corresponds to natural selection'. The double irony was that this was just one year before Nelson and Winter (1982) published their seminal *Evolutionary Theory of Economic Change*, then in apparent ignorance of the earlier evolutionary tradition within institutional economics. For an important discussion of Copeland's work see Rutherford (2002).

This instrumentalist and positivist stance made success in prediction the principal measure of theoretical advance.

Copeland's former teacher, J. M. Clark (1927, p. 221) embraced a broader version of empiricism that relied imprecisely on verification or induction:

> Economics must come into closer touch with facts and embrace broader ranges of data than 'orthodox' economics has hitherto done. It must establish touch with these data, either by becoming more inductive, or by much verification of results, or by taking over the accredited results of specialists in other fields, notably psychology, anthropology, jurisprudence and history. Thus the whole modern movement may be interpreted as a demand for procedure which appears more adequately scientific ...

Clark's position was highly problematic. It is not clear what is meant by theory 'embracing' more data, or why this is desirable. His statement could be interpreted as an injunction to make economics a general theory of everything, in which case it would not be that different from the ahistorical utility analysis and the later 'economic imperialism' of 'orthodox' theory. Alternatively it could be interpreted as an attempt to reconcile economic theory with historical, anthropological, psychological and other specificities. In any case, Clark seemed to have an unwarranted faith in the power of empirical data to validate or generate theory.

Despite their differences, leading institutionalists such as Mitchell, Copeland and Clark shared a broad positivist faith in observation and experiment as sufficient means for obtaining knowledge and confirming hypotheses. They overlooked the prior and necessary role of theory in framing and forming the very questions and methods of all scientific investigation. A positivist spirit infused institutionalism in the interwar years, despite Veblen's earlier warnings of the limits of positivism and empiricism. The mood at the time was for institutionalism to be 'scientific' – in the sense that it should be grounded on empirical methods of enquiry similar to those in the natural sciences (Rutherford, 1997, 1999, 2000a, 2000b). However, instead of emulating the driving role of theory in other sciences, the institutionalists drifted towards a naïve and untenable empiricism, believing that the salvation of their science was in the gathering of yet more data.

For a time, institutionalists were able to exploit the positivist mood, insisting on the need for an empirical foundation for the postulates of economic theory. With funding from the US government and other institutions, leading institutionalists such as Mitchell became engrossed in statistical studies. Others resisted the statistical turn, but Mitchell was resolute in his support of the primacy of this empirical work, emphasizing this point in his 1924 presidential address to the American Economic Association (Mitchell, 1925).

Mitchell had some difficulty in promoting a clear and consistent defence of his empiricist view of the development of scientific knowledge (Seckler, 1975, pp. 108–16). At a subsequent American Economic Association round-table discussion, Viner pressed Mitchell on the necessary assumptions that must precede any quantitative methods. Viner rightly stressed that data alone cannot make a theory. In Viner's words, there would always be 'a metaphysical penumbra to the most concrete of economic problems which will resist tenaciously explorations by the methods of the physical scientist' (Mills *et al.*, 1928, p. 31). In recognizing the unavoidability of metaphysical presuppositions, it was Viner, not Mitchell, who was closer to Veblen on this issue.

By adapting to the positivist climate of the times, institutionalism may have won research grants, but it was ultimately to lose out. The positivist and statistical turn, as represented in particular by Mitchell, reduced the impetus and perceived urgency for institutionalism to further develop its own basic theoretical framework prior to the gathering of data. In any case, even if they had addressed this urgent theoretical task, it was made even more difficult because institutionalism had abandoned much of its philosophical and psychological legacy.

Despite its incompleteness, these Veblenian foundations in psychology and philosophy were not eroded primarily as a result of its own internal weaknesses. Instead, they were displaced by rival approaches that prospered for ideological as much as for scientific reasons. The irony, as elaborated in Chapter 19 below, is that the pillars of pragmatism, instinct–habit psychology and Darwinism are being visibly rebuilt within the social sciences today.

Overall, American institutionalists after 1918 followed several of the changing currents in American social science. Some of these adaptations were less disruptive than others. In particular, the concept of social culture was prominent in institutionalism from the beginning. Veblen himself had pioneered an analysis of culture in his *Theory of the Leisure Class* (1899a). Hence, unlike the Veblenian emphases on instinct and Darwinism, the increasing emphasis on the role of culture by social scientists did not itself embarrass or undermine institutionalism. Like Boas, Veblen argued that both nature and nurture were important. However, by the 1920s, the view became widespread that culture alone determined human attributes and behaviour, without any help or influence from human biology. This affected the prevailing conception of culture within institutionalism itself.

Figure 12.1 charts the appearances of three key concepts – habit, instinct and culture – in articles in anthropology, economics, philosophy, sociology and political science in the JSTOR Internet database of leading journals. The vertical axis shows the percentage of articles in which each

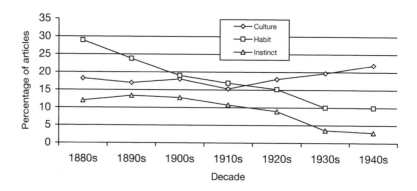

Figure 12.1 Appearances of key concepts in social science journals

concept appears.[14] The figure clearly shows the declining popularity of the concepts of habit and instinct, to the point that they are overtaken by the concept of culture in the 1920s. From the 1920s, the use of the concept of culture increases steadily, to a point well ahead of habit and instinct. These trends continue into the postwar period. Similarly, data show that between 1927 and 1958, listings in *Psychological Abstracts* of entries under the term 'instinct' rapidly declined from 68 per cent to 8 per cent (R. Richards, 1987, p. 509).

Homan alone: early concerns about institutionalism

Despite the aforementioned seismic shifts in thinking in psychology and philosophy, institutionalism did not come under strong and sustained attack until after 1945.[15] What particularly concern us here are the debates within the United States economics profession concerning the viability of institutionalism, from its launch in December 1918 until the outbreak of the Second World War. A highly critical book by Richard Teggart (1932) on Veblen appeared, but was not matched by others of similar hostility. Examining the academic journals in economics from 1919 to 1939, it is remarkable how little space was devoted to criticism of institutionalism. The limited scale of the critical literature in this interwar period makes the task of its assessment much easier. It is possible to identify and analyse a few key persons and prominent themes.

---

14 The number of journal articles in which each term appeared in its singular form was counted. Reviews were excluded.
15 Many critiques of Veblen's institutionalism have been usefully collected together and examined by Rick Tilman (1992). In particular, Tilman (1992, pp. 25–37) documents a pre-1914 debate between I. Fisher and Veblen. But most critiques of Veblen appeared after his death. Post-1945 hostilities against institutionalism began in earnest with Machlup (1946), Koopmans (1947) and Stigler (1947).

The publication of Veblen's (1919a) first and most important set of collected essays brought forth mixed reactions. Knight reviewed the work in a fusion of criticism and praise. Knight (1920, p. 519) wrote of 'the valuable work which Mr. Veblen has done' but remarked that 'he is not a close or clear thinker ... we can hardly follow him as a constructive leader'. There is some truth in the appraisal that Veblen's playful and sometimes opaque style undermined his 'scientific' credentials, but Knight failed to understand Veblen's perceptive and valid connection of Darwinism with a specific materialist and causal ontology. The fault here was as much with the reviewer as with the writer, and showed that even a perceptive and philosophically sophisticated writer such as Knight could fail to grasp the central Darwinian philosophical thrust of Veblen's (1899a, 1914, 1919a) work. Knight made some poignant criticisms of Veblen's distinction between 'pecuniary and industrial employments' and rightly pointed to the need for further clarification of the dichotomy. Knight (1920, p. 520) nevertheless concluded that Veblen's volume was 'interesting and intellectually stimulating'.

Two of the issues highlighted by Knight recur in subsequent critical writings. Other critics allude to Veblen's cryptic style of writing and even suggest that his credentials as a scientist were undermined. Young (1925, p. 183) – another sympathetic critic – wrote of Veblen: 'He is a man of genius, but the term scientist does not fit him.' Both Knight and Young alluded to a deficit of rigorous argument in Veblen's work, but otherwise did not explain what they mean by 'scientific'.

Critics frequently alleged that Veblen's injection of Darwinian evolutionary theory into economics was inappropriate or unjustified. The failure to appreciate the importance and value of Veblen's use of Darwinian philosophy was to be critical for the future development and eventual decline of institutional economics as a whole.

Tugwell (1924) edited a volume of broadly institutionalist essays with contributions by J. M. Clark, Copeland, Knight, Mitchell, Slichter, Wolfe and other leading figures. Young (1925) reviewed the volume in detail, directing a number of criticisms at the positions of individual authors rather than at institutional economics as a whole. Generally, in the interwar period, sustained and detailed attacks in the leading economics journals on the institutionalist movement as a whole were rare. The broad church of institutionalism held sway over American economics.

It is all the more remarkable that the most significant and perceptive attack on institutionalism that emerged in the interwar period was by a young and initially sympathetic scholar. The David who rose up against Goliath was Paul T. Homan. Born in Indianola in Iowa, Homan studied in England at the University of Oxford between 1914 and 1919, where he was awarded a BA. His doctorate was obtained at the Brookings Graduate School of Economics and Government in 1926. After a number of jobs he moved to Cornell University in 1927, where he remained until 1947.

Herbert Davenport – a longstanding friend of Veblen – had moved to Cornell from Missouri in 1916, and he was a major influence on Homan.[16]

Homan (1928a, p. ix) related that he was 'brought up in the faith of Marshall' and afterwards dallied 'for a while in the camp of Veblen'. Homan was no hard-headed defender of neoclassical orthodoxy, but a theoretically astute economist concerned about the development of economics. Homan (1933, p. 481) was highly critical of those, such as Teggart (1932), who misrepresented Veblen and exhibited a 'conscientious refusal to find merit in Veblen's work'. Homan's attitude to Veblen was of 'tolerant scepticism' (Knight, 1928, p. 133) rather than outright attack. Homan (1928a, p. 192) acknowledged that Veblen's achievement was 'to stimulate some of the best scientific work ... in the field of the social sciences'.

Homan's (1927a) first published work was an article on Veblen. Significantly, one of its major complaints concerned Veblen's incorporation of ideas from biology into economics. Homan (1927a, pp. 258–9) remarked that 'in introducing the evolutionary approach, Veblen claimed too much for it'. He accused Veblen of 'an exaggerated insistence on the evolutionary viewpoint'. Homan did not accept that 'scientific social studies must proceed by a method analogous to that of biology' for it is questionable that 'the life of society is compatible to that of a biological organism'. But here Homan missed the point of Veblen's introduction of Darwinian principles into economics, and overlooked the fact that Veblen (1901b, p. 76) himself had rejected the idea that society could be treated as an organism. Like others, Homan (1927a, p. 261) also questioned Veblen's scientific credentials:

> It is obvious that Veblen cannot be rated very high as a scientist. His task is carried out with none of the cold objectivity which, in his own view, distinguishes the scientific spirit. With consummate skill in selecting and coloring his facts ... With his tongue in his cheek under cover of a sophisticated scientific pose he has accomplished a covert ethical damnation of the dominant modern economic institutions.

It is not that all of Homan's criticisms were unjustified. Homan (1927a, p. 260) rightly pointed out that on matters of economic policy Veblen had 'no more concrete suggestion than a vague plan for the supervision of the economic system by a hierarchy of technical experts'. This limitation was exacerbated because Veblen evaded 'the problem of economic guidance and the problem of value and distribution, which lie within the sweep of the price-system'. Hence Veblen failed to advance any 'tenable scheme of social control'.

---

16 From 1947 to 1950, Homan was on the staff of the Council of Economic Advisors to President Truman. Homan became an expert on the National Recovery Administration and the oil industry. He served as managing editor of the *American Economic Review* from 1941 to 1952. In 1950, he moved to the University of California as Professor of Economics. See Samuels (1987).

Continuing his critique in the *Journal of Political Economy*, Homan (1927b, p. 781) noted that Veblen's 'conceptual apparatus is an adaptation to economic studies of certain ideas drawn from biological science. The physical or mechanical analogies are definitely discarded.' Mitchell was seen as 'the apostle of facts and figures'. Homan (1927b, p. 782) then raised the vital question of 'just what complement of general theory is desirable as part of the equipment of a competent modern economist'. Homan was not an advocate of the reckless attempts at theoretical generalization that I have criticized elsewhere (Hodgson, 2001c). He simply and rightly observed that some general framework of ideas was necessary for any theory, and looked to institutionalism to find its theoretical scaffolding. In his search he was disappointed. Homan (1927b, pp. 784–5) himself set out the unavoidable methodological agenda for any economic theorist:

> He is under the necessity of relying upon some general theory of the nature of the social process. And of such theories there is today a glut. He has need of a set of criteria concerning the nature, aims, and methods of scientific inquiry, and must decide which, if any, of the diverse disciplines in the field of natural science furnishes the best basis upon the analogy to which a scientific instrumentality for dealing with social facts may be modeled. No task of his is more fundamental or more difficult than the creation of a terminology in which social facts can be scientifically described. ... Between the limits of an extreme individualistic and an extreme organismic theory of society lies a field for infinite diversity of view.

Homan noted broad sets of economic principles in the works of Alfred Marshall, J. B. Clark and others. Homan (1927b, p. 788) remarked that the institutionalists were 'vaguely bound together' around the 'policy of social control' but as yet had not provided an alternative to the more orthodox theoretical framework. What struck Homan was both the diversity of theoretical approaches within institutionalism and its failure to provide a systematic theoretical alternative. For Homan (1927b, p. 790), John Hobson was the only leading economist 'who has developed any comprehensive body of dissident thought' but 'the abstract character of much of it separates it from the contemporary American impatience with schematic abstractions'. Homan observed that 'effective thinking has been largely turned away from more general theoretical considerations' to concentrate instead on matters of policy and applied economics. In response, Homan rightly argued that all work in economic policy was unavoidably based on theoretical presuppositions. The explicit or implicit theoretical outlook of the applied economist would highlight particular lines of enquiry and interpretation. Even policy-oriented economics cannot be theory-free.

Homan's (1927b) article was less an assault on institutionalism and more a warning that unless it attended to its methodological and theoretical foundations, then it could never become an identifiable alternative to neoclassical orthodoxy. Homan discussed the use of evolutionary ideas from biology within institutional economics but saw little value or meaning in them. Furthermore, 'institutional economics has no tool to substitute for deductive analysis in coping with many problems of economic cause and effect' (Homan, 1927b, p. 801). This was not an argument for wholesale deductivism in economic theory but a valid observation that causal theoretical analysis must make use of logical deductions. Leading historicists such as William Ashley (1891) and Gustav Schmoller (1900) had earlier made the observation that both deduction and induction were essential to economics. Critics of orthodoxy typically rejected 'the exclusive use of the deductive method' (Seligman, 1925, p. 15) rather than dismissing the use of deduction altogether. In calling for a place for deductive analysis, Homan was not then erecting a banner of revolt against institutionalism. It was more a warranted call for serious devotion to the theoretical fundamentals, which was then missing from much institutionalist research.

In his second major article, in the *Quarterly Journal of Economics*, Homan (1928b, p. 337) again accused Veblen of having 'exaggerated the bearing of evolution on economics'. Homan's tone became more aggressive: he referred to Veblen's 'insidious ideas' (p. 338) and 'rather pathetic results' (p. 349). Homan remained unconvinced of any value in the application of evolutionary ideas to economics and threw down an implicit challenge to other institutionalists to explain the theoretical meaning and worth of 'Darwinian' economics.

In the same journal, Overton Taylor (1929, pp. 4–5) declared: 'Veblen's contribution ... brilliant as it is in its way, can hardly be supposed by any one to rank as a serious piece of historical and critical scholarship.' This was merely a repetition of the earlier criticisms by others of Veblen's manner of argumentation. But significantly, Taylor helped to persuade Talcott Parsons to break from his former allegiance to institutionalism (Camic, 1992; Hodgson, 2001c). Parsons (1935) was later to launch a major attack on Veblen and the institutionalists.

We may conjecture that Joseph Schumpeter, while seeking a professorship in Harvard, saw the two critiques of institutionalism by Homan and Taylor in the Harvard-based *Quarterly Journal of Economics*. He may thus have been impelled to declare infamously in a speech in 1931 in Japan: 'Institutionalism is nothing but the methodological errors of German historians ... It is only error and not achievement. This, of course, is the one dark spot in the American atmosphere' (Schumpeter, 1991, p. 292).[17]

---

17 I am unable to explain adequately Schumpeter's motivation for his dismissal of institutionalism, especially after he had published remarks much more sympathetic to institutionalism and the German historical school as late as 1926. Here, as in Hodgson (2001c), I simply lay out the evidence and offer some tentative hypotheses.

Especially through Schumpeter, Homan and Taylor may have had a more significant effect in marginalizing institutionalism than they imagined.

We can sense in Homan's writings a growing frustration with leading institutionalists for making little attempt to justify Veblen's use of Darwinian ideas. As noted above, the only significant institutionalist exception in the interwar period was Copeland (1931), but he failed to capture the full ontological and theoretical significance of Veblen's message. Given this absence of an adequate justification of Darwinian concepts in economics, and a general failure of institutionalists to enunciate a clear and identifiable set of core theoretical principles, Homan was to point increasingly to the lack of identifiable theoretical unity or common theoretical substance in the institutionalist camp. In an encyclopedia article, Homan (1931, p. 388) observed that 'the numerous proponents of the institutional approach to economics differ so markedly in their views concerning the purpose, content and mentality of institutional economics' that 'the use of the term school is justified only if the loosest possible meaning is attached to it'.

Homan was invited to chair the first AEA Round Table devoted to the future of institutional economics (Homan *et al.*, 1931). This Round Table was principally a response to the important papers by institutionalists Eveline Burns (1931) and Copeland (1931). Then a lecturer at Columbia University, the British-born Eveline Burns urged persuasively that institutionalism should overcome its 'vagueness'.[18] In response, however, the American institutionalist Joseph Spengler cast doubt on whether institutionalism required a 'new theoretical framework' at all. Overton Taylor defended neoclassical theory and questioned Copeland's underdeveloped statement that economics was a 'biological' or 'natural science'. William Jaffé urged that institutional economics should be clearly defined. For all concerned, this Round Table must have been a disappointment. Despite the more weighty contributions of Burns and Copeland, insignificant progress was made in dealing with the problem of the definition of institutionalism in general, and in particular the meaning and place of Darwinian evolutionary ideas within it.

Another Round Table was held at the AEA meeting in the subsequent year. It addressed a paper by Homan (1932a) himself. Therein Homan (1932a, p. 10) began by observing that 'Veblen's attempt to make of economics an evolutionary science has been little developed by other economists' and the 'differentiating characteristics of an institutional economics are hard to find'. Homan (p. 15) failed to see why 'the language of the evolutionary process is having or is likely to have any substantial effect upon either the knowledge or the analysis relevant to the solution of our economic problems'. Homan (p. 16) noted forcefully that the meaning of 'institutionalism', and how it differed from any other kind of economics, were entirely unclear:

18 E. Burns's (1931) argument is discussed in more detail in Hodgson (2001c).

Why Clark's studies of costs, Mitchell's studies of cyclical phenomena, Mill's studies of prices, Hamilton's study of the coal industry, Commons's studies of legal institutions should be lumped into one inclusive category which is then married to Hobson, Tawney, Webb, and Sombart is beyond my comprehension. Why not Viner's study of dumping, or Ripley's of railroads, or Watkins's of industrial combinations, or Taussig's of tariffs? If institutional economics be broadly defined, it is practically co-extensive with economics.

Malcolm Rutherford (2000b, p. 302) commented critically on this passage by Homan: 'It is in fact impossible to imagine that anyone could read Hamilton's study of the coal industry or Clark's *Social Control of Business* (1926) and believe the author to have been Viner or Taussig.' Of course, there were differences of approach between 'institutionalists' and others. But what Homan had revealed was the failure of institutionalism to theorize or explain its fundamental differences with 'traditional theory' adequately. In particular, it had neglected to sustain and explain its 'Darwinian' and 'evolutionary' orientation. By 1932, these failures were combined with a complete lack of consensus within institutionalism over their methodological and psychological foundations.

To Homan's forceful arguments the institutionalists had no adequate answer. At the AEA Round Table, J. M. Clark immediately ducked the issue and declared: 'I shall not attempt to define institutional economics' (Kiekhofer *et al.*, 1932, p. 105). In response, Homan argued that an 'institutional economics, differentiated from other economics by discoverable criteria, is largely an intellectual fiction, substantially devoid of content' (op. cit., p. 106). Hugh Fletcher rightly pointed out that the 'methodology of institutional economics has been accorded but little attention' (p. 107). Willard Atkins made an attempt to provide institutionalism with some spine and substance. He pointed out that institutionalists have some agreement on such propositions as 'more attention should be given to uniformities of custom, habit, and law as modes of organizing economic life' and 'economic behavior is constantly changing; therefore, economic generalizations should specify the limits of culture and time to which they apply' (p. 111). But these propositions were vague and insufficient.

Other defenders of institutionalism on the 1932 Round Table relapsed into empiricism. One declared that institutionalism should 'describe rather than explain' (p. 112). Another claimed that institutionalism 'seeks to pursue a more scientific method, aided by statistics, in continuously resubjecting its tentative generalizations to factual verification in the complex actual world' (p. 113). These statements did nothing to provide institutionalism with a discernible theoretical identity. Orthodox economics could also subject its 'generalizations to factual verification'. Finally, Richard Ely attempted to defend institutionalism by pointing out that its emphasis on 'economic evolution, property, contract, custom and competition' was there at the foundation of the AEA in 1885. Intellectual genealogy may be worthwhile, but it is not enough to provide an identity.

Taking the 1931 and 1932 Round Tables as a whole, Homan posed a reasonable and serious challenge concerning the identity and meaning of institutionalism. But there was no adequate answer. In particular, apart from vague allusions to economic 'evolution', there was no explanation or defence of the role of Darwinian evolutionary ideas in institutionalism. While several recognized the importance of psychology, no institutionalist defended instinct–habit psychology or the work of James. There was no mention of emergent properties. Partly as a result of Homan's repeated but legitimate questioning, it became clearly apparent that institutionalism had abandoned its Veblenian foundations and had no developed alternative.

At the time of the soup kitchens and unemployment queues of the Great Depression, the institutionalists faced a catastrophic crisis of self-identification. A reasonable observer might ask: how could institutional economics offer a policy solution to this vast economic and human disaster, when it cannot even define itself, or identify its own core theoretical ideas? This failure is revisited in Chapter 18 below, when the causes of the decline of institutional economics are discussed. Less than thirteen years after its inauguration, and two years after the death of its founder, American institutional economics was in a deep theoretical and identity crisis of its own, aping the calamity in the real world economy.

The assault on emergentist philosophy

It has been shown in Chapter 11 that institutionalists tragically ignored the importance of emergentist philosophy for their own theoretical project. But also in the positivist climate of the 1920s and 1930s, emergentist ideas came under attack from philosophers. Although debates in philosophy seldom have a direct and immediate effect on economics or sociology, this particular philosophical debate was of vital long-term importance for institutionalism. It explains why it became even more difficult for institutionalists to take account of an increasingly beleaguered emergentist philosophy.

Stephen Pepper (1926) was one of the first critics of emergentism. He argued that any failure to predict or explain properties described as emergent was only provisional. It reflected the incompleteness of scientific enquiry; there are no *a priori* grounds that a physical or other lower-level explanation could not eventually be found. The very idea of emergent properties and emergent laws was said to contradict the 'aim of science', which was seen to explain all phenomena in terms of basic units and a few fundamental laws. Paul Henle (1942) later refined this argument.

Bertrand Russell's (1927, pp. 285–6; 1931) critique of emergence was similar and relatively brief. Essentially, Russell defended reductionism.

He argued that it allowed the scientist 'to arrive at a structure such that the properties of the complex can be inferred from those of the parts'. Like Pepper, Russell believed that any apparent emergent could and should eventually be explained in terms of its constituent units and their relations.

Charles Baylis (1929) dissected the concept of emergence, and pointed out that new properties could appear as the result of the disintegration as well as the integration of constituents. Furthermore, there was the additional possibility of 'submergence' where some properties disappeared as the result of either integration or disintegration. For example, just as the combination of hydrogen and oxygen creates water and its properties, gaseous qualities simultaneously disappear. Baylis concluded that both emergence and submergence were ubiquitous. But for Baylis it was precisely this ubiquity that made emergentist philosophy trivial. Like Pepper, Baylis contended that there could be no final assurance that any particular property was emergent. Given that the analysis of a complex system was never complete, there was no guarantee that a property regarded as emergent could not eventually be explained or predicted in terms of the system's parts. 'These two facts, the ubiquity of emergence, and the difficulty of ever being sure that a particular character is an emergent of a particular complex, render the concept almost useless philosophically' (Baylis, 1929, p. 377). In the light of these problems, Baylis believed that the creation of a non-arbitrary ontological hierarchy in terms of emergent levels was impossible. He saw the dispute within emergentist philosophy over the number and denomination of ontological levels as a symptom of these irreconcilable difficulties.

Another critic of emergentism in the interwar period was the psychologist McDougall (1929). McDougall had moved from Oxford University in England to take up chairs of psychology at Harvard in 1920 and at Duke University in 1927. McDougall's criticisms differed radically from those of positivist or reductionist inclinations. Unlike both the emergentist philosophers and the reductionists, McDougall upheld a dualist ontology, within which mind and matter were separated and independent of each other. For McDougall, mental phenomena did not emerge from the interactions of neural matter; instead they were immaterial and irreducible. These assertions of mental irreducibility and mind–body dualism led McDougall to attempt a Custer's Last Stand against the Weismann doctrine. He believed that mental evolution could never be explained in material terms and that the Lamarckian inheritance of acquired characters could occur at the mental level.

After the more influential work of William James (1890), Veblen (1914) also referred to McDougall's (1908) instinct psychology. As noted above, McDougall had been a strong influence on Mitchell (1910). Hence some difficulties were created for institutional economics in disentangling the valuable aspects of McDougall's psychology from his mind–body dualism and his critique of emergentist philosophy.

Two further forces helped to marginalize emergentism in the 1930s. First, important advances in physics and chemistry increased faith in reductionism. Developments in quantum theory in the 1920s suggested that physics could eventually explain a range of physical phenomena in terms of fundamental particles, quantum mechanics and other physical laws. Niels Bohr explained aspects of the periodic table of the elements and some of their chemical properties. It became possible to analyse chemical bonding in terms of electromagnetic forces and to begin to probe the molecular components of organic life. As these discoveries percolated through the scientific community, the hope was raised that biological phenomena could eventually be explained in terms of chemical phenomena, just as the chemical was increasingly explained in terms of the physical. It was increasingly believed that currently unexplained phenomena would eventually be explained, and claims of emergence would thus be undermined.

Second, emergentist philosophy was overcome by the spread of logical positivism, and its scepticism of metaphysical or ontological questions of any kind. One of the leaders of this philosophical movement was Rudolf Carnap, who moved to the United States in 1936. He was confident in the reductionist potential of science, and deemed the erection of higher ontological levels superfluous. Carnap (1934, p. 97) declared that, as the scientific endeavour proceeds, 'the whole of science becomes physics'. This renewed faith in reductionism, within the seemingly elegant analytical clothing of logical positivism, was to sweep emergentist philosophy to the wayside.

When Carl Hempel and Paul Oppenheim (1948) criticized emergentist philosophy in a famous paper, they took it for granted that emergent properties were failures of explanation, rather than ontological claims. This did not simply reflect a widespread neglect of ontology, it also showed the failure of 1920s emergentism to establish generally an ontological conception of emergent properties.

The period from the mid-1930s to the 1950s has been described as the 'eclipse of emergentism' (Blitz, 1992). However, emergentism found a number of refuges, principally in the philosophy of biology, where it maintained some respectability. Despite the synthesis of Darwinism with Mendelian genetics in the 1930s and 1940s and a growing belief that biological phenomena could eventually be explained in terms of molecular biology, the concept of emergence never disappeared from biology. The British embryologist Joseph Needham (1937) proposed levels of organization in reality, ascending in their degree of complexity, giving rise to emergent properties and the cosmological, biological and sociological levels of scientific enquiry. Even more significantly, Julian Huxley defended emergentist ideas, with levels of reality relating to degrees of organizational complexity. In his Romanes lecture of 1943, Huxley argued that: 'Increase in organization is for the most part gradual, but now and again there is a sudden rapid passage to a totally new and more comprehensive type or order of organization, with quite new emergent properties, and involving quite new methods of further evolution' (Huxley and Huxley, 1947, p. 120).[19]

A symposium was organized in 1941 to mark the fiftieth anniversary of the University of Chicago. The sometime university of Veblen, the location of Morgan's inspirational visit in 1896, and the birthplace of American institutional economics, ironically became the venue for a meeting involving biologists and sociologists, on the theme of 'levels of integration in biological and social systems'. This led to a subsequent debate over whether society could be compared with an organism (Redfield, 1942; Gerard and Emerson, 1945; Novikoff, 1945; Sellars *et al.*, 1949). Novikoff (1945) in particular defended the ideas of emergence and the ontology of levels, but argued that societies and organisms were quite different things. While these debates did not have a wide impact, they kept the emergentist discourse alive in the difficult period when logical positivism was triumphant. In general, emergentist philosophy was marginalized until logical positivism waned in influence and a new generation of philosophers revived interest in underlying ontological questions. As shown in Chapter 19 below, this was under way in the 1960s. But this was all too late for institutional economics, which had declined dramatically by that decade.

The next part of this work examines what happened to institutional economics in the absence of adequate philosophical and psychological foundations. The narrative focuses on a few key figures, who reacted to the problems within institutionalism in different and illuminating ways. Despite the philosophical lacunae at its core, institutionalists continued to produce important innovations in both economic theory and policy. But it is ultimately a story of failure and decline. Yet even from errors we can learn much. The history of institutional economics is also a rich quarry for powerful ideas that can play a crucial part in its reconstruction today.

---

19 Julian Huxley was one of the pioneers of the synthesis between Darwinian natural selection and Mendelian genetics. He was the grandson of Thomas Henry Huxley (see Chapter 4 above).

Part IV
Institutionalism into the wilderness

13 John R. Commons and the tangled jungle

> A genius can do in a few years, if he works intensely, more than I can do in fifty years by intensive study. The genius can see through to the bottom of things without digging, but I must dig and re-dig. … Life for me is no longer a physical existence. I do not care much for that. I only care to live long enough to get through the press the last two volumes covering fifty years of work.
>
> John Rogers Commons, *Myself* (1934b)

John Rogers Commons was born in Richmond, Indiana in 1862.[1] After graduating from Oberlin College, in 1888 he began studying his PhD at Johns Hopkins University under Richard T. Ely. However, he failed to complete his PhD and took up a number of teaching positions in economics and sociology. His early life as an academic was marred by difficulties. At Syracuse University in 1899, his chair in sociology was ended by withdrawal of funds, because of his alleged 'radical tendencies'. With no hope of another academic position, Commons entered a period of research work for government, trade unions and political parties. His own thinking was transformed during this period (Gonce, 2002). His writings earned him some fame and respect. Eventually, with the help of Ely, he returned to academia by securing a position at the University of Wisconsin in 1904. He was to remain there until his retirement in 1932.

Commons was elected president of the American Economic Association in 1917 and became one of the most influential economists of the twentieth century. John Maynard Keynes (1931, pp. 303–4) was attracted by some of his ideas (Skidelsky, 1992, p. 229; Hodgson, 2001c, p. 216). In his classic book on *The Functions of the Executive*, the organization theorist Chester Barnard (1938, pp. 202–5) cited Commons at length (Fiorito, 2000, pp. 273–6). In addition, two Nobel Laureates in economics, Gunnar Myrdal (1978, p. 771) and Herbert Simon (1979, p. 499) have claimed to be significantly influenced by Commons (Forest and Mehier, 2001). Finally, Oliver

---

1 This chapter is a revised and extended version of Hodgson (2003d).

Williamson (1975, pp. 3, 254; 1985, pp. 3–5; 2002, pp. 438–9) has repeatedly singled out Commons as an 'old' institutionalist whose work is especially close to his 'new' institutional economics.

Commons was highly involved in the legal and institutional realities of his day. As well as his famous *Legal Foundations of Capitalism*, he led teams of researchers that produced extensive historical studies of American industrial and labour relations (Commons, 1924; Commons *et al.*, 1910–11, 1918–35). Commons probably did more than anyone to establish the importance of legal matters for American economics. In practical terms, he helped to draft a whole series of bills on labour and industrial matters for the State of Wisconsin (Kaufman, 1998). In the first half of the twentieth century, no one had a more sensitive finger on the institutional and juridical pulse of American capitalism than Commons. Indeed, as Marc Tool (2000, p. 122) put it: 'Certainly no institutional economist in the 20th century has had a greater impact on the actual structure of the American economy than has John R. Commons.'

Nevertheless, even a present-day Commons follower, such as Yngve Ramstad (1995), has noted Commons's 'puzzling inconsequentiality as an economic theorist'. Kenneth Boulding (1957, p. 8) described Commons's work as a 'tangled jungle of profound insights, culled by an essentially nontheoretical mind from a life rich with experiences of economic realities'. If we were to characterize Commons's work in no more than twenty words it would be difficult to improve on Boulding's statement. This is not to say that Commons's work was atheoretical or anti-theoretical. But Commons did not have the stature of a major theorist such as Alfred Marshall or Karl Marx. Furthermore, he did not have the aptitude for careful definitions or logical chains of reasoning. As Neil Chamberlain (1963, p. 87) argued of Commons:

> It would be stretching a point … to speak of him as a theorist. If he is intent on conceptualization, he shows little interest in – perhaps even some aversion to – knitting those concepts into a system of thought.

Similarly, Viktor Vanberg (1989, p. 343) has noted that Commons's arguments were hampered by his 'idiosyncratic terminology and unsystematic style of reasoning'. It is in these senses that Commons's work was 'essentially nontheoretical'. This helps to account for the fact that Commons's attempt to provide a theoretical foundation for institutional economics was ultimately a failure.

Elsewhere I have focused on Commons's work on historical periodization and 'ideal types' (Hodgson, 2001c). It would be impossible here to address every remaining aspect of Commons's theoretical work. Among the important remaining omissions are his theory of transactions and his theory of reasonable value. These are significant contributions but they are less central to the argument here. Instead, the priority is to focus on the most fundamental philosophical and theoretical aspects of Commons's work, involving questions of causality, agency and social structure. Some of Commons's greatest achievements were in regard to practical matters of institutional intervention, and these strengths are not necessarily undermined by his theoretical or philosophical failings. By focusing on Commons as a philosopher and theorist, we are addressing the weakest part of his legacy. But because of Commons's crucial role in the development of the theoretical foundations of institutional economics, some audit in this area is appropriate. And because his weakest zone is the sole object of criticism here, no summary claim is made about the deficiencies or merits of Commons's work as a whole.

It has been argued in preceding chapters that an essential feature of the 'old' institutional economics is the recognition that, for the purposes of economic analysis, individual purposes and preferences are to some degree socially formed. Commons (1899, p. 3) recognized this too, seeing institutions 'shaping each individual'. Commons (1934a, pp. 73–4) likewise made it clear that 'the individual with whom we are dealing is the Institutionalized Mind'. By this broad and minimal criterion, Commons was fully in this institutionalist tradition. But, unlike Veblen, Commons did not attempt to examine the causal processes and psychological mechanisms by which an individual is moulded by their circumstances. The purpose of this chapter is to evaluate Commons's attempts to provide institutional economics with a systematic methodological and theoretical foundation.[2]

The main issues involved in this appraisal are: Commons's neglect of the instinct–habit psychology of William James and others; his failure to appreciate the philosophical and other insights of Darwinism; his failure to incorporate the idea of emergent properties; and his failure to give sufficient emphasis to extra-legal institutions, or spontaneous orders that do not involve legal rules.

Commons himself played no significant part in the launch of 'institutional economics' by Walton Hamilton and others in 1918. Remarkably, Commons was not regarded as part of the American institutionalist movement until the appearance of his *Legal Foundations* in 1924. In his extensive review, Wesley Mitchell (1924b, p. 253) saw Commons's book as belonging 'to the institutional type of economics, the type represented in Germany by Sombart, in England by Mr. and Mrs. Webb, in America by Veblen' and others. It was not until after Veblen's death that Commons began to identify himself explicitly as an institutionalist (Rutherford, 2000a, 2000b, 2001). In his *Institutional Economics*, Commons (1934a) made his first comprehensive attempt to provide a systematic theoretical foundation for institutionalism.

---

2 Other evaluations include Bazzoli (1999), Bazzoli and Dutraive (1999), Biddle (1990a, 1990b), Chamberlain (1963), Harter (1962), C. Lawson (1994, 1996), Leathers (1989), Parsons (1985), Perlman and McCann (1998, pp. 547–59), Ramstad (1986, 1990), Rutherford (1983), Van de Ven (1993) and Vanberg (1989, 1997).

Personal contact between Veblen and Commons had been sparse and relatively inconsequential.[3] There are only a few references to Veblen in Commons's works. Significantly, in one of the few passages where Commons discussed Veblen at length, it is where Commons (1934a, pp. 649–77) judged Veblen's approach as inadequate for his theory of 'reasonable value'. For Commons, practical or evaluative issues came first. He was concerned to provide institutionalism with a theory that was an operational guide for economic policy and legislation. In part, these attempts build upon earlier works on 'sociological' theory by Commons in the 1897–1900 period (Commons, 1897, 1899–1900), as well as on his *Legal Foundations*.

Throughout this chapter, comparison is made between Commons and Veblen. There are theoretical similarities between their works, most obviously in their shared focus on institutions and their mutual denial of the 'natural' character of any prevailing social order. The aim is not to show that Veblen was a perfect theorist. Indeed, the works of Veblen are less systematic and sometimes less well structured than those of Commons. It should also be pointed out that even the early institutional economics of the 1920s was far from entirely Veblenian. Instead, the comparison between Veblen and Commons is intended to show that, despite his manifest limitations, Veblen had a deeper understanding of theoretical and philosophical tenets that could serve as a possible foundation for institutional economics. Commons faced the options of *either* improving upon these theoretical and philosophical presuppositions *or* replacing them by something superior. The argument here is that Commons achieved neither.

Commons's tardy attempts to develop a systematic theory for institutionalism emerged in a time when several of the Veblenian theoretical and philosophical tenets had become unfashionable in the social sciences. It has been shown in the preceding chapter that the psychological and philosophical ideas that were central to the work of Veblen and many others had come under attack by the 1920s. Instinct–habit psychology had been largely replaced by behaviourism. Positivism was pushing aside other tendencies in philosophy, including pragmatism, emergentism and anything that smacked of metaphysics.

Commons's work on the theoretical foundations of institutionalism was in this highly difficult context. The limitations of his work must be understood alongside the huge intellectual shifts of his time. He faced a difficult choice: he could attempt to defend the Veblenian foundations from attack, or he could try to find adequate alternative philosophical and

---

3 In a letter to Joseph Dorfman of 24 May 1932, Commons wrote: 'I have no personal relationship with Mr. Veblen except casual visits with him. My conversations with him have been very short and rather incidental to other things. I first met him about twenty years ago in Chicago, but we did not discuss anything of material interest' (quoted in Tilman, 1996, p. 27). By contrast, there was greater contact between Commons and Mitchell (Dorfman, 1958).

psychological foundations for institutionalism. He leaned towards the latter option. But few thinkers could swim so strongly against the torrent, or build so much single-handed on new land. It is not surprising that Commons failed.

The next section proposes that Commons did not incorporate insights from instinct–habit psychology and lacked an adequate causal explanation of human motivation. The section after that discusses Commons's limited appreciation of Darwinism, including his attempt to substitute 'artificial' for 'natural' selection in the social sphere. Another section discusses his treatment of emergent properties. The penultimate section addresses his treatment of social institutions and legal structures.

Commons, psychology and pragmatism

On the whole, and in marked contrast to the writings of Veblen, there are very few references in Commons's works to the instinct–habit psychologies of James or McDougall. Essentially, where Commons generally differed from the instinct–habit psychologists was in his emphasis on the primacy of belief for action. By contrast, Peirce, James and McDougall saw habit as foundational and constitutive for both action and belief. Commons generally differed by seeing beliefs and volitions – as separate from habits and instincts – as the ultimate drivers of human activity. This volitional emphasis persisted in his works.

Commons (1934b, p. 20) candidly admitted that he 'never studied psychology' except with a professor at Oberlin College who ridiculed some of his ideas. Mark Perlman (1996, p. 224) pointed out that Commons was 'not *au courant* with developments in social psychology'. Alexa Albert and Yngve Ramstad (1997, p. 881) asserted that: 'Commons regrettably failed to make his psychological assumptions explicit.' Nevertheless, some attitudes to the pragmatist and behaviourist schools of psychology are apparent from a few key passages in his works.

One passage in Commons's *Legal Foundations* betrays much about his position. Commons (1924, p. 82) wrote: 'Science deals with probabilities and superficialities', rather than underlying causal mechanisms. Here he embraced an interpretation of science that was consistent with positivism. He approvingly reported that 'the behaviorist defines the will as what the will does' and 'passes over to others' the question of what determines and triggers the will. Here Commons showed that his psychological presuppositions were behaviourist in some respects. He endorsed the behaviourist abandonment of any attempt to explain what lies behind human motivation or will. However, in contrast to behaviourism, Commons emphasized the importance of volition or will.

In the first journal article in which Commons clearly proclaimed himself as an institutionalist, Commons (1931, pp. 654–5) proclaimed: 'institutional economics is behavioristic'. He continued: 'If institutional economics is volitional it requires an institutional psychology to accompany it. This is the psychology of transactions, which may properly be named negotiational psychology.' He then noted without qualm that 'negotiational psychology' is 'a behavioristic psychology'. On one page Commons (1934a, p. 637) approvingly quoted Charles Judd, the leading and influential critic of the psychologies of James and McDougall. In three places in the same work, Commons (pp. 91, 95, 640) mentioned John Watson, the father of behaviourism. Commons (p. 640) objected to the treatment of 'the individual in a purely individualist fashion' by behaviourists such as Watson, but he did not object to the behaviourist attack on instinct–habit psychology. He gave the impression that behaviourist psychology was partly consistent with his own view but insufficient for his purposes. Commons followed Mitchell and Ayres in adopting some aspects of behaviourism, and in abandoning instinct–habit psychology.

But in contrast to both behaviourism and pragmatism, Commons erected human volition as if it were an independent causal category. Commons (1950, p. 36) called for 'a science of the human will' and denied that the human will is largely capricious or undetermined. Commons (1934a, p. 741) argued that a 'capricious and lawless' will would be 'incapable of the uniformities required by science'. While Commons (1934a, p. 739) rejected a 'capricious and undetermined' human will, he did not spell out how the will was determined. He merely hinted at a vague process of social conditioning and opened the door for a 'negotiational' and behaviourist psychology. It is evident that Commons saw institutions and customs as affecting human wills. But again there was no clear explanation of the causal processes involved. Are human volitions somehow constructed by institutions or simply channelled and constrained by them? On such questions, Commons was unclear. Above all, there was no systematic theory of the causal origins of human will itself. Commons emphasized volition but gave it no explanatory foundation.

Commons's use of key terms such as instinct, habit and custom yield some clues concerning his reading of pragmatist philosophy and psychology. Commons occasionally mentioned instinct in his earlier works, but he made little of it. Commons (1919, pp. 313–14) noted with scepticism that a 'definition of instinct as a born-disposition that is both variable and adaptive' permits the author 'to combine the instincts in whatever arrangement seems called for by his illustrations'. Behaviourists voiced similar complaints against instinct–habit psychology. Subsequently, the concept of instinct largely disappeared from Commons's discourse. Commons never embraced instinct–habit psychology, and he removed the word 'instinct' from his writing as soon as it became widely unpopular. Commons did accept that some human capacities are inherited, but he gave the concept of instinct no part in the further formation of habits or behaviour.

In contrast, the idea of custom is found in both his early and his later works. One of Commons's (1924, pp. 298–306) extensive discussions of the concept was in his *Legal Foundations*. Commons saw custom as a pattern of similar and enduring behaviour in a social group. Ten years later, in his *Institutional Economics*, the concept of custom was prominent. There Commons (1934a, pp. 155, 701) wrote that 'custom is repetition' and of the 'compulsion of custom'. But this simply underlined his theoretical confusion between behaviour and its underlying causes, and his failure to consider how customs impinge causally upon individual wills. Typically, Commons (1950, p. 110) defined custom as follows: 'Custom is such similarity of behavior as may be expected to continue almost unchanged in the future.'

Commons repeatedly asserted that customs play a role in moulding individual behaviour. Commons (1924, p. 301) wrote: 'The binding power of custom is its security of expectations.' Here he implied that repeated behaviour within a group leads each individual to form stable expectations concerning the future. Somehow this also leads individuals to be bound to the behaviour of the majority. In the same volume, Commons (1924, pp. 300, 349) also mentioned habit, but he did not emphasize any causal connections between habits and customs.

Dewey (1922, p. 58) had written: 'But to a larger extent customs persist because individuals form their personal habits under conditions set by prior customs.' In other words, customs affect habits and these ingrained habits help customs to persist. Belatedly taking part of this on board, Commons (1934a, p. 155) saw customs as group behaviours 'which impose conformity of habitual assumptions upon individuals'. He thus adopted Dewey's idea that there is a causal link from customs to individual habits.

However, Commons did not complete the circle of causation and show, in turn, how habits help 'customs persist'. Dewey (1922) himself pointed to a circular and durable process, through which the imitation and constraint of custom lead individuals to adopt concordant patterns of behaviour. These behaviours give rise to individual habits. These habits help to sustain the same behavioural patterns across the group. These, in turn, become customs, thus completing the circle of causation.

Commons was unable to complete the Deweyian circle of causation because he mangled Dewey's concept of habit. To explain this, let us turn to this third key concept and its role in Commons's thought. While the idea of habit first appeared in his *Legal Foundations*, it played a brief and minor part. Commons (1924, p. 349) there defined habits as 'the sub-conscious setting of body, nerves and brain on the basis of past experience and ready to set off in accustomed directions when touched by stimulus from outside'. He then approvingly quoted Dewey (1922, p. 76): 'Habit is energy organized in certain channels.' What is interesting about the brief and sporadic mention of habit in *Legal Foundations* is that there the concept is defined as a propensity or disposition, rather than repeated behaviour. Likewise, Dewey (1922) made it clear that habits are potentialities and predilections, rather than repeated acts. The pragmatists and instinct–habit psychologists saw habits as bundles of potentialities and dispositions, to be possibly triggered by intentions, perceptions or events. It has been established in Chapter 7 above that Veblen, pragmatist philosophers and instinct–habit psychologists generally adopted the non-behaviourist meaning of habit as an acquired propensity or disposition, which may or may not be actually expressed in behaviour.

Note that the issue of the nature and primacy of habit is quite separate from the issue of the acceptance or otherwise of unintended, non-deliberative or unconsciously motivated behaviour. In a few passages, in both early and later works, Commons (1899, pp. 348, 354; 1934a, p. 698) accepted the possibility of unconsciously motivated behaviour. But Commons did not embrace the pragmatist and Veblenian view that all action and decision is necessarily grounded on habit. Instead of habit, Commons gave universal emphasis to will.

When Commons attempted to systematize institutionalism in the 1930s, he briefly engaged more deeply with pragmatism, particularly in the version developed by Peirce. Commons once explained to Kenneth Parsons (1985, p. 189) how he had been inspired by Peirce's (1878) famous essay: 'How to make our ideas clear'. But it seems that this inspiration came relatively late in Commons's life. There is no reference to Peirce in the *Legal Foundations*. In contrast, Commons's *Institutional Economics* (1934a) contains lengthy references to Peirce. We may conjecture that Commons read Dewey (1922) shortly after its publication, and read Peirce's 1878 essay sometime between 1924 and 1934, while he was writing his *Institutional Economics*. Commons may have also read other works by Peirce, but there is no significant mention of this philosopher until after 1924. Furthermore, Commons's assimilation of these pragmatist ideas was partial and incomplete.[4]

Despite his belated engagement with pragmatism, Commons wanted beliefs and volitions, instead of habits, to retain primacy in the explanation of behaviour. Accordingly, as soon as Commons stressed the idea of habit, he regrettably switched from a dispositional to a behaviourist conception of that term. Commons (1934a, pp. 45, 155, 740) thus wrote repeatedly: 'Habit ... the mere repetition of acts ... Habit is repetition by one person. ... Habit is a repetition of acts'. Hence, for Commons in 1934, habit meant

---

4 In contrast, Albert and Ramstad (1997, 1998) have argued that Commons's ideas were 'congruent' with Dewey (1922) and also 'concordant' with the work of another pragmatist, Mead (1934). In response, it must first be noted that the overwhelming majority of textual references cited in support of these propositions are to *Institutional Economics*, which is admitted here as the high watermark of Commons's incomplete and imperfect engagement with pragmatism. However, in contrast to Albert and Ramstad, some differences between Commons and Dewey have been exposed here. As for the alleged concordance with Mead, Albert and Ramstad (1998, p. 3) themselves admitted that 'Commons was evidently unaware of Mead's work in the areas of philosophy and social psychology.' Personally, I find the Albert and Ramstad (1997, 1998) essays as more an exercise in wishful imputation than a grounded exegesis of what Commons actually wrote and thought.

repeated behaviour or effect, rather than an acquired individual disposition, or propensity. With this definition, the concept of habit itself serves little analytical purpose other than to point to repeated behavioural patterns. This faulty, behaviourist conception of habit contrasted with the more satisfactory notion of James, Veblen and Dewey.

The closest that Commons got to James, Veblen and Dewey on this issue in his *Institutional Economics* was to write in some places of 'habitual assumptions' that are 'taken for granted' and may thus underlie behaviour (Commons, 1934a, pp. 155, 697–702). Such 'habitual assumptions' have some superficial resemblance to Veblen's 'habits of thought'. But for Veblen (1899a, pp. 191–2, 289) 'habits of thought' were 'mental attitudes and aptitudes' that involve some 'mental adaptation' and which make 'up the character of any individual'. In contrast, for Commons (1934a, p. 155) 'habitual assumptions' were related to the 'experiences, feelings, and expectations of an individual'. While Veblen wrote of mental capacities or propensities, Commons wrote more frequently of mental sensations or effects.

As noted above, Commons's concept of custom was also specified in terms of behaviour rather than propensities. Commons (1934a, p. 155) described the difference between habit and custom as follows: 'Habit is repetition by one person. Custom is repetition by the continuing group of changing persons.'[5] Also as noted above, he saw a causal link from custom to habit: customary 'forces' alone somehow built up habits. Commons (1934a, p. 45) wrote that 'custom is … the social habit which creates the individual habit. We do not start as isolated individuals … We start and continue by repetition, routine, monotony – in short by custom.' Here Commons echoed the pragmatist view of the priority of social activity, but he did not go further to embrace further essentials of pragmatism, particularly concerning the causal origins of human motivation.

Customary practices have an effect on individuals and may lead to acquired individual habits. But it is also essential to point to the psychological means and social mechanisms involved in this process. An individual, placed in a complex social world of many rules and customs, requires a set of concepts to make sense of this world and his or her priorities. Furthermore, the individual requires knowledge of a language to converse with others and to understand meanings. A behaviourist psychologist would argue that all this could be developed in the individual through the repeated mechanism of stimulus and response. It is now well established in psychology that this behaviourist mechanism is highly inadequate, at least for the acquisition of language and the cognition of social rules (Degler, 1991; Cosmides and Tooby, 1994a, 1994b; Pinker, 1994; Plotkin, 1994, 1997). For these modern psychologists, and for early pragmatists such as James,

---

5   Here Commons was possibly influenced by Sumner (1906, p. 3) who wrote of 'habit in the individual and custom in the group'.

the acquisition of habit is often triggered by human instincts, as well as by institutional and customary constraints. Accordingly, the earlier outlook of the pragmatist instinct–habit psychologists has now been largely rehabilitated. Although custom is important, custom alone cannot provide the individual with behavioural predispositions, and with a set of concepts and meanings to deal with the world. The individual requires a set of instinctive triggers to act in specific ways so that elemental habits of action and interpretation can be built up, and so that customs and institutions can do their work.

Commons seemed to suggest, in a positivist and behaviourist manner, that the mind is a *tabula rasa* on which customs make their marks. However, learning is more an active, interpretative process of problem formulation and problem solving, and is not confined to the imprinting of information or custom. Prior suppositions and conjectures are necessary to start the learning process. These are programmed into our being, either as inherited instincts or acquired habits. Crucially, in a context where behaviourist psychology and positivism were in the ascendant, Commons failed to appreciate the valuable legacy of the instinct–habit psychologists. Inclining instead toward behaviourism, he lacked an adequate explanation of psychological motivation or volition.

Taking stock of this part of the argument, not only did Commons fail to examine the crucial causal links between custom and habit, and between habit and instinct, but also his concept of habit was itself defective. He emphasized volition but did not see the origin and evolution of these volitions upon substrates of triggering instincts and acquired habits. He never satisfactorily explained, even in principle, the causes of human wills or beliefs.

While reading his *Institutional Economics*, we should not be misled by the many citations of Peirce and the plentiful mentions of habit and custom. Commons embraced a limited version of pragmatism no earlier than the 1930s. It is only in his *Institutional Economics* that the notion of habit acquires prominence. However, his use of this pragmatist intellectual apparatus is bowdlerized and idiosyncratic. Notably, after the 1934 fanfare, the concept of habit drops out of the limelight. In his posthumously published *Economics of Collective Action*, both the concept of habit, and references to pragmatism, play an insignificant role.

In Commons's written output through time, the three concepts of instinct, custom and habit, and the doctrine of pragmatism as a whole, have different citation frequencies, and different citation profiles. First, in contrast to Veblen, instinct played an insignificant role throughout the work of Commons. Second, custom had a contrasting, higher and enduring citation profile, appearing in both his early and later works. Third, habit tentatively appeared in his writings in the 1920s. When it made its full appearance in the 1930s, its definition was changed, in line with Commons's wholly volitional conception of action. But his behaviourist conception of habit played no significant theoretical role, other than as an individual analogue of social custom. Subsequently, habit quickly disappeared from prominence in his work. Concerning pragmatism, James was cited rarely and Dewey occasionally, but Peirce made a sudden and prominent impact in his *Institutional Economics*. He too then virtually disappeared from view, being absent from the quite extensive index of the *Economics of Collective Action*.

On the whole, Commons's attempts to provide institutionalism with a psychological foundation were equivocal and inadequate. Commons was belatedly inspired by pragmatism but this influence was partial and incompletely sustained. He was also influenced by behaviourism, despite his emphasis on volition. Commons's position was not unusual as the social and behavioural sciences were recast in the 1930s. Like many others, he adopted a volitional theory of action in his social science, while tolerating behaviourism in the separated domain of psychology.

Commons and Darwinism

We address here the issue of 'natural' versus 'artificial' selection. While Veblen (1899a, p. 188) called for a theory of the 'natural selection of institutions', Commons (1897, p. 90), declared:

> The term 'natural selection' is a misnomer, as Darwin himself perceived. It means merely survival. 'Selection' proper involves intention, and belongs to human reason. Selection by man we call artificial.

Commons (1934a, pp. 45, 120, 636–8, 657–8, 713) persisted in his view that economic evolution involved 'artificial selection' rather than 'natural selection' (Ramstad, 1994; Bazzoli, 2000). In some passages, Commons (1897, p. 95) saw artificial and natural selection as coexisting in human society: 'Social selection is partly natural and partly artificial.' Elsewhere Commons (1924, p. 376) saw one as replacing the other: 'Economic phenomena … are the result of artificial selection and not of natural selection.'

Commons may have emphasized artificial over natural selection to reinforce his valid insistence that customs and institutions were human creations; they were neither decreed by God nor ordained as optimal by nature. But 'natural selection' implies neither optimality nor lack of human involvement. Furthermore, if an outcome results from 'natural selection' it does not mean that all other possibilities are unnatural. Natural selection does not have the conservative political implications that Commons may have perceived.

As Commons was aware, it was Darwin himself that established a distinction between 'natural' and 'artificial' selection. However, contrary to the impression given by Commons and others, Darwin (1859) rarely used the term 'artificial' selection. He wrote of selection 'applied methodically' by humans to domesticated animals. This was primarily to convince his readers that descent with modification was possible, and thereby to introduce the concept of natural selection. Emphatically, Darwin did not suggest that 'artificial' and 'natural' selection were mutually exclusive. Instead, examples of the former were used to support the idea of the latter. As Darwin's friend George Romanes (1893, p. 296) wrote in explaining Darwin's theory: 'In a word, the proved capabilities of artificial selection furnish, in its best conceivable form, what is called an argument *a fortiori* in favour of natural selection.'

Generally, Commons did not endorse the theoretical role that Veblen had given to Darwinism in the social domain. For instance, Commons (1924, p. 376) referred to 'the natural selection stage of blind evolution that followed Darwin, whose distinguished exponent in economics is Veblen'. He regarded this version of evolution as unacceptable in social theory because it 'attempted to get rid of the human will and to explain economic phenomena as the working out of natural forces'. In contrast with 'blind' natural selection, Commons (1924, p. 376) upheld:

> But volitional theory takes exactly the opposite point of view. Economic phenomena, as we know them, are the result of artificial selection and not of natural selection.

Here Commons denied that social evolution is 'Darwinian' because he saw Darwinism as involving the 'blind' forces of natural selection. Ten years later, in an isolated passage, he modified his position slightly, and admitted some limited scope for the application of Darwinian ideas. Commons (1934a, p. 638) noted that

> transactions, since the principle of scarcity runs through them, have curious analogies to the factors which Darwin discovered in organisms. Custom, the repetition of transactions, is analogous to heredity; the duplication and multiplication of transactions arise from pressure of population; their variability is evident, and out of the variabilities come changes in custom and survival. But here the survival is the 'artificial selection' of good customs and punishment of bad customs.

In this exceptional passage, Commons admitted Darwinian selection as a possible analogy in the social sphere, but only if it were translated into the terms of 'artificial selection'. Commons did not sustain or develop this view that Darwinism could serve as a qualified analogy in social science, but his emphasis on the concept of artificial selection was a constant theme throughout his academic career.[6]

According to Darwin, 'artificial' or 'methodological' selection occurs when a human breeder selects strains of a plant or animal, on the basis of their attributes, for propagation. The essential characteristic of artificial selection is that humans manipulate the process or environment of selection.

The 'artificiality' of the selection process stems principally from the fact that it is under the control of a human agent. But other animals make selections too. There is nothing that especially privileges humans above other animals in this respect. Ants collect live aphids. A tiger selects its prey. A cow eats the tastiest grass. Accordingly, the distinction between social and natural evolution is not so dramatic in this respect as some have supposed.

Contrary to Laure Bazzoli (2000, p. 68) in her attempt to vindicate Commons, natural selection does not necessarily involve 'a given environment, a process which is outside the control of organisms'. First, there are plentiful acknowledgements in the writings of Darwin and other evolutionary biologists of changing environments of selection, including climatic and other changes. Second, animals often change their environment, as well as merely adapting to it (Lewontin, 2000). This phenomenon is associated with thousands of species. Most ants and birds build nests, spiders build webs to snare other insects, and beavers build dams to capture fish. A degree of deliberation and cunning may be involved in the construction of some of these environmental niches. Admittedly, the degree of conscious deliberation and planning that is involved may be much less than in some human activities, but the difference is consistent with the evolution of humans from other species.

There is also evidence of a proto-culture among some animals. For example, a group of macaque monkeys discovered techniques such as washing potatoes in salt water and using water to separate grain from sand. Other macaque groups observed and then copied these behaviours (Degler, 1991, pp. 344–6). A species of British bird learned how to peck through foil milk bottle caps. This innovation then spread by the species through the entire country (Hinde and Fisher, 1951). However, there is some dispute as to the degree to which such cases involve genuine learning by imitation, or merely stimulus enhancement: where the attention of the individual is drawn to the location, the materials and perhaps the reward. But at some stage genuine culture must have emerged among our ancestors. Derek Freeman (1983) analysed the evolution of cultural capacities from animals through to humans. Whenever it developed, the capacity to produce and absorb cultural adaptations is itself a result of natural selection, because that emergent capacity enhanced reproductive success.

Furthermore, the human plant or animal breeder who is doing the selection is also a product of natural evolution. The selector and his or her

---

6 Biddle (1990b, pp. 38–9) argued that Ward, who emphasized human purpose, influenced Commons's view on artificial selection. However, I detect little evidence of the influence of Ward on Commons. For instance, Ward's (1903) central concepts of 'creative synthesis' and 'synergy' are absent from Commons's work. Furthermore, unlike Commons, Ward saw language as an institution and saw it as a member of a substantial class of institutions that are largely spontaneous in origin. In contrast, as noted below, Commons neglected institutions that were spontaneous and did not involve laws.

preferences are also caused, and have to be explained. Human preferences are themselves a product of (social, cultural and biological) evolution. The criteria that the human uses in selecting specimens for 'artificial' selection are also the outcomes of processes of cognitive development and cultural evolution. This opens the door again for the theory of natural selection. Hence it is a misunderstanding to see artificial selection as an alternative to natural selection.

A prominent institutional economist took up this important point very early. In criticizing Commons, Morris Copeland (1936, pp. 343–4) pointed out that Commons's 'artificial selection' of institutions depended on the prior 'natural selection' of the guiding ethical or other principles that were used in the selecting process. Copeland's valid point was that the evolution of the criteria used in any 'artificial' selection must also be explained. Copeland thus identified the same weakness in Commons's theory that is identified above: Commons lacked even a rudimentary account of what causes human motivation, action or choice. Hence Commons could not explain the causal mechanisms behind the 'artificial' selections made by the breeder of animals or plants. For Commons, any backward-in-time, sequential explanation of effect and cause comes to an abrupt stop when it comes to the human will.[7]

Even when 'artificial selection' does take place, that is not the end of the story. Different institutions or societies, in which artificial selection is involved, sometimes compete against each other. Hence some additional processes of evolutionary selection may be involved. In no way can artificial selection replace or demote a broader concept of evolutionary selection in human society.

In *The Hitch Hiker's Guide to the Galaxy* – the wonderful science fiction comedy by Douglas Adams (1979) – it is proposed that humans are the third most intelligent species on Earth, after the white mice and the dolphins.[8] The white mice performed a complex experiment on humans, while just pretending that the humans are performing experiments on them. In such a case, who is artificially selecting whom? As Daniel Dennett (1995, p. 317) reported: 'all the biologists I have queried on this point have agreed with me that there are no sure marks of natural, as opposed to artificial, selection'. Most conceptions of 'artificial selection' artificially and anthropocentrically presume that humans are the choosing agents, but other species are not. The truth is that all reasonably intelligent species are making real choices. These selections may be 'artificial' but 'natural selection' governs the whole.

It may be true that humans are the most intelligent species on Earth and that they have the greatest capacity for conscious prefiguration,

---

7 It should also be pointed out that while Veblen saw the need for a theoretical explanation of the criteria of selection, he did not provide a detailed and adequate theoretical account of these selection processes.

8 The work was originally a radio series, recordings of which are available from the BBC.

deliberation and choice. To a unique extent, we imagine possibilities of choice and action in advance. But these capacities evolved, and also exist to a limited degree in other species (Donald, 1991). As Darwin (1871, vol. 1, p. 46) himself wrote: 'animals possess some power of reasoning. Animals may constantly be seen to pause, deliberate and resolve.' To assume that no trace of judgement or reason occur within other species would be to raise a difficult question: when and how in evolutionary time were these special cognitive and volitional privileges bestowed upon humans? To avoid a religious or mystical answer, we have to assume that these cognitive attributes themselves evolved through time, and existed to some degree in pre-human species.

Commons was wrong to suggest that Darwinian theories of evolution exclude volitional behaviour. On the contrary, Darwin insisted that calculations and intentions had to be explained. This causal explanation has to show how intentions are formed in the psyche and how the capacity to form intentions itself evolved.

As Mitchell (1937, p. 333 n.) pointed out, Commons misunderstood Veblen on this point. Contrary to Commons (1924, p. 376), Veblen did not attempt 'to get rid of the human will' in his explanation of economic phenomena. Such pronouncements are very difficult to reconcile with statements by Veblen (1898b, p. 391) to the effect that: 'Economic action is teleological'. Veblen (1914, pp. 3–6, 31, 334) repeatedly saw human action as purposeful. What Veblen proposed was that intention or 'sufficient reason' had itself to be ultimately explained in terms of cause and effect. Veblen admitted human will, but also tried to explain its causal and evolutionary mechanisms.

Commons (1924, p. 82) abandoned any discussion of the determination of the human will, by proclaiming: 'Whether we hold to "determinism" or "indeterminism," does not matter for economic purposes.' Hence we pass 'over to others the question of whether the will is predetermined'. Commons thus abandoned the principle of determinacy. In contrast, Veblen understood Darwinism as involving an intrinsic commitment to causal explanations. For Veblen and Darwin alike, this commitment applied equally and forcibly to both the natural and the social spheres. Darwinism involves the idea that all outcomes are determined by some cause. It has been shown in Chapter 3 above that this does not imply an adherence to other forms of determinism, such as 'predictability determinism' or 'regularity determinism'.

Commons, emergence and biological reductionism

Commons was writing at a time when it was possible to adopt the concept of emergent properties. In his *Institutional Economics*, Commons (1934a, pp. 17, 96) referred briefly to the philosopher Alfred Whitehead. To some extent, Commons (1950, p. 117) wove the Whiteheadian themes of organicism and relatedness into his writing:

> The modern theory of relativity has superseded the older ideas in physics of the absolute distinctions between time and space, and between the investigator and the materials investigated; it is also urgent that we see the relativities in social action and investigations. ... The individual is a different person according to the nature of the concerns or transactions in which he participates. ... The individual is a system of relations, and changes with the collective action of which he is part and product.

Furthermore, Commons accepted that the relatedness of elements within a society meant that the whole was more than the sum of its parts. Commons (1924, p. 322) wrote, for example: 'A nation is not an addition of atoms but a multiplication of complementary by limiting factors'. But he did not go further to incorporate an explicit concept of emergence. By the late 1920s, emergentist philosophy was strongly challenged by its critics. This may partly explain why the influence of emergentist philosophy on Commons is at best slight. The one passage where Commons belatedly (1950, p. 135) mentioned 'emergent evolution' has been mentioned in Chapter 11.

Like Veblen, Commons made no significant and explicit use of the concept of an emergent property in his work. Where Commons differed from Veblen, however, was that some passages of his works seem to ignore the possibility of emergent properties and are remarkably reductionist in their implications. For example, in his book on *Races and Immigrants in America*, the first edition of which appeared in 1907, Commons (1920, p. 7) wrote of

> the problem of races, the fundamental division of mankind. Race differences are established in the very blood and physical constitution. They are most difficult to eradicate, and they yield only to the slow process of the centuries. Races may change their religions, their forms of government, their modes of industry, and their languages, but underneath all these changes they may continue the physical, mental, and moral capacities and incapacities which determine the real character of their religion, government, industry, and literature.

This passage betrays a remarkable biological reductionism, sustained even in a later edition of this early work. Here Commons reduced the character of social institutions to ethnic and biological terms. Commons believed that 'race differences' were most fundamental and determined 'the real character' of social culture and institutions. There was no recognition here that the emergent properties of diverse social structures might account for real differences in cultures and institutions, which, in turn, may overwhelm any biotic variation due to ethnic differences. Such biological reductionist ideas were not atypical of social scientists around the beginning of the twentieth century, when they were widespread among socialists and radicals as well as conservatives. But by the 1920s, these ideas were rapidly going out of fashion among liberal thinkers in North America and Britain.

In some of his essays, Veblen also discussed ethnic differences. But his conclusions were quite different from Commons. Writing in 1913, Veblen saw 'national and local types of physique and temperament' as 'hybrid types that have been selectively bred into these characteristic forms in adaptation to the peculiar circumstances of environment and culture'. Hence crucially, and in contrast to Commons, 'the local characters in question are of the nature of habits and are therefore to be classed as an institutional element rather than as characteristics of race' (Veblen, 1919a, p. 473). Also, we have already noted that Veblen (1909b, p. 300) argued that if everything was reducible to 'hereditary human nature, then there would be no institutions and no culture'. In contrast to the quoted passage from Commons, Veblen rejected biological reductionism and explicitly acknowledged the importance of multiple levels of analysis in economics and social theory.

Commons, individuals and institutions

In examining Commons's view of institutions, we shall assess three propositions:

1 For Commons, his notions of 'collective action' and 'collective will' involved the notion that institutions have a will of their own that transcends the wills of individuals.
2 Commons ignored the unintended effects of human interaction, including undesigned institutions.
3 Commons emphasized legal, rather than extra-legal institutions. He gave less attention to institutions – including some self-organizing institutions and spontaneous orders – that do not involve legal rules.

I shall explain below that I believe that one of these propositions is true and the two others are false. Several authors have criticized Commons in terms of propositions (1) and (2).[9] Some critics attack the concepts of 'collective action' and 'collective will' for their alleged attribution of intentions to institutions. Others criticize Commons for ignoring unintended consequences. However, several authors have showed that these criticisms are misguided (Rutherford, 1983; Vanberg, 1989; Biddle, 1990b; Ramstad,

9   See Olson (1965), Seckler (1975, pp. 126–30), Schotter (1981, p. 3) and Langlois (1986, p. 4 n.; 1989, pp. 285–7).

1990; C. Lawson, 1996). Commons did not say that organizations or collectives have distinct wills of their own, other than those resulting from the combined wills of individuals. In fact, Commons (1934a, pp. 96, 119) saw the comparison of society with an organism, with a social will of its own, as a 'false analogy'. Also, Commons did not assume that all institutions are the result of conscious design. He acknowledged unplanned outcomes and unintended consequences. Chamberlain (1963, pp. 71–2) summarized Commons's position very well:

> When Commons speaks of collective action, then, he is not referring simply to the activities of organizations such as business firms and labor unions, trade associations and government agencies. ... But in addition to collective action of the organized variety Commons includes unorganized custom, the laws of the state and the common law of the courts, the total bundle of patterns of conduct which a society sanctions or compels of its members. Even when an individual engages in a simple exchange with another individual, he acts within a framework of collective law and custom, so that collective action has in fact structured the relationship. Social custom and law are in fact the product of these interactions. People are not simply adapters to a code of property law, or conformers to a body of customs affecting the scarcity value of property ownership. In the process of dealing with each other, bargaining, negotiating, transacting, compromising, they bend and mold the customs, modify the judicial gloss on the law, help to create the very customs which affect their economic relationships. Collective action thus controls the individual; but the individual has some power (especially in concerted effort with others) to modify the nature of collective control.

In sum, as Jeff Biddle (1990b, p. 31) remarks: 'It is difficult to believe that someone who has read Commons could think that Commons did not appreciate the involuntary or unplanned effects of human action.' Consequently, propositions (1) and (2) are both false. Hence Commons not only accepted the possibility of unconsciously motivated *behaviour*, as noted above, but also he accepted the possibility of unintended *outcomes* of human action.

Having rejected propositions (1) and (2), let us move on to consider proposition (3). I argue, in contrast, that this proposition is true. Note that this proposition *does* admit the possibility of unintended consequences. This proposition does *not* say that Commons believed that all institutional phenomena are intended. But in proposition (3) we find a limitation of Commons's thinking. Commons (1899, p. 170) wrote:

> Social institutions ... are based on the coercive sanctions intrinsic in private property, which is the social expression of self-consciousness

and the origin of social institutions. Herein social organization is fundamentally different from physical or biological organization.

Commons here neglected institutions that involve neither private property nor laws, such as the institution of language. In part this may be a matter of the definition of an institution, but it also betrays a persistent relative neglect by Commons of powerful social structures that work through mechanisms other than (common or statute) law. Although the above quotation is from one of Commons's early essays – and must thereby be treated with due caution – this same neglect is manifest in all of Commons's works. While Commons does accept the importance of informal rules, whenever he wrote of 'institutions' he generally referred to structures involving laws.

Some of the most celebrated theoretical discussions of social institutions address phenomena of the self-organized type. Language is often regarded as such an institution (Searle, 1995). Instead of describing it as an institution, Commons (1934a, p. 73) referred to 'the custom of language'. Incidentally, this is problematic because of his behaviourist conception of custom as 'repetition by the continuing group' (Commons, 1934a, p. 155). Language is much more than repeated sounds or behaviour in a group. It is a complex of referents and meanings, with a syntactic structure that, incidentally, is not typically understood fully by its users. Language is not behaviour; even when conversation ceases the linguistic dispositions, vocabularies and syntactic structures remain.

Commons was right to see common law as a combination of undesigned custom and juridical legitimation. Commons (1924, pp. 298–301; 1934a, pp. 239–43) clearly argued that formal laws are often expressions of pre-existing, informal and undesigned social arrangements or customs. Rightly in my view, he did not depict common law as a purely spontaneous order. He saw it as a stabilizing and regulatory mechanism, as a legal extension and reinforcement of custom itself. In contrast to the writings of several libertarian and Marxian social theorists, Commons (rightly) did not treat the law as a mere epiphenomenon of social reality (Hodgson, 2001c, 2002a). For him, the law was constitutive. In particular, as Commons fully recognized, common law itself requires frequent legal interpretation, choice and judgement. It never works in an entirely spontaneous fashion, entirely outside powerful legal institutions. The outcome was that Commons had a superior understanding of the nature of law, which (rightly) disqualified it as a purely spontaneous mechanism.

His failure was elsewhere. He failed to consider adequately spontaneous orders and systems of rules that function without support or endorsement from the law. For example, consider Commons on working rules in going concerns. In society, many rules are clearly of an extra-legal character and many are not even written down. In one passage, Commons (1924, p. 136) considered the long-term 'evolution' of working rules, including the example of the evolution of the rules of language 'accepted in common by those who enter and remain with the group'. This might be interpreted as an acceptance of the possibility of an extra-legal spontaneous order. However, his use of the term 'evolution' undermines this, because of his repeated statements that evolution in society involves deliberate, 'artificial selection'. At best, there is no more than an undeveloped hint of the possibility of a spontaneous order here. This negative conclusion is further reinforced by another passage, where Commons (1924, p. 332) wrote of 'a working rule of a going concern, laid down by an authority'. Symptomatically, when Commons here considered rules that are not necessarily laws, he simultaneously considered an enforcing authority. And quickly, a few sentences later, his discussion shifted from working rules in general to those working rules that are regulated by laws. Just as Commons required social evolution to work through 'artificial selection' by some legislator or other authority, his discussions of the emergence of social rules depicted them as typically orchestrated by a powerful person or group.

In sum, Commons underestimated the possibility of emergent orders in society that, like self-organization in nature, do not emerge by means of juridical rules, but simply through the (coercive or otherwise) interactions of agents. Some institutions evolve without the use of laws. Carl Menger (1871) described these undesigned structures as 'organic' institutions. For example, a convention might emerge where people travel on one side of the road rather than the other, or a language evolves with its rules or meanings, or a monetary unit might emerge as a widespread medium of exchange. These are familiar examples of coordination outcomes that may emerge without an overall coordinator or a legal apparatus.

It is these cases of coordination equilibria that are most important for our argument here. Coordination rules (language, rules of the road) can differ from other rules involving normative constraints (legal or moral rules). A coordination equilibrium can be self-enforcing; because not only does each player lack any incentive to change strategy, but also each player wishes that other players keep to their strategy as well (Schotter, 1981, pp. 22–3; Schultz, 2001, pp. 64–6). Writers in the spontaneous order tradition – including Smith and Menger – often conflate these two types of rule. They often neglect social interactions where enforcement is neither spontaneous nor endogenous, and thus requires normative constraints (Vanberg, 1994, p. 65). Commons made the opposite error; he stressed problems of enforcement but gave little attention to coordination equilibria or rules.

Commons was right to emphasize that all institutions involve sanctions or coercion. All 'organic' institutions necessarily involve relative disincentives or 'sanctions', in the broad sense that Commons (1899, pp. 21–2, 170; 1900, p. 89; 1934a, p. 713) used the term. In his sense there are clear 'sanctions' against the mispronunciation of language or driving on the wrong side of the road, even if the law is not involved. It is by means of perceived penalties or incentives that 'organic' institutions may emerge. But by neglecting extra-legal self-organization and 'organic' institutions, he diminished the scope and impact of his valid argument. Accordingly, he failed to distinguish between those sanctions or constraints that are consistent with mutual self-interest, and those that have to be (additionally or in contrast) enforced by normative rules.

Hence it is quite misleading to see all institutions as the outcome of subordination to a 'single will' – as Commons (1899, p. 8; 1900, p. 89) put it – whether this 'single will' be of an individual or of a unanimous group. 'Organic' institutional outcomes and spontaneous orders are not only undesigned, but also they do not necessarily involve legal rules. They emerge instead as a result of individuals pursuing their own purposes, by the mutual benefits of coordination and by sanctions or constraints inherent in the evolving structure. Such patterned effects can emerge with automata and insects, as well as with humans. Hence in some respects they are similar to examples of self-organization and spontaneous order in nature (Nicolis and Prigogine, 1977; Prigogine and Stengers, 1984; Kauffman, 1993, 1995, 2000). But order and organization are not the same. It is necessary to understand the difference and analyse them both. While some social scientists over-stress order to the neglect of organization, Commons made the reverse mistake. Throughout his writings, Commons downplayed the phenomenon of spontaneous order or self-organization in society.

In Commons's (1934a, p. 720 ff.) discussion of the *Methodenstreit*, Menger was said to have 'eliminated all conformity to custom' from economic science. The idea of a spontaneous or 'organic' order was central to Menger's attack in the *Methodenstreit*. This suggests that Commons misunderstood Menger's idea of a spontaneous or 'organic' order as excluding any conformity to custom. Menger may have paid insufficient attention to custom, but he did not eliminate it. Obversely, when Commons stressed custom he did not admit the kind of undesigned order explored by Menger.

In a symptomatic passage where he discussed Smith's idea of the 'invisible hand', Commons (1923, p. 110) considered the possibility that an individual might act 'to augment the prosperity of the nation though he did not intend to do so'. But in the very next sentence he dismisses this postulate of unintended consequences as 'a theory of divine providence'. This passage also suggests that Commons did not fully appreciate the Smithian argument and possibility of self-organization or spontaneous order. In contrast, throughout his works, Commons promoted a conception of institutions as necessarily depending on a legal framework and some kind of supreme legal authority. He ignored such potentially spontaneous phenomena as coordination equilibria.

Typically, Commons considered how specific customs, rules and interpretations have evolved. He described how sometimes different customs or interpretations may come into conflict. He then cited cases of how the US Supreme Court has adjudicated on such matters, and the consequences for economic organization and activity. In such cases, the Supreme Court may intend the outcome. In other cases, another legal authority makes a decision: 'Somebody must choose between customs. Whoever chooses is the lawgiver' (Commons, 1924, p. 300). The choice was described as 'artificial selection'. For Commons, then, outcomes were typically represented by one will or more. As Allan Gruchy (1972, p. 41) wrote on Commons's work: 'Individual wills are congealed into a form of collective voliency or will-to-action.'

Commons's notion of a social structure was predominantly legal in character. This legal facet is important for many institutions, especially in societies under the rule of law (Hodgson, 2002c). But it is not true for all institutions, in either the present or the past. Typically, Commons saw institutions as the structured organization of individual wills acting in an evolving legal apparatus; where often a hegemonic group of individual wills coerce many others into obedience. His volitional economics placed an emphasis on individual volitions, either singly or in groups. For Commons, then, the key question is how one will is able to subordinate others. At this point he stressed legal frameworks of institutions and rules.

Another lacuna identified above in his thought is relevant here. Commons (1934a, pp. 73, 638, 698) believed in the 'institutionalized' mind, but he had no developed theory of how the individual mind was institutionalized. Concerning the behavioural functions of institutions, Commons (1931, pp. 648, 651; 1950, p. 21) clearly and repeatedly saw institutions as enabling and 'liberating' for individuals and groups, as well as constraining. This is valid and important. But he had is no psychological or other theory of institutionalization. In this explanatory absence, the temptation for Commons was to place emphasis on legal coercion and constraint.

By contrast, early American sociologists such as Edward Ross (1901) and especially Lester Ward (1903) wrote of 'the spontaneous development of society'. Similarly, Charles Ellwood (1912) adopted a distinction between a 'spontaneous' or 'natural' order, on the one hand, and a 'social order', on the other. Ellwood saw a 'spontaneous' order as underpinned by instinct, habit, custom and tradition. In contrast, a 'social order' was said to involve consciously formulated regulations and institutions, designed to ensure the conformity of the individual to the behaviour of the group. This distinction between designed and spontaneous social institutions was available in the early literature in American social science but seems to have evaded Commons. Commons (1899, pp. 168–70) was clearly aware of Ward and other early sociologists, but does not seem to be especially attracted by their concept of spontaneous order.

In contrast to Commons, Veblen (1899a, 1919a) had a theory of how institutions worked deeply on individual minds and intentions. Although Veblen failed to develop an explicit theory of institutional self-organization, he described institutions as shared habits, rather than behaviour that was always and necessarily under the guidance of a single authority. For

Veblen, the capacity for reason and action depended on the prior acquisition of appropriate habits. In turn, actions take place in institutional and cultural contexts that channel behaviours in specific directions. These new or developing behaviours give rise to new habits, providing a mechanism by which individual preferences and purposes can be moulded by institutional circumstances. Veblen did not take volitions as given for the purposes of institutional analysis. Commons did not adopt a Veblenian or any other theory of human motivation.

Conclusion

Taken as a whole, Commons's contribution to institutional economics is highly significant and important. He also should be given credit for attempting to provide institutional economics with the systematic theory. Neither Veblen, Mitchell nor any other American institutionalist made such a sustained attempt. He was also concerned to make this type of theory a viable tool for policy. But his attempt at theoretical construction was a failure. Commons neither developed a Veblenian approach nor developed an adequate alternative to it.

A successful development of a Veblenian approach was made much more difficult by the shift in prevailing academic opinion away from instinct–habit psychology and Darwinian modes of thinking. In addition, the rise of positivism and behaviourism created adverse conditions for the development of institutionalism along Veblenian lines.

Commons's response to these circumstances was an abandonment of instinct–habit psychology and an admission of some aspects of behaviourism. But he lacked any adequate theory of human motivation. However, this deficit was less visible after about 1930, because the social sciences as a whole were rapidly severing their links with both psychology and biology. Economists such as Lionel Robbins (1932) helped to transform economics into the science of choice, eschewing any explanation of how preferences were determined. Leading sociologists such as Talcott Parsons (1937) helped to turn sociology into a science of society where the psychological and biological aspects of human agency were again neglected. Commons's volitional economics relied on the wills of agents that had no explicit explanation in psychological, biological or other terms. But his line of argument fitted quite well with prominent developments in economics and sociology that emerged in the 1930s and lasted until about the 1970s.

Despite Veblen's celebration of a 'post-Darwinian' economics, Commons failed to incorporate the insights and attitudes of Darwinism. He did not appreciate that 'artificial selection' was no more than a special case of 'natural selection' and not an alternative to it. Unlike Veblen, Commons did not accept the Darwinian injunction to search for explanations of all phenomena, including of the human will itself. Commons's use of volition without explanation reflected the changing preoccupations of social science from the 1930s, but they were based on an ultimately doomed renunciation of Darwinian principles.

Sometime between 1924 and 1934, Commons read some works of Peirce and began to stress the concept of habit. However, *Institutional Economics* represents a forceful but incomplete, brief and unsustained, attempt to incorporate pragmatism. Its conception of habit is a mangled, semi-behaviourist transmutation of the Veblenian and pragmatist legacies. In these and other works, there is an inadequate treatment of the spontaneous and self-organizing aspects of institutions. For institutional economics these were tragic failures. But by the 1930s, American academia would not have been in the intellectual mood to accept an approach based on pragmatist philosophy, instinct–habit psychology or Darwinian principles.

In America in the 1930s, the influence and momentum of institutionalism were themselves sufficient to ensure its prominence and survival for at least two more decades. Enduring movements in economics require theoretical foundations, but they are not popularized by theory alone. An existing momentum is sustainable for a while, especially if it involves a similar policy vision and shared icons of belief. Institutionalism as a whole was concerned with the policy problem of 'social control' and had its enduring theoretical emblems, especially those emphasizing the importance of culture and institutions. These helped to keep institutionalism alive.

But in the absence of a viable theoretical system of the measure of Karl Marx's *Capital*, John Stuart Mill's *Principles*, Léon Walras's *Elements* or Alfred Marshall's *Principles*, it was inevitable that institutionalism would eventually be pushed aside by the emerging formalistic version of neoclassical theory. In the 1930s and 1940s, a younger generation of neoclassical economists – including John Hicks, Alvin Hansen and Paul Samuelson – synthesized Walrasian general equilibrium theory with a formalized version of Keynesian macroeconomics. Where Commons failed to provide an adequate theoretical system, Samuelson and others triumphed. In the circumstances, it would have been very difficult for Commons or any other institutionalist to succeed. As early as 1934 the writing for institutionalism was already on the wall.

14 Wesley Mitchell and the triumph of macroeconomics

> [The] pioneering work of the National Bureau on national income statistics in the twenties ... ushered in a revolution in the economic information system as profound in some ways as the revolution in astronomy caused by the telescope.
>
> Kenneth Boulding, 'A New Look at Institutionalism' (1957)

Despite the underdevelopment of its philosophical and psychological foundations and its lack of a systemic theoretical approach, institutional economics was to achieve a great deal in the 1920s and 1930s. Among the most impressive of its theoretical achievements was to provide some conceptual underpinnings for Keynesian macroeconomics. In this respect the greatest credit is due to Wesley Mitchell and his colleagues at the US National Bureau of Economic Research (NBER). More broadly, at the prestigious Columbia University in New York City, Mitchell built up a tradition of institutional economics that lasted well into the post-1945 era. In large part his career was a success story, and Mitchell thus ranks as the second most important figure in the history of institutional economics.

Institutional economists were responsible for several important theoretical achievements. But it is in the development of macroeconomics that the importance of Veblen's anti-reductionist stance rapidly became apparent. As Veblen established an institutional level of analysis above that of the individual, his student Mitchell developed the foundations of a system-wide, macroeconomic level of analysis. Although Mitchell did not make the ontological foundations of his work explicit, his achievements resonate with emergentist philosophy and modern theories of complexity.

Edwin Gay and Wesley Mitchell set up the NBER in 1920. Providing detailed statistical research for government and business, it received the bulk of its early funding from the Carnegie Corporation and the Commonwealth Fund. Its concentration on detailed facts rather than the promotion of specific policies drew respect from academia. Its strategy succeeded on business, governmental and academic fronts.[1]

Neither Mitchell nor John Maynard Keynes invented macroeconomics. The general idea of focusing on the nation or socio-economic system as a unit, and tracing its flows of goods, services and money from this systemic vantage point is much older. To some extent it is present in the writings of the French physiocrats of the eighteenth century and in the classical economics of Adam Smith and David Ricardo. From the beginning, the idea of *Nationalökonomie*, as prominent in the works of Friedrich List and the German historical school, involved a preoccupation with the wealth and health of the national socio-economic system (Hodgson, 2001c).

As noted in Chapter 10 above, some aspects of Keynesian macroeconomics were foreshadowed in Thorstein Veblen's *Theory of Business Enterprise* (Veblen, 1904; Vining, 1939; Raines and Leathers, 1996). However, the closest precursor to macroeconomics in the Keynesian sense was the work of Karl Marx, particularly his treatment of the circulation of capital and of the capitalist system as a whole, in the second and third volumes of *Capital*, respectively (Marx, 1978, 1981). Marx's 'reproduction schemes' are harbingers of the Keynesian circular flow of income. 'Macroeconomics' was invented and developed long before the word first appeared in 1939.[2]

In the 1920s and 1930s, Mitchell and his NBER colleagues played a vital role in the development of national income accounting. They suggested that aggregate, macroeconomic phenomena have an ontological and empirical legitimacy. Through the development of national income accounting, the work of Mitchell and his colleagues helped to establish modern macroeconomics and in particular influenced and inspired the macroeconomics of Keynes (Mirowski, 1989a, p. 307; Colander and Landreth, 1996, p. 141). A crucial element in their work was the focus on aggregate flows of money as measures of systemic economic activity. By the time Keynes (1936) wrote the *General Theory* he was to take these elements for granted – so much so that he did not even bother to cite Mitchell in this seminal work, despite the fact that they had met at Columbia University in 1934 (Hodgson, 2001c). But if Mitchell and his colleagues had not already demonstrated the feasibility of such aggregate measures, then Keynes would not have taken so many of his readers with him on his theoretical journey.

1 The industrialist Andrew Carnegie had built his wealth upon steel. He had been a friend and devotee of Spencer. Gay had been a pupil of Schmoller, served as the Dean of Harvard Business School for ten years, and influenced Galbraith (Bruce, 2000; Hodgson, 2001c, p. 139). Mitchell (1945, p. 35) later justified the NBER's 'self-imposed rule against expressing opinions on public policy' on the grounds that economists should, first and foremost, 'explain in detail the operation of many processes' and because economists 'have no more and no less claim to set themselves up as ethical judges than chemists or physiologists'.
2 According to Samuelson (1997, p. 157) the word 'macroeconomics' was first used by Lindahl (1939). Its first appearance in a leading English language journal in economics is in Marschak (1945).

The institutionalist policy disposition toward 'social control' has been discussed in a preceding chapter. In 1920, any optimism in the possibility of sustained economic growth as a basis of such policies was shattered by the severe, rapid and unexpected downturn of the US economy. By the early months of 1921, US manufacturing output had contracted by more than 25 per cent from its 1920 peak. The 'problem of controlling business cycles' was placed on the top of the policy agenda.

The United States Secretary of Commerce, Herbert Hoover, organized and chaired the President's Conference on Unemployment in the wake of the severe recession of 1920–1 (Barber, 1988; Biddle, 1998; Bernstein, 2001). The NBER carried out the empirical research for the conference, thus helping to establish its reputation as the leading economics research institute in the country. In 1921, Hoover also set up an Advisory Committee on Statistics, with Edwin Gay, Wesley Mitchell, Edwin Seligman and Allyn Young among its members. The primary conclusion of these economic advisors was that properly timed and well-judged expenditures on public works could reduce the scale of a recession. Such expenditures were said in the 1921 *Report of the President's Conference on Unemployment* to have a 'multiplying effect' on the economy as a whole, reaping rewards in excess of their cost. It was also upheld that the publication of accurate government statistics on the economy could help to educate business to reduce wildly speculative vacillations of investment, thus helping to 'iron out the fluctuations in employment'. This would be no less than a national scheme of indicative planning.

When Hoover became US President in 1929, Mitchell and several of his institutionalist and NBER colleagues were called upon to advise and provide statistical information for the new administration. In 1929, Hoover set up the Research Committee on Social Trends with Wesley Mitchell as its Chairman, Charles Merriam as Vice Chairman and William F. Ogburn as Director of Research. But none of his advisors predicted the Great Crash of late 1929. Hoover subsequently diminished his policy commitment to public works to alleviate recession (Barber, 1988). In the context of mass unemployment, Franklin Roosevelt defeated Hoover in the presidential election of 1932. Nevertheless, institutionalists such as Mitchell continued to be heard in government circles. Mitchell was a member of the National Planning Board (in 1933) and the National Resources Board (in 1934–5). In the early 1930s, institutionalism as a whole was at the zenith of its influence and prestige.

Long before the rise of Keynes, Mitchell (1922a, p. 26) favoured 'the long-range planning of public works, with intent to get the larger part of such undertakings executed in periods of depression'. Mitchell also promoted unemployment insurance as a counter-cyclical mechanism, to maintain demand in a recession and reduce it slightly in an upturn. But at the same time he rightly argued that the implementation of such policies would be haphazard and precarious unless there was greater information and understanding concerning business fluctuations. All remedial measures relied on adequate empirical knowledge of the business cycle. Mitchell (1922a, p. 30) wrote:

> After all, the endless tables of statistics which we need are only raw materials from which we are to construct a more serviceable account of economic behavior – an account that will serve better all efforts to raise the standards of social welfare.

While he suggested that data alone could provide the basis for explanation, Mitchell nevertheless searched for an explanatory account of business cycles and was not content with mere description. As Philip Epstein (1999, p. 527) put it: 'Mitchell's "grand design" was for a comprehensive institutional explanation of economic behavior, derived from critical, quantitatively based examination of all existing theory.' Mitchell saw himself as somehow combining deductive with inductive methods. He wrote to Albert Wolfe on 18 September 1938: 'We cannot do effective thinking without deductive theorizing' (Fiorito, 2000, p. 328).[3]

The institutional economics of aggregates

The problems in Mitchell's project were statistical, methodological and theoretical. On the statistical side, the many problems included the development of methods of data collection, the formulation of index numbers, and so on. On the methodological and theoretical side, a problem was to justify the focus on the theoretical explanation of fluctuations in aggregates rather than the varying dispositions and behaviours of individuals or institutions. Attempting such theoretical analysis at the systemic level using statistical analyses of aggregate data, rather than breaking everything down into microeconomic terms, was something quite new. It differed from both the Marshallian and Austrian School traditions, and from much of 'orthodox' theory at the time.

In his 1924 presidential address to the American Economic Association, and in an article published previously in that year, Mitchell hinted at these methodological issues. Mitchell (1924a, p. 27) upheld that 'it is mass behavior that the economist studies. Hence, the institutions that standardize the behavior of men create most of the openings for valid generalizations.' He thus hinted at the idea of a reconstitutive downward causation from institutions to individuals that would create a sufficient degree of uniformity to make the analytical focus on aggregates plausible. The idea that was thematic to institutional economics as a whole – that individuals are affected

---

3 Hence Williamson (1996a, p. 391) was wrong to suggest that 'Mitchell ... eschewed theory in favour of meticulous empirical investigation.' In his article on Mitchell 'as an economic theorist', Mitchell's student Friedman (1950) converted some of his teacher's theoretical insights into a mathematical model.

by their institutional and cultural environment – became a justification for treating a national complex of institutions as a unit of analysis.

His presidential address expanded slightly on these points. Mitchell (1925, p. 5) argued that economists need not begin with a theory of individual behaviour based on 'imaginary' or 'hypothetical individuals' but with the statistical observation of 'mass phenomena'. Mitchell (1925, p. 8) went on:

> If our present beliefs are confirmed, that the human nature which men inherit remains substantially the same … and that the changes in human life are due mainly to the evolution of culture, economists will concentrate their studies to an increasing degree upon economic institutions … The quantitative workers will have a special predilection for institutional problems, because institutions standardize behavior, and thereby facilitate statistical procedure.

Again Mitchell saw the institutional standardization of behaviour in reality as a basis for 'mass' or aggregate quantitative analysis. In a later passage in the same article, Mitchell (1925, pp. 10–11) looked for a 'counterpart in physics' to his method of aggregates. He found it in the 'statistical view of nature' of James Clerk Maxwell. Mitchell quoted Maxwell's idea that 'uniformities of nature' arise from the statistical 'slumping together of multitudes of cases, each of which is by no means uniform with others'. For Mitchell, the 'statistical view' of nature 'involves the notions of variety, of probability, of approximations'. But Mitchell immediately went on to caution that the correspondence between theory and statistical observation would always be much less in economics than had been achieved in physics: 'the elements of variety, of uncertainty, of imperfect observation are more prominent in the statistical work of the social sciences than in the statistical work of the natural sciences'. For Mitchell, this meant that economists had constantly to compare their theories with the data. In economics there was a lack of 'sameness, of certainty, of invariant laws. … Hence, we must put our ultimate trust in observation.'

In sum, there were two key parts to Mitchell's argument. First, he saw some statistical regularities emerging from large populations of dissimilarly oriented elements. But at the same time he saw the statistical results in economics as being more vulnerable to the higher degrees of variance, uncertainty and imperfect measurement. Second to rescue statistical methods in the haphazard and changing world of economic activity, Mitchell invoked the important additional argument that some standardization was achieved through the effects of institutions on the behaviour of component units in the economy. This strong process of downward causation, where the whole affected the very character and constitution of the parts, was not present in physics.

The first part of Mitchell's argument was unoriginal and fairly commonplace. A number of social scientists (e.g. Edgeworth, 1896) had previously seen large samples as a means of obtaining statistical regularities. But the second part of Mitchell's argument was novel and important. A core assumption of institutional economics became a justification for the methodology of aggregates. A rigorous and detailed exposition was lacking, but for Mitchell the institutionalizing function of institutions implied that macroeconomic order and relative stability was reinforced alongside variety and diversity at the microeconomic level. This institutionalist perspective meant that macroeconomics was not simply built on microeconomic foundations. It was just as important to consider the *macro*-foundations of *micro*economics. The second part of Mitchell's argument saw macroeconomic regularities as not merely statistical in nature. They were results of the institutional structure of society, constraining and moulding the behaviour of individuals.

In other contexts, Mitchell hinted again at this latter aspect of his argument. In addressing the nature and function of money, Mitchell (1916, p. 157) argued: 'Because it thus rationalizes economic life itself, the use of money lays the foundation for a rational theory of that life. Money may not be the root of *all* evil, but it is the root of economic science.' Repeating this theme elsewhere, Mitchell (1924a, p. 24) saw money as 'one of the most potent institutions in our whole culture'. It 'makes us all react in standard ways to the standard stimuli it offers'. Again Mitchell (1936, p. xxxiii) wrote: 'The monetary unit provides us with a common denominator in terms of which the best drilled among us can express all values'. This argument concerning the conformist powers of money could also have been developed as a justification for the use of money as a numeraire in the computation of economic aggregates. Mitchell would then have had to address possible changes in value of the monetary unit, through inflation or whatever. But he did not develop this argument further.

For Mitchell, business cycles were determined by underlying forces and interactions in historically specific institutional frameworks. They were not explained by the actions of given individuals, but by interacting and evolving agents, entwined in largely durable and self-reinforcing institutions.

In developing this argument, Mitchell was also addressing a key theoretical problem on the institutionalist agenda: in relation to their circumstances, how could individual dispositions or preferences be explained? His suggestion was to focus less on the explanation of any given individual and more on the dispositions of a large population of individuals. While the explanation and prediction of individual behaviour is immensely difficult, a great deal can be said about the dispositions of large populations with relevant information concerning social culture and institutional relations. Today, whole commercial and academic departments of marketing and opinion research are devoted to such aggregate investigations. Their work shows that with large groups substantial explanation and predictions are possible.

Institutionalists failed to develop such arguments further. Consequently, the rising generation of Keynesians looked elsewhere for microeconomic foundations. Paul Samuelson (1947, 1948) and others synthesized a version of Keynesian macroeconomics with Walrasian general equilibrium theory. This neoclassical synthesis of given, rational actors with 'Keynesian' aggregate macroeconomic relations – such as aggregate consumption functions, multiplier effects and IS-LM curves – dominated economics from the 1940s to the 1970s. But there were problems in reconciling Walrasian microeconomics with Keynesian macroeconomics. The 'aggregation problems' involved in the neoclassical move from the micro to the macro made an early appearance in the work of Lawrence Klein (1946). It was not demonstrated that Keynesian aggregate macroeconomic regularities could be generally derived from a population of given individuals. This failure to reconcile microeconomic with macroeconomic assumptions paved the way for the Chicago-inspired attack on Keynesianism of the 1960s and 1970s, and the cry that macroeconomics should be placed on the 'sound microfoundations' of neoclassical theory. All other aggregate functional relations were decried as 'ad hoc' and ostensibly abandoned.

Mitchell's alternative approach, if developed and placed on a more explicit and secure methodological foundation, might have placed Keynesian macroeconomics on more secure foundations, even if the more complex phenomena of both upward and downward causation would have been more difficult to place in a mathematical model. But in the absence of adequate theoretical developments, then or now, such verdicts are speculative.

Nevertheless, in Chapter 19 below some recent theoretical results will be raised which encourage the revival of Mitchell's theoretical agenda. It will also be suggested that the institutionalist use of aggregates should be explicitly related to emergent properties of complex, dynamic systems, where, under specific conditions, macro-regularities can emerge out of variety and turbulence at the micro level. Macro-regularities may emerge not despite, but because of, variations at the micro level.

Aggregates without institutions?

This section introduces two other related developments using aggregate variables by institutional economists in the 1920s and 1930s. The purpose of raising them here is threefold. First, I use them as evidence of a continuing focus on aggregate variables and regularities in the institutionalist tradition. Second, I show that problems may arise when the use of aggregates is detached from the kind of institutional structures and mechanisms of downward and upward causation that were hinted at by Mitchell. Third, I suggest that some of the problematic aspects of this conceptual work based on aggregate quantities might have been avoided if institutionalism had developed more adequate methodological and theoretical foundations.

One of the most contentious developments in this period is the famous Cobb–Douglas production function. This has its origins in a paper published by Charles Cobb and Paul Douglas in 1928 in the *American Economic Review*. Douglas was an institutionalist who was also influenced by his neoclassical teacher, J. B. Clark. Douglas (1937, p. 529) greatly admired Veblen, seeing him alongside John Bates Clark 'as perhaps the most penetrating economic thinker that the United States has yet produced'. Douglas attempted to provide measures of aggregate capital, aggregate labour and aggregate output that could be related together in a Clark-type relationship between outputs and factor inputs. The idea was to use a mathematical production function to estimate the effects of marginal changes in aggregate capital or aggregate labour, and of relative changes between the two factors.

They tried to estimate the relative contributions of labour and capital to aggregate manufacturing output. By relatively crude statistical methods, Cobb and Douglas (1928) fitted the arbitrary function $P = 1.01 L^{3/4} C^{1/4}$ to time series data.[4] On this basis they estimated the marginal products of capital and labour. They looked forward to the later possibility of 'including the third factor of natural resources' in their equations (1928, p. 165). Cobb and Douglas (1928, p. 164) were careful to reject an ethical interpretation of marginal productivity theory: 'For while capital may be "productive," it does not follow that the capitalist always is.' Hence, contrary to later apologetic uses of their function, they made a distinction between the contribution of the capitalist and the contribution of capital goods. They also pointed out that the theory did not necessarily support the private ownership of capital. There is more than a whiff of Veblenian sentiment here. But in a non-Veblenian spirit, they also believed that they had discovered ahistorical 'laws of production' (1928, p. 161). They upheld that they had traced relationships that would be applicable to production in any type of economic system. In their intellectual climate, their work appeared as ideologically neutral, empirically grounded, universal and scientific. With rising attempts to turn economics into a universal and ahistorical science, the Cobb–Douglas function made its way into the neoclassical textbooks.

A crucial and contestable step was to regard aggregate capital and aggregate labour as themselves causally effective. Cobb and Douglas saw aggregate capital and aggregate labour as causal inputs into the production function, affecting its output. In contrast, Mitchell focused on aggregate outcomes rather than aggregate causes. For him, the causes of economic change were rooted in the aspirations of individuals, as moulded and standardized by institutional frameworks.

---

4 Wicksell (1958) had suggested a similar formula in Swedish, with land instead of capital, as early as 1900.

While Cobb and Douglas departed from the institutionalist mainstream in some respects, they conformed to it in others. Hence they replicated some of the weaknesses as well as some of the strengths of the Veblenian tradition. In Chapter 10 above I argued that Veblen, like many other thinkers, neglected the fact that production is also unavoidably a matter of organized incentives for individuals. Consequently, the treatment of industrial dynamics cannot be separated from the organizational structures that provide and channel the enticements that are required for production to take place. As Veblen himself sometimes suggested, production technology and institutions are inseparable. But he neglected the organization of production. Beyond the asocial fiction of Robinson Crusoe, any complete specification of the mechanisms of production must involve historically specific organizational structures. Hence the 'laws' of production cannot be considered as ahistorical invariants.

Cobb and Douglas mistakenly treated aggregate capital and aggregate labour as if they were autonomous forces, acting together and producing a resultant output. They explicitly treated their interaction as involving 'laws' that were independent of both individual motivation and any historical context or institutional framework. Their conception was vaguely reminiscent of the 'productive forces' of Marx but otherwise different in its symmetrical treatment of capital and labour. While Veblen had generally stressed the importance of institutions, the overall result of the Cobb–Douglas approach was to downplay the importance of organizations and institutions in economic development.

The statistical work in the Cobb and Douglas (1928) article was later subjected to the devastating criticism of Horst Mendershausen (1938). He argued that the functional regularities and parameter values in Cobb and Douglas (1928) were not supported by their own data. No one took much notice. Later, in the 1960s and 1970s, the theoretical foundations of the aggregate production function were subjected to the powerful and sustained 'Cambridge critique', involving Joan Robinson, Piero Sraffa, Piero Garegnani and several others (Harcourt, 1972; Hunt and Schwartz, 1972; Cohen and Harcourt, 2003). Sraffa (1960) showed that there was no measure of aggregate capital that was independent of the levels of prices, wages and profits. After the dust settled, again no one took much notice. The Cobb–Douglas production function continued to appear, unblemished by any criticism, in all the mainstream textbooks. It endured as the unbelievable, formal surrogate of the process of production. As if it were no longer a vital domain of human agency and social relations, the production process was treated as a simple function or machine.

This theoretical development had roots in J. B. Clark's neoclassical economics but it was not bereft of institutional influences. For instance, in focusing on aggregate measures, in some respects the aggregate production function was an extrapolation of the research programme established by Mitchell. In addition, in their preoccupation with the causes of economic productivity and growth, their work dovetailed with institutionalist concerns about 'social control' as a means to achieve prosperity. The insistence by Cobb and Douglas (1928) that their function was not an attempt to legitimize the existing distribution of income or wealth also bears the marks of Veblen.

On the other hand, Veblen would have objected to their conceptual treatment of capital and the neglect of knowledge and intangible assets. In strong contrast to Mitchell and others, Cobb and Douglas attempted to detach the causal forces at work from the underlying framework of socio-economic institutions. In his studies of business cycles for example, Mitchell (1913, 1927) was always careful to identify the historically specific institutions that enabled and moulded the causal forces at work. Unlike Cobb and Douglas, Mitchell saw these forces as historically specific rather than as universal laws.

Simon Kuznets raised similar concerns. Some time before the Cambridge capital debates had attracted widespread attention, Kuznets (1963, p. 121) reminded his readers of Mitchell's critical 'views on the narrow institutional basis of much economic theorizing'. In particular, Kuznets continued, this 'should put us in a properly critical frame of mind in examining a "theory" in which economic growth is deduced from simple relations of capital to output or Cobb–Douglas production functions'.[5]

Morris Copeland was another institutionalist to make a major contribution in this area. In the 1920s, he became involved in the NBER research programme to measure, understand and control the systemic forces of economic change (Copeland, 1929b). Copeland (1924, 1925, 1926, 1927, 1929a) had already made several significant contributions to economic theory, including economic psychology, methodology and monetary theory. He was closely identified with the institutionalist movement.

Within the broad mode of enquiry developed by Mitchell, Cobb, Douglas and Kuznets, Copeland (1937) proposed a significant innovation. He suggested a comparison through time of aggregate factor inputs with aggregate output. As Copeland and his collaborator Edwin Martin put it, the idea was to 'construct an index of the physical volume of wealth used in production each year' (Copeland and Martin, 1938, p. 104), anticipating that a 'divergence is likely to appear between the movements of a series representing the physical volume of input' and the measure of output and 'this divergence is a rough measure of changes in the efficiency of our economic system' (p. 132). These two papers are the origin of modern growth accounting (Griliches, 1996, p. 1324). A major and continuing theme in modern mainstream economics has its origins in the work of institutionalists such as Copeland.

---

5   Kuznets was a Ukrainian by birth, a former student of Mitchell and one of his colleagues at the National Bureau of Economic Research. In the tradition of Mitchell, Kuznets (1930, 1961) himself made a major contribution to the statistical study of economic aggregates, for which he received the Nobel Prize in 1971.

Many versions of growth accounting are possible. Although most of them today typically use a production function of the Cobb–Douglas type, this does not have to be the case. Rather than explaining production, Copeland and Martin were attempting to measure the overall efficiency of an economic system by comparing an evaluation of its inputs with an evaluation of its outputs. In principle this is an unobjectionable aim. But severe problems arise in the aggregation and measurement of inputs and outputs and the conceptualization of any functional relationship between them. Modern mainstream economics has taken the idea of Copeland and Martin and given it some additional twists. Labour and capital are misleadingly taken as aggregate and symmetrical 'factors' while often downplaying the role of institutions, culture, human agency and the organization of production. In addition, it is often the case that insufficient attention is given to negative 'outputs' such as environmental congestion and degradation. It is an open question whether a growth accounting approach can be developed that avoids all of these pitfalls.

Measurement without theory?

Such was the enduring prestige of Mitchell's approach within American economics that it was not until after 1945 that it came under sustained neoclassical attack. The future Nobel Laureate, Tjalling Koopmans (1947, 1949a, 1949b) criticized Mitchell's attempt to establish an aggregate level of analysis. Koopmans was a migrant from Holland who had originally trained as a physicist. Koopmans's (1947) first broadside was a critical review article of the book by Arthur F. Burns and Wesley Mitchell (1946). The article's title, 'Measurement Without Theory', was somewhat unfair as it ignored the fact that Mitchell had repeatedly attempted to develop a theoretical explanation for business cycles. Koopmans (1947, p. 172) stated that Burns and Mitchell were 'unbendingly empiricist in outlook', argued that there was no theory of economic behaviour of the individual agent in their book, and declaimed the 'pedestrian character of the statistical devices employed'. What Koopmans really meant by his 'measurement without theory' jibe was 'measurement without a theory with individual utility-maximizers'. Koopmans's persistent appeal for a theory of individual behaviour was essentially an appeal for neoclassical theory over any rival, rather than an appeal for any theory. The 'without theory' slur stuck, however, and subsequently Mitchell has wrongly been described as atheoretical or anti-theoretical.[6]

---

6 Mirowski (1989b; 2002, pp. 219–20) argued that the Koopmans–Vining exchange was also a battle between the rival research institutes of the (institutionalist) National Bureau of Economic Research and the (Walrasian and neoclassical) Cowles Commission. Koopmans was appointed as Director of Research at Cowles in 1948 and he subsequently attracted handsome research grants from the RAND Corporation and the US Office of Naval Research.

What Koopmans failed to appreciate was the possibility that there could be a methodological and theoretical basis for focusing on economic aggregates. For him, the matter was quite straightforward: proper economic theory was based on given individuals, not on macroeconomic aggregates. For Koopmans, aggregates involved mere measurement; theory was necessarily based on individuals. Hence the fateful charge against Mitchell: 'measurement without theory'. Mitchell was convicted as charged, but only because of the imposition of a court with neoclassical rules.

Koopmans (1947, p. 164) simply assumed that individuals alone, whose 'modes of action and response ... are the ultimate determinants of the levels of economic variables' provide the invariant foundation for economic analysis. He did not acknowledge the institutionalist maxim that institutions could fundamentally affect individuals, as well as the other way round. And if this was the case, the individual could not serve as an invariant foundation for economic analysis.

The task of defending Burns and Mitchell was taken up by the young Rutledge Vining, a former student of Frank Knight and an admirer of Veblen, then working at the NBER (Vining, 1939). Vining (1949a, 1949b) accepted with Koopmans the general importance of economic theory and that, in particular, any economic theory must start from persistent and stable phenomena. But for Vining this did not mean that the individual should be taken as such an entity. Fully within the institutionalist tradition, Vining (1949a, p. 79) argued that entities such as 'trade fluctuations' were not merely aggregates 'of the economizing units of traditional theoretical economics'. Further,

> we need not take for granted that the behavior and functioning of this entity can be exhaustively explained in terms of the motivated behavior of individuals who are particles within the whole. It is conceivable – and it would hardly be doubted in other fields of study – that the aggregate has an existence apart from its constituent particles and behavior characteristics of its own not deducible from the behavior characteristics of the particles.

Following Mitchell, Vining (1949a, p. 85) considered how 'much orderliness and regularity apparently only becomes evident when large aggregates are observed'. Here was also a possible echo of Knight (1921a, p. 252), who had famously considered the prospect of 'reducing uncertainty by transforming it into a measurable risk through grouping'. Knight thus saw aggregation as a means of overcoming the problem of uncertainty at the microeconomic level. He hinted at the possibility that greater order and predictability may emerge at the macroeconomic level, despite microeconomic disorder or uncertainty. In this manner, Vining made an attack on individual reductionist methods in economics.

However, Vining (1949a, p. 79) made the methodological and strategic blunder of describing his own argument as a 'defense of empiricism', despite his own understanding of the importance of theory. This terminological concession to 'empiricism' played into Koopmans's hands. It was a symptom of a wider and critical failure of Mitchell and his NBER colleagues to adopt or develop a more sophisticated methodological grounding for their theoretical position. Vining thus failed to link his argument with the philosophical literature on emergent properties, albeit then a marginalized concept in both the natural and the social sciences. Neither Mitchell nor Vining had the philosophical expertise to develop such methodological foundations. Vining was perceived to have lost his debate with Koopmans.

However, thirty years later, it became clear that the attempt inspired by Koopmans and others to build up a picture of systemic phenomena from a foundation of given individuals with fixed preference functions had also failed. Eventually, Koopmans's own research programme ran into the sand. This outcome is discussed in Chapter 19.

15 The maverick institutionalism of Frank Knight

> Behind every fact is a theory and behind that an interest.
> Frank Knight, 'Ethics and the Economic Interpretation' (1922)

Frank Knight was born in 1885 in Illinois.[1] His parents were evangelical Protestant farmers of Anglo-Irish descent. Although he reacted against this deeply religious background in his teens, there remain in his teaching some echoes of theological debates, particularly concerning free will and predestination. After attending Milligan College and the University of Tennessee, Knight went to Cornell University in 1913, at first to study philosophy. The lasting influences of Immanuel Kant and Max Weber are detectable in Knight's writings, and in his conception of the relationship between the social and the natural sciences (Schweitzer, 1975). Pragmatist thinkers influenced Knight to some degree (Hammond, 1991; Hands, 1997), but his use of pragmatism was limited and he had reservations about aspects of this philosophy.[2]

In his second year at Cornell, Knight transferred to economics. The economist Alvin S. Johnson suggested to Knight that he write his doctoral dissertation on the problem of explaining the origin of profit.[3] After Johnson left Cornell, Knight's 'A Theory of Business Profit' was partly

---

1 This chapter uses material from Hodgson (2001a).
2 For Knight, in a rather wide and loose interpretation, 'pragmatism' meant principally the valid insight that beliefs about social reality are themselves causal powers within that reality. Hence Knight (1921a, pp. 199–200) saw the importance of understanding 'the nature and function of knowledge' in 'the workings of the economic system'. He then commented in a footnote: 'It will be evident that the doctrine expounded is a functional or pragmatic view, with some reservations.' Similarly, Knight (1927) wrote to Copeland: 'Thought, deliberation, effort ... are quite as *real* as the external physical objective world ... because in practice we can't talk sense or think sense in the ordinary conduct of life without treating them as such. This is to me the philosophy which ought to be called pragmatism, and my criticism of Dewey in particular is that he is not consistently pragmatic.'
3 Johnson had previously taught W. Hamilton at the University of Texas, and had persuaded him to take up graduate study in economics. See Petr (1998).

supervised by institutionalist sympathizer Allyn Young. This dissertation was submitted in 1916. Subsequently it was revised for publication as *Risk, Uncertainty and Profit* under the supervision of John Maurice Clark (Knight, 1921a, p. ix). It became one of the most important books in economics in the twentieth century.

The influence of J. M. Clark is evident in Knight's discussion therein of the costs of deliberation and the limited computational capacity of the human brain. Acknowledging Clark on this point, Knight (1921a, p. 62 n.) wrote: 'One of our most significant "wants" is freedom from the bother of calculating things or making close estimates'. Both Clark and Knight thus prefigured Herbert Simon's concept of bounded rationality.

After a year of teaching economics at Cornell, Knight became an instructor for two years at the University of Chicago. There he was an influential member of a group that gathered together to read and discuss Thorstein Veblen's works.[4] Subsequently, Knight moved to the University of Iowa for eight years. In 1927, Knight returned to Chicago to take up the chair left vacant by J. M. Clark's departure for Columbia University. Knight remained at Chicago for the remainder of his working career.

The main purposes of this chapter are to situate Knight in the broad tradition of American institutional economics, and to consider his views on the relationship between neoclassical and institutional economics, on the problem of agency and structure, on psychology and its relation to economics, and other key aspects of his philosophy. Knight's relationship with the German historical school and his important views on the problem of historical specificity have been discussed in the preceding volume (Hodgson, 2001c).

Neoclassical, Austrian or institutionalist?

What was Knight's relationship to neoclassical, Austrian or institutional economics? There have been attempts to align Knight with the neoclassical and Austrian tenet of methodological individualism. For instance, Ludwig Lachmann (1947, p. 417) wrote: 'For all his strictures on it, Professor Knight is himself a paragon of methodological individualism.' Richard Gonce (1972) and John McKinney (1977) also made this particular methodological claim for Knight. David Seckler (1975, p. 78) saw Knight as 'prominently associated' with the Austrian school of Carl Menger and Ludwig von Mises. Warren Samuels (1977a, p. 485) described Knight's work as 'neoclassicist'. Yuval Yonay (1998) followed Dorothy Ross (1991, p. 425) and portrayed Knight as the leading 'neoclassical' opponent of institutionalism.

---

4   Other members of this group included M. Copeland, C. Goodrich and H. Innis (Neill, 1972, p. 12).

Few have considered a contrary view: that Knight was an institutionalist.[5] Some may dismiss this proposition on the basis of a suggestion that Knight's sympathy for 'free market' policies would rule him out of the institutionalist camp. But it would be a crude mistake to define institutional economics – or any other theoretical approach in social science – simply or mainly in terms of its policy stance, even on the vital question of the role of the market. While many institutionalists favoured government intervention in the economy, other leading and self-confessed institutionalists took pro-market or conservative policy positions. For example, Arthur Frank Burns, the institutionalist and close academic collaborator of Mitchell, advised the conservative President Dwight D. Eisenhower in the 1950s. Another leading institutionalist, Morris Copeland (1958a, p. 1) wrote: 'We in the West are proud – and justly proud – of our free enterprise economic system.' (See also Copeland, 1965.) Institutionalism cannot helpfully be defined in terms of a particular normative stance on the virtues or vices of capitalism.

Keen to recruit someone of Knight's stature, neoclassical and Austrian economists endorse this rejection of Knight by institutionalists, and thereby declare him posthumously as one of their own. Neither institutionalists nor mainstream economists have been eager to describe Knight as an institutionalist.

I accept that there were both neoclassical and Austrian elements in Knight's thinking, and these played no small part. But also, in a strong and meaningful sense, he was an institutionalist. In order to attempt to establish this argument I shall examine Knight's attitudes on five key theoretical issues, namely:

a) neoclassical utility theory,
b) given preference functions and fixed technological possibilities,
c) methodological individualism,
d) the possibility of a synthesis between neoclassical economics and institutionalism, and
e) the place and value of institutional economics.

---

5 Gonce (1992, p. 813) admitted that Knight had 'professed to be in part an institutional economist'. McKinney (1977, pp. 1441–2) went on, somewhat confusingly, to suggest that Knight had shown that the 'fundamental assumptions' of methodological individualism 'are false. In fact, alongside his methodological individualism, coexisting with it in a state of pluralistic contradiction, is an extreme form of sociological determinism.' McKinney claims to identify a paradox in Knight's thought that does not in fact exist. Knight was not a sociological determinist. In fact, Knight was attempting to reconcile the causal role of the individual with broader institutional developments that impinged upon the agent, even changing his or her wants or goals. McKinney was unfortunately afflicted with an – alas still endemic – Austrian disorder that wrongly regards any denial of methodological individualism as an automatic endorsement of methodological collectivism.

Knight's writings show a deeper immersion in economic theory and philosophy than most of his American colleagues at the time. He probed and dissected the methodology and assumptions of received doctrines, including the neoclassical. While being critical of many neoclassical doctrines, he also warned against over-hasty dismissals of neoclassical theory. His writings combine theoretical and philosophical depth with distinctive originality. He fits easily into neither institutionalist nor neoclassical stereotypes. While evolving, his works show a substantial consistency of standpoint, and on many issues his position remained unaltered throughout his long life.

The pernicious concept of utility

In an early essay, Knight (1917, p. 67) criticized 'the pernicious concept of utility dragged into economics by Jevons and the Austrians'. He elaborated this critical view in later writings. In 1921, the *American Economic Review* published the proceedings of a discussion on the state of economic theory, in which several institutionalists had pressed their case. In this discussion, Knight (1921b, p. 145) supported some of the arguments of the institutionalists: 'I fully agree ... that utility is misleading as an explanation of economic behavior.' However, he immediately went on to suggest:

> When we come to pass judgement on the workings of the price system, we have to have a theory of utility as a starting point ... Utility is an ethical category, as indeed is illustrated by the most important conventional application of it, in justifying progressive taxation.

Accordingly, for Knight, the concept of utility was useless as an explanation of human behaviour. However, when it came to matters of normative evaluation or judgement, Knight believed that we are obliged to make rankings consistent with the principles of utility theory. For Knight, the diminishing marginal utility of money was not an explanation of human behaviour but a normative judgement that an extra dollar for a rich person is of less utility than an extra dollar for a pauper. This justified a policy of progressive taxation. Clearly, alternative and more conservative normative standards exist within neoclassical utility theory, such as the Paretian welfare criterion. This allows aid to the poor only if the government does not take from the rich. In policy terms, Knight was more radical and redistributive than the Pareto criterion would allow. Furthermore, his rejection of the explanatory value of utility theory distanced him from mainstream neoclassicism.

Knight believed that the version of individualist utilitarianism that had gained ground within economics had misled marginalism to focus on 'subjective' utility evaluations, rather than 'objective' evaluations of alternative cost. However, to consign utility theory to the normative domain was not to underestimate its significance. A strong lifetime theme through Knight's work is his insistence that economics has to be a moral as well as an ethical science (Nash, 1998). One of his prominent criticisms of mainstream economics was that it downplayed the moral and evaluative dimensions of human behaviour and focused instead on the economic actor as an amoral automaton.

Knight (1935b, p. 283) wrote: 'Economic theory takes all economic individuals in an organization as *data*, not subject to "influence," and assumes that they view each other in the same way.' For him, the idea of the individual with given preferences was of limited use only. As Knight (1961, p. 191) later elaborated:

> Theory on the analogy of mechanics, treating motives as forces, and as 'given,' is illuminating and unavoidable; but the analogy has severe limitations and must not be pressed too far.

Knight regarded the analysis of human motivation or behaviour in terms redolent of mechanics or physics as highly limited. For him, all social actors, including economists themselves, acted on the basis of their own judgements and values. He saw this as creating a theoretical problem. Objective investigations into socio-economic phenomena, with a view to understanding and explaining them, must also deal with the values and judgements that form part of human motivation and behaviour. The fact that human action is always laden with ethical evaluations and judgements of all kinds means that social science is distinguished from the natural sciences. The human social sciences cannot be dissolved into the biological or mechanical. This was clearly a criticism of what more recently has been described as the 'physics envy' of some neoclassical theorists. Knight also criticized some strains within institutionalism for neglecting the moral dimension of human behaviour, by treating people as equivalent to other, non-ethical organisms. Knight (1931, p. 62) wrote:

> the possibility of developing economics along the lines of the natural sciences naturally suggests itself; the possibility, that is, of using objective data exclusively and eschewing all question of motivation as natural science does those of real cause. It is easy to understand the great stir resulting from efforts to rid economics of utility theory and to supplant it by an objective, quantitative science. With the positive part of this program the present analyst is in hearty accord. But ... economics must also continue to develop the older type of theory.

But he was sympathetic to several aspects of institutionalism. For instance, Knight (1921a, p. 113) supported some of John Hobson's criticisms of the concept of the rational actor:

With Hobson's fundamental position, that marginalism is the necessary form of a rational treatment of choice, and that the rational view of life is subject to drastic limitations, the writer is in hearty accord.

A major reason why 'the rational view of life is subject to drastic limitations' was that human decision-making was subject to pervasive uncertainty and a search for novelty. Knight (1921a, pp. 52–4) believed that the explanation of behaviour in terms of the 'satisfaction of wants' could succeed 'only to a limited extent'. He continued:

> The whole interpretation of life as actively directed toward securing anything considered as really wanted, is highly artificial and unreal ... a relatively small fraction of the activities of civilized man are devoted to the gratification of needs or desires ... What men want is not so much to get things that they want as it is to have interesting experiences ... an important condition of our interest in things is an element of the unanticipated, of novelty, of surprise.

Especially in the light of Knight's prominent concept of uncertainty, it is strange that some regard him as a mainstream or neoclassical economist. Uncertainty in a Knightian sense is an anathema to neoclassicism. Uncertainty refers to situations where there is no objective evidence by which to calculate a probability, even if people nevertheless cope by making subjective estimates. Unless salvation is sought in ungrounded subjective utility estimates, uncertainty limits the possibility of formal modelling, neoclassical style (T. Lawson, 1997). Emphasizing objective uncertainty, Knight's theory of the firm is dynamic and open-ended, focusing on the indeterminate outcomes of entrepreneurial decision in the face of uncertainty (Boudreaux and Holcombe, 1989). Faced with its anti-formalist and indeterminate consequences, leading neoclassical Nobel Laureates have thus dismissed uncertainty from economic theory. Kenneth Arrow (1951, p. 417) remarked that 'no theory can be formulated in this case'. Robert Lucas (1981, p. 224) agreed: 'In cases of uncertainty, economic reasoning will be of no value'. Knight would have strongly dissented. For him, theoretical reasoning was still possible. But because of the uncertain, complex and value-driven nature of the human condition, Knight saw formal modelling as having only limited value in economics.

To summarize, Knight rejected utility theory as a basis to explain human behaviour. Its use was essentially normative. Knight thus distanced himself from the neoclassical economists who typically rely on utility theory to model, explain or predict human action. He also saw severe limits in the general use of formal modelling in economic theory. Having established some significant distance between Knight and neoclassical theory, let us turn to the second proposition, as a result of which the gap can be further enlarged.

Tastes and technology as variable

Knight regarded the neoclassical assumption of given preference functions and technological possibilities as inadequate. Concerning the malleability of wants, Knight (1922, pp. 457–8) accepted the influence of John Maurice Clark, Walton Hamilton and Thorstein Veblen:

> the treatment of wants as data from which and with which to reason has already been challenged more than once. More or less conscious misgivings on this point underlie the early protests made by economists of the 'historical' variety against the classical deductive economics, and the same is true in a more self-conscious way of the criticism brought by the modern 'historismus,' the 'institutional economics' of Veblen, Hamilton and J. M. Clark. Thus especially Clark,[6] whose position most resembles that herein taken, observes that the wants which impel economic activity and which it is directed toward satisfying are the products of the economic process itself … Wants, it is suggested, not only *are* unstable, changeable in respect to all sorts of influences, but it is their essential nature to change and grow; it is an inherent inner necessity in them …

Knight was invited by Rexford Tugwell to contribute to a collection of writings on the way forward for economics. Other contributors included institutionalists J. M. Clark, Paul Douglas, Wesley Mitchell, Sumner Slichter and Albert Wolfe. Knight wrote to Mitchell on 18 May 1923 that his own contribution to the volume would be a defence 'of the claims of old-fashioned theory as against institutional economics' (Fiorito, 2000, p. 291). However, Knight's (1924) essay is much closer to institutionalism than he suggested, and if his stance is 'old fashioned' it is nearer to a dynamic version of Marshall than to any static neoclassicism. In his essay, Knight (1924, pp. 262–3) again made it clear that the assumption of given preference functions is not appropriate in long-run theories of economic change:

> Wants are usually treated as *the* fundamental data, the ultimate driving force in economic activity, and in a short-run view of problems this is scientifically legitimate. But in the long run it is just as clear that wants are dependent variables, that they are largely caused and formed by economic activity. The case is somewhat like that of a river and its channel; for the time being the channel locates the river, but in the long run it is the other way round.

Knight (1924, p. 263–5) again emphasized that wants and preferences were subject to change:

---

6 Knight here inserted a footnote referring to J. M. Clark (1918).

The only ultimately independent variables are those features of nature and human nature which are in fact outside the power of economic forces to change, and it would be hard to say what these are. ... The largest reservation called for in assuming the fixity of the data controlling production and consumption over a period of years relates to the permanence of wants.

The notion that individual tastes were both malleable and socially formed was a theme repeated in his later works. Of course, Knight (1956, p. 295) was fully aware of the critical consequences of this for mainstream welfare economics:

But both power and wants or tastes come to the individual chiefly through the processes of the society in which he lives, especially by inheritance, biological and cultural, and through the family. Thus social policy cannot possibly treat the individual as a datum in any of these respects, since he is in fact largely the creation of social action.

In analysing long-period change, Knight (1924, p. 264) saw the role of '"institutional" economics, [as] studying "the cumulative changes of institutions"'. He saw the value of this approach as lying in its capacity 'to predict long-period changes in the factors that applied economics accepts as data'. In a later work, Knight stated a similar position. Concerning what he called 'price-theory economics', Knight (1933, p. xii) admitted that to some extent he was 'in sympathy with the reaction against it'. He explained:

Economic theory based on utilitarian premises ... is purely abstract and formal, without content. It deals, in general, with certain formal principles of 'economy' without reference to what is to be economized, or how; more specifically, price-economics deals with a social system in which every individual treats all others merely as instrumentalities ... a mechanical system of Crusoe economies. It discusses the use of given resources by given 'owners,' in accord with a given system of technology, to satisfy given wants, all organized through a system of perfect markets.

Knight clearly perceived a limitation of neoclassical economics in terms of its assumption of given wants and technology. Knight (1933, p. xii) continued:

Any question as to what resources, technology, etc., are met with at a given time and place, must be answered in terms of institutional history, since all such things, in common with the impersonal system of market relations itself, are obviously culture–history facts and products.

Knight (1933, pp. xii–xiii) then went on to admit that 'economic' motivation was also itself a product of culture and history. In another passage, which suggests a possible influence of John Dewey on his thought, Knight (1956, pp. 295–6) questioned the complete and final separation of means from ends:

> some mention must be made of the limitations of the whole economic view of life and conduct – the view, that is, in terms of the use of means to achieve ends. There really are no 'ends' in any final sense – they are rather milestones on the way ahead and these become means as fast as they are achieved – and the qualities of good and bad belong about as much to means as to ends in any right use of the terms.

Clearly, this placed Knight at some distance from the neoclassical mainstream. Dewey (1939, p. 45) similarly argued at length that 'there is no end which is not in turn a means'. Another feature of Knight's work that was at variance with neoclassical economics was his emphasis on disequilibria in socio-economic systems. Knight (1935b, p. 184) wrote:

> Our general conclusion must be that in the field of economic progress the notion of tendency toward equilibrium is definitely inapplicable to particular elements of growth and, with reference to progress as a unitary process or system of interconnected changes, is of such limited and partial application as to be misleading rather than useful. This view is emphasized by reference to the phenomena covered by the loose term 'institution.' All speculative glimpses at trends in connection with price theory relate to a 'competitive' or 'capitalistic' economic system. But all the human interests and traits involved in this type of economic life are subject to historical change.

Knight's insistence on ongoing changes, including the alteration of human purposes and preferences, all set in a climate of uncertainty, led him to emphasize the limited value of the equilibrium concept and to underline the value of historical and institutional analysis.

Knight and methodological individualism

Was Knight a methodological individualist? The answer clearly depends upon what is meant by the term. For Gonce (1972, p. 552), methodological individualism 'signifies that the subjectivity of the self-interested, rational and free individual is to be used to explain all human conduct and social and economic phenomena'. The problem with this definition is that it does not make it clear whether individual interactions or social structures are also to be used in the explanation, or whether explanations should involve individuals alone. If explanations also involve individual interactions or social structures, then few would disagree with this edict. But such a loose doctrine is unworthy of the title of methodological individualism. Having defined the term vaguely, Gonce (1972, p. 552 n.) made the claim that Knight 'continuously … employed this procedure' and quoted Knight (1921a, pp. 73–4, 264; 1961) in support. But in no case did Knight attempt to explain *all* socio-economic phenomena in terms of individuals alone.

Other claims that Knight was a methodological individualist are based on a different definition of that term. For instance, McKinney (1977, p. 1441) referred to one passage (Knight, 1951, pp. 23–4) alone to support the dubious claim that 'Knight is a methodological individualist'. In this passage Knight argued that 'the organization as a whole has no value in itself or purpose of its own'. However, this statement is about the alleged location of values and wills in individuals rather than organizations; it is not about the explanation of socio-economic phenomena in terms of individuals alone. The passage is not evidence that Knight was a methodological individualist in the narrow sense of reducing all explanations to individuals. The claims of both Gonce and McKinney to have found evidence of methodological individualism in Knight's works do not stand up to critical scrutiny. But the case is not yet closed, because there are other 'individualist' passages to consider. Knight (1941, p. 132) wrote:

> Because human society is an association of consciously purposive individuals rather than an organism to be viewed as a unit and analysed into individual components ... the individual is logically prior to society.

Whether right or wrong, to say that 'the individual is logically prior to society' is not to say that society must be explained entirely in terms of individuals. An emphasis on 'consciously purposive individuals' is not equivalent to methodological individualism. What is contestable in the above statement is the notion that consciousness, choice or purpose are possible without the prior socialization of the individual. Knight (1923, pp. 590–1) himself had argued that

> the freest individual ... is in no sense an ultimate unit or social datum. He is in large measure a product of the economic system, which is a fundamental part of the cultural environment that has formed his desires and needs ...

Alongside this, his inclination was against the reductionist thrust of methodological individualism. Knight (1924, p. 247) wrote: 'the way to improve our technique is not to attempt to analyse things into their elements, reduce them to measure and determinate functional relations, but to educate and train one's intuitive powers'. Furthermore, he rejected any individualist view of knowledge. Knight (1942, p. 46) was much closer to Veblen when he wrote that all knowledge is itself 'social'; it is based on intercommunication between individuals, each of whom is both subject and object, both to himself and to all others in the thinking community in which knowledge has its being.

Knight saw the forces of institutionalization and of indeterminate individuality as *both* being at play. Like the old institutionalists, he stressed the role of habit, imitation and custom. For Knight (1947b, p. 224) the forces that help to mould human society

belong to an intermediate category, between instinct and intelligence. They are a matter of custom, tradition, or institutions. Such laws are transmitted in society, and acquired by the individual, through relatively effortless and even unconscious imitation, and conformity with them by any mature individual at any time is a matter of 'habit'.

Knight's (Knight *et al.* 1957, p. 20) emphasis on the role of customs and institutions was repeated elsewhere:

Human society must always be largely of the original institutional character; custom and habit must rule most of what people feel, think, and do. Institutions, I repeat, are more or less explained historically rather than scientifically and are little subject to control. The ideal type is language, about which we can do so little that we hardly think of trying.

But nowhere does he fall into the methodological collectivist trap of suggesting that human behaviour is *entirely* determined by custom or institutions. In fact, throughout his writings, he attempted to reconcile the non-contradictory propositions of individual 'free will' with the additional notion that individual behaviour was moulded and constrained by institutions. Knight nowhere evades the problem of structure and agency by succumbing to the untenable extremes of either methodological collectivism or methodological individualism. The fact that his solution was incomplete, and even defective, is beyond the point. The point here is to establish that Knight was not a methodological individualist, at least in a sharp and meaningful sense.

Neoclassicism and institutionalism as complements?

Knight favoured a critical synthesis between neoclassical economics and institutionalism. A limited version of neoclassical theory had to be supplemented by studies of history and institutions. He thus recognized the problem of historical specificity, and his contribution in this area has been discussed at greater length elsewhere (Hodgson, 2001c).

Does this limited acceptance of neoclassical theory disqualify Knight as an institutionalist? If so, then we must also indict others, including leading institutionalists such as Commons, Mitchell, J. M. Clark and A. F. Burns. (See Chapter 12 above.) They all saw institutionalism as compatible with aspects of Marshallian price theory. Accordingly, when trying to decide whether person X was or was not an institutionalist, it is difficult to disqualify X simply on the grounds that X accepted elements of neoclassical economics in their theory. If such an overly restrictive criterion is used, then we are left with very few – if any – institutionalists at all. That is one reason why this criterion must be rejected. What is important is whether X accepted neoclassical thinking as *adequate* for economic theory. Those economists that believe it is adequate are best described as neoclassical economists. Those that think that it is inadequate may, subject to further conditions, be described as institutionalists, even if they accept parts of neoclassical economics as valid. Hence to point out that X accepted elements of neoclassical economics in their theory does not necessarily disqualify X from being an institutionalist.

As a result, there is an asymmetry between the two definitions. An institutionalist does not cease to be so if they accept key elements of neoclassical theory. However, a neoclassical economist ceases to be such, once they accept one of the core propositions of institutionalism: that economic theory must take account of changing preferences and purposes and not take them as given. That change of viewpoint is required to remove the 'neoclassical' nametag and install the 'institutionalist' one instead.

For Knight (1924, p. 229), it was necessary for the economist to examine the role of institutions and to also embark on 'an exploration in the field of values'. Institutionalists would agree. Knight (1928, p. 137) did not believe in a gulf between institutional and orthodox economics and declared that the 'discontinuity between the "newer" and the "older" economics is imaginary'. In a letter to Talcott Parsons, dated 1 May 1936, Knight wrote: 'I came to Chicago expecting this "institutionalism" to be my main field of work' (Knight, 1936).[7] He complained that other theoretical controversies and the burdens of teaching had got in the way of this research project.

While at Chicago, Knight taught that institutional economics and Marshallian neoclassical economics had complementary roles. In a letter dated 16 February 1937 to his friend Clarence Ayres, Knight reported that he was giving a course on 'Economics from an Institutional Perspective' at Chicago. In fact, Knight had started giving this course in the summer quarter of 1932. His Reading List for Economics 305, Winter 1937 has the words: 'The task of institutionalism [is] that of accounting historically for the factors treated as *data* in rationalistic, price-theory economics.' He then listed the topics 'individualism and utilitarianism, wants, technology, resources,

---

7   For discussions of Parsons, including his relationship with Knight, Hamilton and Ayres, see Camic (1991) and Hodgson (2001c).

organization, economic institutions as embodied in law' (Samuels, 1977a, p. 503). Knight gave an explicit and extensive place to institutional economics.

James Buchanan (1968, p. 426) summarized Knight as 'that rare theorist who is also an institutionalist, an institutionalist who is not a data collector'. Knight himself should have the last word on the question of his institutionalist credentials. Knight (Knight *et al.* 1957, p. 18) declared: 'I am in fact as "institutionalist" as anyone, in a positive sense.' In a letter to Ayres dated 13 July 1969, Knight wrote 'I've always considered myself an institutionalist ... as far as possible' (Samuels, 1977a, p. 519). His institutionalism was nonconformist, but it was an institutionalism nevertheless.

Empiricism, behaviourism and individual volition

How did Knight react to the rising empiricist philosophy and behaviourist psychology of the interwar period? A version of empiricism is evident in his writing. Knight (1921a, p. 8 n.) declared himself as, 'like Mill, an empiricist, holding that all general truths or axioms are ultimately inductions from experience'. Knight (1924, p. 241) also saw prediction as a principal measure of scientific success. However, he was not a naïve empiricist. Knight (1934) rejected the idea of a 'purely factual economics' and did not believe it would be possible even to give a coherent meaning to the term. Knight (1940) ably criticized the extreme positivist attempt by Terence Hutchison (1938) to ground all assumptions in economics on experience or data alone.

Kant influenced Knight, like many others at the time, including Marshall, Veblen and Weber. Like Kant, Knight insisted that science must unavoidably adopt some core presuppositions that cannot be derived directly from experience. Knight's Kantianism was used to legitimate presuppositions concerning human intentionality that were not derived through induction or empirical generalization.

But Knight did not attempt to synthesize Kant with Darwin, in the manner of Veblen. Any talk of turning economics into a 'Darwinian science' left Knight cold. Knight (1935a, p. 209) responded to Veblen's assertion that he had applied Darwinian principles to economics with the riposte: 'I cannot find anything in particular that he could reasonably have meant by this claim'. Not only did Knight (1951, pp. 23–4) reject the application of evolutionary ideas from biology to society but also he showed no appreciation of the Darwinian metaphysical stance on causality (see Chapter 4 above). Only briefly and belatedly did Knight (1948, pp. 42, 51; 1960, p. 43; 1964, p. 303) acknowledge the doctrine of 'emergent evolution'. It was not given sufficient attention in his writing.

Knight's presuppositions put him closer to Weber than to Veblen. Essentially, like Weber and many others, Knight adopted a dualist position, where human intentionality was elevated into a distinct form of causality, independent of the causality that applied to physical things. Rejecting any Darwinian and Veblian injunctions to the contrary, Knight assumed that human intentionality had a unique causal and entirely independent onto-logical status. Of course, Knight was not alone in taking this view and much of twentieth-century social science has followed the same course. It was Veblen, not Knight, who was exceptional on this point; Veblen saw that Darwinism undermined a dualistic ontology of matter and mind. Knight (1921a, p. 201) argued that human consciousness was beyond the grasp of science:

> It is a mere brute fact that wherever we find complicated adaptations we find consciousness, or at least are compelled to infer it. Science can find no place for it, and no rôle for it to perform in the causal sequence.

Knight abandoned the principle of determinacy; he did not admit that hu-man intentionality was itself caused or that investigation into the causes of intentions was relevant for social science. Knight (1935b, p. 285 n.) wrote:

> 'Institutional Economics' ... is essentially a continuation or revival of the historical standpoint. But if human and social phenomena can be completely explained in terms of their own history, the result is the same as that of a complete mechanical explanation; there is no such thing as purposive action or as practical relevance. ... The view here adopted ... treats social institutions as a product of social choice based on social knowledge of patterns between which choice is made, and has meaning only in so far as such choice may be real.

Here Knight prefigured the 'incompatibilist' position of Buchanan (1969) and others, who alleged that if choice was determined then it cannot be a real choice. This position has been criticized in Chapter 3 above. But Knight was right to warn against some historical and institutional econo-mists who wished to explain all socio-economic phenomena in terms of historical trends, omitting human discretion and creativity. He also rightly stated that institutions must be seen as the result of real social choices. He did not suggest that institutions have to be explained entirely in individual terms, and his emphasis on a free and uncaused will does not itself imply an adherence to methodological individualism. Knight (1942, p. 49) revis-ited these themes:

> As far as science is concerned, free will, which is the only real dyna-mism, is either an illusion or simply a methodological limitation. So-cial science should recognize this limitation and admit that it has nothing to say about it beyond recognizing its existence as a limitation upon regularity and its place in our interpretative thinking. ... Free choice, based on genuine mental activity and not finally explicable in

terms of antecedent conditions, is of very limited scope even in the individual life, even though infinitely important.

Here Knight stresses the reality of 'free will' but again stresses that it
places limits on the explanation and prediction of socio-economic phenomena. In the final sentence of the above quotation, he admits a free will
that is not 'explicable in terms of antecedent conditions' but argues that it
'is of very limited scope'. Knight thus argued that 'free choice' was highly
circumscribed, yet real and important. When 'free choice' was constrained,
the role of custom and habit held sway, creating for Knight a scope for
institutionalist-style arguments concerning the effects of institutions and
culture on human action. Knight (1947b, p. 224) thus attempted to synthesize a conception of the undetermined individual with other propositions
concerning the role 'of custom, tradition, or institutions' in moulding human society.

A notable feature of Knight's position is his attempt to dichotomize individual will, on the one hand, and other factors affecting human behaviour such as habit, culture and institutions, on the other. Not only does this
betray an ontological dualism, but also it shows that he had moved some
distance from pragmatist philosophy and instinct–habit psychology. He
did not seem to accept that habit was foundational for all beliefs and decisions. He did not consider that the 'essence of belief is the establishment of
habit' (Peirce, 1878, p. 294) or that the 'formation of ideas as well as their
execution depends upon habit' (Dewey, 1922, p. 30). In contrast, for
Knight, habit and conscious deliberation were antithetical. In regard to
consciousness, habit and instinct, Knight did not adopt the Darwinian doctrine of continuity.

It is useful to compare the stances of Veblen, Commons and Knight on
these issues. Commons and Knight shared an emphasis on the role of volition and will. Veblen never denied the reality or meaning of 'free will' but
he did not give it any prominence either. What Veblen insisted upon was
the principle of determinacy; human intentions and intentionality are
causally determined, even if such causes are unknown or unknowable.
Similarly, Commons (1934a, p. 739) rejected a 'capricious and undetermined' human will. Unlike Veblen and Commons, Knight abandoned the
principle of determinacy. However, like Knight but unlike Veblen, Commons (1934a, p. 741) argued that a 'capricious and lawless' human will
would be 'incapable of the uniformities required by science'. In contrast to
Veblen and the pragmatists, Knight separated conscious deliberation from
habit and custom. On these issues Commons took an intermediate position
between Veblen and Knight. Nevertheless, Veblen, Commons and Knight
all accepted the role of institutions in affecting human behaviour. Furthermore, Veblen, Commons and Knight all acknowledged the reality and importance of human intentionality. However, as we shall see in the
following chapters, the position of Ayres was quite different; for him

individual volition had no important role in his analysis of socio-economic change.

While other institutionalists after (and excluding) Veblen had accommodated to the rising behaviourist psychology, Knight (1924, 1925a, 1925b, 1931) repeatedly attacked this creed. The thrust of his rebuttal of this psychological doctrine can be anticipated from his aforementioned emphasis on the role of individual consciousness, choice and will. Knight did not accept the positivist and behaviourist argument that the unobservability of human consciousness meant that it was not part of science. Instead, Knight saw consciousness and purpose as an essential part of social science, especially when explanations in terms of motives or values were involved. Knight (1924, p. 243) argued that 'it is surely clear that if consciousness is denied and the behavioristic position assumed, an end is put at once to the possibility of discussing values or motives'.

In taking this view, Knight came into direct conflict with institutionalists such as Ayres and Copeland who had embraced behaviourism (Asso and Fiorito, 2003a). Copeland (1925) published an article that was critical of Knight's treatment of human consciousness, intention and valuation. Copeland argued that economics had to accommodate a behaviourist psychology that was 'scientific' in the narrow and naïve sense of being capable of measurement. Copeland also rejected Knight's causal dualism, arguing that the same kind of causality found in physics should apply also to the human and social sciences. In his subsequent correspondence with Copeland, Knight (1926) wrote: 'It is as futile to pretend that consciousness, desire, effort, error, and the whole list of modalities for that matter, are not as real as the eternal physical world.'

In his critiques of behaviourism, Knight (1931, p. 67) argued that motives and observed behaviour did not necessarily coincide. In particular: 'The indubitable fact of error reinforces the necessity for giving motives recognition separately from behavior'. Elaborating this point, Knight (1941, p. 136) wrote:

> It is of the essence ... of distinctively human behavior ... that, by virtue of being problematic, the course of events involved is not accurately predictable in advance in terms of any positive knowledge. That is, it is conceptually distinct from a mechanical cause-and-effect sequence and so cannot be made the subject matter of any positive science. A problem is not a problem unless the solution involves effort and is subject to error, features or notions which are absolutely excluded from mechanical processes of cause and effect.

The rejection of 'mechanical' notions of cause and effect meant, literally and appropriately, the exclusion from social science of explanations of social phenomena that do not involve human consciousness and intentionality. Knight was right to insist on this point, yet in this critique of behaviourism he was then going against the stream.

Knight understood better than others that human purposes and interpretations of meaning were essential matters for the social sciences and could not be subsumed under the category of mere behaviour. Contrary to behaviourism, beliefs and intentions are real, even if they cannot be directly appraised. But Knight used this insight to create a chasm between the social and natural sciences, rather than attempting to place human purposefulness and intersubjectivity in an overall schema where the two types of science were reconciled. He did not appreciate the importance of Darwinism in this regard. On the other hand, Copeland embraced Darwinism but allowed his behaviourism to drive out all substantial considerations of purposefulness and intersubjective interpretations of meaning. Neither theorist acknowledged that the capacities to think, interact and interpret have themselves evolved and must thus be understood in evolutionary terms (Bogdan, 1997, 2000).

Another interesting feature of the exchange of views between Knight and Copeland is that both writers failed to see the relevance of emergent properties for the discussion of the relationship between human intentionality and materialist causality. Copeland, like many others at that time, adopted a reductionist and monist stance, where human intentionality dissolved into mechanical forces. In contrast, Knight attempted to uphold a dualism where intentionality was treated as different from any other form of causality. It did not occur to either Copeland or Knight that the philosophy of emergent properties might be able to sustain a view that avoided the pitfalls of both dualism and reductionism, by seeing intentionality as real and irreducible but dependent on neural and physical states and relations.

More on Knight and his contemporaries

Knight corresponded extensively with several institutionalists, including his former teacher J. M. Clark, plus Copeland, Mitchell and Ayres. With both Clark and Ayres there was an enduring friendship. Although always a maverick and an independent, Knight applauded many works and ideas from the German historical school and American institutionalism. Knight (1920) sympathetically reviewed Veblen's *Place of Science in Modern Civilization* and supported his nomination as president of the American Economic Association. Reviewing Commons's *Institutional Economics* Knight (1935c, p. 804) declared: 'Much of the content is both profoundly interesting and profoundly illuminating.' Knight also pointed out that Commons's terminology was often obscure and incomprehensible. Overall, Knight encouraged the directions of thought explored by leading institutionalists such as Veblen and Commons, and at the same time made the reasonable request for greater conceptual and theoretical precision.

Leading contemporary institutionalists respected Knight. J. M. Clark gave him strong support and encouragement. Mitchell (1922b) positively reviewed Knight's *Risk, Uncertainty and Profit*. Ayres held Knight in some great esteem, but the theoretical distance between them grew to the point where Knight could not place himself in the institutionalist mainstream.

One of Knight's mentors was Herbert Davenport. Knight made a number of references to Davenport in his work. Davenport was also a close friend and admirer of Veblen. He had been a faculty member with Veblen at two universities: at Chicago for four years and at Missouri for seven years. In 1916, Davenport moved to Cornell and established a close intellectual relationship with Knight. Like Veblen, Davenport objected to the normative and apologetic abuses of economic theory. Like Veblen, Davenport emphasized the tension between finance and industry and denied that the market is an automatic self-righting mechanism: private gain did not necessarily lead to social welfare. Veblen, Knight and Davenport rejected the neoclassical division of economic resources into 'factors of production'. For Davenport, the Austrian theory of alternative costs was essentially correct, but – like Veblen and Knight – he saw the marginalist theory of value and distribution as severely flawed. Like Veblen and Knight, Davenport denied that utility theory could be used as a general explanation of human behaviour. Davenport was elected President of the AEA in 1920.[8]

While Knight endorsed several key institutionalist ideas, he was often critical of the contributions of individual American institutionalists. But Knight was seemingly critical of almost everyone. While he criticized institutionalists such as Commons, Veblen or Slichter, he was also critical of more mainstream thinkers such as Henry Schultz and Henry Simons.

Although I do not believe that it is strictly relevant to the establishment of the proposition that Knight was an institutionalist, we can also dwell briefly on his ethical and policy stance. Knight eschewed Keynesianism and extensive state intervention in the economy. However, while he favoured a market economy he saw the necessity of some substantial reforms. He was an advocate of progressive taxation and the welfare state. He was sceptical of the view that the amassing of an inheritance was an effective spur to the generation of more wealth, and suggested the imposition of an inheritance tax, following 'the Saint-Simonian school of socialists and others' (Knight, 1921a, pp. 373–4).

Throughout his life, Knight was an opponent of complete laissez-faire and the idea that individual preferences in a free market economy should be taken as the ultimate moral standard. Knight (1956, p. 170) argued that 'a really thoroughgoing laissez-faire individualism, accepting individual preferences as absolutely final' had to be ruled out because individuals

---

8   Veblen persuaded Davenport to accept the nomination. Davenport was a pallbearer at Veblen's funeral (Dorfman, 1934, pp. 452, 504).

'are necessarily reared and educated in the society in which they are to live and function as members.' Against neoclassical welfare theory, Knight held that it is 'absurd to treat the individual as a datum for purposes of decisions regarding social policy.' For Knight, the market was 'no agency for improving tastes (wants) or manners or especially for conferring productive capacity to meet wants or needs' (1956, p. 271). He similarly rejected the notion that prices measured values in an ethical sense (Knight, 1935b, pp. 55–6; 1951, pp. 36, 46).

In his famous article on 'The Ethics of Competition', Knight (1923) not only opposed laissez-faire but also accepted that some kind of mixed economy was inevitable. In the early 1930s, Knight was briefly sympathetic to communism. In 1932, he gave a lecture entitled 'The Case for Communism from the Standpoint of an Ex-Liberal' (Patinkin, 1973, p. 800 n.). He then argued that democracy was unable to promote rational government and that communist dictatorship was preferable. Although his flirtation with communism was brief, throughout his life he remained pessimistic about the capabilities of democracy. Accordingly, Knight (1932) was sceptical of both the scientific basis and the political practicality of institutionalist schemes of 'social control'. He also opposed trade unions because they represented a monopoly power in the labour market.

Knight (1956, p. 252) was also critical of the 'fallacious doctrine and pernicious consequences' of the work of John Maynard Keynes, 'who for a decade succeeded in carrying economic thinking well back to the dark age'. Nevertheless, Knight shared Keynes's view that economic recovery from a recession was not automatic, and Knight was in favour of increased public expenditure to alleviate the depression. On 31 January 1932, Knight signed a telegram to President Hoover, urging an increase in expenditure on public works and more vigorous action to protect the banking system. Other signatories included Irving Fisher, Alvin Hansen, Henry Schultz and Henry Simons. In a memorandum of 26 April 1932 to Indiana Congressman Samuel Pettengill, twelve Chicago economists, including Knight, Henry Simons and Jacob Viner, dismissed any faith in the self-righting abilities of the economy. Their advice was that injecting enough new purchasing power through 'generous Federal expenditures' could bring about recovery. On 8 May 1932, Knight himself wrote to Senator Robert Wagner in favour of such a strategy: 'As far as I know, economists are completely agreed that the Government should spend as much and tax as little as possible, at a time such as this.'[9]

Knight's pro-interventionist views were not simply a result of the Great Depression. In the earlier case of the 1924 McNary–Haugen Bill for farm relief, Knight was prepared to run against the bulk of professional opinion by arguing that the proposed farmer subsidy was required to

---

9 For sources, and the opinions of other economists at that time, see Barber (1988, ch. 9) and J. R. Davis (1968, 1971).

counterbalance the protective tariffs placed on industrial goods. In addition, Knight recommended that a government agency, rather than the private banking sector, should deliver additional credit (Dorfman, 1959, pp. 476–7).

The University of Chicago is famous for its pro-market economics, but this 'Chicago School' did not begin to emerge until the late 1940s. Earlier at Chicago, Knight had attracted followers and admirers such as Henry Simons, Paul Samuelson, Milton Friedman and George Stigler. However, Knight's view on the limitations of mathematics within economics and his hostility to Keynesianism created opposition from the rising new technocratic generation of neoclassical economists, many of whom were Keynesian or socialist.

Samuelson was at Chicago from 1932 to 1935. In a 1986 interview, he indicated how his admiration for Knight was later challenged: 'Mathematics, which I was beginning to get interested in, was laughed at by the Knight wing' (Colander and Landreth, 1996, p. 148). Leading mathematical economists such as Samuelson went on to combine neoclassical microeconomics with a bowdlerized Keynesianism. This awkward mixture was nevertheless successful, and ultimately deadly for Knight's reputation.

Within Chicago itself, some additional and distinctive forces were at play. The first was the arrival of the Cowles Commission in October 1939. Having luckily escaped the effects of the 1929 Great Crash, Alfred Cowles offered to finance the new Econometrics Society out of his fortune. His original concern was to develop methods of predicting movements of prices on the stock exchange. Set up in 1932, the Cowles Commission was in the vanguard of the resurgence of neoclassical, mathematical economics in the 1930s and 1940s (R. Epstein, 1987; Mirowski, 1989b, 1998, 2002; M. Morgan, 1990; Hands and Mirowski, 1998). It stayed at Chicago until the 1950s, and despite Knight's resistance, it helped to transform the entire department.

Melvin Reder (1982, p. 10) has argued that the installation of the Cowles Commission in 1939 was one of 'three shocks' that hit Chicago economics in the years 1938–9. The second was the early death in a car accident of Henry Schultz in November 1938, and the third was the election of Schultz's friend, the institutionalist sympathizer Paul Douglas, to the public office of Alderman in November 1939. These three shocks, including the departure of two key personnel, radically changed the balance of opinion within the department against Knight. In addition, in 1938, the young mathematical economist Oskar Lange arrived from Poland as an assistant professor: 'Lange was an up-to-the-minute young theorist, in the vanguard of the Keynesian Revolution who had acquired a considerable reputation as a mathematical economist' (Reder, 1982, p. 4). Lange's economic theory was neoclassical and Walrasian, his style mathematical, and his politics Marxist. Knight was opposed to Lange's economic theory and to his politics. Even in Chicago, it was his theory and its mathematical style that mattered most. Appointed to the Department of Economics against Knight's wishes, Lange declared war against the surviving remnants of Chicago institutionalism and anti-formalism. Lange was 'an excellent expositor' and a persuasive theorist (Patinkin, 1981, p. 8). Lange brought to Chicago the new developments in general equilibrium theory and the formalizations of the 'Keynesian' macroeconomic system pioneered by himself, John Hicks and others. Until his return to Poland in 1945, this 'Marxist' played a leading role in transforming the Chicago department and defeating institutionalism in America. The irony of this has not gone unnoticed. As Donald Patinkin (1995, p. 372) wrote:

> it was the socialist Oskar Lange who extolled the beauties of the Paretian optimality achieved by a perfectly competitive market – and Frank Knight who in effect taught us that the deeper welfare implications of the optimum were indeed quite limited.

The immediate outcome was that: 'By 1944, a fairly intense struggle was underway between Knight and his former students on one side, and the Cowles Commission and its adherents on the other. ... It continued for almost 10 years' (Reder, 1982, p. 10). The result was that Knight, along with his remaining followers, plus the institutionalists, were all the losers: 'After 1945, if not earlier, Knight's outspoken disdain for empirical, especially quantitative, research set him completely apart from the main body of Chicago economists – including his own former students' (Reder, 1982, p. 6).

Furthermore: 'The institutionalist wing of the department was greatly reduced by the retirement of [Harry] Millis (in 1940) and the departure of [Simeon] Leland for Northwestern in 1946' (Reder, 1982, p. 10). Friedman was appointed to Chicago in 1946 and Stigler in 1958. It was not until after Friedman's arrival that the distinctive, modern, anti-Keynesian 'Chicago School' emerged (Bronfenbrenner, 1987; Shils, 1991). Knight (1966, p. 117) saw it as erroneous to take 'the vastly simplified postulates that are legitimate and necessary for the first stage of economic analysis – but which should never be taken as describing reality and still less as normative – and treat them as universal ideals'. Such a criticism applies to the postwar Chicago school. In Chicago, Knight became a revered but isolated figure. His waning influence was a result of forces similar to those that defeated American institutionalism.

The US fought the Second World War with a faith in the powers of technology and quantitative formalism that helped to bring about a radical change in the nature of postwar social science. Both Knight and the institutionalists were the causalities of this transformation. Among the victors after 1945 were the rising generation of mathematical economists and econometricians, including Kenneth Arrow and Paul Samuelson. Chicago took its own distinctive road, promoting its ideologically pro-market version of neoclassical theory.

In a sense, both Knight and Ayres faced the problem of sustaining an institutionalist-inspired economics into the postwar period. For this and other reasons, their correspondence tells a very interesting story (Buchanan, 1976; DeGregori, 1977; Samuels, 1977a). Although Knight and Ayres were friends, in several crucial respects they took very different positions.[10] Despite its important insights and innovations, institutionalism under the leadership of Veblen, Commons and Mitchell had failed to develop a systematic and adequate, theoretical and philosophical base. Knight responded by elevating his central notion of an undetermined individual agency in the context of uncertainty and social institutions. In contrast, Ayres (1935, 1944) almost forgot the individual, and made institutions barriers in the way of the holistic forces of technological and cultural advance.

In one of their critical engagements, Knight (1935a, p. 208) responded to Ayres (1935) by noting that Ayres assumed 'some kind of inner law of progress of an absolute and inscrutable character' for technology and implied that 'there is some equally absolute and inscrutable type of "causality" by which technology drags behind it and "determines" other phases of social change'. For Knight, the ultimate source of causality in the social realm had to be the choosing individual, not technological or historical 'forces' (Knight, 1933, p. xxviii).[11]

From a truly Veblenian perspective, neither Knight's, undetermined individual, nor Ayres's institution-free conception of culture and technology, will do. Institutions constitute human agency just as much as institutions are constituted by human agency. The failure to develop a Veblenian or other suitable perspective led to bifurcation of institutionalism along the diverging Ayresian and Knightian paths of development. Even if they had been followed to the end, both paths led to unsatisfactory destinations. That is part of the tragedy of the story.

Conclusion

By 1950, Knight was isolated from mainstream neoclassicism, Chicago orthodoxy and the surviving remnants of American institutionalism. Knight's opposition to the rising psychology of behaviourism also isolated

---

10 Despite their differences, Ayres wrote in a letter to Charner Perry, dated 9 August 1934: 'I rather think that he [Knight] and I have a good deal more in common than my recent references would suggest' (quoted in Samuels, 1977a, p. 496).

11 In a scathing review of Ayres's *Divine Right of Capital*, Knight (1947a, pp. 238–9) wrote: 'Everything is explained by two opposed principles, a "good" (progressive) one of technology, and its bad "adversary," institutions (Cf. Ormuzd and Ahriman, Jahweh, Satan). The summum bonum is production ... Professor Ayres had already published ample proof that only one of us knows less than nothing about economic theory ... the only question is, which one. ... I may at least observe ... that ... education in economics ... like charity ... should begin at home. The primary issue is whether it shall take the philistine ... view of analysis and replace fact and interpretation with philia and (especially) phobia, and rabble-rousing for some interest or cause'.

him from many psychologists and social scientists. But it is important not to overlook his significant affinities with institutionalism. After all, his work shared the same fate as institutionalism as a whole. As institutionalism declined in influence in the post-1945 period, so too did the prestige of Knight.

Two factors, above all others, categorize Knight as part of the institutionalist camp. First, he accepted the impact social and institutional factors on human wants and behaviour. In this respect, Knight's ideas are still remote from many economists today. Second, he repeatedly described himself as an institutionalist.

Knight differed from mainstream American institutionalism on key points, but he brought to that tradition great insight and rigour. Without reaching a complete solution to the most fundamental and pressing methodological and theoretical problems, he developed an innovative type of economics that maintains its relevance today. He grappled with central problems such as the problem of agency and structure. Inspired by Veblen, Weber and the German historical school, he engaged likewise with the problem of historical specificity in economic theory. He thus addressed two of the most pressing theoretical problems for a revived institutional economics today. Not only was Knight an institutionalist, he was also one of the greatest of all institutionalists after Veblen.

16 The evolution of Clarence Ayres

> His Veblen was no longer anyone else's Veblen and his Dewey was no longer the Dewey of pragmatic philosophy. Ayres emphasized those elements in each man's work that best suited his own purpose and temperament, recreating them both in his own image.
>
> William Breit, 'Clarence Ayres's Theoretical Institutionalism' (1973)

Clarence Ayres was born in 1891 in Lowell, Massachusetts, as the son of a Baptist minister. He studied philosophy at Brown and Harvard Universities. In 1915, he was hired at Amherst College in Massachusetts as an instructor, where the energetic institutionalist Walton Hamilton influenced him. Ayres then went to Chicago, intending to work with Robert Hoxie. But Hoxie committed suicide in 1916, and Ayres switched to philosophy, to specialize in ethics. Wesley Mitchell, Thorstein Veblen and John Dewey had already left the university.

Ayres's PhD dissertation was on *The Nature of the Relationship Between Ethics and Economics* and was published in 1918 (Ayres, 1918a). Other aspects of philosophy, outside ethics, are much less prominent in his writings. After working as an instructor in philosophy at the University of Chicago between 1917 and 1920, Ayres returned to Amherst as a member of its Philosophy Department. Ayres (1973, p. iii) wrote of his early years: 'I ... thought of myself (as perhaps I should still do) more as a would-be philosopher than as even a would-be economist.'

As related elsewhere (Camic, 1991; Hodgson, 2001c), the young Talcott Parsons was a student at Amherst College from 1920 to 1924. There he met Ayres and was taught institutional economics by Hamilton. Under the special guidance of Ayres, Parsons concluded that it was culture rather than nature that was the decisive factor in explaining human behaviour.

In 1923, a dispute at Amherst College led to the sacking of Alexander Meiklejohn, its liberal and progressive President. A substantial number of faculty members, including Hamilton and Ayres, resigned *en masse* in sympathy. Ayres taught at Reed College in 1923 and 1924 and worked as associate editor of the *New Republic* from 1924 to 1927. In 1927, he and his second wife moved to a ranch in New Mexico, where they remained until 1930. That year he accepted a professorship in economics at the University of Texas, where he remained until his retirement in 1968. From 1935 to 1938, Ayres was an active member of the Editorial Board of the *American Economic Review*. At Texas he built up a substantial following among students and faculty.

Ayres's radical critique of all religions and many established institutions led to conflicts with University of Texas administrators and Texas state legislators. He was one of four economics professors threatened with dismissal in 1940. At a Texas Senate hearing in 1949, Ayres called a proposed loyalty oath for University of Texas employees an insult. In 1951, the Texas legislature passed a resolution demanding his dismissal and threatened to block funds for the entire economics department if he stayed. But powerful friends and colleagues who intervened on his behalf saved Ayres. Unrepentant, he continued teaching until well into his seventies.

But Ayres did serve some institutions. He worked for US President Harry Truman's Council of Economic Advisors and was a director of the San Antonio branch of the Dallas Federal Reserve Bank. In the 1960s he was a governor of the Federal Reserve Board. He also helped to found the Association for Evolutionary Economics in 1966. This association, and its quarterly *Journal of Economic Issues*, has played a vital role in keeping American institutionalism alive into the twenty-first century.

Ayres had an enormous influence and was largely responsible for leading American institutionalism into the postwar period. Marc Tool (1994, p. 16) has noted: 'Ayres and his students have been among the most significant contributors to the development of institutional economics in the last half-century.' From his own personal experience, Donald Walker (1979, p. 519) described the spell that Ayres cast over his Texas students:

> The room would be filled with the most unpromising human material imaginable for the sort of purposes that Ayres had – backcountry students from the small towns and ranches of Texas, rich students from Dallas and Houston. Most of them were conservative or reactionary in their social and economic views; most of them were initially supremely indifferent to the issues that agitated Ayres. Yet he would work his magic on them, and by the end of a single semester he would have them ready to leap out into the real world and to start tearing down the old institutions, ready to begin immediately with building a new society free of ceremony, superstition, and myth.

Ayres was a charismatic figure. In the 1960s he received the University of Texas Students' Association award for teaching excellence. Walker (1979, p. 520) himself regarded Ayres as 'Veblen's most creative and theoretically-inclined intellectual descendant, and one of the most important advocates of institutionalism during the years since the Great Depression.'[1]

Downplaying individuals and instincts

In North America today, the Ayresian wing of institutionalism lays claim to the Veblenian title. However, in several significant respects, Ayres's work is a departure from that of Veblen. It is shown in this chapter that while Veblen embraced Darwinism and instinct–habit psychology, Ayres abandoned them. The following chapter addresses the differences between Veblen and Ayres concerning institutions, technology and economic progress.

Ayres (1921a, p. 564 n.) was for some time a member of Jacob Kantor's 'anti-instinct cult at the University of Chicago'. To be admitted, each new member had to invent a new instinct. Kantor had mockingly proposed a supreme instinct for death. Influenced in some respects by Dewey, Kantor (1922a, 1924) combined a stress on natural science method, with a social psychological focus on 'cultural reactions and institutions' and a behaviourist insistence on observable phenomena. As a behaviourist, Kantor (1922b, p. 196) redefined habit as a 'type of behavior' rather than an acquired propensity or disposition, thus rejecting the Veblenian meaning of the concept. Kantor's early influence on Ayres was crucial, at a time when many social scientists still believed in instinct–habit psychology. Ayres (1921a, 1936) thus became committed to the rising behaviourism.

Ayres (1921a, p. 561) believed that the literature on instincts was 'largely self-refuting. ... When instincts fall out, institutions get their due.' As a result: 'The social scientist has no need of instincts; he has institutions' (1921a, p. 565). Ayres saw the drift of scientific opinion from the 1920s as confirming his dismissive view of instincts. Much later, Ayres (1958, pp. 25–9) wrote that 'the very notion of instincts is now scientifically obsolete. ... It is now quite conclusively established that no such complex behavior patterns are in a literal sense "inborn". We now know that such patterns are wholly cultural.' Indeed, between the 1920s and the 1950s, this became the view of the overwhelming majority of social scientists (Stocking, 1968; Cravens, 1978; Degler, 1991). Ayres was an early opinion former in this respect.

As with instinct, the Veblenian concept of habit plays an insignificant part in Ayres's work. Very occasionally, Ayres (1944, p. 84) referred to 'social habits'. But this was a metaphor for social custom, acknowledging that the habits of an individual were entirely (and somewhat mysteriously) a product of 'the mores of his community'.

---

1 Sturgeon (1981) surveyed the enormous influence of Ayres and his students on successive generations of American institutionalists.

Ayres (1921b, p. 606) approvingly quoted the words of the sociologist Charles Cooley (1902, p. 1; 1922, p. 36): 'A separate individual is an abstraction unknown to experience'. But Ayres ignored the rest of Cooley's sentence: 'and so likewise is society when regarded as something apart from individuals.' While Cooley saw the individual and society as equally and symmetrically implicated in social explanation, Ayres in contrast put almost the entire explanatory weight on institutional structures, cultural pressures or the forces of technology.

Indeed, Ayres (1918a, p. 57; 1961, p. 175) went so far as to repeat his exact statement: 'there is no such thing as an individual', after a gap of over forty years. In each case, Ayres went on to attempt to qualify and explain this proposition, but his qualifications cannot undo the damage already done. To put us in little doubt about his extreme position, Ayres (1936, p. 235) wrote that orthodox economists 'conceive the institutions to be an expression of human nature. The institutionalists ... hold precisely the opposite view of human nature, to wit, that it is an expression of institutions.' Much later, and in similar vein, Ayres (1951, p. 49) wrote: 'Social patterns are not the logical consequents of individual acts; individuals, and all their actions, are the logical consequents of social patterns.' Ayres (1952, p. 41) proposed 'a universe of discourse to which the concept "individual" is simply irrelevant'. Overall, Ayres inverted the methodological individualism of neoclassical economics to propose a methodological collectivism. From his youth until his death, Ayres did not waver from this predominantly 'top down' methodological view. This was not the position adopted by Veblen.

Ayres, Veblen and Dewey

The standard view of Ayres today is that he synthesized the thought of Veblen and Dewey. After all, having been educated in a Chicago with recent memories of both writers, it may be expected that Ayres was their obvious, immediate, and diligent synthesizer. Ayres (1973, p. iii) was acquainted with some of Veblen's works by 1915; early articles by Ayres (1918b, 1918c) cite Veblen, whom he later met personally.

But the standard view is far from the truth. Ayres (1923) reviewed Dewey's (1922) *Human Nature and Conduct* and expressed regret that Dewey had not adopted the behaviourist schema of stimulus and response. Both Veblen's and Dewey's adoption of the concept of habit contrasted greatly with Ayres's behaviourism.

Ayres's two books, *Science: The False Messiah* (1927) and *Holier Than Thou* (1929) bear no more than slight possible traces of the influence of Veblen or Dewey. Ayres (1973, p. iii) later admitted: 'When I was writing these two books, I had no thought of contributing to the literature of Institutionalism.' In fact he was countering some of its established propositions. In *Science: The False Messiah*, Ayres dethroned science and scientists, dismissed the value of pure science and described it as an invention of the modern technological culture. Within a few years of its publication, Ayres would reverse his position on this issue. There is no quotation from Veblen or Dewey in these works, and neither Veblen nor Dewey would have agreed with Ayres's attack on science. The point here is not to downgrade Ayres for changing his mind, for most open-minded people do so from time to time. The point is to suggest that Ayres did not begin by building on a bedrock of ideas from Veblen or Dewey.

In *Science: The False Messiah* (1927, p. 277), Ayres wrote that 'habits, formulas, dogmas, and institutional rigidities variously are the antithesis of intelligence and the nemesis of the experimental attitude'. This was in contrast to Veblen (1914, p. 176) who argued that 'the body of knowledge' and 'the facts made use of in devising technological processes and applications, are of the nature of habits of thought'. In Ayres's 1927 book we find the enduring antipathy to all habits and institutions that was to characterize his subsequent writing. This antipathy was not derived from Veblen, and Ayres made no suggestion in his book that it was.

Similarly, in *Holier Than Thou* (1929, p. 239), Ayres condemned 'preposterous beliefs and ... ridiculously solemn rites' because they were opposed to technological and human progress. For Ayres (1929, p. 240) one of the 'most important' things was 'the struggle to make two carrots grow where one has grown before'. This was a hint of the idea of technological progress as the supreme ethical standard, which was to dominate his subsequent work. Ayres (1973, p. x) later acknowledged that it was after reading Dewey's *Theory of Valuation* (1939) that he became convinced of the possibility of such 'absolute' or 'transcultural values'. But Dewey's tract was published ten years after *Holier Than Thou*.

In his mature works, Ayres seemed to incorporate aspects of Dewey's philosophy, but subtly shifted their connotation. As Philip Mirowski (1987, p. 1029) argued: 'Where Dewey wanted to portray scientific enquiry as a continuous questioning procedure, Ayres tried to portray it as the accumulation of certain and final knowledge by means of the accumulation of tools and artefacts.' Ayres read Dewey in curiously empiricist terms, seeing knowledge as a firm and visible construction upon the fixed bedrock of science, untainted by institutions and unencumbered by contingent habits of thought. For Ayres, problems of valuation were resolved by the accumulation of scientific knowledge relating to the provisioning of human needs. Science and technology became the source and bases of normative evaluation. In contrast, Dewey saw science as more experimental, interacting with social institutions and norms. Ayres went further than Dewey, to reach the untenable idea that science and technology could provide a direct and unambiguous means of evaluation. While Dewey was resolutely anti-foundationalist, in seeing no ultimate methodological grounding for knowledge in observation or reason, Ayres differed in seeing the facts of technology as providing the foundationalist bedrock. In his comparison of the views of Ayres and Dewey on science, James Webb (2002, p. 991) thus observed:

> It is ironic that Ayres ended up with what amounts to positivism-with-a-twist. The twist is that Ayres argued that moral questions can be treated in about the same way that positivists treat factual questions. That is, the positivist principle of verification is not rejected but extended to the realm of values, where it is presumed to operate in the same unproblematic way as it does on factual issues.

Overall, Ayres was slow to incorporate ideas from Veblen and Dewey, and when he did so he sometimes modified their meaning. More evidence for this verdict is presented in the following chapter. But first we turn to Ayres's formative views on evolutionary theory.

Ayres, Huxley and Darwin

Ayres published his most successful interwar work in 1932. His *Huxley* was rightly described on its dust jacket as a 'racy' volume. It has the marks of an evangelical tract – but one with the purpose of dethroning rather than upholding religion. This rare and now neglected book tells us a great deal about Ayres and his views. From its pages Thomas Henry Huxley emerges as the radical scientist hero, sweeping away all the stuffy superstition and religious mumbo-jumbo that helped to dupe the masses and keep them in their place. Huxley's debate in Oxford with Bishop Samuel Wilberforce in 1860 is described with relish, as if Ayres had wished to be there himself, striking a smashing blow against superstitions of the British Establishment with all the force of science behind him. In contrast to his earlier tract, science emerged as the Messiah. *Huxley* remained one of Ayres's favourite creations. In his last years, when his sight had become greatly impaired, Ayres would ask his wife to read him passages from this book.

But despite its spirited narrative, the work is in some respects an intellectual embarrassment. Essentially, Ayres's immense admiration for Huxley was largely confined to Huxley's promotion of the (pre-Darwinian) proposition that humans are descended from apes. Ayres also admired Huxley's materialist reductionism and his downgrading treatment of mind as merely an epiphenomenal expression of matter. Furthermore, like Huxley but unlike Veblen, Ayres did not uphold that Darwinian principles applied to the evolution of human society. Ayres acknowledged socio-economic 'evolution' but in a non-Darwinian sense. Ayres (1932, p. 234) outlined three different meanings of the term:

> The word 'evolution' even has come to have a number of meanings. At least three meanings are current today … According to one, evolution means the general theory of development without reference to

particular mechanisms of variation, selection or what not. ... According to another meaning, evolution is taken to be not the general theory of development but the specific mechanisms of variation, mutation, heredity, selection and so forth. ... Still a third evolution is the theory, or fact, of man's descent from anthropoid stock. This is the point of impact of biological facts and principles upon social traditions.

Ayres embraced the term 'evolution' in the first and third senses only, that is in the highly general sense of 'development' and in the sense of asserting human descent from apes. He regarded the second (Darwinian) meaning as controversial and full of 'unanswered questions'. Ayres argued that Darwin's theory of evolution was outmoded and invalid. In his *Holier than Thou*, Ayres (1929, p. 172) had made the familiar but mistaken criticism that Darwin's survival of the fittest is 'a pure tautology'.[2] In *Huxley*, Ayres (1932, p. 95) wrote:

since the opening of this century ... all of Darwin's 'particular views' have gone down wind: variation, survival of the fittest, natural selection, sexual selection, and all the rest. Darwin is very nearly, if not quite, as outmoded today as Lamarck.

For Ayres (1932, p. 96), the primary significance of Darwin's *Origin of Species* was as follows:

All mythology, all superstition, all theology turn upon the assumption of the uniqueness of the human species, its absolute fixity as the lord of the earth, created in the image of God. That is why *The Origin of Species* raised a storm of protest. No one cares about variation or sexual selection. But *The Origin of Species* by implication challenged Genesis, that is to say, the cultural foundation of Christendom. That is why it became 'the gorilla book,' and that is why the infiltration of the idea of evolution is certainly revolutionizing the treatment of morals, politics, and religion. There is a world of difference between the morals, politics, and religion of God's chosen people and a species of super-apes.

Seeing Darwin's principal contribution in these anti-creationist terms, Ayres (1932, pp. 96–7) went on to compare Darwin with Huxley. According to Ayres, Darwin's *Descent of Man* 'is quaint, an outmoded classic' whereas Huxley's *Man's Place in Nature* 'is exciting reading today'. Ayres saw Huxley as making a much greater contribution to the dethronement of religion and the revolutionization of morality: 'this was Huxley's issue, not

2   If fitness is a propensity (or potentiality) and survival an outcome, then the tautology disappears. Indeed, it is possible for units with greater fitness to be unsuccessful (Hodgson, 1993, pp. 94–6). See also S. Mills and Beatty (1979), Sober (1984), Waters (1986) and Brandon (1996).

Darwin's. A comparison of their books tells the whole story.' In a clumsy attempt to argue for Huxley's intellectual superiority over Darwin, Ayres (1932, p. 97) wrote:

> But if evolution were to be defined not in retrospect but as a contemporary force in modern life, the expression of that idea, so defined in modern terms, would be found not in the massive treatises of Charles Darwin but in the essays of Thomas Henry Huxley.

Ayres (1932, p. 97) chided and downgraded Darwin for considering that morality may have some foundation in 'well-marked social instincts' and for believing that some 'moral feelings' could be 'innate' rather than 'acquired'. Against this, Ayres remarked: 'It is a commonplace today that there is no such instinct and that "moral feelings" are "acquired" *in toto.*' But Ayres was too reckless in his dismissal of Darwin's (1871, vol. 1, p. 86) idea of 'social instincts' that disposed individuals to act in accord with others in society. Contrary to Ayres, this idea still prospers in the scientific community. Several scientists have argued that moral emotions – such as those concerning sympathy, protection and reciprocity within social groups – may have a partial foundation in inherited instincts. There are various forms of this argument and it remains controversial.[3] Overall, leaving aside the detailed problems, Ayres's dismissal of the possibility that some limited moral feelings may be inherited as instincts now appears as overly dogmatic and empirically ungrounded.

On the whole, Ayres's critical comparison of Darwin with Huxley is deeply flawed. It betrays a cavalier attitude to evolutionary theory and no recognition of the importance of Darwin's theory of natural selection. The gap between Ayres and Veblen in their understanding of these issues was immense. Veblen not only appreciated the importance of natural selection for the evolution of species but also he saw the possibility that Darwinian mechanisms might also apply to human society and higher-level units of selection. Furthermore, Veblen understood the philosophical impact of Darwin's work and some of its implications for the conduct of the sciences. Ayres saw none of this.

Lamar Jones (1995, p. 419) rightly observed – in the only other detailed commentary on Ayres's *Huxley* of which I am aware – that 'Ayres simply failed to come to effective grips with Darwin's work'. Ayres also failed to appreciate Huxley's intellectual limitations. As noted in Chapter 4 above, Huxley had reservations about the theory of natural selection and gave less emphasis to the importance of adaptation. Ayres was also apparently unaware that Huxley's crude treatment of mind as a mere epiphenomenon of matter had been superseded by developments in emergentist

---

3   See, for example, Ruse (1986), Wright (1994), Pojman (1995), De Waal (1996), Ridley (1996) and Weingart *et al.* (1997).

philosophy in the 1920s (Blitz, 1992). Huxley's treatment of mind as lacking its own causal powers was to some extent reflected in Ayres's own work. Ayres adopted a materialist ontology where the causal powers of the human individual were given relatively little emphasis. Ayres's neglect of individual purposiveness and agency is partly explained by his acceptance of the behaviourist orthodoxy in the psychology of his time.

Although his *Theory of Economic Progress* (Ayres, 1944) may have been 'evolutionary' in some loose sense, it was not Darwinian, in that it did not rely on a mechanism of (natural or cultural) selection. Ayres (1961, pp. 71–4) later adjusted his views on Darwinism, principally by retracting his previous rejection. But even in his later works, Ayres described the impact of Darwinism as principally to do with human descent from apes, and he largely ignored the mechanisms of natural selection. Ayres (1942, p. 353) failed to appreciate the meaning and significance of Veblen's insistence that economics should become a 'post-Darwinian' science.

Evolution does not necessarily connote any reference to biology.[4] There is no Darwinian or other copyright on the word 'evolution'. Despite his differences with Darwinism, Ayres preferred the term 'evolutionary' to 'institutionalist' as a description of his own approach. The reason for his hostility to the 'institutionalist' label became clear in a letter that Ayres wrote to Dewey on 29 January 1930: 'an institution ... is a bad thing from which we are bound to try perpetually to redeem ourselves' (quoted in Tilman, 1990, p. 966). Ayres (1944, p. 155 n.) later repeated similar sentiments, combining these with a rejection of the institutionalist label: 'As a designation of a way of thinking in economics the term "institutionalism" is singularly unfortunate, since it points only at that from which an escape is being sought.' Ayres saw institutions as entirely negative. Unlike Veblen, Dewey, Commons and many others, Ayres did not understand that institutions can enable activity as well as constraining it, and that institutions provide indispensable stuff and structure to social life.

Uneasiness with both of the alternative labels of 'evolutionary' and 'institutionalism' persisted within postwar American institutionalism as a whole. John Gambs (1946, p. 9) saw the title 'institutionalism' as inadequate and preferred 'evolutionary economics' without any Darwinian emphasis. Above all, the Ayresian wing disliked the term 'institutionalism' because they saw institutions in a negative light. Others objected to the term 'evolutionary' because they saw Darwinism as obsolete or spurned any connection between the social sciences and biology. The views of Ayres and Gambs prevailed when the emerging Association for Evolutionary Economics chose its title in 1966. The 'evolutionary' label was not

---

4 Schumpeter's (1954, p. 789) use of the term 'evolution' was also different from the Darwinian conception (Hodgson, 1993, 1997a; Witt, 2002). Ayres and Schumpeter were entitled to use the loose term 'evolution' to denote change. But Witt (2002) invested the word 'evolution' with a relatively narrow meaning that is justified by neither its etymology nor by its wide-ranging past usage.

adopted to highlight any Veblenian connection with Darwinism; instead it was widely interpreted in the shallower sense of development or change. With the notable exceptions of David Hamilton (1953) and Copeland (1958b), few connections between institutionalism and Darwinism were adopted or promoted. A few years after Veblen's death, American institutionalists had abandoned Veblen's research programme to create a 'post-Darwinian' economics.

17 The Ayresian dichotomies
Ayres versus Veblen

History is more or less bunk. It's tradition. We don't want tradition.
Henry Ford, *The Chicago Tribune*, 25 May 1916

After publishing his *Huxley*, Ayres began to develop his theory of economic growth and development.[1] In a letter to Charner Perry of 9 August 1934, Ayres referred to 'the technology–institutional dualism' and 'the tech–inst dichotomy'. Ayres upheld that 'it is only by withdrawing from the institutional basis altogether to the technological side ... that any escape is possible from the relativism of mores-bound standards of value' (quoted in Samuels, 1977a, p. 496). This dichotomy between technology and ceremony became the major theme of Ayres's subsequent work: technology was seen as dynamic and progressive, ceremony and institutions as static and conservative. Technology became the sole motor of progress. Institutions were always its impediment.

Ayres's (1935, 1938) theory of economic development appeared tentatively in the 1930s, but it received its fullest expression in his *Theory of Economic Progress* (1944). Here are laid out the foundations of an institutionalist theory of both analytical and normative dimensions, which was to sustain and become central for the dwindling numbers of American institutionalists for more than fifty years. Ayres (1944, p. 176) wrote:

> The history of the human race is that of a perpetual opposition of these forces, the dynamic force of technology continually making for change, and the static force of ceremony – status, mores, and legendary belief – opposing change.

For Ayres, human behaviour was essentially of two types: tool-using or technological activity leading to production, on the one hand, and ceremonial behaviour reinforcing status and privilege, on the other. Ayres (1944,

---

1   This chapter uses material from Hodgson (1998c).

pp. 178–87) also identified ceremony with institutions. Two possible dichotomies, between technology and ceremony, on the one hand, and between technology and institutions, on the other, were assumed to be one. Ayres (1952, p. 49) wrote:

> By virtue of its peculiar character, the institutional function is essentially static. In the process of social change, institutional function plays a negative part. It resists change.

Ayres (1961, p. 233) persisted in this depiction of technology as dynamic and progressive, while institutions were seen as wholly backward, resistant and serving the *status quo*:

> the technological process is inherently developmental, while the institutional structure of all societies is inherently static and change resistant.

Further, Ayres (1944, p. 220) argued that science and technology provided the normative means of valuation by which economic developments and policies can be assessed: 'It is the technological continuum which is, and has always been, the locus of value; and it has this meaning because of its continuity.' Ayres (1961, p. 21) wrote of 'the genuine values which derive their meaning from clear and certain knowledge of demonstrated cause-and-effect processes' rather than 'the pseudo values which derive their meaning from the fantasies of superstition'.

This statement is problematic because the cause behind an effect is never 'clear and certain'. Events, but not causes, can be observed. Veblen (1908b, p. 398 n.) had repeatedly insisted that causality is 'a matter of metaphysical imputation'. In contrast, but in accord with the prevailing positivism of his day, Ayres (1942, p. 343) described 'metaphysics' as 'nonscience' and upheld that 'science must establish its ascendancy ... leaving nothing whatever to metaphysics'. The contrast could not be greater between Veblen's acceptance of the unavoidability of ontological commitments and Ayres's positivist dismissal of all metaphysics.

Ayres and Veblen also differed on the normative inferences they drew from their discussions of technology. In contrast to Ayres, Veblen rejected the idea that technology was intrinsically worthwhile. Veblen (1908d, p. 109) wrote that 'technological proficiency is not of itself and intrinsically serviceable or disserviceable to mankind, – it is only a means of efficiency for good or ill'. For Veblen (1899a, p. 99) the 'instinct of workmanship' was 'the court of final appeal in any question of economic truth or adequacy'. But Ayres wanted nothing to do with instincts. Veblen and Ayres differed on the intrinsic merits or demerits of technology and on the evaluative use of instincts in this context.

Having argued in general that all institutions had a negative effect on technological change, Ayres had to uphold in particular that the institution of private property provided no aid for technological innovation. If any positive role could be given to any institution, then the Ayresian dichotomy would be undermined. Ayres (1935, p. 189) thus wrote: 'The more we examine the institutions of capitalism, the clearer it becomes that their contribution to the development of industrial society has been permissive rather than creative.' More emphatically, Ayres (1943, p. 166) later remarked: 'The productive powers of industrial society have grown not because of the institutions of capitalism but in spite of them.' In general, Ayres (1944, p. 187) argued: 'There is no such thing as an institution (or set of institutions), that is "appropriate" to a given technology in any but a negative sense.' Ayres (1952, pp. 49–50; 1960, p. 49; 1961, pp. 30–1, 126, 134–7) generally saw institutions as a barrier to technological development.

Ayres alluded to a possible future world virtually free of institutions, and ruled by the principles of technological instrumentalism. Ayres did not acknowledge that some institutions are necessary for social life. In reality, some degree of rule-bound inflexibility is required to create stable expectations, coordinate activities, enable communication and foster social cohesion. On the other hand, some degree of openness and flexibility is necessary to accommodate innovation and change.

Technological change

Making technology the exclusive engine of change, Ayres required a theory of how technology itself developed. Explicitly drawing from Veblen, Ayres (1963, p. 58) saw discovery and invention as resulting from 'the serendipity of the laboratory and the machine shop ... And what else is serendipity but idle curiosity, the free play of the enquiring mind?' Alongside serendipity, he placed his combinatorial principle. Ayres (1944, p. 112) saw great inventions as essentially new combinations of old tools and ideas:

> Thus the airplane is a combination of a kite and an internal combustion engine. An automobile is a combination of a buggy with an internal combustion engine. The internal combustion engine itself is a combination of the steam engine with a gaseous fuel which is substituted for the steam and exploded by the further combination of an electric spark. ... What is presented to the public as a 'new' invention is usually the end-product of a long series of inventions.[2]

---

2 Schumpeter (1934, p. 66) had argued that development involves 'the carrying out of new combinations' of technologies or products. It is not clear whether Schumpeter influenced Ayres on this point.

His twin assertions that technological change results from serendipity or combination have some resemblance to the Darwinian idea of evolution through random mutation and genetic recombination. However, Ayres's theory lacked the crucial Darwinian concept of selection. There was no explanation why one mutation or combination was used more frequently than another. Lacking such an account, Ayres fell back on an unexplained notion of technology as somehow a progressive force in itself. In this respect his evolutionary dynamic was closer to the Spencerian unknowable ultimate cause than to the Darwinian model of detailed causal explanation.

Not only did Ayres's theory fail to explain how particular innovations triumphed over their rivals, but also it lacked an adequate explanation of innovation itself. Partly because he downplayed the role of individual agency, and partly because he overlooked institutional incentives, Ayres did not give a sufficient account of the motives for innovation and creativity (D. Miller, 1944, 1958, 1966; Hill, 1989). Even his combinatorial principle lacked detailed analysis of the (cultural) contexts and mechanisms involved. Although combinations do frequently occur, it is not the case that inventors are regularly or randomly trying to combine everything with everything else. Most inventions are driven by intentions and incentives to create an outcome. Such intentions are formed within and enabled by their social contexts. Sets of highly specific skills, resources, incentives, cues and contexts led the Wright brothers to combine the kite with the internal combustion engine, or the Stephensons to synthesize the stationary steam engine with the coal-mining infrastructure of horse-drawn carts on tracks. Despite being central to his argument, Ayres gave us no detailed analysis of the general process of combination. Ultimately he relied on a mysterious, self-propelled impetus of technological development.

Furthermore, terms requiring precise definition were left unclear. In a devastating omission, Ayres 'never precisely specified the meaning and extension of the term *technology*' (Coats, 1976, p. 29). Ayres repeatedly depicted technology as tool-using behaviour, but this was not enough, especially as Ayres (1961, p. 135) recognized the use of tools in ceremonial activity. Clearly, for his primary dichotomy to remain untangled his concept of technology had to be free of institutional contamination; it must not itself involve institutions.

An adequate definition of an institution was also lacking in his work. In a letter to Frank Knight of 23 February 1937, Ayres described a prominent and relatively sophisticated attempt by Walton Hamilton (1932) to define the key concept of an institution as 'ninetenths piffle' (quoted in Samuels, 1977a, p. 504). Ayres (1944, pp. 178–87) also argued against broad definitions of the term, and for its narrower identification with status and ceremony. In one passage, Ayres (1944, p. 184) vaguely described institutions in behavioural terms as 'segments of social behavior predominantly ceremonial in character'. By suggesting that institutions were essentially 'ceremonial', Ayres passed the burden of definition onto another inadequately defined term.

Technological rigidity and institutional progressiveness

Technology is not always as dynamic or progressive as Ayres upheld. Lock-in can occur, and the literature on technological change brims with examples of this (Kindleberger, 1983; David, 1985; Katz and Shapiro, 1985; Arthur, 1988, 1989). For example, we are still stuck with the anachronistic and inefficient 4 feet and 8½ inches standard railway gauge, originating from ancient horse-drawn carts and applied to wooden railways in Northeast England two hundred years ago. The survival of this inconvenient gauge is a result of the prohibitive costs of changing railway vehicles and entire railway networks.

In other cases, the rigidity of some technological elements can be functional in some respects for technical advance. Even nature's technology depends on rigidity. For example, it is the almost total inertness and slavish reproductive fidelity of the DNA that makes the kind of evolution we observe in earthly organisms possible. In the human economy, without the stability of some established and necessary technological standards or components, investment in further innovation based upon them may be perceived as too risky and thus may be deterred (N. Rosenberg, 1976). The Wrights probably would not have attempted to combine the kite with the piston-based internal combustion engine, and invested their scarce resources in such an uncertain project, if they had thought that the production of a viable rocket engine or anti-gravity machine was soon to happen.

On the other hand, institutions are not as rigid as Ayres suggested. Just as technology is itself conjoined with tradition, institutions can be dynamic and enabling. Indeed, in his writings, Ayres (1944, pp. 186, 188, 198–202; 1952, pp. 58–9) argued that forms of industrial organization and property have changed in response to the imperatives of technology. To be consistent with his theoretical and normative schema, institutions must be portrayed as laggardly respondents to the technological dynamic. However, without any significant and evident 'technological' impetus, some prominent 'non-instrumental' and 'ceremonial' conventions show remarkable fickleness and changeability. We observe frequent changes in fashion, dress and behaviour that have no explanation in terms of technological developments or functional use.

Arguably, some institutions actually help to encourage technological advances. Modern patent laws are a likely example. Patents provide incentives for innovation by preventing others from copying the invention without payment to the inventor. The institutional restrictions of the patent system can thus enable technological innovation.

The Ayresian can circumvent this argument by *defining* the positive or dynamic aspects as technological. But this denial of institutional innovation and progressiveness simply results from an adjusted definition of an institution. As Walker (1979, p. 526) pointed out, Ayres would have difficulty in accepting the progressive possibilities of an institutional innovation:

> If it is true that some institutions stem from the same sources of human inventiveness as science and technology, and are manifestations of a dynamic endogenous social process which contributes to social survival and economic growth, then it is impossible to accept the difference in function that Ayres postulated between technological activities and institutions, and the basis of his entire system collapses.

Furthermore, Ayres never explained why institutional development should be exempt from the same principles of accidental mutation and recombination that supposedly impel technological change. Following Veblen and many others, it is reasonable to suggest that institutions too are subject to evolutionary processes of this type. Ultimately, as Walker (1979, p. 535) argued, Ayres's procedure is tautological:

> Anything that hinders economic development is by definition an institution in Ayres's work. If a habit of thought or behavioral pattern that we would call an institution contributes efficiently to the process of production, Ayres would call it a technological activity.

Malcolm Rutherford (1994, p. 91) made a similar point concerning Ayres's institutionalism:

> there is a tendency to see evolved institutions as *entirely* backward looking, resistant to change and with no positive functions. A substantial part of this comes from Ayres's definition of an institution that seems to associate the term with 'ceremonial' functions only and to exclude any convention, law, or organizational form that is instrumentally effective ...

Both Rutherford and Walker noted that Ayres had simply defined an institution as something that resists change, and likewise defined technology as that which promotes it. Consequently, the Ayresian dichotomy simply follows from these definitions. Other than promoting two (misleading) descriptive terms, the Ayresian dichotomy tells us little of real processes of change.

Ayres's theory led him into conflict with other institutionalists. Morris Copeland (1966) complained that Ayres's distinction between institutions and technology involved a classification of behaviour patterns simply on the basis of a subjective value judgement; the distinction was 'basically one between social structures you consider good in some sense and those you consider bad'. Other critics pointed out that Ayres had described blind ceremony as the main impediment to technological change, neglecting the highly plausible and impeccably Veblenian proposition that new technology could be resisted by vested interests (Dugger and Sherman, 2000, p. 178). In addition to ceremony and superstition, history shows that resistance to technological change may emanate from powerful interest groups, including management and trade unions (Landes, 1969; Kilpatrick and Lawson, 1980).

The technological as institutional

Veblen (1909b, p. 626) famously described institutions as involving 'settled habits of thought common to the generality of men' and being 'an outgrowth of habit'. However, technology itself also involves clusters of common habits, related to industrial know-how and technique. Nowhere did Veblen suggest that technology and institutions are mutually exclusive. Veblen's description of an institution embraces elements that are also common to technology.

This contrasts with the Ayresian proposition that technology and institutions are entirely separated from each other. As Warren Samuels (1977b, p, 872) asked: 'may not technology be considered as a widely prevalent habit of thought, feeling and action?' In contrast, Ayres downplayed the fact that technology was not simply tools but also ideas and habits concerning their use. In his criticism of Ayres, Walker (1979, p. 534) made a related point: 'Technology and institutions interpenetrate each other, and the operation of tools and machines depends upon institutional habits of thought and action, and vice versa.' This echoes the earlier critique of Ayres by David Miller (1944), who argued that technology and institutions were mutually dependent on one another. Indeed, Ayres (1944, p. 99; 1953, p. 283) almost went so far as to admit this point himself. But he never abandoned the wholesale identification of institutions with ceremony, and never denied the view that institutions were essentially a constraint on progress.

Technology, as understood by modern scholars, is deeply impregnated by tacit knowledge and collective habits of thought, which, in Veblen's terms, are themselves institutional and cultural in character (Brinkman, 1997). Richard Nelson and Sidney Winter (1982, pp. 76–82) and Giovanni Dosi (1988) have elaborated the extent to which technology involves both explicit and tacit knowledge, codified and uncodified rules, and organizational routine. Michael Polanyi (1958, 1967) pointed out that technology is often employed without explicit knowledge of its detailed operations. Hence habit, tradition and 'legendary belief' have to be relied upon in the day-to-day practice of a technology. Furthermore, the learning and acquisition of a technology cannot rely wholly on prescription; the necessary codified knowledge is often absent. The learning of a technology typically involves the formation of habit and routine by following the example of others. As a result: 'To learn by example is to submit to authority. ... A society which wants to preserve a fund of personal knowledge must submit to tradition' (Polanyi, 1958, p. 53). Technology involves the accumulated tradition of experiment with complex arrangements that cannot be dissected in every detail. Engineering is a partially conservative evolutionary process that involves the sifting and selection of established conventions (Rosenberg and Vincenti, 1985; Vincenti, 1990).

What can be more 'ceremonial' than the system of master and apprentice that nurtured most of technological achievements of European society from the Middle Ages to the twentieth century? The modern German and Japanese systems of technological training and innovation rely in no short measure on elements of status and deference. Of course, many aspects of these institutions were superfluous to technological efficiency and helped to preserve the power, wealth and status of the masters. On the other hand, some elements of submission and discipline were essential for the transfer of some crucial knowledge. Ayres did not acknowledge that such institutions could sometimes nurture rather than restrain technological advance.

Ayres and Veblen differed in their conceptions of technology and its social transmission. For Ayres, technology was essentially tools, machines and material equipment. Ayres (1935, p. 186) argued that 'the foundation upon which industrial society is built ... is the multiform material equipment of society'. Ayres also mentioned technological knowledge, but it received relatively less emphasis than in the writings of Veblen, who saw technology as essentially a form of knowledge that was embedded in individual habits and social institutions. While Veblen sometimes paid insufficient attention to the institutional integument of productive activity, he repeatedly emphasized that production involved knowledge ingrained in social groups. Veblen (1908a, p. 153) thus saw production as the outcome of 'the accumulated, habitual knowledge of the ways and means involved'. In contrast, 'the "capital goods" needed for putting this commonplace technological knowledge to use are a slight matter'. Veblen regarded institutionalized habits as essential for the preservation and transmission of such knowledge. Ayres's conception was very different.

The institutional as technological

Just as technology is partly 'institutional' in character, even 'ceremonial' institutions can be seen to have instrumental characteristics. As Samuels (1977b, p. 876) has argued, 'technology can include the instrumental role and value of symbols and organizations'. Further, 'institutions (ceremonial thought and behavior) are not always irrational but may function instrumentally to organize behavior'. Examples of such instrumental institutions include language, systems of weights and measures, traffic conventions and the Highway Code. The English language, for example, entails a maze of perplexing rules and spellings. Yet the very rigidity and 'ceremonial' reproduction of many of these rules helps maintain the integrity and usefulness of the language, alongside its fluidity and capacity to evolve in other respects.

Many institutional conventions or rules are often arbitrary, but nevertheless instrumental. There is no reason why one should drive on the right (or left) of the road, other than it is the reigning convention. Similarly, there is no other reason why a female, horned, four-legged mammal that eats grass and is highly productive of milk should be called in English a 'cow' or in French '*une vache*'. Words and other such conventions are arbitrary, rigid and emanate from tradition, but are nevertheless essential. Slavish imitation and repetition, verging on the ceremonial, makes them effective. For much of his life, Ayres railed against rigid and arbitrary institutions, but failed to acknowledge that they were sometimes vital to human interaction.

In a study of technological transfer to less-developed countries, institutionalist writers William Cole and John Mogab (1987, p. 319) argued that under some circumstances 'apparently ceremonial behavior can be a positive factor in the pursuit of progress' if it can overcome other practices that may stifle innovation. They concluded that 'the technology/ceremony dichotomy has little or no operative value'.

Ayres depicted technology as wholly progressive. This can be challenged by many examples of the use of technology for reactionary or repressive purposes, such as the use of military technology to sustain a backward or oppressive regime, or to attack or subdue a civilian population. An Ayresian would address these problems by separating out different aspects of the phenomena and declaring: what is instrumental and progressive is, *by definition*, technology, and what is non-instrumental or ceremonial is, *by definition*, an institution. But again the Ayresian dichotomy becomes tautological: it logically follows from the definitions. To make sense of the real world we have to proceed beyond mere word play.

Shifting Ayres

Perhaps in response to some of the problems outlined above, Ayres's own position itself evolved. Eventually, he came to the view that institutions could aid as well as retard economic development. In *Towards a Reasonable Society* (1961), Ayres attempted 'to show that freedom, equality, security, abundance, excellence, and democracy are all true values contained in and implied by the technological process' (Rutherford, 1981, p. 661). As Ayres (1961, p. 285) himself wrote: 'the democratic process is a process of learning the truth and operating accordingly, and the unanimity towards which the process aims is that of the universality of science and technology'. Was this an admission that democratic institutions aid rather than hinder the progress of technology and science? Such an admission might undermine the Ayresian dichotomy. Anticipating this problem, Ayres (1952, p. 394) declared:

> democratic 'institutions' are not institutions at all, in the strict meaning of that term. They are rather social structures in which considerations of power and status, historic authenticity and ceremonial adequacy, have been replaced by considerations of technically efficient operation.

Hence, to rescue his own dichotomy, Ayres was forced to proclaim that democratic structures were not really institutions. He also had to depict democracy as free of power, status and ceremony to retain its positive appraisal in his theoretical system. This was doubly unconvincing. First, to remove democratic structures from the set of institutions was unjustified. Second, the idea that democratic structures are, or can be, entirely free from power, status and ceremony is mistaken and implausible.

Ayres also shifted his ground in regard to other institutions. Ayres (1968, p. 343) wrote: 'much is to be said to the credit of the institution of property. Its extraordinary flexibility has suited the requirements of industrial revolution to an extraordinary degree'. Property rights, Ayres (1967, p. 174) conceded, 'and the legal system that defined them, were the institutional foundation on which the industrial economy was built. They provided the motivation that impelled common men to build the modern world.' Ayres thus belatedly accepted that institutions can be more than merely permissive – they can provide motivations for agents. However, this overdue admission fatally undermined his earlier and questionable view that all institutions were entirely resistant to change.

As Ayres reflected on these problems and shifted his position, the relationship and boundary between institutions and technology became even more difficult to define. Even in his *Theory of Economic Progress*, Ayres (1944, p. 99) had admitted that activities of a 'technological' and 'a ceremonial character ... not only coexist but condition each other'. Institutions and technology, Ayres (1953, p. 283) suggested in another work, 'overlie each other and interpenetrate, condition, and complement each other'. Ayres (1961, p. 77) later made the important point that 'technology ... is not something separate and distinct from the societal network of personal relationships'. But he failed to note that such a 'societal network' consists essentially of institutions. As the distinction between technology and institutions became increasingly blurred, Ayres in his later writings began to hint at the possibility that institutions could complement or even promote technological change.[3]

---

3 This hint was later taken up and developed by some of Ayres's followers. Crucially, it was fully admitted that institutions could have instrumental as well as ceremonial functions. Ayres's idea that institutions were always constraining or ceremonial, and hence society should get rid of them, was abandoned (J. F. Foster, 1981; Bush, 1987; Tool, 2000).

The false conflation of Veblen and Ayres

Ironically overcoming his own dislike of intellectual tradition or pedigree, Ayres repeatedly asserted that his dichotomy between technology and ceremony was derived from the writings of Veblen. For instance, Ayres (1973, p. v) wrote: 'Veblen made the dichotomy of technology and ceremonialism his master principle'. Ayres's treatment of institutions as largely or wholly ceremonial was also influential within American institutionalism. The so-called – and often loosely defined – 'Veblenian dichotomy' (Waller, 1982, 1994; Klein, 1995) between institutions and technology was thus born. Its Veblenian origins were generally taken for granted. As A. W. (Bob) Coats (1976, p. 25) remarked:

> Veblen's basic dichotomies – between science and ceremonialism, technology and institutions, industry and business, workmanship and waste – recur in Ayres' writings, though he was constantly reformulating, elaborating and synthesizing these elements.

Walker (1977, p. 220) also saw Veblen as arguing that: 'Institutions are static and resist change; new institutions are formed as the result of the dynamic impact of technology.' Similarly, in an important analysis of the history of the dichotomy, William Waller (1982, p. 762) considered it obvious that 'Ayres's concept clearly represents an extension of Veblen's.'[4]

One of the few to question such interpretations of Veblen was Floyd McFarland (1985, p. 100), who noted that 'ostensible followers of Veblen' in the Ayresian tradition 'have handled Veblen's ideas in a strikingly peculiar way ... they define all institutions as imbecile and deleterious'. Consequently 'institutions are bad, having been assumed or defined so; while technology is good, having been assumed or defined so'. McFarland (1985, 1886) hit the Ayresian problem on its head, although he spoilt his case by overlooking the fact that J. Fagg Foster (1981) and other post-Ayresians had abandoned Ayres's idea that institutions were always regressive.

McFarland rightly challenged the idea that the dichotomy between technology and institutions was of Veblenian origins. Veblen established several dichotomies: between business and industry, between making goods and making money, between waste and use, between serviceability and pecuniary gain and so on. In addition, in several passages, there are descriptions of conflicts between technology and ceremony. However, this is not a universal theme; these arguments are specific rather than general. Furthermore, and most significantly, a universal dichotomy between technology and institutions is not to be found. Indeed, it would be inconsistent with Veblen's own conception and analysis of technology and institutions,

---

4 Waller (1999, pp. 836–7) has since modified his view on this point and has adopted a critical position on the 'dichotomy' that is close to my own.

and contrary to his own explicit pronouncements. These controversial points will be addressed in turn.

Veblen argued at length that the machine process could engender a new culture and undermine conservative and anachronistic values. But Ayres (1944, p. 99) said something different when he proposed that Veblen was the first 'to make this analytical distinction between technology and ceremony the point of departure of all further economic analysis'. On the contrary, there is no evidence that Veblen used a 'distinction between technology and ceremony' as an analytical 'point of departure' of any kind. Veblen did not see institutions as wholly non-instrumental, nor did he define them essentially in terms of ceremony. Furthermore, Veblen saw strong institutional elements within technology itself.

Ayres (1961, p. 30) referred to 'the institutional process (or ceremonialism, as Veblen often called it)'. But I have found no case in which Veblen used the word 'ceremonialism', although he occasionally used words such as 'ceremony' and 'ceremonial'. Contrary to Ayres, Veblen *never* described 'the institutional process' as 'ceremonialism'.

The words 'habit' and 'institution' are abundant in Veblen's writings. By contrast, Ayres conflated the category of 'institution' with 'ceremony' and only infrequently mentioned habit. A fundamental methodological (rather than merely terminological) issue is involved here. Veblen attempted to construct a theory of human agency, based in part on instinct–habit psychology, to replace hedonistic or utility-maximizing, neoclassical 'economic man'. Instead, Ayres depicted the human agent as a virtually passive receptacle of culture, and put supreme explanatory emphasis on cultural determination. In contrast, Veblen emphasized that individuals created institutions and culture, just as individuals were moulded by them. Veblen (1901b, pp. 76–77 n.) criticized theories of 'self-determining cultural exfoliation' that treated culture as unfolding 'by inner necessity'. Veblen rejected such theories because they failed to explain the detailed mechanisms of cultural change and did not appreciate the causal role of the individual in the process. Ironically, in these respects, Ayres's version of cultural and technological determination would also be vulnerable to Veblen's criticism.

The alleged Veblenian origins of the dichotomy

Ayres did not provide a detailed analysis of the alleged origins of the 'Veblenian dichotomy'. In one passage, Ayres (1944, p. 176) quoted Veblen's (1914, p. 25) depiction of a 'triumph of imbecile institutions over life and culture' from *The Instinct of Workmanship*. Other authors have claimed that the 'Veblenian dichotomy' is to be found in the first and eighth chapters of *The Theory of the Leisure Class*, or in *The Theory of Business Enterprise* (esp. pp. 311, 322–4), or in *The Place of Science in Modern Civilization* (esp. pp. 279–323) or in *Imperial Germany* (esp. pp. 26–7). Look there or elsewhere in Veblen's writings; a general dichotomy between institutions and technology will not be found.

It is true that Veblen highlighted the conservative facets of *some* institutions. An important and frequently quoted passage is the following, where Veblen (1899a, p. 191) wrote:

> It is to be noted then, although it may be a tedious truism, that the institutions of to-day – the present accepted scheme of life – do not entirely fit the situation of to-day. At the same time, men's present habits of thought tend to persist indefinitely, except as circumstances enforce a change. These institutions which have so been handed down, these habits of thought, points of view, mental attitudes and aptitudes, or what not, are therefore themselves a conservative factor. This is the factor of social inertia, psychological inertia, conservatism.

With no mention of science or technology in this quotation, Veblen noted a mismatch between the inherited 'institutions of to-day' and the general 'situation of to-day', and that some institutions may resist change. Veblen (1899a, p. 192) went on to consider how institutions may in fact be changed:

> Social structure changes, develops, adapts itself to an altered situation, only through a change in the habits of thought of the several classes of the community; or in the last analysis, through a change in the habits of thought of the individuals which make up the community. The evolution of society is substantially a process of mental adaptation on the part of individuals under the stress of circumstances which will no longer tolerate habits of thought formed under and conforming to a different set of circumstances in the past.

Again, there is mention of neither science nor technology here. Instead, Veblen vaguely identified causes of social change in an 'altered situation' or the 'stress of circumstances'. For Veblen, such 'circumstances' included *other institutions* as well as technological practices. Veblen alluded to processes by which one particular institution may adapt to the others, each institution thus interacting with the rest. He depicted several jostling institutions, themselves changing and impelling change in others. Veblen's theory of institutional change was much more a process of sifting, selection and rivalry between different institutions, rather than institutions generally succumbing to the autonomous forces of technology (Edgell, 1975, 2001). Contrary to his interpreters, Veblen did not see technology as the only important factor causing institutional evolution.

Turning to *The Theory of Business Enterprise*, Veblen (1904, p. 303) remarked: 'The factor in the modern situation that is alien to the ancient régime is the machine technology, with its many and wide ramifications.'

This is not evidence of a general dichotomy between institutions and technology but between a specific (machine) technology and specific institutions. In the same work, Veblen wrote of a 'concomitant differentiation and specialization of occupations ... resulting in an ever weakening sense of conviction, allegiance, or piety toward the received institutions' (1904, p. 324). Again there is no universal theory or dichotomy here. The conflict is not between technology and institutions but between the 'differentiation and specialization of occupations' and 'the received institutions'.

Ayres's claim to find a general dichotomy between institutions and technology in *The Instinct of Workmanship* turns out to be invalid. The relevant and often-quoted passage refers to the possibility that instincts such as 'the parental bent or the sense of workmanship' may overturn 'institutional elements at variance with the continued life-interests of the community' and 'the bonds of custom, prescription, principles, precedent' may be broken. 'But history records more spectacular instances of the triumph of imbecile institutions over life and culture' (Veblen, 1914, p. 25).[5]

Here Veblen simply asserted that workmanship and other instincts could come into conflict with some institutions, and with different possible outcomes. In some cases, 'imbecile' institutions block these instinctive drives. In other cases, institutions prove more accommodating. Emphatically, Veblen did *not* suggest that *all* institutions are 'imbecile'. Hence this passage does not give us the general dichotomy associated with Ayres.

Another passage in the same work might seem at first sight to give Ayres's claim more support. There Veblen (1914, p. 148) wrote of changes in 'the technological scheme' and advances in 'workmanlike mastery' being potentially hindered due to 'limitations' including 'the institutional situation'. Veblen clearly admitted that 'institutional factors have doubtless retarded the advance in most cases'. But this statement was in the context of a discussion of 'lower cultures' and even in this case Veblen gave priority to other constraints: 'the insurmountable obstacles to such an advance appear to be those imposed by the material circumstances'. Hence, for Veblen, institutional inhibitions were neither foremost nor universal. Veblen asserted no general dichotomy between all institutions and all technology.

In the preface to his *Vested Interests and the Common Man*, Veblen (1919b) wrote that 'a discrepancy has arisen ... between those accepted principles of law and custom that underlie business enterprise and the businesslike management of industry, on the one hand, and the material conditions which have now been engendered by that new order of industry' on the other. Again there is no general dichotomy between all technology and all

---

5 Contrary to Bush (1986, p. 29) this passage does not lend support to a general principle 'of the dominance of ceremonial patterns of behavior over instrumental patterns of behavior within the culture'. Even if 'instrumental patterns of behavior' can be equated with Veblen's 'parental bent or the sense of workmanship', Veblen clearly also considers their triumph and dominance over ceremonial behaviour, as well as the reverse possibility.

institutions. Instead Veblen wrote of a discrepancy between the 'material conditions' of modern industry and the particular customs and institutions of modern business management.

In his *Absentee Ownership*, Veblen (1923, p. 281) wrote of the 'technology of physics and chemistry' being handicapped by 'an institutional environment ... that is alien to its bent and inhospitable to its free growth'. But if we look at this passage in context, Veblen was not writing of institutions in general. Instead, Veblen (1923, pp. 280–1) was referring to a 'received system of institutions' involving 'a fabric of conventional, sentimental, religious, and magical habits of thought'. Rather than making a statement about institutions in general, Veblen argued that these particular habits of thought inhibited the growth of science and technology.

Veblen frequently suggested that technology might come into conflict with specific institutions or habits of thought. For example, Veblen (1915, p. 26) wrote: 'In many of the lower cultures ... the workday routine of getting a living is encumbered with a ubiquitous and pervasive scheme of such magical or superstitious conceits and observances'. He also considered several cases where technological change had helped to promote or encourage institutional change. What he failed to propose, however, was a notion that technology *always and everywhere* conflicted with *all institutions*. The reason for the absence of such an idea is simple: for Veblen technology itself was also institutional in character.

A passage from *The Instinct of Workmanship* made a decisive point. Veblen (1914, p. 176) wrote: 'the body of knowledge (facts) turned to account in workmanship, the facts made use of in devising technological processes and applications, are of the nature of habits of thought'. Recollecting Veblen's own descriptions of institutions in terms of habits, this was tantamount to a statement that technology itself has institutional features. This was suggested in other places in Veblen's writing. For example, in the *Theory of Business Enterprise*, Veblen (1904, p. 312) asserted: 'The discipline exercised by the mechanical occupations ... is a discipline of the habits of thought.' A similar idea is found in *Absentee Ownership*, where Veblen (1923, p. 280) wrote:

> The technological system is an organisation of intelligence, a structure of intangibles and imponderables, in the nature of habits of thought. It resides in the habits of thoughts of the community and comes to a head in the habits of thought of the technicians.

Science and technology depend on facts, and for Veblen (1914, p. 53) the perception of the facts depends on habits of thought. It again follows that both science and technology are, at least according to Veblen, of an institutional nature. Both institutions and technology are based on habits of thought.

Veblen's implicit denial of the 'Veblenian dichotomy'

Not only is a general 'Veblenian dichotomy' absent from Veblen's writings, but also some passages are inconsistent with the idea. For example, in the *Leisure Class*, Veblen (1899a, p. 193) wrote of 'economic institutions' as 'habitual methods of carrying on the life process of the community'. This suggests that Veblen saw some institutions were instrumental. Veblen (1899a, p. 206) considered 'the leisure class as an exponent and vehicle of conservatism or reversion in social structure. The inhibition which it exercises may be salutary or the reverse.' Here Veblen accepted the possibility that 'conservatism … in social structure' may be considered as 'salutary' – a formulation that would grate with Ayres. Two pages later, Veblen (1899a, p. 208) addressed 'pecuniary or industrial institutions … institutions serving either the invidious or the non-invidious economic interest'. This passage undermines the Ayresian dichotomy, by recognizing that some institutions can serve acceptable economic interests.

Veblen (1899a, p. 266) also wrote of 'the institutional structure required by the economic situation of the collectivity'. This contradicts the Ayresian dichotomy by acknowledging that an 'institutional structure' could be positively 'required' and not necessarily a drag on the economic dynamic. In a similar vein, Veblen (1899a, p. 363) wrote that 'habits of thought which are so formed under the guidance of teachers and scholastic traditions have an economic value'. Bearing in mind Veblen's own view of an institution as common habits, this passage suggests that institutions can have a positive role.

Passages in Veblen's other works support an equivalent verdict. One of the clearest and most dramatic is the following. In an amazingly prescient analysis of the Japanese socio-economic system – written in 1915 – Veblen (1934, p. 251) remarked:

> It is in this unique combination of a high-wrought spirit of feudalistic fealty and chivalric honor with the material efficiency given by the modern technology that the strength of the Japanese nation lies.

Such an observation is commonplace in the literature on the 1945–90 Japanese economic miracle. But Veblen made it well before the rise of modern Japan, and nevertheless saw the root of Japan's future strength. This strength does not lie in technology alone but in its combination with conservative and ceremonial institutions 'of feudalistic fealty and chivalric honor'. This assertion does not simply contradict the Ayresian dichotomy; it turns it inside out and upside-down. In sum, Ayres's notion of a conflict between institutions and technology is not only absent in Veblen's writings but it is contradicted by Veblen's own words and conceptions.[6]

The non-Veblenian origins of the dichotomy

A general dichotomy between institutions and technology is absent in Veblen, but Ayres may have misunderstood or extrapolated some of Veblen's formulations. What else might have influenced Ayres in his creation of the dichotomy? One of the first places to look would be the works of John Dewey. In a typical discussion of the progress of modern science and associated methods of evaluation, Dewey (1939, pp. 61–2) remarked that:

> the difficulties that stand in the way are ... supplied by traditions, customs, and institutions ... Take, as an outstanding example, the difficulties experienced in getting a hearing for the Copernican astronomy a few centuries ago. Traditional and customary beliefs which were sanctioned and maintained by powerful institutions regarded the new scientific ideas as a menace.

Dewey (1935, p. 75) made a similar point elsewhere. However, Dewey did not state that *all* institutions constrain scientific or technological advance. Furthermore, for Dewey, habits and institutions had a positive and enabling function. In words that directly negate Ayres's views on institutions, Dewey (1922, pp. 166–7) wrote:

> To view institutions as enemies of freedom, and all conventions as slaveries, is to deny the only means by which positive freedom in action can be secured. A general liberation of impulses may set things going when they have been stagnant, but ... the released forces ... are bound to be mutually contradictory and hence destructive – destructive not only of the habits they wish to destroy but of themselves, of their own efficacy. Convention and custom are necessary to carrying forward impulse to any happy conclusion. ... Not convention but stupid and rigid convention is the foe.

This made absolutely clear that Dewey saw some but not all institutions or conventions as resistant to change. Similarly, Dewey (1922, pp. 175–6) argued that habits were indispensable to thought and conditions of intellectual efficiency:

> Habit is however more than a restriction of thought. Habits become negative limits because they are first positive agencies. The more numerous our habits the wider the field of possible observation and

---

6   In an important critical discussion of the so-called 'Veblenian dichotomy', T. Lawson (2003a, pp. 194–6) gave further evidence of the incompatibility of this dichotomy with the writings of Veblen himself. More than that, he provided a powerful argument that the dichotomy originated from behaviouristic definitions of institutions and technology and 'a failure to sustain a clear or coherent conception of social structure or culture and of human subjectivity that are ontologically irreducible'.

foretelling. The more flexible they are, the more refined is perception in its discrimination and the more delicate the presentation evoked by imagination.

From such a viewpoint, it is understandable that Dewey directly and explicitly criticized Ayres for his one-sided view of habit. In their letters to each other they were at loggerheads on this matter (Tilman, 1990).

Joseph Dorfman once wrote to Dewey to ask about his interchanges with Veblen. Dewey responded: 'I never had enough personal contact with Dr. Veblen to be able to contribute anything. I got the distinction between business and technology from his writings, I can't tell when' (quoted in Tilman, 1996, p. 140 n.). Note that Dewey here referred to a dichotomy between 'business and technology' (which is found in Veblen) and not institutions and technology, which Ayres wrongly claimed to find in Veblen's writings.

If the influence of Veblen and Dewey on Ayres's thinking is not so great as has been claimed, then we are inclined to ask what other possible influences might there have been on Ayres's thought. Take the Ayresian idea of the conservative nature of custom and ceremony. This idea has a long pedigree. It is particularly prevalent in the liberal reformers of the nineteenth century. For example, John Stuart Mill (1964, pp. 127–8) wrote in 1859: 'The despotism of custom is everywhere the standing hindrance to human advancement, ... progress or improvement.' Ayres took similar liberal ideas on board, and eventually fused them with the scientism of the modern age.

In addition, two then living, but now largely forgotten, American thinkers are likely to have influenced Ayres in the interwar period. There are similarities between the sociologist William Ogburn's (1922) popular theory of 'cultural lag' and the work of Ayres. In his book, Ogburn distinguished between the 'material' and the 'non-material' culture. By material culture he referred to technology and the material environment fashioned by humanity. He included in the non-material culture elements such as laws, conventions, family arrangements and other social relations. He argued that the material culture develops more rapidly than the non-material culture necessarily related to it. The material culture was said to build cumulatively on its own success, but the non-material culture was governed by habit, inertia and tradition. This gave rise to 'cultural lag'. Ogburn argued that the non-material culture was slow to adjust to new technological or material conditions. There are clear resemblances here to Ayres's general dichotomy. But despite some similarities, Ogburn's analysis was not pure Veblen, because Veblen did not develop a substantial or general of a cultural lag. Nevertheless, Ogburn knew Mitchell, and Ogburn's analysis was widely discussed in institutionalist circles.[7]

---

7 Perhaps it was significant that Ayres's former student, Parsons (1935) exaggerated the similarities between Veblen's and Ogburn's ideas. Dugger and Sherman (2000, pp. 175–9) have noted the similarity between Ayres's and Ogburn's conceptions.

Another possible influence on Ayres was Lawrence Kelso Frank, who studied at Columbia under John Dewey and Wesley Clair Mitchell. During the First World War, Frank served as consultant for the War Industry Board with Walton Hamilton, who knew Ayres well. In a prominent journal article, Frank (1925, pp. 184–5) considered the development of 'a new tool or technique' that may conflict with 'traditional group arrangements of ceremonies, rituals, and symbols ... only too frequently acting as impediments and obstacles' to the use of that technique:

> Hence there is an increasing discrepancy between the needs of the technical processes and the possibilities and requirements of the institutional life of the group. To meet the situation there is, later, a bold attempt to rescue and even promote the institutional practices at the expense of the tools and techniques, which is the stage of outright ceremonialism or ritualism, when men cling tenaciously to ancient rites, symbols, and practices, at the expense of their industrial arts.

Frank's rhetoric is uncannily close to the words of Ayres. But Ayres did not establish a clear dichotomy between ceremony and technology until the 1930s.[8]

Another possible precursor of the Ayresian dichotomy is in the writings of Karl Marx. Although Ayres rarely acknowledged Marx, we can read *The Theory of Economic Progress* as a sanitized and Americanized version of Marx's theory of economic development. The genesis of Ayres's mature views in the 1930s coincides with a period when – in reaction to fascism and economic depression – Marxist writings were gaining an increased visibility among American intellectuals. Marx saw technology as a motor of economic change and a prime determinant of fundamental changes of and within economic systems.[9] In his 1847 book *The Poverty of Philosophy*, he wrote:

> Social relations are closely bound up with productive forces. In acquiring new productive forces men change their mode of production; and in changing their mode of production, in changing their way of earning a living, they change all their social relations. The hand-mill gives you society with the feudal lord; the steam-mill, society with the industrial capitalist. ... the mode of production, the relations in which productive forces are developed ... correspond to a definite development of men and of their productive forces, and ... a change in men's productive forces necessarily brings about a change in their relations of production (Marx and Engels, 1976b, pp. 166–75).

---

8 The similarity of the views of Ayres and Frank was brought to my attention by Asso and Fiorito (2003b).

9 For a defence of Marx's view see Cohen (1978).

Marx (1971, pp. 20–21) elaborated the above ideas in his famous 1859 Preface to his *Contribution to the Critique of Political Economy*:

> In the social production of their existence, men inevitably enter into definite relations, which are independent of their will, namely relations of production appropriate to a given stage in the development of the material forces of production. The totality of these relations of production constitutes the economic structure of society, the real foundation, on which arises a legal and political superstructure and to which correspond definite forms of social consciousness. ... At a certain stage of development, the material productive forces of society come into conflict with the existing relations of production or ... with the property relations within the framework of which they have operated hitherto. ... The changes in the economic foundation lead sooner or later to the transformation of the whole immense superstructure. In studying such transformations it is always necessary to distinguish between the material transformation of the economic conditions of production, which can be determined with the precision of natural science, and the legal, political, religious, artistic or philosophic – in short, ideological forms in which men become conscious of this conflict and fight it out.

If we replace 'productive forces' or 'material forces of production' by 'technology', and if we substitute 'institutions' for 'social relations' or 'relations of production', then we have transformed passages from Marx to a point that they could almost have been written by Ayres. The dichotomy between institutions and technology has thus a close precursor in Marx's portrayal of the forces of production pushing up against the relations of production. Both Marx and Ayres believed that technology was a primary and driving force of history. They shared an optimism in the powers of technology and science that is traceable back to eighteenth-century Enlightenment thinkers.

A difference here, however, is that Ayres (1944, p. 187) saw 'no institution ... or set of institutions' as '"appropriate" to a given technology in any but a negative sense'. In contrast, Marx saw some institutions as being periodically brought into harmony with technological development. For Ayres, the conflict between technology and institutions was ubiquitous and continuous. For Marx, the spasmodic conflict was now and then temporarily ameliorated by social revolution and by the subsequent recasting of the economy along new and progressive lines. Then, eventually, the forces of production would again come into conflict with the economic system. Marx analysed change in revolutionary terms; Ayres brought the perspective of a gradualist.

Nevertheless, the similarities between Marx and Ayres go further. Ayres (1944, p. 307) accepted, just like Marx, 'the possibility of abundance' as a result of future technological advance. In their analytical approaches, both Marx and Ayres focused on grand, social forces, to the neglect of micro-socioeconomic processes and details. Ayres largely neglected problems of consciousness and agency. Likewise, in Marx's work as a whole the theory of agency remained underdeveloped, as Veblen himself critically remarked on several occasions.

However, in his stress of the need for social revolution to transform society, Marx differed politically from Ayres. Ayres was more optimistic about the possibility of gradual reform, and less enthusiastic about the goal of general common ownership. Ayres (1946) advocated a limited form of capitalism and defended the 1930s New Deal against its detractors.

With a powerful and unique vision, Ayres nevertheless was a devotee of American libertarianism and technophilia. In downgrading religion he placed himself in an American minority, but in the substitute worship of technology he was true to American cultural form. His creed was characteristically an expression of a deeply rooted tradition of progressive and scientistic American culture, with a pedigree going back to Benjamin Franklin and Thomas Paine, and before that to the European Enlightenment.[10]

Ayres turned the clock back for American institutionalism. Veblen in his critique of Marxism had rejected an exclusive stress on social determination, and asserted that the human agent is 'also an individual, acting out his own life as such'. For Veblen, humans moulded their circumstances just as they are moulded by them. In these respects, Veblen's critique of Marx would apply equally to Ayres. After 1945, the *de facto* leader of American institutionalism brought institutionalism back to the pre-Veblenian 1880s, while at the same time convincing almost everyone that he had absorbed the Veblenian doctrine.

Nevertheless, Ayres's skilful accommodation of American technophilia, his distrust of tradition and institutions, and his adoption of behaviourist psychology gave his school of institutionalism a relatively high survival value in the postwar period. The natural selection of living institutionalist doctrines favoured Ayres first and Commons second. Mitchell and Knight lost out. The notion of two primary traditions of American institutionalism emerged, one based on the work of Commons, and the other seen as emanating from Veblen and passing through Ayres.

The truth was that Ayres's doctrine had much less in common with Veblen than is often supposed. But ironically the postwar success of Ayres helped to keep the name of Veblen alive. Today, in a new intellectual environment – which involves the rejection of behaviourism, the rehabilitation of instinct–habit psychology, and an understanding that institutions are the unavoidable substance of socio-economic life – the survival value of the Ayresian tradition is much diminished. The ultimate achievement of the Ayresian tradition has been to push Veblen again to the fore, while

---

10 For a discussion of Ayres's policy stance see Tilman (1974).

fading itself into obscurity. The natural selection of institutionalist traditions has ultimately favoured the original approach of Veblen, unwittingly sustained by the altruism of their Ayresian relatives.

After Ayres

This book is not intended to address post-1945 American institutionalism, but the focus on Ayres in two chapters here warrants some brief – if inadequate – discussion of some subsequent developments in this important tradition of American institutionalist thought. The development of work in the Ayresian tradition has been discussed and documented elsewhere. I do not intend to address this body of work in detail, other than to focus on one or two aspects.[11]

It has been shown above that Ayres's notion of an institution was very different from that of Veblen. In the post-Ayresian tradition, the definition of an institution was one of the first things to be changed and clarified. John Fagg Foster was one of Ayres's students.[12] Foster taught Tool, who attributed the following definition to his teacher: 'The term *institution* means any prescribed or proscribed pattern of correlated behavior or attitude widely agreed upon among a group of persons organized to carry on some particular purpose' (Tool, 1979, pp. 73–4). This definition is closer to the ideas of Veblen, although it gives too much emphasis to particular institutions involving deliberation, organization and agreement, and too little to institutions that may arise spontaneously, without overall design. It also downplays the structural character of institutions. Nevertheless, this change in definition was of significance because it left open the possibility that institutions may have *both* instrumental and ceremonial aspects, and for that reason it could help to eliminate a series of problems in Ayres's position.

Having redefined the concept of an institution in a manner closer to the Veblen–Hamilton precedents, the next concept that required attention by Ayres's followers was technology. Especially after the rise of the American anti-war and green movements in the 1960s and 1970s, concern was expressed that Ayres had given a positive evaluation to *all* technology, including militaristic, polluting and nuclear technologies. Accordingly, in the writings of J. F. Foster's followers, the emphasis shifted away from technology *per se*, towards more general processes of 'instrumental valuation' (J. F. Foster, 1981; Bush, 1987; Tool, 1995).

Nevertheless, it was still argued that the 'technological process is inherently dynamic' (Bush, 1987, p. 1089). However, Bush argued that all

---

11 See Bush (1986, 1987), Dugger (1995), J. F. Foster (1981), Junker (1982), Tool (1979, 1995, 2000) and Waller (1982, 1994).
12 See Tool (2000). W. D. Williams, another PhD student of J. F. Foster, has informed me that Foster had reservations concerning the way behaviourist psychology encouraged people to treat each other as objects. Foster was thus less devoted to behaviourism than Ayres.

institutions manifest both instrumentally and ceremonially warranted patterns of behaviour. This recognition of instrumentally warranted aspect of all institutions also contrasts with Ayres (1944). Bush (1986, 1987) developed a concept of 'ceremonial encapsulation'. It was argued that dynamic technology may become entwined with and 'encapsulated' within hierarchy, status and other 'ceremonial' institutions.[13]

At least in its treatment of technology and institutions, the work of J. F. Foster, Tool, Bush and others was more sophisticated than that of Ayres himself. Not only was Ayres's inadequate definition of an institution replaced, but also there is a more complex and illustrative taxonomy of possible relations between the instrumental and the ceremonial. To a large degree, the work in this post-Ayresian tradition has been a long retreat from Ayres's strict and questionable dichotomy.

For example, instead of Ayres's (1918a, p. 57; 1961, p. 175) repeated statements suggesting that 'there is no such thing as an individual', Tool (1979, p. 52) took a very different position: 'a person is both a conditioner of culture and is conditioned by the culture, inescapably so'. Instead of the Ayresian, one-sided stress on social forces, Tool and others took a much more balanced stance.

Gradually, writers in the post-Ayresian tradition have qualified and restricted Ayres's idea that technology is inherently progressive, and should be evaluated as such. They have emphasized more that what is 'instrumental' in a Deweyian theory of valuation is essentially with regard to the enhancement of the human condition and human emancipation. Technology can sometimes promote and sometimes undermine those ends. The ultimate welfare criterion is not what serves technology but what serves human life and human development.

Well over two millennia ago, Aristotle in his *Politics* established the distinction between 'use value' and 'exchange value'. 'Use value' meant the usefulness of an item for the sustenance of human society.[14] The distinction between 'use value' and 'exchange value' thus corresponds closely to a distinction between the socially instrumental and the pecuniary. As well as being one of the oldest, it is one of the most important and fundamental distinctions for economic science.

By contrast, ignoring this ancient distinction, modern mainstream welfare economics is founded on the concept of individual utility. Policies are judged not in relation to scientific knowledge concerning, for example, human health or the ecosystem, but exclusively in regard to their ability to increase consumer satisfaction. This subjective and utilitarian approach is so

---

13 In devising the concept of ceremonial encapsulation, Bush (1986, p. 25) generously acknowledged the influence and assistance of L. Junker.

14 In contrast, some neoclassical-inclined writers have wrongly interpreted 'use value' as a precursor of subjective utility. Against this, K. Polanyi *et al.* (1957, pp. 65–7, 80–3) argued convincingly that Aristotle saw use value as an objective quality relating to the usefulness of an item for humankind.

widespread that the alternative and non-utilitarian approaches to problems of welfare – found in the writings of Aristotle, Smith, Ricardo, Marx, the German historical school and the institutionalists – are generally ignored. But work in that ancient, alternative tradition points to a concept of human need that transcends utilitarianism. After leaving behind the misleading Ayresian dichotomies and their tangled technological rhetoric, institutionalist research on the foundations of economic policy and welfare should be in terms of a theory of human need (Doyal and Gough, 1991; Gough, 1994; Corning, 2000b).

18 The decline of institutional economics

> If the outcome of a theoretical confrontation with the institutionalists seemed, in the minds of neoclassical economists, a foregone conclusion, a resolution of the challenges institutionalism posed regarding the practicality and influence of the discipline was not. Wheresoever the twists and turns of academic debate might have led, the force of circumstances could not be denied.
>
> Michael A. Bernstein, *A Perilous Progress* (2001)

John R. Commons died in 1945 and Wesley Mitchell in 1948. The baton of institutionalist leadership passed to the energetic and charismatic Clarence Ayres. As a broad and diverse movement, American institutionalism continued to have some impact in the postwar period (Yonay, 1998). At least thirteen institutionalists or institutionalist sympathizers have been Presidents of the American Economic Association since the Second World War: Paul Douglas (1947), Frank Knight (1950), Calvin B. Hoover (1953), Simon Kuznets (1954), Edwin E. Witte (1956), Morris Copeland (1957), George W. Stocking (1958), Arthur F. Burns (1959), Joseph Spengler (1965), Kenneth Boulding (1968), John Kenneth Galbraith (1972), Robert A. Gordon (1975) and Charles Kindleberger (1985). But the majority of these elections were before 1960. A measure of the rise and decline of American institutional economics is the number of citations in each decade to works by Thorstein Veblen, as shown in Table 18.1.

Table 18.1 compares citations to Veblen by other authors in core American journals of economics, with citations to Veblen in leading American journals in sociology, and with citations to Léon Walras by other authors in the same core American journals of economics.[1] The table shows a relatively high number of citations in articles in three leading American

---

1 Citations to Walras track references to a neoclassical economist who was less well known before the 1930s, but who inspired the rising general equilibrium theory that became the cutting edge of microeconomics from the 1940s. The name of Pareto was relatively frequent because it refers to an efficiency criterion, as well as a person. Marshall was often cited, including in the earlier decades. But several American institutionalists – including Mitchell and J. M. Clark – were partly Marshallian in inclination.

Table 18.1 Number of articles in core journals citing Veblen or Walras

	Number of articles citing Veblen in core American journals of economics*	Number of articles citing Veblen in core American journals of sociology†	Number of articles citing Walras in core American journals of economics
1890s	6	2	8
1900s	15	8	12
1910s	28	9	7
1920s	52	11	19
1930s	54	6	36
1940s	46	10	39
1950s	67	21	62
1960s	35	23	67
1970s	27	23	111
1980s	24	21	84

Notes

* Namely the *Quarterly Journal of Economics* (founded 1886), *Journal of Political Economy* (founded 1892), and the *American Economic Review* (founded 1911).

† Namely the *American Journal of Sociology* (founded 1895) and the *American Sociological Review* (founded 1936)

journals of economics from the 1920s to the 1950s. This was the Veblenian heyday. By comparison, citations to Veblen in the two leading sociological journals were lower in the same four decades, but fewer journals were involved. It is useful to compare citations to Veblen with those to a leading neoclassical economist. Until the 1960s, citations to Veblen in the same three leading American journals of economics were higher than those received by Walras. After the 1950s, citations to Veblen in leading journals of economics declined dramatically, and those to Walras increased considerably. Although this citation comparison between Veblen and Walras has its imperfections, it is consistent with the observation that in the 1960s the victory of neoclassical over institutional economics became complete.[2]

---

2 Cleary and Edwards (1960) analysed the institutional origins of the authors that published articles in the *American Economic Review* in the 1950s. They found that out of the 287 contributors in that decade, 21.6 per cent had their terminal degrees from Harvard, 13.2 per cent from Columbia and 11.8 from Chicago. Columbia then had a few institutionalist sympathizers. The institutional affiliations of these authors told an additional story. In the 1950s, 6.9 per cent of *AER* article pages were by authors from the University of California, 6.4 per cent were from MIT and 5.4 per cent were from Stanford, with no other university exceeding 4 per cent. Universities with little institutionalist presence were attracting leading researchers and rising in prestige. Institutionalism thus lost out in the postwar expansion of the university system.

It would take another entire volume to deal with the development of institutional economics in the postwar period, even in North America alone. Nevertheless, I uphold that Veblenian institutionalism is the most promising basis for the continuation and development of this tradition today. As shown in previous chapters, by the 1930s much of this Veblenian legacy had been discarded. The aim in this chapter is to review the main forces behind the decline in American institutionalism. Chapter 19 will then show that since the 1980s the intellectual conditions for a new Veblenian institutionalist revival have begun to emerge.

Changes in intellectual environment

Several external forces promoted the gradual marginalization of American institutional economics. They are discussed in the approximate historic order of their greatest destructive impact on the institutionalist tradition. We consider some of the strong shifts of opinion among the academic community in the period from 1914 to 1945. But the evolution of ideas is not solely a matter of the merits of the ideas themselves, but also the changing contexts in which some ideas are favoured over others. Some shifts of opinion were obviously linked to major events; others involved more subtle developments in prevailing practice.

A major undermining development was the dissolution of the original philosophical and psychological presumptions of institutionalism. The assault on the pragmatist philosophy and instinct–habit psychology that underlay Veblenian institutionalism has been discussed in Chapter 12 above. It has also been shown that, by the 1930s, leading institutionalists such as Wesley Mitchell, John Maurice Clark, Morris Copeland, John R. Commons and Clarence Ayres were either embracing or deferring to the rising behaviourist psychology, and to the growing empiricist mood in the philosophy of science. Positivism sustained behaviourism, which diverted institutionalism from both the key concept of habituation and causal any discourse on intentionality.

However, behaviourism also bolstered the view that human behaviour was culturally determined, through mechanisms of stimulus and response. The overwhelming importance of culture is undeniable, but to make the individual a mere puppet of cultural conditions would neglect the importance of understanding how culture can mould the deliberations of the individual. The powers of culture are more deeply appreciated if individual agency is also made an adequate part of the picture.

Frank Knight was a maverick institutionalist who resisted these rising positivist and behaviourist doctrines. But he remained an atypical and relatively isolated figure. Furthermore, his version of institutionalism also ditched the Darwinian legacy and contained no adequate evolutionary treatment of human agency.

Another undermining force has also been discussed in Chapter 12. It was the widespread rejection of biological or Darwinian ideas from the social sciences. Even within biology there was a lack of confidence on Darwinian theory, until the success of the synthesis between Darwinism and Mendelian genetics in the 1940s. The growing reaction against links between biology and the social sciences meant that it was much more difficult for social scientists to follow Veblen and develop a 'post-Darwinian' economics.

Furthermore, Darwinism has been widely misinterpreted in terms of teleological progressivism or biological reductionism.[3] The conceptual and philosophical underpinnings of Darwinism were not drawn out fully until the final decades of the twentieth century. Until recently there was a limited understanding of multiple-level evolution, the suboptimality of evolutionary processes and the concept of path dependence. Even for scholars with the courage to continue Veblen's Darwinian research programme in the social sciences, intercourse with biology was not nearly as fruitful as it can be today.

The separation of the Anglophone social sciences from biology was greatly accelerated by the reaction against the rise of Nazism in Europe. Social scientists became increasingly concerned about the Nazi abuse of biological ideas in the pursuit of their racist policies. They drew the conclusion that the social sciences must be separated from biology. Richard Hofstadter's (1944, p. 176) influential critique of 'Social Darwinism' declared: 'the life of man in society, while it is incidentally a biological fact, has characteristics which are not reducible to biology and must be explained in the distinctive terms of a cultural analysis'. He was right, in every word. But it did not occur to him, as it did to Veblen almost fifty years earlier, that some of these distinctive terms might be taken from a generalized Darwinism, untainted by any biological reductionism. The reaction against biology in the social sciences led to the rejection of even nonreductionist applications of Darwinian ideas.

Because of these ideological shifts in Anglophone academia it became nigh impossible to develop the philosophical and psychological foundations of economic theory along Veblenian or Darwinian lines. The rejection of Veblenian core principles left a theoretical void. But at more applied and less fundamental theoretical levels, institutional economics continued for some time, by the ongoing application of existing ideas. Eventually, however, the inner theoretical void meant that institutionalism lost its sense of direction and much of its capacity to innovate. The debilitating consequences took some time to appear. But they resulted from fundamental methodological and theoretical weaknesses that were already there in the 1920s.

---

3   For example, Schumpeter (1934, p. 57) mistakenly associated Darwinism with 'uniform unilinear development'.

It took some time for a rival paradigm to institutionalism to become established in America. A necessary condition for the removal of a prevailing theoretical approach is an alternative set of theoretical ideas. Some new ideas are empowered by great cataclysmic events. They draw their energy from an atmosphere of emergency and from a shared devotion to finding solutions to pressing problems. After Veblen died in 1929, there was no shortage of economic problems and explosive events.

The impact of the Great Crash and Keynesianism

Initially, the Great Crash of 1929 and the subsequent Depression were seen as a triumphant, posthumous vindication of Veblen's (1904) celebrated critique of pecuniary waste and speculation. Attention then turned to the practical problems of dealing with the consequent economic devastation. Mitchell and others had promoted a policy of counter-cyclical public works from 1921. But the extent of government commitment to this policy was insufficient to deal with the massive downturn of the early 1930s. Mitchell himself underestimated the scale and longevity of the Great Depression.[4]

In retrospect, institutionalists should have used their institutional expertise to examine more deeply the way in which the collapse of American banking institutions helped to prolong the Depression. The severe and prolonged downturn was not the natural rhythm of a capitalist machine but the consequence of the breakdown of financial institutions and mechanisms. With the banking system in tatters, attempts to generally stimulate effective demand, and particularly reduce the hoarding of cash, were inevitably of highly limited effect. In this context of institutional collapse, institutionalism failed to play its theoretical trump card.[5]

Furthermore, for simply being in positions of influence, to some extent the institutionalist Establishment was blamed for the failures of the governments that they advised, and for their apparent lack of a remedy. They drew criticism from some young economists, impatient for policy solutions.

---

4 In 1932, Mitchell wrote to his wife that he expected 'a turn for the better' in the 'business outlook'. Considering whether the depression would run on 'for another year' he said: 'I don't think it will; but the wise course is to prepare for that contingency' (quoted in L. Mitchell, 1953, p. 338).

5 For discussions of the way in which the collapse of banking institutions prolonged the Depression see Means (1942), Kindleberger (1973), Bernanke (1983) and Barber (1988). By contrast, Schumpeter (1931) proposed that the global Depression was the unfortunate but unavoidable outcome of the coincidence of the three troughs of the fifty-year Kondratieff cycle, with the seven-year Juglar cycle and the forty-month Kitchin cycle. Schumpeter admitted that other factors had exacerbated the situation, but did not emphasize the collapse of banking institutions. Keynes (1936) promoted discretionary measures to increase aggregate demand but understressed the problems created by the breakdown of American banking institutions.

Gunnar Myrdal (1972, pp. 6–7) recollected that when he came as a young man to the US at the end of the 1920s, institutional economics was still seen by many as the 'wind of the future'. However, at that time Myrdal was at the 'theoretical' stage of his own development and he was 'utterly critical' of this institutionalist orientation in economics. He 'even had something to do with the initiation of the Econometric Society, which was planned as a defense organization against the advancing institutionalists'. Myrdal explained a key event in the decline of the popularity of institutionalism in the United States:

> What I believe nipped it in the bud was the world-wide economic depression. Faced with this great calamity, we economists of the 'theoretical' school, accustomed to reason in terms of simplified macromodels, felt we were on the top of the situation, while the institutionalists were left in a muddle. It was at this stage that economists in the stream of the Keynesian revolution adjusted their theoretical models to the needs of the time, which gave victory much more broadly to our 'theoretical' approach.

This personal testimony is particularly striking because in the 1940s Myrdal converted to institutionalism, and received the Nobel Prize in Economics in 1974. Clarence Ayres (1935, p. 173) implicitly and partially corroborated Myrdal's analysis by his contemporary report that the 'cutting edge of the issue between [the neoclassical economists] and the "Institutionalists" would seem to be the incapacity of the latter to demonstrate the failure of the present economic order which they propose controlling'. Frank Knight (1952, p. 45) came to a similar verdict. He asserted that institutionalism was 'largely drowned by discussion of the depression, or perhaps boom and depression, and especially by the literature of the Keynesian revolution'. A hostile critic of institutionalism took a remarkably similar view when he noted that 'the greatest slump in history finds them sterile and incapable of helpful comment – their trends gone awry and their dispersions distorted' (Robbins, 1932, p. 115). Dorothy Ross (1991, p. 419) corroborates the argument that the Great Depression and the subsequent rise of Keynesianism created difficulties for institutionalism:

> Institutionalism as a movement ... fell victim to the Great Depression and its Keynesian remedy. For self-proclaimed experts in historical change, their inability to come to any better understanding of the Depression than their neoclassical colleagues was a considerable deficit. Mitchell in particular, who predicted like everyone else that the downturn would right itself within a year or two, was driven deeper into his program of empirical research by this proof of ignorance.

On the other hand, the institutionalist played a major role in the design and implementation of New Deal policies. But this important practical contribution could not overcome their theoretical deficit. The institutionalists, while emphasizing the complexity of economic phenomena and the need for careful empirical research, were seemingly out-theorized by the mathematical Keynesians. This group of young and mathematically minded converts to Keynesianism, led by Paul Samuelson and others, developed some simple macroeconomic models. The attraction of this approach was partly its technocratic lure, and partly because it proposed apparent solutions to the urgent problems of the day. It appeared that increasing a variable called G could alleviate the problem of unemployment. The 'solution' was plain and beguiling, dressed up in mathematical and 'scientific' garb, and given all the reverence customarily accorded to such presentations in a technocratic culture.

Ironically, this technocratic view ignored the fact that any practical implementation of a policy to increase government expenditure depended precisely on a detailed knowledge of the workings of government, financial and other institutions. For their concern with such details as pricing procedures and institutional mechanisms, the institutionalists have been overly maligned. However, while many institutionalists were influential and active in US government agencies and New Deal programmes, they did not draw out clear and common, theoretical or strategic guidelines. The immediate problem for institutionalism was its failure to propose a clearly identifiable remedy for economic depression and mass unemployment.

Of course, the rising 'Keynesianism' of the 1930s was different in several key respects from the economics of Keynes. Key contributions in the 1930s and 1940s, notably from Alvin Hansen, John Hicks, Paul Samuelson and Jan Tinbergen, transformed Keynesian ideas to make them mathematically tractable. This was as much a 'formalistic revolution' as a Keynesian one (B. Ward, 1972; Hutchison, 1992). Keynes himself was sceptical of econometrics and mathematical modelling in economics (Moggridge, 1992, pp. 621–3). What did emerge in the 1930s were the foundations of the neoclassical-Keynesian synthesis, based on key developments in neoclassical microeconomics and a crude system of macroeconomic modelling with some Keynesian affinities.

In general, however, institutional economists welcomed Keynes and the Keynesian revolution. Sympathetic economists such as Richard Ely, William Jaffé and Rutledge Vining perceived parallels between the works of Veblen and Keynes (Vining, 1939; Tilman, 1992, pp. 111–12). The young Keynesian James Duesenberry (1949) acknowledged the influence of Veblen while incorporating a concept of habit into his aggregate consumption function.

Leading institutionalists such as Mitchell, Commons, Clark, Copeland and Ayres were very sympathetic to Keynes's theories and policies. For example, Mitchell as early as 1932 applauded Keynes's theory of money as an important step in the development of a 'dynamic theory' and repeatedly acknowledged the importance of Keynes's theoretical contribution (Mitchell, 1969, vol. 2, pp. 825–7). J. M. Clark in 1943 urged his American Economic Association colleagues in their teaching to 'put the Keynesian elements in front, as having more direct and active relevance' (quoted in Bernstein, 2001, p. 85).

To some degree, institutionalism fused with a version of Keynesianism, but institutionalism gave less emphasis to mathematical modelling and more to Keynes's emphasis on 'organic' interactions in economic systems (Gambs, 1946; Dillard, 1948; Gruchy, 1948, 1949). Later, the institutionalist John Fagg Foster (1981) argued at length that institutionalism complemented Keynesianism, by providing the crucial theory of institutional adjustment that is required for Keynesian policies to work. It was not the economics of Keynes that derailed institutionalism; the two doctrines are not rivals but complements. The real theoretical contest within macroeconomics was instead between institutionalism and the bowdlerized, mathematical versions of Keynesianism promoted by Samuelson and others.

Another factor of significance was developments in formalized neoclassical microeconomic theory, particularly in areas of oligopoly or imperfect competition, where institutional economics had previously ruled the roost. In particular, Joan Robinson (1933) developed a formal equilibrium model of imperfect competition that stole much institutionalist thunder, although she later disowned its neoclassical assumptions. In contrast, the theory of Edward Chamberlin (1933) was more dynamic and institutionalist in flavour. But in the contribution of Robinson (1933) and elsewhere, we can observe the broadening of neoclassical economics to deal with phenomena that were previously in the province of heterodoxy.[6]

This expansion of the domain of application of neoclassical economics, while retaining its core assumptions of rationality and equilibrium, steadily continued for the remainder of the twentieth century, even to the point of bringing social institutions to well within its orbit. Institutionalism was thus challenged by the expansion and adaptability of neoclassical theory.

---

6 See Cordell (1972) for supporting arguments. E. Mason was quoted as saying: 'The theory of oligopoly has been aptly described as the ticket of admission to institutional economics' (H. Ellis, 1948, p. 17). Traces of institutionalism in Chamberlin's (1933) theory are discussed in Peterson (1979). It should also be added that Chamberlin's treatment of product and firm differentiation hints at Darwinian 'population thinking' and is more dynamic than that of Robinson. However, oligopoly theory opened up important questions of strategic interaction – involving interpretation of the intentions and interpretations of others – that were treated inadequately by both Chamberlin and Robinson, but later revived within economics through game theory.

The Second World War

The Second World War transformed the economy and society of the USA. In 1939, only 350,000 of its men and women were in military uniform. During the war, this increased to over 10 million uniformed military personnel. The number of civilians employed by the military rose to over 3 million, while an additional 17 million jobs were created in industry and services. America created a huge and unprecedented war machine. National structures and priorities were irrevocably changed.[7]

This massive wartime transformation affected the goals and conduct of US science. In particular, the pervasive militarization of scientific activity gave prestige and resources to research involving particular mathematical and statistical techniques. The military funding of the sciences included the use of economists for wartime operations research, and led to the development and promotion of formalized approaches to optimization problems. The war both accelerated the mathematicization of economics and ensured that particular types of mathematics would prevail (Mirowski, 2002).

The urgencies of war also helped to promote that peculiar synthesis of formalized microeconomics and formalized Keynesianism that dominated economics for three decades after 1945. As Michael Bernstein (2001, p. 81) has argued, the choice-theoretic apparatus of neoclassical microeconomics seemed 'directly applicable to the puzzles facing government and military leaders with respect to defense procurement, production, and mobilization'. Economists in their hundreds were recruited to solve such formalized or statistical problems as the maximization of output with given inputs, or the design of bombing patterns that would maximize the likely destruction of the industrial capacity of the enemy. The greatest armed conflict of the twentieth century promoted a central theme of neoclassical economics – the allocation of scarce resources towards the maximization of a fixed objective function with given institutions and assumed technology. The formalized genre of constrained optimization became the backbone of mainstream microeconomics.

In macroeconomics, the emergency of war swept away any remaining reservations concerning sustained government budget deficits. The Great Depression had already persuaded most US economists that some deficit-financed public spending was required (Barber, 1988). The US entry into the war made the conversion total. Anyone who would preach 'balanced budgets' in a sustained wartime emergency could be accused of being unpatriotic and resisting the war effort. The need for public financing of the

---

7   At the time, the institutionalist Means (1942) saw the end of American laissez-faire policies and the possibly permanent postwar adoption of a measure of national economic planning around military priorities. See also Snyder (1960), Higgs (1999) and US Federal Government statistics. After 1945, the size of the US military did not abate to anywhere near 1939 levels. In 1939, real military purchases of goods and services amounted to 1.4 per cent of US GNP. In 1986, they still amounted to 7.6 per cent of GNP.

war made the whole economics profession 'Keynesian'. Samuelson declared in a 1986 interview: 'Keynesianism at the beginning of the war was a majority view among the active young people at the elite universities, with some exceptions like maybe Chicago. By the end of the war the entire academic profession was Keynesian' (Colander and Landreth, 1996, p. 169). Largely as a result of war, pseudo-Keynesian macroeconomic models took their place on the left hand of Walrasian neoclassical microeconomics.

Samuelson (1944, p. 298) was too flattering to his own profession when he described the Second World War as 'the economist's war'. It was as much an engineer's war, or a physicist's war, or a propagandist's war, or a war of code-breaking mathematicians. It was also the greatest-ever war of *national systems of production*. The overwhelming strategic imperative of over five years of global conflict was to seize more resources, to allocate them efficiently, and to produce more steel, more ships, more tanks, more guns, more aeroplanes, more bombs and more bullets than the enemy. Whichever side won the deadly race of production-net-of-destruction would win the war. This was the first and last major war in history in which the outcome depended principally on the ongoing capacity to produce as well as the military capability to destroy.[8]

The heightened degree of government planning and intervention that became necessary in the wartime emergency brought a particular version of economics to the fore. This version was very much a 'war economics', with Big Government as its central actor and supreme optimizer. Ironically, for much of the second half of the twentieth century, this same theoretical paradigm was used to underpin a different ideology of unfettered markets and free trade. But this mainstream paradigm was much more Big Government 'war economics' than a genuine economic analysis of the structures of market-led capitalism. As several authors have pointed out, (Walrasian) neoclassical economics does not adequately capture the key features of a market economy and is more appropriate as a representation of some system of central planning (Copeland, 1931; Coricelli and Dosi, 1988; Ménard, 1990; Hodgson, 1999b).

It was no accident that the overall nature and scope of economics changed fundamentally during the war, with a greater technocratic bias. The imperatives of production and technology would be taken for granted. Problems of material resource allocation became the hallmark of the mainstream equilibrium microeconomist. A minority would complain and turn

---

8   The military historian J. Ellis (1990, p. xviii) pointed out that 'in the last 18 months of the war the Allies put onto the battlefield 80,000 tanks to the German's 20,000, 1,100,000 trucks and lorries to 70,000 ... between 1942 and 1945 the Japanese built 13 aircraft carriers ... but the Americans built 137' and so on. Ellis argued that despite winning the 'Battle of Production' the Allies repeatedly squandered much of this material advantage in the battlefield and resorted instead to the tactic of 'slowly and persistently battering [the enemy] to death with a blunt instrument'. He not only underlined the fact that the war was one of systems of production, but also showed that as early as 1943 the Allied production advantage was overwhelming.

to problems of economic growth and technical change. Generally among economists there would be a neglect of such theoretical issues as knowledge, psychology, organization and institutions. Such relatively elusive concerns were downplayed in the wartime scramble to produce tangible materials for victory. The theoretical die was cast, for both postwar orthodox and heterodox economics alike.

Hence it was also no accident that the principal version of institutionalism that was to survive these seismic changes was the technological growth theory of Clarence Ayres. It too highlighted the imperative of enhanced production, but unusually within a long-run perspective of technical change and a non-utilitarian ethical framework. Even for institutionalism, production rather than institutions became the centre of attention. But to its credit, Ayresian institutionalism provided a discourse on technological change that contrasted with the short-run optimization perspective of mainstream theory.

Institutional economics was created when the First World War ended, at a time when the energies of economists turned to the urgencies of postwar reconstruction. The version of economics that rose to replace institutionalism came from the crucible of the Second World War, at a time when optimal use of existing resources became the perceived imperative.

This Second World War also destroyed much of what was left of a longstanding foreign ally of institutionalism and rival to neoclassicism – the century-old historical school in Germany. As explained at length elsewhere, what shattered the historical school were the rise of fascism and the destruction of the war (Hodgson, 2001c). But the war changed the economics of the victor as much as that of the vanquished. This volume tells the other half of that story. The war changed American economics, while at the same time the Allied victory shifted the balance of world political power from Europe to America. The United States became the engine of world capitalism and the global leader in economics research. Much as a result of the war, the global balance within economics shifted decisively in favour of an American, formalized version of neoclassical theory.

Other external causes of the decline

However, war itself was not the only factor involved in the mathematicization of economics. In particular, during the interwar years, there was a growing flow of intellectual migrants from a Central Europe dislocated by rising fascism. They included titans such as John von Neumann and Joseph Schumpeter. After the Nazis came to power in Germany in 1933, a greater number of refugees fled from ethnic or doctrinal persecution to the United States. They included the economists Tjalling Koopmans, Oskar Lange, Jacob Marschak, Oskar Morgenstern and many others. Together they had a significant impact on the economics profession (Scherer, 2000). Academic refugees from Continental Europe often had an aptitude in mathematics that was superior to their command of the English language. Mathematical communication and discourse were thus given an increased relative prominence over discursive and conceptual analysis.

As refugees from totalitarian persecution and abuses of science, many of them 'would be infatuated with the vision of an "institution-free" economics, a virtual reality extracted from the disappointments of their own histories' (Mirowski, 2002, p. 285). This virtual reality was created and described in terms of formal models from which explicit institutions were typically banished.

However, although it was given a huge boost during the war, mathematical formalism did not completely overwhelm economics until much later. The pace and extent of this change can be traced in leading journals that have existed for most or all of the century, such as the *American Economic Review*, the *Economic Journal*, the *Journal of Political Economy* and the *Quarterly Journal of Economics*. Before the 1920s, verbal expositions dominated more than 90 per cent of the articles published in these journals. Verbal exposition became less dominant after 1940, falling steadily to about 33 per cent of articles in the 1960s. By the early 1990s, over 90 per cent of the articles in the leading and enduring journals were dominated by algebra, calculus and econometrics (Stigler *et al.*, 1995, p. 342). Mark Blaug (1999, 2003) also argued that the 'formalist revolution' in economics was relatively late, and did not begin in earnest until the late 1950s.[9]

Institutional economists were never hostile to statistics. Indeed, statistical work was central to Mitchell's National Bureau of Economic Research. But they were generally sceptical of the type of mathematical models that emerged in the 1940s. Mitchell and others had argued repeatedly that the reduction of microeconomic or macroeconomic phenomena to just a few variables obscured the essential diversity of economic elements and their interactions. Furthermore, the characteristic 'hot topics' of postwar mathematical economics – from general equilibrium theory, to growth theory, to rational expectations modelling, to game theory – were typically regarded by institutionalists as based on neoclassical or other challengeable assumptions. Some institutionalists reacted against the type of mathematical models that prevailed. Others reacted against the use of mathematics *per se*. In neither case did institutionalists provide an adequate alternative, whether formal or conceptual.

In addition to the external shocks outlined above, the Cold War and McCarthyite persecutions in US academia shook an already fractured and beleaguered institutionalism. When McCarthyism reached its height in the 1950s, the typical institutionalist allegiances to government economic intervention and other left-of-centre policies made institutionalism subject to political persecution.

---

9 Weintraub (2002, ch. 8) expressed a similar view. On the general transformation of American economics see also Morgan and Rutherford (1998).

The picture is complicated, however, because many leading mathematical neoclassical economists also had strong socialist inclinations. In fact, much of the impetus behind general equilibrium theory and linear economic analysis in the 1940s was an attempt to answer the famous demonstration of the unfeasibility of socialism by Ludwig von Mises (1920) and his allies of the Austrian school. Oskar Lange, Tjalling Koopmans and several others were engaged in the development of this 'answer'. Also among those inclined towards socialism were Jacob Marschak and Laurence Klein at the Cowles Commission (Bernstein, 2001, p. 106; Mirowski, 2002, ch. 5). The McCarthyite context endangered all those that dared to promote their leftist views.

But mathematics itself could not be accused of being anti-American. The persecuted economist could take professional refuge in the world of symbols. Hence an effect of McCarthyism was to reinforce the formalization of economics. Furthermore, some formal models were readily adapted to the Cold War paradigm of conflict and deterrence (Bernstein, 2001, pp. 96–9; Mirowski, 2002, ch. 6). Lacking any such core formalization, and always emphasizing conceptual substance over technique, institutional economics had additional difficulties of adaptation and survival in the McCarthy period.[10]

Internal causes of the decline

In the interwar period, institutionalism adapted to the rising empiricist philosophy, behaviourist psychology and cultural anthropology. These adaptations helped institutionalism to survive, but at the cost of most of its original conceptual foundations. The Great Crash, the Great Depression, the Second World War, and McCarthyism hit it successively. Given these devastating events, the question should not be 'why did institutionalism decline?' but 'why did it manage to survive so long?' Institutionalism gradually lost its possession of leading US departments of economics. By the 1970s it was yet another fringe group, alongside Marxian economists, post-Keynesians and others. Its interwar position of dominance was long past and almost forgotten.

There were internal as well as external reasons for this dramatic decline. Previous chapters have considered the theoretical failures of leading institutionalists. The biggest omission was the failure to produce a systematic treatise on institutionalist theory of the calibre of Karl Marx's *Capital*, Léon Walras's *Elements* or Alfred Marshall's *Principles*. The production of such a work required a theorist with a rich understanding of philosophy, psychology and economic theory. Veblen had these qualifications, but he did not attempt to produce such a volume. Commons tried but failed, not

---

10 For one of the very few studies of the impact of McCarthyism on American universities see Schrecker (1986).

only because of his imperfect grasp of theoretical and methodological fundamentals, but also because the rapidly changing intellectual circumstances made the task all the more difficult. Mitchell turned instead to the pressing problems of business cycles and the depression. Knight was intellectually qualified, but he was too far from the institutionalist mainstream and he never attempted such a comprehensive work.

In particular, previous chapters show that leading thinkers, including Paul Homan, John Commons, Wesley Mitchell, Frank Knight and Clarence Ayres, failed to understand the meaning and significance of Veblen's argument that economics should be turned into a 'post-Darwinian' and 'evolutionary' science. In a context where the social sciences were ridding themselves of any links with biology, Darwinian notions of causality and evolution were abandoned as a basis for institutional economics. When Homan (1927a, 1927b, 1928a, 1928b, 1931, 1932a, 1932b) repeatedly questioned the meaning and value of the 'evolutionary' terminology of institutionalism, only Copeland (1931) attempted to defend it in biological terms. Other institutionalists retreated into a bland and pre-Darwinian meaning of 'evolution', where the term meant little else but change. The abandonment by institutionalists of its defining biological metaphor and Darwinian source of inspiration was neither a slight nor a superficial matter. Institutionalism lost a key research programme and much of its own identity. Homan's questions and criticisms made these deficiencies obvious by the 1930s. Even today, with some notable exceptions, American institutionalists have not fully returned to their Darwinian roots.[11]

Veblen, Mitchell, Commons and others were responsible for failing to provide institutionalism with a systematic theory. Ayres bears the additional responsibility of leading postwar American institutionalism into a position where it could survive for a while, but its long-term impact was considerably diminished. Ayres turned to two principal themes: the underlying causes of economic growth and the normative criteria by which economic outcomes may be judged. His contributions were grounded on an inadequate theory and philosophy and led to the simplistic mantra of technology good, institutions bad. This turned upside-down the early institutionalist insight (of Veblen, Dewey, Commons and others) that institutions are not merely constraints but also enablers and regularizers of social activity. Consequently, institutional reform and organizational change, as strategies of economic policy and development, were removed from the institutionalist agenda. Ironically, institutional economics under Ayres's leadership was an economics that wished the world to be entirely rid of institutions.

Other aspects of Ayres's work were also damaging for the future of American institutionalism. Ayres abandoned price theory, industrial

---

11 Prominent postwar exceptions include Copeland (1958b) and D. Hamilton (1953). But both embraced behaviourist psychology as well as Darwinism.

economics and much of microeconomic analysis. While earlier institutionalists (such as W. Hamilton, Mitchell and J. M. Clark) had made major contributions to microeconomics and industrial economics, Ayres paid much less attention to these issues. Ayres (1944, p. 14) believed that 'what has been wrong with economic thinking is its obsession with price'. Significantly, in a review of Ayres's *Theory of Economic Progress*, the radical socialist and neoclassical economist Abba Lerner (1945, p. 163) accused Ayres of the 'surrender of economic theory to the reactionaries'. Ayres also deserted the theoretical problems of institutional analysis and design that are central to considerations of both production and allocation.

Institutionalists had a theory of corporate pricing, notably in the work of Adolf Berle and Gardiner Means (1932). Robert A. Gordon (1945), Richard A. Lester (1946) and others similarly explored real-world processes of pricing, in the context of imperfect competition (Tool, 1995). Their contributions were attacked by Fritz Machlup (1946), George Stigler (1947) and Milton Friedman (1953), who defended neoclassical assumptions of maximization, marginalism and perfect competition. Abandoned by the Ayresian leadership of the institutionalist movement, the defence of institutionalist pricing theory was left to those on its periphery, while resurgent neoclassicism brought its leading generals into the attack. Institutionalism quickly lost its commanding positions.

One striking and impairing feature of twentieth-century institutionalism is its lack of consensus on fundamentals. Table 18.2 overleaf contrasts the methodological views of several leading 'old' institutionalists, arranged individually in the chronological order of their birth. Seven methodological and psychological issues are addressed: the necessity of 'metaphysical presuppositions' for theory, the principle of determinacy, the degree of emphasis on human agency or volition, the degree of application of Darwinian principles to economics, the recognition of the enabling as well as the constraining possibilities of institutions, the degree of acceptance of Jamesian instinct–habit psychology, and the degree of accommodation to behaviourist psychology.

A double positive sign (++) indicates a high degree of explicit assent; a single positive sign (+) indicates partial or moderate, explicit or implicit assent; a single negative sign (–) indicates partial or moderate, explicit or implicit dissent; and a double negative sign (– –) indicates a high degree of explicit dissent. This table shows that a wide diversity of different views emerged within American institutional economics. This lack of consensus on fundamental methodological and psychological issues contributed to its decline.

Table 18.2 completely undermines the widespread supposition of an affinity between Veblen and Ayres. On these issues, Ayres was not the closest to, but one of the furthest from Veblen, taking a position of opposite sign on six out of the seven fundamental issues in the table. The type of Veblenian institutional economics proposed here would follow Veblen in

Table 18.2 Comparing some views of leading institutionalists

	Veblen 1857–1929	Commons 1862–1945	Mitchell 1874–1948	Knight 1885–1972	Ayres 1891–1972	Copeland 1895–1989
Are metaphysical presuppositions required for theory?	+ +	+	–	+ +	–	–
Adoption of the principle of determinacy	+ +	+	+	– –	+	+
Degree of emphasis on human agency or volition	+	+ +	+	+ +	–	+
Application of Darwinian principles to economics	+ +	– –	–	– –	– –	+
Recognition of the enabling possibilities of institutions	+ +	+ +	+	+ +	– –	+
Degree of acceptance of Jamesian instinct–habit psychology	+ +	–	first + then –	–	–	–
Degree of acceptance of behaviourist psychology	–	+	first – then +	– –	+ +	+ +

his six positive and one negative positions, but give all full emphasis. This would result in six emphatic double positives (++) plus an emphatic rejection (– –) of behaviourist psychology.

Having abandoned the Veblenian research agenda, and being divided on questions such as positivism and behaviourist psychology, American institutionalists had little to unite them in terms of theoretical and methodological fundamentals. They began to see their own unity largely in the shared elements in their policy agenda, and in their common dissent from the rising neoclassical formalism. The ideological method of self-definition became especially prominent during the Cold War of 1948–91, when many orthodox economic theorists felt obliged to defend the Western market system against ideological attack. In response, many heterodox critics reacted against mainstream economics in primarily ideological terms. Many wrongly equated orthodox economics with free-market ideology. Accordingly, many heterodox economists saw ideology as the main element in the position that they opposed.

Veblenian priorities: theory and explanation

The more notable attempts to turn American institutionalism primarily into a political and ideological discourse emerged too late to be blamed for the decline of institutionalism as a movement. The causes of this decline are different and of earlier origin. Ideologically strident versions of American institutionalism are much more a reaction to this decline rather than its cause.

Nevertheless, a symptom of the decline of American institutionalism is the degree to which it underplayed the task of fundamental theoretical and methodological development, in favour of ideological pronouncements. This is sometimes justified by the suggestion that facts and values are much the same: that no real distinction exists between the positive and the normative. Of course, all investigation is guided by and infused with judgements of value. But this does not mean that facts and values are equivalent. No social science can or should be free of value judgements. But postwar institutionalism in America has been long on moral pronouncements, and shorter by comparison on adequate theoretical analysis. Morality may be good for the soul, but does relatively little for the theoretical development of institutionalism, as an approach to the understanding and explanation of economic phenomena.[12]

Accordingly, and all too frequently, 'neoclassical economics' is *defined* as a pro-market ideology, rather than a core theoretical position. This not only confuses theory with ideology but also forgets that many neoclassical economists, from Léon Walras to Oskar Lange, were distinctly left of centre (Hodgson, 1999b). Other leading neoclassical economists such as Kenneth Arrow (1962), Frank Hahn (1984), Paul Krugman (1990) and Joseph Stiglitz (1987) have pointed to the limitations of the market mechanism.

Although strong ideological biases are prominent in much mainstream economics, ideology itself does not define the mainstream position. The reduction of economic theory to ideology must be avoided if American institutionalism is to recover from its isolation.

To chart the historical development of this post-Ayres ideological reductionism would take much more space than is available here. I will simply end with the observation that ethical posturing takes us a long way from the theoretical priorities of Veblen. To be sure, Veblen's writings contain many ethically loaded words like 'waste' and 'sabotage'. In the *Leisure Class* he used the extreme word 'invidious' several times but then claimed that 'there is no intention to extol or depreciate, or to commend or deplore any of the phenomena which the word is used to characterise' (Veblen, 1899a, p. 34). I believe that on this occasion at least, Veblen was being ironic, by repeatedly using an ethically loaded word alongside claims of innocent scientific evaluation. But there is no evidence that his irony masked a hidden belief that ideology and science are indistinguishable. Instead, Veblen was satirizing the many apologetic scientists of the Victorian era, who habitually invested their 'scientific' work with claims that it endorsed the established order.

Veblen had strong opinions and clearly upheld many normative propositions. But he repeatedly and rightly argued that for the social scientist, analysis and explanation should have priority over moral pronouncements. Veblen (1899b, p. 116) made clear his desire to disentangle factual and moral issues as much as possible:

> In their discourse and in their thinking, men constantly and necessarily take an attitude of approval or disapproval toward the institutional facts of which they speak, for it is through such everyday approval or disapproval that any feature of the institutional structure is upheld or altered. It is only to be regretted that a trained scientist should be unable to view these categories in a dispassionate light, for these categories, with all the moral force with which they are charged, designate the motive force of cultural development ... A scientist inquiring into cultural growth, and an evolutionist particularly, must take account of this dynamic content of the categories of popular thought as the most

12 For instance, I have so far failed to discover anything proposed under the label of 'radical institutionalism' in recent usage to justify the use of the 'radical' epithet, other than the addition of a set of leftist political positions to an existing version of institutionalist theory. 'Radical institutionalists' are identified primarily by their desire for some kind of leftist radical structural change in society. Although 'radical institutionalism' is distinguished by such declarations concerning what *ought* to happen, it has so far added much less to our understanding of the *existing* world (Dugger, 1989, 1996; Stanfield, 1995; Dugger and Waller, 1996; Dugger and Sherman, 2000). Even the vital theoretical question of the feasibility of these socialist proposals is ignored (D. Lavoie, 1985; Steele, 1992; Hodgson, 1999a). Investing it with a different meaning, Junker (1979) had previously used the term 'radical institutionalism' to denote several ontological, methodological and normative propositions derived from the Ayres–J. F. Foster tradition of institutionalism.

important material with which he has to work. Many persons may find it difficult to divest themselves of the point of view of morality or policy, from which these categories are habitually employed, and to take them up from the point of view of the scientific interest simply. But the difficulty does not set the scientific necessity aside. His inability to keep the cultural value and the moral content of these categories apart may reflect credit upon the state of such a person's sentiments, but it detracts from his scientific competence.

I believe that these words are sincere. After provoking his readers of the *Leisure Class* with ethically loaded terms, Veblen makes good its repeated declarations that the foremost purpose of science is understanding and explanation of the existing and the possible.

In another passage that is difficult to read as ironic, Veblen (1901b, pp. 85–6) criticized Gustav Schmoller when he abandoned a 'dispassionate analysis and exposition of the causal complex at work' and preoccupied himself instead with 'the question of what ought to be and what modern society must do to be saved'. Veblen thought that Schmoller's 'digression into homiletics and reformatory advice means that the argument is running into the sands just at the stage where science can least afford it'. Veblen criticized Schmoller for excessive concentration on what is 'more desirable'. For Veblen, such matters were 'beside the point so far as regards a scientific explanation of the changes under discussion'. Much the same could be said for postwar American institutionalism. Its predilection for 'homiletics and reformatory advice' helped it run 'into the sands' when institutionalism could 'least afford it'. The fact that all analysis is value-laden does not undermine the priority of analysis, at least as a precondition for policy. Neither does it give us licence to treat facts and values as the same.[13]

The use of irony was characteristic of Veblen. However, if the claim that Veblen was ironic is made too recklessly, then we end up treating nothing he wrote with due seriousness. We should take no statement at face value. But there is no basis to assume that Veblen meant the opposite of what he actually and repeatedly wrote, including his criticisms of those who favour 'homiletics and reformatory advice' over hard 'analysis and exposition of the causal complex at work'. If we do not take what he said seriously, on

---

13 Contrary to Bush (1999, p. 143), both Veblen and Dewey acknowledged the difference between 'a truth about what ought to be and a truth about what is'. The claim that Dewey saw no difference is not supported by any adequate quote in Bush's article. Contrary to Bush (1999, p. 145), I find nothing in the writings of Veblen, Peirce, Dewey, James or Mead to support the mistaken view of 'the epistemological equivalence of factual and normative propositions'. However, Tool and Bush (2003, p. 25) themselves wrote later: 'A social problem can be defined as a situation in which the community perceives a difference between "what is" and "what ought to be."' And Bush (2002) himself does 'discern the difference between a factual proposition and a normative proposition'. If so, then how can they be epistemologically equivalent?

the grounds of possible irony or whatever, then we are in danger of abandoning his legacy. We might end up imputing to Veblen a set of propositions that stem from our own imagination, without any possibility of corroboration in his texts.

To repeat, all investigation is guided by and infused with judgements of value. But that does not mean that value and fact have the same meaning or status. The primary task in the reconstruction of a Veblenian institutionalism is to develop a superior explanation of the real world. Of course, Veblen's own normative position must be acknowledged. Where relevant to scientific enquiry, our own values must also be made explicit. But above all, any viable attempt to change the world is premised on a better understanding of how the existing world works. We are unable to propose a feasible future unless we understand the ways in which real institutions exercise their powers. We are unable knowingly to change the world, unless we address and understand the actual and potential forces of both conservatism and change.

Part V

Beginning the reconstruction of institutional economics

19 The potential revival of Veblenian institutionalism

> The novelties of today are a ... later generation of the commonplaces of the day before yesterday.
>
> Thorstein Veblen, *Absentee Ownership* (1923)

The forces that undermined American institutionalism were both doctrinal and institutional. In this chapter it will be argued that, in doctrinal terms at least, the circumstances are now favourable for a revived Veblenian institutionalism. The doctrinal forces that emerged to the detriment of institutionalism included positivism in philosophy, behaviourism in psychology, a reductionist rejection of emergent properties, and the breaking of the links between biology and the social sciences. These forces shook the foundations of institutionalism in the early part of the twentieth century. But remarkably, by the closing decades of that century, every one of these developments had been checked and reversed. We begin this chapter by briefly reviewing these changes. Later sections consider changes in economics and elsewhere that provide openings for a revived Veblenian institutionalism.

The decline of behaviourism and the revival of instinct

Immediately after the end of the Second World War, the nature–nurture controversy was renewed in psychology and anthropology. The idea that some biological factors were significant in human development made a comeback. For example, in 1948 the anthropologist Clyde Kluckhohn declared that biology as well as culture had a part in the explanation of human behaviour. In the 1950s, even Alfred Kroeber abandoned his view that all that mattered was culture, and was ready to acknowledge some biological roots of human nature (Degler, 1991, pp. 218–21).

Also the concept of instinct enjoyed a slow rehabilitation in psychology. Much of the original impetus behind this development came from Europe. In the 1930s, the Austrian ethologist Konrad Lorenz produced scholarly articles on instinctive behaviour. In 1951, the Oxford University ethologist Nikolaus Tinbergen published his *Study of Instinct* in which he argued that much of human behaviour is instinctive. By the 1960s, the concept of instinct had clearly re-emerged in American psychology. In 1973, Lorenz and Tinbergen were awarded, with Karl von Frisch, the Nobel Prize for their work on instinctive behaviour (Degler, 1991, pp. 223–4).

The Second World War transformed psychology, notably giving rise to cognitive approaches (Capshew, 1999). In the 1940s, the development of the first electronic computers involved analysis of the internal structures and processes of computation, with obvious – albeit imperfect – parallels to the human mind. After decades of behaviourist neglect, these developments once again opened the door to legitimate theorizing concerning internal, mental processes. Clark Hull (1943) was a prominent behaviourist psychologist who moved away from orthodox behaviourism by helping to rehabilitate the concept of habit. He evaded the positivist and orthodox behaviourist insistence on observability by comparing habit with the equally unobservable subatomic particle (Hull, 1943, pp. 110–11). Hull proposed a mechanism of habituation, depending on the number of reinforcements and on the timing of the reward or punishment. As another example, George Miller (1966) argued from the 1950s that it was important for psychologists to understand mental planning and prefiguration. By 1960, many psychologists were defying strict behaviourism by constructing theories of how the mind works.

These and other developments put orthodox behaviourism on the defensive. In the 1950s, Harry Harlow performed a set of famous experiments on rhesus monkeys that suggested there was more to monkey behaviour than stimulus and response. An infant monkey would cling to a soft artificial mother in preference to a wire-framed surrogate that dispensed milk. Some instinctive drive must have accounted for this apparently self-destructive behaviour. Another set of experiments, by J. Garcia and R. A. Koelling in 1966, showed that rats could not be conditioned to avoid flavoured water when deterred by electric shocks, but the animals would readily learn to do so when drinking the water was followed by induced nausea. This suggested a functionally specific instinct to avoid nausea-inducing substances, and again undermined the notion of a generally conditioned response. Behaviourism was thus hoist with its own experimentalist petard. Critiques of behaviourism by Noam Chomsky (1959) and Cyril Burt (1962) announced a return of the concept of consciousness to psychology, thus further undermining the hegemony of positivism in that subject.[1]

---

1   The reaction against behaviourism did not always lead to a restoration of habit and instinct. For example, in criticizing behaviourism, Merleau-Ponty (1942) and existentialists such as Sartre fetishized the human will. Postwar humanist philosophy rejected habit (Adorno, 1972). Similarly, there is no significant mention of instinct or habit in the important critique of behaviourism by Hayek (1952a).

The revival of the concept of instinct did not generally mean a return to biological reductionism. Leading biologists themselves argued that explanations could ignore neither the social nor the biotic foundations of human life. For instance, Theodosius Dobzhansky (1955, p. 20) stated: 'Human evolution is wholly intelligible only as an outcome of the interaction of biological and social facts.' The anthropologist Alexander Alland (1967, p. 10) endorsed a related point:

> Biologists now agree that the argument over the primacy of environment or heredity in the development of organism is a dead issue. It is now generally accepted that the function and form of organisms can be understood only as the result of a highly complicated process of interaction.

Accordingly, attempts by economists to explain individual preferences and maximizing behaviour in predominantly biological terms (Becker, 1976; Hirshleifer, 1977; Tullock, 1979; Robson, 2001a, 2001b, 2002) are out of accord with widespread sentiments from within biology and anthropology that much behaviour cannot be explained entirely by the genes (Boyd and Richerson, 1985; Dupré, 1987; Durham, 1991; Sober and Wilson, 1998; Bateson and Martin, 1999).

The shift from behaviourism to cognitive psychology was not itself sufficient to rehabilitate the concept of habit. The crucial rediscovery here was the limited cognitive capacity of the human brain, its 'bounded rationality' and its reliance on triggered responses and acquired rules of interpretation (Cooley, 1902; J. M. Clark, 1918; Simon, 1957; Vanberg, 2002). Habit had to be recognized as not a mere feature of behaviour but an essential part of the mental apparatus in dealing with complexity and large amounts of information (Hodgson, 1997b). Work in artificial intelligence also reinforced this insight: any problem had to be previously interpreted or 'framed' using assumed rules (Pylyshyn, 1984, 1987).

The rehabilitation of instinct and habit was part of a movement to situate the mind in its evolutionary, biological, material and social context. The interactions involved cross the boundaries between the biological and the social, the mental and the material. Accepting that reductionist is generally unattainable, multiple levels of analysis are involved.

The decline of positivism and the revival of pragmatism

Various versions of positivism and empiricism dominated American scientific circles in the first half of the twentieth century. However, the publication in 1951 of Willard van Orman Quine's essay 'Two Dogmas of Empiricism' began to undermine this methodological hegemony. Quine showed that attempts to exclude 'metaphysics' from logical positivism could not work. 'The publication of this essay in 1951 was one of the key events in the collapse of logical positivism' (K. Hoover, 1995a, p. 721). Quine established that every theory necessarily and unavoidably involves an ontology.

Many institutionalists continued to adopt an empiricist epistemology, and did not take sufficient account of the decline of positivism. But with the development of various forms of philosophical realism in the last three decades of the twentieth century, and with most philosophers of science adhering to some form of realism, a suitable alternative philosophical grounding is now possible.[2]

Partly due to Quine's influence, and also to a number of later interventions, pragmatism has eventually re-emerged to become 'if not the most influential, at least one of the fastest growing philosophical frameworks on the intellectual landscape' (Hands, 2001, p. 214). Pragmatism has returned, building on the earlier ideas of Charles Sanders Peirce, William James, John Dewey, George Herbert Mead and others of the Veblenian era.[3]

Pragmatism was eclipsed by the rise of logical positivism in the 1930s and was marginalized until the 1980s. What has helped to bring pragmatism back is the collapse of the received view in the philosophy of science, according to which scientific truth could be readily established by observing some fixed epistemological protocol. The original pragmatism of Peirce and others rejected the traditional epistemological question of how individual beliefs come to reflect the properties of the objective world. The pragmatists saw such a system of workable epistemological rules as unattainable. Instead, the pragmatists saw scientific truth as a process of critical social enquiry, which was both continuous and potentially self-correcting. In addition, pragmatism has typically been regarded as a version of realism, accepting the reality of a world beyond our perceptions.

In the present context, pragmatism seems to offer a way out of the apparent dilemma between, on the one hand, the foundationalist notion that knowledge is grounded on empirical data or deductive reason, and on the other hand, the radical relativism that pervades much of contemporary social theory. In contrast to the methods of induction and deduction, pragmatism points to the causal mechanisms and conditions that give rise to phenomena. Against the relativist and postmodernist view that one discourse is as good as any other, pragmatism upholds the distinctiveness and supreme value of science. Above all, science is distinguished from superstition by its capacity to enhance human life.

Furthermore, pragmatism offers a means of overcoming the Cartesian dualism of body and mind, which still pervades the social sciences. Intellect is not regarded as an independent and ungrounded causal power, but

---

2 See, for example, Bhaskar (1975, 1989), Bunge (1973a), Cartwright (1989), Chalmers (1985), Harré (1986), Humphreys (1989), Lawson (1997, 2003b), Mäki (1998) and Searle (1995).

3 The revival of pragmatism was in part due to Davidson (1980), Apel (1981), Rorty (1982), Habermas (1992), Joas (1993, 1996), Cook (1993), Diggins (1994), Pickering (1995) and Putnam (1995). See also Kilpinen (1998, 1999, 2000) and Hands (2001).

as an emergent and active property of already-engaged dispositions and unfolding actions. The reality and importance of human intentionality and creativity is reconciled with the Darwinian evolutionary legacy and philosophical materialism.

In sum, modern developments in philosophical realism and pragmatism provide fertile intellectual conditions for the redevelopment of the ideas of the early American institutionalists. These ideas were built in part on early pragmatist philosophy and have to be reconsidered in the light of the strong revival of pragmatism today.

Complexity and the re-emergence of emergence

An early sign that the concept of emergence was returning to mainstream philosophy of science was the publication in 1956 of an article co-authored by the son of Roy Wood Sellars. Wilfred Sellars and P. E. Meehl (1956) criticized Stephen Pepper's (1926) earlier argument. They proposed that emergentism was logically consistent and worthy of consideration. As the concept of emergent properties was re-established in philosophy and several sciences, so too was the related idea of a layered ontology. By the 1960s, emergence had re-emerged.[4]

In an influential paper, the philosophers Paul Oppenheim and Hilary Putnam (1968) promoted six ontological levels: social groups, multicellular living things, cells, molecules, atoms, and elementary particles. This involves the 'unity of science' but on the basis of multi-disciplinary 'federalism', rather than an 'imperialism' where one science claims sovereignty over all the others. The 1977 Nobel Laureate and physicist Philip Anderson (1972) likewise insisted on the hierarchical structure of the sciences and the impossibility of reductionist explanations to one level. Anderson (1972, p. 393) wrote: 'At each level of complexity entirely new properties appear. ... At each stage entirely new laws, concepts, and generalizations are necessary.' This was a crucial recognition of the importance of emergent properties by a leading scientist.

It is also fortunate that the revived discourse on emergentism has got rid of many of the theological and mystical trappings that encumbered prominent versions in the 1920s. In contrast to Samuel Alexander (1920) and Conwy Lloyd Morgan (1923, 1926), emergentism no longer points to

---

4 On the post-1956 development of emergentist philosophy see M. Polanyi (1958, 1967, 1968), Bunge (1959, 1973a, 1980), Mayr (1960, 1982, 1988), Sperry (1964, 1969, 1976, 1991), Koestler (1967), Koestler and Smythies (1969), Weiss *et al.* (1971), Popper (1972a), Ayala and Dobzhansky (1974), Bhaskar (1975, 1989), Popper and Eccles (1977), Salk (1983), Salthe (1985), Horgan (1993), Kontopoulos (1993), Cohen and Stewart (1994), Humphreys (1997) and Holland (1998). See also the criticisms of emergentism in Hempel and Oppenheim (1948), Pap (1962), Hempel (1965), Nagel (1961, 1965), Armstrong (1968), Oppenheim and Putnam (1968), Rensch (1971), Klee (1984) and Beckerman *et al.* (1992). Tully (1981), Blitz (1992), Goldstein (1999) and Sawyer (2001, 2002) provide useful summaries of the historical development of emergentist philosophy.

religion. Sunny Auyang (1998, p. 176) represented the modern trend when she associated emergent properties with particular structures: 'Emergent properties mostly belong to the *structural* aspect of systems and stem mainly from the organization of their constituents.' Similarly, David Weissman (2000, p. 17) wrote: '*Emergence* signifies that new properties are generated when relationships are established by a system's proper parts.' These statements are redolent of the earlier materialist definition of emergence by Charlie Broad (1925, p. 61), cited on page 240 above. They also suggest that emergent properties are ontological, deriving from relations and structures, rather than limits of knowledge or prediction, thus circumventing some of the earlier objections to emergentism. In this conception, relations between entities are not mere accidental additions, but partly constitutive of the formed structures or systems. The world does not simply consist of things, but also of causal relations between parts. These causal interactions can give rise to structures and systems, exhibiting emergent properties not found within the parts alone.

In this emergentist conception, agency is differentiated from social structure, partly because of the emergent properties pertaining to the latter. Of course, human agency is unique in its degree of deliberation, prefiguration and self-reflection; while social structures themselves have no such capacity, except perhaps through the occasional aggregation of concordant individual intentions. Nevertheless, social structure is an entity, with its own causal powers. In a layered ontology, every entity (except perhaps the most fundamental physical particle) is a structure, and structure itself can sometimes become an entity. Structures of atoms become cohesive molecules. Upon neural structures emerge the unitary and causal qualities of mind. The interactions of agents capable of mental prefiguration, linguistic communication and purposeful activity, give rise to social structures. The transformation of structures into entities with causal powers likewise warrants the partial autonomy of chemistry from physics, biology from chemistry, psychology from biology, and sociology from psychology.

While macroeconomic systems are not agents – at least in the same sense as individuals – they nevertheless have cohesive and causal properties. Macroeconomic systems are not simply social structures. They have emergent properties and causal powers, they sometimes exhibit empirical regularities, and as national systems they are units of evolutionary selection, alongside others. This means that macroeconomics is a viable scientific discipline, partially autonomous from microeconomics. Noting the limited prospects for a reduction of macroeconomics to microeconomics, Kevin Hoover (1995b, p. 255) reached an allied conclusion:

> Both microeconomics and macroeconomics must refer to irreducible macroeconomic entities. These macroeconomic entities occupy ontologically independent places in economic theory. To the degree that

such theories are empirically successful, the best account of these macroeconomic entities is that they are real.

Hovver thus undermined the idea that the individual is the exclusive and ultimate unit of analysis in economics. His argument can be further sustained within the context of emergentist philosophy.

Broadly, a philosophy of materialist emergentism sustains three ideas that are central to institutional and evolutionary economics. First, the process of evolution can produce qualitative novelties, at all levels of reality. Second, novelty is a result of systemic emergent properties that by definition are not possessed by the parts. Third, reality is appraised and analysed as a structure of irreducible levels, with distinctive and characteristic emergent properties at each level. The first proposition is essential to an evolutionary theory of innovation and change. The second and third propositions establish higher levels and units of analysis, above and in addition to individuals. Without these philosophical ideas, an institutional and evolutionary economics cannot fully develop its identity or core meaning.

The development of chaos theory, complexity theories and agent-based computer simulations in the last two decades of the twentieth century have given a further boost to emergentism and have undermined reductionism. As leading mathematicians of chaos have themselves proclaimed, chaos theory 'brings a new challenge to the reductionist view that a system can be understood by breaking it down and studying each piece' (Crutchfield *et al.*, 1986, p. 48). Chaos theory shows that in some circumstances outcomes can be highly sensitive to initial conditions, making precise or even meaningful prediction difficult or impossible. Consequently, while causes still exist, some causes can be so tiny that the causal trail is difficult to follow. The sciences of complexity emphasize emergent patterns and historically grounded explanations. With emergent properties and path dependent evolution, the positivist emphasis on prediction is undermined

In recent years much work has been done with complex, non-linear computer systems, involving artificial agents interacting to produce systemic order and other 'higher-level' properties. The Santa Fe Institute has been at the centre of much of this research. For example, studies of 'artificial life' in computer simulations reveal emergent properties that are predictable from the rules that govern the behaviour of the individual agents involved (Langton, 1989; Langton *et al.*, 1992). Reviewing the modelling of such 'artificial worlds', David Lane (1993, p. 90) wrote that a main thrust 'is to discover whether (and under what conditions) histories exhibit interesting *emergent properties*'. His extensive review of the literature in the area suggested that there are many examples of artificial worlds displaying such attributes. This lends credence to the idea that emergence is important in the real world.

Auyang (1998) provided a wide-ranging and philosophically informed review of the literature on complex systems in economics, biology and physics. She explained why reductionist ambitions have generally been disappointed. Instead of trying to analyse a system by first presuming its components, then building up a picture of the whole, Auyang proposed that the broad patterns that emerge at the level of the whole system should also be taken into account at the outset. The micro-focus should be on the refinement of assumptions concerning components that are capable of producing the systemic emergent phenomena.

What remains controversial is the extent to which general principles can be derived from complexity theory and its analysis of complex, evolving systems (Kauffman, 1993, 1995, 2000; Cohen and Stewart, 1994; Holland, 1995; Axelrod and Cohen, 1999; Strevens, 2003). There have been some attempts to bring some insights in this area into economics (P. Anderson *et al.*, 1988; Arthur *et al.*, 1997; Louçã, 1997; Albin, 1998; Auyang, 1998; Rosser, 1999; Colander, 2000a, 2000b; J. Potts, 2000). Although the possibility of deriving general principles of complexity is sometimes exaggerated, the impact of the new ideas on complexity is profound. Not only is the common obsession with precise prediction confounded; the whole tradition in science of attempting to reduce each phenomenon to its component parts is placed into question. A reconstructed institutional economics can usefully build on this literature.

The end of the microfoundations project in economics

Problems of tractability and complexity have had an impact in economics as well. Consider the attempt to analyse macroeconomic systems in terms of the attributes of their individual members. One of the consequences of the rise of Walrasian microeconomics in the 1940s was the perception of general equilibrium theory as the cutting edge of mainstream economics for the next 30 years. One of the aims of general equilibrium theorists was to place macroeconomics on the 'sound microfoundations' of given, utility-maximizing individuals. However, it became clear that the derivation of macroeconomic regularities from such individualistic assumptions was much more difficult than originally perceived.

Eventually, leading general equilibrium theorists themselves showed that such theoretical outcomes could not, in general be achieved. Hugo Sonnenschein (1972, 1973a, 1973b), Rolf Mantel (1974) and Gerard Debreu (1974) showed that the excess demand functions in an exchange economy could take almost any form. General equilibrium theory thus provided no basis for the assumption that demand curves are generally downward sloping. This problem is essentially one of aggregation when individual demand functions are combined. As Alan Kirman (1989) reiterated, the consequences for neoclassical general equilibrium theory are devastating. As S. Abu Turab Rizvi (1994a, p. 363) put it, the work of Sonnenschein,

Mantel and Debreu is quite general and is not restricted to counter-examples:

> Its chief implication ... is that the hypothesis of individual rationality, and other assumptions made at the micro level, gives no guidance to an analysis of macro-level phenomena: the assumption of rationality or utility maximisation is not enough to talk about social regularities. This is a significant conclusion and brings the microfoundations project in [general equilibrium theory] to an end.

In general, research into the problems of the uniqueness and stability of general equilibria have shown that they may be indeterminate and unstable unless very strong assumptions are made, such as the supposition that society as a whole behaves as if it were a single individual (M. Lavoie, 1992, pp. 36–41; Screpanti and Zamagni, 1993, pp. 344–53).

It was eventually realized that assumptions of diversity among individuals threatened the feasibility of the microfoundations project. Many types of interaction between the individuals have to be ignored to make the analysis tractable. Ironically, by assuming *given* individuals, the microfoundations project in orthodox economics had typically to assume furthermore that each and every individual was *identical* to attempt to make the analysis tractable. Indeed, it was generally impossible to develop a composite picture from a diversity of types of individual agent. As Kenneth Arrow (1986, p. S388) declared: 'In the aggregate, the hypothesis of rational behaviour has in general no implications.' Consequently, in a desperate attempt to deduce something in the macro-sphere from the micro-tenet of individual rationality, it is widely assumed that all individuals have an *identical* utility function. Apart from ignoring obvious differences in individual tastes, this denies the possibility of 'gains from trade arising from individual differences' (Arrow, 1986, p. S390).

As Kirman (1992, p. 118) wrote: 'there is no plausible formal justification for the assumption that the aggregate of individuals, even maximizers, acts itself like an individual maximizer'. Kirman (1989, p. 138) argued elsewhere: 'If we are to progress further we may well be forced to theorize in terms of groups who have collectively coherent behaviour. ... The idea that we should start at the level of the isolated individual is one which we may well have to abandon.'

The conventional textbooks often go well beyond the confinement and rigour of general equilibrium theory, to make bold and general claims concerning the relationship between wages and unemployment, and inflation and the money supply. The more careful neoclassical theorists have questioned such macroeconomic derivations from microeconomic assumptions. For instance, Arrow (1986, p. S386) stated that he knows 'of no serious derivation of the demand for money from a rational optimization'. As Donald Katzner (1991) has argued, it is impossible to aggregate from individual supply and demand functions to such aggregated functions at the level of the market if considerations of ignorance and historical time are taken into account.

Fabrizio Coricelli and Giovanni Dosi (1988, p. 126) argued that 'the project of building dynamic models with economic content and descriptive power by relying solely on the basic principles of rationality and perfect competition through the market process has generally failed'. Attempts to base macroeconomics on neoclassical microfoundations involve faith in the 'invisible hand' and in the substantive capabilities of individuals to calculate endlessly and make supremely rational choices. Yet the results of this theoretical endeavour show no more than a very crippled hand, incapable of orderly systemic coordination even in relatively simple models. Coricelli and Dosi (1988, p. 136) conclude that 'the attempt to "explain" macroeconomics solely on the basis of some kind of "hyper-rationality" of the agents ... and the (pre-analytical) fundamentals of the economy (i.e. given technology and tastes) has failed'.

It is no exaggeration to say that the microfoundations enterprise has effectively disintegrated, for reasons well understood by leading general equilibrium theorists. The theoretical implications of these results for the microfoundations project and general equilibrium theory are devastating. A fundamental consequence is the breakdown of macroeconomic analysis based on individualistic or atomistic ontologies. The indeterminacy and instability results produced by contemporary theory lead to the conclusion that an economy made up of atomistic agents does not have enough structure to survive, as its equilibria may be evanescent states from which the system tends to depart (Ingrao and Israel, 1985, 1990; Kirman, 1989).

As Rizvi (1994b, 1998) pointed out, it was this crisis in general equilibrium theory in the 1970s that led to the turn to game theory in the 1980s. Today, game theory largely overshadows the general equilibrium approach. However, game theory has only begun to accommodate the notion that the very canons of rational calculation in any individual are socially and culturally formed (Gintis, 2000). A similar problem of deriving systemic conclusions from individualistic and rationalistic suppositions remains. As Martin Shubik (1975, p. 24) put it: 'one of the most important lessons that game theory has to teach is the concept of individual rationality does not generalize in any unique or natural way to group or social reality'. Like general equilibrium analysis, game theory also illuminates the difficulty of generalizing from individuals to social structures.

Emergent properties and heterogenous agents

Discussion of emergent properties is now commonplace in the philosophy of biology and psychology, but it has yet to make a substantial impact in economics. Nevertheless, the ground has now been prepared. In the 1990s, a new approach to the theorization of the relationship between microeconomics and macroeconomics began to emerge. The results remain preliminary and inconclusive, but they suggest a new way of approaching the problem that is redolent of the earlier ideas of Wesley Mitchell and Rutledge Vining.

Francesca Chiaromonte and Giovanni Dosi (1993, p. 93) developed a model in which some macroeconomic regularities, such as the growth in overall labour productivity, were the outcome of far-from-equilibrium interactions among heterogeneous, boundedly rational, agents. Relatively ordered patterns of change emerged as self-organizing properties of the interactions of these agents. They suggested that micro-heterogeneity was of paramount importance for the aggregate behaviour of the system. Behavioural and technological *diversity* among agents was a crucial ingredient of system dynamics. Hence, 'unlike common theoretical wisdom, *more* micro diversity tends to yield *simpler* macro dynamics' (Chiaromonte and Dosi, 1993, p. 61). They conjectured that micro-variety made innovation and change more likely and led to regular patterns of productivity and income growth. They recognized the importance of heterogeneity at the individual level, and noted that macro-order may arise not despite, but because of, such heterogeneity.[5]

Several authors have addressed the problem of how regularities may emerge in the aggregate beyond those derivable from individual optimization (Lesourne, 1992; Lesourne and Orléan, 1998; Kirman and Gérard-Varet, 1999; C. Carroll, 2000). One of the main arguments found in a collection of essays edited by Mauro Gallegati and Alan Kirman (1999) is that models with heterogeneous agents have dynamics that do not show up with representative agents. Elsewhere, Werner Hildenbrand (1999) discusses the emergence of empirical macro-regularities – such as the 'law of demand' – from empirical data relating to heterogeneous agents in a manner that is highly redolent of Mitchell and the interwar National Bureau of Economic Research.

The demonstration that a heterogeneous population of agents can lead to effects that differ from those with representative agents reaffirms the importance of 'population thinking' in social interactions and structures. Significant features of the model emerge precisely because of the diversity at the micro level. If this diversity were removed, by focusing on the 'average' or 'representative' micro units, then the model would have very different properties. The models of Kirman, Hildenbrand and others thus show that the concepts of emergence and population thinking are

5   Using different arguments and models, similar points concerning 'micro-diversity' being at the root of 'macro-order' have been made by Heiner (1983), Eliasson (1984), Cohen and Stewart (1994) and Ngo Mai and Raybaut (1996). The whole literature on self-organization is also relevant here, including Nicolis and Prigogine (1977), Jantsch (1980), Schieve and Allen (1982), Prigogine and Stengers (1984), Witt (1985, 1997), Yates (1987), Lesourne (1992), Kauffman (1993, 1995), Corning (1995), Krugman (1996) and Lesourne and Orléan (1998). The important concept of 'self-organized criticality' is a more recent development (Scheinkman and Woodford, 1994; Bak, 1996; Jensen, 1998; M. Buchanan, 2001).

intimately connected. Their models demonstrate the existence of emergent properties not found in the individual agents themselves. The intimate connection between population thinking and emergence results from the fact that with a heterogeneous population, more complex relations and interactions are possible, creating the potential for richer emergent properties (Allen and McGlade, 1987, 1989; Metcalfe, 1994, 1998).

The collapse of the neoclassical microfoundations project has cleared the way for an exciting new theorization of the micro–macro relationship. Learning lessons from history, we should also attempt to ground this work on a modern philosophy of emergent properties.

The institutional context of rationality

One of the problems that dogged modern microeconomic theory was how to define rationality in the circumstance where the rationality of others has to be taken into account. Another of the achievements of modern game theory is to show that the choices of definition for rationality or for a game equilibrium in such circumstances are neither singular nor obvious (Sugden, 1991; Rizvi, 1994b, 1998; Gintis, 2000). Furthermore, as leading game theorist Kenneth Binmore (1999, p. 137) has acknowledged:

> In brief, the notion of rationality used by economists assumes that agents can decide the logically undecidable. This doesn't matter much until one gets embroiled in the details of reasoning chains of the form, 'If I think that he thinks that I think …' But when one does, one is led to precisely the sort of self-reference that Gödel used.[6]

Binmore (1998a) himself recognized that all of the 'algorithms', norms and boundaries of individual rationality are formed in historically specific processes of biological and cultural evolution. But there is an obvious next step, not yet taken by mainstream game theorists. This would be to abandon the quest for an all-purpose, all-considering, unbounded rationality and replace it with a pluralistic exploration of multiple contextual models of bounded rationality, each of which would reflect historical, cultural and human specificities.

The full-blown models of individual interaction in game theory, where every possible human interaction and defined response is considered, have fallen into widely acknowledged problems of tractability and relevance. In response, some have hinted at an altered direction of research. As

---

6 Other writers had also observed that attempts to define rationality in the interactive, intersubjective and recursive context of guessing what and how others think of what and how you and others think … will come up against Gödelian problems of self-referentiality. See Lewis (1985a, 1985b), Hargreaves Heap and Varoufakis (1995), Conlisk (1996), Albin (1998) and Mirowski (2002). One of the benefits of game theory has been to bring these issues again to the fore. But they were also raised previously in the classic Chapter 12 of Keynes (1936).

Kirman (1999a, p. 10) has pointed out: 'the notion that the structure of the economy, rather than just the parameters of the structural relationship, might be substantially modified over time has received little formal attention'. What cries out for inclusion is an explicit notion of social structure, limiting the available information and human interactions, and thereby restricting the number of possible outcomes in the model (J. Potts, 2000). In a pioneering essay, Kirman (1999b, p. 37) himself tried to show that

> models which take account of the direct interaction between agents allow us to provide an account of macro phenomena which are caused by this interaction at the micro level but are no longer simple blown up versions of individual activity. The network through which the interaction is mediated plays an important role and, the nature of the macroeconomic behaviour will depend on whether interaction is global in the sense that individuals may interact with each other, or whether the interaction is determined by a specific communication structure.

Instead of the macro economy being treated as a 'blown up' individual, social structure has to be introduced in a population of heterogeneous individuals. This is an open door for institutional analysis, whether of a formal or non-formal kind. Indeed, if suitably contrived, both modes of research can usefully complement each other.

Experimental economics has also opened up the requirement of structured individual interactions, with situated rather than context-independent rationality. On the basis of extensive experimental observations, Nobel Laureate Vernon Smith (1991, pp. 881, 894), has gone so far as to consider how 'institutions serve as social tools that reinforce, even induce individual rationality' and 'how decision making is mediated by institutions'. Smith concluded that rationality does not emerge on the basis of cognition alone, but only through 'ongoing social interaction with other agents'.[7]

These remarks are clearly redolent of the old institutionalism, and the arguments of Max Weber, J. M. Clark, Wesley Mitchell and others to the effect that economic rationality is a historically, culturally and institutionally specific phenomenon. They also point to the possibility of a reconstitutive downward causation by which specific institutional contexts engender particular norms and patterns of rational judgement.

---

7   V. Smith was a student of Chamberlin, who pioneered experimental market simulations with human subjects (Mirowski, 2002, pp. 546–7). Smith set out to test Chamberlin's (1948) contention that such experiments show that markets generally fail to reach a competitive equilibrium. Chamberlin, in turn, had been a student of institutionalist sympathizer A. Young, who was discussed at more length in Hodgson (2001c). Chamberlin's famous theory of monopolistic competition was inspired by institutionalist works by Veblen (1904) and J. M. Clark (1923) (Cordell, 1972; Peterson, 1979; Rutherford, 2001), and in turn inspired institutionalists such as Copeland (1940). Regrettably, there is not the space in this volume to consider further Chamberlin's important contribution.

Also reviewing the results of experimental economics, Graham Loomes (1998, p. 486) has proposed that generalized rational preferences should be replaced by 'rules of thumb specific to the particular structure of the decision task in hand'. On the basis of experimental evidence, Loomes (1999, p. F37) abandoned the idea 'that people come to problems armed with a clear and reasonably complete set of preferences, and process all decisions according to this given preference structure'. Both modern experimental economics and game theory have revealed the limitations of all-purpose, context-independent rationality.

These observations tie in closely with some recent work in psychology and elsewhere that has moved away from the 'deliberative thinking paradigm' (Maes, 1991) that dominated postwar cognitive psychology. Researchers have argued that this paradigm downplays both the temporal and the situated aspects of human reason. Instead of assuming that individuals proceed largely by building representative models of their world in their brains, they have emphasized that human cognition depends on its social and material environment and the cues provided by structured interactions with individuals and artefacts. Human cognitive capacities are thus not reducible to individuals alone: they also depend upon social interactions and structures. Scholars in this area have developed concepts such as 'distributed cognition', 'situated cognition' and 'communities of practice'.[8]

In this paradigm shift in the conception of the mind, there has been a move away from seeing the brain as an independent 'rational deliberator,' towards a view of the brain as a controller of embodied activity located in a larger system that includes the body and its social and physical environment. For each individual agent, the material and social context of activity helps to constitute meaning and action. Thought and action are inseparable from their context. In teamwork, for example, individual activity is cued and enabled by its situation, including the behaviours of others. Appropriate cues call forth bursts of activity, which in turn create a new situation, and new cues for action.

The neoclassical idea of the primary and given self, with its all-purpose rationality, is undermined by these developments in psychology. The adoption of a context-dependent, situated rationality is consistent with an institutional economics in which agency and structure are both important and mutually constitutive. Reasoning is impossible without, and inseparable from, its institutional and material context.

These developments in psychology are slowly beginning to affect economics. For example, Douglass North has insisted on the general importance of understanding the context and processes of cognition. In his Nobel

---

8   See Blumer (1969), Rogoff and Lave (1984), Suchman (1987), Lave (1988), Brown and Duguid (1991), Donald (1991), Lave and Wenger (1991), Hutchins (1995), Hendriks-Jansen (1996), A. Clark (1997a, 1997b), Wenger (1998), Nooteboom (2000), Lorenz (2001) and Nelson and Nelson (2002).

lecture, North (1994, p. 362) cautioned on the limits of the rational-choice framework and pointed to the following perspective:

> History demonstrates that ideas, ideologies, myths, dogmas and prejudices matter; and an understanding of the way they evolve is necessary for further progress in developing a framework to understand societal change. ... Learning entails developing a structure by which to interpret the varied signals received by the senses. The initial architecture of the structure is genetic, but the subsequent scaffolding is a result of the experiences of the individual. ... The structures consist of categories – classifications that gradually evolve from earliest childhood to organize our perceptions and keep track of our memory of analytic results and experiences.

North (1994, p. 363) then linked these 'classifications' and 'mental models' – which we use to explain and interpret our environment – with their institutional and cultural context:

> A common cultural heritage provides a means of reducing the divergence in the mental models ... and constitutes the means for the intergenerational transfer of unifying perceptions. ... Belief structures get transformed into societal and economic structures by institutions – both formal rules and informal norms of behavior. The relationship between mental models and institutions is an intimate one. Mental models are the internal representations that individual cognitive systems create to interpret the environment; institutions are the external ... mechanisms individuals create to structure and order the environment.

This recognition of social influences on individual cognition places North very close to – or even within – the 'old' institutionalist tradition.[9] If institutions or a 'common cultural heritage' can somehow reduce divergences between the mental models held by different individuals, or otherwise effect individual beliefs or goals, then we have reconstitutive downward causation in everything but name. What is then required is an elaboration of the causal, social and psychological mechanisms involved in the reconstitutive process. In the following chapter we explore further some of these themes.[10]

---

9 On the convergence of some elements of the 'new institutional economics' with a Veblenian institutionalism, see Dequech (2002) and Hodgson (2002d).

10 In one his last articles, Simon (forthcoming) wrote that 'by far the greatest part of what we come to know and believe has been transmitted to us by social sources that we regard as trustworthy. ... Social learning is by far the predominant concept of human learning'.

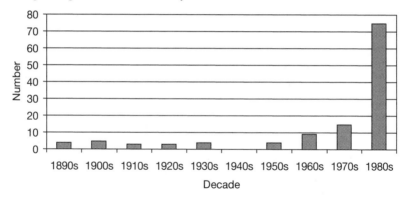

Figure 19.1 Number of works in economics (in English) encountered from the 1890s to the 1980s with the word 'evolution' (or derivatives) in title or subtitle

The evolutionist revival in economics

In 1898, Veblen asked 'why is economics not an evolutionary science?' However, a few years later, evolutionary and Darwinian rhetoric was so unpopular in the social sciences that Joseph Schumpeter (1934, p. 57) repeated in various editions of his *Theory of Economic Development* from 1911 that 'the evolutionary idea is now discredited in our field'. The position is very different today.

Evolutionary thinking and biological analogies reappeared in economics in the 1950s, with works by Armen Alchian (1950) and others. But until the 1980s the use of the term 'evolution' in economics was quite rare. The numbers of books or works in English in economics encountered by the present author, with the word 'evolution' or its derivatives in its title or subtitle, in the decades from the 1890s to the 1980s, are shown in Figure 19.1.[11] The overall number of works published in economics and other sciences has increased explosively since 1945. Nevertheless, 'evolutionary' titles have increased at an even greater exponential rate, with the number published in the 1990s under this category well into the hundreds.

Of course, the mere use of the word 'evolution' is a very crude criterion and does not necessarily indicate the adoption of a biological metaphor. The revival of interest in evolutionary themes in economics was stimulated by the seminal works of Richard Nelson and Sidney Winter (Nelson and Winter 1982; Nelson 1995). Without much explicit reference to Darwinism, they made use of Darwinian principles of selection, variation and replication. Since then, evolutionary modelling along those lines has become commonplace, and evolutionary ideas have been applied to areas ranging from game theory to business economics.

---

11 Subsequent editions of the same book are ignored.

The position in contemporary sociology is different, however. The limited development of evolutionary ideas in sociology has been detailed in Chapter 3 above. Nevertheless, the explosion of interest in Darwinism and evolutionary explanations in economics and elsewhere has created a huge opportunity for the revival of Veblenian themes. As argued in the present book, Veblen offered one of the earliest and most sophisticated applications of Darwinian ideas to the evolution of socio-economic systems.

Moves to generalize Darwinian theory

The Veblenian approach involves the extension of the core Darwinian concepts of variation, replication and selection to socio-economic entities. Its further development can make use of recent work in the philosophy of biology, which has attempted to get at the essence of key Darwinian ideas, to consider if and how they can be applied to spheres outside biology, including to the social sciences.

Consider, for example, the core Darwinian concepts of 'replicator' and 'interactor' as developed in the modern philosophy of biology (Hull, 1981, 1988; Godfrey-Smith, 2000; Sperber, 2000; Aunger, 2002). In brief, a replicator is an entity that copies its structure with some copying fidelity in successive replications. In particular, a replicator is causally implicated in the creation of this copy, the replicator and its copy must be similar in important respects, and much of the crucial information that makes the copy similar must be obtained from the replicator. An interactor is defined as 'an entity that directly interacts as a cohesive whole with its environment in such a way that this interaction *causes* replication to be differential' (Hull, 1988, p. 408). In turn, differential replication is the basis of Darwinian selection processes.

The possibility or otherwise of generalizing Darwinism from biology to the social sciences depends entirely on the creation of meaningful and general definitions of these key Darwinian concepts. But they should not be taken for granted. For Veblenian institutional and evolutionary economics to be developed, they have to be specified in careful detail. This is not an attempt to specify 'gene analogies' but to root out the core meaning of the Darwinian concepts of replication, variation and selection, which were devised by Darwin long before biologists became aware of the gene. These meanings are fixed in highly general terms, to accommodate very different types of evolutionary process, fully recognizing that mechanisms that apply to socio-economic spheres are very different to those in biology.

When these core concepts are defined in general terms, then we may consider candidate 'replicators', 'interactors' and processes of selection in the social domain. These entities and processes must fit generalized Darwinian definitions that also apply to biotic evolution, although (to repeat) social and biotic processes and entities are very different in several important respects. If they do not fit, then Darwinian principles of evolution do not apply.

In social and cultural evolution, what are the replicators? We have several candidates, including Richard Dawkins's (1976) 'memes'. However, recent discussion has cast doubt on whether Dawkins's meme is a genuine and sufficiently well-defined replicator (Godfrey-Smith, 2000; Sperber, 2000; Aunger, 2002). As an alternative, I have argued that habits and routines are replicators, at the individual and group levels respectively (Hodgson, 2001b, 2003c). Habits and routines are replicators by precise criteria, and this further reinforces the viability of a Veblenian-style theory of socio-economic evolution. Further consideration of routines as replicators requires consideration of detailed processes and case studies (Aldrich and Martinez, 2003).

Similar questions should be raised with regard to the general concept of selection. Definitional refinements are required here too, to explore the senses in which the concept of selection is applicable to both biotic and socio-economic evolution. Some initial progress has also been made with this concept (Price, 1970, 1995; Sober, 1984; Knudsen, 2002; Henrich, 2004).

The development of Veblenian institutional and evolutionary economics involves a new conceptual framework as well as novel empirical investigations. Conceptual and theoretical frameworks are necessary prior to empirical investigation, even if they are subsequently modified in the light of new data. Darwinian and Veblenian evolutionary concepts raise new empirical questions and organize the data in different ways. Institutional economics once learned that theory must come first. It then forgot this lesson, as it became overwhelmed by empiricism. However, in recent decades a new opportunity has emerged, with the rapid rise and development of the generalized Darwinian paradigm. To engage with these developments, theory must take priority alongside supportive empirical work. Facts do not speak theory by themselves. This lesson must not be forgotten again.

20 On individuals and institutions

[A]ll narrowly economic activity is embedded in a web of social institutions, customs, beliefs, and attitudes ... different social contexts may call for different background assumptions and therefore for different models. ... If the proper choice of a model depends on the institutional context – and it should – then economic history performs the nice function of widening the range of observation available to the theorist. ... One will have to recognize that the validity of an economic model may depend on the social context.

Robert Solow, 'Economic History and Economics' (1985)

[E]xisting economic theories are not good enough ... We start by studying the behavior of the individual under various conditions of choice. ... We then try to construct a model of the economic society in its totality by a so-called process of aggregation. I now think this is actually beginning at the wrong end. ... Starting with some existing society, we could conceive of it as a structure of rules and regulations within which the members of society have to operate. Their responses to these rules as individuals obeying them, produce economic results that would characterize the society.

Trygve Haavelmo, 'Econometrics and the Welfare State' (1997)

It is of some significance that two Nobel Laureates quoted above, neither of which has a reputation of strong dissent from the mainstream, have pointed to modes of theoretical analysis that would acknowledge institutional and historical specificity. They suggest nothing less than a revival and modernization of some of the core theoretical ideas in the historical school and institutionalist traditions.

The companion and preceding volume (Hodgson, 2001c) related how economics became preoccupied with projects of generalization and purported universality. As a result, important historical and institutional specificities were downplayed or ignored. In the last part of that book I suggested an approach by which different types of socio-economic system could be categorized, as a first step towards enabling the development of historically sensitive theory.

In contrast, in the present volume, the approach is to start from the quite general issues of actor, structure and their coevolution. A major task for a reconstructed institutional economics is to develop a general framework in which particular theories that are sensitive to historical and institutional specificities can be developed more fully. General theorizing has an essential role, but it must be designed to accommodate auxiliary explanations, with historical and institutional sensitivity.

Here biology provides a double lesson. First, biology works without a general theory that unaided can explain everything. Instead, within biology, there is a general (Darwinian) theory of evolution, within which additional explanations of specific biological mechanisms must be fitted. As a kindred science of complex systems, economics should follow this example. A role for the methodology of economics is to scrutinize general explanatory frameworks, and the manner in which more contextually sensitive theories and explanations can fit within them. Second, biology offers a definite general theory of Darwinian evolution that – following Thorstein Veblen – applies forcefully also to the evolution of systems and institutions in the economic domain.

For these and other reasons, social and economic theories have to work at multiple levels, as explained in Hodgson (2001c, ch. 21). The discussion of Darwinian principles in the present volume is situated within what was described in the preceding volume as level 1, involving 'features and principles common to all open, evolving and complex systems'. At higher levels, all that is possible here is to develop a few arguments and guidelines at levels 2 and 3, concerning namely (level 2) 'features and principles common to all human societies' and (level 3) 'features and principles common to all civilized and complex human societies'. The remainder of this chapter concerns analysis at these two relatively abstract levels.

The aim of this chapter is to help develop the core Veblenian concept of an institution and its relevance to understanding individual behaviour. A comprehensive treatment is not possible here; instead I focus on a few key themes. The following section addresses the question of individual rationality in an institutional context, partly in the light of work in modern psychology. The next two sections discuss in general terms the nature and definition of an institution. The two sections after that discuss important differences in types of institution that have been downplayed in much of the literature. A simulation that illustrates reconstitutive downward causation and the role of habit is summarized in the final section.

Situated rationality and institutionalized cognition

As Herbert Simon (1957, 1983) argued at length, once we acknowledge the scarcity of computational powers in the brain, the idea of global rational deliberation is undermined. Any real-world decision-making process involves problems of complexity and combinatorial explosion, which belittle the computational capacities of the human mind. In such real-world circumstances, as Simon argued, we are forced to limit the number of comparisons and to use 'rules of thumb' to help us in our decision-making. For example, we may try to choose a combination of items for a meal by breaking the grocery shopping decision-making algorithm into steps, such as, first choose the meat or fish, then consider compatible vegetables, then compatible forms of carbohydrate, and so on. Such algorithms or 'rules of thumb' can greatly reduce the number of combinations under consideration, reaching an outcome that is satisfactory, rather than necessarily optimal in the sense of resulting from a complete consideration of all possibilities. Simon's work was part of a paradigm shift, where instead of treating the agent as a global calculator and all-purpose utility maximizer, there was a focus on the imperfect guidelines and decision rules that people use to reach outcomes that are 'good enough'.

This paradigm shift involves individual choice in terms of a limited number of discrete and historically given possibilities, rather than optimization through a potentially infinite number of points in a multi-dimensional decision space. This has implications at a formal and a conceptual level. Following Philip Mirowski (1989a), Jason Potts (2000) described general equilibrium analysis as a mathematical 'field theory' where every point in space is connected with every other. Potts argued that, on the contrary, economic reality is characterized by limited interconnectedness, as in a lattice or network. The idea of limited interconnectedness is a response to the reality of both computational limits and institutional constraints.

The problem is to explain a limited number of actual or possible important cases, rather than to attempt to develop a universal theory of every possible instance or configuration. Elsewhere (Hodgson, 1988) it has been argued that Simon's argument needs to be supplemented by explanations of the origins of the 'rules of thumb' or decision algorithms themselves. For example, any disposition to preconceive a meal in terms of a combination of meat or fish with vegetables and carbohydrate is something that is learned in a cultural context. Alternative decision algorithms exist – such as a vegetarian diet – and some of these will have sufficient nutritional value for human survival. The origin and persistence of a decision algorithm in this case involves both cultural and biological factors. It is a result of specific processes of cultural and natural selection. The explanation of 'rules of thumb' or decision algorithms must be consistent with evolutionary principles, and will depend on specific historical, cultural and institutional circumstances.

As noted in the previous chapter, several theoretical and experimental economists are now recognizing the weakness of the universal, utility-maximizing idea. We should take these developments as a cue to create specific, cognitively informed and context-defined models of human decision-making. The key points to take on board are, first, that *all* processes of rational decision-making depend on acquired cognitive frames for the selection, prioritization, interpretation and understanding of the huge volume of sensory stimuli that reaches the human brain (Hodgson, 1988; North, 1994). The attribution of meaning to this apparently chaotic mass of data requires the use of acquired concepts, symbols, rules and signs. It is significant that artificially intelligent systems in moderately complex environments require framing procedures to structure the incoming information (Pylyshyn, 1984, 1987). Any form of rationality in a minimally complex environment relies on cognitive framing, selection and interpretation to make sense of its information inputs.

Second, these rules and means of categorization and understanding have to be learned in a social context. This learning is entirely tacit and involves unconscious reactions to stimuli (M. Polanyi, 1967; Reber, 1993). Through a combination of conscious and unconscious processes, socialization and education help to create the cognitive apparatus that is necessary for 'rational' or any other processes of decision-making. Rationality is not prior to, but requires, an existing social structure. Individual rationality depends on cultural and institutional mechanisms and supports.

Third, as elaborated in Chapter 8 above, the mechanism through which culturally and institutionally specific rules of cognition and action become imprinted in the human mind is through the formation of habits. All reason, deliberation and calculation depend upon the prior formation of habits. Acquired habits of thought involving categories and logical rules are necessary for 'rational' behaviour. Habits are formed through repeated thoughts or behaviours in a specific type of social setting. Issues of behavioural reinforcement or constraint may also be important here, but they relate to how and why behaviour comes to be repetitive. Habits are individual neural connections and mechanisms, but they bear a social imprint. Reconstitutive downward causation, from specific social structure to individual, operates by creating and moulding habits.

Fourth, because cognitive schema are additional to the sense data themselves, different cognitive frameworks are possible with the same sensory input (Choi, 1994). This gives rise to a persistent problem of interpretative ambiguity (March, 1994). Most importantly, different cultures may interpret data in different ways. As Barbara Lloyd (1972, p. 16) put it: 'individuals growing up in different cultures may well learn different rules for processing information from the world around them'. To some degree, differences in cultures and institutional structures will affect the selection, interpretation and understanding of sensory inputs. Reason, in short, is in part culturally specific. Accordingly, the task of the social scientist is to reveal these culturally specific rules of categorization and understanding, as well as the institutional structures through which they are replicated and sustained. The understanding of the (rational) individual presupposes an understanding of specific social structures, just as the understanding of social structures presupposes an understanding of individuals.

Fifth, just as the individual cannot reason or act without a prior repertoire of habits, some conditions and triggers are necessary for habits themselves to be formed. Social institutions mould habits; but that is not sufficient to explain the formation of habits themselves. The infant individual has to be 'programmed' to discern and respond to specific stimuli so that the repeated behaviours that lead to the formation of habits can become possible. This is where instincts come in. Any 'programming' involves inherited instincts, which have slowly evolved over millions of years. The case of language illustrates this forcibly. Although language is largely built up through social interaction in a culturally specific context, the initial acquisition of language requires instinctive mechanisms (Pinker, 1994). Language systems are so complex that their acquisition requires the initial help of instinctive triggers, notwithstanding the immense impact of culture and social environment on each individual. To some degree, this will inevitably be the case with other human capacities. To think and act in social and natural environments, some initial guidances and predispositions are necessary to identify key stimuli and trigger appropriate responses. Once the limited interconnectedness of a rule-system is in place, further habits and rules can be compounded onto this structure.

This treatment of individual capacities complies with the seven Darwinian philosophical principles outlined towards the end of Chapter 4 above, including the principle of evolutionary explanation. It means the end of context-independent rationality. Rationality depends and rests upon a complex foundation of habits, tacit knowledge and experience. This foundation itself depends – at least initially – on instinctive triggers and supports.

In brief, what is involved is linking human reasoning capacities to their evolving social and biological contexts. Rationality is not detached from the world; it is situated in and operates through specific cues, triggers and constraints. These structures and circumstances are part of our biological and social heritage. As Andy Clark (1997a, p. 269) has elaborated:

> These external structures and circumstances act as filters and constraints on the spaces of possible real-time responses. Paramount among such structures and circumstances, in the case of human reason, are the cultural artefacts of language and of social and economic institutions. Models of rational decision making need to situate the reasoning agent as just one element in a complex and time-sensitive feedback system in which such external structures play a major role. It is therefore crucial that we understand the complex and mutually modulatory interplay between individual cognition and the extended environmental loops in which it participates.

A possible response to this challenge is the use of agent-based computer simulations. Faced with the task of creating artificial agents in virtual worlds, it is obvious to the computer programmer that each agent has to be attributed with quite specific decision algorithms. Even if the artificial agent is seen as a utility maximizer, then her utility function has to take on specific attributes. As with the 'frame problem' in artificial intelligence, artificial agents require 'inherited' algorithms to select and structure the incoming information. The issue of importance stems no longer from the ultimately empty debate as to whether agents are really utility maximizers or not. The issue becomes one of considering which specific decision algorithms are appropriate for cognition and action, and of developing a methodological protocol for adjudicating between such algorithms.

In non-computational and conceptual terms, the line of argument here challenges the prevailing wisdom in sociology as well as economics. Just as the all-purpose, context-independent rational utility-maximizing agent of economics has to be discarded in favour of much more specific mechanisms of situated rationality, so too the Berlin Wall between sociology, on the one side, and biology and psychology, on the other, has to come down. As a consequence, social theory is put on a rigorous footing, consistent and engaged with developments in the life sciences, and on which all forms of reductionism, including methodological individualism and methodological collectivism, are regarded as generally unattainable.

Revisiting the nature of institutions

Organized matter has emergent properties that are not explicable in terms of the properties of physical matter alone. In particular, when structured in the human neurosystem (as a result of nature and nurture) and under appropriate stimuli, neural matter can give rise to emergent properties such as consciousness, ideas and beliefs. Beliefs are part of social reality, because human actions not only depend upon beliefs but also have to take into account the supposed beliefs of others.

This has important implications for the nature of institutions.[1] John Searle (1995) explained that mental representations of an institution or its rules are partly constitutive of that institution, since an institution can only exist if people have specifically related beliefs and mental attitudes. Consequently, institutions are simultaneously both structures 'outside' individuals and ideas 'inside' their heads. This does not, however, mean that institutions exist simply in the mind. It means that they depend upon subjective representations, as a necessary but not sufficient condition, as well as other, objective, circumstances.

Institutions are durable systems of established and embedded social rules that structure social interactions. In short, institutions are social rule-systems. They both constrain and enable behaviour. Generally, the

---

1 Some of the points that follow in this section are distilled from the longer discussion in Hodgson (2001c).

existence of rules at least implies constraints. However, such a constraint can also open up possibilities for action or interaction: it may give rise to structures and enable choices that otherwise would not exist. Systems of language, money, law, weights and measures, traffic conventions, table manners, firms (and all other organizations) are all institutions.[2]

Organizations are special institutions that involve (a) criteria to establish their boundaries and to distinguish their members from non-members, (b) principles of sovereignty concerning who is in charge and (c) chains of command delineating responsibilities within the organization.

We need to consider why institutions are durable, how they structure social interactions, and in what senses they are established and embedded. In part, the durability of institutions stems from the fact that they can usefully create stable expectations of the behaviour of others. Generally, institutions enable ordered thought, expectation and action, by imposing form and consistency on human activities. They depend upon the thoughts and activities of individuals but are not reducible to them.

How do people understand rules and choose to follow them? We have to explain not only the incentives and disincentives involved, but how people interpret and value them. This appreciation and valuation of rules is itself a process of social interaction. As Ludwig Wittgenstein (1958, p. 80) pointed out: 'a person goes by a sign-post only in so far as there exists a regular use of sign-posts, a custom'.

The pragmatist philosophers and 'old' institutional economists argued that institutions work only because the rules involved are embedded in shared habits of thought and behaviour. The prevailing rule structure helps to create habits and preferences that are consistent with its reproduction. By reproducing shared habits of thought, institutions create strong mechanisms of conformism and normative agreement. Customary rules acquire the force of moral authority. In turn, these moral norms help to further reinforce the institution in question. Hence institutions are emergent social structures, based on commonly held habits of thought. Upon these structures, actual or potential patterns of social behaviour arise. Habits are the constitutive material of institutions, providing them with enhanced durability, power and normative authority.

---

2 There is a debate within the new institutional economics whether institutions should be regarded essentially as equilibria, norms or rules (Crawford and Ostrom, 1995; Aoki, 2001). But this interpretative conflict arises essentially within an intellectual tradition that takes the individual as given. Being relatively stable, institutions have equilibrium-like qualities, even if their equilibria can be disturbed. Turning to norms and rules, they are not simply the 'environment' in which the (rational) actor must decide and act; they are also internalized in the preferences, and replicated through the behaviour, of the individual. Repeated, conditional, rule-like behaviour acquires normative weight as people accept the customary as morally virtuous, and thus help stabilize the institutional equilibrium. Hence, from the vantage point of Veblenian institutionalism, the three aspects of institutions are complementary and connected.

Habits themselves are rule-like dispositions, conditionally triggered by specific states or stimuli. These circumstances can themselves be natural or social. They can involve specific artefacts or patterns of behaviour that trigger a habituated behavioural response. We are all born into a world of pre-existing institutions, bestowed by history. History provides the resources and constraints, both material and cognitive, in which we think, act and create. Institutions are the kind of structures that matter most in the social realm and make up the stuff of social life.

Some problems with Douglass North's exposition

I now wish to examine aspects of the important work on institutions and organizations by Douglass North, to compare his perspective with mine. He has characterized organizations in a slightly different way. His formulations have been highly influential but I believe that they have led to some problems. The purpose of this section is to expose these difficulties and to maintain my alternative definitions. These difficulties concern North's apparent distinctions (a) between institutions and organizations, and (b) between 'formal rules' and 'informal constraints'. I argue that North has not been sufficiently clear. This has led to many people misinterpreting him as suggesting that organizations are not a type of institution. He is also misinterpreted as making a distinction between formal and informal institutions. Strictly, North upheld neither of these distinctions. I also argue that North has not sufficiently elaborated the nature and functioning of social rules that he rightly identifies as the essence of institutions. His emphasis on the rule-like character of institutions is consistent with my definition, but I believe that something else needs to be added. Concerning institutions in general, North (1990, pp. 3–5) wrote:

> Institutions are the rules of the game in society or, more formally, are the humanly devised constraints that shape human interaction. In consequence they structure incentives in human exchange, whether political, social, or economic. ... Conceptually, what must be clearly differentiated are the rules from the players. The purpose of the rules is to define the way the game is played. But the objective of the team within that set of rules is to win the game ... Modelling the strategies and skills of the team as it develops is a separate process from modelling the creation, evolution, and consequences of the rules.

North rightly insisted that rules must be 'clearly differentiated ... from the players'. The distinction between players and rules is very similar to the distinction between agents and structures, as discussed in Chapter 2 above. Structures depend upon agents, but the two are different and distinct. North (1994, p. 361) also wrote:

It is the interaction between institutions and organizations that shapes the institutional evolution of an economy. If institutions are the rules of the game, organizations and their entrepreneurs are the players. Organizations are made up of groups of individuals bound together by some common purpose to achieve certain objectives.

North reasonably saw organizations as including political parties, firms, trade unions, schools, universities, and so on. Other people have interpreted North as saying that organizations are not institutions. But North did not actually say this. He simply established his own primary interest in economic systems rather than the internal functioning of individual organizations. He was not so interested in the social rules that are internal to organizations, because he wanted to treat them as unitary players and focus on interactions at the national or other higher levels.

There is nothing in principle wrong with the idea that under some conditions organizations can be treated as actors, such as when there are procedures for members of an organization to express a common or majority decision. As Barry Hindess (1989, p. 89) argued, organizations can be treated as social actors as long as 'they have means of reaching decisions and of acting on some of them'. From a different perspective, James Coleman (1982) came to a similar conclusion.

However, a problem arises if we *define* organizations as actors. This would amount to an unwarranted conflation of individual agency and organization. Organizations – such as firms and trade unions – are structures made up of individual actors, often with conflicting objectives. Even if mechanisms for 'reaching decisions and of acting on some of them' are ubiquitous, the treatment of an organization as a social actor should not ignore the potential conflict within the organization. The treatment of the organization as a social actor abstracts from such internal conflicts, but an abstraction should not become a fixed principle or definition that would block all considerations of internal conflict or structure.

Abstraction and definition are entirely different analytical procedures. When mathematicians calculate the trajectory of a vehicle or satellite through space they often treat it as a single particle. In other words, they ignore the internal structure and rotation of the vehicle or satellite. But this does not mean that the vehicle or satellite is *defined* as a particle.

In his work, North did not make it sufficiently clear whether he is *defining* organizations as players or regarding organizations as players as an *analytical abstraction*. This has created much confusion, with other authors insisting that organizations should be *defined* as players. However, North (2002a, 2002b) made it clear that he treated organizations as players simply for the purpose of analysis of the socio-economic system as a whole, and that he did not regard organizations as essentially the same thing as players in all circumstances. In saying that 'organizations are players', North was making an abstraction, rather than defining organizations in this way.

When North wrote that organizations 'are made up of groups of individuals bound together by some common purpose', he simply ignored instances when this may not be the case. He is less interested in the internal mechanisms by which organizations coerce or persuade members to act together to some degree. Crucially, these mechanisms always involve systems of embedded rules. Organizations involve structures or networks, and these cannot function without rules of communication, membership or sovereignty. The unavoidable existence of rules within organizations means that, even by North's own definition of an institution, organizations must be regarded as a type of institution. Indeed, North (2002b) essentially accepted that organizations themselves have internal players and systems of rules, and hence by implication organizations are a special type of institution.[3]

As North acknowledged, it is possible for organizations to be treated as actors in some circumstances *and* generally to be regarded as institutions. Individual agents act within the organizational rule-system. In turn, under some conditions, organizations may be treated as actors within other, encompassing institutional rule-systems. There are multiple levels, in which organizations provide institutional rules for individuals, and possibly in turn these organizations can also be treated as actors within broader institutional frameworks. For example, the individual acts within the nation, but in turn the nation can sometimes be treated as an actor within an international framework of rules and institutions.

Further ambiguities arise with North's distinction between formal 'rules' and informal 'constraints'. Some distinction between the formal and the informal is important, but this distinction is attempted in different and confusing ways by various authors. Some identify the formal with the legal, and see informal rules as non-legal, even if they may be written down. Other authors make the distinction one of explicit versus tacit rules. Although it is rarely acknowledged, we have at least two important distinctions, not one. In his writings, North did not make his intended distinction between 'formal' and 'informal' sufficiently clear.

The picture is further complicated by North's use of the different terms 'rule' and 'constraint'. North (1990, 1991, 1994) wrote most often of formal and informal constraints, rather than formal and informal rules, but he did not indicate why he dropped the word 'rule' and whether or not constraints are also rules. North wrote frequently of 'formal rules' but not of 'informal rules'. But some writers interpret North as making a distinction between formal and informal rules (e.g. Schout, 1991). North's (1994, p. 360) examples of 'formal constraints' are 'rules, laws, constitutions'; and of

---

3 More specifically, in a letter to North of 19 September 2002, I asked if he would agree to 'a definition of organization that accepted that organizations themselves had internal players and systems of rules, and hence organizations were a special type of institution'. North (2002b) expressed 'complete agreement' with this idea. Hence, for both North and myself, organizations are also institutions.

'informal constraints' are 'norms of behavior, conventions, self-imposed codes of conduct'. This suggests that rules are a special kind of formal constraint.

This created a further problem for North: if all rules are formal, and institutions are essentially rules, then all institutions are formal. However, North (1995, p. 15) subsequently redefined institutions in the following terms: 'Institutions are the constraints that human beings impose on human interactions.' By redefining institutions essentially as constraints, rather than rules, this raised the question of a possible distinction between formal and informal constraints. This 1995 definition of an institution neglects the enabling aspect of institutions by emphasizing constraints alone. North (1997, p. 6) then shifted back to a conception of institutions as 'the rules of the game of a society'.

In correspondence with the present author, North (2002b) identified 'formal rules' with legal rules 'enforced by courts'. In contrast: 'Informal norms are enforced usually by your peers or others who impose costs on you if you do not live up to them.' North was thus disposed to identify both rules and institutions with 'formal' (i.e. legal) regulations.[4]

An exclusive emphasis on legal rules and institutions can downplay the existence of rules and institutions, which can constrain and mould human behaviour in ways just as significant as legal rules. Important examples include language and powerful social customs, such as those pertaining to class in Britain, caste in India, and other phenomena elsewhere. Some rules and institutions – such as language and some traffic conventions – can emerge spontaneously as coordination equilibria, which are reproduced principally because it is convenient for agents to conform to them. To some degree, moral beliefs, sanctions and constraints operate in all these cases. Not all powerful rules or institutions are decreed in law.

North rightly emphasizes 'informal constraints' but does not admit the category of informal rules. But all contingent constraints that derive from human action (rather than the laws of nature) are essentially rules.

An overemphasis on the formal and legal aspects can overlook the reliance of legal systems themselves on informal rules and norms. As Émile Durkheim argued in 1893: 'in a contract not everything is contractual' (Durkheim, 1984, p. 158). Whenever a contract exists there are rules and norms that are not necessarily codified in law. The parties to the agreement are forced to rely on institutional rules and standard patterns of behaviour, which cannot for reasons of practicality and complexity be fully established as laws. Legal systems are invariably incomplete, and give scope for custom and culture to do their work (Hodgson, 2001c).

---

4 The similarity in this respect with Commons's limited and predominantly legal conception of an institution (as discussed in Chapter 13 above) should be noted. See Fiori (2002) for a discussion of the role of the distinction between formal rules and informal constraints in North's work.

North fully accepts the importance of the informal sphere, and frequently discusses the informal aspects of formal (i.e. legal) institutions. He emphasizes, for example, the roles of ideology and custom. But he does not sufficiently acknowledge informal institutions that are not decreed in law, including those that arise spontaneously, such as coordination equilibria. North (1990, p. 138) rightly and additionally emphasizes 'informal constraints' and the 'cultural transmission of values' but overly confines his definition of institutions to rules codified in law.

Whether we are dealing with formal or informal rules, we need to consider the ways in which rules are enacted. While it does not necessarily have to enter into the definition of an institution or rule, there has to be some account of how rule-systems affect individual behaviour. Pointing to the incentives and sanctions associated with rules is not sufficient because it would not explain how individuals evaluate the sanctions or incentives involved. We also have to explain why they might, or might not, take incentives or sanctions seriously.

Clearly, the mere codification, legislation or proclamation of a rule is not sufficient to make that rule affect social behaviour. It might simply be ignored, just as many drivers break speed limits on roads, and many Continental Europeans ignore legal restrictions on smoking in restaurants. In this respect, the unqualified term 'rule' may mislead us.

North fully acknowledges that mere rule proclamation is not enough. But in trying to understand how behaviour is fixed or changed, his attention sometimes shifts to the 'informal constraints' of everyday life. Of course, the informal sphere is vital, but ironically, according to North's own definitions, 'informal constraints' are not institutions at all. I prefer a broader conception of institutions that accommodates the informal basis of all structured and durable behaviour. That is why I define institutions as durable systems of established and embedded social rules that structure social interactions, rather than rules as such. In short, institutions are *social rule-systems*, not simply rules.

While broadly subscribing to North's definitions, Pavel Pelikan (1988, p. 372; 1992, p. 45) compared North's 'rules' with the 'genotype' within the 'phenotype' of the organizational structure.[5] If rules are like genes, then this underlines the importance of considering their mechanisms of survival and replication, and the way in which they can affect individuals or organizations. From a Veblenian perspective, the gene-like entities behind rules are individual habits, because these habits are the conditional, rule-like dispositions that marshal behaviour. Rules generally work only because they are embedded in shared habits of thought and behaviour.

---

5   Pelikan's (1988, 1992) definitions are similar but not identical to those of North. He treats institutions as 'rules' but also explicitly considers internal 'institutions' (rules) of organizations.

This section has revealed a lack of definitional consensus over key terms, which has created enormous difficulties. Much further probing and clarification is necessary, partly for matters of explanation and understanding, and partly for the application of institutional analysis to policy design.

Self-enforcement versus external enforcement

We now move on to consider specific aspects and types of institutional reproduction and rule enforcement. This issue also has major implications and lies at the cutting edge of current research in institutional economics today.

It is important to understand the significance of self-organizing institutions and spontaneous orders. The focus on self-organizing aspects of the social system can be traced back to David Hume and Adam Smith, and it is a major theme in the Austrian school of economics from Carl Menger to Friedrich Hayek. The idea of spontaneously self-organizing systems also appeared in works in early American sociology by Edward Ross (1901), Lester Ward (1903) and Charles Ellwood (1912), as noted in Chapters 11 and 12 above. Self-organization is also stressed by modern thinkers such as Ilya Prigogine and Isabelle Stengers (1984) and Stuart Kauffman (1993, 1995, 2000), and by some modern evolutionary economists, including Ulrich Witt (1997) and John Foster (1997).

This literature on self-organization and spontaneous orders provides the essential insight that institutions and other social phenomena can arise in an undesigned way through structured interactions between agents. It provides an important key to the understanding of emergent properties in the social domain, because the emergent order is not itself an intention or property of any single individual or group of individuals. In particular, John R. Commons was criticized in Chapter 13 for his failure to consider spontaneous orders that do not involve legal rules. Veblen too gave it insufficient emphasis. The concept of self-organization is essential to the understanding of the nature and constitution of social institutions.

However, this does not mean that the concepts of self-organization or spontaneous order are sufficient for an understanding of all institutions. They do not tell us the whole story. Indeed, I contend that much of the 'new' institutionalist literature on institutions is disfigured by an overwhelming and relatively excessive emphasis on these (albeit essential) ideas, to the detriment of other vital mechanisms of institutional emergence and sustenance.

It is important not to overlook the fact that different institutions depend on different types of rule, incentive structure, preference stability or normative salience. The first relevant distinction is between coordination-type set-up and other types of incentive structure. Other issues, such as moral pressure and changes in preference functions, will be considered later. First we assume individuals with given preference functions.

Coordination rules typically provide incentives for everyone to conform to the convention. For this reason, a coordination equilibrium can be self-policing and highly stable. Language is an example. Willard van Orman Quine (1960) made the point that language has an error-correcting regime. Individuals have an incentive to make their words clear. As an essential condition of communication, the coding itself (the signifier) must be unmistakable, even if the meaning (the signified) remains partly ambiguous. In communication we have strong incentives and inclinations to use words and sounds in a way that conforms as closely as possible to the perceived norm. Although languages do change through time, there are incentives to conform to, and thus reinforce, the linguistic norms in the given region or context. Norms of language and pronunciation are thus largely self-policing.[6]

Similarly, some (but not all) legal rules have a strong self-policing element. For example, there are obvious incentives to stop at red traffic lights and to drive on the same side of the road as others. Although infringements will occur, these particular laws can be partly enforced by motorists themselves, because infringements can increase perceived personal risks. But even here some variations are possible. Motorists in a 'macho' culture may relish taking such risks. The possibility of self-policing institutions depends on perceived payoffs, and such perceptions can sometimes be moulded by cultural circumstances. This important issue is raised again later below; prior to that point we continue to assume exogenously given preference functions.

A coordination equilibrium can be self-enforcing; not only does each player lack any incentive to change strategy, but also each player wishes that other players keep to their strategy as well (Schotter, 1981, pp. 22–3). If agents have compatible preferences and strategies in this sense, then coordination rules can often emerge spontaneously and be self-reinforcing. For example, if the rule 'drive on the right-hand side' of the road emerges, then each driver has an incentive to stick to this rule and also wishes that other drivers would do likewise. Even if I prefer to drive on the left, but I find myself in a country where driving on the right is the convention, then I will drive on the right, and others will prefer that I do this. I do this because my second-best option is itself much better than a head-on collision! A coordination equilibrium has characteristics of stability and self-enforcement, even when the equilibrium is not ideal for everyone involved. An example is illustrated in Figure 20.1 on page 433.

As an example of a contrasting case, consider the famous Prisoners' Dilemma game, as also illustrated in Figure 20.1. At least in a one-shot play of

---

6 Of course, this does not exclude the possibility of cumulative error and 'drift' in the evolution of language.

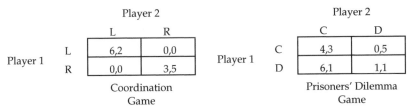

Figure 20.1 A Coordination Game and a Prisoners' Dilemma Game

this game, each player has an incentive to defect. The situation of mutual cooperation (C-C) is not a Nash equilibrium because each player can gain an advantage by shifting from (C) cooperation to (D) defection. The Nash equilibrium is (D-D), where each player gets less than she would if both players cooperated (C-C). A 'spontaneous order' may emerge but it is clearly sub-optimal, by any reasonable criterion. Although a Nash equilibrium may emerge, its social and individual sub-optimality always brings it into question.

Robert Axelrod (1984) has famously argued that with repeated (indefinite or infinite) plays of the Prisoners' Dilemma game, enduring cooperation (C-C) can emerge because each player can learn to reciprocate attempts to cooperate by the other, and punish defection when it occurs by further defection. But this result is not universal and Axelrod's 'tit-for-tat' strategy can be out-competed by alternative behavioural rules (Kitcher, 1987; Lindgren, 1992; Binmore, 1998b). There is no guarantee that cooperation will endure, even in repeated games of this type.

Consider some of the key differences between the two types of game. In the case of a coordination game the incentives to conform to the emergent convention are strong and enduring, even if it is not everyone's first choice. Furthermore, as in the representative cases of languages and rules of the road, normative issues are often secondary to the straightforward incentives and disincentives involved. This is partly because the incentive structure involved is normally sufficient to reach an enduring and acceptable outcome. In a Prisoners' Dilemma game there is also a Nash equilibrium. The equilibrium is stable in the one-shot case, but it will not necessarily endure if the game is repeated. Furthermore, the transparent sub-optimality of the Nash equilibrium, from both the individual and the social point of view, by Paretian and other plausible criteria, raises normative questions including the desirability of third-party intervention to improve the situation for everyone involved. We make a big mistake if we treat these two types of situation as the same, or if we concentrate on models of self-organization based on coordination-type incentive structures, while neglecting other equally important incentive configurations.

With its potential for sub-optimal outcomes, a Prisoners' Dilemma situation would be a candidate for intervention by a third party such as the state. In some circumstances it is conceivable that such a third party could intervene to deter or prevent defection. For example, if the state made defection illegal and subject to a fine of 3 units (or alternatively taxed defection by 3 units), then the Prisoners' Dilemma game in Figure 20.1 would be transformed to the different type of game in Figure 20.2. Clearly, this is no longer a Prisoners' Dilemma game: both players have an incentive to cooperate.[7]

Note also that a similar structure of payoff incentives may be attainable by an alteration in the preferences of the players, as well as by a tax or a fine. If a view prevailed that defection was intrinsically bad or immoral, then agents might internalize such ideas in their own preferences. If these changes in preferences were strong enough, they could lead to changes in perceived payoffs similar to those represented in Figure 20.2, and mutual cooperation would result. Arguably, such changes in preferences could result from a period of mutual cooperation in repeated plays of the game. Without propaganda or coercion, individuals might become freely persuaded that cooperation has a greater relative moral superiority over defection. This would be a case of systemically endogenous enforcement, rather than enforcement from outside. Alternatively, or in addition, a powerful third party could help by example, persuasion or propaganda to shift individual preferences. For example, a democratic state might implore us to fasten seat belts in cars or recycle our garbage, or a totalitarian regime could adopt more sinister methods of propaganda or coercion to reach similar goals.

Of course, such a practical transformation of incentives and outcomes would be very difficult to engineer in complex, real-world circumstances. But this does not mean that state intervention is always dysfunctional. The transformation in Figure 20.2 dramatically oversimplifies the real-world complexities and problems of knowledge involved. But it does show that payoff manipulations can have important qualitative effects. The practical possibility or otherwise of effective state intervention is a matter for detailed theoretical and empirical enquiry in specific circumstances.

Prisoners' Dilemma situations are not exceptional. Their essential features are present in many social interactions. For example, traffic congestion is sub-optimal and often it would be better to use public transport, but people continue to drive their cars, knowing that others are likely to do the

		Player 2	
		C	D
Player 1	C	4,3	0,2
	D	3,0	-2,-2

Figure 20.2 The previous Prisoners' Dilemma Game transformed

---

7   See Ostrom *et al.* (1994, p. 77) for a discussion of the way in which additional rules such as these may 'affect the benefits and costs assigned to actions and outcomes'.

same. This is similar to the famous – and equally real – 'tragedy of the commons' (Hardin, 1968). The employment contract has also been modelled as a Prisoners' Dilemma (Leibenstein, 1982).

While self-organization and spontaneous orders are important and widespread in both nature and society, they rely on specific types of incentive alignment that ensure that most individuals have no reason to deviate from or disrupt the emergent order. Other payoff structures exist that may not lead to optimal or satisfactory outcomes, and additional factors may be necessary to reach a satisfactory result. An option is to rely on the enforcement measures of a third party. Another possibility is that the persistence of a satisfactory solution for a while may lead to a shift of preferences that favours its prolongation. These two possibilities are not mutually exclusive and one process could benefit from the other. The first process involves external enforcement and the second would be an example of systemically endogenous enforcement through reconstitutive downward causation.

Normative issues are clearly raised at this point. Although all rules involve costs and benefits, there is a big difference between following a rule because it is convenient to do so, and following a rule because of a normative belief. Coordination rules are foremost examples of rules that are followed primarily because of convenience. Viktor Vanberg (1994, p. 65) has rightly pointed out that writers in the spontaneous order tradition – from Hume and Smith through Menger to Hayek – have failed to account adequately for the difference between coordination rules and rules involving normative constraints (legal or moral rules). Walter Schultz (2001, pp. 64–6) stressed a similar distinction in his powerful discussion of the problem of enforcement of social rules.

Until recently, the problem of enforcement has been neglected in much of the 'new' institutionalist tradition. As noted above, some institutions are largely self-enforcing. But things are even more different with many other laws and institutions. Laws that restrict behaviour, where there are substantial, perceived net advantages to transgression, are the ones that require the most policing. Hence people frequently evade tax payments or break speed limits. Without some policing activity the law itself is likely to be infringed, debased and 'brought into disrepute'.

For example, there are incentives to debase money. With potential quality variation, individual agents have an obvious incentive to use a less costly, poor quality or fake version of the medium of exchange. Given that traders cannot readily detect all variations, then forgeries and debasements are possible. If they are allowed to endure, then bad money will drive out the good. Money is not self-policing in the same way as language.[8]

---

8 Menger (1909) acknowledged this himself. See the discussion of Menger's theory of money in Hodgson (1993, 2001c).

Self-policing mechanisms can be undermined if there is the possibility of undetected variation from the norm and there is sufficient incentive to exert such variations. Language and money differ in this respect. There are always incentives to under-pay but not always to under-inform. The argument for enforcement by a third party such as the state is thus stronger in the case of money and some laws, than in the case of language.[9]

Furthermore, the boundary between potentially self-policing and other institutional arrangements depends on perception, which in turn may depend on the cultural context. While self-organization is an extremely important phenomenon in both nature and human society, it cannot account for all the peculiar features of human social organization. To treat human society as closely analogous to the spontaneous emergence of order in a chemical system or a slime mould is to belittle the reality of human agency. It would ignore the importance of reconstitutive downward causation on human agents, including the human capacities to prefigure, imitate and adopt the dispositions of their neighbours. These factors become more important in the case of 'agent sensitive institutions' as discussed below.

Attempts to explain the evolution of several important types of social institutions in entirely spontaneous terms have failed. Consider the institutions of contract and private property. Elsewhere (Hodgson, 2001c, ch. 20) I have noted some attempts by economists and economic historians to explain the enforcement of property rights by means of such devices as 'hostages' and trading coalitions. Several authors, including Avner Greif (1993), have used game theory to illustrate these arguments. I have also discussed the critique of some of the arguments in this literature by Itai Sened (1995, 1997). However, because of its relevance and importance, I will summarize it again here. Sened (1995, p. 162) wrote:

> Like traditional economists, most game theorists systematically overlook the role of law enforcement..... Many important social institutions do not emerge as equilibria in games among equal agents, but as equilibria in games among agents who control old institutions and agents who challenge such institutions with new demands. In particular, governments play a crucial role in the evolution of institutions that protect individual rights.

In his extended critique of the notion of property without statute law, Sened (1997) argued that true individual rights are established only when a territorial institution establishes its monopoly over the use of force. Sened's argument departs significantly from that of Robert Sugden (1986,

---

9 However, there has been some limited institutional regulation of language in France, and spelling reforms have been inaugurated (relatively successfully) in the Netherlands and (less successfully) in Germany. After independence, some changes in English spelling were made in the United States.

p. 5) and others, who argue that legal codes 'merely formalize … conventions of behaviour' that have evolved spontaneously out of individual interactions. However, to accept the role of the state in the evolution of property and contract is not to romanticize this institution. Sened saw the state as neither a benevolent nor a disinterested legislator, but as an institution whose members pursue their own interests. For Sened, governments weigh the benefits of granting rights against the cost of enforcement. Sened (1997, p. 123) further wrote:

> Governments do not erect such structures out of benevolence or moral concern. They grant and protect rights in order to promote their own interests. But in doing so, they fulfil two crucial social functions. The function of maintaining law and order that is a necessary condition for economic growth and affluence, and the function of arbitrage between conflicting interests.

In addition, Sened showed the limitations in this context of game-theoretical models involving a few agents. With a larger number of players it is more difficult for individuals to establish mutual and reciprocal arrangements that ensure contract compliance. If trading coalitions do emerge, then these themselves take upon state-like qualities to enforce agreements and protect property. In a world of incomplete and imperfect information, high transaction costs, asymmetrically powerful relations and agents with limited insight, powerful institutions are necessary to enforce rights. These institutions result from a complex bargaining process. Sened uses an n-person Prisoners' Dilemma to show that the introduction of a government, enforcing rights, can often improve on a suboptimal outcome.[10]

It is an open question as to whether another strong institution, apart from the state, could fulfil this necessary role. However, it is not to endorse or glorify the state if we start analytically from the likelihood and reality of a legislative state, and analyse its role and limits in the establishment and protection of property. Clearly, the state has the capacity to appropriate, as well as to protect, private property. For private property to be relatively secure, a particular form of state had to emerge, countered by multiple powerful interest groups in civil society. This meant a pluralistic state with some separation of powers, backed up by a plurality of group interests in the community at large. Accordingly, the emergence of a powerful institution like the state is a necessary but not a sufficient condition for the protection of property and other individual rights.

Given that some institutions require exogenous enforcement, it is important to analyse the complementary and structured sets of institutions,

---

10 Mantzavinos (2001, ch. 8) also emphasized the problem of dealing with large numbers of agents in obtaining autonomous enforcement, and reached a conclusion similar to Sened.

where one institution can provide enforcement or other supportive mechanisms for another. For example, the market and the state are not always substitutes, but in some respects can be complements (Hodgson, 1984). A major agenda for enquiry is to explore the extent of such complementarities and understand their mechanisms in depth.

Agent-sensitive and agent-insensitive institutions

In the preceding section I discussed the differences between institutions that required external enforcement and those that were largely self-enforcing. Here I introduce a different dichotomy, with the terms 'agent-sensitive' and 'agent-insensitive' institutions. An agent-sensitive institution is one in which the reigning equilibria or conventions can be significantly altered if the preferences or dispositions of some agents are changed, within a feasible set of personality types. This issue is best approached by considering some examples of agent-insensitive institutions.

Strikingly, in one of his earliest papers, Gary Becker (1962) demonstrated that behaviour ruled by habit and inertia is just as capable as rational optimization of predicting the standard downward-sloping demand curve and the profit-seeking activity of firms. He showed how the negatively inclined market demand curve could result from habitual behaviour, up against a moving budget constraint. A constraint means that agents, whether super-rational or sluggish and habit-driven, have to stay on one side of the line. With agents of each type, rotations in the budget constraint can bring about downward-sloping demand curves. Becker (1962, p. 4) concluded that:

> negatively inclined market demand curves result not so much from rational behavior per se as from a general principle which includes a wide class of irrational behavior as well. Therefore, households can be said to behave not only 'as if' they were rational but also 'as if' they were irrational: the major piece of empirical evidence justifying the first statement can equally well justify the second.

Much later, Dhananjay Gode and Shyam Sunder (1993) showed that experiments with agents of 'zero intelligence' produce behaviours that differ little from those with human traders. Gode and Sunder thus suggest that structural constraints can produce similar outcomes, whatever the objectives or behaviour of the individual agents. As in Becker's (1962) model, systemic constraints prevail over micro-variations. Ordered market behaviour can result from the existence of resource and institutional constraints, and may be largely independent of the 'rationality', or otherwise, of the agents. Structural constraints, not individuals, do much of the explanatory work. We thus face the possibility of a study of markets that focuses largely on institutions and structures, to a degree independent of the assumptions made about agents.[11]

From these previous studies, two conclusions follow. First, the 'accuracy of the predictions' or other familiar criteria for theory selection do not give outright victory to rational choice models. Second, these models suggest that ordered and sometimes predictable behaviour can sometimes result largely from institutional constraints. The explanatory burden is carried by system structures rather than the preferences or psychology of individuals. We describe such cases as 'agent-insensitive' institutions, because outcomes are insensitive to individual psychology.

However, it would be a serious error to suggest that all institutions are agent insensitive as in the illustrations of Becker (1962) and Gode and Sunder (1993). Mirowski (2002) uses the Gode and Sunder (1993) results to argue for the treatment of the market itself as a computational entity, with no detailed attention to the computational capacities or psychologies of the agents that operate within markets. These arguments may apply to some institutional structures, including some markets, and to that extent they are important and worthwhile. But they do not constitute a general theoretical strategy, unless agent insensitivity is itself general among institutions.

Agent insensitivity is not general. What is common to the Becker (1962) and Gode and Sunder (1993) models is the existence of hard and insurmountable (budget) constraints. These models are agent insensitive because the constraints are solid. They push the agents into position and offer them few alternatives. The constraints thus do most of the explanatory work. Such hard constraints do exist in reality, but they are a rather special case. Other institutional constraints operate through disincentives or legal penalties. But in such cases it may be possible to cross the line or break the law. The propensity to break rules or transgress constraints will in part depend on the preferences and personality of each individual agent. If the constraints were softer, then the agents would have more discretion, and it would be likely that the personalities of the agents will have to be taken into account.

Some possibilities for agent-sensitive institutions are considered below. By wrongly suggesting that agent insensitivity is a general case, Mirowski's (2002) research strategy carries the danger of a general conflation of agency into the structure.

There are multiple types of agent-insensitive institution. In addition to the possibility of hard constraints we should consider the alternative possibility of relatively high incentives to conform to a convention. A

---

11 For useful discussions of these results see Denzau and North (1994), Mirowski (2002) and Mirowski and Somefun (1998). Grandmont (1992) has similarly demonstrated that aggregate demand can be well behaved under certain distributional restrictions, merely by assuming that individual behaviour satisfies budget constraints, without any reference to utility maximization. See also Hildenbrand (1994).

coordination game is ostensibly agent insensitive, because the players have an incentive to conform to the reigning convention, even if it is not their most favoured option. British drivers will drive on the right in America and Continental Europe, even if they find it easier to drive on the left. To a degree, such traffic conventions are agent insensitive.

However, a convention can be overturned if a sufficient number of people defy it. As long as the relative benefits of coordination are finite, the possibility exists of a relatively extreme personality type that will not perceive any advantage in conforming to the prevalent convention. In contrast, in the case of hard constraints, all agents are required to comply, whatever their personality.

Strictly, in game-theoretic terms, all coordination games are agent insensitive. This is because the game payoffs express the preferences of all the players involved, and intrinsically a coordination game results in a Nash equilibrium. However, to consider agent sensitivity in a game-theoretic framework we have to consider a game of n players, where n is the number of feasible personality types. If such an n-person game is a coordination game, then its structure and payoffs will result in a Nash equilibrium where every player plays the same strategy. This is a feasible but rather extreme case. The overturning of a reigning convention can be modelled only by the introduction of a group of players with perceived payoffs that bring the n-person payoff matrix outside the strict category of a coordination game.

Coordination games are a subset of agent-insensitive institutional configurations. The models of Becker (1962) and Gode and Sunder (1993) are relatively agent insensitive but they are not coordination games.

A number of configurations are agent sensitive. Consider, for example, a reigning pattern of cooperation in a repeated Prisoners' Dilemma game. This cooperation results from a population dominated by units playing the tit-for-tat strategy. But they can be invaded by an influx of others who always cooperate. If this occurs, then the consequent population of cooperators would clearly be vulnerable to an invasion by a species that consistently defects. In turn, if this invasion was incomplete, or subject to a slight amount of error, then a new invasion of tit-for-tat players could take advantage of the fact that consistent defection was not absolute. And so on: each outcome is unstable (Kitcher, 1987; Lindgren, 1992; Binmore, 1998b). The prevailing conventions are sometimes sensitive to the types of player that are involved. Another possibility of agent sensitivity results from the existence of multiple (Nash) equilibria. Even if the constraints are hard, slight differences between the personalities of agents may matter if there is a choice between two or more (near) optimal positions.

If we introduce greater variance in personality and observe the stability of reigning conventions, then we can gauge the agent sensitivity of the institutional set-up involved. Agent sensitivity is a matter of degree.

Institutions involve a range of degrees of agent sensitivity and insensitivity, and investigations should not be confined to extreme or particular values.

Modelling habit and institutional evolution

Thorbjørn Knudsen and myself developed the simulation described in this section (Hodgson and Knudsen, 2004). This agent-based simulation with heterogeneous agents casts light on several of the themes raised in this book. In our model we chose one of the most straightforward of conventions: whether the rule is to drive on the right or on the left side of the road. In this model, artificially intelligent 'drivers' in 'cars' are programmed to negotiate a circular road configuration along with a number of other, similar vehicles.

Each driver is boundedly rational. To negotiate the road and avoid collision, it would seem to be rational for each driver at least to consider *conformity* with the perceived distribution of traffic to the left and right, and *avoidance* of cars that are close ahead. In the model these particular dispositions are fixed at birth, like instincts or a given preference function. To these factors, our model adds *habit*.

The simulations show that strength of habit and processes of habituation can play a vital role alongside rational deliberation and selection pressure. This not only raises important questions concerning the role of habit in decision-making but also it challenges the frequent assumption that preference functions should always be taken entirely as exogenously given.

In the model, 40 agents drive in cars around a ring, with two lanes and 100 zones in each lane. The drivers are unique individuals, born to drive either clockwise or counter-clockwise around the ring. Half of the agents drive clockwise and the other half counter-clockwise. For each car, the direction of its lengthways movement cannot be changed.

Initially the drivers are randomly assigned a zone and a position on one of the two sides of the ring. Each car is addressed and moves sequentially. With no simultaneous moves, some associated problems of interpretation of the intentions of others are thus avoided. All drivers in turn make a (subjective) decision based on the (objective) information about the traffic ahead. The driver looks 10 increments ahead and counts in that region the number of cars in each lane and the number of cars going in each direction. Their decision algorithm combines decision elements that vary according to the cognitive personality of the driver and the global parameter weights. Based on this information, and given its behavioural and cognitive dispositions, the driver decides on which side of the ring to drive in its next move.

The final element to be taken into consideration is the possibility of error. An error probability variable is fixed at the beginning of the simulation. A random number generator was used to determine whether each car, with this probability, makes the move opposite to its subjective evaluation. At this final stage, the left or right inclination of the car in the upcoming move is determined.

Each car drives around the ring until it is involved in a collision. If there is a collision, then – regardless of blame or circumstances – the two drivers die and are replaced by two new cars and drivers. As a result, the number of cars on the grid is always 40. The replacement routine also ensures that the number of cars moving clockwise and counter-clockwise is always 20. After a collision, the two newborn drivers acquire a new set of fixed cognitive and behavioural dispositions, chosen randomly in the same manner as the cars at the beginning of the simulation, likewise with a habituation level set initially to zero. Their cognitive and behavioural characteristics being determined, each new car is allocated to a random position on the track.

If there is neither birth nor death, then the pool of fixed characteristics among the population cannot change. At least a small amount of death and replacement is necessary to select the combinations of fixed cognitive and behavioural dispositions that are conducive to survival. However, the overwhelming majority of deaths generally occur in the early, transition phase of the simulations. This selection process leads to surviving decision algorithms which are relatively fit and adaptive.

Generally, when an equilibrium outcome emerges, whether the resulting convention is drive-on-the-right or drive-on-the-left can be highly sensitive to initial conditions. Once the system begins to swing decisively and permanently one way or the other, and a convention begins to emerge, then it can become locked in to a process that is the cumulative result of tiny initial movements (Arthur, 1994).

Error can disturb this process of convergence to a left/right convention. The effects of error can be particularly disruptive in the early phases of this process. However, even in later phases, errors can trigger deaths that lead to replacements that are ill-adapted for the road conditions, leading to further collisions, and so on. It is possible for such processes of positive feedback to destroy an established convention.

Many simulations were performed, with many different parameter weights. Generally, as the strength of habit increases from zero, mean convergence levels improve, for all levels of error. Increases in the levels of error have a significant and opposite effect. No other variable emerged to generally improve convergence in our simulations. For instance, while the avoidance coefficient can help the drivers to survive, it does not significantly assist convergence.

In this boundedly rational situation, where drivers are unable to see the whole ring, habit emerges as the single most significant factor improving convergence. This improvement in convergence does not come at the cost of increased death rates. We show that if drivers can see further ahead, habit still has a positive effect. In addition, 'conformist' factors become significant and more important when there is more information concerning the traffic ahead. The relative importance of habit is inversely related to omniscience.

The most important result of our simulations concerns the effect of introducing processes of habituation into the modelling of agent behaviour. In a substantial region of parameter space, strength of habit can increase the systemic rate of convergence towards a left/right convention. In some circumstances it can also enhance systemic resistance to error. In short, habit helps agents to deal with uncertainty, complexity and change.

In some simulations we replaced habit by a factor we describe as 'inertia'. Each driver knows its current position and remembers two preceding periods. According to fixed coefficients acquired by each driver at birth, each driver is disposed to some degree to continue with its current inclination or an inclination it has assumed in the recent past. The inertia values reflect a memory vector of behavior in a finite set of present and past periods. By contrast, habit in the model is a single-value, weighted summation of behaviours in an unbounded set of present and past periods. Habits are like a crude, summarized memory. Habits are built up steadily once a repeated behaviour emerges.

It would be possible to extend the number of preceding periods in the calculation of the inertia values, from two to a much higher number. A (weighted) summation of these values could then approximate to habit. But with inertia and unlike habit any informational significance in the values of the individual elements in the inertia vector is retained. However, the cost of this is an increase in memory and computational capacity.

In a more complex world, the number of scalar values represented by multiple inertia vectors relating to multiple past behaviours and behavioural variables would be vastly increased. The storage limits of any finite memory could be readily challenged. By contrast, habit is a cruder summary of past behaviour but requires much less memory.

We showed that with three inertia variables the convergence characteristics of the model are inferior to those in the model with habit instead. Habit not only economizes on memory and computational capacity, it also is a superior aid to convergence.

The conception and role of habit in this model contrast greatly with the definition and conception of habit elsewhere. Becker (1992, p. 328) wrote: 'I define *habitual* behavior as displaying a positive relation between past and current consumption'. Becker here defines habit not as a behavioural propensity but as sequentially correlated behaviour. A car may manoeuvre to the left to avoid oncoming traffic, but its propensity may still be to drive on the right. In this case, the right-driving propensity is overridden, creating a degree of left-driving inertia. If there is an observed succession of left-driving behaviour, this is not necessarily the underlying disposition of the agent. Becker's definition confuses propensity with actuality. However, if past behaviour were taken to mean a potentially infinite sequence of past events, then a propensity acquired through habituation could approximate to mean past behaviour. In this extreme case, propensity could coincide with actuality. But in general, and in contrast to Becker, we distinguish between habit and behaviour by defining habit as a disposition or propensity, rather than correlated behaviour.

It is true that habit removes some actions from conscious deliberation and helps the agent to focus on other, more strategic or immediate, decisions. However, the model here suggests that there is something more to habit than economizing on decision-making. After all, each car in the model makes only one simple binary decision at each point of time. Habit is doing much more in our model than simply economizing on the time taken to search for, and process, information.

The model suggests that a crucial role played by habit is to build up and reinforce an enduring disposition in each agent, concerning the appropriate side of the road on which to drive, especially in a situation where information concerning the traffic ahead is limited. The development of habits amounts to an element of endogenous preference formation. A sequence of similar and repeated behaviours creates in each agent a habitual predilection, which can stimulate a 'belief' or 'conviction' that a particular behaviour is appropriate.

Again this is reminiscent of the arguments of the pragmatists, who saw acquired habits as the basis of firmly held beliefs. For Peirce (1878, p. 294) the 'essence of belief is the establishment of habit'. Similarly, in our model, habit differs from mere inertia, in that it creates stubborn 'beliefs' in the appropriateness of an action, that weigh heavily in the decision-making process of each agent. The evolution of an equilibrium convention depends largely on one set of stubborn 'beliefs' triumphing over the other. Once a stable convention forms, it is encoded in the dispositions of the majority and it can resist the intrusion of a substantial amount of erratic behaviour. Accordingly, habit is more than a means of economizing on decision-making for individuals, it is a means by which social conventions and institutions are formed and preserved.[12]

Another heuristic use of our model is that it provides a framework to consider the nuanced interpretations and meanings of the concept of 'downward causation'. As noted in Chapter 8 above, the notion of 'downward causation' has weak and strong forms. In our model, this weaker form of downward causation is clearly present. Evolutionary selection acts on the population of agents, causing a shift in the characteristics of the population as a whole. In the population as a whole, this evolutionary selection works on the fixed parameters and on the single variable expressing habit.

---

12 The model also raises questions concerning the conceptual distinction between preference exogeneity and endogeneity. See Hodgson and Knudsen (2004) for a discussion of this point.

In the population as a whole, the fixed parameters change by means of the death of the unsuccessful and the birth of the new agents. However, for any individual agent, evolutionary selection does not cause a change in the values of the fixed parameters.

In our model, this stronger form of downward causation is also present. More and more surviving cars develop the habit to drive on the left or the right, according to the emerging convention. Strength of habit is based on two of the five variables that form the 'preference function' of each agent. For each individual, one of these preference elements can change. In this way, emerging and enduring systemic properties reconstitute 'downwards' the preferences of the agent. This causal mechanism amounts to reconstitutive downward causation. Part of the achievement here is to show that both forms of downward causation can be represented in an agent-based model.

Another crucial point is to recognize the specific mechanism by which reconstitutive downward causation operates. It is on *habits*, rather than merely on behaviour, intentions or other preferences. Clearly, the definitional distinction between habit (as a propensity or disposition) and behaviour (or action) is essential to make sense of this statement.

The existence of a viable mechanism of reconstitutive downward causation contrasts with other, untenable 'top-down' explanations in the social sciences where there are unspecified 'cultural' or 'economic' forces controlling individuals. Crucially, the mechanism of reconstitutive downward causation that is outlined here affects the dispositions, thoughts and actions of human actors. Hence this model illustrates the Veblenian process by which emergent institutions work on individual habits and give rise to new preferences and intentions.

In addition, the model reinforces Mitchell's insight that the circular, positive feedback from institution to individuals and from individuals to institutions can help to enhance the durability of the institutional unit. In some institutional circumstances there may be stable emergent properties at the institutional level that exist not despite, but because of, endogenous preference formation. Where these institutional reinforcements work effectively, there is a case for treating institutions as units of analysis, as outlined in Chapter 14 above. Hence, more generally, this heuristic model thus opens up an agenda of agent-based modelling of institutional formation and endurance, on Veblenian conceptual foundations.

It has been noted in this chapter that the emphasis in the 'spontaneous order' tradition, from Hume and Smith to Hayek, has been on situations similar to coordination games. A likely reason why the predominant emphasis has been on coordination rules has been to retain the notion that institutions are largely matters of rational consent – or a 'social contract' – for the actors involved. It has been argued here, however, that coordination games are not typical of all institutional set-ups, and many institutions rely on external, third-party enforcement, typically from the impositions of other institutions. The model discussed here further undermines the notion that institutions are predominantly matters of rational consent, by showing that, even in the case of a simple coordination situation, habit plays a crucial role in underscoring the emergent convention. This is again consistent with the Veblenian insight that all institutions rely on habit and custom, and these factors help to explain their inertia, their historical persistence, and the difficulties involved in institutional change.

Game theory has revived interest in the problems of intersubjective interpretation of the intentions of others through observation of their behaviour. Questions concerning common beliefs and the assumption of common rationality have come to the fore. But in a world of many players, with pervasive ignorance and nagging uncertainty, severe limits are placed on the rational analysis of the interactions of rational agents. Historically formed constraints impinge on individuals and mould their habits, and can often tell us more than the best game-theoretic analysis. Individuals may make rational choices, but their options and preferences are historically and socially formed. Habit is the means of escape from the hermeneutic regress of interpretation of others' interpretations of others' interpretations ... .

Habits are both 'subjective' springs of human agency 'in the human head' and the basis of 'objective' institutions 'out there'. Like Klein bottles, the subjective 'inside' is simultaneously the objective 'outside'. Actor and structure, although distinct, are connected in a circle of mutual interaction and interdependence. Habit is the key. Veblen was right, after all.

21 Conclusion and beginning

In my end is my beginning.

T. S. Eliot, *East Coker* (1944)

If the reader has studied *How Economics Forgot History* as well as this present volume, he or she will have traversed almost 800 pages and about 400,000 words to come to this point. It is a long story, relating how economics has lost many of its past insights and even disowned its own past. It has aspects of a Greek tragedy. But expectations may also be raised after such a long journey, for sustenance and riches at its end. But our expedition has been into the past, and we have merely returned to the present day. Hopefully we have become enriched by this experience, but the greater and more difficult expedition stretches into the uncertain future. The past has provisioned us for this passage. This final chapter is an exhortation to begin the journey, with a few meagre thoughts on some of the problems ahead.

The foregoing discussion of recent intellectual developments in the social sciences suggests an enormous potential for future development along the lines suggested in this book. At the same time there are enormous constraints, and many of these are due to the institutions and culture of academia itself. One of the most severe problems for a revived institutional and evolutionary economics is the existing compartmentalization of the social sciences.[1] However, the boundary between economics and sociology that has endured since the 1940s is now being violated on both sides. The Robbinsian line of demarcation defined by 'the science of rational choice' is thus losing its legitimacy, and the most reasonable alternative is to attempt once again to redefine economics as the intellectual discipline concerned with the study of economic systems. In other words, it should be defined,

---

1 See Colander (2003) for a discussion of additional problems involved in raising the academic status of institutionalism.

as in other sciences, in terms of its object of analysis, rather than by any set of prior tenets.

Perhaps this loss of the reigning twentieth-century boundaries between the social sciences foreshadows a great centennial climacteric in these intellectual disciplines. For long the butt of the critic from the heterodox fringes, 'rational economic man' has increasingly come under an additional challenge from the mainstream in recent years, principally because of developments in game theory, experimental economics and psychology. Optimizing activity will be recognized as no more than a special case of a larger set of possible modes of behaviour, with all of them being required to render viable explanations of their origin and evolution.

It is now widely acknowledged that once such factors as uncertainty, the costs of decision-making, and appraisals of the rationality of others, are brought into the picture, the meaning of rationality becomes problematic (Sugden, 1991; Conlisk, 1996). Consequently, this core element in the neoclassical paradigm is being questioned. Eirik Furubotn (1997, p. 452) – a prominent contributor to the new institutional economics – argued that

> the New Institutional Economics has reached a watershed in its development. Although there are still writers who seek to deal with institutional questions through the use of extended neoclassical theory, this approach is coming under increasing criticism and would seem to be unsustainable in the long run.

Furthermore, 'the orthodox neoclassical model has proved to be an essentially misleading guide for modern institutional economics.' Consequently, the new institutional economics 'must lose its connections with neoclassicism' (Furubotn, 1997, pp. 454–8). This is evidence of the extent of a rethink now being considered in some quarters. As economics in general, and the new institutional economics in particular, search for a new set of core principles, the possibility of a fruitful dialogue with other traditions of social thought becomes enlarged.

Biology is widely seen as the science of the twenty-first century. We may conjecture that the renewed social sciences will find some of their fundamental precepts in principles of evolution, taking strong inspiration from the methodology and approach of Darwin, but with due sensitivity to the differences between evolution in the social and the natural sphere. We shall thereby take a huge step back in time and visit the evolutionary controversies of the 1890s and early 1900s – and the intellectual world of Peirce, James, Veblen, and Commons – and discover that much of what we want to say has already been said before. Only then will we be able to read the works of the 'old' institutionalists and fully appreciate their achievement.

Neoclassical economics as a special case of institutional economics

Where would a revived institutional and evolutionary economics stand in relationship to the neoclassical economics that prevailed for much of the twentieth century? In at least two senses, institutional economics is more general than neoclassical economics. First, at the centre of neoclassical economics is the idea of rational choice in the context of scarcity. The concept of scarcity is typically used in overly loose and general terms. In reality, not all resources are scarce, at least in the Robbinsian sense of being 'limited' in supply. For example, factors such as trust and human skill can sometimes be enhanced rather than diminished by their use. The concept of scarcity is relevant in a *relative* sense, concerning immediate availability of resources for an agent. In an *absolute* sense scarcity applies to natural resources, but it does not apply to all resources. Lionel Robbins (1932) and others conflated these two meanings, overlooking the fact that resource scarcity in an absolute sense is not universal (Hodgson, 2001c, pp. 277–9).

Following Herbert Simon (1957, 1979), it is now widely acknowledged that human computational capacities are scarce (in a relative sense). For those that wish to employ them, human skills and competences are also of limited immediate availability (Pelikan, 1988, 1992). Furthermore, especially since the 1970s and the rise of the 'new' institutional economics, it is now realized that the essential institutional context of human activity cannot be established without costs: institutions are neither immediately available nor a free good. Institutional construction is costly, in terms of time, resources and human effort. As shown in this volume, the 'old' institutional economics recognized the computational limitations of the human brain, the importance of institutions, and the costs and difficulties involved in their establishment and maintenance. In these senses, both rationality and institutions are scarce (Pagano, 2000). Consequentially, institutional economics involves an extension and deeper understanding of the principle of relative scarcity and thus, in this respect at least, is more general than the neoclassical position.

Furthermore, because rationality always depends on prior habits and instincts as props, rational optimization alone can never supply the complete explanation of human behaviour and institutions for which some theorists seem to be striving (Vanberg, 2002). For this reason, neoclassical economics is a restricted explanatory discourse; it assumes rationality without explaining its genesis. In contrast, before addressing rationality itself, Veblenian institutional economics takes the more general starting point of Darwinian evolution, thereby explaining the ubiquity and primacy of habits, instincts and rules.

In contrast to their image as myopic and anti-theoretical data-gatherers, institutionalists have the potential to achieve a higher level of theoretical generality in this respect, and in a sphere where some general observations are appropriate. Sidney Winter (1971) has argued that neoclassical economics is a special case of the behavioural economics of Simon (1957) and others. Institutional economics attempts to add to behavioural economics an explanation of the cultural evolution of the heuristic rules of decision-making that are employed by boundedly rational agents. On these additional grounds, both behavioural economics and neoclassical economics are special cases of institutional economics. As the Indian institutionalist Radhakamal Mukerjee (1940, p. 89) wrote: 'Institutional economics deals not only with the abstract laws governing the relations between restricted or scarce goods and satisfactions or services, but also with the entire social and institutional structure'. At its theoretical foundations, institutional economics has greater generality; it encompasses neoclassical economics as a special case, where the habitual and instinctive basis of rationality, along with much of the natural and institutional environment, are all taken as given, and where the principle of scarcity is not itself applied to human rationality and social institutions. Institutionalism is more general, in that it has a deeper explanatory scope and that scarcity is also applied to institutions and rationality.

The promise of Darwinism for the social sciences

In another respect, Veblenian institutional and evolutionary economics attains a higher degree of generality. It adopts Darwinian principles, which ostensibly apply not only to economic evolution but also to all open, complex and evolving systems. As argued in the preceding volume (Hodgson, 2001c), Darwinism combines a general theoretical framework with pointers to historically and context specific analysis that is highly relevant for the social sciences.

Despite considerable resistance to its radical message from within both economics and sociology, the Darwinian movement within the sciences has now built up such a huge momentum that it is unstoppable. A vital task for the social sciences is to come to grips with the nature and importance of Darwinism. Above all, Darwinism is a new philosophical system, signalling an unwavering commitment to causal explanation. It involves algorithmic explanations of process, rather than an exclusive focus on the properties of equilibria. It moves us from an equation-based towards an algorithm-based science.

Another feature of Darwinism that is insufficiently acknowledged, even by resolute Darwinians, is its reliance on an irreducibly layered ontology involving emergent properties. Consequently, despite several impressions to the contrary, Darwinism itself prescribes some limits to reductionism.

A brief explanation is necessary. Even in its simplest form, Darwinism involves a conceptualization of three domains: the individual organism or unit, the population of organisms or units, and their environment. Darwinian laws or principles apply to whole populations, but have implications concerning the characteristics of individuals in relation to their population. Natural selection is a case of 'downward causation' in that it posits laws concerning populations and systems that bear down upon individuals. Hence, even in the simplest presentation of Darwinian theory, there are at least two ontological levels: concerning individuals and regarding a whole population of varied individuals.

Any population of entities has emergent properties that are not reducible to component individuals alone. Most trivially, the statistical concepts of mean and variance are emergent in that they relate to a set of individuals, rather than to any individual alone. More profoundly, if there are causal interactions between (varied) individuals themselves, and between them and their environment, then we should expect further emergent properties in the system. For these reasons, Darwinism involves a commitment both to an irreducibly layered ontology and to the possibility of emergent properties at higher levels.

Matters become even more complicated when we bring the human mind into the picture, along with the mysteries of consciousness and intentionality and the causal explanations of their emergence. A Darwinian approach to the mind–body problem (dubbed in Chapter 4 above as the 'second Darwinian philosophical principle') is an 'emergentist materialism' where human intentions are regarded as emergent properties of materialist interactions within the human nervous system (Bunge, 1980). The relationship between nature and mind is thus addressed within the philosophical framework of emergence. There is a mental level above that of matter. Neural configurations or ideas themselves become possible units of replication and selection in an evolutionary process at this second level (Edelman, 1987; Plotkin, 1994). In some respects this is an old approach to understanding the human mind, elements of which were proposed by several authors in the nineteenth century, including Darwin himself (R. Richards, 1987).

The incorporation of social structures and institutions into the picture adds yet another dimension. Just as mind depends on matter but is not reducible to it, society depends on individuals but cannot be explained in terms of individuals alone. This adds yet another ontological layer: above the material and the psychic is the social. Furthermore, complex societies themselves may consist of subsystems and multiple ontological layers. In general, properties of societies or institutions cannot be entirely reduced to those of individuals.

How can we help to resolve the problem of agency and structure from a Darwinian perspective? First, the implicit anti-reductionism of this generalized Darwinism rules out both methodological individualism and methodological collectivism, as defined in this work. The obverse and positive side of this anti-reductionism is the multi-level character of Darwinian evolutionary theory. This points to the possibility of macroeconomics and the necessity of levels of analysis above that of the individual. Second, as noted above, Darwinism involves a conceptual shift from statical comparisons to causal, algorithmic processes. The relationship between agents and structures must be considered as a causal process through time, rather than a static relationship. How do individuals change in their interaction with structures, and how do interactions between individuals give rise to structural changes? Third, Darwinism emphasizes both the interactions between individuals and their with interactions between individuals and their social and natural environment. Fourth, Darwinism requires, at least in principle, an evolutionary explanation of origin. The individual, individual rationality, individual aims and social structure must all be causally explained. This implies that human intentions and intentionality cannot be regarded as a permanent explanatory starting point. Explanation in terms of intentions is provisional but never sufficient. Both individual intentions and the human capacity of intentionality have to be causally explained, even if we abstract from this explanation on a provisional basis in some spheres of enquiry.

Darwinism does not provide all the answers. With its explicit recognition of historical processes and context dependence, it points to the irreplaceable requirement for historically sensitive theory (Blute, 1997). The previous volume has explored this issue in greater detail (Hodgson, 2001c). The further development of the Darwinian perspective outlined here provides us with a full theoretical research agenda. Ironically, at the beginning of the twenty-first century, long after the birth of institutional economics, we are in a position to begin the task of constructing a systematic foundation for this approach. Much belatedly, but in a modern scientific context that is much more conducive to its development, we can begin to provide the systematic theoretical foundation that was so tragically and precariously lacking in institutional economics in the twentieth century.

We are both natural and social beings, and social science cannot advance without full recognition of this fact. As investigators into our own legacy, we marvel at the wonders of both natural and social evolution; we acknowledge both the majesty and mystery of our inheritance and the challenges of our future. It is in this spirit that institutional economics was born. Rehabilitated as a genuinely interdisciplinary science – despite a global academia unfortunately inhibited by its extreme disciplinary compartmentalization and its obsession with technique over substance – institutionalism can once again make a difference.

Bibliography

Adams, Douglas (1979) *The Hitch Hiker's Guide to the Galaxy* (London: Barker).

Adorno, Theodor (1972) *The Jargon of Authenticity* (Chicago: Northwestern University Press).

Agazzi, Evandro (ed.) (1991) *The Problem of Reductionism in Science* (Dordrecht: Kluwer).

Åkerman, Johan (1932) *Economic Progress and Economic Crises*, translated from the Swedish edition of 1931 by Elizabeth Sprigge and Claude Napier (London: Macmillan).

Åkerman, Johan (1938) *Das Problem der sozialökonomischen Synthese* (Lund: Gleerup).

Åkerman, Johan (1942) 'Ekonomisk Kalkyl och Kausalanalys', *Ekonomisk Tidskrift*, No. 1. Translated as 'Economic Plans and Causal Analysis', *International Economic Papers*, no. 4, 1954, pp. 181–96.

Albert, Alexa and Ramstad, Yngve (1997) 'The Social Psychological Underpinnings of Commons's Institutional Economics: The Significance of Dewey's *Human Nature and Conduct*', *Journal of Economic Issues*, **31**(4), December, pp. 881–916.

Albert, Alexa and Ramstad, Yngve (1998) 'The Social Psychological Underpinnings of Commons's Institutional Economics II: The Concordance of George Herbert Mead's "Social Self" and John R. Commons's "Will"', *Journal of Economic Issues*, **32**(1), March, pp. 1–46.

Albin, Peter S. (1998) *Barriers and Bounds to Rationality: Essays on Economic Complexity and Dynamics in Interactive Systems* (Princeton: Princeton University Press).

Alchian, Armen A. (1950) 'Uncertainty, Evolution and Economic Theory', *Journal of Political Economy*, **58**(2), June, pp. 211–22.

Aldrich, Howard E. (1999) *Organizations Evolving* (London: Sage).

Aldrich, Howard E. and Martinez, Martha (2003) 'Entrepreneurship as Social Construction: A Multi-Level Evolutionary Approach', in Acs, Z. C. and Audretsch, David B. (eds) *Handbook of Entrepreneurial Research* (Boston: Kluwer), pp. 359–99.

Alexander, Samuel (1892) 'Natural Selection in Morals', *International Journal of Ethics*, **2**(4), July, pp. 409–39.

Alexander, Samuel (1920) *Space, Time and Deity*, 2 vols (London: Macmillan).

Alland, Alexander, Jr (1967) *Evolution and Human Behavior* (New York: Natural History Press).

Allen, Garland (1968) 'Thomas H. Morgan and the Problem of Natural Selection', *Journal of the History of Biology*, **1**, pp. 113–39.

Allen, Peter M. and McGlade, J. M. (1987) 'Evolutionary Drive: The Effects of Microscopic Diversity, Error-Making and Noise', *Foundations of Physics*, **17**(7), pp. 723–38.

Allen, Peter M. and McGlade, J. M. (1989) 'Optimality, Adequacy and the Evolution of Complexity', in Christiansen, P. and Parmentier, R. (1989) *Structure, Coherence and Chaos in Dynamical Systems* (Manchester: Manchester University Press), pp. 3–21.

Allport, Floyd H. (1924) 'The Group Fallacy in Relation to Social Science', *American Journal of Sociology*, **29**(6), May, pp. 688–706.

Allport, Floyd H. (1927) 'The Psychological Nature of Political Structure', *American Political Science Review*, **21**(3), August, pp. 611–18.

Alpert, Harry (1938) 'Operational Definitions in Sociology', *American Sociological Review*, **3**(6), December, pp. 855–61.

Althusser, Louis and Balibar, Étienne (1970) *Reading Capital*, translated from the French edition of 1968 by Ben Brewster (London: NLB).

Ammon, Otto (1895) *Die Gesellschaftsordnung Und Ihre Natürlichen Grundlagen* (Jena: Fischer).

Anderson, Karl L. (1933) 'The Unity of Veblen's Theoretical System', *Quarterly Journal of Economics*, **47**(4), August, pp. 598–626.

Anderson, Philip W. (1972) 'More is Different: Broken Symmetry and the Nature of the Hierarchical Structure of Science', *Science*, **177**, no. 4047, 4 August, pp. 393–6.

Anderson, Philip W., Arrow, Kenneth J. and Pines, David (eds) (1988) *The Economy as an Evolving Complex System* (Reading, MA: Addison-Wesley).

Ansoff, H. Igor (1965) *Corporate Strategy* (New York: McGraw-Hill).

Aoki, Masahiko (2001) *Toward a Comparative Institutional Analysis* (Cambridge, MA: MIT Press).

Apel, Karl-Otto (1981) *Charles S. Peirce: From Pragmatism to Pragmaticism* (Amherst, MA: University of Massachusetts Press).

Archer, Margaret S. (1995) *Realist Social Theory: The Morphogenetic Approach* (Cambridge: Cambridge University Press).

Archer, Margaret S. (2000) *Being Human: The Problem of Agency* (Cambridge: Cambridge University Press).

Argyrous, George and Sethi, Rajiv (1996) 'The Theory of Evolution and the Evolution of Theory: Veblen's Methodology in Contemporary Perspective', *Cambridge Journal of Economics*, **20**(4), July, pp. 475–95.

Aristotle (1956) *Metaphysics*, edited and translated by John Warrington with an introduction by W. David Ross (London: Dent).

Armstrong, D. M. (1968) *A Materialist Theory of the Mind* (London: Routledge and Kegan Paul).

Arnold, A. J. and Fristrup, K. (1982) 'The Theory of Evolution by Natural Selection: A Hierarchical Expansion', *Paleobiology*, **8**, pp. 113–29.

Aronson, Jerrold L. (1984) *A Realist Philosophy of Science* (Basingstoke: Macmillan).

Arrow, Kenneth J. (1951) 'Alternative Approaches to the Theory of Choice in Risk-Taking Situations', *Econometrica*, **19**(4), pp. 404–37.

Arrow, Kenneth J. (1962) 'Economic Welfare and the Allocation of Resources to Invention', in Nelson, Richard R. (ed.) *The Rate and Direction of Inventive Activity: Economic and Social Factors* (Princeton: Princeton University Press), pp. 609–25. Reprinted in Arrow, Kenneth J. (1972) *Essays in the Theory of Risk-Bearing* (Amsterdam: North Holland).

Arrow, Kenneth J. (1968) 'Mathematical Models in the Social Sciences', in Brodbeck, May (ed.) *Readings in the Philosophy of the Social Sciences* (New York: Macmillan), pp. 635–67.

Arrow, Kenneth J. (1974) *The Limits of Organization* (New York: Norton).

Arrow, Kenneth J. (1986) 'Rationality of Self and Others in an Economic System', *Journal of Business*, **59**(4.2), October, pp. S385–S399. Reprinted in Hogarth and Reder (1987) and in Eatwell, John, Milgate, Murray and Newman, Peter (eds) (1987) *The New Palgrave Dictionary of Economics* (London: Macmillan), vol. 2.

Arrow, Kenneth J. (1994) 'Methodological Individualism and Social Knowledge', *American Economic Review (Papers and Proceedings)*, **84**(2), May, pp. 1–9.

Arthur, W. Brian (1988) 'Self-Reinforcing Mechanisms in Economics', in Anderson, Philip W., Arrow, Kenneth J. and Pines, David (eds) *The Economy as an Evolving Complex System* (Reading, MA: Addison-Wesley), pp. 9–31.

Arthur, W. Brian (1989) 'Competing Technologies, Increasing Returns, and Lock-in by Historical Events', *Economic Journal*, **99**(1), March, pp. 116–31.

Arthur, W. Brian (1994) *Increasing Returns and Path Dependence in the Economy* (Ann Arbor, MI: University of Michigan Press).

Arthur, W. Brian, Durlauf, Steven N., Lane and David A. (eds) (1997) *The Economy as an Evolving Complex System II* (Redwood City, CA: Addison-Wesley).

Ashley, William J. (1891) 'The Rehabilitation of Ricardo', *Economic Journal*, **1**(3), September, pp. 474–89.

Asso, Pier Franceso and Fiorito, Luca (2003a) 'Waging War Against Mechanical Man: The Knight–Copeland Controversy Over Behaviorism in Economics', *Research in the History of Economic Thought and Methodology*, **21-A**, pp. 65–104.

Asso, Pier Franceso and Fiorito, Luca (2003b) 'Lawrence Kelso Frank's Proto Ayresian Dichotomy', unpublished mimeo.

Augros, Robert and Stanciu, George (1987) *The New Biology: Discovering the Wisdom in Nature* (Boston: Shambhala).

Ault, Richard W. and Ekelund, Robert B., Jr (1988) 'Habit in Economic Analysis: Veblen and the Neoclassicals', *History of Political Economy*, **20**(3), Fall, pp. 431–45.

Aunger, Robert (ed.) (2000) *Darwinizing Culture: The Status of Memetics as a Science* (Oxford and New York: Oxford University Press).

Aunger, Robert (2002) *The Electric Meme: A New Theory of How We Think* (New York: Free Press).

Auyang, Sunny Y. (1998) *Foundations of Complex-System Theories: In Economics, Evolutionary Biology, and Statistical Physics* (New York and Cambridge: Cambridge University Press).

Axelrod, Robert M. (1984) *The Evolution of Cooperation* (New York: Basic Books).

Axelrod, Robert M. and Cohen, Michael D. (1999) *Harnessing Complexity: Organizational Implications of a Scientific Frontier* (New York: Free Press).

Ayala, Francisco J. and Dobzhansky, Theodosius (eds) (1974) *Studies in the Philosophy of Biology* (London, Berkeley and Los Angeles: Macmillan and University of California Press).

Ayres, Clarence E. (1918a) *The Nature of the Relationship Between Ethics and Economics* (Chicago: University of Chicago Press).

Ayres, Clarence E. (1918b) 'The Function and Problems of Economic Theory', *Journal of Political Economy*, **26**(1), January, pp. 69–90.

Ayres, Clarence E. (1918c) 'The Epistemological Significance of Social Psychology', *Journal of Philosophy, Psychology and Scientific Methods*, **15**(2), January, pp. 35–44.

Ayres, Clarence E. (1921a) 'Instinct and Capacity – I: The Instinct of Belief-in-Instincts', *Journal of Philosophy*, **18**, No. 21, October 13, pp. 561–5.

Ayres, Clarence E. (1921b) 'Instinct and Capacity – II: Homo Domesticus', *Journal of Philosophy*, **18**, No. 22, October 27, pp. 600–6.

Ayres, Clarence E. (1923) 'John Dewey: Naturalist', *The New Republic*, April 4, pp. 158–60.

Ayres, Clarence E. (1927) *Science: The False Messiah* (Indianapolis: Bobbs-Merrill).

Ayres, Clarence E. (1929) *Holier Than Thou: The Way of the Righteous* (Indianapolis: Bobbs-Merrill).

Ayres, Clarence E. (1932) *Huxley* (New York: Norton).

Ayres, Clarence E. (1935) 'Moral Confusion in Economics', *International Journal of Ethics*, **45**(2), January, pp. 170–99.

Ayres, Clarence E. (1936) 'Fifty Years' Developments in Ideas of Human Nature and Motivation', *American Economic Review (Papers and Proceedings)*, **26**(1), March, pp. 224–36.

Ayres, Clarence E. (1938) *The Problem of Economic Order* (New York: Farrar and Rinehart).

Ayres, Clarence E. (1942) 'Economic Value and Scientific Synthesis', *American Journal of Economics and Sociology*, **1**(4), July, pp. 343–60.

Ayres, Clarence E. (1943) 'The Twilight of the Price System', *Antioch Review*, **3**, Summer, pp. 162–81.

Ayres, Clarence E. (1944) *The Theory of Economic Progress*, 1st edn (Chapel Hill, NC: University of North Carolina Press).

Ayres, Clarence E. (1946) *The Divine Right of Capital* (Boston: Houghton Mifflin).

Ayres, Clarence E. (1951) 'The Co-ordinates of Institutionalism', *American Economic Review (Papers and Proceedings)*, **41**(2), May, pp. 47–55.

Ayres, Clarence E. (1952) *The Industrial Economy: Its Technological Basis and Institutional Destiny* (Cambridge, MA: Houghton Mifflin).

Ayres, Clarence E. (1953) 'The Role of Technology in Economic Theory', *American Economic Review (Papers and Proceedings)*, **43**(2), May, pp. 279–87.

Ayres, Clarence E. (1958) 'Veblen's Theory of Instincts Reconsidered', in Dowd, Douglas F. (ed.) (1958) *Thorstein Veblen: A Critical Appraisal* (Ithaca, NY: Cornell University Press), pp. 25–37.

Ayres, Clarence E. (1960) 'Institutionalism and Economic Development', *Southwestern Social Science Quarterly*, **41**(2), June, pp. 45–62.

Ayres, Clarence E. (1961) *Towards a Reasonable Society: The Values of Industrial Civilization* (Austin: University of Texas Press).

Ayres, Clarence E. (1963) 'The Legacy of Thorstein Veblen', in Dorfman *et al.* (1963, pp. 46–62).

Ayres, Clarence E. (1967) 'Guaranteed Income: An Institutionalist View', in Theobald, Robert (ed.), *The Guaranteed Income: Next Step in Socioeconomic Evolution?* (New York: Doubleday), pp. 169–82.

Ayres, Clarence E. (1968) 'The Price System and Public Policy', *Journal of Economic Issues*, **2**(3), September, pp. 342–44.

Ayres, Clarence E. (1973) 'Prolegomenon to Institutionalism', introduction to the combined reprint of Ayres (1927, 1929) (New York: Augustus Kelley).

Babbage, Charles (1832) *On the Economy of Machinery and Manufactures*, 1st edn (London: John Murray).

Bagehot, Walter (1872) *Physics and Politics, or, Thoughts on the Application of the Principles of 'Natural Selection' and 'Inheritance' to Political Society* (London: Henry King).

Bain, Alexander (1859) *The Emotions and the Will* (London: Longmans, Green, Reader and Dyer).

Bain, Alexander (1870) *Logic*, 2 vols (London: Longmans, Green, Reader and Dyer).

Bak, Per (1996) *How Nature Works: The Science of Self-Organized Criticality* (Oxford: Oxford University Press; and New York: Copernicus).

Baldwin, James Mark (1894) 'Imitation: A Chapter in the Natural History of Consciousness', *Mind*, **3**(9), January, pp. 26–55.

Baldwin, James Mark (1896) 'A New Factor in Evolution', *American Naturalist*, **30**, pp. 441–51, 536–53.

Baldwin, James Mark (1909) *Darwin and the Humanities*, 1st edn (Baltimore: Review Publishing).

Bandura, Albert (1986) *Social Foundations of Thought and Action: A Social Cognitive Theory* (Englewood Cliffs, NJ: Prentice-Hall).

Bannister, Robert C. (1973) 'William Graham Sumner's Social Darwinism: A Reconsideration', *History of Political Economy*, **5**(1), Spring, pp. 89–108.

Bannister, Robert C. (1979) *Social Darwinism; Science and Myth in Anglo-American Social Thought* (Philadelphia: Temple University Press).

Barber, William J. (1988) *From New Era to New Deal: Herbert Hoover, the Economists, and American Economic Policy, 1921–1933* (Cambridge: Cambridge University Press).

Barber, William J. (1994) 'The Divergent Fates of Two Strands of "Institutionalist" Doctrine During the New Deal Years', *History of Political Economy*, **26**(4), Winter, pp. 569–87.

Barber, William J. (1996) *Design Within Disorder: Franklin D. Roosevelt, the Economists, and the Shaping of American Economic Policy* (Cambridge: Cambridge University Press).

Barnard, Chester I. (1938) *The Functions of the Executive* (Cambridge, MA: Harvard University Press).

Barrett, Paul H., Gautrey, Peter J., Herbert, Sandra, Kohn, David and Smith, Sydney (eds) (1987) *Charles Darwin's Notebooks, 1836–1844: Geology, Transmutation of Species, Metaphysical Enquiries* (Cambridge: Cambridge University Press).

Bateson, Patrick and Martin, Paul (1999) *Design for a Life: How Behaviour Develops* (London: Jonathan Cape).

Baylis, Charles A. (1929) 'The Philosophic Functions of Emergence', *Philosophical Review*, **38**(4), July, pp. 372–84.

Bazzoli, Laure (1999) *L'économie politique de John R. Commons: Essai sur l'institutionnalisme en sciences sociales* (Paris: Éditions L'Harmattan).

Bazzoli, Laure (2000) 'Institutional Economics and the Specificity of Social Evolution: About the Contribution of J. R. Commons', in Louçã and Perlman (2000, pp. 64–82).

Bazzoli, Laure and Dutraive, Véronique (1999) 'The Legacy of J. R. Commons' Conception of Economics as a Science of Behaviour', in Groenewegen, John and Vromen, Jack (eds), *Institutions and the Evolution of Capitalism: Implications of Evolutionary Economics* (Cheltenham: Edward Elgar), pp. 52–77.

Becker, Gary S. (1962) 'Irrational Behavior and Economic Theory', *Journal of Political Economy*, **70**(1), February, pp. 1–13.

Becker, Gary S. (1976) 'Altruism, Egoism, and Genetic Fitness: Economics and Sociobiology', *Journal of Economic Literature*, **14**(2), December, pp. 817–26.

Becker, Gary S. (1992) 'Habits, Addictions and Traditions', *Kyklos*, **45**, Fasc. 3, pp. 327–46.

Becker, Gary S. and Murphy, Kevin M. (1988) 'A Theory of Rational Addiction', *Journal of Political Economy*, **96**(4), pp. 675–700.

Beckerman, Ansgar, Flohr, Hans and Kim, Jaegwon (eds) (1992) *Emergence or Reduction? Essays on the Prospects of Nonreductive Physicalism* (Berlin: De Gruyter), pp. 49–93.

Bellomy, Donald C. (1984) '"Social Darwinism" Revisited', *Perspectives in American History*, New Series, **1**, pp. 1–129.

Benedict, Ruth (1934) *Patterns of Culture* (New York: New American Library).

Ben-Ner, Avner and Putterman, Louis (2000) 'Some Implications of Evolutionary Psychology for the Study of Preferences and Institutions', *Journal of Economic Behavior and Organization*, **43**(1), September, pp. 91–9.

Bennett, A. W. (1870) 'The Theory of Selection from a Mathematical Point of View', *Nature*, **3**, pp. 30–31.

Bentley, Arthur F. (1908) *The Process of Government: A Study of Social Pressures* (Bloomington, IN: Principia Press).

Berger, Peter and Luckmann, Thomas (1966) *The Social Construction of Reality: A Treatise on the Sociology of Knowledge* (Harmondsworth: Penguin).

Bergson, Henri (1911) *Creative Evolution*, translated from the French edition of 1907 (New York: Henry Holt).

Bergstrom, Theodore C. (2002) 'Evolution of Social Behavior: Individual and Group Selection', *Journal of Economic Perspectives*, **16**(2), Spring, pp. 67–88.

Berle, Adolf A. and Means, Gardiner C. (1932) *The Modern Corporation and Private Property* (New York: Commerce Clearing House).

Bernal, John Desmond (1957) *Science in History* (London: Watts).

Bernanke, Ben S. (1983) 'Nonmonetary Effects of the Financial Crisis in the Propagation of the Great Depression', *American Economic Review*, **73**(3), June, pp. 257–76.

Bernard, Luther L. (1924) *Instinct: A Study in Social Psychology* (New York: Holt).

Bernstein, Michael A. (2001) *A Perilous Progress: Economists and Public Purpose in Twentieth-Century America* (Princeton, NJ: Princeton University Press).

Bhaskar, Roy (1975) *A Realist Theory of Science*, 1st edn (Leeds: Leeds Books).

Bhaskar, Roy (1989) *The Possibility of Naturalism: A Philosophic Critique of the Contemporary Human Sciences*, 2nd edn (Brighton: Harvester).

Biddle, Jeff E. (1990a) 'The Role of Negotiational Psychology in J. R. Commons's Proposed Reconstruction of Political Economy', *Review of Political Economy*, 2(1), March, pp. 1–23.

Biddle, Jeff E. (1990b) 'Purpose and Evolution in Commons's Institutionalism', *History of Political Economy*, 22(1), Spring, pp. 19–47.

Biddle, Jeff E. (1998) 'Social Science and the Making of Social Policy: Wesley Mitchell's Vision', in Rutherford (1998b, pp. 43–79).

Biddle, Jeff E. and Samuels, Warren J. (1998) 'John R. Commons and the Compatibility of Neoclassical and Institutional Economics', in Holt, Richard P. F. and Pressman, Steven (eds) *Economics and its Discontents: Twentieth Century Dissenting Economists* (Cheltenham: Edward Elgar), pp. 40–55.

Binmore, Kenneth (1994) *Playing Fair: Game Theory and the Social Contract. Volume 1* (Cambridge, MA: MIT Press).

Binmore, Kenneth (1998a) *Just Playing: Game Theory and the Social Contract. Volume 2* (Cambridge, MA: MIT Press).

Binmore, Kenneth (1998b) Review of *Complexity and Cooperation* by Robert Axelrod, *Journal of Artificial Societies and Social Situations*, 1(1). http://jasss.soc.surrey.ac.uk/JASSS/1/1/review1.html

Binmore, Kenneth (1999) 'Goat's Wool', in Heertje, Arnold (ed.) (1999) *Makers of Modern Economics*, vol. 4 (Cheltenham: Edward Elgar), pp. 119–39.

Blanshard, Brand (1958) 'The Case for Determinism', in Hook, Sidney (ed.) (1958) *Determinism and Freedom in the Age of Modern Science* (New York and London: Collier Macmillan), pp. 19–30.

Blau, Peter (ed.) (1975) *Approaches to the Study of Social Structure* (New York: Free Press).

Blaug, Mark (1999) 'The Formalist Revolution or What Happened to Orthodox Economics After World War II?', in Backhouse, Roger E. and Creedy, John (eds) *From Classical Economics to the Theory of the Firm: Essays in Honour of D. P. O'Brien* (Cheltenham: Edward Elgar), pp. 257–80.

Blaug, Mark (2003) 'The Formalist Revolution of the 1950s', in Samuels *et. al.* (2003, pp. 395–410).

Blitz, David (1992) *Emergent Evolution: Qualitative Novelty and the Levels of Reality* (Dordrecht: Kluwer).

Blumer, Herbert (1969) *Symbolic Interactionism: Perspective and Method* (Chicago: University of Chicago Press).

Blute, Marion (1979) 'Sociocultural Evolutionism: An Untried Theory', *Behavioral Science Research*, 24, pp. 46–59.

Blute, Marion (1997) 'History Versus Science: The Evolutionary Solution', *Canadian Journal of Sociology*, 22(3), pp. 345–64.

Boakes, Robert (1984) *From Darwin to Behaviourism: Psychology and the Minds of Animals* (Cambridge and New York: Cambridge University Press).

Boas, Franz (1894) 'Human Faculty as Determined by Race', *Proceedings of the American Association for the Advancement of Science*, 43, pp. 301–27. Reprinted in Ryan (2001, vol. 2).

Bode, B. H. (1922) 'Critical Realism', *Journal of Philosophy*, 19(3), February, pp. 68–78.

Boesiger, Ernest (1974) 'Evolutionary Theories after Lamarck and Darwin', in Ayala, Francisco J. and Dobzhansky, Theodosius (eds) *Studies in the Philosophy of Biology* (London, Berkeley and Los Angeles: Macmillan and University of California Press), pp. 21–44.

Bogdan, Radu (1997) *Interpreting Minds: The Evolution of Practice* (Cambridge, MA: MIT Press).

Bogdan, Radu (2000) *Minding Minds: Evolving a Reflexive Mind in Interpreting Others* (Cambridge, MA: MIT Press).

Boring, Edwin G. (1950) 'The Influence of Evolutionary Theory Upon American Psychological Thought', in Persons (1950, pp. 267–98).

Boudon, Raymond (1981) *The Logic of Social Action* (New York: Routledge and Kegan Paul).

Boudreaux, D. J. and Holcombe, R. G. (1989) 'The Coasian and Knightian Theories of the Firm', *Managerial and Decision Economics*, **10**, pp. 147–154.

Boulding, Kenneth E. (1957) 'A New Look at Institutionalism', *American Economic Review (Papers and Proceedings)*, **47**(2), May, pp. 1–12.

Boulding, Kenneth E. (1981) *Evolutionary Economics* (Beverly Hills, CA: Sage Publications).

Bourdieu, Pierre (1990) *The Logic of Practice*, translated by Richard Nice from the French edition of 1980 (Stanford and Cambridge: Stanford University Press and Polity Press).

Bourdieu, Pierre and Wacquant, Loïc J. D. (1992) *An Invitation to Reflective Sociology* (Cambridge: Polity Press).

Bovill, Edward W. (1958) *Golden Trade of the Moors* (Oxford: Oxford University Press).

Bowie, Norman E. (1988) 'The Paradox of Profit', in N. Dale Wright (ed.) (1988) *Papers on the Ethics of Administration* (Provo, UT: Brigham Young University Press).

Bowler, Peter J. (1983) *The Eclipse of Darwinism: Anti-Darwinian Evolution Theories in the Decades around 1900* (Baltimore: Johns Hopkins University Press).

Bowler, Peter J. (1988) *The Non-Darwinian Revolution: Reinterpreting a Historical Myth* (Baltimore: Johns Hopkins University Press).

Bowles, Samuel (2002) *Economics, Institutions and Behavior: An Evolutionary Approach to Microeconomic Theory* (Princeton, NJ: Princeton University Press).

Boyd, Robert and Richerson, Peter J. (1980) 'Sociobiology, Culture and Economic Theory', *Journal of Economic Behavior and Organization*, **1**(1), March, pp. 97–121.

Boyd, Robert and Richerson, Peter J. (1985) *Culture and the Evolutionary Process* (Chicago: University of Chicago Press).

Brace, Charles Loring (1863) *The Races of the Old World* (London: Murray).

Brandon, Robert N. (1996) *Concepts and Methods in Evolutionary Biology* (Cambridge and New York: Cambridge University Press).

Brandon, Robert N. and Burian, Richard M. (eds) (1984) *Genes, Organisms, Populations: Controversies Over the Units of Selection* (Cambridge, MA: MIT Press).

Breit, William (1973) 'Clarence Ayres's Theoretical Institutionalism', *Social Science Quarterly*, **54**(2), September, pp. 244–57.

Brightman, Edgar S. (ed.) (1927) *Proceedings of the Sixth International Congress of Philosophy, Harvard University, 13–17 September 1926* (London and New York: Longmans, Green).

Brinkman, Richard (1997) 'Toward a Culture-Conception of Technology', *Journal of Economic Issues*, **31**(4), December, pp. 1027–38.

Broad, Charlie D. (1925) *The Mind and Its Place in Nature* (London: Routledge and Kegan Paul).

Broda, Philippe (1998) 'Commons versus Veblen on the Place of the Individual in the Social Process', in Rutherford (1998b, pp. 210–30).

Bronfenbrenner, Martin (1987) 'A Conversation with Martin Bronfenbrenner', *Eastern Economic Journal*, **13**(1), January–March, pp. 1–6.

Bronowski, Jacob (1973) *The Ascent of Man* (Boston: Little Brown).

Brooks, Daniel R. and Wiley, E. O. (1988) *Evolution as Entropy: Toward a Unified Theory of Biology*, 2nd edn (Chicago: University of Chicago Press).

Brown, John Seely and Duguid, Paul (1991) 'Organizational Learning and Communities of Practice: Toward a Unified View of Working, Learning and Innovation', *Organizational Science*, **2**(1), pp. 40–57.

Brown, Roger W. (1973) *A First Language: The Early Stages* (Cambridge, MA: Harvard University Press).

Bruce, Kyle (2000) 'Conflict and Conversion: Henry S. Dennison and the Shaping of J. K. Galbraith's Economic Thought', *Journal of Economic Issues*, **34**(4), December, pp. 949–67.

Bruce, Kyle and Nyland, Chris (2001) 'Scientific Management, Institutionalism, and Business Stabilization: 1903–1923', *Journal of Economic Issues*, **35**(4), December, pp. 955–78.

Buchanan, James M. (1968) 'Knight, Frank H.', *International Encyclopaedia of the Social Sciences*, vol. 8, pp. 424–8.

Buchanan, James M. (1969) 'Is Economics the Science of Choice?', in Erich Streissler (ed.) *Roads to Freedom: Essays in Honour of Friedrich A. von Hayek* (London: Routledge and Kegan Paul), pp. 47–64.

Buchanan, James M. (1976) 'Methods and Morals in Economics: The Ayres–Knight Discussion', in Breit, William and Culbertson, William P., Jr (eds) *Science and Ceremony: The Institutional Economics of C. E. Ayres* (Austin: University of Texas Press), pp. 164–74.

Buchanan, Mark (2001) *Ubiquity: The Science of History ... or Why the World is Simpler Than We Think* (New York: Crown).

Buckle, Henry Thomas (1858) *History of Civilization in England*, 2 vols (London: Longmans Green).

Bukharin, Nikolai (1969) *Historical Materialism: A System of Sociology*, translated from the Russian edition of 1921 (Ann Arbor: University of Michigan Press).

Bunge, Mario A. (1959) *Causality: The Place of the Causal Principle in Modern Science* (Cambridge, MA: Harvard University Press).

Bunge, Mario A. (1973a) *Method, Model and Matter* (Dordrecht, Holland: Reidel).

Bunge, Mario A. (1973b) *The Philosophy of Physics* (Dordrecht, Holland: Reidel).

Bunge, Mario A. (1980) *The Mind–Body Problem: A Psychobiological Approach* (Oxford: Pergamon).

Bunge, Mario A. (1998) *Social Science Under Debate: A Philosophical Perspective* (Toronto: University of Toronto Press).

Burge, Tyler (1986) 'Individualism and Psychology', *Philosophical Review*, **95**(1), January, pp. 3–45.

Burkhardt, Richard W., Jr (1984) 'The Zoological Philosophy of J. B. Lamarck', in Lamarck (1984, pp. xv–xxxix).

Burnham, John C. (1972) 'Instinct Theory and the German Reaction to Weismannism', *Journal of the History of Biology*, **5**, pp. 321–8.

Burns, Arthur Frank and Mitchell, Wesley C. (1946) *Measuring Business Cycles* (New York: National Bureau of Economic Research).

Burns, Eveline M. (1931) 'Does Institutionalism Complement or Compete with "Orthodox Economics"?', *American Economic Review*, **21**(1), March, pp. 80–7.

Burt, Cyril (1962) 'The Concept of Consciousness', *British Journal of Psychology*, **53**, pp. 229–42.

Bush, Paul Dale (1986) 'On the Concept of Ceremonial Encapsulation', *The Review of Institutional Thought*, vol. 3, December, pp. 25–45.

Bush, Paul Dale (1987) 'The Theory of Institutional Change', *Journal of Economic Issues*, **21**(3), September, pp. 1075–116.

Bush, Paul Dale (1999) 'Veblen's "Olympian Detachment" Reconsidered', *History of Economic Ideas*, **7**(3), pp. 127–51.

Bush, Paul Dale (2002) Email communication to G. M. Hodgson, dated 31 December 2002.

Buss, David M. (1999) *Evolutionary Psychology: The New Science of the Mind* (Needham Heights, MA: Allyn and Bacon).

Buss, Leo W. (1987) *The Evolution of Individuality* (Princeton, NJ: Gordon and Breach).

Butler, Samuel (1878) *Life and Habit* (London: Trübner).

Caldwell, Bruce J. (1982) *Beyond Positivism: Economic Methodology in the Twentieth Century* (London: Allen and Unwin).

Calvin, William H. (2002) *A Brain for All Seasons: Human Evolution and Abrupt Climate Change* (Chicago: University of Chicago Press).

Camic, Charles (1986) 'The Matter of Habit', *American Journal of Sociology*, **91**(5), March, pp. 1039–87.

Camic, Charles (ed.) (1991) *Talcott Parsons: The Early Essays* (Chicago: University of Chicago Press).

Camic, Charles (1992) 'Reputation and Predecessor Selection: Parsons and the Institutionalists', *American Sociological Review*, **54**(4), August, pp. 421–45.

Campbell, Donald T. (1965) 'Variation, Selection and Retention in Sociocultural Evolution', in Barringer *et al.* (1965, pp. 19–49). Reprinted in *General Systems*, **14**, 1969, pp. 69–85.

Campbell, Donald T. (1974a) 'Evolutionary Epistemology', in P. A. Schilpp (ed.) *The Philosophy of Karl Popper* (Vol. 14, I & II). *The Library of Living Philosophers* (La Salle, IL: Open Court), pp. 413–63.

Campbell, Donald T. (1974b) '"Downward Causation" in Hierarchically Organized Biological Systems', in Ayala, Francisco J. and Dobzhansky, Theodosius (eds) *Studies in the Philosophy of Biology* (London, Berkeley and Los Angeles: Macmillan and University of California Press), pp. 179–86.

Campbell, John H. (1987) 'The New Gene and Its Evolution', in Campbell, K. and Day, M. F. (eds) *Rates of Evolution* (London: Allen and Unwin), pp. 283–309.

Capshew, James (1999) *Psychologists on the March* (Cambridge and New York: Cambridge University Press).

Carnap, Rudolf (1934) *The Unity of Science* (London: Kegan Paul).

Carroll, Christopher D. (2000) 'Requiem for the Representative Consumer? Aggregative Implications of Microeconomic Consumption Behavior', *American Economic Review (Papers and Proceedings)*, **90**(2), May, pp. 110–15.

Carroll, Glenn R. (1984) 'Organizational Ecology', *Annual Review of Sociology*, **10**, pp. 71–93.

Cartwright, Nancy (1989) *Nature's Capacities and Their Measurement* (Oxford: Oxford University Press).

Chalmers, Alan F. (1985) *What is This Thing Called Science?* (Milton Keynes: Open University Press).

Chamberlain, Neil W. (1963) 'The Institutional Economics of John R. Commons', in Dorfman *et al.* (1963, pp. 63–94).

Chamberlin, Edward H. (1933) *The Theory of Monopolistic Competition: A Re-orientation of the Theory of Value*, 1st edn (Cambridge, MA: Harvard University Press).

Chamberlin, Edward H. (1948) 'An Experimental Imperfect Market', *Journal of Political Economy*, **56**(2), April, pp. 95–108.

Chattoe, Edmund (2002) 'Developing the Selectionist Paradigm in Sociology', *Sociology*, **34**(4), November, pp. 817–33.

Chiaromonte, Francesca and Dosi, Giovanni (1993) 'Heterogeneity, Competition, and Macroeconomic Dynamics', *Structural Change and Economic Dynamics*, **4**(1), June, pp. 39–63.

Childe, V. Gordon (1951) *Man Makes Himself* (New York: Mentor).

Choi, Young Back (1994) *Paradigms and Conventions: Uncertainty, Decision Making, and Entrepreneurship* (Ann Arbor, MI: University of Michigan Press).

Chomsky, Noam (1959) 'Review of *Verbal Behavior* by B. F. Skinner', *Language*, **35**, pp. 26–58.

Chugerman, Samuel (1939) *Lester F. Ward: The American Aristotle* (Durham, NC: Duke University Press).

Churchland, Patricia S. (1986) *Neurophilosophy: Toward a Unified Science of the Mind–Brain* (Cambridge, MA: MIT Press).

Churchland, Paul M. (1984) *Matter and Consciousness* (Cambridge, MA: MIT Press).

Churchland, Paul M. (1989) *A Neurocomputational Perspective: The Nature of Mind and the Structure of Science* (Cambridge, MA: MIT Press).

Clark, Andy (1997a) 'Economic Reason: The Interplay of Individual Learning and External Structure', in Drobak, John N. and Nye, John V. C. (eds) *The Frontiers of the New Institutional Economics* (San Diego and London: Academic Press), pp. 269–90.

Clark, Andy (1997b) *Being There: Putting the Brain, Body and World Together Again* (Cambridge, MA: MIT Press).

Clark, John Bates (1885) *The Philosophy of Wealth: Economic Principles Newly Formulated* (London and New York: Macmillan).

Clark, John Bates (1887) 'The Limits to Competition', *Political Science Quarterly*, **2**(1), March, pp. 45–61. Republished in Clark, John Bates and Giddings, Franklin H. (1888) *Modern Distributive Process* (Boston: Ginn).

Clark, John Maurice (1917) 'Business Acceleration and the Law of Demand: A Technical Factor in Economic Cycles', *Journal of Political Economy*, **25**(1), March, pp. 217–35. Reprinted in Clark (1967).

Clark, John Maurice (1918) 'Economics and Modern Psychology', parts I and II, *Journal of Political Economy*, **26**(1–2), January–April, pp. 1–30, 136–66. Reprinted in Clark (1967).

Clark, John Maurice (1923) *Studies in the Economics of Overhead Costs* (Chicago: University of Chicago Press).

Clark, John Maurice (1925) 'Problems of Economic Theory – Discussion', *American Economic Review (Papers and Proceedings)*, **15**(1), Supplement, March, pp. 56–8.

Clark, John Maurice (1926) *Social Control of Business* (Chicago: University of Chicago Press).

Clark, John Maurice (1927) 'Recent Developments in Economics', in Hayes, Edward C. (ed.) *Recent Developments in the Social Sciences* (Philadelphia: Lippencott), pp. 213–306.

Clark, John Maurice (1967) *Preface to Social Economics* (New York: Augustus Kelley).

Cleary, Frank R. and Edwards, Daniel J. (1960) 'The Origins of the Contributors to the AER During the Fifties', *American Economic Review*, **50**(5), December, pp. 1011–14.

Cloak, F. T. (1975) 'Is a Cultural Ethology Possible?', *Human Ecology*, **3**(3), pp. 161–82.

Closson, Carlos C. (1896a) 'Dissociation by Displacement: A Phase of Social Selection', *Quarterly Journal of Economics*, **10**(2), January, pp. 156–86.

Closson, Carlos C. (1896b) 'Social Selection', *Journal of Political Economy*, **4**(4), September, pp. 449–66.

Coase, Ronald H. (1937) 'The Nature of the Firm', *Economica*, **4**, November, pp. 386–405.

Coase, Ronald H. (1984) 'The New Institutional Economics', *Journal of Institutional and Theoretical Economics*, **140**, pp. 229–31.

Coats, A. W. (1976) 'Clarence Ayres' Place in the History of American Economics: An Interim Assessment', in Breit, William and Culbertson, William P., Jr (eds) *Science and Ceremony: The Institutional Economics of C. E. Ayres* (Austin: University of Texas Press), pp. 23–48. Reprinted in Coats, A. W. (1992), *On the History of Economic Thought: British and American Economic Essays, Volume I* (London: Routledge).

Cobb, Charles W. and Douglas, Paul H. (1928) 'A Theory of Production', *American Economic Review (Papers and Prodeedings)*, **18**(1) Supplement, March, pp. 139–65.

Cohen, Avi J. and Harcourt, Geoffrey C. (2003) 'Whatever Happened to the Cambridge Capital Theory Controversies?', *Journal of Economic Perspectives*, **17**(1), Winter, pp. 199–214.

Cohen, Gerald A. (1978) *Karl Marx's Theory of History: A Defence* (Oxford: Oxford University Press).

Cohen, Jack and Stewart, Ian (1994) *The Collapse of Chaos: Discovering Simplicity in a Complex World* (London and New York: Viking).

Colander, David C. (ed.) (2000a) *The Complexity Vision and the Teaching of Economics* (Cheltenham: Edward Elgar).

Colander, David C. (2000b) *Complexity and the History of Economic Thought* (London and New York: Routledge).

Colander, David C. (2003) 'Are Institutionalists an Endangered Species?', *Journal of Economic Issues*, **37**(1), March, pp. 111–22.

Colander, David C. and Landreth, Harry (eds) (1996) *The Coming of Keynesianism to America: Conversations with the Founders of Keynesian Economics* (Aldershot: Edward Elgar).

Cole, William E. and Mogab, John W. (1987) 'The Transfer of Soft Technologies to Less-Developed Countries: Some Implications for the Technology/Ceremony Dichotomy', *Journal of Economic Issues*, **21**(1), March, pp. 309–20.

Coleman, James S. (1982) *The Asymmetric Society* (Syracuse: Syracuse University Press).

Coleman, James S. (1990) *Foundations of Social Theory* (Cambridge, MA: Harvard University Press).

Coleman, William (2001) 'The Strange "Laissez Faire" of Alfred Russel Wallace: The Connection Between Natural Selection and Political Economy Reconsidered', in Laurent and Nightingale (2001, pp. 36–48).

Commons, John R. (1897) 'Natural Selection, Social Selection, and Heredity', *The Arena*, **18**, July, pp. 90–7. Reprinted in Hodgson (1998e).

Commons, John R. (1899–1900) 'A Sociological View of Sovereignty', *American Journal of Sociology*, **5**(1–3) (1899), pp. 1–15, 155–71, 347–66; **5**(4–6) (1900), pp. 544–52, 683–95, 814–25; **6**(1) (1900), pp. 67–98. Reprinted as John R. Commons (1965) *A Sociological View of Sovereignty*, edited with an introduction by Joseph Dorfman (New York: Augustus Kelley).

Commons, John R. (1919) Review of 'Instincts in Industry. A Study of Working-Class Psychology' by Ordway Tead and 'Creative Impulse in Industry' by Helen Marlot, *American Economic Review*, **9**(2), June, pp. 312–16.

Commons, John R. (1920) *Races and Immigrants in America*, 2nd edn (New York: Macmillan).

Commons, John R. (1923) 'Wage Theories and Wage Policies', *American Economic Review (Papers and Proceedings)*, **13**(1), March, pp. 110–17.

Commons, John R. (1924) *Legal Foundations of Capitalism* (New York: Macmillan).

Commons, John R. (1925) 'Marx Today: Capitalism and Socialism', *Atlantic Monthly*, pp. 686–7.

Commons, John R. (1931) 'Institutional Economics', *American Economic Review*, **21**(4), December, pp. 648–57.

Commons, John R. (1934a) *Institutional Economics – Its Place in Political Economy* (New York: Macmillan).

Commons, John R. (1934b) *Myself: The Autobiography of John R. Commons* (New York: Macmillan).

Commons, John R. (1950) *The Economics of Collective Action*, edited by K. H. Parsons (New York: Macmillan).

Commons, John R., Phillips, U. B., Gilmore, E. A., Sumner, H. L. and Andrews, J. B. (eds) (1910–11) *A Documentary History of American Industrial Society*, 10 vols (Cleveland: Arthur H. Clark).

Commons, John R., Saposs, David J., Sumner, Helen L., Mittleman, H. E., Hoagland, H. E., Andrews, John B. and Perlman, Selig (1918–35) *History of Labor in the United States*, 4 vols (New York: Macmillan).

Comte, Auguste (1853) *The Positive Philosophy of Auguste Comte*, 2 vols, translated by Harriet Martineau from the French volumes of 1830–42 (London: Chapman).

Conlisk, John (1996) 'Why Bounded Rationality?', *Journal of Economic Literature*, **34**(2), June, pp. 669–700.

Cook, Gary A. (1993) *George Herbert Mead: The Making of a Social Pragmatist* (Urbana: University of Illinois Press).

Cooley, Charles Horton (1902) *Human Nature and the Social Order*, 1st. edn (New York: Scribner's).

Cooley, Charles Horton (1918) 'Economic Factors: The Classes Above Poverty', *Social Process*, pp. 218–25. Reprinted in Ryan (2001, vol. 2).

Cooley, Charles Horton (1922) *Human Nature and the Social Order*, 2nd edn (New York: Scribner's).

Copeland, Morris A. (1921) 'Some Phases of Institutional Value Theory', PhD Thesis, University of Chicago. Morris A. Copeland Papers, Box 8, Manuscripts by M. A. Copeland Folder, Butler Library, Columbia University.

Copeland, Morris A. (1924) 'Communities of Economic Interest and the Price System' in Tugwell (1924, pp. 105–50).

Copeland, Morris A. (1925) 'Professor Knight on Psychology', *Quarterly Journal of Economics*, **40**(1), November, pp. 134–151.

Copeland, Morris A. (1926) 'Desire, Choice, and Purpose from a Natural-Evolutionary Standpoint', *Psychological Review*, **33**(4), July, pp. 245–67.

Copeland, Morris A. (1927) 'An Instrumental View of the Part–Whole Relation', *Journal of Philosophy*, **24**(4), 17 February, pp. 96–104.

Copeland, Morris A. (1929a) 'Money, Trade and Prices – A Test of Causal Primacy', *Quarterly Journal of Economics*, **43**, August, pp. 648–66.

Copeland, Morris A. (1929b) 'The National Income and its Distribution', in National Bureau of Economic Research (1929) *Recent Economic Changes in the United States*, vol. 2 (New York: National Bureau of Economic Research).

Copeland, Morris A. (1931) 'Economic Theory and the Natural Science Point of View', *American Economic Review*, **21**(1), March, pp. 67–79.

Copeland, Morris A. (1936) 'Commons's Institutionalism in Relation to the Problem of Social Evolution and Economic Planning', *Quarterly Journal of Economics*, **50**(2), February, pp. 333–46.

Copeland, Morris A. (1937) 'Concepts of National Income', in National Bureau of Economic Research (1937) *Studies in Income and Wealth*, vol. 1 (New York: National Bureau of Economic Research), pp. 3–63.

Copeland, Morris A. (1940) 'Competing Products and Monopolistic Competition', *Quarterly Journal of Economics*, **55**(1), November, pp. 1–35.

Copeland, Morris A. (1958a) 'Institutionalism and Welfare Economics', *American Economic Review*, **48**(1), March, pp. 1–17.

Copeland, Morris A. (1958b) 'On the Scope and Method of Economics', in Douglas F. Dowd (ed.) (1958) *Thorstein Veblen: A Critical Reappraisal* (Ithaca, NY: Cornell University Press), pp. 57–75.

Copeland, Morris A. (1965) *Our Free Enterprise System* (New York: Macmillan).

Copeland, Morris A. (1966) Letter to Clarence Ayres, dated 24 August 1966, Clarence E. Ayres Papers, Center for American History, University of Texas.

Copeland, Morris A. (1981) *Essays in Socioeconomic Evolution* (New York: Vantage Press).

Copeland, Morris A. and Martin, Edwin M. (1938) 'The Correction of Wealth and Income Estimates for Price Changes', in National Bureau of Economic Research (1938) *Studies in Income and Wealth*, vol. 2 (New York: National Bureau of Economic Research), pp. 85–135, including a comment by Milton Friedman.

Cordell, Arthur J. (1972) 'Imperfect and Monopolistic Competition: The Role of the Robinson–Chamberlin Theories in the Demise of Institutionalism', *American Journal of Economics and Sociology*, **31**(1), pp. 41–60.

Coricelli, Fabrizio and Dosi, Giovanni (1988) 'Coordination and Order in Economic Change and the Interpretative Power of Economic Theory', in Dosi, Giovanni, Freeman, Christopher, Nelson, Richard, Silverberg, Gerald and Soete, Luc L. G. (eds) *Technical Change and Economic Theory* (London: Pinter), pp. 124–47.

Corning, Peter A. (1983) *The Synergism Hypothesis: A Theory of Progressive Evolution* (New York: McGraw-Hill).

Corning, Peter A. (1995) 'Synergy and Self-Organization in the Evolution of Complex Systems', *Systems Research*, **12**(2), pp. 89–121.

Corning, Peter A. (2000a) '"The Synergism Hypothesis": On the Concept of Synergy and its Role in the Evolution of Complex Systems', *Journal of Social and Evolutionary Systems*, **21**(2), pp. 133–72.

Corning, Peter A. (2000b) 'Biological Adaptation in Human Societies: A "Basic Needs" Approach', *Journal of Bioeconomics*, **2**, pp. 41–86.

Cosmides, Leda and Tooby, John (1994a) 'Beyond Intuition and Instinct Blindness: Towards an Evolutionary Rigorous Cognitive Science', *Cognition*, **50**(1–3), April–June, pp. 41–77.

Cosmides, Leda and Tooby, John (1994b) 'Better than Rational: Evolutionary Psychology and the Invisible Hand', *American Economic Review (Papers and Proceedings)*, **84**(2), May, pp. 377–432.

Costall, Alan P. (1993) 'How Lloyd Morgan's Canon Backfired', *Journal of the History of the Behavioral Sciences*, **29**, April, pp. 113–22.

Craib, Ian (1992) *Anthony Giddens* (London: Routledge).

Cravens, Hamilton (1978) *The Triumph of Evolution: American Scientists and the Hereditary–Environment Controversy, 1900–1941* (Philadelphia: University of Pennsylvania Press).

Crawford, Sue E. S. and Ostrom, Elinor (1995) 'A Grammar of Institutions', *American Political Science Review*, **89**(3), September, pp. 582–600.

Cronin, Helena (1991) *The Ant and the Peacock: Altruism and Sexual Selection from Darwin to Today* (Cambridge: Cambridge University Press).

Crutchfield, James P., Farmer, J. Doyne, Packard, Norman H. and Shaw, Robert S. (1986) 'Chaos', *Scientific American*, **255**(6), December, pp. 38–49.

Cummins, Denise Delarosa (1998) 'Social Norms and Other Minds', in Cummins and Allen (1998, pp. 30–50).

Cummins, Denise Delarosa and Allen, Colin (eds) (1998) *The Evolution of Mind* (Oxford and New York: Oxford University Press).

Cushing, James (1994) *Quantum Mechanics: Historical Contingency and the Copenhagen Hegemony* (Chicago: Chicago University Press).

Cziko, Gary (1995) *Without Miracles: Universal Selection Theory and the Second Darwinian Revolution* (Cambridge, MA: MIT Press).

Damasio, Antonio R. (1994) *Descartes' Error: Emotion, Reason, and the Human Brain* (New York: Putnam).

Darwin, Charles R. (1859) *On the Origin of Species by Means of Natural Selection, or the Preservation of Favoured Races in the Struggle for Life*, 1st edn (London: Murray). Facsimile reprint 1964 with an introduction by Ernst Mayr (Cambridge, MA: Harvard University Press).

Darwin, Charles R. (1868) *The Variation of Animals and Plants Under Domestication*, 2 vols, 1st edn (London and New York: Murray and Orange Judd).

Darwin, Charles R. (1871) *The Descent of Man, and Selection in Relation to Sex*, 2 vols, 1st edn (London: Murray and New York: Hill). Facsimile reprint 1981 with an introduction by John T. Bonner and Robert M. May (Princeton, NJ: Princeton University Press).

Darwin, Charles R. (1883) *The Variation of Animals and Plants Under Domestication*, 2 vols, 2nd edn (London and New York: Murray and Appleton).

Daugert, Stanley Matthew (1950) *The Philosophy of Thorstein Veblen* (New York: Columbia University Press).

David, Paul A. (1985) 'Clio and the Economics of QWERTY', *American Economic Review (Papers and Proceedings)*, **75**(2), May, pp. 332–7.

David, Paul A. (1994) 'Why are Institutions the "Carriers of History"? Path Dependence and the Evolution of Conventions, Organizations and Institutions', *Structural Change and Economic Dynamics*, **5**(2), pp. 205–20.

David, Paul A. (2001) 'Path Dependence, its Critics, and the Quest for "Historical Economics"', Garrouste, Pierre and Ioannides, Stavros (eds) *Evolution and Path Dependence in Economic Ideas: Past and Present* (Cheltenham: Edward Elgar), pp. 15–40.

Davidson, Donald (1980) *Essays on Actions and Events* (Oxford: Oxford University Press).

Davies, Michael and Humphreys, Glyn W. (1993) *Consciousness: Psychological and Philosophical Essays* (Oxford: Blackwell).

Davis Allen F. (1967) 'Welfare, Reform and World War I', *American Quarterly*, **19**(3), Autumn, pp. 516–33.

Davis, J. Ronnie (1968) 'Chicago Economists, Deficit Budgets, and the Early 1930s', *American Economic Review*, **58**(3), Part 1, June, pp. 476–82.

Davis, J. Ronnie (1971) *The New Economics and Old Economists* (Ames, IA: Iowa State University Press).

Davis, John B., Hands, D. Wade and Mäki, Uskali (eds) (1998) *Handbook of Economic Methodology* (Cheltenham: Edward Elgar).

Dawkins, Richard (1976) *The Selfish Gene*, 1st edn (Oxford: Oxford University Press).

Dawkins, Richard (1983) 'Universal Darwinism', in Bendall, D. S. (ed.) *Evolution from Molecules to Man* (Cambridge: Cambridge University Press), pp. 403–25.

Dawkins, Richard (1986) *The Blind Watchmaker* (Harlow: Longman).

Debreu, Gerard (1974) 'Excess Demand Functions', *Journal of Mathematical Economics*, **1**(1), March, pp. 15–21.

Degler, Carl N. (1991) *In Search of Human Nature: The Decline and Revival of Darwinism in American Social Thought* (Oxford and New York: Oxford University Press).

DeGregori, Thomas R. (1977) 'Ethics and Economic Inquiry: The Ayres–Knight Debate and the Problem of Economic Order', *American Journal of Economics and Sociology*, **36**, pp. 41–50.

Dennett, Daniel C. (1984) *Elbow Room: The Varieties of Free Will Worth Wanting* (Cambridge, MA: MIT Press).

Dennett, Daniel C. (1995) *Darwin's Dangerous Idea: Evolution and the Meanings of Life* (London: Allen Lane).

Dennett, Daniel C. (2003) *Freedom Evolves* (London: Allen Lane).

Denzau, Arthur T. and North, Douglass, C. (1994) 'Shared Mental Models: Ideologies and Institutions', *Kyklos*, **47**, Fasc. 1, pp. 3–31.

Depew, David J. and Weber, Bruce H. (1995) *Darwinism Evolving: Systems Dynamics and the Genealogy of Natural Selection* (Cambridge, MA: MIT Press).

Dequech, David (2002) 'The Demarcation Between the "Old" and the "New" Institutional Economics: Recent Complications', *Journal of Economic Issues*, **36**(2), June, pp. 565–72.

Desmond, Adrian and Moore, James R. (1991) *Darwin* (London: Michael Joseph).

De Vries, Hugo (1901) *Die mutationstheorie: Versuche und Beobachtungen über die Entstehung der Arten im Pflanzenreich*, 2 vols (Leipzig: Von Veit).

De Waal, Frans B. M. (1996) *Good Natured: The Origin of Right and Wrong* (Cambridge, MA: Harvard University Press).

Dewey, John (1894) 'The Ego as Cause', *Philosophical Review*, **3**(3), May, pp. 337–41.

Dewey, John (1896) 'The Reflex Arc Concept in Psychology', *Psychological Review*, **3**, July, pp. 357–70.

Dewey, John (1898) 'Evolution and Ethics', *Monist*, **8**, April, pp. 321–41. Reprinted in Ryan (2001, vol. 1).

Dewey, John (1910a) *The Influence of Darwin on Philosophy and Other Essays in Contemporary Philosophy* (New York: Holt).

Dewey, John (1910b) 'The Short-Cut to Realism Examined', *Journal of Philosophy, Psychology and Scientific Methods*, **7**(20), 29 September, pp. 553–7.

Dewey, John (1922) *Human Nature and Conduct: An Introduction to Social Psychology*, 1st edn (New York: Holt).

Dewey, John (1926) *Experience and Nature* (Chicago: Open Court).

Dewey, John (1935) *Liberalism and Social Action* (New York: G. P. Putnam's Sons).

Dewey, John (1938) *Logic: The Theory of Enquiry* (New York: Holt).

Dewey, John (1939) *Theory of Valuation* (Chicago: University of Chicago Press).

Dewey, John and Bentley, Arthur F. (1949) *Knowing and the Known* (Boston: Beacon Press).

Dewey, John and Spaulding, Edward G. (1911) 'Joint Discussion with Articles of Agreement and Disagreement', *Journal of Philosophy, Psychology and Scientific Methods*, **8**(21), October 12, pp. 574–9.

Diggins, John Patrick (1978) *The Bard of Savagery: Thorstein Veblen and Modern Social Theory* (Brighton and New York: Harvester and Seabury).

Diggins, John Patrick (1994) *The Promise of Pragmatism: Modernism and the Crisis of Knowledge and Authority* (Chicago: University of Chicago Press).

Dillard, Dudley (1948) *The Economics of John Maynard Keynes: The Theory of a Monetary Economy* (London: Crosby Lockwood).

Dobriansky, Lev E. (1957) *Veblenism: A New Critique*, with an introduction by James Burnham (Washington, DC: Public Affairs Press).

Dobzhansky, Theodosius (1955) *Evolution, Genetics and Man* (London: Wiley).

Dobzhansky, Theodosius, Ayala, Francisco J., Stebbins, G. Ledyard and Valentine, James W. (1977) *Evolution* (San Francisco: Freeman).

Donald, Merlin (1991) *Origins of the Modern Mind: Three Stages in the Evolution of Culture and Cognition* (Cambridge, MA: Harvard University Press).

Dorfman, Joseph (1934) *Thorstein Veblen and His America* (New York: Viking Press).

Dorfman, Joseph (1949) *The Economic Mind in American Civilization, Volume 3, 1865–1918* (New York: Viking Press).

Dorfman, Joseph (1958) 'The Mutual Influence of Mitchell and Commons', *American Economic Review*, **48**(3), June, pp. 405–8.

Dorfman, Joseph (1959) *The Economic Mind in American Civilization, Volumes 4–5, 1918–1933* (New York: Viking Press).

Dorfman, Joseph (1963) 'The Background of Institutional Economics', in Dorfman *et al.* (1963, pp. 1–44).

Dorfman, Joseph (1974) 'Walton Hamilton and Industrial Policy' in Hamilton, Walton H. (1974) *Industrial Policy and Institutionalism: Selected Essays*, with an introduction by Joseph Dorfman (New York: Augustus Kelley), pp. 5–28.

Dorfman, Joseph, Ayres, Clarence W., Chamberlain, Neil W., Kuznets, Simon and Gordon, Robert A. (1963) *Institutional Economics: Veblen, Commons, and Mitchell Reconsidered* (Berkeley, CA: University of California Press).

Dosi, Giovanni (1988) 'The Sources, Procedures, and Microeconomic Effects of Innovation', *Journal of Economic Literature*, **26**(3), September, pp. 1120–71.

Dosi, Giovanni and Metcalfe, J. Stanley (1991) 'On Some Notions of Irreversibility in Economics', in Saviotti and Metcalfe (1991, pp. 133–59).

Dosi, Giovanni, Freeman, Christopher, Nelson, Richard, Silverberg, Gerald and Soete, Luc L. G. (eds) (1988) *Technical Change and Economic Theory* (London: Pinter).

Douglas, Mary (1990) 'Converging on Autonomy: Anthropology and Institutional Economics', in Williamson, Oliver E. (ed.) *Organization Theory: From Chester Barnard to the Present and Beyond* (Oxford: Oxford University Press), pp. 98–115.

Douglas, Mary T. (1986) *How Institutions Think* (London and Syracuse: Routledge and Kegan Paul and Syracuse University Press).

Douglas, Paul H. (1937) Review of *Thorstein Veblen and his America* by Joseph Dorfman, *Economic Journal*, **47**(3), September, pp. 529–31.

Dow, Sheila C. (1990) 'Beyond Dualism', *Cambridge Journal of Economics*, **14**(2), June, pp. 143–57.

Doyal, Leonard and Gough, Ian (1991) *A Theory of Human Need* (London: Macmillan).

Drake, Durant, Lovejoy, Arthur O., Pratt, James Bisset, Rogers, Arthur K., Santayana, George, Sellars, Roy Wood and Strong, G. A. (1920) *Essays in Critical Realism* (London: Macmillan).

Driesch, Hans (1908) *The Science and Philosophy of the Organism*, 2 vols (London: Black).

Drummond, Henry (1894) *The Ascent of Man* (London: Hodder and Stoughton).

Duesenberry, James S. (1949) *Income, Saving and the Theory of Consumer Behavior* (Cambridge MA: Harvard University Press).

Dugger, William M. (1984) 'Veblen and Kropotkin on Human Evolution', *Journal of Economic Issues*, **18**(4), December, pp. 971–85.

Dugger, William M. (ed.) (1989) *Radical Institutionalism: Contemporary Voices* (Westport, CT: Greenwood Press).

Dugger, William M. (1995) 'Veblenian Institutionalism: The Changing Concepts of Inquiry', *Journal of Economic Issues*, **29**(4), December, pp. 1013–27.

Dugger, William M. (ed.) (1996) *Inequality: Radical Institutionalist Views on Race, Gender, Class, and Nation* (Westport, CT: Greenwood Press).

Dugger, William M. and Sherman, Howard J. (1994) 'Comparison of Marxism and Institutionalism', *Journal of Economic Issues*, **28**(1), March, pp. 101–27.

Dugger, William M. and Sherman, Howard J. (2000) *Reclaiming Evolution: A Dialogue Between Marxism and Institutionalism on Social Change* (London and New York: Routledge).

Dugger, William M. and Waller, William J., Jr (1996) 'Radical Institutionalism: From Technological to Democratic Instrumentalism', *Review of Social Economy*, **54**(2), Summer, pp. 169–89.

Dunlap, Knight (1922) *The Elements of Scientific Psychology* (St Louis: Mosby).

Dupré, John A. (ed.) (1987) *The Latest on the Best: Essays on Evolution and Optimality* (Cambridge, MA: MIT Press).

Dupré, John A. (1993) *The Disorder of Things: Metaphysical Foundations of the Disunity of Science* (Cambridge, MA: Harvard University Press).

Durham, William H. (1991) *Coevolution: Genes, Culture, and Human Diversity* (Stanford: Stanford University Press).

Durkheim, Émile (1982) *The Rules of Sociological Method*, translated from the French edition of 1901 by W. D. Halls with an introduction by Steven Lukes (London: Macmillan).

Durkheim, Émile (1984) *The Division of Labour in Society*, translated from the French edition of 1893 by W. D. Halls with an introduction by Lewis Coser (London: Macmillan).

Dutta, Prajit K. and Radner, Roy (1999) 'Profit Maximization and the Market Selection Hypothesis', *Review of Economic Studies*, **66**(4), October, pp. 769–98.

Dyer, Alan W. (1986) 'Veblen on Scientific Creativity', *Journal of Economic Issues*, **20**(1), March, pp. 21–41.

Earman, John (1986) *A Primer on Determinism* (Boston: Reidel).

Eby, Clare Virginia (1998) 'Veblen's Assault on Time', *Journal of Economic Issues*, **32**(3), September, pp. 689–707.

Eby, Clare Virginia (2001) 'Boundaries Lost: Thorstein Veblen, The Higher Learning in America, and the Conspicuous Spouse', *Prospects: An Annual of American Cultural Studies*, **26**, pp. 251–93.

Edelman, Gerald M. (1987) *Neural Darwinism: The Theory of Neuronal Group Selection* (New York: Basic Books).

Edgell, Stephen (1975) 'Thorstein Veblen's Theory of Evolutionary Change', *American Journal of Economics and Sociology*, **34**, July, pp. 267–80.

Edgell, Stephen (2001) *Veblen in Perspective: His Life and Thought* (Armonk, NY: M. E. Sharpe).

Edgell, Stephen and Tilman, Rick (1989) 'The Intellectual Antecedents of Thorstein Veblen: A Reappraisal', *Journal of Economic Issues*, **23**(4), December, pp. 1003–26.

Edgerton, Robert B. (1992) *Sick Societies: Challenging the Myth of Primitive Harmony* (New York: Free Press).

Edgeworth, Francis Y. (1896) 'A Defence of Index-Numbers', *Economic Journal*, **6**(1), March, pp. 132–42.

Edie, Lionel D. (1922) *Principles of the New Economics* (New York: Cromwell).

Eff, E. Anton (1989) 'History of Thought as Ceremonial Genealogy: The Neglected Influence of Herbert Spencer on Thorstein Veblen', *Journal of Economic Issues*, **23**(3), September, pp. 689–716.

Eggen, J. B. (1926) 'The Fallacy of Eugenics', *Social Forces*, **5**(1), September, pp. 104–9.

Einstein, Albert, Podolsky, Boris and Rosen, Nathan (1935) 'Can Quantum-Mechanical Descriptions of Physical Reality be Considered Complete?', *Physical Review*, **47**, pp. 777–80.

Eldredge, Niles (1985) *Unfinished Synthesis: Biological Hierarchies and Modern Evolutionary Thought* (Oxford: Oxford University Press).

Elias, Norbert (1991) *The Society of Individuals* (Oxford: Basil Blackwell).

Elias, Norbert (2000) *The Civilizing Process*, revised edn, translated from the German edition of 1939 (Oxford: Blackwell).

Eliasson, Gunnar K. (1984) 'Microheterogeneity of Firms and the Stability of Industrial Growth', *Journal of Economic Behavior and Organization*, **5**(3–4), September–December, pp. 249–74.

Ellis, H. S. (ed.) (1948) *Survey of Contemporary Economics*, vol. I (Philadelphia: Blakiston).

Ellis, John (1990) *Brute Force: Allied Strategy and Tactics in the Second World War* (London: Andre Deutsch).

Ellwood, Charles A. (1912) *Sociology in its Psychological Aspects* (New York: Appleton).

Ellwood, Charles A. (1918) 'Theories of Cultural Evolution', *American Journal of Sociology*, **23**(6), May, pp. 779–800.

Elster, Jon (1982) 'Marxism, Functionalism and Game Theory', *Theory and Society*, **11**(4), pp. 453–82. Reprinted in Roemer, John E. (ed.) *Analytical Marxism* (Cambridge: Cambridge University Press).

Elster, Jon (1983) *Explaining Technical Change* (Cambridge: Cambridge University Press).

Elster, Jon (1986) *The Multiple Self* (Cambridge: Cambridge University Press).

Engels, Frederick (1964) *Dialectics of Nature* (London: Lawrence and Wishart).

Epstein, Philip (1999) 'Wesley Mitchell's Grand Design and Its Critics: The Theory and Measurement of Business Cycles', *Journal of Economic Issues*, **33**(3), September, pp. 525–53.

Epstein, R. J. (1987) *A History of Econometrics* (Amsterdam: North-Holland).

Etzioni, Amitai (1988) *The Moral Dimension: Toward a New Economics* (New York: Free Press).

Faris, Robert E. L. (1950) 'Evolution and American Sociology', in Persons (1950, pp. 159–80).

Faulkner, Philip (2002) 'Some Problems With the Conception of the Human Subject in Critical Realism', *Cambridge Journal of Economics*, **26**(6), November, pp. 739–51.

Fayazmanesh, Sasan and Tool, Marc R. (eds) (1998) *Institutionalist Method and Value: Essays in Honour of Paul Dale Bush, Volume 1* (Cheltenham: Edward Elgar).

Ferri, Enrico (1896) *Socialisme et Science Positive* (Paris: Giard et Brière).

Ferri, Enrico (1906) *Socialism and Positive Science (Darwin–Spencer–Marx)*, translated by Edith C. Harvey from the French edition of 1896 (London: Independent Labour Party).

Field, Alexander J. (1979) 'On the Explanation of Rules Using Rational Choice Models', *Journal of Economic Issues*, **13**(1), March, pp. 49–72.

Field, Alexander J. (1981) 'The Problem with Neoclassical Institutional Economics: A Critique with Special Reference to the North/Thomas Model of Pre-1500 Europe', *Explorations in Economic History*, **18**(2), April, pp. 174–98.

Field, Alexander J. (1984) 'Microeconomics, Norms and Rationality', *Economic Development and Cultural Change*, **32**(4), July, pp. 683–711.

Field, Alexander J. (2001) *Altruistically Inclined? TheBehavioral Sciences, Evolutionary Theory, and the Origins of Reciprocity* (Ann Arbor: University of Michigan Press).

Fiori, Stefano (2002) 'Alternative Visions of Change in Douglass North's New Institutionalism', *Journal of Economic Issues*, **36**(4), December, pp. 1025–43.

Fiorito, Luca (ed.) (2000) 'The Mitchell Correspondence', in Samuels, Warren J. (ed.) *Research in the History of Economic Thought and Methodology*, **18-C**, pp. 263–335.

Fiorito, Luca (2001) 'John Maurice Clark's Contribution to the Genesis of the Multiplier Analysis (With Some Related Unpublished Correspondence)', *History of Economic Ideas*, **9**, pp. 7–37.

Fiorito, Luca (2003) 'John Maurice Clark and Frank H. Knight on Marginal Productivity Theory: A Note With Some Unpublished Correspondence', *Research in the History of Economic Thought and Methodology*, **21-A**, pp. 49–64.

Fischer, David Hackett (1989) *Albion's Seed: Four British Folkways in America* (Oxford and New York: Oxford University Press).

Fisher, Irving (1919) 'Economists and the Public Service', *American Economic Review (Papers and Proceedings)*, **9**(1), Supplement, March, pp. 5–21.

Fishman, L. (1958) 'Veblen, Hoxie and American Labor', in Dowd, Douglas F. (ed.) *Thorstein Veblen: A Critical Appraisal* (Ithaca, NY: Cornell University Press), pp. 221–36.

Fleck, Ludwik (1979) *Genesis and Development of a Scientific Fact*, translated by F. Bradley and T. J. Trenn from the German edition of 1935 (Chicago: University of Chicago Press).

Foley, Vernard (1973) 'An Origin of the Tableau Economique', *History of Political Economy*, **5**(2), Summer, pp. 121–50.

Fontana, Andrea, Roe, Linda and Tilman, Rick (1992) 'Theoretical Parallels in George H. Mead and Thorstein Veblen', *Social Science Journal*, **29**(3), pp 241–57.

Forest, Joëlle and Mehier, Caroline (2001) 'John R. Commons and Herbert Simon on the Concept of Rationality', *Journal of Economic Issues*, **35**(3), September, pp. 591–605.

Foster, John Fagg (1981) 'The Papers of J. Fagg Foster', *Journal of Economic Issues*, **15**(4), December, pp. 857–1012.

Foster, John (1997) 'The Analytical Foundations of Evolutionary Economics: From Biological Analogy to Economic Self-Organisation', *Structural Change and Economic Dynamics*, **8**, pp. 427–51.

Frank, Lawrence Kelso (1925) 'The Significance of Industrial Integration', *Journal of Political Economy*, **33**(2), April, pp. 179–95.

Frank, Robert H. (1988) *Passions Within Reason: The Strategic Role of the Emotions* (New York: Norton).

Freeman, Christopher (1992) *The Economics of Hope: Essays on Technical Change, Economic Growth and the Environment* (London and New York: Pinter).

Freeman, Derek (1983) *Margaret Mead and Samoa: The Making and Unmaking of an Anthropological Myth* (Cambridge, MA: Harvard University Press).

Freeman, Derek (1992) *Paradigms in Collision: The Far-Reaching Controversy Over the Samoan Researches of Margaret Mead and Its Significance for the Human Sciences* (Canberra: Research School of Pacific Studies).

Friedman, Milton (1950) 'Wesley C. Mitchell as an Economic Theorist', *Journal of Political Economy*, **58**(6), December, pp. 465–93.

Friedman, Milton (1953) 'The Methodology of Positive Economics', in M. Friedman, *Essays in Positive Economics* (Chicago: University of Chicago Press), pp. 3–43.

Furubotn, Eirik G. (1997) 'The Old and the New Institutionalism in Economics', in Koslowski, Peter (ed.) *Methodology of the Social Sciences, Ethics, and Economics in the Newer Historical School: From Max Weber and Rickert to Sombart and Rothacker* (Berlin: Springer), pp. 429–63.

Furubotn, Eirik G. and Richter, Rudolf (1997) *Institutions in Economic Theory: The Contribution of the New Institutional Economics* (Ann Arbor: University of Michigan Press).

Galbraith, John Kenneth (1958) *The Affluent Society* (London: Hamilton).

Galbraith, John Kenneth (1969) *The New Industrial State* (Harmondsworth: Penguin).

Gallegati, Mauro and Kirman, Alan P. (eds) (1999) *Beyond the Representative Agent* (Cheltenham: Edward Elgar).

Gambs, John S. (1946) *Beyond Supply and Demand* (New York: Columbia University Press).

Gerard, Ralph W. and Emerson, Alfred E. (1945) 'Extrapolation from the Biological to the Social', *Science*, **101**, no. 2632, 8 June, pp. 582–5.

Ghent, William J. (1902) *Our Benevolent Feudalism* (New York: Macmillan).

Ghiselin, Michael T. (1974) *The Economy of Nature and the Evolution of Sex* (Berkeley: University of California Press).

Giddens, Anthony (1976) *New Rules of Sociological Method* (London: Hutchinson).

Giddens, Anthony (1979) *Central Problems in Social Theory* (Berkeley and Los Angeles: University of California Press).

Giddens, Anthony (1982) *Profiles and Critiques in Social Theory* (London: Macmillan).

Giddens, Anthony (1984) *The Constitution of Society: Outline of the Theory of Structuration* (Cambridge: Polity Press).

Giddens, Anthony (1989) 'A Reply to My Critics', in Held, David and Thompson, John B. (1989) *Social Theory of Modern Societies: Anthony Giddens and His Critics* (Cambridge: Cambridge University Press), pp. 249–301.

Giddings, Franklin Henry (1888) *The Sociological Character of Political Economy* (Baltimore: American Economic Association).

Giddings, Franklin Henry (1896) *The Principles of Sociology: An Analysis of the Phenomena of Association and of Social Organization* (New York: Macmillan).

Gigerenzer, Gerd, Todd, Peter M. *et al.* (1999) *Simple Heuristics That Make Us Smart* (Oxford and New York: Oxford University Press).

Gintis, Herbert (2000) *Game Theory Evolving: A Problem-Centred Introduction to Modeling Stategic Interaction* (Princeton: Princeton University Press).

Glass, Bentley, Temkin, Owsei and Strauss, William L., Jr (eds) (1959) *Forerunners of Darwin, 1745–1859* (Baltimore: Johns Hopkins University Press).

Gode, Dhananjay K. and Sunder, Shyam (1993) 'Allocative Efficiency of Markets with Zero-Intelligence Traders: Market as a Partial Substitute for Individual Rationality', *Journal of Political Economy*, **101**(1), February, pp. 119–37.

Godfrey-Smith, Peter (2000) 'The Replicator in Retrospect', *Biology and Philosophy*, **15**(3), June, pp. 403–23.

Goertzel, Ben (1992) 'What is Hierarchical Selection?', *Biology and Philosophy*, **7**(1), January, pp. 27–33.

Goldstein, Jeffrey (1999) 'Emergence as a Construct: History and Issues', *Emergence*, **1**(1), pp. 49–72.

Golomb, Jacob and Wistrich, Robert S. (2002) *Nietzsche, Godfather of Fascism? On the Uses and Abuses of Philosophy* (Princeton: Princeton University Press).

Gonce, Richard A. (1972) 'Frank H. Knight on Social Control and the Scope and Method of Economics', *Southern Economic Journal*, **38**(4), April, pp. 547–58.

Gonce, Richard A. (1992) 'F. H. Knight on Capitalism and Freedom', *Journal of Economic Issues*, **26**(3), September, pp. 813–44.

Gonce, Richard A. (2002) 'John R. Commons's "Five Big Years": 1899–1904', *American Journal of Economics and Sociology*, **61**(4), October, pp. 755–77.

Gordon, Robert A. (1945) *Business Leadership in the Large Corporation* (Washington, DC: Brookings Institution).

Gough, Ian (1994) 'Economic Institutions and the Satisfaction of Human Needs', *Journal of Economic Issues*, **28**(1), March, pp. 25–66.

Gould, Stephen Jay (1978) *Ever Since Darwin: Reflections in Natural History* (London: Burnett Books).

Gould, Stephen Jay (1980) *The Panda's Thumb: More Reflections in Natural History* (New York: Norton).

Gramsci, Antonio (1971) *Selections from the Prison Notebooks* (London: Lawrence and Wishart).

Grandmont, Jean-Michel (1992) 'Transformations of the Commodity Space, Behavioral Heterogeneity and the Aggregation Problem', *Journal of Economic Theory*, **57**(1), pp. 1–35.

Gray, John (1984) *Hayek on Liberty* (Oxford: Basil Blackwell).

Greif, Avner (1993) 'Contract Enforceability and Economic Institutions in Early Trade: The Maghribi Traders' Coalition', *American Economic Review*, **83**(3), June, pp. 525–48.

Griliches, Zvi (1996) 'The Discovery of the Residual: A Historical Note', *Journal of Economic Literature*, **34**(3), September, pp. 1324–30.

Groenewegen, Peter (1995) *A Soaring Eagle: Alfred Marshall 1842–1924* (Aldershot: Edward Elgar).

Gruber, Howard E. (1974) *Darwin on Man: A Psychological Study of Scientific Creativity, Together with Darwin's Early and Unpublished Notebooks*, transcribed and annotated by P. H. Barret (New York: Dutton).

Gruchy, Allan G. (1947) *Modern Economic Thought: The American Contribution* (New York: Prentice-Hall).

Gruchy, Allan G. (1948) 'The Philosophical Basis of the New Keynesian Economics', *International Journal of Ethics*, **58**(4), July, pp. 235–44.

Gruchy, Allan G. (1949) 'J. M. Keynes' Concept of Economic Science', *Southern Economic Journal*, **15**(3), January, pp. 249–66.

Gruchy, Allan G. (1972) *Contemporary Economic Thought: The Contribution of Neo-Institutional Economics* (London and New York: Macmillan).

Guillen, Mauro F. (1997) 'Scientific Management's Lost Aesthetic: Architecture, Organization, and the Taylorized Beauty of the Mechanical', *Administrative Science Quarterly*, **42**(4), December, pp. 682–715.

Haavelmo, Trygve (1997) 'Econometrics and the Welfare State' (Nobel Lecture), *American Economic Review*, **87**(Supplement), December, pp. 13–17.

Habermas, Jürgen (1992) *Postmetaphysical Thinking: Philosophical Essays* (Cambridge, MA: MIT Press).

Haeckel, Ernst (1874) *Anthropogenie oder Entwicklungsgeschichte des Menschen* (Leipzig: Engelmann).

Hahn, Frank H. (1984) *Equilibrium and Macroeconomics* (Oxford: Basil Blackwell).

Haken, Hermann (1977) *Synergetics* (Berlin: Springer-Verlag).

Haken, Hermann (1983) *Advanced Synergetics* (Berlin: Springer-Verlag).

Halton, Eugene (1995) *Bereft of Reason: On the Decline of Social Thought and the Prospects for its Renewal* (Chicago: University of Chicago Press).

Hamilton, David B. (1953) *Newtonian Classicism and Darwinian Institutionalism* (Albuquerque: University of New Mexico Press).

Hamilton, Walton H. (1915) 'Economic Theory and "Social Reform"', *Journal of Political Economy*, **23**(6), June, pp. 562–84. Reprinted in Hamilton (1974).

Hamilton, Walton H. (1916) 'The Development of Hoxie's Economics', *Journal of Political Economy*, **24**(9), November, pp. 855–83. Reprinted in Hamilton (1974).

Hamilton, Walton H. (1918) 'The Requisites of a National Food Policy', *Journal of Political Economy*, **26**(6), June, pp. 612–37.

Hamilton, Walton H. (1919) 'The Institutional Approach to Economic Theory', *American Economic Review*, **9**, Supplement, pp. 309–18. Reprinted in Hamilton (1974).

Hamilton, Walton H. (1923) Review of H. D. Henderson *Supply and Demand*, *American Economic Review*, **13**(1), March, pp. 92–5.

Hamilton, Walton H. (1932), 'Institution', in Seligman, Edwin R. A. and Johnson, A. (eds) *Encyclopaedia of the Social Sciences*, Vol. 8, pp. 84–9.

Hamilton, Walton H. (1944) 'The Control of Strategic Materials', *American Economic Review*, **34**(2), June, pp. 261–79.

Hamilton, Walton H. (1974) *Industrial Policy and Institutionalism: Selected Essays*, with an introduction by Joseph Dorfman (New York: Augustus Kelley).

Hammond, J. Daniel (1991) 'Frank Knight's Antipositivism', *History of Political Economy*, **23**, pp. 359–81.

Hammond, John L. and Hammond, Barbara (1920) *The Skilled Labourer 1760–1832* (London: Longmans, Green).

Hands, D. Wade (1997) 'Frank Knight's Pluralism', in Salanti, Andrea and Screpanti, Ernesto (eds) *Pluralism in Economics: New Perspectives in History and Methodology* (Aldershot: Edward Elgar), pp. 194–206.

Hands, D. Wade (2001) *Reflection Without Rules: Economic Methodology and Contemporary Science Theory* (Cambridge and New York: Cambridge University Press).

Hands, D. Wade and Mirowski, Philip (1998) 'Harold Hotelling and the Neoclassical Dream', in Backhouse, Roger E., Hausman, Daniel M., Mäki, Uskali and Salanti, Andrea (eds) *Economics and Methodology: Crossing Boundaries* (London: Macmillan), pp. 322–97.

Hannan, Michael T. and Carroll, Glenn R. (1992) *Dynamics of Organizational Population: Density, Legitimation and Competition* (Oxford and New York: Oxford University Press).

Hannan, Michael T. and Freeman, John (1989) *Organizational Ecology* (Cambridge, MA: Harvard University Press).

Harcourt, Geoffrey C. (1972) *Some Cambridge Controversies in the Theory of Capital* (Cambridge: Cambridge University Press).

Hardin, Garrett (1968) 'The Tragedy of the Commons', *Science*, **162**, pp. 1243–8.

Hardy, Alister C. (1965) *The Living Stream: A Restatement of Evolution Theory and its Relation to the Spirit of Man* (London: Collins).

Hargreaves Heap, Shaun P. and Varoufakis, Yanis (1995) *Game Theory: A Critical Introduction* (London: Routledge).

Harré, Rom (1986) *Varieties of Realism* (Oxford: Basil Blackwell).

Harré, Rom and Madden, Edward H. (1975) *Causal Powers: A Theory of Natural Necessity* (Oxford: Basil Blackwell).

Harris, Abram L. (1932) 'Types of Institutionalism', *Journal of Political Economy*, **40**(4), December, pp. 721–49.

Harris, Abram L. (1934) 'Economic Evolution: Dialectical and Darwinian', *Journal of Political Economy*, **42**(1), February, pp. 34–79.

Harrod, Roy F. (1936) *The Trade Cycle* (Oxford: Clarendon Press).

Harter, Lafayette G., Jr (1962) *John R. Commons: His Assault on Laissez Faire* (Corvallis: Oregon State University Press).

Hawkins, Mike (1997) *Social Darwinism in European and American Thought, 1860–1945: Nature as Model and Nature as Threat* (Cambridge: Cambridge University Press).

Hayek, Friedrich A. (1943) 'Scientism and the Study of Society, Part II', *Economica*, **10**, pp. 34–63. Reprinted in Hayek (1952).

Hayek, Friedrich A. (1948) *Individualism and Economic Order* (London and Chicago: George Routledge and University of Chicago Press).

Hayek, Friedrich A. (1952a) *The Sensory Order: An Inquiry into the Foundations of Theoretical Psychology* (London: Routledge and Kegan Paul).

Hayek, Friedrich A. (1952b) *The Counter-Revolution of Science: Studies on the Abuse of Reason*, 1st edn (Glencoe, IL: Free Press).

Hayek, Friedrich A. (1967) 'Notes on the Evolution of Systems of Rules of Conduct', *Studies in Philosophy, Politics and Economics* (London: Routledge and Kegan Paul), pp. 66–81.

Hayek, Friedrich A. (1979) *Law, Legislation and Liberty; Volume 3: The Political Order of a Free People* (London: Routledge and Kegan Paul).

Hayek, Friedrich A. (1988) *The Fatal Conceit: The Errors of Socialism, the Collected Works of Friedrich August Hayek*, Vol. I, ed. Bartley, W. W., III (London: Routledge).

Hayes, Edward C. (1907) Comment on 'Points of Agreement Among Sociologists' by Albion W. Small, *American Journal of Sociology*, **12**(5), March, pp. 652–5.

Hayes, Edward C. (1911) 'The "Social Forces" Error', *American Journal of Sociology*, **16**(5), March, pp. 613–25.

Hearn, William Edward (1863) *Plutology, or, The Theory of the Efforts to Satisfy Human Wants* (Melbourne: George Robertson).

Hegel, Georg Wilhelm Friedrich (1976) *Science of Logic*, translated from the German edition of 1830 by A. V. Miller (London: George Allen and Unwin).

Heiner, Ronald A. (1983) 'The Origin of Predictable Behavior', *American Economic Review*, **73**(4), December, pp. 560–95.

Hempel, Carl G. (1965) *Aspects of Scientific Explanation and Other Essays in the Philosophy of Science* (New York: Free Press).

Hempel, Carl G. and Oppenheim, Paul (1948) 'Studies in the Logic of Explanation', *Philosophy of Science*, **11**, pp. 209–21.

Hendriks-Jansen, Horst (1996) *Catching Ourselves in the Act: Situated Activity, Interaction, Emergence, Evolution and Human Thought* (Cambridge, MA: MIT Press).

Henle, Paul (1942) 'The Status of Emergence', *Journal of Philosophy*, **39**(18), pp. 486–93.

Hennis, Wilhelm (1988) *Max Weber, Essays in Reconstruction* (London: George Allen and Unwin).

Henrich, Joseph (2004) 'Cultural Group Selection, Coevolutionary Processes and Large-Scale Cooperation', *Journal of Economic Behavior and Organization* (forthcoming).

Henrich, Joseph, Boyd, Robert, Bowles, Samuel, Camerer, Colin, Fehr, Ernst, Gintis, Herbert and McElreath, Richard (2001) 'In Search of Homo Economicus: Behavioral Experiments in 15 Small-Scale Societies', *American Economic Review (Papers and Proceedings)*, **91**(2), May, pp. 73–84.

Hickman, C. Addison (1975) *J. M. Clark* (New York: Columbia University Press).

Higgs, Robert (ed.) (1999) *Arms, Politics and the Economy: Historical and Contemporary Perspectives* (Oakland, CA: Independent Institute).

Hildenbrand, Werner (1994) *Market Demand: Theory and Empirical Evidence* (Princeton, NJ: Princeton University Press).

Hildenbrand, Werner (1999) 'On the Empirical Content of Economic Theories', in Kirman and Gérard-Varet (1999, pp. 37–54).

Hill, Forest G. (1958) 'Veblen and Marx', in Dowd, Douglas F. (ed.) *Thorstein Veblen: A Critical Appraisal* (Ithaca, NY: Cornell University Press), pp. 129–49.

Hill, Lewis E. (1989) 'Cultural Determinism or Emergent Evolution: An Analysis of the Controversy Between Clarence Ayres and David Miller', *Journal of Economic Issues*, **23**(2), June, pp. 465–71.

Himmelfarb, Gertrude (1959) *Darwin and the Darwinian Revolution* (London: Chatto and Windus).

Hinde, R. A. and Fisher, James (1951) 'Further Observations on the Opening of Milk Bottles by Birds', *British Birds*, **44**, December, pp. 393–6.

Hindess, Barry (1977) *Philosophy and Methodology in the Social Sciences* (Brighton: Harvester).

Hindess, Barry (1989) *Political Choice and Social Structure: An Analysis of Actors, Interests and Rationality* (Aldershot: Edward Elgar).

Hirshleifer, Jack (1977) 'Economics from a Biological Viewpoint', *Journal of Law and Economics*, **20**(1), April, pp. 1–52.

Hirshleifer, Jack (1985) 'The Expanding Domain of Economics', *American Economic Review*, **75**(6), December, pp. 53–68.

Hirst, Paul Q. and Woolley, Penny (1982) *Social Relations and Human Attributes* (London: Tavistock).

Hobson, John A. (1896) *The Problem of the Unemployed* (London: Methuen).

Hobson, John A. (1902) *The Social Problem: Life and Work* (London: James Nisbet).

Hobson, John A. (1914) *Work and Wealth: A Human Valuation* (London: Macmillan).

Hobson, John A. (1926) *The Evolution of Modern Capitalism: A Study of Machine Production*, revised edn (London: Walter Scott, and New York: Charles Scribner's).

Hobson, John A. (1936) *Veblen* (London: Chapman and Hall).

Hodder, H. J. (1956) 'The Political Ideas of Thorstein Veblen', *Canadian Journal of Economics and Political Science*, **22**(3), August, pp. 347–57.

Hodge, Charles (1874) *What Is Darwinism?* (New York).

Hodge, M. J. S. and Kohn, David (1985) 'The Immediate Origins of Natural Selection', in Kohn, David *The Darwinian Heritage* (Princeton: Princeton University Press), pp. 185–206.

Hodgson, Geoffrey M. (1984) *The Democratic Economy: A New Look at Planning, Markets and Power* (Harmondsworth: Penguin).

Hodgson, Geoffrey M. (1988) *Economics and Institutions: A Manifesto for a Modern Institutional Economics* (Cambridge and Philadelphia: Polity Press and University of Pennsylvania Press).

Hodgson, Geoffrey M. (1993) *Economics and Evolution: Bringing Life Back Into Economics* (Cambridge, UK and Ann Arbor, MI: Polity Press and University of Michigan Press).

Hodgson, Geoffrey M. (1994) 'Optimisation and Evolution: Winter's Critique of Friedman Revisited', *Cambridge Journal of Economics*, **18**(4), August, pp. 413–30.

Hodgson, Geoffrey M. (1997a) 'The Evolutionary and Non-Darwinian Economics of Joseph Schumpeter', *Journal of Evolutionary Economics*, **7**(2), June, pp. 131–45.

Hodgson, Geoffrey M. (1997b) 'The Ubiquity of Habits and Rules', *Cambridge Journal of Economics*, **21**(6), November, pp. 663–84.

Hodgson, Geoffrey M. (1998a) 'The Approach of Institutional Economics', *Journal of Economic Literature*, **36**(1), March, pp. 166–92.

Hodgson, Geoffrey M. (1998b) 'On the Evolution of Thorstein Veblen's Evolutionary Economics', *Cambridge Journal of Economics*, **22**(4), July, pp. 415–31.

Hodgson, Geoffrey M. (1998c) 'Dichotomizing the Dichotomy: Veblen versus Ayres', in Fayazmanesh and Tool (1998, pp. 48–73).

Hodgson, Geoffrey M. (1998d) 'Veblen's *Theory of the Leisure Class* and the Genesis of Evolutionary Economics', in Warren J. Samuels (ed.) *The Founding of Evolutionary Economics* (London and New York: Routledge), pp. 170–200.

Hodgson, Geoffrey M. (ed.) (1998e) *The Foundations of Evolutionary Economics: 1890–1973*, 2 vols (Cheltenham: Edward Elgar).

Hodgson, Geoffrey M. (1999a) *Economics and Utopia: Why the Learning Economy is not the End of History* (London and New York: Routledge).

Hodgson, Geoffrey M. (1999b) *Evolution and Institutions: On Evolutionary Economics and the Evolution of Economics* (Cheltenham: Edward Elgar).

Hodgson, Geoffrey M. (2000a) 'What is the Essence of Institutional Economics?', *Journal of Economic Issues*, **34**(2), June, pp. 317–29.

Hodgson, Geoffrey M. (2000b) 'From Micro to Macro: The Concept of Emergence and the Role of Institutions', in Burlamaqui, Leonardo, Castro, Ana Célia and Chang, Ha-

Joon (eds) *Institutions and the Role of the State* (Cheltenham: Edward Elgar), pp. 103–26.

Hodgson, Geoffrey M. (2001a) 'Frank Knight as an Institutional Economist', in Biddle, Jeff E., Davis, John B. and Medema, Steven G. (eds), *Economics Broadly Considered: Essays in Honor of Warren J. Samuels* (London and New York: Routledge), pp. 64–93.

Hodgson, Geoffrey M. (2001b) 'Is Social Evolution Lamarckian or Darwinian?', in Laurent and Nightingale (2001, pp. 87–118).

Hodgson, Geoffrey M. (2001c) *How Economics Forgot History: The Problem of Historical Specificity in Social Science* (London and New York: Routledge).

Hodgson, Geoffrey M. (2001d) 'Darwin, Veblen and the Problem of Causality in Economics', *History and Philosophy of the Life Sciences*, **23**, pp. 383–422.

Hodgson, Geoffrey M. (2002a) 'Reconstitutive Downward Causation: Social Structure and the Development of Individual Agency', in Fullbrook, Edward (ed.) *Intersubjectivity in Economics: Agents and Structures* (London and New York: Routledge), pp. 159–180.

Hodgson, Geoffrey M. (ed.) (2002b) *A Modern Reader in Institutional and Evolutionary Economics: Key Concepts* (Cheltenham: Edward Elgar).

Hodgson, Geoffrey M. (2002c) 'The Legal Nature of the Firm and the Myth of the Firm-Market Hybrid', *International Journal of the Economics of Business*, **9**(1), February, pp. 37–60.

Hodgson, Geoffrey M. (2002d) 'The Evolution of Institutions: An Agenda for Future Theoretical Research', *Constitutional Political Economy*, **13**(2), June, pp. 111–27.

Hodgson, Geoffrey M. (2002e) 'Darwinism in Economics: From Analogy to Ontology', *Journal of Evolutionary Economics*, **12**(2), June, pp. 259–81.

Hodgson, Geoffrey M. (2003a) 'Darwinism and Institutional Economics', *Journal of Economic Issues*, **37**(1), March, pp. 85–97.

Hodgson, Geoffrey M. (2003b) 'The Hidden Persuaders: Institutions and Individuals in Economic Theory', *Cambridge Journal of Economics*, **27**(2), March, pp. 159–75.

Hodgson, Geoffrey M. (2003c) 'The Mystery of the Routine: The Darwinian Destiny of *An Evolutionary Theory of Economic Change*', *Revue Économique*, **54**(2), Mars, pp. 355–84.

Hodgson, Geoffrey M. (2003d) 'John R. Commons and the Foundations of Institutional Economics', *Journal of Economic Issues*, **37**(3), September, pp 547–76.

Hodgson, Geoffrey M. (2004) 'Thorstein Veblen and the Machine Process', in Argyrous, George, Forstater, Mathew and Mongiovi, Gary (eds) *Growth, Distribution and Effective Demand: Essays in Honor of Edward J. Nell* (Armonk, NY: M. E. Sharpe), pp. 261–78.

Hodgson, Geoffrey M. (unpublished) 'Social Darwinism in Anglophone Academic Journals: A Contribution to the History of the Term'.

Hodgson, Geoffrey M. and Knudsen, Thorbjørn (2004) 'The Complex Evolution of a Simple Traffic Convention: The Functions and Implications of Habit', *Journal of Economic Behavior and Organization* (forthcoming).

Hodgson, Geoffrey M., Warren J. Samuels and Marc R. Tool (eds) (1994), *The Elgar Companion to Institutional and Evolutionary Economics*, 2 vols (Aldershot: Edward Elgar).

Hofstadter, Richard (1944) *Social Darwinism in American Thought, 1860–1915*, 1st edn (Philadelphia: University of Pennsylvania Press).

Hofstadter, Richard and Hardy, C. DeWitt (1952) *The Development and Scope of Higher Education in the United States* (New York: Columbia University Press).

Holland, John H. (1995) *Hidden Order: How Adaptation Builds Complexity* (Reading: Helix Books).

Holland, John H. (1998) *Emergence: From Chaos to Order* (Oxford: Oxford University Press).

Holmes, Oliver Wendell (1881) *The Common Law* (Boston and London: Little, Brown and Macmillan).

Holt, Edwin B., Marvin, Walter T., Montague, William P., Perry, Ralph Barton, Pitkin, Walter B. and Spaulding, Edward Gleason (1910) 'The Program and First Platform of Six Realists', *Journal of Philosophy, Psychology and Scientific Methods*, **7**(15), 21 July, pp. 393–401.

Homan, Paul T. (1927a) 'Thorstein Veblen', in Odum, Howard W. (ed.) *American Masters of Social Science* (New York: Holt), pp. 231–70.

Homan, Paul T. (1927b) 'The Impasse in Economic Theory', *Journal of Political Economy*, **35**(6), December, pp. 776–803.

Homan, Paul T. (1928a) *Contemporary Economic Thought* (New York: Harper and Brothers).

Homan, Paul T. (1928b) 'Issues in Economic Theory: an Attempt to Clarify', *Quarterly Journal of Economics*, **42**(3), May, pp. 333–65.

Homan, Paul T. (1931) 'Economics: The Institutional School', in Edwin R. A. Seligman and Alvin Johnson (eds) *Encyclopaedia of the Social Sciences* (New York: Macmillan), Vol. 7, pp. 387–92.

Homan, Paul T. (1932a) 'An Appraisal of Institutional Economics', *American Economic Review*, **22**(1), March, pp. 10–17.

Homan, Paul T. (1932b) Contribution to 'Round Table Conferences: Institutional Economics', *American Economic Review*, **22**(1), Supplement, March, pp. 106–7.

Homan, Paul T. (1933) Review of *Thorstein Veblen: A Chapter in American Thought* by Richard V. Teggart, *American Economic Review*, **23**(3), September, pp. 480–1.

Homan, Paul T., Copeland, Morris A., Burns, Eveline M., Spengler, Joseph J., Taylor, Overton H., and Jaffé, William (1931) 'Economic Theory – Institutionalism: What It Is and What It Hopes to Become', *American Economic Review (Papers and Proceedings)*, **21**(1), Supplement, March, pp. 134–141.

Honderich, Ted (1993) *How Free Are You?* (Oxford: Oxford University Press).

Hookway, Christopher (1985) *Peirce* (London and New York: Routledge).

Hoover, Kevin D. (1995a) 'Why Does Methodology Matter for Economics?', *Economic Journal*, **105**(3), May, pp. 715–34.

Hoover, Kevin D. (1995b) 'Is Macroeconomics for Real?', *Monist*, **78**, pp. 235–57.

Horgan, Terence (1993) 'From Supervenience to Superdupervenience: Meeting the Demands of a Material World', *Mind*, **102**, no. 408, pp. 555–86.

Hoxie, Robert F. (1917) *Trade Unionism in the United States* (New York: Appleton).

Hull, Clark L. (1943) *Principles of Behavior: An Introduction to Behavior Theory* (New York: Appleton-Century).

Hull, David L. (1980) 'Individuality and Selection', *Annual Review of Ecology and Systematics*, **11**, pp. 311–32.

Hull, David L. (1981) 'Units of Evolution: A Metaphysical Essay', in Jensen, U. L. and Harré, Rom (1981) *The Philosophy of Evolution* (Brighton: Harvester Press), pp. 23–44.

Hull, David L. (1982) 'The Naked Meme', in Henry C. Plotkin (ed.) *Learning, Development and Culture: Essays in Evolutionary Epistemology* (New York: Wiley), pp. 273–327.

Hull, David L. (1988) *Science as a Process: An Evolutionary Account of the Social and Conceptual Development of Science* (Chicago: University of Chicago Press).

Humphreys, Paul (1989) *The Chances of Explanation: Causal Explanation in the Social, Medical and Physical Sciences* (Princeton: Princeton University Press).

Humphreys, Paul (1997) 'How Properties Emerge', *Philosophy of Science*, **64**(1), March, pp. 1–17.

Hunt, E. K. and Schwartz, Jesse G. (eds) (1972) *A Critique of Economic Theory* (Harmondsworth: Penguin).

Hutchins, Edwin (1995) *Cognition in the Wild* (Cambridge, MA: MIT Press).

Hutchison, Terence W. (1938) *The Significance and Basic Postulates of Economic Theory* (London: Macmillan).

Hutchison, Terence W. (1992) *Changing Aims in Economics* (Oxford: Basil Blackwell).

Hutchison, Terence W. (1996) 'On the Relations Between Philosophy and Economics. Part I: Frontier Problems in an Era of Departmentalized and International "Professionalism"', *Journal of Economic Methodology*, 3(2), December, pp. 187–213.

Hutter, Michael (1994) 'Organism as a Metaphor in German Economic Thought', in Mirowski, Philip (ed.) *Natural Images in Economic Thought: Markets Read in Tooth and Claw* (Cambridge and New York: Cambridge University Press), pp. 289–321.

Huxley, Thomas Henry (1894) *Collected Essays*, 9 vols (London: Macmillan).

Huxley, Thomas Henry (1900) *The Life and Letters of Thomas Henry Huxley* (London: Macmillan).

Huxley, Thomas Henry and Huxley, Julian (1947) *Evolution and Ethics, 1893–1943* (London: Pilot Press).

Ingrao, Bruna and Israel, Giorgio (1985) 'General Economic Equilibrium: A History of Ineffectual Paradigmatic Shifts', *Fundamenta Scientiae*, 6, pp. 1–45, 89–125.

Ingrao, Bruna and Israel, Giorgio (1990) *The Invisible Hand: Economic Equilibrium in the History of Science* (Cambridge, MA: MIT Press).

Jacoby, Sanford M. (1990) 'The New Institutionalism: What Can it Learn from the Old?', *Industrial Relations*, 29(2), Spring, pp. 316–59.

James, William (1880) 'Great Men, Great Thoughts, and the Environment', *Atlantic Monthly*, 46, pp. 441–59. Reprinted in James (1897).

James, William (1890) *The Principles of Psychology*, 2 vols, 1st edn (New York and London: Holt and Macmillan).

James, William (1892) *Psychology: Briefer Course* (New York and London: Holt and Macmillan).

James, William (1897) *The Will to Believe and Other Essays in Popular Philosophy* (New York and London: Longmans Green).

James, William (1900) *Psychology* (New York: Holt).

Jantsch, Erich (1980) *The Self-Organizing Universe: Scientific and Human Implications of the Emerging Paradigm of Evolution* (Oxford and New York: Pergamon Press).

Jenkin, Fleeming (1867) 'The Origin of Species', *North British Review*, 46, pp. 149–71.

Jennings, Ann L. and Waller, William J. (1998) 'The Place of Biological Science in Veblen's Economics', *History of Political Economy*, 30(2), Summer, pp. 189–217.

Jensen, Hans E. (1990) 'Are There Institutionalist Signposts in the Economics of Alfred Marshall?', *Journal of Economic Issues*, 24(2), June, pp. 405–13.

Jensen, Henrik J. (1998) *Self-Organized Criticality: Emergent Complex Behavior in Physical and Biological Systems* (Cambridge and New York: Cambridge University Press).

Joas, Hans (1991) 'Mead's Position in Intellectual History and the Early Philosophical Writings', in Aboulafia, Mitchell (1991) *Philosophy, Social Theory and the Thought of George H. Mead* (Albany, NY: State University of New York Press).

Joas, Hans (1993) *Pragmatism and Social Theory* (Chicago: University of Chicago Press).

Joas, Hans (1996) *The Creativity of Action* (Chicago: University of Chicago Press).

Johnson, Gary R. (1998) Review of *Social Darwinism in European and American Thought, 1860–1945: Nature as Model and Nature as Threat* by Mike Hawkins, *American Political Science Review*, 92(4), December, pp. 930–2.

Jones, Greta (1980) *Social Darwinism and English Thought* (Brighton and Atlantic Highlands, NJ: Harvester and Humanities Press).

Jones, Stephen R.G. (1984) *The Economics of Conformism* (Oxford: Basil Blackwell).

Jones, Lamar B. (1995) 'C. E. Ayres's Reliance on T. H. Huxley: Did Darwin's Bulldog Bite?', *American Journal of Economics and Sociology*, 54(4), October, pp. 413–20.

Jorgensen, Elizabeth W. and Jorgensen, Henry I. (1999) *Thorstein Veblen: Victorian Firebrand* (Armonk, NY: M. E. Sharpe).

Junker, James A. (1982) 'The Ceremonial-Instrumental Dichotomy in Institutional Analysis', *American Journal of Economics and Sociology*, **41**(2), pp. 141–50.

Junker, Louis (1979) 'Genuine or Spurious Institutionalism? Veblen and Ayres Seen from a Neo-Classical Perspective Raises the Question', *American Journal of Economics and Sociology*, **38**(2), April, pp. 207–23.

Kagel, John H. and Roth, Alvin E. (eds) (1995) *The Handbook of Experimental Economics* (Princeton: Princeton University Press).

Kahneman, Daniel, Slovic, Paul and Tversky, Amos (eds) (1982) *Judgement Under Uncertainty: Heuristics and Biases* (Cambridge and New York: Cambridge University Press).

Kaldor, Nicholas (1985) *Economics Without Equilibrium* (Cardiff: University College Cardiff Press).

Kallen, Horace M. (1930) 'Behaviorism', in Edwin R. A. Seligman and Alvin Johnson (eds) *Encyclopaedia of the Social Sciences* (New York: Macmillan), Vol. 2, pp. 495–8.

Kantor, Jacob Robert (1922a) 'An Essay Toward an Institutional Conception of Social Psychology', *American Journal of Sociology*, **27**(5), March, pp. 611–627; **27**(6), May, pp. 758–779.

Kantor, Jacob Robert (1922b) 'The Integrative Character of Habits', *Journal of Comparative Psychology*, **2**(3), pp. 195–226.

Kantor, Jacob Robert (1924) 'The Institutional Foundation of a Scientific Social Psychology', *American Journal of Sociology*, **29**(6), May, pp. 674–687.

Katz, Michael L. and Shapiro, Carl (1985), 'Network Externalities, Competition, and Compatibility', *American Economic Review*, **75**(3), June, pp. 424–40.

Katzner, Donald W. (1991) 'Aggregation and the Analysis of Markets', *Review of Political Economy*, **3**(2), April, pp. 220–31.

Kauffman, Stuart A. (1993) *The Origins of Order: Self-Organization and Selection in Evolution* (Oxford and New York: Oxford University Press).

Kauffman, Stuart A. (1995) *At Home in the Universe: The Search for Laws of Self-Organization and Complexity* (Oxford and New York: Oxford University Press).

Kauffman, Stuart A. (2000) *Investigations* (Oxford and New York: Oxford University Press).

Kaufman, Bruce E. (1993) *The Origins and Evolution of the Field of Industrial Relations in the United States* (Ithaca, NY: Cornell University Press).

Kaufman, Bruce E. (1998) 'Regulation of the Employment Relationship: The "Old" Institutional Perspective', *Journal of Economic Behavior and Organization*, 34(3), March, pp. 349–85.

Keller, Albert G. (1915) *Societal Evolution: A Study of the Evolutionary Basis of the Science of Society* (New York: Macmillan).

Keller, Albert Galloway (1923) 'Societal Evolution', in Baitsell, George Alfred (ed.) *The Evolution of Man* (New Haven: Yale University Press), pp. 126–51. Reprinted in Ryan (2001, vol. 2).

Keller, Laurent (ed.) (1999) *Levels of Selection in Evolution* (Princeton: Princeton University Press).

Kerr, Benjamin and Godfrey-Smith, Peter (2002) 'Individualist and Multi-Level Perspectives in Structured Populations', *Biology and Philosophy*, **17**(4), September, pp. 477–517.

Keynes, John Maynard (1931) *Essays in Persuasion* (London: Macmillan).

Keynes, John Maynard (1936) *The General Theory of Employment, Interest and Money* (London: Macmillan).

Khalil, Elias L. (1995) 'The Socioculturalist Agenda in Economics: Critical Remarks on Thorstein Veblen's Legacy', *Journal of Socio-Economics*, **24**(4), Winter, pp. 545–69.

Khalil, Elias L. (1997) 'Biological Metaphors, Socio-Economic Theory, and Reductionism', *Economic Issues*, **2**(2), September, pp. 45–57.

Kidd, Benjamin (1894) *Social Evolution* (London and New York: Macmillan).

Kiekhofer, W. H., Clark, John Maurice, Homan, Paul T., Fletcher, Hugh M., Wasserman, Max J., Atkins, Willard E., Tyson, Francis D., Hewett, William W. and Ely, Richard T. (1932) 'Institutional Economics', *American Economic Review (Papers and Proceedings)*, **22**(1), Supplement, March, pp. 105–116.

Kilminster, Richard (1991) 'Structuration Theory as a World-View', in Bryant, Christopher G. A. and Jary, David (eds) *Giddens' Theory of Structuration: A Critical Appreciation* (London: Routledge), pp. 74–115.

Kilpatrick, Andrew and Lawson, Tony (1980) 'On the Nature of the Industrial Decline in the UK', *Cambridge Journal of Economics*, **4**(1), March, pp. 85–102.

Kilpinen, Erkki (1998) 'The Pragmatic Foundations of the Institutionalist Method: Veblen's Preconceptions and their Relation to Peirce and Dewey', in Fayazmanesh and Tool (1998, pp. 23–47).

Kilpinen, Erkki (1999) 'What is Rationality? A New Reading of Veblen's Critique of Utilitarian Hedonism', *International Journal of Politics, Culture and Society*, **13**(2), pp. 187–206.

Kilpinen, Erkki (2000) *The Enormous Fly-Wheel of Society: Pragmatism's Habitual Conception of Action and Social Theory* (Helsinki: University of Helsinki).

Kim, Jaegwon (1978) 'Supervenience and Nomological Incommensurables', *American Philosophical Quarterly*, **15**, pp. 149–56.

Kim, Jaegwon (1992) '"Downward Causation" in Emergentism and Nonreductive Physicalism', in Beckerman, Ansgar, Flohr, Hans and Kim, Jaegwon (eds) *Emergence or Reduction? Essays on the Prospects of Nonreductive Physicalism* (Berlin: De Gruyter), pp. 119–38.

Kim, Jaegwon (1993) *Supervenience and Mind* (Cambridge and New York: Cambridge University Press).

Kincaid, Harold (1997) *Individualism and the Unity of Science: Essays on Reduction, Explanation, and the Social Sciences* (Lanham, ML: Rowman and Littlefield).

Kincaid, Harold (1998a) 'Methodological Individualism/Atomism', in Davis *et al.* (1998, pp. 294–303).

Kincaid, Harold (1998b) 'Supervenience', in Davis *et al.* (1998, pp. 487–8).

Kindleberger, Charles P. (1973) *The World in Depression 1929–1939* (London: Allen Lane).

Kindleberger, Charles P. (1983) 'Standards, as Public, Collective and Private Goods', *Kyklos*, **36**, pp. 377–96.

Kirman, Alan P. (1989) 'The Intrinsic Limits of Modern Economic Theory: The Emperor Has No Clothes', *Economic Journal (Conference Papers)*, **99**, pp. 126–39.

Kirman, Alan P. (1992) 'Whom or What Does the Representative Individual Represent?', *Journal of Economic Perspectives*, **6**(2), Spring, pp. 117–36.

Kirman, Alan P. (1999a) 'The Future of Economic Theory', in Kirman and Gérard-Varet (1999, pp. 8–22).

Kirman, Alan P. (1999b) 'Interaction and Markets', in Gallegati and Kirman (1999, pp. 1–44).

Kirman, Alan P. and Gérard-Varet, Louis-André (eds) (1999) *Economics Beyond the Millennium* (Oxford: Oxford University Press).

Kitcher, Philip (1987) 'Why Not the Best?', in Dupré, John A. (ed.) *The Latest on the Best: Essays on Evolution and Optimality* (Cambridge, MA: MIT Press), pp. 77–102.

Klaes, Matthias (2000a) 'The History of the Concept of Transaction Costs: Neglected Aspects', *Journal of the History of Economic Thought*, **22**(2), pp. 191–216.

Klaes, Matthias (2000b) 'The Birth of the Concept of Transaction Costs: Neglected Aspects', *Industrial and Corporate Change*, **9**(4), pp. 567–93.

Klee, Robert (1984) 'Micro-Determinism and Concepts of Emergence', *Philosophy of Science*, **51**, pp. 44–63.

Klein, Lawrence R. (1946) 'Macroeconomics and the Theory of Rational Behavior', *Econometrica*, **14**(2), pp. 93–108.

Klein, Philip A. (1995) 'Ayres on Institutions – A Reconsideration', *Journal of Economic Issues*, **29**(4), December, pp. 1189–96.

Klein, Richard G. and Edgar, Blake (2002) *The Dawn of Human Culture* (New York: Wiley).

Knight, Frank H. (1917) 'The Concept of Normal Price in Value and Distribution', *Quarterly Journal of Economics*, **32**, pp. 66–100.

Knight, Frank H. (1920) Review of Thorstein Veblen, *The Place of Science in Modern Civilization*, *Journal of Political Economy*, **28**(6), June, pp. 518–20.

Knight, Frank H. (1921a) *Risk, Uncertainty and Profit* (New York: Houghton Mifflin).

Knight, Frank H. (1921b) 'Discussion: Traditional Economic Theory', *American Economic Review*, **11**, Supplement, pp. 143–6.

Knight, Frank H. (1922) 'Ethics and the Economic Interpretation', *Quarterly Journal of Economics*, **36**(3), May, pp. 454–81. Reprinted in Knight (1935b).

Knight, Frank H. (1923) 'The Ethics of Competition', *Quarterly Journal of Economics*, **37**, August, pp. 579–624. Reprinted in Knight (1935b).

Knight, Frank H. (1924) 'The Limitations of Scientific Method in Economics', in Tugwell (1924, pp. 229–67). Reprinted in Knight (1935b).

Knight, Frank H. (1925a) 'Fact and Metaphysics in Economic Psychology', *American Economic Review*, **15**(2), June, pp. 247–66.

Knight, Frank H. (1925b) 'Economic Psychology and the Value Problem', *Quarterly Journal of Economics*, **39**(3), May, pp. 372–409.

Knight, Frank H. (1926) Letter to Morris A. Copeland, dated 9 November 1926. Knight Papers, Department of Special Collections, University of Chicago. Reprinted in Asso and Fiorito (2003).

Knight, Frank H. (1927) Letter to Morris A. Copeland, dated 25 January 1927. Knight Papers, Department of Special Collections, University of Chicago. Reprinted in Asso and Fiorito (2003).

Knight, Frank H. (1928) 'Homan's Contemporary Economic Thought', *Quarterly Journal of Economics*, **43**(1), November, pp. 132–41.

Knight, Frank H. (1931) 'Relation of Utility Theory to Economic Method in the Work of William Stanley Jevons and Others', in Rice, Stuart A. (ed.) *Methods in Social Science* (Chicago: University of Chicago Press), pp. 59–69.

Knight, Frank H. (1932) 'The Newer Economics and the Control of Economic Activity', *Journal of Political Economy*, **40**(4), August, pp. 433–76.

Knight, Frank H. (1933) 'Preface to the Re-Issue', in *Risk, Uncertainty and Profit*, 2nd edn (London: London School of Economics), pp. xi–xxxvi.

Knight, Frank H. (1934) Letter to Joseph Mayer dated 15 March 1934. W. C. Mitchell Papers, Rare Book and Manuscript Library, Columbia University.

Knight, Frank H. (1935a) 'Intellectual Confusion on Morals and Economics', *International Journal of Ethics*, **45**(1), January, pp. 200–20.

Knight, Frank H. (1935b) *The Ethics of Competition and Other Essays* (New York: Harper).

Knight, Frank H. (1935c) Review of J. R. Commons (1934) *Institutional Economics*, *Columbia Law Review*, May, pp. 803–5.

Knight, Frank H. (1936) Letter to Talcott Parsons, dated 1 May 1936, Talcott Parsons Papers.

Knight, Frank H. (1940) '"What is Truth" in Economics?', *Journal of Political Economy*, **48**(1), February, pp. 1–32. Reprinted in Knight (1956).

Knight, Frank H. (1941) 'Social Science', *Ethics*, **51**(2), January, pp. 127–43. Reprinted in Knight (1956).

Knight, Frank H. (1942) 'Social Causation', *American Journal of Sociology*, **49**(1), July, pp. 46–55. Reprinted in Knight (1956).

Knight, Frank H. (1947a) Review of *The Divine Right of Capital* by Clarence E. Ayres, *American Sociological Review*, **12**(2), April, pp. 238–9.

Knight, Frank H. (1947b) *Freedom and Reform: Essays in Economic and Social Philosophy* (New York: Harper and Brothers).

Knight, Frank H. (1948) 'Free Society: Its Basic Nature and Problem', *Philosophical Review*, **57**(1), January, pp. 39–58. Reprinted in Knight (1956).

Knight, Frank H. (1951) *The Economic Organization* (New York: Sentry Press). First published privately in 1933.

Knight, Frank H. (1952) 'Institutionalism and Empiricism in Economics', *American Economic Review (Papers and Proceedings)*, **42**, May, pp. 45–55.

Knight, Frank H. (1956) *On the History and Method of Economics* (Chicago: University of Chicago Press).

Knight, Frank H. (1960) *Intelligence and Democratic Action* (Cambridge, MA: Harvard University Press).

Knight, Frank H. (1961) 'Methodology in Economics' Parts I and II, *Southern Economic Journal*, **27**(3–4), January–April, pp. 185–93, 273–82.

Knight, Frank H. (1964) Review of Sidney Hook (ed.) (1963) *Philosophy and History: A Symposium*, *Ethics*, **74**(4), July, pp. 302–4.

Knight, Frank H. (1966) 'Abstract Economics as Absolute Ethics', *Ethics*, **76**(3), April, pp. 163–77.

Knight, Frank H. *et al.* (1957) 'A New Look at Institutionalism: Discussion', *American Economic Review (Supplement)*, **47**(2), May, pp. 13–27.

Knight, Jack (1992) *Institutions and Social Conflict* (Cambridge: Cambridge University Press).

Knight, Jack and Sened, Itai (eds) (1995) *Explaining Social Institutions* (Ann Arbor, MI: University of Michigan Press).

Knoedler, Janet T. (1997) 'Veblen and Technical Efficiency', *Journal of Economic Issues*, **31**(4), December, pp. 1011–26.

Knoedler, Janet T. and Mayhew, Anne (1999) 'Thorstein Veblen and the Engineers: A Reinterpretation', *History of Political Economy*, **31**(2), Summer, pp. 213–36.

Knudsen, Thorbjørn (2001) 'Nesting Lamarckism within Darwinian Explanations: Necessity in Economics and Possibility in Biology?', in Laurent and Nightingale (2001, pp. 121–59).

Knudsen, Thorbjørn (2002) 'Economic Selection Theory', *Journal of Evolutionary Economics*, **12**(3), September, pp. 443–70.

Koestler, Arthur (1967) *The Ghost in the Machine* (London: Hutchinson).

Koestler, Arthur and Smythies, J. R. (eds) (1969) *Beyond Reductionism: New Perspectives in the Life Sciences* (London: Hutchinson).

Koford, Kenneth J. and Miller, Jeffrey B. (eds) (1991) *Social Norms and Economic Institutions* (Ann Arbor, MI: University of Michigan Press).

Kontopoulos, Kyriakos M. (1993) *The Logics of Social Structure* (Cambridge: Cambridge University Press).

Koopmans, Tjalling C. (1947) 'Measurement Without Theory', *Review of Economics and Statistics*, **29**(3), August, pp. 161–72.

Koopmans, Tjalling C. (1949a) 'Identification Problems in Economic Model Construction', *Econometrica*, **17**, pp. 125–44.

Koopmans, Tjalling C. (1949b) 'Methodological Issues in Quantitative Economics: A Reply', *Review of Economics and Statistics*, **31**(2), May, pp. 86–91.

Kottler, Malcolm Jay (1985) 'Charles Darwin and Alfred Russel Wallace: Two Decades of Debate over Natural Selection', in Kohn, David (ed.) *The Darwinian Heritage* (Princeton: Princeton University Press), pp. 367–432.

Krabbe, Jacob Jan (1996) *Historicism and Organicism in Economics: The Evolution of Thought* (Dordrecht: Kluwer).

Kroeber, Alfred L. (1915) 'The Eighteen Professions', *American Anthropologist*, **17**, pp. 283–9.

Kroeber, Alfred L. (1917) 'The Superorganic', *American Anthropologist*, **19**, pp. 163–213.

Kroeber, Alfred L. (1923) *Anthropology*, 1st edn (New York: Harcourt Brace Jovanovich).

Kropotkin, Petr A. (1902) *Mutual Aid: A Factor of Evolution*, 1st edn (London: Heinemann).

Krugman, Paul R. (1990) *Rethinking International Trade* (Cambridge, MA: MIT Press).

Krugman, Paul R. (1996) *The Self-Organising Economy* (Oxford: Blackwell).

Kuhn, Thomas S. (1970) *The Structure of Scientific Revolutions*, 2nd edn (Chicago: University of Chicago Press).

Kuznets, Simon (1930) *Secular Movements of Production and Prices: Their Nature and Their Bearing upon Cyclical Fluctuations* (Boston: Houghton Mifflin).

Kuznets, Simon (1961) *Capital in the American Economy* (Princeton, NJ: Princeton University Press).

Kuznets, Simon (1963) 'The Contribution of Wesley C. Mitchell', in Dorfman *et al.* (1963, pp. 95–122).

Labriola, Antonio (1897) *Essais sur la conception materialiste de l'histoire* (Paris: Giard et Brière).

Labriola, Antonio (1908) *Essays on the Materialist Conception of History*, translated by Charles H. Kerr from the Italian edition of 1896 (Chicago: Kerr).

Lachmann, Ludwig M. (1947) Review of Knight, F. H. (1947) *Freedom and Reform*, *Economica*, **14**, November, pp. 314–17.

Lachmann, Ludwig M. (1969) 'Methodological Individualism and the Market Economy', in Streissler, Erich W. (ed.) *Roads to Freedom: Essays in Honour of Friedrich A. von Hayek* (London: Routledge and Kegan Paul), pp. 89–103. Reprinted in Lachmann, Ludwig M. (1977) *Capital, Expectations and the Market Process*, edited with an introduction by W. E. Grinder (Kansas City: Sheed Andrews and McMeel).

Lamarck, Jean Baptiste de (1984) *Zoological Philosophy: An Exposition with Regard to the Natural History of Animals*, translated by Hugh Elliot from the 1st French edn of 1809 with introductory essays by David L. Hull and Richard W. Burkhardt (Chicago: University of Chicago Press).

Landa, Janet (1999) 'Bioeconomics of Some Nonhuman and Human Societies: New Institutional Economics Approach', *Journal of Bioeconomics*, **1**(1), pp. 95–113.

Landes, David S. (1969) *The Unbound Prometheus* (Cambridge: Cambridge University Press).

Lane, David A. (1993) 'Artificial Worlds and Economics, Parts I and II', *Journal of Evolutionary Economics*, **3**(2), May, pp. 89–107; and **3**(3), August, pp. 177–97.

Lane, David, Malerba, Franco, Maxfield, Robert and Orsenigo, Luigi (1996) 'Choice and Action', *Journal of Evolutionary Economics*, **6**(1), pp. 43–76.

Langlois, Richard N. (ed.) (1986) *Economics as a Process: Essays in the New Institutional Economics* (Cambridge: Cambridge University Press).

Langlois, Richard N. (1989) 'What Was Wrong With the Old Institutional Economics (and What is Still Wrong With the New)?', *Review of Political Economy*, **1**(3), November, pp. 270–98.

Langlois, Richard N. (2001) 'Knowledge, Consumption, and Endogenous Growth', *Journal of Evolutionary Economics*, **11**(1), pp. 77–93.

Langton, Christopher G. (ed.) (1989) *Artificial Life* (Redwood City, CA: Addison-Wesley).

Langton, Christopher G., Taylor, Charles, Farmer, J. Doyne and Rasmussen, Steen (eds) (1992) *Artificial Life II* (Redwood City, CA: Addison-Wesley).

Lapouge, Georges Vacher de (1896) *Les sélections sociales* (Paris: Fontemoing).

Lapouge, Georges Vacher de (1897) 'The Fundamental Laws of Anthropo-Sociology', *Journal of Political Economy*, **6**(1), December, pp. 54–92.

Latta, Robert (1905) 'Memoir', in Ritchie, David G. (1905) *Philosophical Studies*, ed. Latta, Robert (London and New York: Macmillan), pp. 1–65. Reprinted in Ritchie (1998, vol. 5).

Laurent, John (2000) 'Alfred Marshall's Annotations on Herbert Spencer's *Principles of Biology*', *Marshall Studies Bulletin*, **7**, pp. 1–6.

Laurent, John and Nightingale, John (eds) (2001) *Darwinism and Evolutionary Economics* (Cheltenham: Edward Elgar).

Lave, Jean (1988) *Cognition in Practice: Mind, Mathematics, and Culture in Everyday Life* (Cambridge: Cambridge University Press).

Lave, Jean and Wenger, Etienne (1991) *Situated Learning: Legitimate Peripheral Participation* (Cambridge: Cambridge University Press).

La Vergata, Antonello (1995) 'Herbert Spencer: Biology, Sociology, and Cosmic Evolution', in Maasen, Sabine, Mendelsohn, Everett and Weingart, Peter (eds) *Biology as Society, Society as Biology: Metaphors*, Sociology of the Sciences Yearbook, **18**, 1994 (Boston: Kluwer), pp. 193–229.

Lavoie, Donald (1985) *Rivalry and Central Planning: The Socialist Calculation Debate Reconsidered* (Cambridge: Cambridge University Press).

Lavoie, Marc (1992) *Foundations of Post-Keynesian Economic Analysis* (Aldershot: Edward Elgar).

Lawson, Clive (1994) 'The Transformational Model of Social Activity and Economic Analysis: A Reconsideration of the Work of J. R. Commons', *Review of Political Economy*, **6**(2), April, pp. 186–204.

Lawson, Clive (1996) 'Holism and Collectivism in the Work of J. R. Commons', *Journal of Economic Issues*, **30**(4), December, pp. 967–84.

Lawson, Tony (1997) *Economics and Reality* (London and New York: Routledge).

Lawson, Tony (2002) 'Should Economics Be an Evolutionary Science? Veblen's Concern and Philosophical Legacy', *Journal of Economic Issues*, **36**(2), June, pp. 279–92.

Lawson, Tony (2003a) 'Institutionalism: On the Need to Firm up Notions of Social Structure and the Human Subject', *Journal of Economic Issues*, **37**(1), March, pp. 175–207.

Lawson, Tony (2003b) *Reorienting Economics* (London and New York: Routledge).

Layton, Edwin (1962) 'Veblen and the Engineers', *American Quarterly*, **14**(1), Spring, pp. 64–72.

Leathers, Charles G. (1989) 'New and Old Institutionalists on Legal Rules: Hayek and Commons', *Review of Political Economy*, **1**(3), November, pp. 361–80.

Le Conte, Joseph (1892) *The Race Problem in the South* (New York: Appleton).

Leibenstein, Harvey (1982) 'The Prisoners' Dilemma in the Invisible Hand: An Analysis of Intrafirm Productivity', *American Economic Review (Papers and Proceedings)*, **72**(2), May, pp. 92–7.

Lenski, Gerhard and Lenski, Jean (1987) *Human Societies: An Introduction to Macrosociology*, 5th edn (New York: McGraw-Hill).

Leplin, Jarrett (ed.) (1984) *Scientific Realism* (Berkeley: University of California Press).

Lerner, Abba P. (1945) Review of *The Theory of Economic Progress* by C. E. Ayres, *American Economic Review*, **35**(1), March, pp. 160–4.

Lesourne, Jacques (1992) *The Economics of Order and Disorder: The Market as Organizer and Creator* (Oxford: Clarendon Press).

Lesourne, Jacques and Orléan, André (1998) *Advances in Self-Organization and Evolutionary Economics* (London and Paris: Economica).

Lester, Richard A. (1946) 'Shortcomings of Marginal Analysis for Wage- Employment Problems', *American Economic Review*, **36**(1), March, pp. 63–82.

Lévi-Strauss, Claude (1962) *The Savage Mind* (Chicago: University of Chicago Press).

Levitt, Barbara and March, James G. (1988) 'Organizational Learning', *Annual Review of Sociology*, **14**, pp. 319–40.

Lewes, George Henry (1874) *Problems of Life and Mind: First Series: The Foundations of a Creed*, vol. 1 (London: Trübner).

Lewes, George Henry (1875) *Problems of Life and Mind: First Series: The Foundations of a Creed*, vol. 2 (London: Trübner).

Lewes, George Henry (1877) *Problems of Life and Mind: Second Series: The Physical Basis of Mind*, vol. 3 (London: Trübner).

Lewes, George Henry (1879) *Problems of Life and Mind: Third Series*, 2 vols (London: Trübner).

Lewin, Roger (1992) *Complexity: Life at the Edge of Chaos* (New York: Macmillan).

Lewin, Shira B. (1996) 'Economics and Psychology: Lessons for Our Own Day From the Early Twentieth Century', *Journal of Economic Literature*, **34**(3), September, pp. 1293–323.

Lewis, Alain (1985a) 'On Effectively Computable Realizations of Choice Functions', *Mathematical Social Sciences*, **10**, pp. 43–80.

Lewis, Alain (1985b) 'The Minimum Degree of Recursively Representable Choice Functions', *Mathematical Social Sciences*, **10**, pp. 179–88.

Lewontin, Richard C. (1970) 'The Units of Selection', *Annual Review of Ecology and Systematics*, **1**, pp. 1–18.

Lewontin, Richard C. (1978) 'Adaptation', *Scientific American*, no. 239, pp. 212–30.

Lewontin, Richard C. (2000) *The Triple Helix* (Cambridge, MA: Harvard University Press).

Lindahl, Erik R. (1939) *Studies in the Theory of Money and Capital* (London: Allen and Unwin).

Lindgren, Kristian (1992) 'Evolutionary Phenomena in Simple Dynamics', in Langton *et al.* (1992, pp. 295–312).

Lipton, Peter (1991) *Inference to the Best Explanation* (London: Routledge).

Lloyd, Barbara B. (1972) *Perception and Cognition: A Cross-Cultural Perspective* (Harmondsworth: Penguin).

Lluch, C. (1974) 'Expenditures, Savings and Habit Formation', *International Economic Review*, **15**, pp. 786–97.

Loasby, Brian J. (1976) *Choice, Complexity and Ignorance: An Enquiry into Economic Theory and the Practice of Decision Making* (Cambridge: Cambridge University Press).

Loasby, Brian J. (2001) 'Cognition, Imagination and Institutions in Demand Creation', *Journal of Evolutionary Economics*, **11**(1), January, pp. 7–21.

Loeb, Jacques (1900) *Comparative Physiology of the Brain and Comparative Psychology* (New York: Putman's Sons).

Loeb, Jacques (1912) *The Mechanistic Conception of Life: Biological Essays* (Chicago: University of Chicago Press).

Long, Stewart (2002) 'Lewis Mumford and Institutional Economics', *Journal of Economic Issues*, **36**(1), March, pp. 167–82.

Loomes, Graham (1998) 'Probabilities vs Money: A Test of Some Fundamental Assumptions About Rational Decision Making', *Economic Journal*, **108**(1), March, pp. 477–89.

Loomes, Graham (1999) 'Some Lessons from Past Experiments and Some Challenges for the Future', *Economic Journal*, **109**(2), February, pp. F35–45.

Lopreato, Joseph and Crippen, Timothy (1999) *Crisis in Sociology: The Need for Darwin* (New Brunswick, NJ: Transaction).

Lorenz, Edward H. (2001) 'Models of Cognition, the Development of Knowledge and Organisational Theory', *Journal of Management and Governance*, **5**, pp. 307–30.

Lorenz, Max (1896) *Die Marxistische Socialdemokratie* (Leipzig: George M. Wigand).

Loria, Achille (1895) *Problemi Sociali Contemporanei* (Milano: Kantorowicz).

Loria, Achille (1897) *La proprieta fondiaria a la questione sociale* (Verona: Fratelli Drucker).

Louçã, Francisco (1997) *Turbulence in Economics: An Evolutionary Appraisal of Cycles and Complexity in Historical Processes* (Aldershot: Edward Elgar).

Louçã, Francisco and Perlman, Mark (eds) (2000) *Is Economics an Evolutionary Science? The Legacy of Thorstein Veblen* (Cheltenham, UK and Northampton, MA: Edward Elgar).

Lovejoy, Arthur O. (1927) 'The Meanings of "Emergence" and Its Modes', in Brightman (1927, pp. 20–33).

Lovejoy, Arthur O. (1936) *The Great Chain of Being* (New York: Harper).

Lucas, Robert E., Jr (1981) *Studies in Business Cycle Theory* (Cambridge, MA and Oxford, UK: MIT Press and Basil Blackwell).

Lukes, Steven (1973) *Individualism* (Oxford: Basil Blackwell).

Lukes, Steven (1974) *Power: A Radical View* (London: Macmillan).

Lyotard, Jean-François (1984) *The Postmodern Condition: A Report on Knowledge*, translated by G. Bennington and B. Massumi (Minnesota and Manchester: University of Minnesota Press and Manchester University Press).

Machlup, Fritz (1946) 'Marginal Analysis and Empirical Research', *American Economic Review*, **36**(3), September, pp. 519–54.

Maddison, Angus (1964) *Economic Growth in the West: Comparative Experience in Europe and North America* (New York: Twentieth Century Fund).

Maddison, Angus (1991) *Dynamic Forces in Capitalist Development: A Long-Run Comparative View* (Oxford: Oxford University Press).

Maes, Pattie (ed.) (1991) *Designing Autonomous Agents* (Cambridge, MA: MIT Press).

Maine, Henry Sumner (1961) *Ancient Law, Its Connection with the Early History of Society, and Its Relation to Modern Ideas* (London: Murray).

Mäki, Uskali (1998) 'Aspects of Realism About Economics', *Theoria*, **13**(2), pp. 301–19.

Mäki, Uskali (ed.) (2001) *The Economic World View: Studies in the Ontology of Economics* (Cambridge: Cambridge University Press).

Mäki, Uskali (ed.) (2002) *Fact and Fiction in Economics: Models, Realism and Social Construction* (Cambridge: Cambridge University Press).

Mani, G. S. (1991) 'Is There a General Theory of Biological Evolution?', in Saviotti and Metcalfe (1991, pp. 31–57).

Manicas, P. T. (1987) *A History and Philosophy of the Social Sciences* (Oxford: Basil Blackwell).

Mantel, Rolf R. (1974) 'On the Characterization of Aggregate Excess Demand', *Journal of Economic Theory*, **12**(2), pp. 348–53.

Mantzavinos, Chris (2001) *Individuals, Institutions and Markets* (Cambridge and New York: Cambridge University Press).

March, James G. (1994) *A Primer on Decision Making: How Decisions Happen* (New York: Free Press).

Marchant, James (ed.) (1916) *Alfred Russel Wallace: Letters and Reminiscences* (New York: Harper).

Margolis, Howard (1982) *Selfishness, Altruism, and Rationality: A Theory of Social Choice* (Chicago: University of Chicago Press).

Margolis, Howard (1987) *Patterns, Thinking and Cognition: A Theory of Judgment* (Chicago: University of Chicago Press).

Margolis, Howard (1994) *Paradigms and Barriers: How Habits of Mind Govern Scientific Beliefs* (Chicago: University of Chicago Press).

Marschak, Jacob (1945) 'A Cross Section of Business Cycle Discussion', *American Economic Review*, **35**(3), June, pp. 368–81.

Marsden, Paul (2000) 'Forefathers of Memetics: Gabriel Tarde and the Laws of Imitation', *Journal of Memetics - Evolutionary Models of Information Transmission*, **4**, www.cpm.mmu.ac.uk/jom-emit/2000/vol4/marsden_p.html.

Marshall, Alfred (1890) *Principles of Economics: An Introductory Volume*, 1st edn (London: Macmillan).

Marshall, Alfred (1923) *Money Credit and Commerce* (London: Macmillan).

Marshall, Alfred (1949) *The Principles of Economics*, 8th (reset) edn (London: Macmillan).

Martindale, Don (1976) 'American Sociology Before World War II', *Annual Review of Sociology*, **2**, pp. 121–43.

Marvin, Walter T. (1912) *A First Book in Metaphysics* (New York: Macmillan).

Marx, Karl (1867) *Das Kapital: Kritik der politischen Ökonomie*, vol. 1 (Hamburg: Meissner).

Marx, Karl (1971) *A Contribution to the Critique of Political Economy*, translated from the German edition of 1859 by S. W. Ryazanskaya and edited with an introduction by Maurice Dobb (London: Lawrence and Wishart).

Marx, Karl (1973) *Surveys From Exile: Political Writings – Volume 2*, edited and introduced by David Fernbach (Harmondsworth: Penguin).

Marx, Karl (1976) *Capital*, vol. 1, translated by Ben Fowkes from the fourth German edition of 1890 (Harmondsworth: Pelican).

Marx, Karl (1978) *Capital*, vol. 2, translated by David Fernbach from the German edition of 1893 (Harmondsworth: Pelican).

Marx, Karl (1981) *Capital*, vol. 3, translated by David Fernbach from the German edition of 1894 (Harmondsworth: Pelican).

Marx, Karl and Engels, Frederick (1975) *Karl Marx and Frederick Engels, Collected Works, Vol. 4, Marx and Engels: 1844–45* (London: Lawrence and Wishart).

Marx, Karl and Engels, Frederick (1976a) *Karl Marx and Frederick Engels, Collected Works, Vol. 5, Marx and Engels: 1845–47* (London: Lawrence and Wishart).

Marx, Karl and Engels, Frederick (1976b), *Karl Marx and Frederick Engels, Collected Works, Vol. 6, Marx and Engels: 1845–48* (London: Lawrence and Wishart).

Marx, Karl and Engels, Frederick (1977) *Karl Marx and Frederick Engels, Collected Works, Vol. 8, Marx and Engels: 1848–49* (London: Lawrence and Wishart).

Marx, Karl and Engels, Frederick (1987) *Karl Marx and Frederick Engels, Collected Works, Vol. 42, Letters 1864–68* (London: Lawrence and Wishart).

Maryanski, Alexandra and Turner, Jonathan H. (1992) *The Social Cage: Human Nature and the Evolution of Society* (Stanford, CA: Stanford University Press).

Maslow, Abraham H. (1954) *Motivation and Personality* (New York: Harper and Row).

Maudsley, Henry (1887) 'The Physical Conditions of Consciousness', *Mind*, **12**, no. 48, October, pp. 489–515.

Mayhew, Anne (1987) 'The Beginnings of Institutionalism', *Journal of Economic Issues*, **21**(3), September, pp. 971–98.

Maynard Smith, John (1975) *The Theory of Evolution*, 3rd edn (Harmondsworth: Penguin).

Maynard Smith, John (1989) *Evolutionary Genetics* (Oxford: Oxford University Press).

Maynard Smith, John and Szathmáry, Eors (1995) *The Major Transitions in Evolution* (Oxford: W. H. Freeman).

Maynard Smith, John and Szathmáry, Eors (1999) *The Origins of Life: From the Birth of Life to the Origin of Language* (Oxford: Oxford University Press).

Mayr, Ernst (1960) 'The Emergence of Evolutionary Novelties', in Tax, Sol (ed.) *Evolution After Darwin (I): The Evolution of Life* (Chicago: University of Chicago Press).

Mayr, Ernst (1963) *Animal Species and Evolution* (Cambridge, MA: Harvard University Press).

Mayr, Ernst (1964) 'Introduction', in Darwin, Charles, *On the Origin of Species*, facsimile of the first edition (Cambridge, MA: Harvard University Press), pp. vii–xxvii.

Mayr, Ernst (1976) *Evolution and the Diversity of Life: Selected Essays* (Cambridge, MA: Harvard University Press).

Mayr, Ernst (1982) *The Growth of Biological Thought: Diversity, Evolution, and Inheritance* (Cambridge, MA: Harvard University Press).

Mayr, Ernst (1985a) 'How Biology Differs from the Physical Sciences', in Depew, David J. and Weber, Bruce H. (eds) *Evolution at a Crossroads: The New Biology and the New Philosophy of Science* (Cambridge, MA: MIT Press), pp. 43–63.

Mayr, Ernst (1985b) 'Darwin's Five Theories of Evolution', in Kohn, David (ed.) *The Darwinian Heritage* (Princeton: Princeton University Press), pp. 755–72. Reprinted in Mayr (1988).

Mayr, Ernst (1988) *Toward a New Philosophy of Biology: Observations of an Evolutionist* (Cambridge, MA and London: Harvard University Press).

Mayr, Ernst (1992) *One Long Argument: Charles Darwin and the Genesis of Modern Evolutionary Thought* (London: Allen Lane).

McDougall, William (1908) *An Introduction to Social Psychology*, 1st edn (London: Methuen).

McDougall, William (1924) 'Can Sociology and Social Psychology Dispense With Instincts?', *American Journal of Sociology*, **29**(6), May, pp. 657–73.

McDougall, William (1929) *Modern Materialism and Emergent Evolution* (London: Methuen).

McFarland, Floyd B. (1985) 'Thorstein Veblen Versus the Institutionalists', *Review of Radical Political Economics*, **17**(4), Winter, pp. 95–105.

McFarland, Floyd B. (1986) 'Clarence Ayres and his Gospel of Technology', *History of Political Economy*, **18**(4), Winter, pp. 593–613.

McKelvey, William (1982) *Organizational Systematics: Taxonomy, Evolution, Classification* (Berkeley, CA: University of California Press).

McKinney, John (1977) 'Frank Knight on Uncertainty and Rational Action', *Southern Economic Journal*, **43**(4), April, pp. 1438–52.

McLaughlin, Brian (1992) 'The Rise and Fall of British Emergentism', in Beckerman, Ansgar, Flohr, Hans and Kim, Jaegwon (eds) *Emergence or Reduction? Essays on the Prospects of Nonreductive Physicalism* (Berlin: De Gruyter), pp. 49–93.

McNulty, Paul J. (1973) 'Hoxie's Economics in Retrospect: The Making and Unmaking of a Veblenian', *History of Political Economy*, **5**(3), Fall, pp. 449–84.

McNulty, Paul J. (1980) *The Origins and Development of Labor Economics* (Cambridge, MA: MIT Press).

Mead, George Herbert (1932) *The Philosophy of the Present* (Chicago: Open Court).

Mead, George Herbert (1934) *Mind, Self and Society – From the Standpoint of a Social Behaviorist* (Chicago: University of Chicago Press).

Mead, George Herbert (1938) *The Philosophy of the Act* (Chicago: University of Chicago Press).

Mead, Margaret (1928) *Coming of Age in Samoa: A Psychological Study of Primitive Youth for Western Civilization* (New York: William Morrow).

Means, Gardiner C. (1942) 'Economic Institutions', *American Journal of Sociology*, **47**(6), May, pp. 941–57.

Medawar, Peter B. (1982) *Pluto's Republic* (Oxford: Oxford University Press).

Menand, Louis (2001) *The Metaphysical Club: A Story of Ideas in America* (London: Flamingo).

Ménard, Claude (1990) 'The Lausanne Tradition: Walras and Pareto', in Hennings, Klaus and Samuels, Warren J. (eds) *Neoclassical Economic Theory, 1870 to 1930* (Boston: Kluwer), pp. 95–136.

Mendershausen, Horst (1938) 'On the Significance of Professor Douglas' Production Function', *Econometrica*, **6**(2), April, pp. 143–53.

Menger, Carl (1871) *Grundsätze der Volkswirtschaftslehre* (Tübingen: J. C. B. Mohr). Published in English as *Principles of Economics*, edited by J. Dingwall and translated by B. F. Hoselitz from the German edition of 1871 (New York: New York University Press).

Menger, Carl (1909) 'Geld', reprinted in *The Collected Works of Carl Menger, Vol. IV, Schriften über Geldtheorie und Währungspolitik* (London: London School of Economics, 1936), pp. 1–116.

Merleau-Ponty, Maurice (1942) *La Structure de Comportement* (Paris: PUF).

Merton, Robert K. (1949) *Social Theory and Social Structure*, 1st edn (Glencoe, IL: Free Press).

Metcalfe, J. Stanley (1993) 'Some Lamarckian Themes in the Theory of Growth and Economic Selection: A Provisional Analysis', *Revue Internationale De Systemique*, **7**, pp. 487–504.

Metcalfe, J. Stanley (1994) 'Competition, Fisher's Principle and Increasing Returns in the Selection Process', *Journal of Evolutionary Economics*, **4**(4), November, pp. 327–46.

Metcalfe, J. Stanley (1998) *Evolutionary Economics and Creative Destruction* (London and New York: Routledge).

Mill, John Stuart (1843) *A System of Logic: Ratiocinative and Inductive, Being a Connected View of the Principles of Evidence and the Methods of Scientific Investigation*, 1st edn, 2 vols (London: Longman, Green, Reader and Dyer).

Mill, John Stuart (1964) *Utilitarianism, Liberty and Representative Government*, Everyman edition (1st edn 1859) (London: Dent).

Miller, David L. (1944) 'The Theory of Economic Progress', *Southwestern Social Science Quarterly*, **25**(3), December, pp. 159–77.

Miller, David L. (1958) *Modern Science and Human Freedom* (Austin: University of Texas Press).

Miller, David L. (1966) *Individualism* (Austin: University of Texas Press).

Miller, George A. (1966) *Psychology: The Science of Mental Life* (Harmondsworth: Penguin).

Miller, Richard W. (1981) 'Productive Forces and the Forces of Change: A Review of Gerald A. Cohen, Karl Marx's Theory of History: A Defense', *Philosophical Review*, **90**(1), January, pp. 91–117.

Mills, C. Wright (1963) *The Marxists* (Harmondsworth: Penguin).

Mills, Frederick C., Hollander, Jacob H., Viner, Jacob, Wilson, E. B., Mitchell, Wesley C., Taussig, F. W., Adams, T. S., Black, John D. and Cobb, John Candler (1928) 'The Present Status and Future Prospects of Quantitative Economics', *American Economic Review (Papers and Proceedings)*, **18**(1), Supplement, March, pp. 28–45.

Mills, Susan and Beatty, John (1979) 'The Propensity Interpretation of Fitness', *Philosophy of Science*, **46**(2), pp. 263–86.

Mirowski, Philip (1987) 'The Philosophical Bases of Institutional Economics', *Journal of Economic Issues*, **21**(3), September, pp. 1001–38. Reprinted in Philip Mirowski (1988), *Against Mechanism: Protecting Economics from Science* (Totowa, NJ: Rowman and Littlefield).

Mirowski, Philip (1989a) *More Heat Than Light: Economics as Social Physics, Physics as Nature's Economics* (Cambridge: Cambridge University Press).

Mirowski, Philip (1989b) 'The Measurement Without Theory Controversy: Defeating Rival Resarch Programs by Accusing Them of Naive Empiricism', *Économies et Sociétés*, **11**, pp. 65–87.

Mirowski, Philip (1998) 'Machine Dreams: Economic Agents as Cyborgs', in *New Economics and its History, annual Supplement to Volume 29 of History of Political Economy*, edited by John B. Davis (Durham, NC: Duke University Press) pp. 13–40.

Mirowski, Philip (2002) *Machine Dreams: Economics Becomes a Cyborg Science* (Cambridge and New York: Cambridge University Press).

Mirowski, Philip and Somefun, Koye (1998) 'Markets as Evolving Computational Entities', *Journal of Evolutionary Economics*, **8**(4), pp. 329–56.

Mises, Ludwig von (1920) 'Die Wirtshaftsrechnung im sozialistischen Gemeinwesen', *Archiv für Sozialwissenschaften und Sozialpolitik*, **47**(1), April. Translated and reprinted as 'Economic Calculation in the Socialist Commonwealth', in Hayek, Friedrich A. (ed.) *Collectivist Economic Planning* (London: George Routledge), pp. 87–130.

Mises, Ludwig von (1949) *Human Action: A Treatise on Economics* (London: William Hodge).

Mitchell, Lucy Sprague (1953) *Two Lives: The Story of Wesley Clair Mitchell and Myself* (New York: Simon and Schuster).

Mitchell, Wesley C. (1910) 'The Rationality of Economic Activity', *Journal of Political Economy*, **18**(2–3), parts I and II, February–March, pp. 97–113, 197–216.

Mitchell, Wesley C. (1913) *Business Cycles* (Berkeley: University of California Press).

Mitchell, Wesley C. (1914) 'Human Behavior and Economics: A Survey of Recent Literature', *Quarterly Journal of Economics*, **29**(1), November, pp. 1–47.

Mitchell, Wesley C. (1916) 'The Role of Money in Economic Theory', *American Economic Review (Papers and Proceedings)*, **6**(1), pp. 140–61. Reprinted in Mitchell (1937).

Mitchell, Wesley C. (1917) 'Wieser's Theory of Social Economics', *Political Science Quarterly*, **32**(1), March, pp. 95–118.

Mitchell, Wesley C. (1922a) 'The Crisis of 1920 and the Problem of Controlling Business Cycles', *American Economic Review (Papers and Proceedings)*, **12**(1), March, pp. 20–32.

Mitchell, Wesley C. (1922b) Review of *Risk, Uncertainty, and Profit* by Frank Knight, *American Economic Review*, **12**(2), June, pp. 274–5.

Mitchell, Wesley C. (1924a) 'The Prospects of Economics', in Tugwell (1924, pp. 3–34). Reprinted in Mitchell (1937).

Mitchell, Wesley C. (1924b) 'Commons on the Legal Foundations of Capitalism', *American Economic Review*, **14**(2), June, pp. 240–53.

Mitchell, Wesley C. (1925) 'Quantitative Analysis in Economic Theory', *American Economic Review*, **15**(1), March, pp. 1–12. Reprinted in Mitchell (1937).

Mitchell, Wesley C. (1927) *Business Cycles: The Problem and its Setting* (New York: National Bureau of Economic Research).

Mitchell, Wesley C. (ed.) (1936) *What Veblen Taught* (New York: Viking). Mitchell's introduction is reprinted in Mitchell (1937).

Mitchell, Wesley C. (1937) *The Backward Art of Spending Money and Other Essays* (New York: McGraw-Hill).

Mitchell, Wesley C. (1945) 'The National Bureau's First Quarter-Century', *Twenty-Fifth Annual Report of the National Bureau of Economic Research* (New York: National Bureau of Economic Research).

Mitchell, Wesley C. (1969) *Types of Economic Theory: From Mercantilism to Institutionalism*, 2 vols, ed. Joseph Dorfman (New York: Augustus Kelley).

Moggridge, Donald E. (1992) *Maynard Keynes: An Economist's Biography* (London: Routledge).

Moore, A. W. (1922) 'Some Logical Aspects of Critical Realism', *Journal of Philosophy*, **19**, October, pp. 589–96.

Morgan, Conwy Lloyd (1885) *The Springs of Conduct: An Essay in Evolution* (London: Kegan Paul).

Morgan, Conwy Lloyd (1891) *Animal Life and Intelligence* (London: Edward Arnold).

Morgan, Conwy Lloyd (1894) 'Dr Weismann on Heredity and Progress', *Monist*, **4**(1), pp. 17–30.

Morgan, Conwy Lloyd (1896a) *Habit and Instinct* (London and New York: Edward Arnold).

Morgan, Conwy Lloyd (1896b) 'On Modification and Variation', *Science*, **4**, No. 99, 20 November, pp. 733–40.

Morgan, Conwy Lloyd (1896c) 'Naturalism', *Monist*, **6**, pp. 76–90.

Morgan, Conwy Lloyd (1913) *Spencer's Philosophy of Evolution* (Oxford: Clarendon Press).

Morgan, Conwy Lloyd (1919) *Eugenics and Environment* (London: Bale).

Morgan, Conwy Lloyd (1923) *Emergent Evolution*, 1st edn (London: Williams and Norgate).

Morgan, Conwy Lloyd (1926) *Life, Mind and Spirit* (London: Williams and Norgate).

Morgan, Conwy Lloyd (1927) *Emergent Evolution*, 2nd edn (London: Williams and Norgate).

Morgan, Lewis Henry (1877) *Ancient Society* (Chicago: Charles Kerr).

Morgan, Mary S. (1990) *The History of Econometric Ideas* (Cambridge: Cambridge University Press).

Morgan, Mary S. and Rutherford, Malcolm H. (eds) (1998) *The Transformation of American Economics: From Interwar Pluralism to Postwar Neoclassicism, Annual*

Supplement to Volume 30 of History of Political Economy (Durham, NC: Duke University Press).

Mouzelis, Nicos (1995) *Sociological Theory: What Went Wrong? Diagnosis and Remedies* (London and New York: Routledge).

Mukerjee, Radhakamal (1940) *The Institutional Theory of Economics* (London: Macmillan).

Mumford, Lewis (1934) *Technics and Civilization* (New York: Harcourt, Brace and World).

Murphey, Murray G. (1990) 'Introduction to the Transaction Edition', in Veblen, Thorstein B. (1914) *The Instinct of Workmanship, and the State of the Industrial Arts*, reprint of 1990 (New Brunswick, NJ: Transaction Books), pp. vii–xlv.

Murphree, Idus L. (1959) 'Darwinism in Thorstein Veblen's Economics', *Social Research*, **26**(2), June, pp. 311–24.

Murphy, James Bernard (1994) 'The Kinds of Order in Society', in Mirowski, Philip (ed.) *Natural Images in Economic Thought: Markets Read in Tooth and Claw* (Cambridge and New York: Cambridge University Press), pp. 536–82.

Murray, David J. (1988). *A History of Western Psychology*, 2nd edn (Englewood Cliffs, NJ: Prentice-Hall).

Myrdal, Gunnar (1939) *Monetary Equilibrium*, translated from the Swedish edition of 1931 and the German edition of 1933 (London: Hodge).

Myrdal, Gunnar (1957) *Economic Theory and Underdeveloped Regions* (London: Duckworth).

Myrdal, Gunnar (1972) *Against the Stream: Critical Essays in Economics* (New York: Pantheon Books).

Myrdal, Gunnar (1978) 'Institutional Economics', *Journal of Economic Issues*, **12**(4), December, pp. 771–84.

Nagel, Ernest (1961) *The Structure of Science* (London and Indianapolis: Routledge and Hackett Publishing).

Nagel, Ernest (1965) 'Mechanistic Explanation and Organismic Biology', in Hook, Sidney (ed.) *American Philosophers at Work: The Philosophical Scene in the United States* (New York: Criterion).

Nash, Stephen J. (1998) *Cost, Uncertainty, and Welfare: Frank Knight's Theory of Imperfect Competition* (Aldershot: Ashgate).

Nasmyth, George (1916) *Social Progress and Darwinian Theory: A Study of Force as a Factor in Human Relations* (New York and London: Putnam).

Needham, Joseph (1937) *Integrative Levels: A Reevaluation of the Idea of Progress* (Oxford: Clarendon Press).

Neill, Robin (1972) *A New Theory of Value: The Canadian Economics of H. A. Innis* (Toronto: University of Toronto Press).

Nelson, Alvin F. (1968) *The Development of Lester Ward's World View* (Fort Worth, TX: Branch-Smith).

Nelson, Richard R. (1995) 'Recent Evolutionary Theorizing About Economic Change', *Journal of Economic Literature*, **33**(1), March, pp. 48–90.

Nelson, Richard R. and Nelson, Katherine (2002) 'On the Nature and Evolution of Human Know-How', *Research Policy*, **31**(5), July, pp. 719–33.

Nelson, Richard R. and Winter, Sidney G. (1982) *An Evolutionary Theory of Economic Change* (Cambridge, MA: Harvard University Press).

Nelson, Richard R. and Winter, Sidney G. (2002) 'Evolutionary Theorizing in Economics', *Journal of Economic Perspectives*, **16**(2), Spring, pp. 23–46.

Nicholson, Peter P. (1998) 'Introduction', to Ritchie (1998, vol. 1, pp. vii–xxviii).

Nicolis, Gregoire and Prigogine, Ilya (1977) *Self-Organization in Non-Equilibrium Systems: From Dissipative Structures to Order Through Fluctuations* (New York: Wiley).

Niman, Neil B. (1998) 'Marshall, Veblen, and the Search for an Evolutionary Economics', in Rutherford (1998b, pp. 190–209).

Ngo Mai, Stéphane and Raybaut, Alain (1996) 'Microdiversity and Macro-Order: Toward a Self-Organization Approach', *Revue Internationale de Systémique*, **10**(3), pp. 223–39.

Nooteboom, Bart (2000) *Learning and Innovation in Organizations and Economies* (Oxford and New York: Oxford University Press).

North, Douglass C. (1981) *Structure and Change in Economic History* (New York: Norton).

North, Douglass C. (1990) *Institutions, Institutional Change and Economic Performance* (Cambridge: Cambridge University Press).

North, Douglass C. (1991) 'Institutions', *Journal of Economic Perspectives*, **5**(1), Winter, pp. 97–112.

North, Douglass C. (1994) 'Economic Performance Through Time', *American Economic Review*, **84**(3), June, pp. 359–67.

North, Douglass C. (1995) 'Five Propositions about Institutional Change', in Knight and Sened (1995, pp. 15–26).

North, Douglass C. (1997) 'Prologue', in Drobak, John N. and Nye, John V. C. (eds) *The Frontiers of the New Institutional Economics* (San Diego and London: Academic Press), pp. 3–28.

North, Douglass C. (2002a) Letter to G. M. Hodgson dated 10 September 2002.

North, Douglass C. (2002b) Letter to G. M. Hodgson dated 7 October 2002.

Novikoff, Alex B. (1945) 'The Concept of Integrative Levels in Biology', *Science*, **101**, no. 2618, 2 March, pp. 209–15.

Nozick, Robert (1977) 'On Austrian Methodology', *Synthese*, **36**, pp. 353–92.

Nyland, Christopher (1996) 'Taylorism, John R. Commons, and the Hoxie Report', *Journal of Economic Issues*, **30**(4), December, pp. 985–1016.

O'Donnell, John M. (1985) *The Origins of Behaviorism: American Psychology, 1870–1920* (New York: New York University Press).

O'Hara, Phillip Anthony (1999) 'Thorstein Veblen's Theory of Collective Social Wealth, Instincts and Property Relations', *History of Economic Ideas*, **7**(3), pp. 153–79.

O'Hara, Phillip Anthony (2000) *Marx, Veblen, and Contemporary Institutional Political Economy: Principles and Unstable Dynamics of Capitalism* (Cheltenham: Edward Elgar).

Oberschall, Anthony (1972) 'The Institutionalization of American Sociology', in *The Establishment of American Sociology* (New York: Harper and Row), pp. 187–251.

Ogburn, William F. (1922) *Social Change: With Respect to Culture and Original Nature* (New York: Huebsch).

Olson, Mancur, Jr (1965) *The Logic of Collective Action* (Cambridge, MA: Harvard University Press).

Oppenheim, Paul and Putnam, Hilary (1968) 'Unity of Science as a Working Hypothesis', in Feigl, Herbert, Scriven, Michael and Maxwell, G. (eds) *Concepts, Theories, and the Mind–Body Problem*, Minnesota Studies in the Philosophy of Science, Vol. 2 (Minneapolis: University of Minnesota Press), pp. 3–36.

Ostrom, Elinor (1986) 'An Agenda for the Study of Institutions', *Public Choice*, **48**, pp. 3–25.

Ostrom, Elinor, Gardner, Roy and Walker, James (1994) *Rules, Games, and Common-Pool Resources* (Ann Arbor, MI: University of Michigan Press).

Outhwaite, William (1987) *New Philosophies of Social Science: Realism, Hermeneutics and Critical Theory* (London: Macmillan).

Pagano, Ugo (2000) 'Bounded Rationality, Institutionalism and the Diversity of Economic Institutions', in Louçã and Perlman (2000, pp. 95–113).

Pap, Arthur (1962) *An Introduction to the Philosophy of Science* (Glencoe, IL: Free Press).

Parker, Carleton H. (1918) 'Motives in Economic Life', *American Economic Review (Papers and Proceedings)*, **8**(1), Supplement, March, pp. 212–31.

Parsons, Kenneth H. (1985) 'John R. Commons: His Relevance to Contemporary Economics', *Journal of Economic Issues*, **19**(3), September, pp. 755–78.

Parsons, Talcott (1932) 'Economics and Sociology: Marshall in Relation to the Thought of his Time', *Quarterly Journal of Economics*, **46**(2), February, pp. 316–47. Reprinted in Camic (1991).

Parsons, Talcott (1934) 'Some Reflections on "The Nature and Significance of Economics"', *Quarterly Journal of Economics*, **48**(3), May, pp. 511–45. Reprinted in Camic (1991).

Parsons, Talcott (1935) 'Sociological Elements in Economic Thought, Parts I & II', *Quarterly Journal of Economics*, **49**(3–4), May–August, pp. 414–53, 646–67. Reprinted in Camic (1991).

Parsons, Talcott (1937) *The Structure of Social Action*, 2 vols (New York: McGraw-Hill).

Patinkin, Donald (1973) 'Frank Knight as a Teacher', *American Economic Review*, **63**(5), December, pp. 787–810. Reprinted in Patinkin (1981).

Patinkin, Donald (1981) *Essays On and In the Chicago Tradition* (Durham, NC: Duke University Press).

Patinkin, Donald (1995) 'The Training of an Economist', *Banca Nazionale del Lavoro Quaterly Review*, **48**, pp. 359–95.

Patten, Simon Nelson (1894) 'The Failure of Biologic Sociology', *Annals of the American Academy of Political and Social Science'*, **4**, pp. 919–47.

Paul, Diane (1984) 'Eugenics and the Left', *Journal of the History of Ideas*, **45**(4), October–December, pp. 567–590.

Peckham, George (1896) Letter to C. Lloyd Morgan dated 28 January 1896, C. Lloyd Morgan Papers, University of Bristol Library.

Peirce, Charles Sanders (1878) 'How to Make Our Ideas Clear', *Popular Science Monthly*, **12**, January, pp. 286–302. Reprinted in Peirce (1958).

Peirce, Charles Sanders (1891) 'The Architecture of Theories, *Monist*, January, pp. 161–76. Reprinted in Peirce (1958).

Peirce, Charles Sanders (1892) 'The Doctrine of Necessity', *Monist*, April, pp. 321–37. Reprinted in Peirce (1958).

Peirce, Charles Sanders (1935) *Collected Papers of Charles Sanders Peirce, Volume VI, Scientific Metaphysics*, ed. C. Hartshorne and P. Weiss (Cambridge, MA: Harvard University Press).

Peirce, Charles Sanders (1958) *Selected Writings (Values in a Universe of Chance)*, edited with an introduction by Philip P. Wiener (New York: Doubleday).

Pelikan, Pavel (1988) 'Can the Innovation System of Capitalism be Outperformed?', in Dosi *et al.* (1988, pp. 370–98).

Pelikan, Pavel (1992) 'The Dynamics of Economic Systems, Or How to Transform a Failed Socialist Economy', *Journal of Evolutionary Economics*, **2**(1), March, pp. 39–63.

Penrose, Edith T. (1952) 'Biological Analogies in the Theory of the Firm', *American Economic Review*, **42**(4), December, pp. 804–19.

Penrose, Roger (1994) *Shadows of the Mind: A Search for the Missing Science of Consciousness* (Oxford: Oxford University Press).

Pepper, Stephen C. (1926) 'Emergence', *Journal of Philosophy*, **23**(9), April, pp. 241–5.

Perlman, Mark (1996) *The Character of Economic Thought, Economic Characters and Economic Institutions: Selected Essays by Mark Perlman* (Ann Arbor, MI: Michigan University Press).

Perlman, Mark and McCann, Charles R. (1998) *The Pillars of Economic Understanding: Ideas and Traditions* (Ann Arbor: University of Michigan Press).

Perry, Charner M. (1928) 'Habit as an Explanatory Concept in the Social Sciences', *International Journal of Ethics*, **38**(3), April, pp. 269–83.

Perry, Ralph Barton (1918) *The Present Conflict of Ideals: A Study of the Philosophical Background of the World War* (New York: Longmans Green).

Perry, Ralph Barton (1935) *The Thought and Character of Willam James* (Boston: Little, Brown).

Persons, Stow (ed.) (1950) *Evolutionary Thought in America* (New Haven: Yale University Press).

Peterson, R. D. (1979) 'Chamberlin's Monopolistic Competition: Neoclassical or Institutional?', *Journal of Economic Issues*, **13**(3), September, pp. 669–86.

Petr, Jerry L. (1998) 'The Social Conscience of an American Economist: Alvin S. Johnson as Advocate/Reformer', in Rutherford (1998b, pp. 258–71).

Pfaffenberger, Bryan (1988) 'Fetishised Objects and Humanised Nature: Towards an Anthropology of Technology', *Man*, **23**(2), June, pp. 236–52.

Pfeifer, Edward J. (1965) 'The Genesis of American Neo-Lamarckism', *Isis*, **56**(2), no. 184, pp. 156–67.

Pfeiffer, John E. (1969) *The Emergence of Man* (New York: Harper and Row).

Phlips, Louis and Spinnewyn, F. (1984) 'True Indexes and Rational Habit Formation', *European Economic Review*, **24**, pp. 209–23.

Piaget, Jean (1979) *Behaviour and Evolution*, translated from the French edition of 1976 by D. Nicholson-Smith (London: Routledge and Kegan Paul).

Pickering, Andrew (1995) *The Mangle of Practice: Time, Agency and Science* (Chicago: University of Chicago Press).

Pigou, Arthur C. (1907) 'Social Improvements in the Light of Modern Biology', *Economic Journal*, **17**(3), September, pp. 358–69.

Pingle, Mark (1992) 'Costly Optimization: An Experiment', *Journal of Economic Behavior and Organization*, **17**(1), January, pp. 3–30.

Pinker, Steven (1994) *The Language Instinct: The New Science of Language and Mind* (London and New York: Allen Lane and Morrow).

Plotkin, Henry C. (1994) *Darwin Machines and the Nature of Knowledge: Concerning Adaptations, Instinct and the Evolution of Intelligence* (Harmondsworth: Penguin).

Plotkin, Henry C. (1997) *Evolution in Mind: An Introduction to Evolutionary Psychology* (Harmondsworth: Penguin).

Pojman, Louis P. (ed.) (1995) *Ethical Theory: Classical and Contemporary Readings*, 2nd edn (Belmont, CA: Wadsworth).

Polanyi, Karl (1944) *The Great Transformation: The Political and Economic Origins of Our Time* (New York: Rinehart).

Polanyi, Karl, Arensberg, Conrad M. and Pearson, Harry W. (eds) (1957) *Trade and Market in the Early Empires* (Chicago: Henry Regnery).

Polanyi, Michael (1958) *Personal Knowledge: Towards a Post-Critical Philosophy* (London: Routledge and Kegan Paul).

Polanyi, Michael (1967) *The Tacit Dimension* (London: Routledge and Kegan Paul).

Polanyi, Michael (1968) 'Life's Irreducible Structure', *Science*, **160**, no. 3834, 21 June, pp. 1308–12.

Popenhoe, Paul and Johnson, Roswell H. (1918) *Applied Eugenics* (New York: Macmillan).

Popper, Karl R. (1945) *The Open Society and Its Enemies*, 2 vols (London: Routledge and Kegan Paul).

Popper, Karl R. (1960) *The Poverty of Historicism* (London: Routledge and Kegan Paul).

Popper, Karl R. (1972a) *Objective Knowledge: An Evolutionary Approach* (Oxford: Oxford University Press).

Popper, Karl R. (1972b) *The Logic of Scientific Discovery*, 3rd edn, translated and revised from the German edition of 1935 (London: Hutchinson).

Popper, Karl R. (1982) *The Open Universe: An Argument for Indeterminism*, in *Postscript to the Logic of Scientific Discovery*, ed. William W. Bartley, III (London: Hutchinson).

Popper, Karl R. (1990) *A World of Propensities* (Bristol: Thoemmes).

Popper, Karl R. and Eccles, John C. (1977) *The Self and Its Brain* (Berlin: Springer International).

Posner, Richard A. (1973) *Economic Analysis of Law* (Boston: Little, Brown).

Potts, Jason (2000) *The New Evolutionary Microeconomics: Complexity, Competence and Adaptive Behaviour* (Cheltenham: Edward Elgar).

Potts, Richard (1996) *Humanity's Descent:The Consequences of Ecological Instability* (New York: William Morrow).

Price, George R. (1970) 'Selection and Covariance', *Nature*, **227**, pp. 520–1.

Price, George R. (1995) 'The Nature of Selection', *Journal of Theoretical Biology*, **175**, pp. 389–96.

Prigogine, Ilya and Stengers, Isabelle (1984) *Order Out of Chaos: Man's New Dialogue With Nature* (London: Heinemann).

Putnam, Hilary (1995) *Pragmatism* (Oxford: Blackwell).

Pylyshyn, Zenon W. (1984) *Computation and Cognition* (Cambridge, MA: MIT Press).

Pylyshyn, Zenon W. (ed.) (1987) *The Robot's Dilemma: The Frame Problem in Artificial Intelligence* (Norwood, NJ: Ablex).

Quine, Willard van Orman (1951) 'Two Dogmas of Empiricism', *Philosophical Review*, **60**(1), January, pp. 20–43. Reprinted in Quine (1953).

Quine, Willard van Orman (1953) *From a Logical Point of View* (Cambridge, MA: Harvard University Press).

Quine, Willard van Orman (1960) *Word and Object* (Cambridge, MA: Harvard University Press).

Raines, J. Patrick and Leathers, Charles G. (1996) 'Veblenian Stock Markets and the Efficient Markets Hypothesis', *Journal of Post Keynesian Economics*, **19**(1), Fall, pp. 137–51.

Ramstad, Yngve (1986) 'A Pragmatist's Quest for Holistic Knowledge: The Scientific Methodology of John R. Commons', *Journal of Economic Issues*, **20**(4), December, pp. 1067–106.

Ramstad, Yngve (1990) 'The Institutionalism of John R. Commons: Theoretical Foundations of a Volitional Economics', *Research in the History of Economic Thought and Methodology*, **8**, pp. 53–104.

Ramstad, Yngve (1994) 'On the Nature of Economic Evolution: John R. Commons and the Metaphor of Artificial Selection', in Magnusson, Lars (ed.) *Evolutionary and Neo-Schumpeterian Approaches to Economics* (Boston: Kluwer), pp. 65–121.

Ramstad, Yngve (1995) 'John R. Commons's Puzzling Inconsequentiality as an Economic Theorist', *Journal of Economic Issues*, **29**(4), December, pp. 991–1012.

Rasmussen, Charles and Tilman, Rick (1992) 'Mechanistic Physiology and Institutional Economics: Jacques Loeb and Thorstein Veblen', *International Journal of Social Economics*, **19**(10–12), pp. 235–47.

Rasmussen, Charles and Tilman, Rick (1998) *Jacques Loeb: His Science and Social Activism and Their Philosophical Foundations* (Philadelphia, PA: American Philosophical Society).

Reber, Arthur S. (1993) *Implicit Learning and Tacit Knowledge: An Essay on the Cognitive Unconscious* (Oxford and New York: Oxford University Press).

Reder, Melvin W. (1982) 'Chicago Economics: Permanence and Change', *Journal of Economic Literature*, **20**(1), March, pp. 1–38.

Redfield, Robert (ed.) (1942) *Levels of Integration in Biological and Social Systems* (Lancaster, PA: Cattell).

Rensch, Bernhard (1971) *Biophilosophy* (New York: Columbia University Press).

Richards, Janet Radcliffe (2000) *Human Nature After Darwin: A Philosophical Introduction* (London and New York: Routledge).

Richards, Robert J. (1987) *Darwin and the Emergence of Evolutionary Theories of Mind and Behavior* (Chicago: University of Chicago Press).

Richardson, R. Alan and Kane, Thomas C. (1988) 'Orthogenesis and Evolution in the 19th Century: The Idea of Progress in American Neo-Lamarckism', in Nitecki, Matthew H. (ed.) *Evolutionary Progress* (Chicago: University of Chicago Press), pp. 149–67.

Richerson, Peter J. and Boyd, Robert (2001) 'Built For Speed, Not for Comfort: Darwinian Theory and Human Culture', *History and Philosophy of the Life Sciences*, **23**, pp. 423–63.

Richerson, Peter J., Boyd, Robert and Bettinger, Robert L. (2001) 'Was Agriculture Impossible During the Pleistocene But Mandatory During the Holocene? A Climate Change Hypothesis', *American Antiquity*, **66**, pp. 387–411.

Ridley, Matt (1996) *The Origins of Virtue* (Harmondsworth: Penguin).

Riesman, David (1963) *Thorstein Veblen: A Critical Interpretation* (New York: Charles Scribner's).

Ritchie, David G. (1889) *Darwinism and Politics*, 1st edn (London: Swan Sonnenschein).

Ritchie, David G. (1891) *Darwinism and Politics*, 2nd edn (London: Swan Sonnenschein).

Ritchie, David G. (1896) 'Social Evolution', *International Journal of Ethics*, **6**(2), pp. 165–81. Reprinted in Ritchie, David G. (1902) *Studies in Political and Social Ethics* (London and New York: Swan Sonnenschein and Macmillan) and Ritchie (1998, vol. 4).

Ritchie, David G. (1901) *Principles of State Interference: Four Essays on the Political Philosophy of Mr. Herbert Spencer, J. S. Mill and T. H. Green* (London: Swan Sonnenschein). Reprinted in Ritchie (1998, vol. 1).

Ritchie, David G. (1998) *The Collected Works of D. G. Ritchie*, 6 vols, ed. and introduced by Peter P. Nicholson (Bristol: Thoemmes).

Rizvi, S. Abu Turab (1994a) 'The Microfoundations Project in General Equilibrium Theory', *Cambridge Journal of Economics*, **18**(4), August, pp. 357–77.

Rizvi, S. Abu Turab (1994b) 'Game Theory to the Rescue?', *Contributions to Political Economy*, **13**, pp. 1–28.

Rizvi, S. Abu Turab (1998) 'Responses to Arbitrariness in Contemporary Economics', in Davis, John (ed.) *The New Economics and its History* (Durham, NC: Duke University Press) pp. 273–88.

Robbins, Lionel (1932) *An Essay on the Nature and Significance of Economic Science*, 1st edn (London: Macmillan).

Robinson, Joan (1933) *The Economics of Imperfect Competition* (London: Macmillan).

Robson, Arthur J. (2001a) 'The Biological Basis of Human Behavior', *Journal of Economic Literature*, **39**(1), March, pp. 11–33.

Robson, Arthur J. (2001b) 'Why Would Nature Give Individuals Utility Functions?', *Journal of Political Economy*, **109**(4), August, pp. 900–14.

Robson, Arthur J. (2002) 'Evolution and Human Nature', *Journal of Economic Perspectives*, **16**(2), Spring, pp. 89–106.

Rogoff, E. and Lave, Jean (1984) *Everyday Cognition: Development in Social Context* (Oxford: Oxford University Press).

Romanes, George John (1883) *Mental Evolution in Animals* (London: Kegan Paul, Trench).

Romanes, George John (1893) *Darwin and After Darwin: An Exposition of the Darwinian Theory and a Discussion of Post-Darwinian Questions*, vol. 1, 2nd edn (London: Longmans, Green).

Rorty, Richard (1982) *The Consequences of Pragmatism: Essays* (Minneapolis: University of Minnesota Press).

Rose, Hilary and Rose, Steven (2000) *Alas, Poor Darwin: Arguments Against Evolutionary Psychology* (London: Jonathan Cape).

Rosenberg, Alexander (1995) *The Philosophy of Social Science*, 2nd edn (Boulder, CO: Westview Press).

Rosenberg, Alexander (1998) 'Folk Psychology', in Davis *et al.* (1998, pp. 195–7).

Rosenberg, Nathan (1976) 'On Technological Expectations', *Economic Journal*, **86**(3), September, pp. 523–35.

Rosenberg, Nathan and Vincenti, Walter (1985) *The Britannia Bridge, the Generation and Diffusion of Technological Knowledge* (Cambridge, MA: MIT Press).

Ross, Dorothy (1991) *The Origins of American Social Science* (Cambridge: Cambridge University Press).

Ross, Edward Alsworth (1901) *Social Control: A Survey of the Foundations of Order*, 1st edn (New York: Macmillan).

Rosser, J. Barkley, Jr (1999) 'On the Complexities of Complex Economic Dynamics', *Journal of Economic Perspectives*, **13**(4), Fall, pp. 169–92.

Royce, Josiah (1903) *Outlines of Psychology: An Elementary Treatise with Some Practical Applications* (New York and London: Macmillan).

Royce, Josiah (1969) *The Basic Writings of Josiah Royce*, 2 vols, edited with an introduction by J. J. McDermott (Chicago: University of Chicago Press).

Runciman, Walter G. (1989) *A Treatise on Social Theory. Volume 2: Substantive Social Theory* (Cambridge: Cambridge University Press).

Runciman, Walter G. (1998) 'The Selectionist Paradigm and Its Implications for Sociology', *Sociology*, **32**(1), February, pp. 163–88.

Runde, Jochen H. (1998) 'Assessing Causal Economic Explanations', *Oxford Economic Papers*, **50**(1), pp. 151–72.

Ruse, Michael (1979) *The Darwinian Revolution: Science Red in Tooth and Claw*, 1st edn (Chicago: University of Chicago Press).

Ruse, Michael (1981) 'Philosophical Aspects of the Darwinian Revolution', in Sumner, L. W., Slater, John G. and Wilson, Fred (eds) *Pragmatism and Purpose: Essays Presented to Thomas A. Goudge* (Toronto: University of Toronto Press), pp. 220–235.

Ruse, Michael (1986) *Taking Darwin Seriously: A Naturalistic Approach to Philosophy* (Oxford: Basil Blackwell).

Russell, Bertrand (1927) *The Analysis of Matter* (London: George Allen and Unwin).

Russell, Bertrand (1931) *The Scientific Outlook* (New York: Norton).

Russett, Cynthia Eagle (1976) *Darwin in America: The Intellectual Response 1865–1912* (San Francisco: W. H. Freeman).

Rutherford, Malcolm H. (1981) 'Clarence Ayres and the Instrumentalist Theory of Value', *Journal of Economic Issues*, **15**(3), September, pp. 657–74.

Rutherford, Malcolm H. (1983) 'J. R. Commons's Institutional Economics', *Journal of Economic Issues*, **17**(3), September, pp. 721–44.

Rutherford, Malcolm H. (1984) 'Thorstein Veblen and the Processes of Institutional Change', *History of Political Economy*, **16**(3), Fall, pp. 331–48.

Rutherford, Malcolm H. (1992) 'Thorstein Veblen and the Problem of the Engineers', *International Review of Sociology*, **3**, pp. 125–50.

Rutherford, Malcolm H. (1994) *Institutions in Economics: The Old and the New Institutionalism* (Cambridge: Cambridge University Press).

Rutherford, Malcolm H. (1997) 'American Institutionalism and the History of Economics', *Journal of the History of Economic Thought*, **19**(2), Fall, pp. 178–95.

Rutherford, Malcolm H. (1998a) 'Veblen's Evolutionary Programme: A Promise Unfulfilled', *Cambridge Journal of Economics*, **22**(4), July, pp. 463–77.

Rutherford, Malcolm H. (ed.) (1998b) *The Economic Mind in America: Essays in the History of American Economics* (London and New York: Routledge).

Rutherford, Malcolm H. (1999) 'Institutionalism as "Scientific Economics"', in Backhouse, Roger E. and Creedy, John (eds) *From Classical Economics to the Theory of the Firm: Essays in Honour of D. P. O'Brien* (Cheltenham: Edward Elgar), pp. 223–42.

Rutherford, Malcolm H. (2000a) 'Institutionalism Between the Wars', *Journal of Economic Issues*, **34**(2), June, pp. 291–303.

Rutherford Malcolm H. (2000b) 'Understanding Institutional Economics: 1918–1929', *Journal of the History of Economic Thought*, **22**(3), pp. 277–308.

Rutherford, Malcolm H. (2001) 'Institutional Economics: Then and Now', *Journal of Economic Perspectives*, **15**(3), Summer, pp. 173–94.

Rutherford, Malcolm H. (2002) 'Morris A. Copeland: A Case Study in the History of Institutional Economics', *Journal of the History of Economic Thought*, **24**(3), September, pp. 261–90.

Rutherford, Malcolm H. (2003) 'American Institutionalism in the Interwar Period', in Samuels *et al.* (2003, pp. 360–76).

Ryan, Frank X. (ed.) (2001) *Darwin's Impact: Social Evolution in America, 1880–1920*, 3 vols (Bristol: Thoemmes).

Salamon, Sonya (1992) *Prairie Patrimony: Family, Farming and Community in the Midwest* (Chapel Hill, NC: University of North Carolina Press).

Salk, Jonas (1983) *Anatomy of Reality: Merging Intuition and Reason* (New York: Columbia University Press).

Salmon, Wesley C. (1998) *Causality and Explanation* (Oxford: Oxford University Press).

Salthe, Stanley N. (1985) *Evolving Hierarchical Systems* (New York: Columbia University Press).

Samelson, Franz (1981) 'Struggle for Scientific Authority: The Reception of Watson's Behaviorism, 1913–1920', *Journal of the History of the Behavioral Sciences*, **17**, pp. 399–425.

Samuels, Warren J. (1977a), 'The Knight–Ayres Correspondence: The Grounds of Knowledge and Social Action', *Journal of Economic Issues*, **11**(3), September, pp. 485–525.

Samuels, Warren J. (1977b) 'Technology vis-à-vis Institutions in the JEI: A Suggested Interpretation', *Journal of Economic Issues*, **11**(4), December, pp. 871–95.

Samuels, Warren J. (1987) 'Homan, Paul Thomas', in Eatwell, John, Milgate, Murray and Newman, Peter (eds) *The New Palgrave Dictionary of Economics* (London: Macmillan), vol. 2, p. 668.

Samuels, Warren J. (1990) 'The Self-Referentiability of Thorstein Veblen's Theory and the Preconceptions of Economic Science', *Journal of Economic Issues*, **24**(3), pp. 695–718.

Samuels, Warren J., Biddle, Jeff E. and Davis, John B. (eds) (2003) *A Companion to the History of Economic Thought* (Malden, MA and Oxford, UK: Blackwell).

Samuelson, Paul A. (1939) 'Interactions Between the Multiplier Analysis and the Principle of Acceleration', *Review of Economics and Statistics*, **21**(2), May, pp. 75–8.

Samuelson, Paul A. (1944) 'A Warning to the Washington DC Expert', *New Republic*, **11**, September 11, pp. 297–9.

Samuelson, Paul A. (1947) *Foundations of Economic Analysis* (Cambridge, MA: Harvard University Press).

Samuelson, Paul A. (1948) *Economics*, 1st edn (New York: McGraw-Hill).

Samuelson, Paul A. (1997) 'Credo of a Lucky Textbook Author', *Journal of Economic Perspectives*, **11**(2), Spring, pp. 153–60.

Sanderson, Stephen K. (1990) *Social Evolutionism: A Critical History* (Oxford: Blackwell).

Saviotti, Pier Paolo and Metcalfe, J. Stanley (eds) (1991) *Evolutionary Theories of Economic and Technological Change: Present Status and Future Prospects* (Reading: Harwood).

Sawyer, R. Keith (2001) 'Emergence in Sociology: Contemporary Philosophy of Mind and Some Implications for Sociological Theory', *American Journal of Sociology*, **107**(3), November, pp. 551–85.

Sawyer, R. Keith (2002) 'Emergence in Psychology: Lessons From the History of Non-Reductionist Science', *Human Affairs*, **45**(1), pp. 2–28.

Sayer, Andrew (1984) *Method in Social Science: A Realist Approach* (London: Hutchinson).

Schaffer, Mark E. (1989) 'Are Profit-Maximizers the Best Survivors?: A Darwinian Model of Economic Natural Selection', *Journal of Economic Behavior and Organization*, **12**(1), March, pp. 29–45.

Scheiber, Henry N., Vatter, Harold G. and Faulkner, Harold U. (1976) *American Economic History*, 9th edn (New York: Harper and Row).

Scheinkman, José A. and Woodford, Michael (1994) 'Self-Organized Criticality and Economic Fluctuations', *American Economic Review (Papers and Proceedings)*, **84**(2), May, pp. 417–21.

Scherer, Frederick M. (2000) 'The Emigration of German-Speaking Economists After 1933', *Journal of Economic Literature*, **38**(3), September, pp. 614–26.

Schieve, W. C. and Allen, Peter M. (eds) (1982) *Self-Organization and Dissipative Structures: Applications in the Physical and Social Sciences* (Austin: University of Texas Press).

Schlicht, Ekkehart (1998) *On Custom in the Economy* (Oxford and New York: Clarendon Press).

Schmoller, Gustav (1900) *Grundriss der allgemeinen Volkswirtschaftslehre, Erster Teil* (München und Leipzig: Duncker und Humblot).

Schotter, Andrew R. (1981) *The Economic Theory of Social Institutions* (Cambridge: Cambridge University Press).

Schout, Adriaan (1991) Review of *Institutions, Institutional Change and Economic Performance* by Douglass C. North, *Economic Journal*, **101**(5), November, pp. 1587–9.

Schrecker, Ellen W. (1986) *No Ivory Tower: McCarthyism and the Universities* (Oxford and New York: Oxford University Press).

Schultz, Walter J. (2001) *The Moral Conditions of Economic Efficiency* (Cambridge and New York: Cambridge University Press).

Schumpeter, Joseph A. (1908) *Das Wesen und der Hauptinhalt der theoretischen Nationalökonomie* (München und Leipzig: Duncker und Humblot).

Schumpeter, Joseph A. (1931) 'The Present World Depression: A Tentative Diagnosis', *American Economic Review (Papers and Proceedings)*, **21**(1), Supplement, March, pp. 179–82.

Schumpeter, Joseph A. (1934) *The Theory of Economic Development: An Inquiry into Profits, Capital, Credit, Interest, and the Business Cycle*, translated by Redvers Opie from the second German edition of 1926 (Cambridge, MA: Harvard University Press).

Schumpeter, Joseph A. (1942) *Capitalism, Socialism and Democracy*, 1st edn (London: George Allen and Unwin).

Schumpeter, Joseph A. (1954) *History of Economic Analysis* (New York: Oxford University Press).

Schumpeter, Joseph A. (1991) *The Economics and Sociology of Capitalism*, ed. Richard Swedberg (Princeton: Princeton University Press).

Schwartz, Jordan A. (1993) *The New Dealers: Power Politics in the Age of Roosevelt* (New York: Knopf).

Schweber, Silvan S. (1977) 'The Origin of the *Origin* Revisited', *Journal of the History of Biology*, **10**(2), Fall, pp. 229–316.

Schweber, Silvan S. (1980) 'Darwin and the Political Economists: Divergence of Character', *Journal of the History of Biology*, **13**(2), Fall, pp. 195–289.

Schweber, Silvan S. (1985) 'The Wider British Context in Darwin's Theorizing', in Kohn, David (ed.) *The Darwinian Heritage* (Princeton: Princeton University Press), pp. 35–69.

Schweitzer, Arthur (1975) 'Frank Knight's Social Economics', *History of Political Economy*, **7**(3), Fall, pp. 279–92.

Screpanti, Ernesto and Zamagni, Stefano (1993) *An Outline of the History of Economic Thought* (Oxford: Clarendon Press).

Searle, John R. (1995) *The Construction of Social Reality* (London: Allen Lane).

Searle, John R. (1997) *The Mystery of Consciousness* (London: Granta Books).

Seckler, David (1975) *Thorstein Veblen and the Institutionalists: A Study in the Social Philosophy of Economics* (London: Macmillan).

Seligman, Edwin R. A. (1925) *Essays in Economics* (New York: Macmillan).

Sellars, Roy Wood (1908) 'Critical Realism and the Time Problem', *Journal of Philosophy*, **5**(20, 22), September, pp. 542–8 and October, pp. 597–602.

Sellars, Roy Wood (1916) *Critical Realism: A Study of the Nature and Conditions of Knowledge* (Chicago: Rand-McNally).

Sellars, Roy Wood (1918) 'An Approach to the Mind–Body Problem', *Philosophical Review*, **27**(2), March, pp. 150–63.

Sellars, Roy Wood (1922) *Evolutionary Naturalism* (Chicago: Rand-McNally).

Sellars, Roy Wood (1926) *The Principles and Problems of Philosophy* (New York: Macmillan).

Sellars, Roy Wood (1955) 'My Philosophical Position: A Rejoinder', *Philosophy and Phenomenological Research*, **16**(1), September, pp. 72–97.

Sellars, Roy Wood (1959) 'Levels of Causality: The Emergence of Guidance and Reason in Nature', *Philosophy and Phenomenological Research*, **20**(1), September, pp. 1–17.

Sellars, Roy Wood, McGill, Vivian J. and Farber, Marvin (eds) (1949) *Philosophy for the Future: The Quest for Modern Materialism* (New York: Macmillan).

Sellars, Wilfred and Meehl, P. E. (1956) 'The Concept of Emergence', in Feigl, Herbert and Scriven, Michael (eds) *Minnesota Studies in the Philosophy of Science, Vol. 1: The Foundations of Science and the Concepts of Psychology and Psychoanalysis* (Minneapolis: University of Minnesota Press), pp. 239–52.

Sened, Itai (1995) 'The Emergence of Individual Rights', in Knight and Sened (1995, pp. 161–88).

Sened, Itai (1997) *The Political Institution of Private Property* (Cambridge: Cambridge University Press).

Shackle, George L. S. (1961) 'Time, Nature, and Decision', in Hegeland, Hugo (ed.) *Money, Growth, and Methodology; and Other Essays in Economics in Honor of Johan Åkerman* (Lund: C. W. K. Gleerup), pp. 299–310.

Shackle, George L. S. (1967) *The Years of High Theory: Invention and Tradition in Economic Thought 1926–1939* (Cambridge: Cambridge University Press).

Shackle, George L. S. (1976) 'Time and Choice', *Proceedings of the British Academy*, **66**, pp. 309–29. Reprinted in Shackle, George L. S. (1990) *Time, Expectations and Uncertainty in Economics: Selected Essays of G. L. S. Shackle*, ed. J. L. Ford (Aldershot: Edward Elgar).

Shaw, George Bernard (1921) *Back to Methuselah: A Metabiological Pentateuch*, 1st edn (London: Constable).

Sherwood, John M. (1985) 'Engels, Marx, Malthus, and the Machine', *American Historical Review*, **90**(4), October, pp. 837–65.

Shils, Edward (ed.) (1991) *Remembering the University of Chicago* (Chicago: University of Chicago Press).

Shubik, Martin (1975) *The Uses and Methods of Gaming* (Amsterdam: Elsevier).

Shubik, Martin (1982) *Game Theory in the Social Sciences: Concepts and Solutions* (Cambridge, MA: MIT Press).

Shute, Daniel K. (1896) 'Racial Anatomical Peculiarities', *American Anthropologist*, **9**, April, pp. 123–7. Reprinted in Ryan (2001, vol. 2).

Shute, Laurence (1996) *John Maurice Clark: A Social Economics for the Twenty-First Century* (London and New York: Macmillan and St. Martin's Press).

Simon, Herbert A. (1957) *Models of Man: Social and Rational. Mathematical Essays on Rational Human Behavior in a Social Setting* (New York: Wiley).

Simon, Herbert A. (1979) 'Rational Decision Making in Business Organizations', *American Economic Review*, **69**(4), September, pp. 493–513.

Simon, Herbert A. (1981) *The Sciences of the Artificial*, 2nd edn (Cambridge, MA: MIT Press).

Simon, Herbert A. (1983) *Reason in Human Affairs* (Oxford and Stanford: Basil Blackwell and Stanford University Press).

Simon, Herbert A. (1996) Letter to G. M. Hodgson of 26 January 1996.

Simon, Herbert A. (forthcoming) 'Darwinism, Altruism and Economics', in Dopfer, Kurt (ed.) *The Evolutionary Foundations of Economics* (Cambridge and New York: Cambridge University Press).

Simon, Herbert A., Egidi, Massimo, Marris, Robin and Viale, Riccardo (1992) *Economics, Bounded Rationality and the Cognitive Revolution* (Aldershot: Edward Elgar).

Singh, Jitendra V. (ed.) (1990) *Organizational Evolution: New Directions* (London: Sage).

Skidelsky, Robert (1992) *John Maynard Keynes: Volume Two: The Economist as Saviour, 1920–1937* (London: Macmillan).

Small, Albion W. (1903–04) 'Note on Ward's "Pure Sociology"', *American Journal of Sociology*, 9(3), November, pp. 404–7; 9(4), January, pp. 567–75; 9(5), March, pp. 703–7.

Smith, Norman E. (1979) 'William Graham Sumner as an Anti-Social Darwinist', *Pacific Sociological Review*, 22, pp. 332–47.

Smith, Vernon L. (1991) 'Rational Choice: The Contrast Between Economics and Psychology', *Journal of Political Economy*, 99(4), August, pp. 877–96. Reprinted in Smith (1992).

Smith, Vernon L. (1992) *Papers in Experimental Economics* (Cambridge: Cambridge University Press).

Smuts, Jan Christiaan (1926) *Holism and Evolution* (London and New York: Macmillan).

Snyder, Loius L. (1960) *The War: A Concise History, 1939–1945* (New York: Messner).

Sober, Elliott (1981) 'Holism, Individualism, and the Units of Selection', in Asquith, P. D. and Giere, R. N. (eds) *Philosophy of Science Association 1980*, Vol. 2 (East Lansing, MI: Philosophy of Science Association), pp. 93–121.

Sober, Elliott (1984) *The Nature of Selection: Evolutionary Theory in Philosophical Focus* (Cambridge, MA: MIT Press).

Sober, Elliott and Wilson, David Sloan (1998) *Unto Others: The Evolution and Psychology of Unselfish Behavior* (Cambridge, MA: Harvard University Press).

Solow, Robert M. (1985) 'Economic History and Economics', *American Economic Review (Papers and Proceedings)*, 75(2), May, pp. 328–31.

Sonnenschein, Hugo F. (1972) 'Market Excess Demand Functions', *Econometrica*, 40(3), pp. 549–63.

Sonnenschein, Hugo F. (1973a) 'Do Walras's Identity and Continuity Characterize the Class of Community Excess Demand Functions?', *Journal of Economic Theory*, 6(4), pp. 345–54.

Sonnenschein, Hugo F. (1973b) 'The Utility Hypothesis and Market Demand Theory', *Western Economic Journal*, 11(4), pp. 404–10.

Sosa, Ernest and Tooley, Michael (eds) (1993) *Causation* (Oxford: Oxford University Press).

Souter, Ralph W. (1933) *Prolegomena to Relativity Economics: An Elementary Study in the Mechanics and Organics of an Expanding Economic Universe* (New York: Columbia University Press).

Spaulding, Edward Gleason (1906) 'Driesch's Theory of Vitalism', *Philosophical Review*, 15(5), September, pp. 518–27.

Spaulding, Edward Gleason (1912) 'A Defense of Analysis', in Holt, Edwin B., Marvin, Walter T., Montague, William P., Perry, Ralph Barton, Pitkin, Walter B. and Spaulding, Edward Gleason (1912) *The New Realism: Cooperative Studies in Philosophy* (New York: Macmillan).

Spencer, Herbert (1851) *Social Statics* (London: Chapman).

Spencer, Herbert (1862) *First Principles*, 1st edn (London: Williams and Norgate).

Spencer, Herbert (1868) *Essays: Scientific, Political and Speculative*, 1st edn (London: Williams and Norgate).

Spencer, Herbert (1877) *The Principles of Sociology*, vol. 1, 1st edn (New York: Appleton).

Spencer, Herbert (1881) *The Study of Sociology*, 10th edn (London: Kegan Paul).

Spencer, Herbert (1893) 'The Inadequacy of Natural Selection', *Contemporary Review*, 63, pp. 153–66, 439–56.

Spencer, Herbert (1904) *An Autobiography*, 2 vols (London: Williams and Norgate).

Spengler, Joseph J. (1950) 'Evolutionism in American Economics, 1800–1946', in Persons (1950, pp. 201–66).

Sperber, Dan (1996) *Explaining Culture: A Naturalistic Approach* (Oxford: Basil Blackwell).

Sperber, Dan (2000) 'An Objection to the Memetic Approach to Culture', in Aunger (2000, pp. 162–73).

Sperry, Roger W. (1964) *Problems Outstanding in the Evolution of Brain Function* (New York: American Museum of Natural History).

Sperry, Roger W. (1969) 'A Modified Concept of Consciousness', *Psychological Review*, **76**(6), pp. 532–6.

Sperry, Roger W. (1976) 'Mental Phenomena as Causal Determinants in Brain Function', in Globus, Gordon G., Maxwell, Grover and Savodnik, Irwin (eds) *Consciousness and the Brain: A Scientific and Philosophical Inquiry* (New York and London: Plenum), pp. 163–77.

Sperry, Roger W. (1991) 'In Defense of Mentalism and Emergent Interaction', *Journal of Mind and Behavior*, **12**(2), pp. 221–46.

Spiller, Gustav (1914) 'Darwinism and Sociology', *Sociological Review*, **7**, pp. 232–53.

Sraffa, Piero (1960) *Production of Commodities by Means of Commodities: Prelude to a Critique of Economic Theory* (Cambridge: Cambridge University Press).

Stanfield, James Ronald (1995) *Economics, Power and Culture: Essays in the Development of Radical Institutionalism* (London: Macmillan).

Steele, David Ramsay (1992) *From Marx to Mises: Post-Capitalist Society and the Challenge of Economic Calculation* (La Salle, IL: Open Court).

Sterba, James P. and Kourany, Janet A. (1981) 'How to Complete the Compatibilist Account of Free Action', *Philosophy and Phenomenological Research*, **41**(4), June, pp. 508–23.

Stern, Bernhard J. (1946) 'The Ward–Ross Correspondence II 1897–1901', *American Sociological Review*, **11**(6), December, pp. 734–48.

Stern, Bernhard J. (1947) 'The Ward–Ross Correspondence III 1902–1903', *American Sociological Review*, **12**(6), December, pp. 703–20.

Stewart, Ian (1989) *Does God Play Dice? The Mathematics of Chaos* (Oxford: Basil Blackwell).

Stich, Stephen P. (1983) *From Folk Psychology to Cognitive Science* (Cambridge, MA: MIT Press).

Stich, Stephen P. (1996) *Deconstructing the Mind* (Oxford and New York: Oxford University Press).

Stigler, George J. (1947) 'Professor Lester and the Marginalists', *American Economic Review*, **37**(1), March, pp. 154–7.

Stigler, George J. and Becker, Gary S. (1977) 'De Gustibus Non Est Disputandum', *American Economic Review*, **76**(1), March, pp. 76–90.

Stigler, George J., Stigler, Stephen M. and Friedland, Claire (1995) 'The Journals of Economics', *Journal of Political Economy*, **105**(2), pp. 331–59.

Stiglitz, Joseph E. (1987a) 'The Causes and Consequences of the Dependence of Quality on Price', *Journal of Economic Literature*, **25**(1), March, pp. 1–48.

Stocking, George W., Jr (1962) 'Lamarckianism in American Social Science, 1890–1915', *Journal of the History of Ideas*, **23**, pp. 239–56. Revised and reprinted in Stocking (1968).

Stocking, George W., Jr (1968) *Race, Culture, and Evolution: Essays in the History of Anthropology* (New York: Free Press).

Stoneman, William (1979) *A History of the Economic Analysis of the Great Depression* (New York: Garland).

Storper, Michael and Salais, Robert (1997) *Worlds of Production: The Action Frameworks of the Economy* (Cambridge, MA: Harvard University Press).

Strevens, Michael (2003) *Bigger Than Chaos* (Cambridge, MA: Harvard University Press).

Sturgeon, James I. (1981) 'The History of the Association for Institutionalist Thought', *Review of Institutionalist Thought*, 1, December, pp. 40–53.

Suchman, Lucy (1987) *Plans and Situated Actions: The Problem of Human–Machine Communication* (Cambridge: Cambridge University Press).

Sugden, Robert (1986) *The Economics of Rights, Co-operation and Welfare* (Oxford: Basil Blackwell).

Sugden, Robert (1991) 'Rational Choice: A Survey of Contributions from Economics and Philosophy', *Economic Journal*, 101(4), July, pp. 751–85.

Sumner, William Graham (1885) *Collected Essays in Political and Social Science* (New York: Holt).

Sumner, William Graham (1906) *Folkways: A Study of the Sociological Importance of Usages, Manners, Customs, Mores and Morals* (Boston: Ginn).

Tarde, Gabriel (1884) 'Darwinisme naturel et Darwinisme social', *Revue Philosophique*, 17, p. 607.

Tarde, Gabriel (1890) *Les lois de l'imitation: étude sociologique* (Paris: Alcan).

Tarde, Gabriel (1899) *Social Laws: An Outline of Sociology*, translated from the French edition of 1898 by Howard C. Warren, with a Preface by James M. Baldwin (New York: Macmillan).

Tarde, Gabriel (1903) *The Laws of Imitation*, translated from the French edition of 1890 by E. C. Parsons with introduction by F. H. Giddings (New York: Henry Holt).

Tattersall, Ian (1998) *Becoming Human: Evolution and Human Uniqueness* (New York: Harcourt Brace).

Taylor, Frederick Winslow (1911) *The Principles of Scientific Management* (New York: Harper).

Taylor, Overton H. (1929) 'Economics and the Idea of Natural Laws', *Quarterly Journal of Economics*, 44(1), November, pp. 1–39.

Teggart, Richard V. (1932) *Thorstein Veblen: A Chapter in American Economic Thought* (Berkeley, CA: University of California Press).

Thomas, Brinley (1991) 'Alfred Marshall on Economic Biology', *Review of Political Economy*, 3(1), January, pp. 1–14.

Thomas, William and Znaniecki, Florian (1920) *The Polish Peasant in Europe and America*, vol. 2 (New York: Octagon).

Thompson, Edward P. (1968) *The Making of the English Working Class*, 2nd edn (Harmondsworth: Penguin).

Thomson, Garrett (1987) *Needs* (London: Routledge and Kegan Paul).

Tichi, Cecelia (1987) *Shifting Gears: Technology, Literature, Culture in Modenist America* (Chapel Hill, NC: University of North Carolina Press).

Tiles, J. E. (1988) *Dewey* (London: Routledge).

Tilman, Rick (1974) 'Value Theory, Planning, and Reform: Ayres as Incrementalist and Utopian', *Journal of Economic Issues*, 8(4), December, pp. 689–706.

Tilman, Rick (1990) 'New Light on John Dewey, Clarence Ayres, and the Development of Evolutionary Economics', *Journal of Economic Issues*, 24(4), December, pp. 963–79.

Tilman, Rick (1992) *Thorstein Veblen and His Critics, 1891–1963: Conservative, Liberal, and Radical Perspectives* (Princeton: Princeton University Press).

Tilman, Rick (1996) *The Intellectual Legacy of Thorstein Veblen: Unresolved Issues* (Westport, CT: Greenwood Press).

Tilman, Rick (1998) 'John Dewey as User and Critic of Thorstein Veblen's Ideas', *Journal of the History of Economic Thought* 20(2), June, pp. 145–60.

Todd, Emmanuel (1985) *The Explanation of Ideology: Family Structures and Social Systems* (Oxford: Basil Blackwell).

Todd, Peter M. and Gigerenzer, Gerd (2000) 'Précis of *Simple Heuristics that Make Us Smart*', *Behavioral and Brain Sciences*, 23(5), October, pp. 727–41.

Tool, Marc R. (1979) *The Discretionary Economy: A Normative Theory of Political Economy* (Santa Monica, CA: Goodyear).

Tool, Marc R. (1994) 'Ayres, Clarence E.', in Hodgson *et al.* (1994, vol. 1, pp. 16–22).

Tool, Marc R. (1995) *Pricing, Valuation and Systems: Essays in Neoinstitutional Economics* (Aldershot: Edward Elgar).

Tool, Marc R. (2000) *Value Theory and Economic Progress: The Institutional Economics of J. Fagg Foster* (Boston: Kluwer).

Tool, Marc R. and Bush, Paul Dale (eds) (2003) *Institutional Analysis and Public Policy* (Boston: Kluwer).

Tugwell, Rexford G. (1922) 'Human Nature in Economic Theory', *Journal of Political Economy*, **30**(3), June, pp. 317–45.

Tugwell, Rexford G. (ed.) (1924) *The Trend of Economics* (New York: Alfred Knopf).

Tugwell, Rexford G. (1930) 'Human Nature and Social Economy', *Journal of Philosophy*, **27**(17–18), August 14–28, pp. 449–57, 477–92.

Tugwell, Rexford G. (1949) 'Variation on a Theme by Cooley', *Ethics*, **59**(4), July, pp. 233–43.

Tullock, Gordon (1979) 'Sociobiology and Economics', *Atlantic Economic Journal*, September, pp. 1–10.

Tullock, Gordon (1994) *The Economics of Non-Human Societies* (Tuscon, AZ: Pallas Press).

Tully, R. E. (1981) 'Emergence Revisited', in Sumner, L. W., Slater, John G. and Wilson, Fred (eds) *Pragmatism and Purpose: Essays Presented to Thomas A. Goudge* (Toronto: University of Toronto Press), pp. 261–77.

Twomey, Paul (1998) 'Reviving Veblenian Economic Psychology', *Cambridge Journal of Economics*, **22**(4), July, pp. 433–48.

Tylor, Edward Burnett (1871) *Primitive Culture: Researches into the Development of Mythology, Philosophy, Religion, Language, Art, and Custom*, 2 vols (London: John Murray).

Udéhn, Lars (2001) *Methodological Individualism: Background, History and Meaning* (London and New York: Routledge).

Urban, Wilbur M. (1926) 'Progress in Philosophy in the Last Quarter Century', *Philosophical Review*, **35**(2), March, pp. 93–123.

Urmston, J. O. (1989) 'Determinism', in Urmston, J. O. and Rée, Jonathan (eds) *The Concise Encyclopedia of Western Philosophy and Philosophers* (London: Unwin Hyman), p. 78.

Vanberg, Viktor J. (1986) 'Spontaneous Market Order and Social Rules: A Critique of F. A. Hayek's Theory of Cultural Evolution', *Economics and Philosophy*, **2**(1), April, pp. 75–100. Reprinted in Vanberg (1994).

Vanberg, Viktor J. (1989) 'Carl Menger's Evolutionary and John R. Commons' Collective Action Approach to Institutions: A Comparison', *Review of Political Economy*, **1**(3), November, pp. 334–60. Reprinted in Vanberg (1994).

Vanberg, Viktor J. (1994) *Rules and Choice in Economics* (London: Routledge).

Vanberg, Viktor J. (1997) 'Institutional Evolution Through Purposeful Selection: The Constitutional Economics of John R. Commons', *Constitutional Political Economy*, **8**, pp. 105–22.

Vanberg, Viktor J. (2002) 'Rational Choice versus Program-Based Behavior: Alternative Theoretical Approaches and Their Relevance for the Study of Institutions', *Rationality and Society*, **14**(1), Summer, pp. 7–53.

Van den Berghe, Peter L. (1990) 'Why Most Sociologists Don't (and Won't) Think Evolutionarily', *Sociological Forum*, **5**(2), pp. 173–85.

Van de Ven, Andrew H. (1993) 'The Institutional Theory of John R. Commons: A Review and Commentary', *Academy of Management Review*, **18**, January, pp. 139–52.

Veblen, Thorstein B. (1884) 'Kant's Critique of Judgement', *Journal of Speculative Philosophy*, **43**, July, pp. 260–74. Reprinted in Veblen (1934).

Veblen, Thorstein B. (1892) 'The Price of Wheat Since 1867', *Journal of Political Economy*, **1**(1), December, pp. 68–103.

Veblen, Thorstein B. (1893) 'The Food Supply and the Price of Wheat', *Journal of Political Economy*, **1**(3), June, pp. 365–79.

Veblen, Thorstein B. (1896) Review of *Socialisme et Science Positive* by Enrico Ferri, *Journal of Political Economy*, **5**(1), December, pp. 97–103. Reprinted in Veblen (1973).

Veblen, Thorstein B. (1897a) Review of Antonio Labriola, *Essais sur la conception matérialiste de l'histoire*, *Journal of Political Economy*, **5**(3), June, pp. 390–1. Reprinted in Veblen (1973).

Veblen, Thorstein B. (1897b) Review of Max Lorenz, *Die Marxistische Socialdemokratie*, *Journal of Political Economy*, **6**(1), December, pp. 136–7. Reprinted in Veblen (1973).

Veblen, Thorstein B. (1898a) Review of William H. Mallock, *Aristocracy and Evolution: A Study of the Rights, the Origins and the Social Functions of the Wealthier Classes*, *Journal of Political Economy*, **6**, June, pp. 430–5.

Veblen, Thorstein B. (1898b) 'Why Is Economics Not an Evolutionary Science?', *Quarterly Journal of Economics*, **12**(3), July, pp. 373–97. Reprinted in Veblen (1919a).

Veblen, Thorstein B. (1898c) 'The Instinct of Workmanship and the Irksomeness of Labor', *American Journal of Sociology*, **4**(2), September, pp. 187–201. Reprinted in Veblen (1934).

Veblen, Thorstein B. (1898d) 'The Beginnings of Ownership', *American Journal of Sociology*, **4**, November, pp. 352–65. Reprinted in Veblen (1934).

Veblen, Thorstein B. (1899a) *The Theory of the Leisure Class: An Economic Study in the Evolution of Institutions* (New York: Macmillan).

Veblen, Thorstein B. (1899b) 'Mr. Cummings's Strictures on "The Theory of the Leisure Class"', *Journal of Political Economy*, **8**(1), December, pp. 106–17. Reprinted in Veblen (1934).

Veblen, Thorstein B. (1899c) 'The Preconceptions of Economic Science: I', *Quarterly Journal of Economics*, **13**(2), January, pp. 121–50. Reprinted in Veblen (1919a).

Veblen, Thorstein B. (1900a) 'The Preconceptions of Economic Science: III', *Quarterly Journal of Economics*, **14**(2), February, pp. 240–69. Reprinted in Veblen (1919a).

Veblen, Thorstein B. (1900b) Review of *Social Laws: An Outline of Sociology* by Gabriel Tarde, *Journal of Political Economy*, **8**(4), September, pp. 562–3. Reprinted in Veblen (1973).

Veblen, Thorstein B. (1901a) 'Industrial and Pecuniary Employments', *Publications of the American Economic Association*, Series 3, pp. 190–235. Reprinted in Veblen (1919a).

Veblen, Thorstein B. (1901b) 'Gustav Schmoller's Economics', *Quarterly Journal of Economics*, **16**, November, pp. 69–93. Reprinted in Veblen (1919a).

Veblen, Thorstein B. (1902) Review of *Psychologie économique* by Gabriel Tarde, *Journal of Political Economy*, **11**(1), December, pp. 146–8. Reprinted in Veblen (1973).

Veblen, Thorstein B. (1903) Review of *Pure Sociology: A Treatise Concerning the Origin and Spontaneous Development of Society* by Lester Ward, *Journal of Political Economy*, **11**(4), September, pp. 655–6. Reprinted in Veblen (1973).

Veblen, Thorstein B. (1904) *The Theory of Business Enterprise* (New York: Charles Scribners).

Veblen, Thorstein B. (1905) 'Credit and Prices', *Journal of Political Economy*, **13**(3), June, pp. 460–72. Reprinted in Veblen (1934).

Veblen, Thorstein B. (1906a) 'The Place of Science in Modern Civilisation', *American Journal of Sociology*, **11**(1), March, pp. 585–609. Reprinted in Veblen (1919a).

Veblen, Thorstein B. (1906b) 'The Socialist Economics of Karl Marx and His Followers I: The Theories of Karl Marx', *Quarterly Journal of Economics*, **20**(3), August, pp. 578–95. Reprinted in Veblen (1919a).

Veblen, Thorstein B. (1907) 'The Socialist Economics of Karl Marx and His Followers II: The Later Marxism', *Quarterly Journal of Economics*, **21**(1), February, pp. 299–322. Reprinted in Veblen (1919a).

Veblen, Thorstein B. (1908a) 'Professor Clark's Economics', *Quarterly Journal of Economics*, **22**(2), February, pp. 147–95. Reprinted in Veblen (1919a).

Veblen, Thorstein B. (1908b) 'The Evolution of the Scientific Point of View', *University of California Chronicle*, **10**(4), pp. 396–416. Reprinted in Veblen (1919a).

Veblen, Thorstein B. (1908c) 'On the Nature of Capital I', *Quarterly Journal of Economics*, **22**(4), August, pp. 517–42. Reprinted in Veblen (1919a).

Veblen, Thorstein B. (1908d) 'On the Nature of Capital II: Investment, Intangible Assets, and the Pecuniary Magnate', *Quarterly Journal of Economics*, **23**(1), November, pp. 104–36. Reprinted in Veblen (1919a).

Veblen, Thorstein B. (1909a) 'Fisher's Rate of Interest', *Political Science Quarterly*, **24**(2), June, pp. 296–303. Reprinted in Veblen (1934).

Veblen, Thorstein B. (1909b) 'The Limitations of Marginal Utility', *Journal of Political Economy*, **17**(9), November, pp. 620–36. Reprinted in Veblen (1919a).

Veblen, Thorstein B. (1913) 'The Mutation Theory and the Blond Race', *Journal of Race Development*, April, pp. 491–507. Reprinted in Veblen (1919a).

Veblen, Thorstein B. (1914) *The Instinct of Workmanship, and the State of the Industrial Arts* (New York: Macmillan).

Veblen, Thorstein B. (1915) *Imperial Germany and the Industrial Revolution* (New York: Macmillan).

Veblen, Thorstein B. (1918) *The Higher Learning in America: A Memorandum on the Conduct of Universities by Business Men* (New York: Huebsch).

Veblen, Thorstein B. (1919a) *The Place of Science in Modern Civilization and Other Essays* (New York: Huebsch).

Veblen, Thorstein B. (1919b) *The Vested Interests and the Common Man* (New York: Huebsch).

Veblen, Thorstein B. (1921) *The Engineers and the Price System* (New York: Harcourt Brace and World).

Veblen, Thorstein B. (1923) *Absentee Ownership and Business Enterprise in Recent Times* (New York: Huebsch).

Veblen, Thorstein B. (1925) 'Economic Theory in the Calculable Future', *American Economic Review (Papers and Proceedings)*, **15**(1), March, pp. 48–55. Reprinted in Veblen (1934).

Veblen, Thorstein B. (1934) *Essays on Our Changing Order*, ed. Leon Ardzrooni (New York: Viking Press).

Veblen, Thorstein B. (1973) *Essays, Reviews and Reports*, ed. with an introduction by Joseph Dorfman (New York: Augustus Kelley).

Veysey, Laurence R. (1965) *The Emergence of the American University* (Chicago: University of Chicago Press).

Vincenti, Walter (1990) *What Engineers Know and How They Know It: Analytical Studies from Aeronautical History* (Baltimore: Johns Hopkins University Press).

Vining, Rutledge (1939) 'Suggestions of Keynes in the Writings of Veblen', *Journal of Political Economy*, **47**(5), October, pp. 692–704.

Vining, Rutledge (1949a) 'Methodological Issues in Quantitative Economics', *Review of Economics and Statistics*, **31**(2), May, pp. 77–86.

Vining, Rutledge (1949b) 'Methodological Issues in Quantitative Economics: A Rejoinder', *Review of Economics and Statistics*, **31**(2), May, pp. 91–94.

Vorzimmer, Peter J. (1977) *Charles Darwin: the Years of Controversy; The Origin of Species and Its Critics, 1859–1882* (Philadelphia: Temple University Press).

Vromen, Jack J. (2001) 'The Human Agent in Evolutionary Economics', in Laurent and Nightingale (2001, pp. 184–208).

Vroom, Victor H. and Deci, E. L. (eds) (1970) *Management and Motivation* (Harmondsworth: Penguin).

Waddington, Conrad H. (1953) 'Genetic Assimilation of an Acquired Character', *Evolution*, **7**, pp. 118–26.

Waddington, Conrad H. (1969) 'The Theory of Evolution Today', in Koestler, Arthur and Smythies, J. R. (eds) *Beyond Reductionism: New Perspectives in the Life Sciences* (London: Hutchinson), pp. 357–74.

Waddington, Conrad H. (1976) 'Evolution in the Sub-Human World', in Jantsch, Erich and Waddington, Conrad H. (eds) *Evolution and Consciousness: Human Systems in Transition* (Reading, MA: Addison-Wesley), pp. 11–15.

Walker, Donald A. (1977) 'Thorstein Veblen's Economic System', *Economic Inquiry*, **15**(2), April, pp. 213–37.

Walker, Donald A. (1979) 'The Institutionalist Economic Theories of Clarence Ayres', *Economic Inquiry*, **17**(4), October, pp. 519–38.

Wallace, Alfred Russel (1869) 'Geological Climates and the Origin of Species', *Quarterly Review*, **126**, pp. 359–94.

Wallace, Alfred Russel (1870) *Contributions to the Theory of Natural Selection: A Series of Essays* (London: Macmillan).

Waller, William J., Jr (1982) 'The Evolution of the Veblenian Dichotomy: Veblen, Hamilton, Ayres, and Foster', *Journal of Economic Issues*, **16**(3), September, pp. 757–71.

Waller, William J., Jr (1994) 'The Veblenian Dichotomy and its Critics', in Hodgson *et al.* (1994, vol. 2, pp. 368–72).

Waller, William J., Jr (1999) 'Institutional Economics, Feminism, and Overdetermination', *Journal of Economic Issues*, **33**(4), December, pp. 835–44.

Ward, Benjamin (1972) *What's Wrong With Economics* (London: Macmillan).

Ward, Lester Frank (1883) *Dynamic Sociology, Or Applied Social Science, as Based Upon Statical Sociology and Less Complex Sciences*, 2 vols (New York: Appleton).

Ward, Lester Frank (1891) 'The Transmission of Culture', *The Forum*, **11**, pp. 312–19.

Ward, Lester Frank (1892) 'Neo-Darwinism and Neo-Lamarckism', *Proceedings of the Biological Society of Washington*, **6**, pp. 45–50.

Ward, Lester Frank (1893) *The Psychic Factors of Civilization* (Boston: Ginn).

Ward, Lester Frank (1900) Review of *The Theory of the Leisure Class* by Thorstein Veblen, *American Journal of Sociology*, **5**(6), May, pp. 829–37.

Ward, Lester Frank (1903) *Pure Sociology: A Treatise Concerning the Origin and Spontaneous Development of Society* (New York: Macmillan).

Ward, Lester Frank (1906) *Applied Sociology* (Boston: Ginn).

Ward, Lester Frank (1907) 'Social and Biological Struggles', *American Journal of Sociology*, **13**(3), November, pp. 289–99. Reprinted in Ryan (2001, vol. 2).

Waters, C. Kenneth (1986) 'Natural Selection Without Survival of the Fittest', *Biology and Philosophy*, **1**(2), April, pp. 207–25.

Watson, John B. (1913) 'Psychology as the Behaviorist Views It', *Psychological Review*, **20**, pp. 158–77. Reprinted in Watson (1914).

Watson, John B. (1914) *Behavior: A Textbook of Comparative Psychology* (New York: Henry Holt).

Watson, John B. (1919) *Psychology from the Standpoint of a Behaviorist* (Philadelphia: J. B. Lippincott).

Watson, John B. (1924) *Behaviorism* (New York: W. W. Norton).

Watson, John B. (1936) 'Autobiography', in Murchison, Carl (ed.) *A History of Psychology in Autobiography, Volume 3* (Worcester, MA: Clark University Press), pp. 273–84.

Webb, James L. (2002) 'Dewey: Back to the Future', *Journal of Economic Issues*, **36**(4), December, pp. 981–1003.

Webb, Sidney J. (1889) 'The Historic Basis of Socialism', in Shaw, George Bernard (ed.) *Fabian Essays in Socialism* (London: Fabian Society), pp. 33–61.

Weber, Bruce H. and Depew, David J. (1996) 'Natural Selection and Self- Organisation: Dynamical Models as Clues to a New Evolutionary Synthesis', *Biology and Philosophy*, **11**, pp. 33–65.

Weber, Bruce H., Depew, David J., Dyke, Charles, Salthe, Stanley N., Schneider, E. D., Ulanowicz, R. E. and Wicken, Jeffrey S. (1989) 'Evolution in Thermodynamic Perspective: An Ecological Approach', *Biology and Philosophy*, **4**(4), October, pp. 373–405.

Weber, Max (1978) *Max Weber: Selections in Translation*, edited and introduced by W. G. Runciman (Cambridge: Cambridge University Press).

Weingart, Peter, Mitchell, Sandra D., Richerson, Peter J. and Maasen, Sabine (eds) *Human By Nature: Between Biology and the Social Sciences* (Mahwah, NJ: Lawrence Erlbaum Associates).

Weintraub, E. Roy (2002) *How Economics Became a Mathematical Science* (Durham, NC: Duke University Press).

Weismann, August (1889) *Essay Upon Heredity and Kindred Biological Problems*, ed. Edward B. Poulton, Selmar Schonland and Arthur E. Shipley (Oxford: Clarendon Press).

Weismann, August (1893) *The Germ-Plasm: A Theory of Heredity*, translated by W. Newton Parker and Harriet R. Ronnfeldt (London and New York: Walter Scott and Scribner's).

Weiss, Paul A., Buechner, H. K., Coleman, J. S., Forrester, J. W., Lorenz, K., McNeill, D. and Ozbekhan, H. (1971) *Hierarchically Organized Systems in Theory and Practice* (New York: Hafner).

Weissman, David (2000) *A Social Ontology* (New Haven, CT: Yale University Press).

Wells, Alan (1970) *Social Institutions* (London: Heinemann).

Wells, D. Collin (1907) 'Social Darwinism', *American Journal of Sociology*, **12**(5), March, pp. 695–708. Reprinted in Ryan (2001, vol. 2).

Wenger, E. (1998) *Communities of Practice: Learning, Memory and Identity* (Cambridge: Cambridge University Press).

Werkmeister, William H. (1937) 'Seven Theses of Logical Positivism Critically Examined II', *Philosophical Review*, **46**(4), July, pp. 357–76.

Werkmeister, William H. (1949) *A History of Philosophical Ideas in America* (Westport, CO: Greenwood Press).

Wheeler, William Morton (1921) 'The Organization of Research', *Science*, **53**, no. 1360, 21 January, pp. 53–67.

Wheeler, William Morton (1926) 'Emergent Evolution and the Social', *Science*, **66**, no. 1662, 5 November, pp. 433–40. Reprinted in Wheeler (1926, 1928) and Brightman (1927, pp. 33–45).

Wheeler, William Morton (1928) *Emergent Evolution and the Development of Societies* (New York: Norton).

Wheeler, William Morton (1930) *Social Life Among the Insects* (New York: Harcourt).

Wheeler, William Morton (1939) *Essays in Philosophical Biology* (Cambridge, MA: Harvard University Press).

Whitaker, John K. (ed.) (1996) *The Correspondence of Alfred Marshall, Volume 2* (Cambridge: Cambridge University Press).

Whitehead, Alfred N. (1926) *Science and the Modern World* (Cambridge: Cambridge University Press).

Wicken, Jeffrey S. (1987) *Evolution, Thermodynamics, and Information: Extending the Darwinian Paradigm* (Oxford and New York: Oxford University Press).

Wicksell, Knut (1958) *Selected Papers in Economic Theory* (London: Allen and Unwin).

Wiener, Philip P. (1949) *Evolution and the Founders of Pragmatism* (Cambridge, MA: Harvard University Press).

Williamson, Oliver E. (1975) *Markets and Hierarchies: Analysis and Anti-Trust Implications: A Study in the Economics of Internal Organization* (New York: Free Press).

Williamson, Oliver E. (1985) *The Economic Institutions of Capitalism: Firms, Markets, Relational Contracting* (London: Macmillan).

Williamson, Oliver E. (1996a) 'Revisiting Legal Realism: The Law, Economics, and Organization Perspective', *Industrial and Corporate Change*, **5**(2), pp. 383–420.

Williamson, Oliver E. (1996b) Review of Jack Vromen *Economic Evolution*, *Economic Journal*, **106**(6), November, pp. 1791–3.

Williamson, Oliver E. (2002) 'The Lens of Contract: Private Ordering', *American Economic Review (Papers and Proceedings)*, **92**(2), May, pp. 438–43.

Wills, Christopher (1989) *The Wisdom of the Genes: New Pathways in Evolution* (New York: Basic Books).

Wilson, Edward O. (1971) *The Insect Societies* (Cambridge, MA: Harvard University Press).

Wilson, Edward O. (1975) *Sociobiology: The New Synthesis* (Cambridge, MA: Harvard University Press).

Wilson, Edward O. (1978) *On Human Nature* (Cambridge, MA: Harvard University Press).

Wilson, Edward O. (1998) *Consilience: The Unity of Knowledge* (New York and London: Alfred Knopf and Little, Brown).

Wilson, Raymond J. (1967) *Darwinism and the American Intellectual* (Homewood, IL: Irwin).

Wiltshire, David (1978) *The Social and Political Thought of Herbert Spencer* (Oxford: Oxford University Press).

Winter, Sidney G., Jr (1964) 'Economic "Natural Selection" and the Theory of the Firm', *Yale Economic Essays*, **4**(1), pp. 225–72. Reprinted in Hodgson (1998e).

Winter, Sidney G., Jr (1971) 'Satisficing, Selection and the Innovating Remnant', *Quarterly Journal of Economics*, **85**(2), May, pp. 237–61.

Witt, Ulrich (1985), 'Coordination of Individual Economic Activities as an Evolving Process of Self-Organization', *Economie appliquée*, **37**(3/4), pp. 569–95.

Witt, Ulrich (1997) 'Self-Organisation and Economics – What is New?', *Structural Change and Economic Dynamics*, **8**, pp. 489–507.

Witt, Ulrich (2002) 'How Evolutionary is Schumpeter's Theory of Economic Development?', *Industry and Innovation*, **9**(1/2), pp. 7–22.

Wittgenstein, Ludwig (1958) *Philosophical Investigations*, 2nd edn (Oxford: Basil Blackwell).

Wolfe, Albert B. (1924) 'Functional Economics', in Tugwell (1924, pp. 443–82).

Wrege, Charles D. and Greenwood, Ronald J. (1991) *Frederick W. Taylor, The Father of Scientific Management: Myth and Reality* (Homewood, IL: Irwin).

Wright, Robert (1994) *The Moral Animal: Why We Are the Way We Are: The New Science of Evolutionary Psychology* (New York: Vintage).

Wunderlin, Clarence E., Jr (1992) *Visions of a New Industrial Order: Social Science and Labor Theory in America's Progressive Era* (New York: Columbia University Press).

Wundt, Wilhelm (1895) *Logik: Eine Untersuchung der Principien der Erkenntniss und der Methoden wissenschaftlicher Forschung*, 2 vols (Stuttgart: Enke).

Yates, F. Eugene (ed.) (1987) *Self-Organizing Systems: The Emergence of Order* (New York: Plenum Press).

Yonay, Yuval P. (1998) *The Struggle Over the Soul of Economics: Institutionalist and Neoclassical Economists in America Between the Wars* (Princeton, NJ: Princeton University Press).

Young, Allyn A. (1911) 'Some Limitations of the Value Concept', *Quarterly Journal of Economics*, **25**(3), pp. 409–28.

Young, Allyn A. (1925) 'The Trend of Economics, as Seen by Some American Economists', *Quarterly Journal of Economics*, **39**(2), February, pp. 155–83.

Young, Allyn A. (1928) 'Increasing Returns and Economic Progress', *Economic Journal*, **38**(4), December, pp. 527–42.

Young, Gary (1976) 'The Fundamental Contradiction of Capitalist Production', *Philosophy and Public Affairs*, **5**(2), Winter, pp. 196–234.

Young, H. Peyton (1996) 'The Economics of Convention', *Journal of Economic Perspectives*, **10**(2), Spring, pp. 105–22.

Young, Robert M. (1985) *Darwin's Metaphor: Nature's Place in Victorian Culture* (Cambridge: Cambridge University Press).

Index